1/5/98
Hamilton
6.95

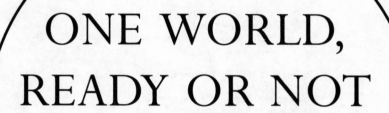

ONE WORLD, READY OR NOT

The Manic Logic of Global Capitalism

WILLIAM GREIDER

Simon & Schuster

SIMON & SCHUSTER
Rockefeller Center
1230 Avenue of the Americas
New York, NY 10020

Designed by Edith Fowler
Manufactured in the United States of America

10   9   8   7   6   5   4   3   2   1

Library of Congress Cataloging-in-Publication Data

Greider, William.
   One world, ready or not : the manic logic of
global capitalism / William Greider.
      p.   cm.
   Includes bibliographical references and index.
   1. Capitalism.   2. Economic history—1945–
I. Title.
HB501.G647   1997
330.12'2—dc20   96-33202   CIP
ISBN 0-684-81141-3

For my brothers and sisters:

Nancy and Julius Gluck, Richard and Mary Greider, Diane Furry and Todd Stiles.

And in memory of my brother David McClure Greider, who led the way and taught us generosity.

Contents

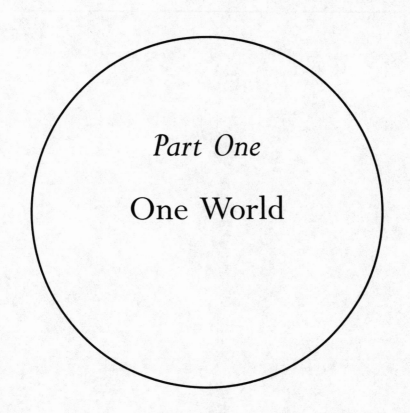

Part One

One World

One

The Storm Upon Us

IMAGINE A WONDROUS new machine, strong and supple, a machine that reaps as it destroys. It is huge and mobile, something like the machines of modern agriculture but vastly more complicated and powerful. Think of this awesome machine running over open terrain and ignoring familiar boundaries. It plows across fields and fencerows with a fierce momentum that is exhilarating to behold and also frightening. As it goes, the machine throws off enormous mows of wealth and bounty while it leaves behind great furrows of wreckage.

Now imagine that there are skillful hands on board, but no one is at the wheel. In fact, this machine has no wheel nor any internal governor to control the speed and direction. It is sustained by its own forward motion, guided mainly by its own appetites. And it is accelerating.

The machine is the subject of this book: modern capitalism driven by the imperatives of global industrial revolution. The metaphor is imperfect, but it offers a simplified way to visualize what is dauntingly complex and abstract and impossibly diffuse—the drama of a free-running economic system that is reordering the world.

The logic of commerce and capital has overpowered the inertia of politics and launched an epoch of great social transformations. Settled facts of material life are being revised for rich and poor nations alike. Social understandings that were formed by the hard political struggles of the twentieth century are put in doubt. Old verities about the rank ordering of nations are revised and a new map of the world is gradually being drawn. These great changes sweep over the affairs of mere governments and destabilize the established political orders in both advanced and primitive societies. Everything seems new and strange. Nothing seems certain.

Economic revolution, similar to the impulse of political revolution, liberates masses of people and at the same time projects new aspects of tyranny. Old worlds are destroyed and new ones emerge. The past is up-ended and new social values are created alongside the fabulous new wealth. Marvelous inventions are made plentiful. Great fortunes are accumulated. Millions of peasants find ways to escape from muddy poverty.

Yet masses of people are also tangibly deprived of their claims to self-sufficiency, the independent means of sustaining hearth and home. People and communities, even nations, find themselves losing control over their own destinies, ensnared by the revolutionary demands of commerce.

The great paradox of this economic revolution is that its new technologies enable people and nations to take sudden leaps into modernity, while at the same time they promote the renewal of once-forbidden barbarisms. Amid the newness of things, exploitation of the weak by the strong also flourishes again.

The present economic revolution, like revolutions of the past, is fueled by invention and human ingenuity and a universal aspiration to build and accumulate. But it is also driven by a palpable sense of insecurity. No one can be said to control the energies of unfettered capital, not important governments or financiers, not dictators or democrats.

And, in the race to the future, no one dares to fall a step behind, not nations or major corporations. Even the most effective leaders of business and finance share in the uncertainty, knowing as they do that the uncompromising dynamics can someday turn on the revolutionaries themselves.

As history confirms, every revolution gradually accumulates its own tensions and instabilities, the unresolved contradictions that deepen and eventually lead it to falter or break down. Likewise, this revolution is steadily creating the predicate for its own collapse. This book roams the world to capture instructive glimpses of the action, but its main purpose is to explore and explain the underlying dynamics of the revolution, the imperatives driving enterprise and finance and leading to great social transformations. These imperatives reveal, in turn, the inherent contradictions that are also propelling the world toward some new version of breakdown, the prospect of an economic or political cataclysm of unknowable dimensions.

In this book, the central message takes the form of a reasoned warning: our wondrous machine, withal its great power and creativity, appears to be running out of control toward some sort of abyss. Amid revolutionary fervor, such warnings may sound far-fetched and, as history tells us, usually go unheeded until one day, sometimes quite suddenly, they are confirmed by reality.

Before the machine can be understood, one must first be able to see it. The daunting shape and scope of the global system are usually described by opaque statistics from business and economics, but only the most sophisticated can grasp the explosive dynamics in those numbers. To visualize this great drama in its full dimensions, one must also see the people. The economic revolution astride the world will be made visible in these pages through images of human endeavor and struggle—from peasants entering industrial life for the first time to operators in the most exalted realms of finance, across nations from Eastern Europe to Asia and across industrial sectors from aircraft to semiconductors.

When I visited Bangkok, in Thailand, the newspapers were preoccupied with the melancholy saga of Honey, a work elephant who was severely injured when a truck sideswiped her on the highway. As doctors tried to mend the elephant's smashed hip, contributions poured in from heartsick citizens, including the king. Elephants have been the emblem of Thai culture for at least seven centuries, but are now gradually dying out. Honey's death prompted editorial reflections on the price of prosperity.

The new national symbol of Thailand, one could say, is the traffic jam. Bangkok's are the worst in Asia, citizens remark with an air of disgusted pride. Their daily commuting routines are the longest in developing Asia and Thais manipulate schedules endlessly to try to avoid the hours of steaming in tropical congestions of cars. The problem is that Thais are buying cars much faster than the government is building a modern transportation system. Thailand may emerge as Toyota's biggest overseas market aside from the United States.[1]

In Poland, the newly chartered Warsaw Stock Exchange was under way in a stately old pre-Communist building on Aleje Jeroszolimskie. Trading was quite thin since only two dozen companies had their shares listed and Poles were already experiencing the turbulence of Adam Smith's *niewidzialna ręka rynku,* "the invisible hand of the market." Stock prices rose fabulously in 1993, and many of the pioneer investors became instantly wealthy, zloty millionaires, at least on paper. The stock market crashed the following spring. As shares fell 40 to 70 percent in ten days, the Polish traders adopted the style of gallows humor familiar to mature financial markets around the world. Watching stocks plunge 27 percent in a single day, a broker observed: "The Warsaw Stock Exchange still awaits its first suicide."[2]

The lobby of Warsaw's Victoria Intercontinental Hotel, a favorite of foreign business travelers, was filled with hopeful plungers. Each morning Polish entrepreneurs would spread their business prospectuses across the broad coffee tables and sit back, a bit fidgety, while visiting investors from Frankfurt or New York or Milan inspected the numbers.

On the city's industrial outskirts, meanwhile, workers at the Huta Luchini steelworks were on strike. They closed down the mill to demand a share of the ownership. These steelworkers had once been revolutionaries themselves, among the militant members of Solidarity, the free trade union that arose to confront the Polish Communist regime in the early 1980s and had campaigned for the autonomy of workers and enterprises organized on principles of self-management. The Warsaw steelworks is now owned by an Italian conglomerate.

In China, as the November days turned crisp and cold, the citizens of Beijing shopped at sidewalk markets for the traditional supplies of winter cabbage. High, squared-off mounds of cabbages attended by merchants in blue smocks with white kerchiefs on their heads were stacked at street corners along Chang An—Avenue of Eternal Peace—the mainstem boulevard. Farmers hauled cabbages into the city every day, stacked on trucks, bicycle-powered wagons and overloaded handcarts. The ritual reflects a national memory of poverty and famine. Every autumn a family acquires its store of winter cabbages as insurance against the ancient threat of scarcity. One can see the cabbages hanging atop communal walls or outside apartment windows, their outer leaves blackened by Beijing's sooty air.

Meanwhile, traffic on the boulevard was abruptly interrupted to make way for a caravan of important personages—a fleet of limousines and police escorts racing down the center lanes, with blue lights flashing. It was Jean Chrétien, the Canadian prime minister, and a trade delegation from Ottawa and the provinces. Kohl, Mitterrand, Major, Balladur, Bentsen, Brown, Christopher—visiting political leaders from the most advanced economies, statesmen seeking contracts for home companies and access to China's explosive market, have become a commonplace.

As usual, McDonald's was already there, selling burgers to consumers. From Kuala Lumpur to Moscow, the company acts like an advanced scout for the global revolution, somehow able to detect the emergence of disposable incomes before other firms see it. Chinese buy their winter cabbages and also fast food. McDonald's measures its market potential with numbers like these: In the United States, there is a McDonald's restaurant for every 29,000 Americans. In China, despite rapid expansion, there is one McDonald's for every 40 million Chinese.

In Indonesia, four Korean businessmen, perhaps managers or salesmen in the garment industry, were dining at a Jakarta restaurant and indulging in a self-important routine. Each of them held a cellular telephone and made periodic phone calls while they ate and continued to talk with one another.

Mobile phones are a nearly universal artifact of revolution. The diversity of the world's peoples is converging in this common experience: the delight of encountering new inventions, magical gadgets or electronic machines that seem smarter than people. Traveling in Berlin, I made a telephone call to Warsaw by dialing AT&T Direct, which would automatically bill my home in Washington, D.C. Before the operator disappeared, I asked where she was located. "Richmond, Virginia." How does this work? She laughed uncertainly. "It's amazing, isn't it?" she said. The operator explained the technology, sort of, but the truth is that neither of us had a need to understand how it works. It just works.

In Stuttgart, Germany, a local leader of the metalworkers union, Alois Süss, described the oppressive power of multinational corporations and the new pressures imposed on German workers, but his talk kept drifting back to another subject, his recent trip to Paris. Süss is the elected chairman of the workers council at a major communications-equipment factory formerly owned by ITT of the United States, now owned by Alcatel Alsthom of France. He was a small boy in Bavaria during World War II and now he has marched through the streets of Paris, arm in arm with Frenchmen. The metalworkers unions from both nations decided to mount a joint demonstration against their common adversary, Alcatel's corporate headquarters, and Alois Süss went to Paris to participate. "I never thought I would see that," he said several times, wonder in his voice.

In Tokyo, the Sony Corporation, an authentic symbol of Japan's manufacturing excellence, is on the verge of becoming an un-Japanese company. The human resources manager, Yasunori Kirihara, lamented the prospect but explained it as an inevitable consequence of global economic integration. At present, he said, Sony's employees are split roughly fifty-fifty between Japanese and foreigners. As Sony continues to relocate its factories elsewhere, from Southeast Asia to Mexico, the substantial majority of its workforce, about 60 percent, will soon be outside Japan.

A new Japanese word, *kudoka,* has been popularized in business and political circles to describe this phenomenon. *Kudoka,* I was told, did not exist in the language before the 1980s. Its meaning should be familiar to American industrial workers who have seen their manufacturing jobs disappear. In English, it means "hollowing out."

In Everett, Washington, just north of Seattle, workers on the assembly line for Boeing's new 777, the company's latest addition to its line of large-body aircraft, gossiped that they might be shut down by the earthquake in Kobe, Japan. The main body section of the "Triple Seven," as Boeing people call their new plane, is manufactured by Mitsubishi Heavy Industries, though its plant, as it turned out, was not damaged by the quake. The 777 is a brilliant expression of America's productive prowess in advanced technologies, but the aircraft is manufactured, piece by piece, in twelve different countries.

As these scattered glimpses suggest, the symptoms of upheaval can be found most anywhere, since people in distant places are now connected by powerful strands of the same marketplace. The convergence has no fixed center, no reliable boundaries or settled outcomes. As enterprise opens up new territories, the maps keep changing—changing so rapidly that it has already become commonplace to speak of "one world" markets for everything from cars to capital. The earth's diverse societies are being rearranged and united in complicated ways by global capitalism. The idea evokes benumbed resignation among many. The complexity of it overwhelms. The enormity makes people feel small and helpless.

The essence of this industrial revolution, like others before it, is that commerce and finance have leapt inventively beyond the existing order and existing consciousness of peoples and societies. The global system of trade and production is fast constructing a new functional reality for most everyone's life, a new order based upon its own dynamics and not confined by the traditional social understandings. People may wish to turn away from that fact, but there is essentially no place to hide, not if one lives in any of the industrialized nations.

The only option people really have is to catch up with the reality. The only way to escape a sense of helplessness is to confront this new world on its own terms and try to understand its larger implications. This book is intended to assist people in doing that—by taking the machine apart, breaking it down to its underlying mechanics and explaining how it really works. The actual system, as we shall see, does not conform to the economic theory it presumes to follow. Nor are people and nations actually powerless to influence its behavior, as conventional wisdom asserts. But people and nations may restore a sense of control over their own destinies only if they are willing to face the complexity, only by grasping the operating imperatives that drive the global system and the full scope of human consequences that it yields.

To make these matters visible, this book roams selectively around the world, both to savor the human variety and to illuminate the system's functional realities. The inquiry is organized into three distinct but interconnected realms—the industrial system of multinational production, the global market of finance capital and the altered social reality for both rich and poor. These first three chapters describe the context and scope in which all those activities are grounded, a framework that may be read as an introduction to "one world."

The present-day upheaval is fundamentally similar to the great industrial revolutions of the past, yet distinctive in its size and scope. At its outset the English industrial revolution launched in the late 1700s—steam power, steel, mechanized textile looms, the first railroads—involved a handful of cities and probably at most a few hundred thousand people. The great wave of industrial inventions in the latter nineteenth century—electrical generation, internal combustion engines, cars, telephones, radio, flight— also spawned globalization of industry, but engaged only a minor percentage of the world's population. The current revolution counts recruits in the billions.

The idea of nations converging into "one world" is not new, of course. Half a century ago, while World War II raged across several continents, it was an immensely popular theme among Americans. A conservative corporate lawyer named Wendell L. Willkie, the Republican presidential nominee defeated by Franklin D. Roosevelt in 1940, wrote a best-selling book with that title. At FDR's behest, Willkie undertook a flying tour of various Allied war fronts around the globe. His dramatic account of that trip, published in early 1943, connected with America's growing self-confidence, generated by the wartime mobilization, and beckoned Americans to embrace a new internationalist outlook.

"The world has become small and completely interdependent," Willkie reported. He was presciently optimistic about the postwar future, generously progressive in his view of humanity. Once the war was won, Willkie predicted, nations would work together to construct a new, more stable and prosperous international economic system. The "race imperialism" of European colonialism, as well as America's own racial caste system, would be confronted. Above all, America would lead.

Willkie's book became an important marker in American politics, signaling a generational shift away from the isolationism and nativist hostilities that had traditionally shuttered America's perspective toward the larger world. Fifty years later his prophecy is remembered mainly by right-wingers who continue to rant occasionally about "one worlders" subverting American sovereignty.[3]

The "one world" Willkie envisioned did emerge after World War II, more or less as he predicted, energetic and abundant, with America at the vital center (though also burdened by the costly Cold War conflict he did not foresee). It is Willkie's postwar world order that is now coming unhinged, eclipsed by a brave new vision for "global convergence" that is far more radical than anything he imagined.

"One world" now evokes a different, more ambivalent set of emotions among Americans, especially among those whose livelihoods are threatened by the implications. Unlike Willkie's world, the United States is not the foreordained center of this new one. America's basic superlatives endure— the richest, largest, most powerful market economy—but the essence of what is forming now is an economic system of interdependence designed to ignore the prerogatives of nations, even the most powerful ones.

In that spirit, this book is not about nations per se, not even my own, but about the terms of convergence. It is focused primarily on business and finance and the commercial imperatives driving them, on people trying to cope with the great social transformations visible across many societies. Governments and the usual policy debates come into the story only secondarily as politics also tries to deal with these great changes.

Grasping the meaning of this new order requires one to set aside reflexive national loyalties in order to see the system whole. I have tried at least to do that. Above all, I avoid the standard nationalist complaints (most often aimed at Japan) that preoccupy so many books about the global economy, especially books written by Americans.*

"Universality means taking a risk in order to go beyond the easy certainties provided us by our background, language, nationality, which so often shield us from the reality of others," Edward W. Said, the Palestinian-American scholar, has written. "It also means looking for and trying to uphold a single standard for human behavior when it comes to such matters as foreign and social policy."[4]

Willkie's title is borrowed for the obvious sense of historical irony, but

---

* While I have tried to stand outside national identity and see things in a spirit of universality, I do not imagine for a moment that I succeeded fully. Like most people, I am bound by culture and personal experience, by limitations of language and native biases, to one nation. Thus, the reporting in this book relies disproportionately on American commerce and political economy since those realms are most familiar and accessible to me. Further, anyone familiar with my previous work knows of my fervent attachment to America and its possibilities, pro patria convictions I did not entirely suppress in this book.

also with admiration for his humane optimism. Like Willkie, I traveled the world to capture instructive glimpses of the action—to a dozen or so "fronts" in Asia, Europe and North America. My arbitrary itinerary inevitably left out much more than it included, such as the very poorest nations on the periphery that are not yet engaged by the revolutionary dynamics. Each time I returned home I was exhilarated—and also overwhelmed—by contradictory feelings of wonder and dread.

The usual question—is America winning or losing?—can be disposed of quickly. The answer is yes. America is winning, and yes, it is losing. Some sectors of Americans are triumphant and other sectors are devastated, but not in equal measures. The same rough answer applies in differing degrees throughout most of the world, especially among the wealthiest nations—Germany, France or Britain, even Japan.

Books that nominate one country or another as "the winner" of global competition have a very short shelf life since these things change so rapidly. In 1992, a best-selling author heralded Europe, led by Germany, as the likely champion for its superior economic system; eighteen months later Europe and Germany were mired in gloomy forecasts from their own business leaders, complaining about their failure to keep up with American flexibility. Likewise, the United States has been written off and revived a number of times. Even Japan, so wealthy that many thought it had already won the race, is now experiencing its own tangible crisis of self-doubt.[5]

The obsession with nations in competition misses the point of what is happening: The global economy divides every society into new camps of conflicting economic interests. It undermines every nation's ability to maintain social cohesion. It mocks the assumption of shared political values that supposedly unite people in the nation-state.

That is the fundamental reason politics has become so muddled in the leading capitalist democracies. In recent years voters have turned on established parties and leaders, sometimes quite brutally, in the United States, Canada, Italy, France, Sweden and Japan, to name the most spectacular cases. Nor is there any ideological consistency to these voter rebellions. Socialists were tossed out in socialist Sweden, then restored to power a few years later. In a single election, the Conservative Party of Canada was reduced from governing majority to a remnant of two parliamentary seats. The business party that ruled Japan without interruption for four decades, the Liberal Democrats, was ousted by dissident reformers, then regained power in an unstable coalition of its own, this time led by a socialist.

Deeper political instability lies ahead for these societies because the global economy has put a different political question on the table: What exactly is the national interest in these new circumstances? No elected government in the richest countries, neither right nor left, has produced a definition that convinces its own electorate. Indeed, some important governments, clinging to the inherited postwar orthodoxy, are pursuing economic strategies that arguably do injury to majorities of their own citizens. This reflects not only the heavy hand of defunct theory, but also that insecure politicians do not know what else to do.

Political confusion in the dominant economies is set against a fundamental countervailing reality: For most people living in most parts of the world, the global economy began in 1492. In their history, the centuries of conquest and economic colonization were integral to the rise of industrial capitalism in Europe and North America, but the returns were never really shared with them. Books by Americans proclaiming "one world" may seem quite precious and self-centered to those people. For them, the global economy long ago consigned most regions of the world to lowly status as commodity producers—the hewers and haulers, the rubber tappers, tin miners and cane cutters. What William Faulkner said of the American South applies as well to those colonialized nations that used to be known as the Third World: the past is never dead, it is not even past.*

From the perspective of most of these countries, the present industrial revolution is a rare opening in history, a chance to get out from under. Some of them are succeeding, climbing rapidly in wealth and establishing at least a fragile basis for national self-sufficiency. Dozens of others are trying to do the same. All of them approach the present with deep historical skepticism, the memory of how many times their aspirations were thwarted by the leading economic powers, how many previous openings turned out to be illusory.

For now, some of the world's superlatives are on the march. The fastest elevator in the world is in Yokohama. The tallest building is in Kuala Lumpur. Or is it in Jakarta, as Indonesians claim? The largest exporter of semiconductor chips, air conditioners and videocassette recorders is Malaysia. Asian markets now count 33 million "affluent consumers" spread across ten countries—that is, people whose incomes of $30,000 or more place them above the American family median. By 2000, these Asian affluents are expected to number 50 million, a market still less rich than the United States but coming up smartly.[6]

When all the larger economic and political questions are exhausted, the heaviest legacy of this new "one world" may be the psychological blow to national arrogance. Americans reflexively think of themselves as without any real peers. Number One. In their own racialist ways so do the Japanese and the Germans. Tribal assumptions of inherited superiority are embedded in the cultures of the French and Chinese and Muslims, among many others. These folk illusions are now under vigorous assault, contradicted by the emerging economic reality.

* The global economy has a language problem: The old labels for categories of nations are confused or obsolete. "Third World," a condescending term coined for the Cold War, is now meaningless. Even the "West" is useless if it is meant to designate the advanced economies, since Japan is among them and booming Asia lies west of the United States, not east. We are reduced to cruder terms like rich and poor nations, advanced and primitive economies.

During my travels I experienced certain small epiphanies, intense moments of realization that are described in various places in this book: The amazement of watching a great modern industrial factory at work. The anguish of encountering exploited young people, peasant children turned into low-wage industrial workers, struggling to understand their own condition. The simple delight any tourist feels at glimpsing the weird variety of human life and also the underlying sameness.

The most powerful moments, however, were the recurring experience of witnessing poor people who dwell in marginal backwaters doing industrial work of the most advanced order. People of color, people who are black, yellow, red, brown, who exist in surroundings of primitive scarcity, are making complex things of world-class quality, mastering modern technologies that used to be confined to a select few. The tools of advanced civilization are being shared with other tribes. Multinational corporations, awesomely powerful and imperiously aloof, are the ironic vehicle for accomplishing this generous act of history.

The confident presumption that certain high-caliber work can be done only by certain people (mainly, it is assumed, by well-educated white people in a few chosen countries) is mistaken, and this book visits a few of the many places where the workers daily prove it wrong. Observing these scenes of industrial activity, I thought first of the explosive implications for the future of work and prosperity in the advanced economies, including America. The portents are stark and threatening. Yet the meaning also has to be understood in the broader sweep of human history. Watching former peasants making high-tech goods for the global market, I eventually reached a simpler, more nourishing understanding. Of course, I thought. People are capable, everywhere in the world.

Is it conceivable that commerce, pursuing narrow self-interested ends, might accomplish what idealistic politics has never been able to achieve— defeating stubborn ideas of racial superiority? I returned from my travels imagining it might someday be possible. Certainly, enormous conflicts lie ahead for the peoples of the world, political and economic collisions, possibly including the violence of wars between rival economies. Nevertheless, the process of globalization is visibly dismantling enduring stereotypes of race and culture, ancient assumptions of supremacy. In the progressive spirit of Wendell Willkie, this transformation will someday be understood as the most radical dimension of the revolution.

The raw energies of the global system, its power of excitement, can be glimpsed in the daily headlines about important business deals. Anheuser-Busch buys a stake in Kirin, Japan's biggest brewery, also a 5 percent share of China's Tsingtao, then acquires 10 percent of Antarctica, the leading beer of Brazil. Siemens of Germany forms a partnership with Skoda Plzen to manufacture steam turbines in the Czech Republic. Volvo opens an assembly line near Xian, China, with Chinese machinists making Swedish tour buses. Taiwan Aerospace Corporation considers buying a major stake in a troubled American company, McDonnell Douglas, then decides to dicker instead with another weakening firm, British Aerospace. Switzerland's Roche bids $5.3 billion for the U.S. pharmaceutical Syntex, while Smith-Kline Beecham buys another American company for $2.3 billion. NEC, the Japanese electronics giant, agrees to collaborate with Samsung, the Korean multinational, to make DRAM memory chips, probably at a plant in Portugal, to supply the $5 billion European market.

The problem, of course, is that the stories are too diverse and plentiful to make the motivating principles very clear. As the announcements of new ventures accumulate in breathtaking number, the effect is like the blur of a major blizzard. IBM announces quarterly losses of $8 billion and plans to cut 35,000 jobs. Bausch & Lomb begins making contact lenses and Ray-Ban sunglasses in India. Colgate-Palmolive opens a toothbrush factory in Colombia. AT&T forms an alliance with the national telephone companies of Sweden, Switzerland and the Netherlands; its American rival MCI pairs off with British Telecommunications.

Coca-Cola returns to Vietnam, this time without the U.S. military forces. Toyota picks Kentucky to make automobiles, BMW picks South Carolina, Mercedes picks Alabama. Ford and General Motors hope the Chinese government will pick them to make cars in China.[7]

John F. Welch Jr., CEO of General Electric and widely admired for hardheaded corporate strategies, has warned fellow executives not to be lulled by self-congratulations or press clippings about how American companies have regained an edge over foreign competitors. "Things are going to get tougher," he predicted in mid-1994. "The shakeouts will be more brutal. The pace of change more rapid." What lies ahead, Welch said, is "a hurricane."[8]

The accumulating evidence supports this warning. After two decades of dramatic changes the revolutionary pressures are not abating or leveling off into familiar patterns. The dynamics appear to be accelerating. What is the nature of the storm upon us? A new structure of power is gradually emerging in the world, forcing great changes everywhere it asserts itself. The broad dimensions are defined by a baseline of unsettling facts:

1. During the last generation the world's 500 largest multinational corporations have grown sevenfold in sales. Yet the worldwide employment of these global firms has remained virtually flat since the early 1970s, hovering around 26 million people. The major multinationals grew in sales from $721 billion in 1971 to $5.2 trillion in 1991, claiming a steadily growing share of commerce (one third of all manufacturing exports, three fourths of commodity trade, four fifths of the trade in technology and management services). Yet the human labor required for each unit of their output is diminished dramatically.

While this galaxy of major global firms grew in size, its center of gravity also shifted. America's flagship companies, from du Pont and IBM to GE and General Motors, were the modern progenitors of globalized manufacturing after World War II, but the United States has lost its dominance. In 1971, 280 of the largest 500 multinationals were American-based. By 1991, the United States had only 157 on the list.

Europe's largest companies surpassed America's in number and sales volume during the last half of the 1980s. By 1991, Europe had 168 of the largest 500. Japan, meanwhile, had risen in twenty years from 53 to 119. A few important multinational corporations have even emerged in countries that were once very poor—Korea, Taiwan, even Thailand. The corporate girth of nations is gradually dispersing, leveling out.[9]

2. The basic mechanism of globalization—companies investing capital in foreign countries, buying existing assets or building new factories—has accelerated explosively during the last fifteen years. The volume of foreign direct investment nearly quadrupled during the 1980s, reaching $2 trillion in the 1990s. The largest portion of that capital flow, about 25 percent, actually went into the United States during the 1980s, reversing the historic pattern. The United States became a debtor nation and sold off domestic assets to foreign investors; Japanese auto companies, among others, prudently located assembly plants in the States.[10]

Direct investing across borders cooled off for several years amid the major recessions of the early 1990s, but as it resumed the heaviest flows of capital were aimed in a different direction—building new production in the so-called emerging markets of Asia and selected nations in Latin America and Eastern Europe. Indeed, another historic relationship seemed broken: the utter dependence of poor nations on the prosperous. This time around, while the advanced economies remained stagnant or mired in recession, a league of poorer economies was enjoying a spectacular investment boom.

The growth of transnational corporate investments, the steady dispersal of production elements across many nations, has nearly obliterated the traditional understanding of trade. Though many of them know better, economists and politicians continue to portray the global trading system in terms that the public can understand—that is, as a collection of nations buying and selling things to each other. However, as the volume of world trade has grown, the traditional role of national markets is increasingly eclipsed by an alternative system: trade generated within the multinational companies themselves as they export and import among their own foreign-based subsidiaries.

According to one scholarly estimate, more than 40 percent of U.S. exports and nearly 50 percent of its imports are actually goods that travel not in the open marketplace, but through these intrafirm channels. A U.S. computer company ships design components to its assembly plant in Malaysia, then distributes the finished hardware back to the United States and to other buyers in Asia and Europe. A typical Japanese plant located in America "imports" most of its components from its parent corporation and allied suppliers, then "exports" products back to the parent in Japan or sister affiliates in other countries.[11]

All of this intrafirm traffic is counted in the national trade statistics, but national identities are increasingly irrelevant to the buyers and sellers. Nation-to-nation trade flows are driven more and more by the proprietary strategies of the multinational corporations organizing their own diversified production, less and less by traditional concepts of comparative advantage among nations or the economic policies of home governments.

The shifting content of trade has led many leading governments, including the one in Washington, to embrace a strategy that might confound some citizens (if it were explained to them clearly) because it seems to offend nationalist intuition. The governments are actively promoting the dispersal of capital investment and production to foreign locations on the assumption that this will lead to increased exports for home-based production (and more jobs for domestic workers). As the flagship multinationals make more things overseas, they will presumably ship more homemade goods to their overseas affiliates. That, anyway, is the logic governments embrace.

3. Finance capital—the trading of stocks, bonds, currencies and more exotic forms of financial paper—has accelerated its movements around the world at an astonishing pace. International bank loans more than quadrupled from 1980 to 1991, reaching $3.6 trillion. Global bond financing expanded likewise. Cross-border stockholdings in the so-called Triad—Europe, Japan and the United States—nearly doubled during a few years in the late 1980s.

The global exchange markets in national currencies—swapping dollars for yen or deutschemarks for francs or scores of other such trades—are moving faster still. Foreign-exchange trading totaled more than $1.2 trillion a day by the early 1990s, compared to only $640 billion a day as recently as 1989. Since financial traders usually move in and out of different currencies in order to buy or sell a nation's stocks or bonds, this furious pace of currency exchange reflects the magnifying presence of borderless finance.

The entire global volume of publicly traded financial assets (about $24 trillion) turns over every twenty-four days. The International Monetary Fund, which attempts to monitor such matters, claims that this quickening pace is unexceptional since, it points out, the trading in U.S. government bonds is even faster. The entire traded volume of U.S. Treasury debt ($2.6 trillion) turns over every eight days.[12]

Despite the staggering volume the financial trading across borders is mostly transacted by a very small community: the world's largest thirty to fifty banks and a handful of major brokerages that do the actual trades in behalf of investor clients—wealthy individuals and the various pools of private capital, smaller banks and brokerages, pension funds, mutual funds and so on—as well as the banks' own portfolios.

As the volume has swelled, the global financial markets have become much more powerful—and much more erratic. Sentiment and prices can shift suddenly and sharply, cascading losses across innocent bystanders like the multinational corporations that depend on predictable currency values for their cross-border trade or national governments that watch helplessly as global finance raises their domestic interest rates or devalues their currencies. "Crisis" has become an overworked word. Market economists speak more politely of "disturbances." These are the decisive breaks in prices that occur when global investors suddenly lose confidence in one investment sector or an entire country and abruptly shift huge amounts of capital elsewhere, quick as the electronic impulses of modern banking.

The results are harrowing for national pride. The United Kingdom, Italy, Mexico, Malaysia, Sweden and Spain, even the twelve-nation European Community and the United States, have all experienced the shock of going up against the "global speculators" to defend their currencies and economies. National governments and their central banks discover from these episodes that private finance capital, once it is in motion collectively, can sometimes veto the counterweight of governments, even when the leading governments act in concert. During the first half of the 1990s such humbling "disturbances" occurred with greater frequency and growing consequence.

To make sense out of these bewildering facts, it helps to think of the global system in cruder terms, as a galaxy of four broad, competing power blocs—each losing or gaining influence over events. The biggest, most obvious loser in these terms is labor, both the organized union workers and wage earners in general. Wages are both rising and falling around the world, but workers at both ends of the global economy have lost substantial control over their labor markets and the terms of employment. "Now capital has wings," as New York financier Robert A. Johnson explained succinctly. "Capital can deal with twenty labor markets at once and pick and choose among them. Labor is fixed in one place. So power has shifted."

National governments, likewise, have lost ground on the whole, partly because many have retreated from trying to exercise their power over commerce and finance, implicitly ceding to the revolutionary spirit. In the advanced economies, most governments have become mere salesmen, promoting the fortunes of their own multinationals in the hope that this will provide a core prosperity that keeps everyone afloat. The clearest evidence that this strategy is not working is the condition of labor markets in the wealthiest nations: either mass unemployment or declining real wages (nominal pay adjusted for inflation), and, in some cases, both of these deleterious effects.

The more subtle evidence of the dilemma of leading governments is their deteriorating fiscal condition: most are threatened by rising, seemingly permanent budget deficits and accumulating debt. The swollen fiscal deficits of the United States are the largest in size, but far from the worst in relative

terms. The general fiscal crisis of rich nations is driven by the same fundamental—disappointing economic growth that, year after year, fails to generate the tax revenues needed to keep up with the public obligations
established in more prosperous times. The modern welfare state, the social
protections that rich nations enacted to ameliorate the harsh inequalities of
industrial capitalism, is now in peril. Some would say it is already obsolete.

Ironically, the governments of developing countries, at least the most
successful ones, are less enthralled by the global system's theory and rhetoric
and more willing to impose their own terms on capital and trade. Given
their own historical memory, poor countries attempt, if they can, to bargain
within the system—making nationalistic trade-offs with global firms and
investors. Some succeed; many are overwhelmed.

The multinational corporations are, collectively, the muscle and brains
of this new system, the engineers who are designing the brilliant networks
of new relationships. It is their success at globalization that has inevitably
weakened labor and degraded the control of governments. Some smart
organizations are even reconfiguring themselves into what business futurists
have dubbed "the virtual corporation," a quick-witted company so dispersed that it resembles the ganglia of a nervous system, a brain attached to
many distant nodes but without much bodily substance at the center.[13]

Despite their supple strengths the great multinationals are, one by one,
insecure themselves. Even the most muscular industrial giants are quite
vulnerable if they fail to adapt to the imperatives of reducing costs and
improving rates of return. Critics who focus on the awesome size and
sprawl of the global corporations find this point difficult to accept, but
the executives of Volkswagen, GM, Volvo, IBM, Eastman Kodak and Pan
American Airlines can attest to it. Those well-known firms, among many
others, have experienced the harsh consequences of straying from the path
of revolution. Their stocks were hammered, their managements ousted, tens
of thousands of employees discarded. Behind corporate facades, the anxiety
is genuine.

The Robespierre of this revolution is finance capital. Its principles are
transparent and pure: maximizing the return on capital without regard
to national identity or political and social consequences. Global finance
collectively acts as the disinterested enforcer of these imperatives, like a
Committee of Public Safety presiding over the Terror (though historians
would note that Robespierre's revolutionaries pursued the opposite objective of reducing the great inequalities of wealth).

Financial investors monitor and punish corporations or whole industrial sectors if their returns weaken. Finance disciplines governments or even
entire regions of the globe if those places appear to be creating impediments
to profitable enterprise or unpleasant surprises for capital. If this sounds
dictatorial, the global financiers also adhere to their own rough version of
egalitarian values: they will turn on anyone, even their own home country's
industry and government, if the defense of free capital seems to require it.

As the Jacobins learned during the French Revolution, it is the most zealous, principled advocates of new values who are ultimately most at risk in a revolutionary environment. Master financiers seem to appreciate this, too. George Soros, the Hungarian-American billionaire who became fabulously wealthy by grasping the new principles of global investing before others, often emphasizes his own fallibility. In early 1994, when Soros got things wrong, he lost $600 million during two days of brisk disturbance in global bond markets. When Robespierre got things wrong, he was guillotined before a cheering mob in the Place de la Révolution.

In other words, even the most powerful players—titans of finance or the multinationals regularly demonized in popular lore—are themselves dwarfed by the system and subject to its harsh, overwhelming consequences. To describe the power structure of the global system does not imply that anyone is in charge of the revolution. The revolution runs itself. This point is critical to understanding its anarchic energies and oblivious disregard for parochial victims or, for that matter, the seeming impotence of enterprises themselves to control things. This revolution, as the next chapter explores, is following historical patterns of behavior that industrial capitalism has reiterated across the centuries—an explosive cycle of renewal, migration and destruction that is typically ignited by human invention.

Two

The New Against the Old

ECONOMIC REVOLUTION always originates with the invention of a new power source—a machine that can do the work previously done by human toil but cheaper, faster, more effectively. In those terms, the origins of this revolution can be dated, quite confidently, as the autumn of 1958 and early winter of 1959.

Within a few months of each other, working independently, two Americans, Jack Kilby at Texas Instruments and Robert Noyce at Fairchild Semiconductor, each arrived at the same breakthrough: the silicon chip. Kilby and Noyce conceptualized the device that inscribes electronic circuitry in a tiny space much too small to see—a device that has become exponentially smaller as technology continues to perfect their idea.

This new integrated circuit was the inventive watershed because it literally liberated computers from their bulky limitations of size and cost, and allowed them to become ubiquitous in modern life. The chip led eventually to fabulous powers of memory and complex calculation, to the miniaturization and precision of microprocessing—powers that now routinely control everything from a car window to financial spreadsheets to industrial assembly lines.

The inventions are new and amazing, but the consequences of upheaval are not. In fact, many present aspects of change that seem shocking and unprecedented are actually following the long-established patterns of capitalism. Understanding this historical context will be comforting for some and dispiriting to others, but it is essential in order to appreciate how little these deeply driven forces depend upon the nationalist virtues claimed by different societies or the particular decisions of mere governments.

The arrival of radical inventions typically spawns two other fundamental dimensions of industrial revolution. An important new technology encourages the migration of capital. Production moves to new locations, undeveloped territories where it will be easier (and cheaper) for enterprises to build the new production systems, free of the old restraints like established laws and social commitments, including taxes and wages.

Thus, second, business and finance mobilize to play an aggressive form of politics. Their first great political goal is escape—escape from the past. Commerce either persuades a society to relax its laws and social obligations or it exits to another society. As production moves elsewhere, a second great political task emerges: persuading the developing territories themselves to adopt new rules, laws to protect the free flow of commerce and, above all, to protect the property rights of capital.

Technology, geography, politics. These same patterns have played out repeatedly during the previous episodes of industrial upheaval, across five or six centuries of capitalism. This time, what is obvious to foreign observers is not so well understood by many Americans: the revolutionary order was born in the United States and has been promoted by it ever since.

Neither Noyce nor Kilby ever won the celebrity of an Edison or Bell or Ford, despite the great transformations their invention has launched. T. R. Reid speculated in *The Chip*, his narrative account of their inventive breakthrough, that a tiny semiconductor chip that does the work of the human brain is perhaps more threatening to people than a lightbulb or telephone or automobile that augments human physical strengths.[1]

The essential difference of the new information technology—its capacity to amplify human intellect rather than muscle—is integral to the social and economic consequences that are unfolding. Among other things, computers have reversed the logic of mass-production work systems, the classic assembly line devised by people like Henry Ford in the preceding era of industrial breakthroughs. Ford's assembly-line system, by standardizing manufacturing into mechanical repetitions, had the effect of displacing the individualistic skills of the craftsmen, the mechanics and artisans who made things by hand. "Before Henry Ford, you had to be an engineer to make an automobile," economist Lawrence Summers observed.

Mass assembly imposed dehumanizing clockwork routines, treating workers like moving parts in a larger machine, but it was also strangely egalitarian: the unskilled and ill educated could enter, too, to work at jobs in which they focused on narrow, regularized functions in a complex process they themselves did not have to understand or manage. In many sectors, this efficient process added high value to the manufactured product, so the production could support higher wages. Huge mills and centralized factories, in any case, provided a convenient setting for workers trying to organize themselves to demand a larger share of the returns.

In those terms, the new technology is more individualistic and anti-egalitarian: it restores a premium for the higher technical skills held by the best-educated people, it demands more sophistication and flexibility, even from many routine jobs. At least in theory, decision-making can be decentralized in reformed workplaces and production jobs can be scattered across many distant places, even at a computer terminal in one's home.

Yet, paradoxically, the easy flow of reliable information also strengthens the hand of the managers at the very top. Thanks to reliable data collected by computerization, a CEO and his team can skip over the company's middle-rung bureaucracy and directly command operations from afar, including factories and markets dispersed around the world. The new work system tells workers to get smarter and promises to empower them with more authority on the shop floor. Yet it also creates a steeper pyramid between them and the commanding heights.

None of this was obvious in the fall of 1958 (though some astute social thinkers were already warning that "automation" would someday lead to a crisis of mass unemployment). Like previous industrial transformations, this one has taken nearly two generations to reach full acceleration. The reason the pace of change proceeds slowly at first is partly that it waits upon the follow-on inventions, technological elaborations based on the new power source. These continue to appear robustly each year.

Another delay is the trial and error of business enterprises figuring out what these new technologies can do. Some major American companies wasted billions buying new computers in the 1980s before they realized that they were missing the point. The managerial challenge was not to put a computer on everyone's desk. It was to deploy computers so as to eliminate many of the desks.

But the heaviest drag on the rise of new technologies is the weight of what is. The routines of the status quo, the inertia of existing factories, social arrangements and political commitments—all these stand in the way of new processes and yield but slowly. This reality leads to the second great source of upheaval: the migration of capital. Sooner or later, ambitious business minds realize that rather than trying to reform the old, it is much easier to move somewhere else and begin anew.

The modern industrial world's first great center for iron- and steel-making was located in several villages of South Wales. Starting in the late 1700s, the Welsh industry expanded to a production peak in 1830 and then fell back, surpassed by the larger mills of England in places like Sheffield and Leeds. A generation or so later, steel moved again, this time to the United States, where, after the Civil War, Pittsburgh emerged as the vital center of the world's steel production. The younger steel industries rising in America and Germany borrowed the technology first devised by an Englishman, Henry Bessemer, and perfected its application. By World War I, British steelmaking was eclipsed by both.

Steel moved again after the devastations of World War II. This time Japan borrowed some American ideas and built new, more efficient integrated rolling mills that by the 1970s were able to outproduce and underprice Pittsburgh. South Korea followed along the same path, and its massive works at Pohang became the largest steel mill in the non-Communist world.

The center of steelmaking may be on the move again. The Shanghai No. 5 steelworks is said to be as efficient as the most advanced mills in the world and is one of the largest, able to turn out eight million tons a year.

With help from German engineering, China's steel output has been expanding rapidly, growing by 50 percent in a recent five-year period. The world leader, Japan, is steadily declining in size. South Wales, meanwhile, has settled into marginal status as an outpost for low-wage, light-assembly factories, most of them owned by foreign companies.

These patterns of industrial migration, based on borrowed technology and investments in what the modern planners call "greenfield" production sites, are as old as capitalism. The great French historian Fernand Braudel, author of an epic three-volume history of capitalism, described how the productive dominance moved around Europe in the centuries before it migrated to the United States.

Venice was the center in 1380, until a gigantic shift in 1500 that favored Antwerp. Economic dominance then returned briefly to the Mediterranean around 1560, this time to Genoa. When the northern countries of Europe gained permanent ascendancy, Amsterdam became the new capital of commerce and held it for nearly two centuries. By 1815, invigorated by the English industrial revolution, the center moved to London. In 1929, when Britain's fading hegemony was conclusively destroyed by the great crash, the capital of capitalism moved decisively to New York.[2]

Has it already moved again, this time to Tokyo? The lopsided accumulation of the 1980s, when Japan became very wealthy and the United States became a debtor nation and the dollar lost its undisputed primacy as an international currency, certainly indicates the drift of events. But there is not as yet a settled answer to the question. For the moment, global capitalism is pulled by numerous competing centers—New York, Tokyo, Frankfurt, London, Hong Kong and some others—converging with each other and at the same time contesting for dominance. If China succeeds in its grandest ambitions, one can imagine that many years from now the capital might find its next home not in Tokyo or Hong Kong, but in Shanghai.

To the distress of mature economies, the energetic boomers who borrow their ideas and improve upon them often neglect to follow the established rules of capitalism, especially patent and copyright laws. Along the sidewalks of Beijing and Shanghai and in other cities throughout Asia, the best recordings of American pop culture are on sale cheap, compact discs mass-produced in knockoff factories. In the central market stalls of Kuala Lumpur, I bought Rolexes by the fistful, only $6 or $7 apiece. "Genuine copy," the teenage peddler assured me with a smile. The fake watches seemed to work okay except the "gold finish" will turn green after a year or two.

The periphery borrows from the center and makes cheap copies. This widespread piracy not only ignites the outrage of established businesses and governments, but it is also a very old trait of migrating capitalism. Stolen technology and stolen markets were the foundation of America's earliest industry.

Braudel described how northern European merchants in the sixteenth century aggressively ripped off the superior craftsmanship of the Italians: "They flooded the area with clever imitations of the excellent southern textiles and even marked them with the universally reputed Venetian seals in order to sell them under that 'label' on the usual Venetian markets. As a result, Mediterranean industry lost both its clientele and its reputation. Imagine what would happen if, over a period of 20, 30 or 40 years, new nations were regularly able to undercut the foreign—and even the domestic —markets of the United States by selling their products under the label 'Made in U.S.A.' "

Dynamic capitalism has its unforgiving aspects: the new become enemy of the old, the upstart offspring devour their parents. Americans recall how Japanese consumer electronics triumphed over the established U.S. companies that had originated most of the products. Swedes remember when their shipbuilding industry was second in the world until Japan and Korea came along and wiped it out.

The emergence of new economic rivals resembles a kind of inverted food chain in which the little fish try to eat the big fish and sometimes succeed. Multinational firms both take advantage of this play and are sometimes victimized by it. The big-fish nations, having forgotten how they got big themselves, complain bitterly about the unfairness. Poorer nations tend to see their success as the long-deferred flowering of economic justice.

Actually, the United States, playing the generous role that Wendell Willkie had envisioned for it, had a lot to do with stimulating the rise of East Asian economies, starting with Japan. In the early tumult of the Cold War, the U.S. military provided billions in procurement contracts, creating the aggregate demand needed to launch infant industries in Japan, Korea, Taiwan and Thailand. More important, America's superb system of higher education was opened to the aspiring engineers and scientists of these countries as well as to many of their future political leaders. As more than one Asian confided to me in my travels, the "Asian miracle" got its start in the classrooms at MIT, Stanford and Berkeley.

When capitalism migrates in this brutal way, social theorists follow along and develop cultural explanations for why it has happened. Four centuries ago, the rise of industrial power in northern Europe was attributed to the Protestant work ethic, the moral rigor and frugality of Lutherans and Calvinists who supposedly loved money and hard work more than did the Catholic cultures of the Mediterranean. The industrial hegemony of England, and later the United States, was sometimes explained as a Darwinian triumph of the Anglo-Saxon character.

Now that commerce is flourishing in Asia, some scholars are discovering unique traits in the cultures of Confucianism, Buddhism and Islam to explain why certain Asian nations outperform spoiled, spendthrift places like the United States or Germany. All that this new migration really establishes is that the seeds of capitalist development—adventurous minds, acquisitive desires—can be found among people almost everywhere.

A great shift of productive wealth is under way, reflected in the extraordinary growth rates of some developing nations. Korea and Taiwan follow Japan up the ladder, then attention shifts to Indonesia, Chile, Malaysia, Thailand or Turkey. Who's next? Maybe Vietnam and Myanmar, maybe Bangladesh. As multinationals survey the world, China, India and Brazil are seen as the main contenders racing to become the world's next major manufacturing economy. Mexico was also on the list until its financial economy abruptly collapsed in early 1995.

The heady prospects for these new producing nations are real in the long term, but can also be exaggerated. The stunning statistics from emerging markets have produced some fanciful projections that obscure the fundamental realities of relative wealth and poverty in the world. China's economy, for instance, has been growing annually by double-digit percentages, but it starts from a very weak base—per capita income of $490 compared with $24,750 in the United States.

By extrapolating from the relative purchasing power of China's 1.2 billion citizens, some economists have excitedly proclaimed that China is actually the third or fourth largest economy in the world and can even catch the United States in ten to fifteen years. Measured in hard currency, the only measure that matters in global commerce, this claim is nonsense. In American dollars, China's Gross National Product in 1993 was about $580 billion —roughly equal to New York State's, considerably smaller than California's.[3]

The developing nations (never mind the many more that remain stagnant) would point out further that the expanding global system still seems to be rewarding the same old folks in the same economic centers. As global trade expanded vigorously through the 1980s, the most advanced countries substantially increased their share of the total exports from 63 to 72 percent between 1980 and 1991, while most regions suffered shrinkage in exports. Among all the other nations, only Asia claimed a larger share, growing from 9 to 15 percent.[4]

Anyway, economic history never proceeds neatly like the trend lines on an economist's graph. It encounters crisis—booms and crashes, surpluses and scarcities. It also confronts constantly the troublesome interferences from politics. That is why revolutionary capital, empowered by new inventions and pursuing geographic dispersal, must also struggle to get free of what it considers outmoded legal restraints imposed by governments.

The Grand Cayman Islands, population 30,000, is the fifth largest nation in the world in terms of booking bank loans. The Netherlands Antilles is a leading supplier of capital to the United States and legal home for some of the world's wealthiest investors, including George Soros's Quantum Fund. Hong Kong banks hold $500 billion in foreign assets, yet this British crown colony refuses to reveal its balance-of-payments data to the International Monetary Fund.

As the IMF admits, its own nation-by-nation reports on international capital flows are seriously flawed because the six largest offshore banking centers as well as Hong Kong will not provide an honest accounting of their banking activities. Money flows out of those islands, but the auditors cannot figure out where all the money flowed in from. "Choke points in the world's financial system," the IMF called them.[5]

Big money hides itself in the global economy. Respectable capital mingles alongside dirty money from illegal enterprise (drugs, gambling, illicit arms sales) because the offshore banking centers allow both to hide from the same things: national taxation and the surveillance of government regulators. Major governments, including the United States, are not likely to help the IMF get these financial entrepôts to open up their books since major governments actively encouraged the rise of offshore banking as a convenience for global companies and investors.

Tax havens are merely a flagrant example of a much larger and exceedingly complicated political agenda—the politics of escape. Transnational commerce, either to defend against price competition or to maximize the potential returns of globalization, has aggressively campaigned over three or four decades to free itself from various social controls imposed by home governments. These political contests, commonly described as deregulation, continue, and the issues generate great controversy across virtually every sector of public policy, from environmental protection to wage-and-hour laws, from food-safety regulation to interest-rate controls and banking codes.

The most important breakthrough, by far, was in an obscure realm of high finance that is utterly unfamiliar to most citizens and, for that matter, to most politicians: the decontrol of capital movement itself. Thirty years ago every major economy and many minor ones regulated both the inflows and outflows of capital at their borders, often through tax measures on the currency-exchange transactions. One by one, nations surrendered this power, sometimes in the midst of a financial crisis, sometimes because it offered obvious advantage to domestic interests.

The United States, originally the main source of multinational expansion and the largest exporter of capital, has been the leading advocate for reform, pushing other countries to deregulate their financial markets. In the 1980s, when Germany and France finally abandoned capital controls and even insular Japan began opening its financial system to foreigners, the process was largely complete: capital is free to cross and recross the major borders (though not without various strategic restrictions). This political retreat helps explain why the movement of global finance has accelerated so dramatically in recent years.

The politics of deregulation does not usually involve a straightforward policy debate on the pros and cons, but is instead driven by opening wedges in the marketplace. The first nation that relaxes its rules, whether for banking controls or labor law, can create a temporary price advantage for local enterprises and thereby increase the pressure on other governments to do the same. Once the Netherlands and Britain established tax havens for capital, American bankers demanded similar arrangements for themselves and U.S. bank regulators claimed they had no choice but to yield.

For obvious reasons, business interests do not talk about escaping from the law (it sounds unpatriotic). Instead, they promote the goal of greater efficiency—a "harmonization" of national laws that will remove barriers and thus encourage greater trade. Harmonization cuts in different directions. Bayer, the German pharmaceutical firm, is moving its biotechnology research to the United States because U.S. regulation of biotech is friendlier than Germany's. American agriculture complains that Europe's ban on growth hormones in cattle is really a subterfuge to keep out American beef. In one area after another, the harmonization of regulatory standards usually pulls the law downward in a search for the lowest common denominator.*

The most alarming aspect of how globalization degrades law is in the conditions for work. The new information technology has been popularized as the dawn of a "postindustrial age," but that blithe vision ignores what is actually happening to industrial workers. In the primitive legal climate of poorer nations, industry has found it can revive the worst forms of nineteenth-century exploitation, abuses outlawed long ago in the advanced economies, including extreme physical dangers to workers and the use of children as expendable cheap labor. Indeed, the powerful strands of the global market also undermine legal protections for workers in some advanced economies. Sweatshops are back in the United States, visible from Los Angeles to New York and across the rural South.

Global business and finance seem to be astride a giant contradiction: while they campaign to dismantle legal restraints in one part of the world, the wealthiest societies, they are simultaneously urging poorer nations to adhere to the "rule of law." From their point of view, there is no contradiction. The laws they urge the underdeveloped nations to adopt are mainly ones that will protect private property from political interferences.

The simplest versions of this campaign involve persuading nations like China to observe international patents and copyrights or to create a court system that will enforce business contracts in an honest manner. Likewise, global capital demands that nations adopt a monetary system they can trust, one that does not manipulate money and credit for political purposes. The IMF and the World Bank help enforce this demand by withholding major loans from countries whose currencies do not seem reliable.

The more complex versions of global lawmaking are the major trade agreements among nations that promote what is called trade liberalization —getting nations to play by the same rules and not to interfere with free

---

* *The implications for national sovereignty, the ability of nations to determine social standards, were explored in "The Closet Dictator," a chapter in my book* Who Will Tell the People *(New York: Simon & Schuster, 1992).*

commerce. Trade law expresses the free-market dogma in concrete terms, but as we shall see it also has a fictitious quality. Major parties, from the major multinationals to leading governments, remain free to ignore the agreed-upon rules whenever it suits their interests. They regularly do so, even while proclaiming their dedication to the concept. The General Agreement on Tariffs and Trade (GATT), revised and renewed most recently in 1994, has the densely argued texture of biblical scholarship, but it is better understood as a theological treatise than as enforceable law.

In a revolutionary atmosphere, law always suffers. The bonds of social consent have been torn asunder and people find themselves free to make their own rules. That leads to another recurring feature of economic revolutions—corruption. Corrupt money deals between business and politics are epidemic around the world.

Something like five thousand Italian businessmen and politicians have been formally accused in the past few years. American politics has experienced so many money scandals that they now seem routine. Businessmen sometimes grumble, in a low voice, about the bribery extracted by political leaders in the poorest nations—the *guanxi* in China, the military partnerships required to do business in Indonesia—but this is not peculiar to the poor. Every major capital is regularly scandalized by more sophisticated versions of the same thing. Corruption is yet another, ironic form of convergence.

Something else happened—the end of an empire—that has compounded and quickened the revolutionary forces. As the impact of new technology, capital migration and political deregulation approached full acceleration, the collapse of Soviet communism occurred, perhaps hastened by those forces, and acted like a supercharger in the engine. The abrupt demise of Russia's vast, self-contained economic system greatly expanded the field of play for capitalism and further unsettled assumptions about the future.

Depending on how one counts them, another billion or two people have joined the ranks of potential workers in the free market of global industrial production. In terms of reducing costs, enterprises in Western Europe quickly recognized that they can move plants a few miles eastward and develop their own version of a *maquiladora* zone, the belt of low-wage factories that U.S. companies have established along the border in Mexico. Except Hungary, Poland, the Czech Republic and others are not lowly commodity producers, populated mainly by peasants, but experienced industrial societies with deep ranks of skillful workers and well-educated engineers.

Eventually, when the political turmoil of Eastern Europe's painful transition subsides, these new entrants should become competing producers, too, quite capable of adopting borrowed technology and matching world-class quality. The established firms are already compelled to ponder the possibilities. Will Russia's huge aircraft industry someday sell cheaper airplanes into the world market, preempting market shares of Boeing or Europe's Airbus consortium? Will cheap aluminum or steel, abundantly produced in states of the former Soviet Union, drive down world prices still further? More little fish have suddenly entered the pond, eager to go after big fish.

But the truly profound consequence is ideological: Marxism is utterly vanquished, if not yet entirely extinct, as an alternative economic system. Capitalism is triumphant. The ideological conflict first joined in the midnineteenth century in response to the rise of industrial capitalism, the deep argument that has preoccupied political imagination for 150 years, is ended.

The right has seized the revolutionary banner from the left. Political forces depicted through most of the twentieth century as the reactionaries —wealth holders and business enterprise—are now cast as the progressives, the reformers busily designing the future. The remnant left, from European social democrats to American labor-liberals, finds itself pinned down in rearguard battles, defending social structures built by the past.

"For years, socialists used to argue among ourselves about what kind of socialism we wanted," said Denis MacShane, British Labour MP and an official of the International Metalworkers Federation based in Geneva. "The choice of the left is no longer what kind of socialism it wants, but what kind of capitalism it can support."

As MacShane suggests, the most important arguments are now located on the right, among the competing strands of capitalism. The internationalist camp, led by multinational enterprise and establishment politics, promotes an unregulated supranational economic system, with open borders and reduced social obligations for capital. The nationalist strand of capitalism, articulated by such eccentric figures as Italy's Silvio Berlusconi or the populist billionaire from Texas, Ross Perot, or the Anglo-French tycoon James Goldsmith, wants to defend the home country first.

Some of the nationalist strands are frankly protectionist, some exude a reactionary temperament, but patriotic capitalists constitute an important storm warning for politicians in the advanced societies. Rising nationalist emotions range from the ill-focused anxieties of the American middle class to the darker, racist fantasies of neofascism that are gaining political voice across the nations of Europe and in some quarters of America.

Meanwhile, ascendant Asia offers several competing variations of its own. These include an authoritarian state capitalism that fosters economic prosperity by requiring citizens to forgo such decadent Western luxuries as free speech, free press, free assembly and other liberties.

The city-state of Singapore, a former colony whose per capita income ($19,300) now exceeds its former imperial master, Great Britain, is much admired in American business circles for its bootstrapping ascent, though it is neither a free market nor a free society. Singaporeans are comfortably provided for by a harshly autocratic government that administers paranoid control over press and politics and an effective welfare state that keeps everyone well housed and fed, but not free.[6]

The ideological confusion within capitalism poses a crucial question about the nature of global convergence: Will nations gravitate toward civil democracy something like America's or will they decide instead that success in the marketplace requires the productive efficiency of a regime more like Singapore's? The answer is not as self-evident as many Americans may suppose. Political freedom, like regulatory laws, may conceivably be harmonized downward, as competition quickens.

One of the striking qualities of the post–Cold War globalization is how easily business and government in the capitalist democracies have abandoned the values they putatively espoused for forty years during the struggle against communism—individual liberties and political legitimacy based on free elections. Concern for human rights, including freedom of assembly for workers wishing to speak for themselves, has been pushed aside by commercial opportunity. Multinationals plunge confidently into new markets, from Vietnam to China, where the governments routinely control and abuse their own citizens. In Singapore, some leading tribunes of the free press—the *Wall Street Journal, Newsweek, The Economist*—have published meek apologies to the ruling politicians who were offended by certain news items, rather than lose access to Singapore's burgeoning market.[7]

This retreat from principle begs a question: What was the Cold War really all about? Was it about securing freedom for enslaved peoples, as every patriot believed, or was it about securing free markets for capitalism, as Marxist critics often argued? The goal of human rights that leading governments once described as universal has been diluted by a new form of commercial relativism.

The triumphant dogma of free-market capitalism has an explanation for this inconsistency: industrial capitalism leads to democracy by a process of gradual evolution. This rationale, though not supported by history, provides a comforting refuge for policy thinkers in many leading nations, especially the United States, as they back away from the Cold War's moral principles. Once people begin to enjoy the rising incomes generated by industrial development, it is argued, they will begin to demand individual freedoms. In time, a newly prosperous middle class emerges with the influence to insist upon free expression and the equitable power sharing of a stable democracy. Thus, the wisest course is to do business with these repressive regimes and let things evolve, engaging them in the wealth-creating process that eventually will unravel their monopoly on power.

South Korea and Taiwan are frequently cited as proof that authoritarian regimes did indeed evolve into more open and democratic societies, though civil rebellions were required to force matters and neither has yet accepted a genuinely open economy and society. Promoters of the evolutionary thesis do not cite opposite examples—nations like Iran, Chile or Singapore—where rapid industrialization led to varieties of anti-democracy.

The conventional faith that democracy follows inevitably from industrial capitalism is simply wrong as historical fact—oblivious to the actual experience of industrial societies and the richly complicated social origins of political freedom. England, the United States, France and some other societies did evolve to systems of civil democracy and popular sovereignty, though the consolidation of individual rights was tortuously slow and imperfect, spread across centuries and regularly advanced only by political upheaval or violent conflict. England's Parliament was a self-perpetuating "committee of landlords" that for centuries protected propertied wealth against disenfranchised workers and peasants. Basic rights of citizenship in the American republic were secured for all men (though not for women) only in the crucible of civil war. France required political revolution.

In Germany and Japan, the rise of industrial capitalism did not lead to democracy, but to twentieth-century fascism. The repressive corporate states that emerged in those societies were able to supervise enormously productive economic systems without the bother of individual freedoms or electoral accountability. These fascist systems did not evolve into democracies or reform themselves voluntarily. They changed because they were destroyed by World War II.

In Russia and China, the turmoil of industrialism led eventually to a different political resolution for those vast, agrarian societies—state communism. The centralized bureaucratic regimes in China and Russia failed as modern economic systems and, in hindsight, were not so different from the feudal structures that had always ruled over those countries. A mandarin class continues to run things in China, only the mandarins are called Communists. They describe their newly reformed economic system as "market socialism with Chinese characteristics." [8]

The point of these historical citations is wariness. Facile theories about the inevitability of democracy skip over not just the visible facts of history, but also the individual dynamics of societies, the complicated interplay of culture and class structures that in some places leads to a politics based on individual freedom, in other places to the opposite.

The promise of a democratic evolution requires special skepticism if the theory is being promoted by economic players who actually benefit from the opposite conditions—the enterprises doing business in low-cost labor markets where the absence of democratic rights makes it much easier to suppress wages. A corporation that has made strategic investments based on the cost advantages offered by repressive societies can hardly be expected to advocate their abolition.

In fact, the most threatening political question facing the global system, as the next chapter explains, is whether it will restart history along the same bloody path created by previous industrial revolutions. The twentieth century's ideological conflict has been deflated by events, but the seeds of great new social and economic conflict are being planted now by the contradictions inherent in our "one world" revolution.

Three

The Ghost of Marx

MARXISM IS DEAD, the Communist system utterly discredited by human experience, but the ghost of Marx hovers over the global landscape, perhaps with a knowing smile. The gross conditions that inspired Karl Marx's original critique of capitalism in the nineteenth century are present and flourishing again. The world has reached not only the end of ideology, but also the beginnings of the next great conflict over the nature of capitalism.

The fundamental struggle, then as now, is between capital and labor. That struggle is always about control of the workplace and how the returns of the enterprise shall be divided. In both dimensions, capital is winning big again, claiming a steadily larger share of returns and asserting greater control over employees, just as it did in Marx's time. The inequalities of wealth and power that Marx decried are marching wider almost everywhere in the world. The imbalances of power lead today to similar excesses and social abuses.

"An army of Luddites is assembling around the world—55 or 60 million by official estimates but probably more like 75 million—the people whose lives have been destroyed by technological progress," the Canadian writer John Ralston Saul observed. "When the world went through this the last time in the early 1800's, the decision made then was that the technology was right and the Luddites were wrong, so these people had to be pushed aside, jailed or hung or whatever. What's the modern phrase? Reeducate them. But the Luddites weren't against progress. They were against their exclusion from progress. Had things been worked out differently back then, the world might have avoided the most violent century in history." [1]

The Luddites are history's symbol of violent resistance to technology—smashing the new machines to protect jobs—and of the futility of resisting progress. Luddites were not a rabble army of drifters, as many suppose, but highly skilled craftsmen in the English Midlands displaced by the steam engine and mechanization in the textile industry. Starting around 1810, unable to win concessions from mill owners, they raided factories at night, burning and smashing the looms, clandestine rebels who followed a mythical leader, Ned Lud. The revolt was crushed swiftly, its leaders hung or jailed. English industrialization rolled forward.

Where would the latter-day Luddites go if they wished to smash the new machines? In the information age, everything melts into electronic streams—workplaces, financial wealth, even behemoth corporations. In any case, the redundant workers accumulating across nearly every industrial sector, white collar as well as blue collar, are not mobilizing for violent counterattack. Most are quite passive, sullenly resigned, perhaps because many are cushioned in their fall by modern social protections that did not exist in 1810: severance pay, early pensions or unemployment benefits.

The true incendiaries of this age may be found among the gathering masses of younger people—Europeans call them "marginalized youth"— who have never had a real job and perhaps never will. Unlike the Luddites, they are detached from communities and rudderless, without skills or prospects, without any genuine stake in the social order except perhaps a welfare check.

"Powerlessness gets expressed in different ways," remarked Stephen J. Silvia, an American political scientist who studies European labor markets and social systems. "In America, it's drive-by shootings. In Germany, it's burning down the homes of foreigners."

In Britain, he might have added, it is violent rioting at soccer matches. In Italy and Mexico, kidnapping rich people. In Brazil, looting supermarkets. In Indonesia, job riots. These various disorders are all marginal events and unthreatening to the larger economic order, but they should be thought of as another warning signal. Governments treat them as police problems.

The accumulating social dislocations, as Saul and others have warned, reflect the same preconditions that ultimately deranged nations a century ago. The refusal to confront the human destruction and deal with it justly sowed the ground for the great ideological divisions of left and right. The rise of communism and its totalitarian twin, fascism. The recurring social disorders. Finally, eventually, the devastation of wars among nations.

"That was the basic result of our decision to choose unregulated technology and capital over human beings," Saul said. "The world finally gets to the end of that ideological conflict and what do we do? We start over again with the same decision."[2]

Opinion leaders in the advanced nations, especially in business circles, read the history of the last century quite differently, of course, as a seamless story of ascendant prosperity. Across the last century, they point out, modern invention and industrial expansion delivered fabulous abundance and unprecedented standards of living that were enjoyed by all classes of citizens. The present transformations will lead inevitably to the same happy outcome.

After all, in the late nineteenth century, America was still a nation of farmers and farm laborers. When their work disappeared almost completely in the technological revolution of agriculture, those displaced people streamed into other, more rewarding occupations in the new manufacturing industries. Now that technology is shrinking manufacturing work in a similar fashion and these jobs may virtually disappear in some nations, people can look forward again to greater abundance as new industries arise to employ them.

Peter F. Drucker, a favorite management guru of American business, is a leading apostle of this view. "The extreme social transformations of this century have caused hardly any stir," Drucker wrote. "They have proceeded with a minimum of friction, a minimum of upheavals. . . . Indeed, if this century proves one thing, it is the futility of politics. . . . [T]hese enormous transformations in all developed free-market countries were accomplished without civil war and, in fact, in almost total silence." [3]

The problem with this self-satisfied optimism is that it lobotomizes history, mainly by separating the epic economic changes from their political consequences. New inventions that reduce human toil do lead, in the long run, to higher plateaus of economic well-being, and, certainly, eventually, they should do so again. But what is Drucker leaving out? The terrible history that lies in between, the wrenching politics in which societies assert themselves against the destabilizing impact of unregulated commerce.

Business commentators exclude from the history of progress such matters as the violent rise of national socialism in Drucker's own native Germany, the decades of frustrated struggles everywhere in the industrial world to redress the inequalities of income and wealth, the conflicts that recurred as laboring ranks organized their collective power and demanded higher wages, the reform campaigns to impose humane standards on industrial production, the misery and social disintegration and powerlessness that ignited revolutions from the left and from the right. That is the history Drucker describes as "a minimum of friction."

To imagine, for instance, that America's middle-class prosperity in the second half of the twentieth century sprang inevitably from wonderful inventions and the bounty distributed by modern manufacturing requires one to forget the hard parts of American political history—seventy-five years or more when pained voices were raised and suppressed, when social movements mobilized to campaign for decent working standards, when much political energy and some blood were expended to correct the inequities of industrial capitalism. In the sanitized version of American history, the labor movement did not happen, nor the agrarian Populists, the Progressive reformers, the New Deal. Neither did the Great Depression nor World War II.

The relevance of this contentious political history to the widely shared prosperity that eventually emerged is largely forgotten now, especially among the better-educated classes in the industrialized nations. The unfettered marketplace, not political action, is now understood as the only reliable vehicle for assuring both prosperity and social justice. This forgetfulness suggests that some hard lessons of history will be substantially repeated.

○

The difficult challenge, more difficult than remembering the past accurately, is to see the future in its own new terms. Unless one subscribes to vulgar determinism, there is no need to suppose that the patterns of the past must be slavishly replicated. Human actors may determine different outcomes. The past reasserts itself when people and societies fail to see things clearly and grasp the new understandings.

The world economy is now leveraged on a fulcrum that is profoundly different from the straightforward contest of labor and capital that Marx described. This new fulcrum is the shifting of opportunities for wealth and incomes from the older, richer societies to the poorer ones. Even given its ugliest exploitative aspects, the process of productive dispersal has the potential to produce a dramatic departure from the past, an opening for greater equality on a global scale. Yet this same opening feeds the economic loss and growing social distress of the older and wealthier nations, where inequalities deepen and marginalized people forfeit control of their own lives.

"The world is experiencing an enormous improvement in standards of living, just not here in the United States," said Albert Wojnilower, retired chief economist at CS First Boston, the Wall Street brokerage. The gradual decline of average real wages in the United States, for instance, has been under way unevenly for twenty years or more, driven by the deep pressures of the global marketplace toward wage equilibrium. The same erosion of incomes is beginning to appear in other leading nations. As this occurs, inequalities widen severely among the citizens of advanced societies, even as the gross inequality between richer and some poorer nations is reduced.

Given the free run of globalizing commerce, informed observers like Wojnilower expect this form of harmonization to continue for many years, probably for decades. "I don't think the Good Lord himself could stop this trend, short of nuking Southeast Asia," Wojnilower quipped.

The tension between these two realities constitutes the profound dilemma for convergence. The tension provokes ambivalent reactions, a theme of conflicting aspirations that recurs in many places in this book. The famous old question of organized labor—which side are you on?—posed a straightforward choice, capital versus labor, that has been perversely complicated by new circumstances. In crude outline, the new world sets up a conflict between peoples who, at least in abstract theory, have been on the same side—workers against workers. Older, more prosperous workers versus the newly recruited, poorer workers. Which side are you on?

The history of industrial development has taught societies everywhere to think of the economic order as a ladder. Some people are high up on the ladder, others are struggling to climb it. The new dynamic of globalization plants a different metaphor in people's minds—a seesaw—in which some people fall in order that others may rise.

Neither the ladder nor the seesaw is a satisfying metaphor since both excite explosive resentments and rivalries. Neither promises to lead to a global system that is both prosperous and stable, equitable and tolerant, since both rely inherently on exploiting the inequalities among peoples and societies. The political temptation to interrupt the globalizing process—to stop the erosion by somehow smashing the system—is sure to grow stronger in the advanced economies because the losses are growing larger.

A Luddite remedy, a self-defensive political upheaval, might staunch the deterioration, at least temporarily and for some people, but it could also wreck the system for almost everyone. The possibility of such a political rebellion constitutes a significant threat to the free-running revolution, one of the ways in which it might break down. If some nations impose self-protective measures on their markets, as many now do, the system can still function. But if every nation tries to do the same, then commerce implodes. When this has happened in the past, it led to general suffering and eventually to great wars.

The nationalist solution, in any case, condemns vast portions of the earth to the status of permanent losers. This is neither a just outcome nor a reliable solution, even if it were possible to make the striving peoples accept it. Thanks to globalizing capital, the dominant nations are slowly losing their ability to impose such harsh terms on all the others. Commercial power still resides overwhelmingly among the small number of rich nations, but the dispersal of productive wealth may already preclude a neocolonialist resolution.

The only way out of the dilemma is to think anew, to reject the choice between one side and the other. The political values known as human rights are not, as we explore later on, marginal matters reserved for idealistic reformers. These issues are integral to how the global economy functions and how it imposes consequences on wage earners everywhere, in rich nations as well as poor. In crude terms, the top of the ladder will continue to fall if the bottom is not brought up more rapidly. Bringing the bottom up would be very difficult to achieve in the best circumstances. It is impossible to imagine so long as people at the bottom lack the political freedom to demand it.

For the first time in human history, though most people don't yet grasp it, a fateful connection is emerging between the first and the last. One end of the ladder (or seesaw) cannot defend its own general prosperity without attending to human conditions at the other end. For masses of people in the global marketplace, economic self-interest is converging with altruism.

Understanding this new reality will be very difficult for people, especially in the richest nations, especially among political and business leaders, since it suggests a very different conception of the national interest. In order to escape from the dilemma, people have to reimagine an economic order based on different metaphors. They have to slip the bonds of inherited ideologies and begin the task of discovering a more expansive framework for thinking about human possibilities. Not a ladder or seesaw. Perhaps a vast playground where many different children are playing, together and separately, but all playing in the same game.

The final section of this book focuses directly on people engaged in trying to confront the social and economic consequences of the global revolution in different ways and in different places. The objective is to explain by example some aspects of the deeper transformations under way among rich and poor. The facts are abundantly bleak: how some societies are upended by industrialization, how free-running commerce revives brutalities that shocked public morality in the nineteenth century, how politics and business sometimes conspire to treat people as mere commodities.

For Americans and Europeans, some of this action may seem like an old film loop, replaying events from their own national histories. Casual indignation is not a sufficient response since the advanced societies all passed through similar eras of exploitation and upheaval on their way to wealth. The deeper challenge is to consider the market connections that enable people on one end to enjoy a prosperity that is based on the abuse of others who are weak. Around the world, a halting search for political reforms is under way, and some of the solutions are found in unexpected places.

Revolution offers the opportunity to rethink the largest questions and, in fact, compels people to reexamine what they have always taken for granted.

What is a nation, after all, if commerce has destroyed the meaning of national boundaries? For that matter, what is a citizen? Are people confined by accident of birth to certain geographical locations or are they as free as business and finance? What is the future of work and workers when machines make things and also do much of the thinking? What is the meaning of wealth and economic growth if the world is someday choking on its own luxuriously wasteful consumption?

This book does not presume to provide answers, but offers some ways in which people might approach the questions. The later chapters can be thought of as rough field notes on the future, contributing to the great task of formulating a new ideology.

The exploration begins in the marketplace, not the social realm, because that is where the imperatives of revolution are at work. To understand how this wondrous machine functions, one is required to listen seriously to the insecurities, even desperation, expressed by major business enterprises. This book asks respectfully: What is driving their anxieties? What are the underlying business realities that motivate their actions and explain the larger economic consequences that flow from their collective behavior? The approach is grounded not in Marx or macroeconomics, but in the practical, adventurous life of business firms.

As economist Thorstein Veblen taught several generations ago, the problem of capitalist enterprise is always the problem of supply: managing the production of goods in order to maximize profit and the return on invested capital. Beneath the dazzling technologies, the blizzard of business deals, the wrenching social effects, the present economic upheaval revolves around old-fashioned questions that have always been the basics of capitalism. The challenge of managing supply to match the market demand and to maintain profit levels is the heart of what preoccupies every business manager from the corner shop to the largest industrial corporation. Revolutionary change has unhinged those basic calculations.[4]

The fundamentals are easier to understand in the simple setting of a localized, self-contained market: An enterprise tries to produce enough goods to meet the visible consumer demand, but not much more than that. As demand rises and a firm's productive capacity is eventually exhausted, then the company invests in building more plant capacity to increase its output. In the meantime, its rate of profit should increase because, as rising demand exceeds the supply of goods, a firm is able to raise its prices, restrained only by competing firms that might capture the new sales by keeping their prices a bit lower.

In the opposite case, when demand is weak, a company's returns are threatened if its production consistently outruns the market of available buyers. A firm has to limit its supply of goods or else be stuck with unsold inventories, surpluses that must be disposed of at discount or perhaps a dead loss. Excess production threatens to drive down prices and thus narrow the profit margins on the company's output. When a firm's profits decline, owners of capital typically respond by moving their investment capital elsewhere, dumping the company's stock and searching for others that will deliver a better return.

Eventually, in order to halt the damage, the company has to shrink supply and even its productive capacity—closing the factory, either temporarily or permanently. In simplified terms, these are the main variables that managers try to keep in balance as they respond to changing conditions in the market.

The great virtue of capitalism—the quality that always confounded socialist critics and defeated rival economic systems—is its ability to yield more from less. Its efficient organization of production strives to produce more goods from less input, whether the input is capital, labor or raw resources. Assuming markets are stable, the rising productivity increases the profit per unit, the yields that get distributed as returns to invested capital or as rising wages for labor or in lower product prices for consumers and, in the happiest circumstances, all three.

But this expanding potential to produce more goods also poses the enduring contradiction for capitalist enterprise: how to dispose of the surplus production. You can make more things, but can you sell them? An undisciplined expansion of productive capacity will be self-defeating, even dangerous for a firm, if all it accomplishes are continuing supply surpluses that degrade prices and undermine the rate of return. The problem of surplus capacity drives not only the competition among firms for market shares but also the imperative to discover new markets.

The point of elaborating these fundamentals is to make the following clear: The global revolution has deranged the logic of standard business calculations. The conventional decision-making is not only greatly accelerated (and complicated) by globalization, but also gravely altered. The new machines introduce dramatic opportunities both to reduce costs and to increase output—more for less—but on an exponential scale. The same machines have given capital wings and allowed firms to disperse globally, going after shares in markets that were once securely local. Above all, by steadily expanding the potential supply, the breakout of new production methods and products creates pervasive downward pressures on prices.

The old standard logic is thus destabilized: the imperative to modernize must be heeded lest a company lose out in the price competition, but the modernizing process also makes the supply problem worse. When companies adopt the technologies that reduce costs and protect their market shares, the inescapable result is to enlarge productive capacity. They do this to keep up, though it means supply surpluses will steadily accumulate somewhere in the marketplace—goods that can't be sold, plants that can't be operated at full capacity. Someone somewhere will have to eat the losses. Business people hope it is not their company.

All companies are thus caught in a continuing scramble to avoid holding the surpluses, protecting themselves by closing factories in a timely manner or unloading excess goods at prices that injure their rivals. To preserve their position, they are compelled to keep doing more of the same: more cost reduction and price-cutting and, in turn, more expansion of potential supply. The circle continues, with its destructive element concealed by the fabulous expansiveness of the system.

The dirty little secret about technological revolution is that it typically depresses a firm's rate of return per unit, whether the firm is making cars or computers. Falling prices, as always, threaten profit margins. Production costs may fall dramatically, sales volumes may expand robustly. Yet the rate of return remains in jeopardy.

In rough outline, these imperatives describe the fierce spiral that enthralls major businesses across nearly every sector of production, across the complicated landscape of the global marketplace. The supply problem is not the only way global revolution upends standard practices, but it is the one most central to everything else that happens. The supply factor and ancillary dislocations explain the desperate edge to the global competition, where even the strongest firms sometimes sound paranoid about the future.

Motorola, one of America's most successful multinationals, has a standing rule, applied to every division, that productive efficiency will be increased by 15 percent a year, every year—that is, doubled every five years. Boeing, the world leader in aircraft manufacturing, sets a hard target of 25 percent reductions in its overall operating costs. Chrysler, after a decade of painful but effective streamlining, enunciates new "stretch goals" for its managers, including an additional 50 percent improvement in efficiency.

A tangible illustration of what this means was provided by Chrysler's chief corporate economist, Wynn Van Bussman. "To develop the K-car in the late seventies and early eighties, it took 54 months and 3,100 people," he said. "A few years later, to develop the Neon took 33 months and 700 people. Those are real numbers. Now, we're not going to make that same type of improvement again, but that's a new way of doing business."

Fast, lean, flexible—these familiar buzzwords are modern corporate management's response to the revolutionary conditions. Rigorous contests for design efficiency. Continuous suppression of costs, including labor costs. Redeploying elements of production overseas to capture local advantages, from low wages and taxes to other political favors. Securing access to the hot new markets in the world where rising demand exceeds supply and per unit profit margins can be widened. Reducing the fixed costs by dismantling corporate assets—selling plants and properties, shrinking middle-level bureaucracies, converting jobs to temporary status. Sharing cost burdens by forming alliances with putative rivals who will jointly finance the overhead of research and development, even share production.

These and other strategies are the new standard in business and some will be explored later on, but they are not the only realm of competition. Facing the same market pressures, nations and regions respond with their own fierce contests: bidding for scarce jobs with tax subsidies and other favors. Pushing surpluses off on other nations through measures to protect the home producers. Suppressing domestic wages and other costs to attract investment capital. Using the leverage of their fast-growing consumer market to demand a share of the production and jobs.

Winners and losers—the conventional understanding of what's unfolding is that smart, quick companies will flourish and the slow-footed will perish. Energetic, entrepreneurial nations will thrive and the lazy ones won't. Citizens are expected to get smarter, work harder and cheer for the home team. The trouble is, the more everyone behaves in this virtuous manner, the more likely the underlying supply problem will be compounded for the system as a whole.

What if the expanding system is moving further and further out of balance as it grows? That is the global experience to date. Enormous supply surpluses are accumulating across nearly every major sector of industry, from cars to steel, from chemicals to aircraft. Millions of people are earning more money and buying more things. Some people are becoming fabulously wealthy and committing their fortunes to the global stream of capital. Companies are deploying advanced production systems and plunging into undeveloped markets. World trade continues to expand, as does overall economic growth. Yet this haunting gap between supply and demand keeps growing steadily wider, too.

The global acceleration of recent years, the restructurings of firms and migrations of capital, did not correct these imbalances, but added greatly to their dimensions. As we explore in detail later on, the supply problems in major sectors are more serious than a decade ago, yet the investment in new capacity naturally continues as a key ingredient of competition. Companies and industrial sectors seem powerless, one by one, to reverse the overall direction or even manage it successfully. Individual nations may succeed at protecting their own markets from the world glut of goods, but, of course, their success only compounds the global problem for others.

Economic orthodoxy teaches that markets always come into balance —excess supply shrinks to match demand, or vice versa—so it is assumed that, in time, this problem resolves itself, quite naturally, by market forces. Sophisticated business leaders may grumble regularly about the overcapacity problems in their own sectors, but generally they avoid addressing the larger implications, at least in public. In the daily affairs of business, surpluses and overcapacity are thought of as the other guy's problem. The supply surpluses will work themselves out when the other guy closes his factory. Besides, corporate leaders cannot withdraw from the chase, even if they are concerned by its direction, without sacrificing their own firm's position.

Free-market theory is not really a science so much as a value-laden form of prophecy, so it is not subject to definitive proofs of right or wrong except in those cataclysmic moments when reality provides the crushing refutation. Two observations, derived from reality rather than abstract theory, argue that, once again, the widespread faith in self-regulating markets is a dangerous illusion, awaiting a correction by reality.

The first observation is from economic history: The run-up to the 1929 financial crash and the Great Depression was also an era of robust industrialization distinguished by the same sort of huge imbalances between excess supply and inadequate demand. Despite assurances from orthodox economics, the market did not arrive at an eventual balance; the market collapsed. The event was seen as the crash of a speculative bubble in financial-market prices, as indeed it was. But the underlying economic cause was the supply problem. The false expectations driving up the stock prices were based on the euphoric assumption that all those new factories being built with the investors' capital would somehow be able to sell all the things they could make.

The second observation is based on the present: The global economy, as it accelerates, is not moving toward the economist's golden mean but in the opposite direction. As greater surpluses accumulate in industry, the optimistic assumptions of finance capital become visibly more tenuous, with widening gyrations of market prices leading to the occasional financial disorders. None of this proves, of course, that the global market is certain to crash again someday. But it ought to encourage great skepticism about the future of free-running commerce.

Unless the fundamentals of capitalist enterprise have somehow been repealed, the system cannot continue on its present trajectory, not without sooner or later facing a substantial, perhaps sudden adjustment in expectations and returns. To put it crudely, capital is being invested in new factories to make more things when the market is already struggling with a mounting shortage of buyers. One way or another, losses will multiply—for firms or nations or global investors. But when? When the realization takes hold that the expected returns from these new productive investments are grossly overvalued against the actual market prospects.

If the adjustments to reality occur quite abruptly, the recognition can induce a panicky rush to prudence. Everybody starts dumping assets and marking things down all at once, goods and factories or financial paper. Governments rush to bail out losers or protect their own markets against outsiders. Every major enterprise is then trapped in self-defensive moves, cutting losses by shrinking excess output, so the downward pressure feeds upon itself. The wider the gap becomes between productive capacity and realistic market demand, the more likely it is that the collapse of optimism will be sharp and shocking.

This is the nature of catastrophe that the global system is flirting with at present. I do not presume to predict with certainty that it will occur, much less when or how it might start. I do assert that the risk is visible and large and that it is growing. In the globalized setting, such an implosion might be triggered by any number of odd events—an obscure market disturbance, an unexpected failure of major banking interests, a debt crisis in a major market like the United States, anything that triggers a wholesale retreat from the optimistic assumptions.

The leading nations have institutional safeguards in place that did not exist in 1929, including international financial pools like the International Monetary Fund, and conceivably these governments might be able to respond with rescue measures that staunch a crisis before it turns into a general unwinding. It is equally conceivable that the scale of a global retreat, spread across dozens of economies and financial markets simultaneously, could overwhelm the existing capacities of governments. The world is on new ground. Nobody really knows the likely outcome.

The present facts could also support an alternative supposition that might be less cataclysmic: a gradual unwinding of the supply problem as firms fail and consolidate, as nations forfeit their shares in the global industrial base. Possibly, over many years, this could reduce the imbalances and avoid severe ruptures. That is what conventional economics believes— hopes—will occur. In a sense, this process has been under way for many years, as some nations give up manufacturing industries and others claim them, though so far these adjustments have been insufficient to reverse the overall trend toward greater surplus.

Thus, even in the best scenario for adjustment, a much greater "shakeout" lies ahead for the major industrial sectors, for firms and nations. That is the "hurricane" GE's Jack Welch sees ahead. It is what makes business leaders so anxious.

The main problem with the gradualist scenario is politics: people generally do not passively accept their losses but try instead to defend themselves against the market forces by imposing irregular solutions. In theory, the market might adjust in a gradual manner, picking out the losers and disposing of them. In reality, the scale of adjustment is likely to excite grave political reactions, and major economic players, both firms and governments, will be challenged to stop the losses.

For governments, if their own factories are closed and the ranks of jobless citizens grow, the political fallout invites nationalist measures to protect markets, limiting the intrusion of foreign goods. Despite the reigning free-market dogma, governments already do this in different ways, including in Europe and North America. As long as the supply problem persists, the threat of greater protectionism hangs over the system.

For companies, solving the supply problem also might lead them eventually to form producer cartels—agreements among rivals to limit overall production and divide up the available sales in the global market, thus escaping the revolutionary logic that drives down prices and leads to the continuing surpluses. This outcome may seem improbable, given the bracing rhetoric of free-market competition, but preliminary sketches toward such a solution are already visible in the thousands of alliances that competing producers are forming among themselves, sharing everything from product lines to advanced research. If they emerge, cartelized markets might be governed by subtle understandings among the suviving giants that they will compete in certain areas but not in others.

Both forms of political intrusion—nationalist barriers to free commerce or cartelized industrial sectors—were widely employed in the early-twentieth-century history of capitalism. These solutions may have temporarily protected individual producers and nations but generally made things worse for the system as a whole. Either approach effectively brings the free-running revolution to an end. However, the globalization of production makes either response much more difficult to imagine, given that so much is now dispersed across so many different nations with competing interests.

In the meantime, multinational corporations are pursuing what might be called hedging strategies, trying to deploy elements of production to protect themselves against the unpredictable lurches of markets and politics. By creating regionalized production in many parts of the world, including North America and Europe, a firm may insulate itself against the variables of shifting currency values or up-and-down economic cycles. By locating plants and employment in potentially hostile regions, a company hopes to immunize itself against the present danger of national or regional protectionism. If a global firm exists everywhere, it figures it cannot be shut out anywhere.

Major multinationals also have a hedging strategy designed to protect them against the surpluses: they are learning to operate profitably while employing a smaller portion of their productive capacity. The great goal of corporate managers is to lower the "break-even point" in the company's capacity utilization rate. That is, a lean, flexible enterprise arranges its elements to sustain profits while operating far below its real potential—even when a third or more of its production base is idle.

To achieve this, firms must become truly globalized, not American or German or Japanese, but flexible hydras with feet planted in many different markets, making so-called world products that are adaptable across different cultures. Multinationals are already positioning themselves so they may effortlessly shift production activity from nation to nation, continent to continent, maximizing profit by continually adjusting the sources of output to capitalize on the numerous shifting variables: demand, price, currency values, politics. To function on this global plane, managers must be prepared to sacrifice parts of the enterprise, even the home base, at least temporarily, to protect themselves against the transient tides that undermine profit margins.

It is not yet clear whether they will succeed at this, but if they do, the multinational enterprises may have found a way to insulate their rates of return against the storm of change. The supply problem would still have to be dealt with, of course, but the decision-making could be stabilized around rational market choices from the firm's point of view.

For nations, however, the consequences would diminish further the leverage of their governments, communities and workforces. A vast and permanent redundancy would be built into the global system, shifted here and there in response to factors far beyond the influence of a nation's policy makers, not to mention its workers. Karl Marx's famous "reserve army of the unemployed" may come to resemble an assemblage of global transients, scattered everywhere and nowhere, as portable as the "virtual corporation" itself.

The other way out of the supply problem, as history also recommends, is the fundamental alternative of addressing the other side of the market equation—inadequate demand—through government intervention to increase the purchasing power of consumers worldwide. This activist doctrine was enunciated sixty years ago by John Maynard Keynes to refute the same free-market orthodoxy that was then prevailing. Keynes argued that markets cannot extricate themselves from permanent stagnation, high unemployment and underutilized capacity without the artificial demand stimulus of government spending. The new spending creates market demand for goods and labor; governments promote rising wages and schemes that redistribute incomes downward to those who will spend the money. As a means to recover from the Great Depression, the idea of demand stimulus more or less worked for many nations, including Hitler's Germany and eventually the United States.

The Keynesian economic logic intersects with the social dimension of today's global marketplace. The approach would attack global inequalities in order to enhance economic prospects for everyone in the system. An aggressive effort aimed at rapidly bringing up the bottom of the global wage ladder would directly contribute to the greater purchasing power needed worldwide to consume the world's surpluses of goods and thus narrow the supply gap. Various advocates, myself included, have been describing versions of "global Keynesianism" for some years.

The Keynesian solution, however, encounters great obstacles of its own. The most obvious one is its political improbability in an era of conservative hegemony. Intent on shrinking governments and devoted to the efficacy of unregulated markets, free-market reformers in most industrial nations naturally dismiss an alternative doctrine that describes their faith in markets as a dangerous illusion. In history, the alternative of government-led regeneration of economies has become a tolerable choice to business and banking interests only when their economies were thoroughly ruined. Until then, the idea seems wasteful and intrusive. Lacking a visible disaster, the doctrine is very difficult to sell.

The more formidable obstacle to the Keynesian solution of stimulating global demand and growth is quite threatening: the dangerous collision it engenders between mass consumption and the natural environment. In crude terms, if everyone owns a car and refrigerator, if every nation becomes rich enough to throw off vast quantities of industrial waste, can the earth stand it? The answer is already visible: if the industrial system proceeds further along its conventional path of expansion, the ecological consequences will someday overwhelm everyone, rich and poor alike. This dilemma was not created by the present revolution, but its energy and mobility have greatly enlarged the implications. The solution will require a profound reordering of industrial processes, both in production and consumption, even reforming the market's price system. Like other large questions, this is not a matter the marketplace is disposed to address.

Nonetheless, if my analysis is correct, then the world's nations must eventually turn to political solutions of this nature: collective reforms to ameliorate or slow down the destructive forces, to correct the economic imbalances of supply and demand, to reassert controls on capital and restore the social understandings, to foster a more stable promise of prosperity. In subsequent chapters I describe some of these reform possibilities, the actions that governments can take, the measures that might allow the creative energies of commerce to proceed in a more humane and less dangerous fashion.

The next section of this book proceeds to explore the multinational industrial system itself, across various sectors and nations, to identify the working imperatives behind the action and the sources of underlying contradictions. Most dimensions of this inquiry reflect, one way or another, the core problem of supply that I have described in outline, but also the strategic dilemmas confronting the largest global firms. In the brave new world we explore, the action does not much resemble the "free trade" orthodoxy that is exalted in political debate, especially in American politics. For that reason, this book does not expend great energy arguing with the dogma, except to point out occasionally how the theory does not conform to the reality.

The following section will focus directly on the commanding heights of finance capital, the anarchic forces of global investors who strive to rule over both corporations and nations. The "one world" financial market that some visionaries foresee is still emerging, but has already become an unruly, insecure place. Governments are hostage to its random enthusiasms and yet compelled to rush to its rescue when the market's illusions are suddenly shattered.

The final section, as I have already explained, attempts to restate the issues that Bismarck and other nineteenth-century leaders called "the social question," but in the new terms that have been created by globalizing commerce. Can people discover their social connections to distant others around the world and act upon them? Or is the global system doomed to repeat the pathologies of the past, the conflict and exploitation, until one day the Luddites or others explode into violent rebellion?

A frail basis for optimism lies in the fact that these economic forces are not new to the world, but have all been experienced before. Perhaps, through conscientious self-knowledge, people can find ways to avert tragedy. Perhaps.

There are as well ample grounds for pessimism. To escape from these perils and others, nations would have to find the courage to reclaim control over free-running capital. That will require an assertion of governing power that lies far beyond present-day political imagination or will. Respectable opinion is now enthralled by the secular faith that Austrian economist Karl Polanyi long ago described as "the utopian endeavor" to establish a system of self-regulating markets. Today, there is the same widespread conviction that the marketplace can sort out large public problems for us far better than any mere mortals could. This faith has attained almost religious certitude, at least among some governing elites, but, as Polanyi explained, it is the ideology that led the early twentieth century into the massive suffering of global depression and the rise of violent fascism. So long as the dogma reigns unchallenged, this revolution will continue to hurtle forward, fatefully out of control.[5]

In fact, there is not much evidence from economic history of societies that have acted in an alert, timely manner to avert similar catastrophes. Usually, it is the opposite story. Contradictions and instabilities accumulate, but no one in power has the presence to act. Warnings are sounded, but pass by unheeded.

The world is a wondrous place, filled with gorgeous, striving, capable people who are endlessly interesting in their differences and likenesses. Still, it is true, neither technological invention nor economic revolution has yet managed to eliminate folly and error from the human condition.

Part Two

Desperate Enterprise

Four

"Gleiche Arbeit, gleicher Lohn" *

ARBITRAGE IS an ancient and honorable routine in market economies—the practice of buying a commodity in one local market where it is cheap, then selling it in a neighboring market where the price is higher and profiting from the fractional difference. These transactions, whether for grain or precious metals or financial assets, provide a continuous discipline on prices and create the informal limits of market equilibrium among distant buyers and sellers. If the producers of corn or copper set their prices too high, the arbitrageurs move in and flood their market with cheaper corn or copper purchased elsewhere. The effect is swift and sure: the out-of-line prices are driven downward.

In the globalizing economy, arbitrage is applied to a vastly different purpose: the commodity is human labor, the price is wages. Wage arbitrage (though companies do not call it that) functions more or less in reverse: It moves the production and jobs from a high-wage labor market to another where the labor is much cheaper. The producers thus reduce their costs and enhance profits by arbitraging these wage differences, usually selling their finished products back into the high-wage markets.

The cost of transporting things between distant markets has always been the practical obstacle to successful arbitrage, but modern technologies have greatly reduced these costs, even for moving entire factories. Transportation is a trivial factor alongside the potential gains of exploiting the vast disparities that exist among wage levels in different parts of the world.

A crude equilibrium system for labor wages is thus gradually emerging in global commerce: a discrete form of price discipline that links the best-paid, most prosperous industrial workers in the world with the cheapest and poorest. Like corn or copper, the practice of wage arbitrage drives the price of human labor downward.

The great hall where workers of the world assembled in reunion was the Kongresshaus in Zurich, a neoclassical marble palace facing the Zü-

* German: "same work, same pay."

richsee, the narrow lake that bends away from the city toward dim snowy peaks in the distant Alps. At the back of the hall was the heart of the city, an elegant congestion of crooked little streets with fine shops and important banks, gabled split-timber houses and stone churches dating from the Reformation. More than four hundred union leaders were gathered from six continents, and for many who came from impoverished nations the city of Zurich must have seemed quaint, pristine and very rich. On their way to the hall, they strolled the Bahnhofstrasse, one of the world's most pleasing shopping boulevards, and some paused to snap pictures of one another before the banks and boutiques with world-famous names.

A century before, thirty leaders of young labor had met in a Zurich hotel to found the International Metalworkers Federation. That was 1893, the infancy of modern industrialization, and the delegates were sent from embattled unions in Germany, France, Hungary, Britain and some other European nations, as well as the United States. They were all struggling for recognition, drawn together by a new spirit of international labor solidarity.

In early summer of 1993, leaders of more than ninety metalworker unions from around the world came back to Zurich to commemorate the IMF's 100th Congress and to adopt an "action programme" to confront global capitalism. Their reunion seemed more melancholy than celebratory, for it mainly delineated how the globalization of production has dismantled a century's work, the collective mobilization of workers.

In the assembly hall, some of the labor delegates had the familiar, beefy look of men who had once worked with their hands and still appeared slightly uncomfortable in business suits. Others, especially among the younger Europeans, had the appearance of smart, trim technocrats, interchangeable in style with modern management. Diminutive Asians from places like Sri Lanka or Thailand looked frail and ascetic alongside well-fed Germans and Americans. The Japanese were the largest contingent, eighty-two men in identical dark suits, who, unlike other delegates, sat patiently and listened through all the speeches.

The program opened with an original musical interlude, a romantic composition by a young Norwegian (under the influence of Leonard Bernstein). The theatrical music was intended to evoke proud memory with a *tableau vivant* of labor's glorious past. Mimes and dancers acted out the history of organized labor: workers on barricades struggling against police truncheons, workers confronting industrial pollution and other dangers, workers embracing across race and cultural differences. The composition included familiar snatches of the "Marseillaise" and the "Battle Hymn of the Republic" and a popular march song of the Italian Communists. At a triumphant moment in the performance, the dancers ascended a broad staircase, waving four huge red flags.

Evocations of Red revolution seemed especially dated. "All this romantic Communist crap," a British unionist muttered to me. "The East Europeans must be gagging on the red flag stuff." Indeed, the free labor unions of the West had stood in staunch opposition to the controlled unionism of Communist regimes in the Soviet sphere. With the end of the Cold War, the Zurich congress reunited some labor organizations from East and West that had not spoken to one another for forty years. The metalworkers federation was growing rapidly as a result and now included seventy countries, with members who spoke a babble of languages that required nineteen interpreters.

Solidarity was never an easy matter. It has become much more complicated than it seemed in the 1890s.

China was absent. Its workers are not free. The All-Chinese Federation of Labor claims 125 million members, which would make it the largest in the world, but everyone knows the union is inauthentic. The membership is not voluntary. The Chinese union is but an appendage of the Communist Party that helps control workers rather than speaking for them.

The cardinal principle of free trade unions is autonomy—a free voice for workers, independent of government control. When Solidarity asserted that principle in Poland, supported by the IMF and other free labor federations, it fostered civil upheaval that led eventually to the collapse of the Communist state.

Now the spirited rhetoric from labor leaders was aimed in an opposite direction, at "the market radicals" of capitalism who were reordering the world. They denounced the "social dumping" of companies that exit from their home countries and leave behind unemployment and social decay. They deplored the "neo-Americanism" of unregulated capital. They pledged earnestly and unanimously to mobilize workers worldwide to confront the power of multinational corporations and "put finance back in its place."

Labor's loss was capital's gain. The gathering at Zurich provided a convenient snapshot of functional reality in the global economy: the imperative of reducing labor costs. As business people frequently pointed out, reducing labor costs was only one among many factors behind the dispersal of production (others will be described in subsequent chapters). But the wage question was central to everything else. It set up the most powerful and convenient incentive for global commerce: the opportunity to capture savings at home and abroad by taking advantage of the gross surpluses of human labor that exist around the world.

In the crude logic of markets, labor's loss was simply a matter of supply exceeding demand and thus driving down the price. The supply of willing workers who were now available to industry worldwide far exceeded the industrial world's need for them. The essence of organized labor's power in the twentieth century had always been grounded in its ability to limit the supply of workers—by strikes or boycotts or seizing the factory, through legal guarantees of exclusive bargaining status. That control gave unions their leverage over wages and working conditions, but it has been decimated by the mobility of capital. From labor's standpoint, the snapshot from Zurich looked like a negative.

Despite the presumptions of a "postindustrial age," metalworking remained the prosaic core in the world's industrial production: autos, steel, electronics and computers, machine tools, aircraft, shipbuilding and some others. Workers liked to call these the "metal-bending" industries, and nearly half of the world's largest five hundred corporations were centered in those sectors. National governments, rich and poor, strove to acquire these industries (or as many elements as they could get) because they knew that "metal-bending" production brought with it both advanced technologies and higher wages, the high value-added employment that has centrifugal benefits for entire economies.

In America, the manufacturing unions traditionally divided their jurisdictions along product lines—autos or steel or aircraft—but major unions in other nations, especially in Europe, encompassed the entire span of metalworking sectors and therefore often became larger and stronger organizations. The lion among them was Germany's IG Metall with 3.4 million members, from cars and aerospace to electronics and machine tools, a union that was smart, aggressive and self-confident or, as adversaries would say, stubborn.*

IG Metall's president, Klaus Zwickel, accepted the gavel as the IMF's new president. Zwickel was a man of overbearing dimensions with a stern demeanor and burr-short hair. He promptly reported to the congress on IG Metall's latest victory—an industry-wide strike that shut down factories across East Germany, the first free-labor action in that territory since Hitler came to power in 1933.

The issue was equal pay for equal work. In 1990, the leaders of German business, government and labor had agreed upon grand terms for swift reunification of the divided nation, including an explicit timetable for bringing wages in the crippled eastern zone up to the much higher level in productive and prosperous West Germany. Helmut Kohl, the conservative prime minister who was running for reelection that year, campaigned through the collapsed industrial towns in the eastern states with a popular slogan: *"Gleiche Arbeit, gleicher Lohn"*—"Same work, same pay." Germany would not be truly unified, he declared, until all German workers were treated on an equal footing. Kohl's Christian Democrats swept to reelection, carrying districts that for forty years had been governed by Communists.

But the promise foundered on reality. As East German wages advanced rapidly, industry rebelled. In the spring of 1993, the employers' federation that speaks for German manufacturing in the metalworking sectors announced that it would unilaterally abrogate the agreement. Union leaders were shocked. In all the postwar years of national bargaining, a German business federation had never tried to renege on a wage contract. In May,

---

* *The union's full name, seldom used for obvious reasons, is Industriegewerkschaft Metall.*

IG Metall called the strike to defend its position in the old order, though many of its own members were hostile to the idea. "Sisters and brothers," Zwickel reported to the labor congress, "there was a lot of ill feeling between our members in East and West Germany. But we felt we had no choice."

Industry backed down and the unification agreement was upheld, but the union's victory was more hollow than it wished to admit. The terms were compromised and opened the way for deviations; as many as half of the employers shifted to lower wage scales anyway. Indeed, Germany's national unions, including IG Metall, were themselves beginning to accept new wage contracts that were either flat or negative. For the first time in more than a decade, the highest industrial wages in the world were headed downward. Meanwhile, unemployment remained high across Germany, horrendously so in the East.

Germany was evolving not toward equality in wages, but toward greater inequality. A two-tiered wage structure was emerging, closer to the gross disparities of income in America. Established workers with high-end jobs in the western states would come to be known colloquially as the "gold card workers."

Swift reunification was a noble act in historic terms, but utterly illogical in terms of the global free market for labor. As their wages rose according to schedule, the labor costs for manufacturing workers in East Germany quickly reached $17.30 an hour—higher than in Japan or the United States, not to mention other advanced economies of Europe. In theory at least, unification would bring them up to the same level as West Germany, where labor costs averaged $24 an hour.

Yet German and American companies were already hiring the skilled metalworkers who lived a few miles away in Hungary or the Czech Republic, who would do the same work for $2 or $3 an hour or even less. It didn't make sense. Aside from national loyalty, why hire expensive Germans when Hungarians or Czechs or Poles were so much cheaper?[1]

"Gleiche Arbeit, gleicher Lohn," in fact, no longer seemed to make sense in the context of globalizing wages, not for employers but also not for powerful labor unions. Organized labor everywhere had always endorsed the egalitarian ideal (or at least paid lip service to it), but the concept was now producing disastrous consequences for its own rank-and-file members. The idea of equal pay for equal work mocked labor's idealism because the global marketplace was already moving toward that objective, with devastating effect. In practical terms, the slogan has come to mean: pay cuts, from the top down.

The formal speeches at a labor convention are usually predictable boilerplate, but the more revealing moments are impromptu "interventions" scattered in between—brief remarks offered at random by various leaders describing their homegrown struggles. At Zurich, these informal voices inadvertently revealed the underlying tension that divides labor, the industrial crossruff that pits workers against workers.

Bill Jordan of Britain's Amalgamated Engineering and Electrical Union delivered a fiery denunciation of Timex, the U.S. company, for sacking 343 striking workers at its plant in Dundee, Scotland. Jordan urged the IMF unions to rally around these Scottish victims of "social dumping." The Timex production was being relocated in Dijon, France.

Per-Erik Lund of Finland reported on the troubled shipbuilding industry. Growth stagnating, traditional ship-building countries continuing to lose jobs and market share. Meanwhile, Brazil up 50 percent, China up 15 percent, Taiwan up 20 percent. Shipyards in Eastern Europe were swiftly entering the competition.

An official of the U.S. machinist union, representing aerospace workers at Boeing and McDonnell Douglas, announced plans for closer cooperation with Airbus Industrie unions and the 250,000 employees in Italy, France, Britain and Germany who also make large-body aircraft. Offstage, the Americans grumbled about the unfair subsidies with which European governments supported those 250,000 Airbus jobs.

A Swiss leader, Agostino Tarabusi, exclaimed over a shocking announcement from Asea Brown Boveri (ABB), the giant Swiss-Swedish engineering conglomerate, that it planned to lay off a thousand Swiss workers and invest $1 billion in Asia. "In Switzerland, it used to be that we knew the names of each of the unemployed," Tarabusi said. "But now there are too many of them." Asians sat silent through his remarks.

The German leader, Zwickel, criticized the Japanese for trying to export their model of "enterprise unions" to the rest of Asia—unions that are closely aligned with company managements, if not controlled by them. The Japan delegation returned the volley. "Our Japanese colleagues didn't like it one bit," said Albert Schunk, IG Metall's international secretary, "but we have to open that debate. We can't just keep singing 'Solidarity Forever.' "

The lone delegate from Hungary, László Paszternák, complained in private conversation that European and American multinationals—GE, GM, Audi, VW and others—were pressuring "to make a union-free zone in Hungary." Paszternák has pleaded for united labor action to thwart the companies, but confided to me that unity is difficult. "I was at a conference with U.S. machinists and the people there complained that American wealth is being exported to Russia and the Eastern Bloc—they meant us," he said.

The Swedish metalworkers were helping the Hungarians deal with Electrolux. IG Metall contributed two million deutschemarks to strengthen Hungarian labor as it confronts VW or Audi. Still, Paszternák observed: "It would be an illusion for us to believe that any Western union would go on strike to support a sister union in Eastern Europe. Basically, we have to fight it through on our own."

These random facts, whether drawn from Europe or Asia, described a terrible conflict that no one wished to acknowledge very directly because it was painfully at odds with principle. Whatever they said or felt, however sincerely they might embrace the idea of global solidarity, these unions were not entirely on the same side. As a practical matter, some would benefit from the others' losses. Some were wealthy, in the process of becoming less so. Others were very poor and weak, hoping to get out from under. They needed each other, certainly, against the multinational companies, but they had not yet fully absorbed the implications of that mutual struggle.

Klaus Zwickel, despite his confident manner, came closest to expressing the despair that lurked beneath the brave talk. "Brothers and sisters, what can we do?" he asked the assembly. "Fine calls for solidarity will not be sufficient. Simple calls for protectionism will not work either. The strong trade union organizations expect more action from the weak. And the weak expect more help from the strong."

This desperate gulf between them—the wage disparities so easily arbitraged by capital investment—was exquisitely expressed in a chance moment during the week-long discourse. Two speakers, separately and innocently, described the distance between East Peoria, Illinois, and Kuala Lumpur, Malaysia.

A burly American in a pale blue jacket, Bill Casstevens, came to the microphone to report on the brutal wage conflict between the United Auto Workers and Caterpillar Inc. The UAW vice president thanked unions from France, Belgium and elsewhere for fraternal support. When Caterpillar demanded drastic wage reductions at the midwestern factories where its famous earthmovers are made, it provoked a UAW strike that closed twelve plants. The union felt cornered, he said, knowing Caterpillar intended to hire replacement workers at lower wages and to shift some production to overseas plants in Brazil, Europe or Japan.

"There is no way we can accept the company demands," Casstevens explained. "They want a two-tiered wage system: when workers get laid off at $17 an hour, they want to call them back at $7 an hour."

His remarks caused a stir in the hall, murmured expressions of disbelief. The harshness of Caterpillar's terms made many of the other labor complaints seem small and manageable.

But then Rajasekaran of Malaysia was at the same microphone, describing a quite different reality. A small, dark-skinned man, with a fine gray moustache and a high-colonial English accent, Rajasekaran resembled a distinguished professor more than a union leader, though he led the Malaysian Trade Union Congress. He described the futile twenty-year struggle to establish unions in Malaysia's burgeoning electronics industry, where the 150,000 workers, mostly young women, assemble everything from Japanese cameras to American semiconductor chips. Wages did rise, but generally they are paid only $130 to $150 a month around Kuala Lumpur, he said, sometimes much less in remote rural factories.

The Malaysian government, acting on demands from the multinational corporations, has prohibited all attempts to organize independent unions in the electronics factories so that workers might collectively demand higher wages. The companies have warned that if unions are allowed, they may be compelled to move their factories to other markets where wages are even lower. Indeed, a few have already moved. To Vietnam, where workers may be paid one tenth of the Malaysian wage. To China, where officials established a new minimum wage for the Shanghai industrial zones: $24 a month.[2]

Rajasekaran described the repeated appeals to international authorities, including the U.S. government, that were fruitless. Once more, he urged the metalworkers federation to insist upon a single global standard: "the recognition of human dignity everywhere." But he also politely expressed his deepening frustration.

"We must come up with something that will be truly effective," he pleaded. "Otherwise, we will come back to the 150th Congress of the IMF and we will still be talking about the power of the multinational corporations. Most of us will not be here. But our children will be here, still talking about the same things."

Auto workers in Illinois earned in a day or two what the electronics workers of Malaysia earned in a month, not to mention those in China or Vietnam who worked for far less. The Anglo-French investor James Goldsmith has calculated that the cost of one Frenchman was equivalent to forty-seven Vietnamese. If humanity was to be measured on that rude scale, one American machinist was worth about sixty Chinese machinists.[3]

Yet, despite the great distances between their different circumstances, each group of workers was experiencing the power of the global wage system. Each was ensnared and blocked by the same market dynamics. Whose grievances should be redressed? If one were forced to choose among them, which group would have first claim on sympathies: auto workers in Illinois whose middle-class livelihoods were collapsing or peasant women in Southeast Asia who have been transformed into cheap industrial labor?

The choice might seem unbearable to many people of conscience because the human dilemma it posed was truly global in dimension, a social equation beyond the easy loyalties of national borders. Social sensibilities, especially in the most prosperous nations, were not yet prepared to take in such extremes and sort them out confidently.

These disparities (and many others even more dramatic) constituted the new social fact that global commerce has put before citizens of the world, confronting rich and poor nations alike. The wage differences were also, of course, the fundamental economic fact that animated the action in global commerce and finance.

Many middle-class managers and professionals, who were oblivious to the impact on blue-collar factory workers, were beginning to discover that wage arbitrage might also be applied to their jobs in the front office. Graduate engineers in India, for instance, earned less than $10,000 a year, compared with $60,000 to $80,000 for typical American counterparts. The

Indian engineers were skillful and abundant (plus they spoke English). Many were employed by leading U.S. electronics companies. Middle-class Americans, who were largely indifferent when the job losses were concentrated among blue-collar workers, became conscious of the implications for themselves when the wave of corporate downsizings in 1990s turned on the front office—eliminating broad swaths of middle-level managers and professionals.

The stark wage disparities were not new, of course, to the poorer countries around the world, where many people would say the answer to the social question is self-evident. Some months after the Zurich congress, I was recounting my experience to a financial-market analyst who is based in Hong Kong, a smart young New Zealander named Rodney Jones who surveys Asian economies and financial markets for George Soros's Quantum Fund. Jones was married to a Sri Lankan, and from his Asian-Anglo perspective he was briskly impatient with the complaints from the prosperous working class of Europe or America.

"Where is it written that white guys in Britain are entitled to $15 an hour and five weeks of holiday while Asians are supposed to work for $3 a day?" Jones asked. "What is the difference between an unskilled worker living in Germany and an unskilled worker living in India? Not much, really. These Asian workers are now part of the global economy and the West will simply have to adjust to that fact."

George Kourpias was a first-generation Greek-American who went to work as a teenager in an Iowa packinghouse, then got a better job as a machinist at Zenith in the days when it was still making TV sets in the United States. A short, muscular man, with an unpretentious manner, Kourpias became active in the union and, over thirty-five years, worked his way up the ladder of various positions. When he finally became president of the International Association of Machinists and Aerospace Workers, the IAM's domain was in collapse.

"What happened to us over the last twelve years is now happening to everyone else—closed plants, lost memberships," Kourpias reflected over dinner in Zurich. "We had 831,000 members in '81. We lost 300,000. We're down to 469,000 in the U.S., another 50,000 in Canada. For years, you could count on us dropping 1,500 to 2,000 members every month. And that was before the defense industry was hit. For every layoff at Pratt & Whitney, you can bet there's another five or six people in the small supplier shops who get bumped, too."

American labor leaders of Kourpias's generation had the melancholy fate of experiencing in their youth the glorious upside for American labor —the bountiful postwar decades when U.S. wages led the world's—and in their later years the brutal downside when American labor began its long slide, a decline that was not yet ended. The last twenty years resembled a game of king of the mountain, played in slow motion, as American workers were gradually pulled down from the top of the hill. In 1975, hourly wages for production workers in U.S. manufacturing were double Japan's and exceeded everyone else's except Norway, Sweden, Belgium and the Netherlands. By 1980, American factory wages were below those in eight other countries, including West Germany. By 1992, the United States was behind thirteen countries, including Japan.

The same dynamic, as Kourpias observed, had begun to hammer on European jobs and wages and, in a somewhat different context, even on Japan's. German production workers in manufacturing were earning $25.56 an hour by 1993 (compared to $16.79 in the United States), but the German industrial unions were already accepting wage cutbacks. Japan's average factory worker was paid $19.20 an hour in 1993, but Japanese multinationals were busy shipping tens of thousands of manufacturing jobs offshore. In Italy, France and Britain, even in Sweden and Norway, wages were already falling.[4]

No one could say exactly how far the top must fall, but clearly the new wage leaders were being disciplined by the same forces of market equilibrium that had decimated American labor a decade before. The downward pressures were intensified by the general recession in the early 1990s—a recession was always an opportunity for employers to close less productive factories and extract concessions from labor—but did not let up when economies recovered.

The emerging restructuring in Western Europe would likely be less swift and violent than the American experience, but this force was much more fundamental than the ups and downs of business cycles. As Americans have learned, once wage depression gets under way, the pattern may persist for many years, even decades.

ABB, the engineering giant, was establishing forty new joint ventures in the low-wage East, from Slovakia and Hungary to Russia and Ukraine, taking on 25,000 cheaper workers. As its co-chairman pointed out, the former Soviet sphere has more engineers than Western Europe and 60 million industrial workers compared to 40 million.

Swissair began shipping its used airplane tickets, 20 million of them, to Bombay for processing by Indian computer specialists who make one tenth the salaries in Switzerland.

IBM was considering shifting its disc-drive manufacturing from Mainz, Germany, and Havant, England, to somewhere in Eastern Europe. It had already moved 1,100 disc-drive jobs from San Jose, California, and Rochester, Minnesota, to Asian locations.

Some movements of capital were designed to capture minor advantages in labor terms within Europe. Hoover closed a plant in France and moved the work to its plant in Scotland, where pay was less and the union would accept concessions to improve productivity. Thomson Electronics closed a plant in Gosport, England, because the redundancy payments were cheaper there than if it had laid off its workers in Holland and Germany.

Ikea of Sweden moved some furniture production to Poland and opened a new store in Warsaw. The head of Ikea's East European operations boasted to the *Wall Street Journal:* "Costs of raw materials and labor are going to be cheaper in eastern Europe for the next 25 years. Once they get efficient, they'll beat the hell out of anything in the West."

Daimler-Benz, the titan of German manufacturing, decided to play hardball with its powerful labor adversary, IG Metall. Daimler's Mercedes-Benz division conducted a sort of international bidding contest for its new small-car plant, visiting sites in Britain, the Czech Republic, France and Germany. Meanwhile, Daimler's aerospace division announced it was closing six factories. And the corporation revealed plans to eliminate 44,000 jobs, 27,000 of them at Mercedes.

IG Metall got the message. The union acceded to cutbacks totaling 200 million deutschemarks, concessions said to have saved 3,000 jobs. Having made its point, Daimler-Benz picked Germany as the location for its new small-car factory. Over three years the corporation would eliminate more than 80,000 jobs, about 25 percent of its global workforce.

"Competition in the global village is like a tidal wave," Daimler Chairman Edzard Reuter said. "No one can escape."[5]

American workers (and union leaders) might find a grim sense of confirmation in these facts. Starting in the late 1970s, when U.S. workers in autos, steel and other sectors were being hammered by job losses and giveback contracts, the conventional explanation blamed the workers themselves. Their unions had gotten too greedy. Americans were said to be lazy or insufficiently skilled to compete. At that time American business leaders and economists often cited the example of German and Japanese workers as the model of productivity and discipline that Americans must emulate.

A decade later European business leaders and economists were disparaging their own workers in the very same terms and urging their governments to adopt what they called the "American solution." They meant: Europe must reduce social protections like unemployment benefits, weaken the labor laws and lower the minimum-wage levels to make labor cheaper. The American approach, they said, would create the "flexibility" needed to create more jobs and reduce Europe's persistently larger ranks of unemployed.

Lower wages, in other words, would encourage employers to hire more people. As a market principle, this was irrefutable. But Americans working at "temp jobs," which now composed an expanding share of the new job creation, or who worked at two or three places to keep up with car payments or the mortgage might not regard America's flexibility as a satisfying solution. They thought falling income was the problem.

In fact, European business was confronting the paradoxical consequence of its long political campaign to create a unified European market: eliminating the national commercial borders made Europe's producers and their workers more vulnerable to the effects of transnational wage arbitrage, Charles I. Clough Jr., Merrill Lynch's chief investment strategist, explained in a blunt essay entitled "The Meek Inherit the Earth."

The single European market meant many Western European factories must close, Clough wrote, because "it exposes a tremendous amount of redundancy in that continent's manufacturing and distribution infrastructure. Growth and employment will suffer. That continent's excess savings will find use in the emerging capitalist economies to their east."[6]

In past decades, unlike American labor, the self-confident European unions have looked positively on the trend of global dispersal because they recognized that offshore production could strengthen their companies and support their export production at home. Since European labor law requires companies to consult labor on major decisions, labor leaders had a much more intimate grasp of corporate strategies than their American counterparts. As exporting nations, Germany or Sweden or Italy were comfortable with economic interdependence and accepted the companies' assurances that, in the end, the workers at home benefit, too.

That was still European labor's general outlook, but the confidence was weakening. The new rush of capital flight, accompanied by massive job losses, was hinting that maybe the insular Americans were not altogether wrong. "VW has located all of the subsidiary production of gears in Hungary," said IG Metall's Albert Schunk. "If you look at the tax breaks and other incentives and the wage levels, it looks like a sound choice. But we ask the company: How are they going to defend jobs in Germany? They always assure us that they will, but our works councils are very concerned. We're trying to get certain bottomline agreements, but we know it is not easy."

In Sweden, industry has always thrived on trade, so the nation has no choice but to match or surpass global standards. "Our sixteen largest corporations export 80 to 90 percent of their production, so we are terribly vulnerable," said Bengt Jakobsson, international secretary of the Swedish Metalworkers Union. "This is the reality—more co-production with other countries. This is very, very dangerous, but I don't see what choice we have. This is a terrible question to face, but what's the alternative? If you don't do it, you might lose everything."

In Japan, meanwhile, major manufacturers were also closing mills and plants. Nissan shut its Zama plant, 5,000 jobs. Toshiba cut 5,000. Honda 3,000. Nippon Steel 7,000. The Japanese dispersal was driven less directly by wage levels and more obviously by the rising value of its national currency, but the consequences were the same: wage arbitrage became a compelling strategy by which the producing companies could hold down their costs and prices.[7]

As the yen appreciated steadily in exchange value against the dollar, the price of made-in-Japan goods automatically rose proportionately in export markets, especially the United States. The companies had to find a way to offset the rising yen and keep prices competitive. Reducing labor costs was the obvious choice. Starting in 1986, as the dollar-yen relationship began to shift dramatically, the Japanese companies adjusted by moving more and more production offshore, partly to the United States and Europe but primarily to other nations in Asia.

This process accelerated in the 1990s as the dollar continued to weaken against the yen. Just as consumer electronics production exited America for Japan, it was now exiting Japan for Malaysia or Thailand or other places. Sony's most celebrated product, the Walkman, was now made entirely in Korea, Malaysia and Indonesia.

The basic trade-off was explained by Yasunori Kirihara, Sony's general manager of corporate human resources: "The issue of shifting production to underdeveloped countries is the question of whether it's cheaper to use people or machines. If it's located in Japan, it has to be based on machines because wages are so high. But if you're too quick to invest the capital in machines, you may lose to competition that is relying relatively more on manual labor in some other country where labor is much cheaper."

Cheap people versus expensive machines—the same basic calculation was embedded somewhere in the decision-making of virtually every multinational corporation regardless of its national origin. Even domestic producers might face the same imperative if their products competed in price with a company that had already seized the labor-cost advantage of globalizing production.

In some circumstances, for various reasons including old-fashioned loyalty, companies would choose the machines, invest the necessary capital to create more advanced production systems and stick with the high-wage workers at home, though usually a reduced number of them. The potential alternative of cheaper labor still served, however, as a cautionary message to labor: don't push too hard or capital will take wing.

In all these decisions, the corporations were supervised by the flinty oversight of financial markets and capital investors. The miseries of industrial giants like IBM or GM, when their stock prices were smashed, were driven by many problems, but one of the thunderous complaints from finance capital was that these companies were being too sentimental about their workforces. As in other less spectacular cases, the corporations responded by shedding tens of thousands of employees, lest they lose the ability to raise the capital needed for new investments.

In Europe, banking has always been intimately interwoven with corporate managements and thus more patient about disappointing returns, but similar confrontations were becoming more common, as the values of global finance began to displace traditional loyalties. Thomas Mayer, a German who is chief economist for Goldman Sachs in Frankfurt, put the wage imperative bluntly: "Only a correction of the misaligned cost of labor relative to capital will provide a lasting solution to the [European] unemployment problem."

Finance was less beholden to national loyalties, more oblivious to the potential social consequences. Etienne Davignon, chairman of Société Générale de Belgique, Belgium's largest holding company, complained to the *Financial Times* about the lopsided perspective of investors. "You see it in our companies," he said. "If you want $300 million for layoffs and restructuring, you get approval in 15 seconds. But if you want to go out and buy something, your share price goes down."[8]

The food chain of wages, in which cheaper workers replaced expensive ones, did not stop with the most advanced economies, however. On the low end, the swiftly growing Asian nations were subject to similar pressures. Wages were usually rising in the new industries, but were also held back by the threat of capital flight. When labor rebellions forced wages up dramatically in South Korea, the cheaper light-assembly or garment factories were moved down the chain to other Asian countries, often taking the machines and managers with them. If these industries were replaced by higher value-added production like cars or steel or advanced electronics, as they were in Korea, the effects were quite positive. But the insecurity of wage arbitrage still stalked even the thriving economies.

"Look at Thailand," said Quantum Fund's Rodney Jones. "They are raising the minimum wage, and that has decimated their textile sector. The production is moving to China, to Indonesia, to Vietnam. Something that started out as well-meaning is costing jobs. In five years, Thailand won't have a textile sector."

Sony's Kirihara observed: "We should not think only of Japan but Korea and Taiwan. If we compare Korea with China, nobody can compete. Even Malaysia or Singapore is weaker than China or India because of wages. The question is whether they can produce more sophisticated products."

At the bottom of the global wage ladder is a seemingly inexhaustible supply of new recruits: peasants leaving the bleak circumstances of rural subsistence for the cash incomes offered by factory work. This ever-growing pool of available industrial labor has produced a paradoxical consequence: economic growth in poor nations increased unemployment.

Even the fast-growing economies, India or Indonesia or China, faced swelling accumulations of people searching for wage work, not to mention the tens of millions who left their homelands to become job-seeking immigrants. In China, where the statistics always seemed staggering, the state labor agency reported its estimate that Chinese unemployment a decade hence will total 268 million people.

Capital flight was general in the advanced economies, but Japan's was distinctive for one reason: The Japanese companies felt bad about it. Executives frequently expressed regrets. Japan's multinationals lamented the economic necessities that compelled them to disperse manufacturing jobs offshore and, in most instances, went to extraordinary lengths to make sure that the displaced workers were made whole. When Nissan closed its Zama plant, it found new work for the town to replace lost jobs and keep the community afloat. Japan's unemployment rate had reached an unprecedented level of 3 percent, but Japanese manufacturers were avoiding harsher layoffs by keeping some 1.2 million surplus workers on the payroll.

The explanation was social cohesion, not economics. Japan had to cope with the same market realities, but Japanese firms were governed by social understandings that barely existed in the United States and were visibly weakening in European nations: a sense of shared responsibility, group loyalty, collective identity with the nation, from top to bottom. The social terms that different nations have set for commerce were under assault everywhere and visibly unraveling in many places, but these implicit bonds could still be decisive in altering the consequences of globalization (the question of global pressures on social systems is addressed directly in Chapter 16).

Kudoka became the popular term for Japan's industrial hollowing out, but Japanese business executives did not fear that this trend would someday make Japan poor or even that it might lead to massive unemployment. Japan was sure to remain very wealthy. The demographics of its aging population meant that, if anything, the future problem might be a shortage of workers.

The anxieties over *kudoka* were more about the core identity of the nation: Japanese understand themselves as a people who know how to make fine things. What would happen to the next generation if the excellent products were no longer made in Japan? Where would younger workers learn the skills? How could they be expected to inherit the tradition?

In America, a self-respecting multinational did not apologize to its workers when it closed the factory—more often it blamed them—nor did it accept responsibility for the depressed community it was leaving behind. As a people, Americans had a different understanding of themselves: freestanding individuals who could each take care of themselves.

George Kourpias spoke for a different, lesser tradition in American life: a working-class understanding that only collective action could counter the powerful advantages of corporate and financial wealth. This social sensibility was never that strong in the United States, especially compared to European societies with their class-ridden histories, but it had weakened substantially during the last two decades as its principal advocate, organized labor, was decimated. Kourpias was still searching for countervailing strategies because the losses for machinists continued. He thought he knew the long-term answer, but was less sure about how to achieve it.

"One of these days," Kourpias said, "we're going to have to get a truly international union. Maybe it's the IMF, I don't know. This may not come in my lifetime, but we are going to do it. We've got to do it to survive."

Some years ago I spent an evening drinking beer and conversing with several young UAW members who described in great detail how their workplace, a General Motors foundry in the Buffalo area, coped with the global economy. The various castings produced by the foundry competed, order by order, with rival suppliers scattered around the world. The auto workers named five or six of them in Europe, Asia and Latin America. The differing wage and price structures might determine, by a few pennies, where GM acquired engine mounts or transmission housings. The workers recalled the modernizing machinery GM had brought in to boost productivity as well as the depressing struggles over wage contracts and layoffs. I regret that I cannot recall their names. I do know that GM subsequently closed their foundry.

For most of the last twenty years, academic economists have typically denied what those young auto workers understood to be true: that the globalization of production was eliminating U.S. jobs and depressing wages. The typical economist who studied trade and employment data could not find much of a correlation, so he or she offered the conventional conclusion: it wasn't the global economy that hurt American blue-collar workers but the new labor-saving technologies. Since the new machines required more sophisticated skills, the solution seemed obvious to the economists: unskilled workers must simply get smarter.

Economists, as the best of them would cheerfully admit, were prisoners of their data and sometimes had difficulty grasping realities that did not appear in tabular form—dynamics like the continuous trade-offs companies made between cheap people and expensive machines. As the young auto workers understood, the explanation for what caused labor's losses was not a choice between technology or capital flight. The answer was both, interacting with each other. If the foundry failed to modernize, it lost orders to a distant, low-wage competitor. If it did modernize, some jobs were eliminated and even the survivors remained vulnerable.

In any case, in recent years some respectable economists have begun to conclude that the auto workers had it about right. One of these, Professor Adrian Wood of Britain's University of Sussex, a former senior economist at the World Bank, published a controversial study in 1994 arguing that conventional economic analysis has underestimated the job losses in advanced economies attributable to the expanding global trade by a factor of 10. Wood calculated that by 1990 the reduced demand for less skilled manufacturing workers was six to twelve million "person-years."

The job losses from "defensive innovation," as Wood called it, added still further to that total but were impossible to measure. As a crude estimate, he suggested that competitive modernization doubled the impact, and that the losses from the trade in nonmanufacturing services might double it again. Thus, the overall loss in demand for unskilled labor, relative to the skilled, was about 20 percent.

Some higher-skilled workers lost, too, and even more dramatically, Wood pointed out, if they happened to be working in the industrial sectors that were wiped out. This compounded the job and wage problems for blue-collar industrial workers since the displaced workers, skilled and un-skilled, were left to compete for the same dwindling pool of jobs—a phe-nomenon of downward mobility familiar in the United States where recent college graduates have begun to seek jobs on auto assembly lines.[9]

Many mainstream economists resisted Wood's conclusions for good reason: If he was correct, then a central tenet supporting unregulated global capitalism was in doubt—namely, that the free-trade regime was good for everyone, every society and almost everyone in it. The profession acknowl-edged temporary dislocations, of course, but argued that the great benefits generated by free commerce and expanding trade far offset the localized losses. By insisting that technology, not the global trading system, was responsible for the displacements, economists and political leaders could argue that it was the workers, not the system, that had to be corrected.

Thus, supported by sound economics, government and business leaders delivered a reassuring lecture to working people: They will survive and flourish in the global economy once they have acquired higher skills. Most of the displacements, they pointed out, had hit the less skilled industrial workers, from garment making to auto assembly, while engineers and vari-ous technicians were prospering. If workers improved their productivity so their labor added more value to the finished product, then their wages would begin to increase, too, instead of steadily declining.

On the shop floor, the familiar mantra of training and productivity may have sounded like a high-tech version of "let them eat cake." If the peasants cannot afford bread, Marie Antoinette suggested, let them eat cake. If your job as a steelworker vanishes, why not become a computer engineer or chemist or stock-market analyst?

More to the point, the economic facts did not exactly support these reassurances. Many orthodox economists oddly neglected the supply ques-tion: the global overabundance of cheaper labor. This surplus was most obviously threatening to highly paid factory workers, but it was beginning to claim highly skilled workers in the front office as well—engineers and other industrial professionals. Their work was portable, too.

"There are excellent engineers in China, graduate engineers, but they don't have many opportunities," said Yuri Momomoto of Fujitsu. "So we are developing software centers in Beijing and Fujian."

GM was opening a technical center in Shanghai for China's infant auto industry. Motorola was locating a new corporate R&D center in Sydney, Australia, where the engineers earned 50 to 60 percent of U.S. salaries.

"There's no question that engineering talent is much lower cost in Asia," said Richard W. Heimlich, who was Motorola's corporate vice presi-dent for international strategy before taking charge of Southeast Asia opera-tions in Singapore. "We have a software center in Bangalore, India, but that's not the only place. For the new technologies in software, it's much more portable."

Jeffrey Henderson, a British scholar who studied the globalization of high-tech production, concluded: "What is becoming important . . . is the relative cheapness (and availability) of skilled, technical labor power." [10]

Educational improvement was self-evidently a good thing for anyone to do, regardless of the economics, but the assumption that better training would somehow rescue Americans or Europeans from the global market pressures carried with it an unstated (and perhaps unconscious) implication of racial or cultural superiority. The subliminal message, crudely translated, was: these other people are catching up with us, climbing up higher on the ladder, but we will be okay—still on top—if we just scramble a bit higher on the ladder ourselves. Cultural egotism, as later chapters make clear, is a provincial illusion mocked by the global marketplace.

In any case, the fundamental assumption in the economists' optimistic assurances—that workers would be rewarded if they increased their productivity—was also wrong. For several decades, that had been the expected outcome, but reality no longer conformed with the comforting theory. For many years, wages had not kept up with productivity increases in the United States and many other leading countries. In fact, productivity has been uncoupled from wage levels, starting with the great upheavals of industrial restructurings.

U.S. manufacturing productivity increased cumulatively by about 35 percent from the late 1970s to 1990, while manufacturing wages were stagnant or falling in real terms, discounted for inflation. From 1989 to 1994 output per hour in all nonfarm business rose just under 10 percent; the real compensation per hour rose less than 4 percent.

"In the 1980's, higher skills have simply not led to higher wages," David R. Howell wrote in the *American Prospect*. "In industry after industry, average educational attainment rose while wages fell. Indeed, wages fell more rapidly for younger workers, despite their higher educational attainment." [11]

The pattern varied widely in other industrial economies, especially if the nations had strong unions and had not yet undergone the kind of wrenching deindustrialization that American industries experienced. As the industrial shakeouts and wage-cutting labor contracts rolled forward in Western Europe, their workers and unions likewise discovered that rising productivity no longer guaranteed rising wages.

The primary explanation was the global wage arbitrage. The general presumption that low-wage workers in backward countries were crudely unproductive was simply not true. In fact, dollar for dollar, the cheaper workers often represented a better buy for employers than the more skillful workers who were replaced. Their productivity was lower but it also improved rapidly—much faster than their wages. In order to attract foreign capital, their governments often made certain this was the case.

In Mexico, for instance, the new auto workers for Ford or GM or

VW might perform at 50 to 70 percent of the efficiency of workers in the companies' home plants. But their wages were one sixth or one eighth as much. Throughout the 1980s and again in the financial crisis of early 1995, Mexico's domestic wages were effectively collapsed by the government's financial policies. The peso devaluations literally rendered the Mexican workers twice as cheap for foreign employers.

Harley Shaiken, a University of California economist, studied auto production in Mexico and, like American company managers, came away impressed by the abilities of the Mexican workers. "When advanced manufacturing combines with artificially depressed wages, the labor costs are disconnected from productivity," Shaiken explained. "In Mexico, manufacturing productivity is up 40 percent since 1980, but real wages in pesos are down 40 percent. That's quite a wide divergence." [12]

Similar divergences were commonplace around the world, even in the Asian labor markets where wages were rising smartly. The classic case was shirts: American garment workers could make a shirt with 14 minutes of human labor, while it took 25 minutes in Bangladesh. But the average U.S. wage was $7.53 an hour, while in Bangladesh it was 25 cents, an edge that would not be erased even if the Bangladeshi wages were doubled or quadrupled. Or steel: U.S. industry required 3.4 hours of human labor to produce a ton of steel, while Brazil took 5.8 hours. But the wage difference was 10 to 1: $13 an hour versus $1.28. [13]

The bottom line came down to this: capital was claiming a larger share of the returns from production, and not just in America. International comparisons were difficult, but this reality was reflected in the World Bank's nation-by-nation calculations of wages as a percentage of manufacturing's value-added gains. In the United States, the earnings share of the value-added production had fallen over twenty years from 45 to 35 percent. In Germany, though wages remained higher, the wage share of production returns had declined from 47 to 42 percent. Even in Japan, where labor's share had grown robustly for many years, a decline set in during the last decade. [14]

In the fast-developing poor countries, the multinational managers who resisted unions for their workers often smugly argued that—with or without unions—local wages were rising rapidly as workers and industries improved their productivity (and that unions might get in the way of this process). The evidence from the World Bank's tables did not support their claim. In places like Malaysia and Indonesia, wages were indeed rising, but the workers' share of the value-added returns was falling—just like their better-off counterparts in American and European factories.

One spectacular exception was South Korea, where labor's share has risen from 23 to 30 percent. One of the explanations was that, after several decades of brutal repression, Korean workers had rebelled. With help from free trade unions in the United States and Europe, Korean unions had helped to spark the civil upheaval that upended the authoritarian military regime. After the workers won new political freedoms, Korean manufacturing wages rose spectacularly.

The unhinging of wages from productivity was driven by a fundamental structural change: the mass production system that for many years had guaranteed a happy convergence of interests between workers and owners was itself being dismantled—smashed by the technological revolution and by the global dispersal of production. In the postwar decades, what economists described as a "virtuous circle" had operated in the core manufacturing sectors, a self-reinforcing prosperity that, in effect, shared the gains of rising productivity among owners, workers and consumers, distributed in the form of profits, wages and prices.

The old system resembled a splendidly harmonious wheel: economies of scale in mass production fostered rapidly rising productivity (that is, per unit labor costs were reduced as the volume of production grew). These cost savings permitted steady wage increases for workers (and lower unemployment) as well as cheaper prices for consumers. The rising incomes for workers made possible the robust growth in consumer spending which, in turn, fed back into supporting the more profitable economies of scale.[15]

The "virtuous circle" did not vanish entirely, but it was gravely destabilized by the industrial revolution. New producers from the poorer nations flooded into the marketplace, offering cost advantages based on an opposite premise: lower wages. Simultaneously, the new technologies undermined the simplicities and standardization of the mass-production assembly lines. Rapid change, a stream of newly differentiated products and constant competition to elaborate their quality, undercut the cost savings that companies expected to derive automatically from repetitive mass production.

In the old era, industrial managers spoke of the "learning curve" in which a company (and its workers) increased their efficiency savings (the productivity gains that fed into profits and wages) the longer they produced something and the greater its volume. In the new era, the "learning curve" could turn against them. Instead of extracting more returns from a long production run that turned out more and more of the same standardized stuff, managers and workers discovered they must continuously "move up" the learning curve: constantly getting smarter, customizing products and refining the production processes to keep up with price competitors doing the same.

In short, the emerging system produced less surplus to share, and as profits were squeezed the owners of capital stopped sharing with the workers. The erosion of middle-class incomes in affluent nations like America was directly connected to this breakdown of the "virtuous circle." In the long run, restoring a stable prosperity to the broad working populations of advanced nations would depend upon creating a new core that revived the harmonious wheel—new elements of production and consumption that could support rising incomes. Whether this future involved new, as-yet-unimagined products or new economic and social arrangements, it was still no more than a fuzzy vision at present.

Labor leaders might not dispute the profit-productivity account of why manufacturing wages declined, but they would perhaps put it differently: the capital owners stopped sharing gains with labor because they found they had the power to do so. Starting in the 1970s, U.S. companies gravitated toward a different strategy in which global price pressures were offset by extracting more from labor. Corporations discarded their long postwar truce with unions and began moving jobs, first to the low-wage South and then offshore. They closed factories and demanded wage contracts that depressed wages. They mobilized both political and economic power to weaken labor's bargaining position.

American corporate managers might point out that they themselves were driven to these defensive actions by the global economic forces. The "virtuous circle" of the 1950s and 1960s had also been sustained by the existence of industrial oligopolies—a few big companies that dominated major sectors like autos, steel and aircraft and were powerful enough to set prices and wages in a clubby, arbitrary fashion. The rise of foreign producers, especially from Japan, broke up that comfortable arrangement forever.

As firms shifted production to lower-wage workers, organized labor lost members and became steadily less able to discipline managements. The decline in wages was not confined to union members, however, but was more general. Retail sales workers, for instance, experienced a much sharper fall than manufacturing. In 1970, wages constituted 67 percent of all personal income in the United States, a ratio that had held constant for decades. By 1994, wages were less than 58 percent of total incomes. In 1960, wages were about 26 percent of total sales. By 1994, they were about 20 percent.[16]

Labor unions have always argued that while unionized workers enjoyed higher wages that seemed inequitable to others, their collective power in labor markets provided the wage discipline that was the floor holding up all working incomes, except, perhaps, for the upper tier of well-educated professionals. Without this core of union power, labor argued, wages would fall generally for union and nonunion workers alike, but especially for the least skilled. The events of the last two decades seemed to confirm that claim.

The American experience was now being tested in other affluent nations where the levels of unionization were stronger, but were also coming under attack. The "American solution" would meet more resistance in Europe certainly, but capital was employing the same form of discipline: exit to other labor markets. Among European business leaders, there was admiration for the way in which U.S. politics had solved the jobs problem.

"The Wobblies were right, but they were about a hundred years ahead of their time," said William Goold, a Washington labor-rights activist. Wobblies were the early homegrown radicals of the American labor movement, formally organized as Industrial Workers of the World and proclaiming an all-encompassing, transnational challenge to corporate capitalism. Goold meant that their global perspective did not really fit the 1890s, when national corporations were unifying national economies, but was more appropriate to the late twentieth century, when capital became truly global. "Workers of the world, unite," the Wobblies had declared.

If that sounded romantic, contemporary labor organizations like the International Metalworkers Federation were trying, somewhat haphazardly, to invest new meaning in the old slogan. From different continents some major unions were beginning to support each other in actions against multinational corporations and these cross-border tactics sometimes succeeded. Still, the labor apparatus for cooperation was pathetically primitive and nationalistic alongside the cosmopolitanism of modern commerce and finance.

"People still think nationally or even locally," Marcello Malentacchi, an Italian who is the IMF's general secretary, conceded. "Steelworkers still think about steelworkers, auto workers about auto workers. The trouble is, the multinational corporations don't think European or American any more, they haven't for a long time. They think globally.

"If you go back a hundred years, we started to organize our people in one plant. It took us a few years to understand that there was another plant that also needed to be organized before we could prevail. Now we are at the stage where you have to teach people that there is another country and another region and that we have to organize there, too. It will take a generation."

The barriers to global labor action were formidable, more formidable than many labor people could bring themselves to acknowledge. The most wrenching, fundamental obstacle was the stark gulf between the interests of rich and poor. Solutions that protected the living standards of the prosperous simply by shutting out the aspirations of impoverished nations were denounced, correctly, as a new expression of colonialism.

A new labor movement was indeed struggling to be born across the developing nations of Asia, but it was weak and often defenseless against overbearing political and economic forces. High-minded measures that reformers advanced to help those workers were often denounced as "moral protectionism," schemes to insulate European and American labor by robbing the poor nations of their principal attraction—cheap workers.

Labor's principal answer was a campaign to incorporate universal labor rights in the global trading system, a so-called social clause in trade agreements that would allow workers everywhere to organize their own collective power and punish exports from those nations that did not honor the new rules. Over time, this would redefine the global labor market and stop the erosion or at least slow it down. In a crude sense, it meant bringing up the bottom.

Political opposition to this approach was overwhelming: Global corporations and finance were naturally against it, joined by the governments of developing nations, but many governments in advanced economies were also indifferent or hostile. Many leading politicians lent rhetorical support to labor's goal, but, in reality, most were aligned, one way or another, with the imperatives of the multinationals. Perhaps that would change as the mainstream political parties in the wealthier nations continued to decline.

Even among the prosperous nations, however, organized labor was itself profoundly divided by history and perspective. If a global labor movement were to arise, what would it look like—the European model or the American or the Japanese? Each form had developed vastly different ways of relating to companies: the sectoral and confrontational style of U.S. unions; the broader, more participatory social systems of Europe where workers sat on corporate boards and multinational companies shared strategic information with the elected works councils; the Japanese collaborative style in which cooperative union leaders often went on to become company managers.

Perhaps none of these forms would be right for an Indonesia or a China, if the day ever arrived when workers in those countries were free to organize themselves. Some other model might emerge instead, perhaps an organization that was broader than industrial sectors, closer to the social life of communities, less narrow in its objectives. After all, it was clear everywhere that a hundred years after the birth of industrial unions, organized labor had not yet devised an enduring and satisfactory response to corporate capitalism.

An alternative future was also plausible for labor: obsolescence. As manufacturing migrated, it was conceivable that industrial unions would continue to atrophy and eventually become empty remnants, at least in the most advanced economies. After all, agriculture was once the major employer in America and the Grange had once been a major force in U.S. politics. Many business and political leaders, at least privately, expected the same fate for unions: virtual extinction.

That possibility begged the social question in new terms: if unions disappeared, might something else arise to replace them, some new form of collective voice that could counter the unfettered force of the marketplace? As an economic imperative driving global commerce, wage arbitrage was an opportunity. As a social imperative, it sowed deepening disarray and anger. While business and finance pursued the economics, it was the deteriorating social conditions that in the long run might become more threatening to free capital than unions.

In the meantime, some elements of labor were belatedly trying to catch up with the action. In the fall of 1994, the IMF sent an exploratory committee to China to survey the burgeoning industry there and to meet with Chinese labor leaders. Trade-union principle dictated that solidarity with China's unions was impossible since China's workers were involuntary members of the state-controlled labor federation.

On the other hand, the major multinationals that employed Swedes and Germans, Japanese and Americans were already in China, already making deals and building factories. To protect its own workers, a union must keep track of its companies—where they are headed, what they are making, how they treat their workers. The metalworker unions reluctantly decided they could no longer stand aloof on principle. After anguished debate, the IMF decided it must enter China, too.

Five

"Wawasan 2020" *

THE PROCESS of global economic integration is broadly driven by market forces, in particular the competitive price pressures to reduce costs, but the actual events of industrial movement depend crucially upon political transactions—irregular deals that often offend the reigning principles of free-market enterprise. When a multinational corporation seeks to shift production to low-wage labor markets, a process of political bargaining ensues with the governments competing for the new factories. Concessions are offered, deals are made, investment follows.

Given the worldwide thirst for economic development and the abundance of willing governments, these political arrangements are now so commonplace that almost everyone regards them as normal. The multinational companies usually have the leverage to stipulate terms for their capital investments, but the leverage is reversed in some important cases and nations can dictate terms to the firms (conditions of market leverage that are examined in later chapters).

A corporation's power is naturally strongest if it is dealing with a small, very poor country desperate for industrial development. The terms typically involve special political favors not available to others in commerce: state subsidies, exemption from taxation, government suppression of workers, special status as export enclaves free of import duties.

With these protective benefits, commerce is able to leap across the deepest social and economic divisions, bringing advanced production systems to primitive economies, disturbing ancient cultures with startling elements of modernity. Governments of developing nations may be nervous about the cultural disruption, but they usually suppress doubts and dissent. Starting from positions of weakness, the poor states hope this exchange will start them on an upward track toward higher levels of industrialization and an escape from general poverty. Some are succeeding in those terms and with spectacular results; many others eagerly offer themselves as the new greenfields for migrating production.

* Bahasa Malaysia: "vision 2020."

Even successful nations discover, however, that a basic insecurity lingers in their economic advance. A prosperity based on the strategies of multinational corporations remains hostage to them. If a country manages to graduate from low-wage status and establish a self-sustaining industrial base, its achievement may become permanent. But the very process of moving up also threatens to drive away the global investors. If capital does eventually move on, a relationship intended to be a mutually rewarding symbiosis may prove to have been parasitic.

An ironic and debilitating form of global convergence is under way between rich and poor: a global jobs auction. The irregular political leverage that commerce first employed in the weak countries is now being applied to the wealthy and powerful as well, especially the United States. Multinationals are, in effect, conducting a peripatetic global jobs competition, awarding shares of production to those who make the highest bids— that is, the greatest concessions by the public domain. If a poor country like Malaysia grants public favors to capital in exchange for scarce jobs, then so will Ohio or Alabama.

In the industrial zone at Petaling Jaya outside Kuala Lumpur, a line of dingy blue buses began delivering workers for the 2 P.M. shift change at the Motorola plant. Motorola's blue logo was visible from the freeway, along with some other celebrated names of electronics like Canon, Sanyo, Panasonic and Minolta. Its factory looked like a low-slung office building facing an asphalt parking lot that was bordered by palms and giant yews. The white facade was temporarily decorated with dozens of red paper lanterns and gilded banners in honor of the Chinese New Year. Above the front entrance, a billboard invited workers to enter the "Motorola 10K Run," winners to compete at the U.S. Austin marathon.

The arriving workers passed through glass doors and headed down a long gleaming corridor toward the changing room, past the library and health center and an automatic banking machine. All of them were women, and most were young, small and delicate by American standards. They were dressed in the modesty of Islam—flowing ankle-length dresses, heads and shoulders draped by the Muslim *tundjung,* silken scarves of pale blue, orange and brown. A few wore the fuller, more conservative black veils that closely framed their faces like pale brown hearts and encased the upper body like shrouds.

"Good afternoon, ladies." Roger Bertelson, Motorola's country manager, was showing me around, and the two of us towered above the stream of women. They passed by, eyes down, barely nodding. Bertelson had brush-cut hair and a sunny American forwardness, like a taller version of Ross Perot. He was explaining the "I Recommend" board on the wall, a display covered with snapshots of employees who had made successful suggestions.

"We had to change the culture," Bertelson said, "because the Malay home does not encourage women to speak out. The daughter is supposed to have babies and take care of her husband. The idea was to break down the resistance to speaking out. We use positive reinforcement, just like you would work with schoolchildren. First, convince them that you are going to listen to them. Then have them stand up before their peers for recognition."

The automatic teller machine also disturbed the culture. "We had to change the pattern," he said. "She had to go home and tell her father: 'I'm not going to bring my money home in a pay envelope any more. It's going into the bank.' "

Farther along the hallway, the women passed by a collection of Norman Rockwell paintings—warm, nostalgic scenes of American life—each accompanied by an inspirational aphorism in English. "People Will Take Note of Excellent Work." "You'll Be Prepared for Anything with Enthusiasm." "What We Say Is as Important as How We Say It." It was hard to know what meaning these homey American images might have in this setting.

At the changing room, the women removed shoes and veils and proceeded to the gowning room across the hall. A few minutes later they emerged cloaked in ghostly white jumpsuits, wearing surgical masks and hooded bonnets. They looked like otherworldly travelers, more chaste than they would appear in the most severe Islamic garments. At the air shower, blasts of purified air cleansed them of any remaining particles of dust. Then they entered the sealed operations room, where the rows of complex machines and monitors awaited the next shift.

Once inside, the women in space suits began the exacting daily routines of manufacturing semiconductor chips. They worked in a realm of submicrons, attaching leads on devices too small to see without the aid of the electronic monitors. Watching the women through an observation window, Bertelson remarked: "She doesn't really do it, the machine does it."

The manufacturing process for semiconductors literally bounced around the world. Larger silicon wafers that included the circuitry for multiple chips had been designed and fabricated back in the States (or perhaps in Scotland, where the industry had also located a major production base). Then the wafers were flown by 747 to Malaysia (or perhaps Singapore or the Philippines or elsewhere in Asia) for final assembly—sawed into individual chips, wired, tested and packaged. The finished chips were shipped back to North America, Asia and Europe to become the functional guts of TV sets, computers, cars, portable phones, missile control systems and countless other products.

The spectacle of cultural transformation at Motorola was quite routine —three times a day, seven days a week—but it conveyed the high human drama of globalization: a fantastic leap across time and place, an exchange that was banal and revolutionary, vaguely imperial and exploitative, yet also profoundly liberating. In the longer sweep of history, the social intrusions of modern technology might be as meaningful as the economic upheavals. Motorola and the other semiconductor companies settled in Malaysia have managed to unite the leading edge of technological complexity with shy young women from the *kampong*, rural villages where destiny was defined as helping peasant fathers and husbands harvest the rice or palm oil.

At lunch in the company cafeteria, Bertelson and his management staff talked about the complexity. "We improve our productivity 15 percent a year, that's company policy," he said. "We have a road map for each one of our operations that calls for a 10x improvement by the year 2000, by automating and by improving worker efficiency. We will do that."

Malaysian production was not exempt from the same steep "learning curve" that drove price competition throughout the global industry, a standing assumption that costs and prices will fall by roughly 30 percent every time the volume doubles. To defend market share, every producer must continuously squeeze out more waste and imperfection or develop the new materials and production methods that could keep up with the curve. "Our technology, the miniaturization, is growing so fast that we really need to get the human element out of the process as fast as we can," Bertelson said.

Around the lunch table Bertelson's department managers looked like a visionary's ideal of multicultural cooperation. Chinese, Malay, Indian, black, yellow, pale brown, Christian, Buddhist, Muslim, Hindu. The only white guys were Bertelson and a Scottish engineer named Dave Anderson, hired from Singapore. Longinus Bernard, an Indian from Johore whose father had worked on colonial estates, described the early days in 1974 when Motorola started up. "We were so small, everybody knows everybody," he said. "It was really—how do you call it—a good feeling."

Hassim Majid, manager of government affairs, explained how the racial diversity had been achieved. "We were advised by the government to play an active role in restructuring the ethnic composition of the company," he said. "We were told to hire *x* number of Malay people like me, Chinese and Indians, just like your affirmative action in the United States. Motorola did well in meeting the government requirement."

The Kuala Lumpur operations, Motorola's largest outside the United States, had 5,000 employees, 80 percent Malay and 3,900 ladies, as the managers called them. The company had plans to double this facility, though not its employment. It represented one of the ripe anomalies of global economic revolution: while conservative ideologues in America fiercely contested the threat of multiculturalism, conservative American corporations were out around the world doing it. In the global context, the preoccupation of American politics with race and cultural superiority seemed ludicrous, out of touch and perhaps also dangerous.

At night, downtown Kuala Lumpur looked a little like a theme park celebrating postcolonial Asian prosperity. Some important buildings were fancifully lit with streamers of sparkling lights, giving outline to an eclectic collection of architecture. The clock tower of an old British administrative building was reminiscent of Westminster, but with oriental grace notes. The railway station looked like a Moorish fantasy imported from some other colonial outpost, as indeed its design was. Dozens of modern office towers formed a dense cluster that dwarfed remnants of the past. The city's oldest mosque, Bandaraya, one of its pale domes in collapse, sat at the foot of the thirty-story Bank Bumiputra.

By the river, the old central market hall had been renovated into artisans' stalls and tourist boutiques, with a U.S. fast-food franchise nearby that sold "Prosperity Burgers." In the early evening, young professionals from the office towers gathered at the outdoor cafes for beer or tea. One night I watched six Malay boys entertaining the sidewalk patrons with an acrobatic hip-hop routine that seemed straight out of Compton, California, the lyrics in Bahasa.

On the headquarters building of the state-owned television station, the Malaysian national imperative—"2020"—was spelled out in huge red lights two stories high and framed by two glittering butterflies. The full slogan, *"Wawasan 2020,"* appeared frequently around the city and was otherwise embedded in everyday consciousness. It stood for the shared "vision" of what Malaysia intended to become: a self-sufficient industrial nation, with an economy that will grow eight times larger by 2020, with a people who will be, as Prime Minister Mahathir Mohamad often emphasized, "psychologically subservient to none."

To that end, the government in the last decade force-fed the development of a national car, the Proton Saga, a smart-looking sedan that relied heavily on Mitsubishi of Japan for design and components, but now claimed 70 percent local content. Mahathir rode in one with "2020" on the license plate. Proton was selling 102,000 cars a year at home and abroad, and has spawned an infant components industry. It was moving into Vietnam with a co-production venture, and a second national car, the Kancil, named for a small jungle deer, was planned with Daihatsu.[1]

The essence of *"Wawasan 2020"* was rapid growth—7 percent a year, every year for the next twenty-five years—and government industrial strategies to foster homegrown industries and a new middle class of talented managers and professionals. Per capita income was supposed to quadruple by 2020. Mahathir talked somewhat airily about launching ventures in telecommunications and aerospace, forming industrial consortia with Asian neighbors like Indonesia or Thailand that could become freestanding rivals to the most advanced economies.

That was the plan. It sounded improbably optimistic, even for the dynamic economies of Southeast Asia, and grandiose in some elements. But Malaysia had earned its self-confidence. Since 1971 its economy had expanded yearly at about the same phenomenal pace: GNP rose from 13 million ringgits in 1971 to 123 million twenty years later. Per capita income had exploded from an impoverished level of $410 a year to more than

$3,000. In more basic terms, Malaysian life expectancy increased in two decades from 62.3 to 70.5 years.[2]

In some ways Malaysia was the best-case illustration of globalization, though it was also unrepresentative because its development was more mature than others and the country was quite small, only twenty million people in territory the size of Florida and Georgia combined. The spectacular growth occurred under a one-party regime that Mahathir had led for nearly fifteen years.

The wealth accumulation produced the usual corruption of political deal-making and centralized ownership, though regular elections were held and Malaysian civil repression was more benign than in many other places. The government had not made mass political arrests since 1989. As Malaysians pointed out, the Internal Security Act set severe limits on political dissent, but the original statute was drafted by the British raj.

Indeed, Malaysia's most striking accomplishment was defusing what Mahathir called the "multi-racial time-bomb we inherited from our colonial past."[3] About 61 percent of the people were the native *bumiputras,* "sons of the soil," the Malay peasantry and some small tribal groups. Across several centuries of colonial rule, the Malays had been confined to the bottom rung in their own country, subsistence agriculture and fishing.

The Chinese, about 30 percent of the population, were part of the vast Chinese diaspora that had spread millions of migrants across nations of Asia and other continents, driven by famine or political upheavals or brought in as "coolie" labor. In Malaysia as elsewhere, the ethnic Chinese became the dominant merchant class (and were sometimes called, with admiration and derision, the "Jews of Asia"). A tenacious sense of community produced their own schools and stores and family-centered wealth, an entrepreneurial self-sufficiency derived from adversity.

The remaining Malaysian population was Indian, mostly Tamils, whom the British had imported, some as adolescent children, to do the lowly work of commodity production—rubber tappers, cane cutters, coffee workers—or to serve as petty civil servants.

The British had ruled Malaysia by exploiting these ethnic divisions. After independence the unstable mix exploded in deadly racial riots in 1969, in which two hundred Chinese were killed.* The racial history was central to the economics: the multi-ethnic political coalition that took power in the early 1970s set out to redress the economic imbalances and bring the Malay people into the action. Sensitive racial tensions remained, but by 1990 the *bumiputras* held roughly 20 percent of the economic assets, compared to 2 percent in the 1960s. Common poverty declined dramatically, from 49 percent of households to 16 percent. Affirmative action was working, most

---

* "Amok," a frenzy of violence, is said to be one of the very few words from Bahasa that has entered regular English usage.

visibly in the profusion of *"kampong* boys" who emerged as well-connected millionaires.[4]

The historic wounds of colonialism, often neglected in the economic literature of advanced nations, were central to understanding the economics and purposeful political strategies that shaped globalization. Though the facts varied in each situation, other Asian nations had experienced similar postcolonial traumas and shared a lingering paranoia about the intentions of Western powers. In all of them, the memory of imperial economic exploitation, including by U.S. interests, produced an abiding wariness, even as these nations rushed to secure a place in the global system.

The most successful Asian nations were not following the laissez-faire capitalism preached by the Americans; they were following Japan (though it had brutally occupied many of these countries during World War II) because the Japanese model for development seemed to work. Whatever else the Malay felt toward the Japanese, Japan's economic triumph had reversed five centuries of world history: the European-American economic hegemony was at last upended by people of color. The Japanese approach meant a strong central government that would command or protect or subsidize markets and enterprises. It meant nationalistic strategies that imposed controls and sacrifices on individual citizens in order to foster rapid economic momentum.

To soften social conflict and compensate for the low industrial wages, Asian governments also typically constructed elaborate social-subsidy systems, public housing and income supports that both ameliorated and controlled. Singapore provided public housing apartments for nearly half of its industrial workers with the understanding: if you do not work, you lose your home. The Asians' development strategies were logically consistent with their own historic grievances and aspirations. The great contradiction was in American orthodoxy: U.S. free-market economists, business leaders and politicians praised the energies of these heretical Asian systems while they denounced similar ideas at home as dangerously socialistic.

Prime Minister Mahathir played to the Pan-Asian sensibilities by offering himself as an acerbic "bad boy" who would say aloud what others were thinking and feeling. While he collaborated with the American multinationals, Mahathir also delivered regular rebukes to the arrogant Western powers, especially the United States. In Beijing, he congratulated the Chinese leaders on the wisdom of their "socialist market economy" and advised them to disregard "sanctimonious pronouncements" from the West on such matters as human rights, low wages or environmental protection. These, he said, were merely self-interested attempts to block Asian progress. "They made a mistake with Japan," he warned. "They are not going to make any more mistakes."[5]

The paranoia also resonated with cultural insecurities. Many young women in Malaysia, I was told, had typically not worn the *tundjung* in everyday life before industrialization arrived. Amid the confusion of rapid changes, it became a way to affirm identity. Mahathir complained bitterly about the corrupting cultural influences of global media and seemed particularly to resent the intrusive presence of Michael Jackson (though not Motorola's).

"The people who decide what we should see and hear hold terrible power," he declared. "They can have us dancing in the streets or they can have us rioting in the streets with firebrands in our hands, burning, looting and killing." It was indeed bizarre to observe the young Malay girls in *tundjung,* riding behind boyfriends on motorcycles, wearing jeans and T-shirts with saucy Americanisms like: "The Night Is Still Young—Party Hard."

A "massive taste transfer" under way from the West to non-Western civilization visibly threatened to overwhelm what was distinctively native in places like Malaysia. Chandra Muzaffar, a Malaysian human-rights advocate, argued that defending cultural pluralism would eventually be understood as an essential dimension of establishing universal human rights. A globalized culture, words and pictures controlled from afar, he said, could deprive people of their independent ability to think and act as surely as imperial armies.[6]

Mahathir's combative posture, nevertheless, may have originated from a deeper source of insecurity: the new form of dependency that the global system had delivered to his country, along with the rising incomes. Social reforms aside, Malaysia's prosperity was really based upon a singular decision by American semiconductor companies in the early 1970s to find a new locale for low-wage final assembly. Malaysians celebrated their progress, but also sometimes wondered if a new raj had taken power.

Seventeen U.S. companies—Fairchild, National Semiconductor, Texas Instruments, Intel, Hewlett-Packard and others—had moved chip production to Kuala Lumpur and Penang, a northern island in the Straits of Malacca, in rapid succession. In time, they were joined by their principal competitors, the Japanese electronics companies, producing semiconductors and a wide array of consumer products, from VCRs to air conditioners.

These foreign producers were the core of the new Malaysian economy, not the Proton Saga. Between the Japanese and the Americans, electronics produced half of all Malaysia's manufacturing exports and employed as many as 150,000 people. Their presence expanded most dramatically, roughly by half, from 1988 to 1993, when Japanese companies began moving assembly work offshore to offset the price effects of the rising yen and falling dollar.[7]

Malaysia's gamble was that this huge core of multinational companies, using the country as an export platform, would stimulate the spin-off development of domestic firms and create a lasting infrastructure of economic activity alongside the privileged export zones. Despite twenty years of robust expansion it was still not certain that the gamble was succeeding.

"Despite the most rapid development in the free trade zones, insignificant demand has been generated for local intermediate products," Mahathir himself acknowledged to the Malaysian Business Council. "There is inadequate development of indigenous technology. There is too little value-added, too much simple assembly and production."[8]

In fact, despite Malaysia's brave claims of nationhood, its economy appeared to be trapped in the middle—not fully self-sufficient, yet compelled to compete downward with the new low-wage entrants from below, poorer nations also struggling to get out from under. Malaysia enjoyed full employment and rising productivity, yet these virtues could also undermine the progress if they led to the usual consequence of rising wages.

"The prime minister talks very tough, very radical, but watch what he does, not what he says," Jeffrey E. Garten, U.S. Undersecretary of Commerce, confided to me in Washington. "Malaysia did all of this major development with tremendous growth in electronics. But it could move on a dime, move on a dime. There are seven or eight countries waiting in the wings if the companies ever decide to leave. So Malaysia is stuck. It could lose the electronics industry overnight if it makes the wrong move."

Semiconductor chips, as a basic commodity in every modern industrial product, were sometimes described as the "crude oil of the information age," but that comparison obscured the fabulous mobility and complexity. Malaysia was but one important outpost in a dizzying network of production locations, from Scotland to California and Texas to the belt of East Asian nations that runs southward from Korea and Taiwan to Indonesia and Thailand.[9]

"The longer we stay in this business and grow," Motorola's Roger Bertelson said, "the easier we find it is to take a new factory and set it up in an underdeveloped country. We use the same training methodology and technology we perfected in Malaysia to go into China."

These movements were originally driven by a straightforward search for cheaper workers, but the rationale evolved into more sophisticated strategies as the rising complexity reduced the labor dimension and greatly multiplied the capital costs of building new semiconductor plants. Locating production elements in different regions became a hedge play for multinationals of all kinds, protecting prices and profits against the constant storm of currency changes or market shares against the growing threat of protectionism. If major consumer markets were to close access to outside producers, the semiconductor industry had already established itself as a ubiquitous insider.

At the outset, competing among themselves, the U.S. companies had followed one another to Asian locations and then worked out the deal with Malaysia for its burgeoning assembly base. When the Japanese producers came on strong as price rivals in the late 1970s, the Americans moved still more production abroad to keep up. But the Japanese preferred to automate rather than move jobs offshore (thus improving quality as well as price), so American companies were compelled to automate more themselves.

"The original logic was labor costs," said Richard W. Heimlich, formerly Motorola's corporate vice president for international strategy. "Now the logic is transformed into a core competence in different parts of the world that doesn't get transferred. The original logic was: keep the highest technology in the home country and the rest went to countries where you could find low-cost labor. Now it's a matter of accumulated capability in different regions, centers of excellence."

The bargaining process with host governments sounded like a high-stakes poker game. "You've got a bunch of governments with chips they can play and a bunch of multinational corporations with chips they can play, and, basically, they sit down and negotiate," Heimlich explained. "Obviously, the multinational corporation is going to try to do things that optimize their situation, market share or profitability or whatever. In the case of the governments, the question is what's it going to do for jobs or exports or technology."

The politics of multinationals was much more ambidextrous than that, however. Like other sectors, the semiconductor industry pursued politics at home and away, extracting benefits from governments on both ends of the production network (indeed from many ends at once). In the United States, Motorola has been especially aggressive and successful in using the federal government as a market-opening wedge for itself. From Carter to Clinton, the company offered itself as a test case for U.S. trade policy and persuaded the White House to mobilize against Japan's closed domestic markets.

During the Reagan administration, as Japanese semiconductor producers threatened to monopolize the global market, the White House went to battle for American firms and produced a formal semiconductor agreement with Japan in 1986 that provided a guaranteed market share to the U.S. industry. While the American firms regained their balance, the government also financed a research consortium, Sematech, to help enhance their technological edge. The rationale for these political interventions was that semiconductors constituted a critical advanced technology and the United States could not afford to lose these capabilities.

As an employer, however, the American semiconductor industry was a declining asset, at least for Americans. American employment in semiconductors peaked in 1985 and had fallen 23 percent by 1993, even though the industry's global market share was rebounding. The job losses were heavier in the front office than on the factory floor.

During those years when Republican and Democratic presidents were going to bat for the semiconductor industry, the multinationals were shifting their employment base abroad. This was reflected in Commerce Department reporting on electronic components, a broader category that included semiconductors but excluded firms that were solely domestic. Among those multinationals, American jobs declined by 37 percent from 1982 to 1991, from 290,000 to 184,000, while those same global firms increased their offshore employment by nearly one third. Though some Japanese companies were simultaneously moving some production to the United States, the overall effect was still negative: jobs at the foreign-owned plants also declined in the United States, from 85,000 to 52,000.[10]

While Motorola was especially adept at enlisting the U.S. government to advance its global interests, the company was steadily becoming less "American" itself. Its workforce was growing robustly, reaching 142,000 worldwide by 1995, but the U.S. share has declined to only 56 percent, according to a company spokesman. Intel, another major employer in Malaysia, was down to 17,000 employees at home in America. A new $750 million wafer fabrication plant Motorola announced in 1995 could have been located in the United States, an industry source said, but the company chose to put it in China for strategic reasons.

In the orthodox theory guiding the U.S. government's economic policy, these shifts of production were regarded as beneficial to the United States, despite the job losses, because they strengthened the companies and would presumably stimulate U.S. exports. By establishing elements of production in other nations, the global manufacturers would increase their intrafirm trade and thus support the jobs back home.

That was the theory promoting greater globalization. For the United States, the theory was not exactly supported by the trade statistics: Asian economies absorbing new U.S. investments were also running persistent, substantial trade surpluses with the United States. Malaysia, for instance, bought $4.4 billion in goods from the United States in 1992 and sold it $8.3 billion. When the trade flows from all of Asia's developing countries, including China, were combined, they represented a U.S. trade deficit rivaling the one with Japan.[11]

In any case, given the extreme wage differences, the production jobs that had left the United States were not likely to ever come back. If anything, according to Heimlich and others, the globalization strategies meant the dispersal of more high-end engineering jobs as software design centers were located in Malaysia, India and elsewhere. "The only way those assembly jobs would come home is if the industry fully automates," said Clyde V. Prestowitz Jr., president of the Economic Strategy Institute. "But if it does that, there won't be any jobs anyway."

Malaysia, in order to secure its status as a major export platform, had offered the semiconductor industry, among other things, a lengthy holiday from taxes. Plants in the economic zones were given "pioneer" status for five to ten years. That meant no taxation on earnings in the country, exemptions from import duties and other forms of state subsidies. These tax holidays would eventually expire, but could be renewed and extended if a company made new investments. Other tax breaks kicked in later.

A more controversial benefit was the government's guarantee that electronics workers would be prohibited from organizing independent unions. Though organized labor functioned with some freedom in other sectors, including electrical manufacturing, the government decreed that the goal of national development required a union-free environment for the "pioneers" in semiconductors. The original restriction, supposedly temporary, was regularly protested by groups of workers, but nearly twenty-five years later the ban was still enforced. It now covered not just semiconductors but every other electronics product as well, including at the Japanese firms, which, unlike the American firms, were unionized at home.

Whenever the labor rights issue arose, leading companies professed not to care one way or the other, but the same message always got delivered to the government: unions will jeopardize investment. The government always backed off. On one occasion in the 1980s a delegation from American companies warned the minister of labor: "If unionization is forced upon them, some companies that are already operating here will close down their local operations while others would cease to continue investment, thereby moving to obsolescence."

In 1988, pressured by complaints from the AFL-CIO and the threat of trade sanctions, the labor minister announced an opening. Given the robust growth in Malaysia's electronics sector, he was lifting the restrictions and would recognize a new national union of electronics workers. Five hundred workers gathered from Kuala Lumpur factories to begin an organizing drive. A few days later a delegation from the Malaysian-American Electronics Industry Association met with the labor minister to express their disappointment. Simultaneously, U.S. executives collared Mahathir at a trade conference he was attending in New York. The policy change was rescinded. The labor minister retired.[12]

Instead of the national union, the government offered a weaker alternative, company-by-company "in-house unions." When workers organized one at Harris Electronics, the twenty-one leaders were fired and the new union evaporated. The French-owned Thomson Electronics, which had acquired elements of the old RCA from General Electric, inherited a factory with a union with three thousand members. It closed the plant and moved to Vietnam.[13]

Bruno Petera, a forty-two-year-old supervisor at Harris and one of the union organizers who lost his job, thought the union movement would eventually persevere, regardless of the obstacles, as Malaysians became more confident about themselves. The nation was building not only a new middle class, but also a new working class. In time, he said, people would object to their own powerlessness.

"Once you meet your material needs, you want the dignity," Bruno said. "The dignity to ask a question, to file a complaint, to speak for yourself. It will happen, little by little. Nothing is given free without a struggle."

○

If Malaysians were capable of manufacturing American semiconductor chips, could Alabamians make a German Mercedes? The question was not entirely frivolous because the state of Alabama awarded a huge package of subsidies to Daimler-Benz in exchange for a small Mercedes factory that will be located at Tuscaloosa. The Alabama government put up more than $300 million in tax breaks and subsidies for a plant that would employ only 1,500 people—that is, $200,000 per job.

Alabama citizens were enormously proud of their acquisition, as proud as Malaysians had been when Motorola arrived. Alabamians were used to being disparaged as backward and passed over by new industrial development because of the state's ugly, racist history. Perhaps the Mercedes name would make them respectable, modern. The boastful governor announced that the interstate highway from Montgomery to Birmingham was being renamed the Mercedes-Benz Autobahn. He dispatched National Guard troops to begin clearing the factory site. The Mercedes emblem was placed atop the scoreboard at the university football stadium, though even Alabamians flinched at that excess, and it was taken down.

The terms that Alabama provided Daimler made Malaysia's tax deals seem frugal. In addition to $253 million in direct incentives, the state promised to buy 2,500 of the newly designed sports utility vehicles, priced at $30,000 each. Alabama taxpayers would pay $60 million in travel and hotel costs to send their fellow citizens to Germany for training. Given the generous tax holiday, the taxpayers would be paying the wages of the future Mercedes workers for some years to come.[14]

To justify this, boosterish state leaders spun out a fanciful economic scenario in which Alabama might become, if not Stuttgart or Detroit, at least a major center for auto-components production. The vision ignored the fact that auto components were routinely shipped across continents and oceans or that Daimler's supplier base was moving eastward to Hungary and the Czech Republic, where industrial labor was even cheaper than in Alabama. Several months after Alabama's expensive triumph, Daimler announced that it also had made a deal with Vietnam to locate a new assembly plant for light trucks and cars at Ho Chi Minh City. Terms were not disclosed, but it seemed likely that Hanoi had gotten a better deal than Alabama.[15]

The larger point was that the United States and some other advanced nations were now mimicking the Third World—bidding for jobs with public money, offering irregular favors to migrating capital. The dispersal of manufacturing might be driven by other imperatives, but companies naturally collected whatever was available from the process. In Britain, Ford threatened to locate production of a new Jaguar model and a thousand jobs in the United States if the United Kingdom did not provide an additional $150 million in state aid for the plant. Ford CEO Alexander Trotman, who was British himself, allowed that Americans "could build Jaguars just fine."[16]

The jobs auction in America, already generous, was escalating absurdly. Ohio had paid $16 million in direct incentives to Honda for a plant at Marysville in 1982. Kentucky spent $125 million to lure Toyota to Georgetown in 1988. "The package that won the last Japanese factory becomes the opening bid for the next plant," the Office of Technology Assessment observed. Tennessee gave Nissan $11,000 per job for a plant in Smyrna in 1980. South Carolina put up $79,000 per job for a BMW plant at Spartanburg in 1992. Alabama's $200,000 per job in 1993 shocked even the other southern states competing for the plant. Bill Bishop, a columnist for the *Lexington Herald-Leader,* dubbed Kentucky "the free lunch state" because it had set a new record with tax exemptions for a small Canadian steel producer worth $350,000 per job.[17]

Alongside the auction, migrating capital has further refined a domestic form of jobs blackmail: pay up or we leave. The blackmail was given a polite name, "corporate retention," just as the jobs auction has been dignified as "economic development."

Owens-Corning, which has made glass in Toledo, Ohio, for nearly sixty years, extracted $90 million from the city and state when it threatened to leave. Pratt & Whitney shook down Connecticut for $32 million. Minnesota put up $828 million to keep Northwest Airlines based there (and to finance two new repair facilities that were subsequently put "on hold"). Illinois gave $240 million in suburban land and bonuses to Sears for staying put in the Chicago area (though Sears announced large Illinois job layoffs shortly thereafter). Morgan Stanley, Merrill Lynch and many others have collected millions in public money in return for not leaving New York. The state of Virginia put up $165 million to get IBM to return to the town of Manassas with a new semiconductor plant—a town that had lost 10 percent of its jobs when IBM abandoned it a few years before.

"We in the economic development profession have created a monster that is devouring us," Mark Waterhouse, chairman of the American Economic Development Council, told the *Wall Street Journal.*[18]

The bidding war for employment was a convenient window on the new power relationships that globalization has fashioned: capital took the money because it could, because capital controlled a world of scarcity—scarce jobs, overabundant labor. Governments did not resist on principle; they raised their bids. Given the steady loss of prime manufacturing jobs and the quiet desperation sown by declining wages, neither state nor national governments dared to challenge the practice, though it amounted to a corporate form of brigandage.

Like freebooters on the highway, some companies walked away from the local tax deals when it suited them, without penalty. Volkswagen abandoned its plant in Westmoreland County, Pennsylvania, despite the millions it had received in taxpayer support. For more than a decade, General Motors received a 50 percent holiday from property taxes in Ypsilanti, Michigan, for its Willow Run assembly plant. When GM closed Willow Run, citizens sued and discovered that there wasn't any real contract covering the deal, only a GM press release promising that many jobs would result. GM settled the lawsuit essentially by promising not to do it again, at least not to Ypsilanti.

The lost tax revenue was significant, but the larger loss was the degradation of the commonweal. It amounted to a perverse form of industrial policy: In the context of an advanced economy, the irregular awarding of public favors inevitably did injury to other competitors who did not get the same tax breaks, whether they were small domestic firms or major auto companies. For that reason, not surprisingly, the practice spread as other businesses realized they, too, could shake down the government. Some states and communities were struggling to impose rules or form a mutual pact against the most egregious demands, but they were bargaining from weakness.[19]

The indifference of the U.S. government was especially contradictory since it regularly promoted new international free-trade agreements ostensibly aimed at prohibiting such irregular market subsidies. Washington was offended on principle by state subsidies provided to industry by the governments of Asia or Europe. Why was it silent about the same practices in Ohio or Alabama? Until the national government imposed orderly limits, the plundering was sure to continue.

Alongside the jobs auction, globalization has provided another, far more lucrative window of opportunity for the multinationals: escaping taxation by gaming the tax codes of various nations. Just as firms arbitraged the wage differences between labor markets, they also arbitraged governments.

The dispersal of production opened the door to complicated accounting strategies in which companies shifted corporate tax liabilities from high-tax to low-tax nations, taking the business deductions where tax rates were high and claiming the income where rates are low. No one has succeeded, so far as I could discover, in estimating the total revenue losses to governments around the world, but it amounted to scores of billions of dollars, probably hundreds of billions.

BMW, for instance, claimed in 1993 that 95 percent of its profit (1.5 billion marks) was made overseas. From 1988 to 1992, BMW reduced its taxes paid to German authorities from 545 million marks to 31 million. Its chief financial officer, Volker Doppelfeld, bluntly told *Der Spiegel:* "We're trying to incur our expenditures where the taxes are highest and that is in Germany."[20]

American companies played the same game. IBM reported to its stockholders that a third of its worldwide profits in 1987 were earned by U.S. operations, but it told the Internal Revenue Service that it earned almost nothing in the United States. By deducting its R&D expenditures against its U.S. income, IBM virtually wiped out its federal tax liability, despite $25 billion in American sales that year.

Intel, the leading semiconductor producer, treated profits from U.S.-

made chips as Japanese income for U.S. tax purposes because "title" to the goods was transferred in Japan. Meanwhile, the tax treaty between the two countries explicitly required the Japanese government to treat the profits as American. The result, according to Michael J. McIntyre, an authority on international tax law at Wayne State University, "was to exempt at least half of Intel's export income from U.S. tax. That income became 'nowhere income'—income not taxable in any country." [21]

Foreign companies gamed the U.S. tax code, too. A 1993 Commerce Department study estimated that foreign multinationals evaded one half of their U.S. taxes, $30 billion a year by one estimate. An IRS study of 1989 tax data found that 72 percent of the foreign companies paid no U.S. taxes at all and, as a group, reported taxable income that was only .9 percent of sales, compared to 3.1 percent for American firms. [22]

Nissan paid 17 billion yen in tax penalties to the IRS ($170 million in 1993 dollars), but Japanese auto companies like Nissan and Toyota appeared to play the game in reverse, McIntyre observed. Though operating highly successful U.S. factories, they routinely claimed not to make a profit on their American transplants. They were accused of shipping their profits home, even though that meant facing higher tax rates in Japan. The apparent motivation was that reporting higher corporate profits in Japan stimulated higher stock prices. [23]

The more a multinational dispersed itself to many countries, the more opportunity it had to avoid taxation. The evasions involved the complexities of intrafirm trade in which the company, as both buyer and seller, decided for itself the "price" of goods moving between its subsidiaries and assigned the "costs" of overhead and debt deductions to suit its own convenience. Tax collectors struggled to unwind the manipulations of so-called transfer pricing, but without much success.

One study of two hundred U.S. corporations found that "the average multinational firm with subsidiaries in more than five regions uses income shifting to reduce its taxes to 51.6 percent of what they would otherwise be." American companies with subsidiaries in low-tax countries paid relatively low U.S. taxes per sales or assets, lower than the multinationals with branches in high-tax countries, according to the 1993 study published by four economists. Thus, tax arbitrage provided another incentive, alongside cheaper labor, to relocate in such low-tax places as Singapore, Hong Kong, South Korea and Taiwan. [24]

The leading national governments, if they had the will, could put a stop to this erosion of their tax bases, but none had found the nerve to challenge the globalizing corporations. The obvious solution was a worldwide unitary taxation system that stopped the accounting games. Taxable incomes from multinationals would be apportioned to the nations where they operated, based on where their sales or assets or employees were located. Nations could tax that income at any rate they chose, but companies could no longer move it around to escape taxation. [25]

The use of a global tax formula would not be difficult to devise, but politics blocked reform. Though every major industrial government was in fiscal crisis, politicians found it easier to raise taxes on consumers or workers or to reduce government spending. The political scandal of multinational tax avoidance was a visible marker of who held power in the new world order.

At least in Alabama's case, the state could claim that it, too, was a "developing country" and, like Malaysia, needed to take extraordinary measures. The generous subsidies were not, however, the essence of why the migrating multinationals went to places like Tuscaloosa or Spartanburg or Smyrna. In the southeastern United States, average manufacturing wages were less than half of Germany's. At BMW's new plant in South Carolina, workers would start at $12 an hour and rise to $16, with ten days of paid vacation instead of thirty days for German workers.[26]

Just as capital migration allowed companies to start over with a new, modernized "greenfield" factory, it also enabled them to begin anew, tabula rasa, with "greenfield" workers. "We are leaving behind our bad habits," a manager from Ford told me, describing a components plant in Hungary where, unlike in Detroit, the new workforce was organized into floating teams, with no foremen. When Japanese and German auto companies set up new factories in the United States, they chose small towns in rural areas, usually in southern states where organized labor was weak.

Could Alabamians make a Mercedes? When I was in Stuttgart, Germany, I put the question to Erich Klemm, leader of the works council at Sindelfingen, Daimler's largest assembly plant. The parking lot at Sindelfingen was filled with Mercedeses because every auto worker drove one. Klemm made a tight, pained grin at my question and reflected for a moment. "With our support," he answered finally.

IG Metall and the works council had endorsed the Mercedes move to Alabama, Klemm explained, because the new recreation vehicles to be made there were mainly aimed at the American market anyway. The German union also pledged to support the United Auto Workers in efforts to organize workers at the new German factories in America, but recognized that the resistance will be formidable, especially from American workers grateful to get a paycheck from Mercedes.

Introducing Germany's sophisticated system of industrial relations into anti-union states like Alabama or South Carolina would constitute a revolutionary intrusion on the local culture, as extreme as introducing Malay women to automatic teller machines. In Germany, IG Metall representatives sat on the supervisory board of Daimler-Benz and were kept informed of corporate strategies. At Sindelfingen, the managers consulted Klemm and the worker-elected works council on every important decision.

Could anyone imagine workers in an Alabama factory electing their own works council? Or that the company would be required by law to consult the workers? Was the United States ready for such radical innovations? Probably not, Klemm acknowledged, but the German union was determined to support the rights of the American workers, even if some American workers did not appreciate the help. It was another ripe anomaly: Germans offering to show Americans how to deal with their new boss from Stuttgart.

"We told the company: when you go to the States, you shouldn't behave like ugly capitalists, but be more responsible," Klemm said. "We certainly would not tolerate a situation where Mercedes was actively fighting unions or a works council by using American law. If the company fired workers for trying to organize, then we would get very belligerent."

Semiconductor production, despite the presumed maturity of a high-tech industry, still traveled around the world on the backs of women, most of whom were young and inexperienced, lacking the status or self-awareness to speak for themselves. As Jeffrey Henderson observed in his study of the global semiconductor industry, its strategy of recruiting women for the low-wage assembly jobs was employed worldwide, from Scotland to Silicon Valley to Southeast Asia.[27]

On factory gates in Petaling Jaya, the recruiting banners sought workers with particular qualifications. At Toko Electronics: "Female Production Worker, Age 16–30 Years, Not Married, Should Be Able to Read and Write." At Minolta: "Female Production Operators, 17–27, Completely Furnished Hostels, Free Transportation, Subsidized Meals." In this realm, workers regarded Motorola, with its "empowerment teams" and higher wages and benefits, as a much-admired employer.

As a practical matter, the young women in most electronics factories were not likely to advance. Henderson concluded from his survey: "Whether the women are employed by, say, National Semiconductor or Motorola in the U.S. or Scotland, Hong Kong or Malaysia, they are likely to remain the unskilled recipients of relatively low wages . . . For the employment of skilled (and predominantly male) technicians and engineers, however, the prospects seem to be more rosy."

The global economy was a feminist issue. Across Asia and other developing regions, foreign-owned factories, from electronics to textiles, were typically "manned" by workforces that were 80 to 90 percent female. This was not an accident of the marketplace. The companies deliberately recruited younger women, Henderson noted, for "the sense of discipline that women have acquired through subjection to patriarchal domination in the household." As new industrial workers, not unlike the new auto workers in the American South, the women would not bring "bad work habits," including familiarity with trade unions.

In Malaysia, the younger women were regarded as better hires precisely because they were not likely to be permanent. "I call electronics our evergreen industry," said Arunasalam, leader of the Malaysian Electrical Workers Union. "It's been here for twenty years, but the workers never age."

For these women in Malaysian electronics factories, the feminist question was set in a profoundly different context, with social implications that were more ambiguous but still explosive. I spent an evening at a union-subsidized hostel in Kuala Lumpur, conversing with six young women who lived together in the small house and worked at various electronics factories. Some had just come in from evening prayers at the mosque; some would depart later for the 11 P.M. shift. They did not talk about labor rights or consciousness. They recounted homely details of their lives, mildly stated complaints and modest ambitions.

Rosita: "I had no intention of working for the company [a Japanese electronics plant], but the company came to my *kampong* and approached my father and he suggested that I work. . . . The basic pay was 270 ringgit ($100 a month), now it is 300. . . . The problem is when they want more production, if we don't reach the target, they are unhappy with us. . . . I would like to take care of my brothers and sisters. I took a computer course, but I quit halfway."

Raziah: "I changed jobs three times because the salary was not as big as it was promised. . . . It was not a happy place and my supervisors were very rude and pressured me. . . . I want to better myself, but I've got no money for classes."

Sansiah: "Initially, I was helping my father in the paddies. When my friends started leaving, I felt lonely and bored, so I went, too."

Rakimah: "I have put away some savings. I might even start a small business, like a nursery for children. That is my plan. I love to cook, so if not a nursery, I will open a restaurant."[28]

Dutiful daughters in Asian families, each sent some money home every month to father and mother. One girl was getting married and would quit the factory. Another talked about a friend who had been overwhelmed by the fast life of Kuala Lumpur and returned to her village. They discussed the relative merits of the foreign employers and agreed that Koreans were the worst, Americans were the best and Motorola was the best among the Americans.

The discussion reminded me of something Roger Bertelson had said: "The government would like to maintain Islamic principles and protect people from Western values, but whether the government likes it or not, the people are becoming westernized."

These young women could be seen as pawns in the industrial system, as indeed they were. But they were also the first generation of women from their villages to receive cash incomes of their own, however meager, and to live apart from their families, single and unsupervised amid the perils and pleasures of a big modern city. They were starting out—only starting—on a complicated journey of self-discovery that was utterly different from the traditional past. This experience was sure to clash with what they had been taught to think about themselves.

The multinational corporations were, in a sense, standing on both sides of the women's issue. If industrial globalization exploited the weak status of young women in Malay society, as it certainly did, the globalization was also, potentially, their engine of liberation.

Anwar Ibrahim, a thin, ascetic-looking man with a slight moustache and fuzzy chin whiskers, was deputy prime minister and presumed to be Mahathir's successor if ever the seventy-one-year-old prime minister decided to retire. Anwar was the hope of reformers because, in his militant youth, he had led a Muslim youth organization and spent twenty-two months in detention for protesting against government policies. He is the same age as Bill Clinton.

"People mature and become more critical and ask questions and demand more rights," Anwar reflected. "I think that is perfectly natural. I am of that generation of the sixties and this is the lingo of my generation. Power has to yield. The political process has to be more open."

In the meantime, however, Malaysia would proceed cautiously. Workers should have a vehicle to express themselves, Anwar allowed, but not the aggressive sort of unions that might upset the companies or disrupt political unity. "If we start playing that kind of game, then we will soon be in trouble," he said, "because nobody will come to invest here."

Some low-wage assembly factories would probably migrate to poorer nations, he continued, but that would not be a problem so long as the economy moved up to higher production. "In my youth, I was detained because of my fight for the poor," he reminded me. "But you mature in the process. You don't abdicate your ideals, but you learn to face reality. There is no equity without growth and so we are pro-growth."

The strategy of pursuing rapid growth was more plausible when only a limited number of Asian nations were pursuing it, but it became less so as the poker game was widened to take in many more players. Malaysia was now surrounded by struggling nations engaged in a fierce competition for capital, for any industries that would move them up the ladder.

Malaysia's economic vulnerability had two dimensions. First, the domestic shortage of labor put upward pressure on wages at all skill levels, despite one million foreign workers brought in temporarily from Indonesia and elsewhere. If wage levels were allowed to rise too rapidly, it would drive capital elsewhere. Yet reformers on the other end of the global system in America and Europe were pushing in that direction: campaigning for labor rights in countries like Malaysia in order to foster rising wages that might lessen the downward pressures on high-wage nations and also increase worldwide consumer demand for everyone's products.

In Malaysia, the low wages were frankly regarded as a national asset. Mahathir complained about the Western intruders: "They know very well this is the sole comparative advantage of the developing countries. They know that all the other comparative advantages—technology, capital, rich domestic markets, legal framework, management and marketing network —are with the developed countries." [29]

Those qualities of advancement were the other dimension of Malaysia's vulnerability: the frustrating struggle to acquire higher levels of technological development for the domestic economy. The threat was crisply summarized in a December 1993 economics report cabled from the U.S. Embassy: The "concern is waning foreign interest in Malaysia as a site for investment, especially in high-tech, capital intensive industries. . . . The i , is technology transfer. Unless Malaysia manages to attract increasingly sophisticated manufacturers, it risks getting caught in a medium-tech trap, finding itself saddled with a low-growth industrial base." [30]

The poker game continued, but on a more sophisticated level. American companies like Motorola and Intel were regarded as cooperative players because they were locating software design centers in Malaysia and spreading technological competence to the local population. The Japanese, on the other hand, "are very, very difficult," Anwar said. "No technology transfers, no locals hired for management, no research centers. The Americans are very different."

Malaysia's supposed "comparative advantage" of cheap labor did not help much in the advanced fields. Malaysian engineers with master's degrees were in overabundance and cost only one fourth of U.S. engineers. But the Indian engineers in Bangalore were twice as cheap as the Malaysians. There were too many bidders for too few jobs.

"These guys are competing for the best airports," Jeffrey Garten remarked in Washington. "It sounds crazy, but this is going to boil down to infrastructure and which country provides the most convenient modern airport for businesses."

In broader outline, the political insecurities of a Malaysia were not as different from Alabama or Ohio or industrial countries in general as people in those places wished to imagine. All were stuck in different aspects of the same poker game. The global revolution put labor wages in play, but it also put governments in play. The shift in power that drove the irregular bargaining was eroding the public realm, as well as private incomes, and stimulated a race to the bottom: lower wages, lower taxes, less accountability. To borrow an old cliché from the ideology of laissez-faire capitalism, the multinationals were freely pursuing beggar-thy-neighbor politics.

That debilitating process would continue until nations found the sovereign means to confront the marketplace or collaborated on asserting new terms for how commerce was allowed to function. Or the process would continue until the system broke down, destabilized by its own freewheeling behavior.

In the meantime, the major powers, led by the United States, promoted further liberalization of the global trading regime, encouraged the competence of their own multinationals and promoted the objective of greater globalization. Increasing numbers of citizens were unconvinced. The U.S. government, among others, lacked a coherent, concrete vision of how this globalization was expected to benefit the general population.

The Malaysian government at least had its own *"Wawasan 2020,"* a concrete plan for what the nation intended to become. Americans might ask, What was the American *wawasan*?

Six

Jidoka[*]

THE GREAT CONTEST of technology sweeps across every industrial sector, a harrowing competition that discards the old way of making things and invents future benchmarks for quality and efficiency. No enterprise can stand aside and none can feel permanently triumphant. The race for technological improvement drives on two levels at once: improving the product itself and improving the processes by which it is made. On one level, engineers add refinements and complexity to their product while, on the other level, they try to extract time and cost from the design and manufacturing processes. The new industrial leaders are those brilliantly managed firms that do both simultaneously, and a vast literature is devoted to recounting their achievements.

There is another dimension to the technological revolution, however, that is seldom discussed in the business books: the gathering vulnerability of an industrial system that is ruled by persistent excess supply. The same technological imperative that continuously reduces costs and improves quality has also generated a seemingly permanent and expanding surplus in the productive capacity of the world.

Crudely stated, the technology competition leads companies to invest in more output of goods than the global marketplace of consumers can possibly absorb. New factories, designed to produce more from less, naturally increase the capacity for production, but the output potential expands faster than older, less efficient factories are being closed. This underlying imbalance is compounded by the accelerating drive for globalization, as firms both modernize and rush to build new production in the developing markets.

A perverse syllogism is thus at work, company by company, sector by sector: the burdensome presence of overcapacity quickens the price competition and threatens market shares, but the only obvious response is to create more new capacity—that is, to build new factories that will be more

Japanese: "automation." Toyota Motor Corporation defines the word more precisely: "investing machines with human-like intelligence."

cost-efficient than one's rivals. The resulting surpluses are often lamented by business leaders but generally regarded as a revolutionary condition beyond anyone's control.

From a manager's viewpoint, the challenge is to make sure that the market's overcapacity becomes the other guy's problem, that some other firm will be compelled to swallow losses in sales and close down its factories. Meanwhile, it is hoped that the newly developing economies will create enough new consumers so that the market eventually comes back into balance. Economists conventionally assume the same. As orthodox theory teaches, markets are always self-correcting, so the surpluses are a temporary consequence of competition and will work themselves out as supply comes into balance with demand.

Theory notwithstanding, the global system is headed in roughly the opposite direction for most major manufacturing sectors. The productive overcapacity is neither temporary nor diminishing. Autos are the leading example of the dilemma—too many cars chasing too few buyers—but the same trend is visible in steel, aircraft, chemicals, computers, consumer electronics, drugs, tires and some others. The particulars vary from one sector to another, but the overriding fact is gross surplus of capacity, despite the many years of plant closings, and the overhang grows steadily larger in most cases. Of all the imperatives driving the behavior of global enterprises, this constitutes a central source of their anxiety.

For the global system as a whole, it represents a fundamental disorder, threatening to destabilize the free-running commerce. At a minimum, the growing imbalance between supply and demand guarantees that the storm of dislocations and shakeouts must continue. Whether these are described as restructuring or deindustrialization, more factories must be closed, more employees discarded, more production moved elsewhere. The scale of adjustments that will be inescapable grows larger as the industrial overcapacity expands. No one can predict who exactly must absorb these losses—which companies or which nations—but the usual pattern is that the old gives way to the new, more costly locales cede to less expensive ones.

A calamitous possibility also lurks in these facts: the threat that accumulating overcapacity will lead to some sort of decisive breakdown, a financial crisis or an implosion of global commerce, perhaps precipitated by emergency measures enacted by nations desperate to protect their home producers. In the 1920s, similar imbalances developed from similar causes, and the root cause of the eventual market breakdown was excess supply and inadequate demand. Capital was being invested in new productive capacity based on expectations that could not possibly be fulfilled by a marketplace already burdened by plentiful goods and scarce buyers. When that reality could no longer be denied, the optimism of financial investors collapsed; so did financial prices. The Great Depression followed.

An alternative threat that these surpluses pose for the free-running global system is political: How much more loss and upheaval can be absorbed by the political systems of advanced nations before the popular stress generates a reactionary counterrevolution? No one, of course, can know the answer, but the symptoms of rebellion are already visible in many leading economies. One foreboding fact is the evasion and denial of political leaders in those nations. None is yet willing even to discuss the global economy in these terms.

The No. 4 Assembly Shop at Toyota's Tahara plant was not the absolute pinnacle of manufacturing perfection, but it stood among the awesome heights constructed by Japanese ingenuity. Tahara was a vast gray industrial complex situated on a narrow peninsula alongside Mikawa Bay and the Pacific Ocean, two hours southeast of Toyota's corporate headquarters at Nagoya. The Lexus 400s that rolled off the No. 4 line were test-driven, then loaded straight aboard ships bound for the American market. Inside the plant, fantastic machines were making cars. There did not seem to be many people.

In the body shop, where the car frames were constructed, scores of long-necked welding robots swayed back and forth like white storks in a mating ritual, performing a mechanical ballet of bending and dipping and flashing sparks. Computers controlled the factory's three hundred welders who, unlike human welders, always torched the frames at precisely the right spots.

The assembly line known as No. 4 looked like a mad mechanic's concoction of Erector set pieces, with huge and plodding industrial equipment that moved things around, eerily confident about what it was doing. A greenish fluorescent glow emanated from the line's complex superstructure as various disconnected elements of an automobile floated silently through the dimness. The empty shell of a blue car body glided forward overhead, hood up, doors and engine missing. Down below, its power train, the engine and transmission, proceeded independently on the shop floor, carried by a low-slung driver-less vehicle. While overhead hydraulics lowered the body to meet up with the chassis, the package of the car's electronics controls traveled a parallel route through the maze, waiting for its moment.

A robot came forward to install the seats. Another with camera eyes attached doors. Another bolted on front wheels. As the elements of a Lexus came together, a huge conveyor device turned the vehicles sideways, more conveniently positioned for the finishing operations to be done by human hands. Machines did all of the heavy lifting and most of the precision work as well.

Watching the contraption's effortless motions, I found myself wondering: Where are the workers? Some were around. Now and then, one or two of them appeared from the shadows, wearing bright blue safety helmets and white shirts, to complete an installation task or often to perform a quick test on what the machines had done. A small robot carried their tools for them, from car to car. If something was amiss, the workers could pull a cord that signaled error. In an instant, the machine would stop briefly while things were corrected. The autos were moved forward on an accordion lift so workers could adjust things to function at a natural posture. Less back strain.

"How far can we go making human life and invention pleasant?" a management text asked. "This is our quest at Tahara plant." At five o'clock an electronic chime filled the shop with cheery music, announcing the end of the shift.

The auto workers themselves became more visible at the point where the finished cars rolled off the line because all of their pictures were posted there on a large bulletin board, accompanied by personal messages from each of them, expressing their enthusiasm for the enterprise. "I will do my best to make this the No. 1 car which will be loved by our customers." "I stick to the car-making which can satisfy our users."

Bottom line: Tahara No. 4 assembled the Lexus LS 400, a complex and luxuriously equipped automobile, with only 18.4 hours of human labor. In Hamtramck, Michigan, at the plant where General Motors assembled Cadillacs, each car required 38.8 hours of labor. A Buick from GM's Buick City plant took 32 hours. At Ford's Wixom, Michigan, plant, where Continentals and Mark VIIIs were assembled, each one consumed 34 hours of labor.

Sweden's Volvo, a long-lasting car because it was made with great care, required 47 hours of labor (reduced from 70 hours, Volvo officials proudly noted). Germany's luxury cars—Mercedes, BMW, Audi—were said to involve labor inputs of more than 100 hours per car. Even Volkswagens—the simpler, less expensive cars made at VW's mammoth industrial works in Wolfsburg, Germany—required an average of 36 hours' labor each—that is, half as efficient as Toyota's luxury-car production at Tahara.[1]

The Tahara plant provided a visual marker of how the technological contest was proceeding and some obvious implications. James E. Harbour, an independent authority in Detroit, estimated that Toyota's engineering prowess translated, roughly speaking, into a cost advantage of $600 or $700 per car because of the more efficient production, plus another $300 or so in savings from the higher quality—that is, cars with fewer defects and thus lower warranty costs to the company. Labor input was the most convenient measure for comparisons of productivity, but reducing labor costs was, of course, only one dimension of this competition. And robotic automation was only one of the ways in which the company reduced production costs.

Still, Line No. 4 offered an intimidating demonstration of what was possible at the extremes: when machines were substituted for people and systematically organized to produce a better automobile. Toyota had a reputation, even among its own people, as a company that will "squeeze a dry towel," and it was not as relentless as some of the other Japanese companies. To glimpse the implications, one need only imagine: What if every auto producer in the world might someday be capable of matching Toyota's efficiency? And what would happen to those producers who remained far behind? In crude outline, the questions defined the global chase: catching up with the best.

Formulating the broad strokes of history was assumed to be the province of statesmen or great generals, but the work of shaping the future was also done, more concretely, by engineers—people who know how to make things work. Their decisions also determined the social reality at least as profoundly as the politicians who ostensibly governed.

One of those people was Tadaaki Jagawa, a Toyota vice president and the engineer who designed Tahara. Jagawa was tall and lean like an athlete, with gray-flecked black hair and a flat, hawk-like face. He managed Tahara and two other Toyota plants, and while we talked, he was waiting on a helicopter ride to one of his other outposts. His manner was direct and precisely engaged, though perhaps slightly impatient with familiar questions. The engineer's commanding presence was reflected in the body language of those around him. When Jagawa uttered a guttural aside, their heads bobbed and bowed anxiously.

"When we introduced automation systems, people thought it was only for labor saving," he said, "but that was kind of misunderstood. Actually our concept has always been the same—quality. To improve the quality is the key to winning, and to improve the quality you must improve the system."

When launched in 1991, Tahara No. 4 was described as "experimental"—an opportunity to see how far the engineers could go with capital-intensive automation—but Toyota managers preferred to emphasize the humanistic aspects. "Probably the labor saving was about 20 percent," Jagawa said, "but our main purpose was to reduce the turnover rate among the workers on the assembly line. At that time, turnover was very high. Why? Because the physical work was too hard, too heavy, maybe too complicated. So we have to change that. The longer the workers stay on with the company, the better quality they will produce."

Actually, during the latter half of the 1980s, when Japanese capital was abundant and cheap and its auto sales were booming, Toyota and leading rivals Nissan, Mazda and Mitsubishi had indulged in a kind of capital-spending binge—a test of manhood in which the auto companies competed to see which one could develop the highest levels of automation. "Other engineers would say, hey, Toyota, we're at 60 percent robots and you're only at 40 percent—what's the problem?" a Toyota official recalled. "Engineers cannot resist such competition and so they all wanted to show, hey, we can do that."

The contest consumed billions in capital, built some of the world's first-class factories and also greatly expanded Japan's capacity to produce cars (more cars than it could sell). In hindsight, this was widely regarded as an expression of hubris. Toyota had been more restrained than others, but it concluded that Tahara had gone too far. Even Jagawa acknowledged that some of the investment was wasteful.

"The engine-and-chassis automated assembly machines reduced labor to only four operators, but to do that we had to spend 600 million yen—not a very efficient investment," he said. "When I introduced this automation, I knew it would not be a good investment for the moment. But it would be a good experiment for the future. The knowledge of labor saving was in place."

Furthermore, the intensive automation produced unanticipated discontent on the line: surrounded by dazzling machines, workers felt impotent and ignorant, cut out of the car-making process. So Toyota backed off a bit. At its new factory at Kyushu, the work system was redesigned to give the workers a greater sense of control and a more comfortable knowledge of what was happening around them. "In a sense, the full automation at Tahara was cut in half at Kyushu," Jagawa said.

The Kyushu plant was still extraordinarily efficient, and a similar approach was being followed in Toyota's U.S. transplant at Georgetown, Kentucky, a factory that has become the second most efficient assembly plant in North America, with 19.5 hours of labor per car. In first place was Nissan's plant at Smyrna, Tennessee, where the labor input per vehicle matched Tahara's No. 4 line.

Inevitably, these leaders have become the new benchmark for the American companies. By 1994, Ford had several car plants that were operating with 20 hours' labor per car, very nearly as good as the Japanese transplants, and Chrysler was closing fast with several of its own. Despite large gains General Motors still lagged behind: the most efficient GM factory required 24.8 hours per car.[2]

The ascendance of Toyota as a front-ranking American manufacturer represented one of the great role reversals in industrial history. In the early 1930s, when Sakichi Toyoda announced his desire to manufacture cars, his own son, Kiichiro, thought it sounded far-fetched. The elder Toyoda was a self-taught engineer and successful manufacturer of automated looms, but there were no Japanese auto companies back then. GM and Ford virtually owned Japan's market, operating knockdown assembly plants with the mass-produced parts imported from the United States. The son, with an engineering degree, pursued his father's dream. Fifty years later GM was inviting Toyota to form a joint venture at a plant in Fremont, California, so Japanese managers could teach Americans how to make a car with the "just-in-time" techniques.*

Company lore subsequently attributed all of Toyota's basic concepts to

---

* The Toyoda family has continued to manage the enterprise through three generations, but the company name was altered in 1936 when the first logo was designed. In Japanese script, Toyota required eight brush strokes, instead of ten for Toyoda, and eight was regarded as a lucky number, signifying growth.

the founding patriarch—*jidoka,* the automation premised on machines with human-like reflexes, or *kaizen,* the systems for continuous improvement. But the saga of invention was necessarily more complicated than that, a mix of borrowed ideas and brilliant insights across several decades. The first Toyota engine in 1934 was a knockoff patterned after a Chrysler model and was so poorly cast it produced only 30 horsepower. Taiichi Ohno, the engineer who developed the "just-in-time" organization of production, was said to be inspired by his visit to an American supermarket in 1956.

The ambitions of Japan's infant car companies also converged with the nationalistic agenda of the military regime that took power in the thirties. As it prepared for war, the Japanese government provided a subsidized market for the new made-in-Japan cars and trucks, while it simultaneously squeezed out the American companies. Toyota trucks went to war in China and across the Pacific Rim; its Koroma factory was bombed by B-29s near the close of World War II. Afterwards, amid Japan's postwar devastation, the car companies got help from another government—the victorious Americans—as procurement by the U.S. military occupation provided new demand stimulus and helped Toyota and the others to recover and grow.[3]

This history might not seem especially relevant to the technological competition under way at century's end, except the story of defeat and triumph was the past embedded in Japanese national memory. It was one of the reasons people like Tadaaki Jagawa were determined to be winners.

On the other side of the world, the chase quickened in different directions. The German car makers, hailed in the past for their high quality and skilled workforces, were engaged in wrenching restructurings and massive layoffs. Sweden's struggling Volvo arranged a corporate merger with Renault of France, but when Swedish shareholders and workers realized they would be junior partners to the French, they vetoed the marriage. Volkswagen, Europe's largest producer, negotiated a labor contract that provided for a four-day workweek and reduced pay for German workers, meanwhile shifting more production to Portugal, Mexico and the Czech Republic.

VW was described by its own chairman as "a duck grown too fat to fly." In an age of flexibility, it was stuck with a huge centralized complex of foundries and factories at Wolfsburg, 57,000 employees and forty-three miles of its own railroad tracks. "An industrial dinosaur," one business professor called it. To make matters more difficult, the state government of Lower Saxony was a major shareholder and defended local jobs almost as zealously as the union, IG Metall, both of which sat on VW's supervisory board. Nonetheless, swamped with losses in 1993, Volkswagen set out to get lean and mean.

The Germans hired away a Spanish engineer named López from General Motors, where he had saved billions by streamlining GM's supplier base first in Europe, then in North America. José Ignacio López de Arriortúa preached reform with revolutionary fervor and enunciated a grandiose vision—a manufacturing scheme called Plateau Six that he said would eclipse even the Japanese.

López pounded VW suppliers to reduce component prices, just as he had done at GM, and organized ten thousand young German workers as "warriors" in training for revolutionary conflict. He also dreamed aloud about a factory of the future he wanted VW to build in his native Basque country: an assembly plant that could make an automobile with less than ten hours of labor. The world is in the midst of the Third Industrial Revolution, López told audiences, and manufacturers and nations must mobilize for the struggle. "Only those that don't realize they are in a revolution will disappear," he promised.[4]

A car made with only eight hours of human labor? That would indeed be a revolutionary breakthrough, but managers at other companies remained quite skeptical. Volkswagen was not about to build López's "dream factory" in Spain, they figured, not while it wanted to shed some thirty thousand surplus workers at home. The company was, in fact, still struggling with costs at a much more primitive stage: VW's average labor input per car, according to one industry authority, was reduced from 40 hours to 36 hours, and its near-term goal was 32 hours. In other words, before the Germans surpassed the Japanese, they would have to catch up with the Americans.[5]

López's central idea—assembling autos from modular components built by suppliers elsewhere—also did not sound altogether new, but merely an intensification of an approach the Japanese and others had already explored. Still, VW and GM thought enough of the man's talent to conduct a very nasty legal controversy over his abrupt shift in employment.

If López's vision should prove to be right or even half right, VW might clip 20 to 30 percent off the Japanese system—an accomplishment that would doubtless set off another global round of competitive improvements. Meanwhile, the other companies were not especially nervous. They would wait and watch and, if necessary, borrow freely from López's playbook, just as they had borrowed from Toyota and other Japanese companies.

Oscar B. Marx III, a former Ford vice president for components production and now president of an independent global supplier, Electro Wire Products, explained: "There's an inability to keep a process advantage for very long. We're just too nimble. I'm not saying we always were, but we are now."

The American scramble to catch up had already produced striking accomplishments, as the Big Three reorganized production during the 1980s to counter the Japanese imports. In 1979, Ford's average labor input for all of its North American cars and trucks was just under 40 hours per vehicle. By 1993, it was down to 25.4 hours. Chrysler reduced its average from 45 to 29.5 hours. GM improved from 41 hours to 32.5 hours. The Japanese average still was lower, about 20 hours per vehicle, but the U.S. companies had substantially closed the gap. To illustrate what this great leap meant, a

Ford plant in 1979 made 960 Granadas a day with 4,270 workers. By 1990, a Ford plant was making 1,200 Escorts a day with only 1,880 workers.[6]

Chrysler, the smallest and weakest of the three, became the most profitable, car for car, by the mid-1990s. It had devoted less capital to automating production and concentrated instead on drastically reducing its fixed costs and the time and expense of design cycles. Its reformed system could design a new model nearly twice as fast and with one fourth as many people. More important, the design process was integrated with the manufacturing process so a new model would be easier to assemble, and as old models were replaced, the cost reductions would continue steadily. *The Harbour Report* on industry productivity observed: "Chrysler is literally designing people out of the manufacturing process."

Chrysler's triumphant chairman, Robert Eaton, liked to say: In the past, it was the Big swallowing the Small. Now it's going to be the Fast swallowing the Slow.

Yet, despite these advancements, the chase must continue because there is no finish line. The competitive imperative is sure to intensify not only for the Americans and for the Germans, but also for the Japanese. The reason was obvious to the industry: After fifteen years of dramatic adjustments, relentless modernizations and scores of plant closings, the global market for motor vehicles was still grossly out of balance in supply and demand. The industry's unused capacity to make cars was not gradually diminishing. It was growing much larger.

Engineering brilliance might help an individual producer protect its market share and restore profitability, but it did not lead to a stable industrial structure. Some companies would have to eat the surplus—that is, shrink or fail. So anxieties continued, as did the planning for the next new stage of competition, like the so-called global cars that some companies planned to produce. While automobile executives lamented this reality, they had more or less learned to accept it, and they regularly warned business audiences not to expect the storm to abate.

"Over-capacity will cause the consolidation and restructuring of the auto industry worldwide," Alex Trotman predicted when he became Ford's new CEO. "Not everyone will be around by the end of the century, certainly not in their current configurations."[7]

The dimensions of overcapacity were roughly stated in these terms: In 1985, if operating at full tilt, the industry's potential production was about 25 percent more than the market's existing demand. That is, if companies had been running every plant at three shifts, they could have turned out about 60 million cars and trucks for a global market that bought only 44.8 million that year. A decade later the condition of oversupply was worse: about 30 percent. Worldwide demand had risen, but so had the gap of overcapacity.

These estimates, like most statistics on industrial capacity, were necessarily inexact, in part because companies typically underreported their true production capabilities. If anything, these numbers probably erred on the conservative side. They were derived from confidential projections on global supply and demand prepared by the planners at one of the U.S. auto companies (made available with the understanding I would not identify the company). The point was not to claim great precision for these estimates, but to give readers a concrete sense of the industry's gathering problems.

The explanation for this trend was straightforward: Overcapacity grew because productive supply was expanding faster than demand. Based on the U.S. company's market projections, the global demand for motor vehicles grew by about 20 percent from 1985 to 1995, while the productive capacity grew by 25 percent. Thus, even with the burgeoning new consumer markets emerging in Asia, the global auto industry was digging a deeper hole for itself.

Nor was there any expectation that this trend would somehow be reversed. On the contrary, the production base was expanded, not only by the technological competition, but also by the global dispersal of auto plants, as companies raced to secure a foothold in the growing new markets. Many new nations were entering the field as future producers. Korea, Taiwan, Thailand, India and China, even Vietnam, were forming joint production ventures with the major companies from Japan, Europe and North America.

Indeed, in 1995 the major American car company recalculated its supply-demand projections as so many new producers were entering the global market and it found the imbalance much worse—a worldwide productive capacity that would exceed demand in 2000 by 36 percent. With expanding production expected in Korea, China, Eastern Europe and Latin America, the world auto industry would be able to produce 79 million vehicles. But worldwide demand would provide buyers for only 57 million vehicles.

The gulf was staggering. The global overcapacity in cars by 2000 would be equivalent to the entire North American industry—only larger. To bring supply and demand into balance, the industry would have to discover a new consumer market that was bigger than the United States. Put another way, one quarter of the world's auto factories were redundant —unneeded by the market and unable to sell any cars they produced. Yet more new auto factories were in the works.

Honda was building new capacity in Mexico and Thailand. India had signed deals with GM, Chrysler, Ford, Peugeot, Daimler-Benz, Volvo, Hyundai, Mitsubishi, Daewoo and Volkswagen. VW planned to expand U.S. sales by 30 percent with cars produced in Puebla, Mexico.[8]

Whether these new cars were targeted for domestic markets or export, the effect was the same: more capacity was added to an already glutted market. A new auto factory in Mexico, it was true, might be less efficient than many in the United States or Japan, but the workers were also much, much cheaper. And some Mexican plants were already first-rate. Ford's

Cuautitlán plant made Cougars with a labor input of nearly 50 hours per vehicle, but Ford produced Escorts at Hermosillo with only 24.8 hours' labor per car—more efficient than twenty U.S. assembly plants.

Moreover, developing nations recognized that a national auto industry would help them generate a broad, mature economy. Korea, building on its new, muscular industrial base, was using its own multinationals like Daewoo and Samsung to launch an aggressive drive for global auto exports. Korean companies intended to produce five million cars by the year 2000, about twice the size of Chrysler and five times Korea's own domestic market.

"It boggles the mind—Korea will someday be making more cars than Germany," said Maryann Keller, an author and automotive analyst at the Wall Street brokerage of Furman Selz. "Korea has the No. 1–selling car in Peru and Chile, they are selling cars in Romania. They're going where nobody else wanted to go, heading off the Americans. Do they really care what happens to us? The car industry used to be a Western Hemisphere business and it's becoming an Eastern Hemisphere business and we don't understand that. It's not going to be answerable to our wonderful Western economic philosophy."

The larger implications were described by Wynn Van Bussman, chief corporate economist at Chrysler: "The big question you may ask is, gee, isn't this going to mean too much new capacity? I would answer: yes. What everybody wants to do with their excess capacity is export it, but it is still the case that in a lot of Asian countries there are substantial restrictions on imports because those countries want to develop their own domestic auto sectors. So what you have is a permanent situation of excess supply and downward pressure on prices and wages. That's certainly still true in the United States."

The consequences of this permanent oversupply have bounced around the globe unevenly during the last twenty years, visiting crises on different companies and countries, but the first, most devastating encounter was in the United States. From 1980 to 1994, thirty-two car and truck assembly plants were closed in North America, wiping out 5.4 million units of production capacity. Another thirteen plants were either scheduled for closing or considered likely candidates. During this onslaught of creative destruction U.S. auto employment shrank by 180,000 jobs, most in assembly work.[9]

Yet, the oversupply problem actually grew worse for the American market—roughly doubled—during this same period. Demand increased but slightly, while millions of new units of production were added, targeted at American buyers. This was driven mainly by the influx of Japanese companies locating factories in the United States to protect themselves against the threat of American import barriers. But the American companies also contributed significantly with the new, more efficient factories they were building. Bottom line: the stunning transformation of North American auto production had greatly improved efficiency, displaced many workers and crippled some communities, but it left the producers still fighting over scarce buyers.

The storm visited Europe next, and it was continuing there. The waves of retrenchments were accompanied by a vigorous expansion of more efficient production, just as in the United States. Marcello Malentacchi, general secretary of the International Metalworkers Federation, expressed the bewilderment of organized labor: "We know the European auto industry has a 22 percent overcapacity," he said. "We said that three years ago. We knew it six years ago. But we waited for the governments to act, we waited on the companies. What can you do now when Mercedes lays off 25,000? What can you do when Volkswagen lays off 28,000? It's too late. I wonder also why the Japanese companies and the Korean companies have so much interest in investing in Europe while, at the same time, the European companies are moving production from here to Southeast Asia. Why?" One reason, as Malentacchi knew, was that producers everywhere feared that the glutted markets would lead to regional protectionism, so they built new factories to get in the door before it was closed.

Next was Japan. By 1995, the supply problem was stalking the Japanese auto industry too, forcing even the strongest companies like Nissan and Toyota to accept the unprecedented (and deeply embarrassing) measure of closing assembly plants at home and perhaps laying off some Japanese workers. Japan's producers were said to be over capacity by as much as 50 percent; its nine companies were simply too numerous for a stagnant domestic market. The weakest among them were imperiled. The triumphant Japanese were themselves hurting.[10]

This ironic turn of events contained an element of rough justice: After all, for two decades Japan had provided considerable fuel to the global problem of oversupply. Operating from a market sanctuary that foreign rivals could not penetrate, the Japanese auto companies vastly overbuilt their own productive capacity and aggressively exported the surplus into the U.S. and other foreign markets, grabbing market share from the domestic producers. Now the global problem was at their doorstep: as output fell, Toyota's capacity utilization dipped below 80 percent.

Two things happened to undermine the market dominance of Toyota and the others: First, the collapse in 1989 of Japan's booming, easy credit era known as the bubble economy had severely depressed their home market. Car sales in Japan were flat for four straight years. Second, every Japanese foreign sale suffered as the U.S. dollar steadily declined in value against the yen, sharply raising the cost and price of made-in-Japan exports. The Japanese, it could be argued, had partly done this to themselves since it was Japan's huge, persistent trade surpluses with the United States that centrally contributed to weakening the dollar in foreign exchange. In any case, when the dollar sank to 80 yen in 1995, Japanese car companies started looking in earnest for factories to close.

Engineering brilliance would not solve this problem and, indeed, may have compounded it. The appreciating yen automatically raised the cost of their home-based production, but Toyota and others had just sunk vast amounts of capital in the new highly automated plants like Tahara. When the cheap capital of the 1980s boom vanished, those investment decisions increasingly looked self-indulgent, at least in hindsight. Toyota's ability to make a luxurious Lexus with only 18 hours of labor was valuable only if it could sell them.

The Japanese strategy of emphasizing high-tech content also had its downside. When the yen was at 150 to the dollar in the 1980s, Toyotas could be loaded up with advanced engines and elaborate automatic features and still be highly profitable. When the dollar sank below 100 yen, so did Toyota's profit per car. James Harbour, the Detroit industry analyst, calculated that by 1995 Toyota was making only about $50 on each car it sold in the United States, while Chrysler's profit margin was about $1,200 per car. "Toyota loaded up with high-technology production and equipment," Harbour said, "but when the dollar took a dive, they're sitting there sucking gas."

Americans who found shortsighted pleasure in Toyota's comeuppance were misguided, however. In the global system, Toyota's problem would eventually become everyone's. Toyota, a wealthy and brilliantly managed multinational that would make the necessary adjustments, was already moving to do so. Production at its American transplants was to be doubled, Toyota announced. Meanwhile, it was breaking the traditional understandings of Japan's domestic market and aggressively going after greater sales at home—threatening the market shares of other, weaker Japanese car companies.

An adroit producer could make the surplus become the other guy's problem. As Toyota and others repositioned their production, that would create new jobs for some Americans while some Japanese auto workers were prematurely retired, but it could also intensify the surplus problem for the American companies, displacing their production and adding to the downward pressures on American wages and prices. If there were too many auto factories, there were also too many auto workers, especially the kind with high wages.

The larger consequence for the global system was to keep the surpluses moving around, adding and destroying, renewing the desperate chase.

In Clermont-Ferrand, France, headquarters of Michelin, the world's largest tire manufacturer has made a great leap forward. A new and secretive plant went on-line in early 1994, producing tires with an integrated system of automation so advanced that rival companies rushed to check out the patents. Michelin would not reveal the factory's capacity, but it employed only fifty workers. The design was said to approach the futuristic vision that industrialists liked to call a "lights out" factory: The last worker to depart turns out the lights.

François Michelin, the sixty-seven-year-old patriarch and grandson of the company founder, told an audience: "Tires will never again be an industry of manual labor." Clermont-Ferrand had lost half of its Michelin jobs and the company's worldwide employment was shrinking from 140,000 to 125,000, with more losses to come. The global tire industry, dominated by six companies, had already invested billions in modernized plants but was operating worldwide in 1994 at about 70 percent of potential capacity.[11]

Chemicals struggled with a similar imbalance, driven less by technology and more by the new production sources coming on stream in so many new places, from Asia to Eastern Europe. Bayer of Germany was investing one billion deutschemarks in new Asian output; its chairman, Manfred Schneider, was warning European politicians that they did not yet grasp how brutal the international competition was about to become.[12]

Allen J. Lenz, economics director at America's Chemical Manufacturers Association, described his industry's dilemma: "With everyone trying to build their own chemical industry, we have in many basic industrial chemicals a global oversupply. That has kept prices down and profit margins low." Individual companies could survive, he said, but the most advanced economies, like the United States, will probably continue to lose production to other parts of the world where wages were much lower.

"It seems safe to predict," Lenz reported, "that generally the world supply of many basic industrial chemicals will, from the standpoint of producers, trend toward an oversupply situation during much of the rest of the decade and perhaps beyond. That's because every developing country wants to have its own chemical industry to obtain the value-added and technology transfer benefits of domestic production.

"Inevitably, as the number of producers grows, the tendencies toward global oversupplies will be enhanced, competition will get tougher, rates of return may decline and U.S.-based production and the production of other major developed-country producers will become an even smaller portion of total world production. . . . [T]he tendency toward a diminished role for U.S.-based production in total global production seems quite inevitable. . . ."[13]

The pharmaceutical industry was experiencing its own shakeout, a flurry of global mergers among leading drug companies as they tried to shore up their consumer base by acquiring discount distributors. Overcapacity in drug manufacturing was expressed in somewhat different terms, not as idle factories but as the overinvestment in research and development that leads eventually to new products. The competitive R&D spending by pharmaceutical companies had risen from $5.4 billion in 1981 to $26.5 billion in 1993. Then the optimistic expectations gave way to reality and the multibillion-dollar mergers began.

Professor Jürgen Drews, head of research at Roche, the Swiss firm, told the *Financial Times:* "Global prescription sales would need to reach about $280 billion a year within 10 years [more than twice the current sales] to justify the present levels of investment. The chances of reaching that figure are more than low—they are non-existent." Dr. Leon Rosenberg, president of Bristol-Myers Squibb's research institute, described the outlook: "The worst case scenario would be that the pharmaceutical industry as we know it disappears because companies no longer believe that there is a likelihood of generating a reasonable return on money put into research." [14]

Or the example of steel, where global capacity exceeded demand by 20 percent. Or commercial aircraft, where the capacity was approximately twice the market demand. Or consumer electronics. Or textiles. Or computers. The facts varied in each marketplace, as did the driving elements. But the overwhelming condition of the global system was oversupply. The major exceptions were the fast-developing advanced technologies, like semiconductors or communications, where the old products were rapidly eclipsed by new inventions, and the demand for them rose so steeply that producing companies could hardly keep up. Across most industries, however, the fact of surplus was the revolutionary storm cloud that never went away.

Some multinational managers responded to the reality with admirable pluckiness. "Consumer electronics suffers from overcapacity, but that's why we are living in an interesting world," Yasunori Kirihara of Sony remarked. "Somebody is winning and somebody is losing. If there's no overcapacity, we would have a less exciting capitalism."

Or managers responded with resilient optimism, a conviction that somehow or other things would work out. Dean Thornton, as Boeing's president for commercial aircraft production, lamented that Boeing could turn out forty-five to fifty airliners a month but would produce and sell only half as many. "If something doesn't get better before the end of the century, do we have a big risk? The answer is, hell yes," Thornton said. Still, he expected things would get better, though "not dramatically better, not 180 degrees better." [15]

Meanwhile, these surpluses were a driving force behind the capital migration. Multinationals moved production to new locations (including within the advanced economies) in part to offset the risks created by the permanent overcapacity. A new location might protect their market position by introducing more efficient technology or by employing cheaper labor or by avoiding the possibility of protectionist import barriers or by hooking up with a national industry to exploit a fast-developing market. Over time, the net effect of all these motivations was a gradual, geographical shift of industrial structures, usually from old places to the new, from high wages to low wages.

The U.S. steel industry, for instance, was booming in 1995, newly modernized and operating at close to its full capacity, but it was about one third smaller than its peak size twenty years before. Japan's steel production was now shrinking, too. The steel industry was gradually moving to Korea, Taiwan, India, Brazil and, above all, China. This transition was generally regarded as a natural evolution for a basic industry (unless you happened to be an American steelworker). The process was devastating for some, but roughly consistent with industrial history across several centuries.

But the implications became more difficult to absorb—and more threatening to the long-term prosperity—when the same general trend was observed across so many sectors, both the basic industries and the advanced. The fashionable futuristic view was that the wealthier nations would simply cease manufacturing things. Their people would move onward and upward to a postindustrial age where the work was cleaner and more rewarding, less muscular and more cerebral. The vast literature devoted to this sunny vision had so far not succeeded in persuading most people or nations to believe in it or welcome the consequences. If Americans or Europeans surrendered their manufacturing industries and jobs, what exactly would replace them? Across two decades the main answer for most people appeared to be greater risk of unemployment, declining wages and part-time work.

In a sense, that was the global impasse the free-market economists failed to acknowledge, the reason their theory failed to match the reality. Just as poor countries made special efforts to acquire a steel industry or auto sector, aircraft or electronics, the citizens and governments of wealthy nations naturally wished to hold on to theirs. The surplus capacity was, therefore, bound to grow as a function of the accelerating globalization, sure to produce more wrenching consequences.

If everyone would just cooperate with the free-market theory and accept their fate, then markets might come effortlessly into balance. The global industrial structure could be reallocated to this place or that to achieve maximum efficiency of production, based on the market requirements of the multinational corporations. But, in the here and now, people generally did not acquiesce to abstract theories, not when they could see that the tangible outcomes for themselves were starkly different from what the theorists had promised.

The historical portents of oversupply were visible, but unacknowledged by authorities. Perhaps things will work out, as the managers assumed, but twentieth-century history taught that the accumulating surpluses could also lead to a general breakdown.

A Canadian economist who did not share the orthodox view of things, J. H. Hotson of the University of Waterloo, succinctly described the situation: "The central irrationality of the Great Depression years has reappeared in our times. In a depressed world of inadequate demand, each firm, industry and nation attempts to save itself by competitive deflation. Some can 'win' in this struggle by cutting their costs and boosting their efficiency the most. However, the more the winners win, the more the losers lose as this is a negative sum game."[16]

Peter Schavoir, the IBM director of strategy before his retirement, was one manager who saw similar gloomy outlines in his industry and expressed anxiety about the larger system: "I've been worried for a long time that there's too much capacity, and as a result, there are very few people in the computer industry making much money. It's true in other industries, too— they are all losing money. The computer industry is like that and yet people are pouring into it. They figure they can make money if they find a niche that's protected for a time, while IBM or Unisys are stuck with the losses.

"Don't get me wrong. I believe in competition, but when you get too much of it and it's just a matter of price, price, price, it's very difficult to keep yourself afloat. For those whose jobs are destroyed in the process, they aren't ever going to get them back. You can't become so efficient that all this stuff is made without any labor content. Because then you have nobody with the money to buy anything."

Consumers were the winners in this revolution. Or so it was said. Consumers were presumed to benefit because the same technological contest that hammered labor wages and corporate profits also delivered a plentitude of cheaper, better products to the people who buy things. The global surpluses created a buyer's market for nearly every good; the producer's loss was a customer's gain. Thus, it was claimed, the global system really was positive sum.

This was a frequently expressed article of faith that appeared to be both true and not true at the same time. Certainly, the technological revolution had generated a wide variety of remarkable products, from video recorders to advanced microprocessors, that became dramatically cheaper to buy, especially for newly developed products riding the steep growth curve of a new market. Around the world, people in many places were able to buy things unimagined in their societies only a few years before. The main reason pirated compact discs were sold so freely on the streets of Beijing or Kuala Lumpur was that so many citizens of China or Malaysia now had CD players in their homes.

Yet, if everything was cheaper, why didn't the consumers feel better about it? Their usual complaint, at least in advanced economies like America's, was that prices were too high and rising, that it was more difficult, not less, for them to acquire the standard things of modern life. As it happened, this complaint was also correct. People felt this way because their incomes were on average losing real value faster than any price benefits delivered by the marketplace. Indeed, their ability to purchase things was gradually shrinking relative to the price of things. Mass consumption, in other words, was generally not able to keep pace with the new abundance. That was the meaning of the industrial surpluses and inadequate demands, the consequence of declining real wages.

This general paradox was illustrated explicitly by the auto industry itself: the industrial revolution depressed prices and profits, yet nonetheless most people found it harder to buy a new car. In 1975, an average American family needed 18 weeks of earnings to buy an average-priced car; by 1995, the cost of this new car consumed 28 weeks of income. People typically coped with the growing gap by borrowing more: an average new car loan ran for 36 months in 1975, and twenty years later it was stretched out to 54 months.[17]

Part of the explanation was in the improved quality: The companies often protected profit margins per car by adding options and refinements (and new safety features required by law), all of which allowed them to charge higher prices. Thanks to the production innovations, the automobile manufactured in the 1990s was also better made and longer lasting. Probably, it was also true that without the global competition, car prices would have been even higher than they were. Still, the residual fact for most consumers was "sticker shock" and a growing recognition that they could no longer buy as much as they had previously assumed.

Meanwhile, auto companies, from the quick to the slow, were confronted with a relentless squeeze of their own—the downward pressure on profit margins. The fortunes of individual companies might rise or fall from one season to the next, according to their own nimbleness, but the general long-term reality was that making cars was a less profitable enterprise than it had been during the auto industry's halcyon years, the robust and stable decades after World War II.

Around the world the companies struggled to restore a condition of dependable profitability and thought they knew the way: by lowering the break-even point in their capacity utilization—that is, restructuring so they would make a profit even in bad times, if one fourth or one third of their productive capacity was unused. The main way to do this was to shrink themselves: sell off fixed assets, trim down managerial and factory-floor employees, write off the weaker investments. If market demand expanded, it could be met by hiring temporary workers, easily shed when slack times returned.

Unprofitable Volkswagen's break-even point had been above 90 percent of its capacity utilization, but VW was rapidly reducing this by shedding redundant workers, shooting for a goal of 70 percent. Toyota and other Japanese companies, used to operating profitably at very high capacity levels, were reluctantly beginning to shrink some of their base. Americans, for a change, appeared to be at the head of the chase.[18]

"Every manufacturer would like to reduce their break-even point as far as they can," said Van Bussman, the Chrysler chief economist. "For us, our target in 1993 was 70 percent. In 1994, it was 65 percent. We are shooting for 60 percent in 1996. You keep restraining fixed costs and you strive for more efficiency increases. You can only do that by lowering your fixed costs in relation to everything else, and, of course, you don't do that by building new plants. Everyone is now attuned to that reality. . . . The short-run effect is some pain because one of the ways to reduce the break-even point is to trim the workforce and eliminate redundant tasks."

Something similar was occurring across other sectors, as companies wrote off disappointing investments and slimmed down: going for profit margin instead of growth. Charles I. Clough, chief investment strategist at Merrill Lynch, called it "a sea change in corporate behavior."

"There is too much of everything and returns on investment are declining," Clough explained. "If a surplus persists in everything from auto plants to retail selling space, write-offs will not cease. Increasingly, managements will realize that growth in this sluggish world is out of the question unless they are willing to risk sharp declines in profitability. Going for market share means giving money away. Particularly in liquidating industries, such as department store retailing and mainframe computer manufacturing, it is critical to salvage cash flow by downsizing the corporation before revenues run down. Even in less threatened situations, it makes more sense to manage a mature business for cash." [19]

If Clough was correct and this represented a new strategic response to the revolutionary pressures of constant surplus, then the implications for long-term prosperity in the global system were bleak, particularly for the mature economies. The essence of this strategy, after all, was companies' learning how to live with weak markets. Individual enterprises might find the ways to do this and prosper, in effect restoring the "virtuous circle" that had existed in the postwar boom for themselves and their shareholders, though not for their employees and communities.

The larger economic meaning was ominous: If the companies succeeded, it meant a system that routinely accumulated a reserve of idle people and unused production, that found a profitable operating level far short of the economy's full potential. These blighted conditions—inadequate demand, oversupply of goods, permanent underemployment, falling wages and lackluster investment—already existed in many leading economies, but no one was ready to congratulate the self-correcting markets.

Ordinary people sometimes described these circumstances as recession. Economists, who employ a narrower definition, always corrected them, explaining that recession could not exist so long as the overall economy was expanding. But the popular understanding was not wrong in the broader sense: something fundamental was amiss in the global system. If such conditions persisted year after year, the period might eventually be described, more accurately, as depression.

Seven

"Scratching Their Itch"

IN A WORLD of glutted markets, the leverage naturally shifts from producers to buyers, so even the most successful global corporations find themselves cast as humble supplicants before prospective customers. To gain access to promising markets, multinational firms are engaged, quite literally, in trading away domestic jobs in exchange for sales. Struggling to unload over-abundant goods, companies are compelled to bargain with nations for entry into their markets, especially those fast-growing economies where demand is rising rapidly. In these transactions, the manufacturers will typically agree to consign a portion of their home-based production system—and technological prowess—to the buyers, the foreign country and its fledgling industrial enterprises.

The fulcrum for these negotiations is not the traditional economic question of comparative advantage—where will things be produced most efficiently?—but the particular ambitions of both companies and nations. Multinational corporations, faced with continuing surpluses, desperately need entry into the burgeoning markets. National governments, meanwhile, aim to secure a foothold in the advanced-technology sectors—aircraft, electronics, automobiles, telecommunications and others—that provide the core of modern, high-wage economies. These motivations converge in a familiar, blunt demand from the customers: if we buy your airplanes (or cars or telephone systems), you have to give us a share of the production, jobs and also industrial expertise.

This bargaining is always done discreetly and seldom discussed very openly by either governments or multinational corporations because it directly violates the reigning spirit of free trade. The deals regularly flout or circumvent the numerous global trade agreements negotiated among nations, ostensibly to prohibit such political interferences with the free marketplace. Despite the supposed rules, these government-corporate trade-offs are commonplace around the world, regularly demanded in different forms by rich and poor nations alike.

The contest for market entry constitutes another fundamental imperative shaping the behavior of enterprises in the global system. In the case of the most advanced technologies, it is probably a more powerful incentive driving the globalization of industry than the search for lower labor costs (though frequently the two objectives merge). In poorer countries, as we have seen, companies have the leverage to set the terms for their investments and to extract special benefits. But the bargaining power shifts to the governments if they control access to a "hot market" like China or India or even smaller nations like Indonesia where the economic growth is robust.

Market leverage—using a sheltered home market as a base to gain advantage in global commerce—provokes moral indignation among free-trade advocates, especially in the United States, but there are no innocent parties in this story. Employing a country's market leverage to promote its domestic welfare is an ancient practice of trading nations. Across the centuries it has been regularly used by both mature and developing economies, including the United States whenever the strategy seemed to serve American economic interests.

Moral objections, in any case, do not dissuade either nations or companies from pursuing self-interest in this manner, and neither have the much-heralded trade agreements known as GATT. The political management of trade and foreign industrial investment is not gradually receding, as many suppose, but actually expanding and refining its dimensions. Overall, the global system is more accurately described as a market-access regime, despite the familiar rhetoric about free trade and open markets. This reality helps explain further why firms are driven to globalize and why the migration of industrial jobs will continue.

As multinationals parcel out elements of production and share their skills with other firms, they inevitably invite a large risk: the possibility that they are helping to create their future competitors. From the standpoint of developing nations, that, of course, is the idea. Their goal is to become world-class producers themselves—to get out from under the domination of a handful of industrial states. In the broader sweep of human history, redistributing the world's industrial structure among many new nations may eventually be understood as a great act of economic justice—sharing not only jobs and incomes, but also capitalism's power of wealth creation. But, in the here and now, this process adds stress to the accumulating social and economic contradictions.

Corporations hedge against the risk of future rivals by globalizing—forming partnerships with their potential competitors, the new producers in emerging markets. The major multinationals hope to guide their evolution and, if it comes to that, to share the future markets with them in transnational corsortia of producers. Even if this corporate strategy should succeed, it still leaves out one group: the industrial workers back home whose jobs were traded away.

The Boeing Company of Seattle, the world's preeminent manufacturer of large-body commercial aircraft and America's number one exporter, was astride an awkward paradox. The company appeared to be shrinking and booming at the same time.

Around Puget Sound, where most of Boeing's domestic production was located, employment was contracting dramatically, down 50,000 jobs company-wide since 1990 when the aircraft-building boom of the 1980s collapsed. The company shrank by nearly one third, and thousands more layoffs were scheduled as managers pursued the concrete goal of reducing overall costs by 25 percent. With many of its lines idle, Boeing's awesome assembly plant just north of Seattle at Everett, Washington, was working at about half strength.

Yet, in fundamental ways, Boeing was booming. Profits topped $1.5 billion and were growing robustly. Boeing's brilliant menu of different models claimed 60 percent or more of the worldwide airliner sales. Its newest addition, the 320-seat 777, rolled out on schedule in May 1994 with 150 firm orders already booked, priced upward from $116 million each. United Airlines ordered thirty-four "Triple Sevens" over rival models offered by McDonnell Douglas and Airbus. Three Japanese airlines—ANA, JAL and JAS—bought thirty-two of them. Korean Air Lines and Thai Airways wanted eight each. China Southern and Cathay Pacific bought seventeen between them.[1]

When Boeing announced a new package of $5 billion in future sales from China, President Clinton personally celebrated the deal at the White House. This was evidence, the President said, that his administration's aggressive trade policies were working. If any multinational corporation could properly be called a "national champion," Boeing certainly qualified as America's.

Yet, back in Seattle, the machinists and engineers who made the airplanes were not cheered by the news. Having lived through them before, they understood the familiar boom-and-bust cycles of aircraft production and employment. But what they saw unfolding now was different and deeply troubling—the steady, gradually escalating relocation of Boeing's manufacturing work to other shores, other factories.

The company announced that complete tail sections for Boeing's most popular model, the mid-range 737, usually produced at Boeing's Wichita, Kansas, plant, would soon also be fashioned in China. Chinese factories and foundries had been making some minor components for selected Boeing aircraft for at least a decade—cargo doors or engine struts—but this was a major leap forward in the manufacturing process. When Boeing first announced the new outsourcing for the 737, it said only one hundred tail sections would be made in China and no U.S. jobs would be lost. Two years later, Beijing announced that Boeing had expanded the commitment to cover tail sections for fifteen hundred airplanes—"the biggest contract in the history of China's aviation industry," the official new agency boasted. Boeing confirmed the announcement.[2]

Indeed, Boeing also began dickering with Chinese officials about assembling some 757s there. When that idea stalled, the talks shifted to a possible consortium in which Boeing might coordinate between old enemies —China and Japan—to produce a new 100-seat regional jet, a smaller plane than Boeing models that would be made mainly in Asia, presumably China.

Even more unsettling was Boeing's decision to do in China what it had always declined to do in other countries—establish a foreign subsidiary, Boeing China, based in Beijing with a $600 million commitment of capital. This looked like another important step in the evolving process by which large and small elements of Boeing aircraft were one by one assigned to foreign producers, from Ireland and Italy to South Korea and Brazil, but especially to Japan.

"Sure, we're frightened, frightened beyond belief," said Lois I. Holton, who worked on mock-ups for tube development at the Everett plant. "I hear people saying, if they hadn't offloaded all these jobs to all the foreign countries, I'd still be working for Boeing."

"It's shameful," declared June Moen, who has worked fifteen years at Boeing's Seattle center. "A lot of this technology was basically paid for by us taxpayers through the defense work and then Boeing turns around and gives it away to another country. Up in Everett, they're ripping machine tools right out of the factory and sending them to Korea."

"And the jobs go with them," added Mark A. Blondin, a young tool and die maker at Boeing's Renton assembly plant. "One day, when the Japanese and Koreans start making their own aircraft, Boeing will turn around and say to us, if you workers had been team players and made more concessions, this wouldn't have happened. You watch. They'll blame it on the workers and the union."

Boeing employees could see the disturbing trend line in their own factories. Boeing's original triumph—the 707 launched back in the late 1950s —was fully made in America and was the twin of a military transport of the same design that Boeing built for the U.S. Air Force. The 727 that followed had only 2 percent foreign content. The best-selling 737 was originally less than 10 percent foreign-made. In the early 1980s, the 767 reached 15 percent. The new "Triple Seven" that rolled out in 1994 was 30 percent foreign content, 21 percent made in Japan.[3]

Mitsubishi Heavy Industries, Kawasaki and Fuji were enrolled as "risk-sharing" partners in the 777's $5 billion financing and the design. Five hundred work stations in Japan were connected in real time to the Boeing design center in Seattle. Two hundred Japanese engineers came to Boeing headquarters in 1991 for instruction. This intimate relationship prompted one project engineer to resign in protest. The technology sharing "should inevitably lead to a gradual transfer of most of Boeing's know-how to Japan," a Boeing engineer complained anonymously to an MIT professor. "That is quite a price to pay to keep Airbus out and get quality hardware on schedule."[4]

The employees' anxieties were deepened by an ominous precedent set by America's other commercial aircraft producer, McDonnell Douglas. Perceptibly losing ground, McDonnell seemed to be selling off the family jewels in the process. In the mid-1980s, McDonnell Douglas agreed to provide an assembly plant for China: Shanghai Aviation would set up a line to assemble two dozen MD-80s, airliners designated for the Chinese market, with most of their content manufactured in the United States. Despite the company's original promises five of those aircraft were sold back into the U.S. market —bought by TWA in 1993 at discount prices.

When McDonnell Douglas renewed the co-production deal for twenty more airplanes in 1994, the assembly work returned to Long Beach, California, but China demanded and got better terms for the long run: these new planes were to be 85 percent Chinese-made by the end of their production run in 2000. McDonnell Douglas was a desperate case, having fallen to 10 percent of the global market, and many in the industry assumed it would eventually be driven from the field. In the meantime, it was offering itself to foreign bidders. Taiwan Aerospace, a mere shell of a corporation but with global ambitions, looked it over and decided to pass; Taiwan instead bought a chunk of British Aerospace.

Indeed, from Moscow to Hamburg to Beijing, the aircraft industry was aswarm with private discussions of such globalizing partnerships—tentative schemes being negotiated among governments and companies to work together on production in exchange for new market shares. McDonnell's China president, Peter K. Chapman, explained the purpose to Patrick Tyler of the *New York Times:* "We're in the business of making money for our shareholders. If we have to put jobs and technology in other countries, then we go ahead and do it." [5]

In addition to the Asian market, Russia was on everyone's mind, not so much as a customer but as a rival producer. If Russia's aircraft industry entered the global market as a low-cost competitor, the potential to upset market shares and add to worldwide surpluses would be enormous. Established players like Boeing were trying to develop cooperative relationships and it opened a technical center in Moscow. Pratt & Whitney was already making engines for a new 300-seat Russian jetliner that would be 25 to 50 percent cheaper. The American company persuaded the U.S. Export-Import Bank to support the project with a $1 billion loan guarantee for Aeroflot. [6]

These actions in the aircraft industry contradicted the pious sermons from business and government leaders about the benefits of free trade and how it was supposed to work. Expanding global trade would advance the well-being of all nations, it was said, because free markets rewarded price efficiency. Therefore, over time, the sales would gravitate to nations that each produced what they did best and at the lowest cost, whether it was textiles or automobiles. If that was true, then why was commercial aircraft migrating, too?

"This isn't supposed to be happening," Barbara Shailor, the international affairs representative for the American machinists union, pointed out. The International Association of Machinists and Aerospace Workers (IAM), already losing heavily from the defense industry's retrenchment, was mobilizing to challenge the erosion of commercial aircraft jobs. "We're not talking about shirts or shoes moving to low-wage countries," Shailor said. "We're talking about the most advanced manufacturing technologies in the world. These are the high-skilled jobs, remember, that were going to be our future, that were supposed to save us in the global economy. Now they're leaving, too."

The aircraft industry offered a better window on the global reality than other sectors precisely because its migration was not complicated by the standard issues of comparative wage levels or which company held the high ground in the technological contest. Boeing was already, without dispute, the best. It was the world's most efficient low-cost producer, even with the $20-an-hour wages for machinists. Boeing products and especially its design capabilities were without peer. If the economists' logic of comparative advantage ruled the world, then Boeing could be making all of the world's jet airliners.

And given the escalating migration of these prized high-tech jobs, the familiar lectures on job training sounded ludicrously naive. American workers were repeatedly told that they must improve their skills in order to survive in the global economy; the Clinton administration had made this uplifting notion a cornerstone of its economic strategy. But Boeing machinists and engineers did not need higher technological skills; they were already acknowledged to be the most advanced workforce in the global industry. And tens of thousands of them were losing their jobs, many permanently. In the global context, the reality was that the United States had too many skilled aircraft workers. In the future, it was sure to have fewer of them.

The IAM pressured Boeing for job-security language in the new labor contract, but the union also challenged the U.S. government's passive acquiescence in the trade deals by which Boeing's workforce was gradually being globalized. The machinists raised some provocative questions: If the United States was so committed to free trade, why did it allow these irregular deals that drained America of its best jobs? And why was President Clinton celebrating? Why, for that matter, should U.S. taxpayers be asked to subsidize such transactions? The public helped underwrite sales by Boeing and other multinationals through the low-cost financing provided by the Export-Import Bank. The government lending agency did not question the offloading of American industrial structure in these transactions or even know the real terms.

"We are flying into the side of a mountain," IAM president George Kourpias warned. "If we continue trading away our finest jobs and industrial secrets, we are headed for certain disaster."

The Boeing Company had an answer for all this: its managers were trying to cope with reality rather than theory. The company strategy was to do whatever was necessary in a difficult situation to win new sales and defend market share and, yes, to hang on to as many American jobs as possible. But that meant sharing the work with the customers. Dean D. Thornton, the recently retired president of Boeing's commercial airplane group, described the trade-off in his plainspoken manner: "What people need to understand is that 60 percent of something is a helluva lot better than 100 percent of nothing."

The cavernous assembly plant at Everett was one of the great wonders of the industrial world and, in its way, beautiful to behold. The factory encompassed ninety-eight acres of manufacturing activity under a single roof and was said to be the largest building on earth. The ceiling was ten stories above the factory floor and covered by an intricate grid of pale green girders, like a steel spiderweb. Yellow cranes crept forward and sideways through this network, dangling pieces of wing or tail section beneath them on long, slender threads. There were forty of these cranes working overhead in the building, orchestrating construction of the wide-body craft known as the 747, 767 and 777. An air-traffic control center was required to coordinate their movements.

The dimensions of the place were overwhelming. From an observation loft, the huge aircraft below looked like glistening toys. The disconnected shells of fuselages, forward and aft sections, nose cones, tails and wings resembled pieces from a fabulous model airplane kit fastidiously arranged as though a precocious child had lined them up. Every seven days these pieces were methodically, miraculously brought together by the yellow cranes, fitted and fastened by the people down below, wings and center section joined to fuselage, electronics wired in, jet engines attached, every week a new airplane that weighed as much as 400 tons.

On the shop floor, the perspectives were reversed and the workers were dwarfed by what they were making. People bicycled from one behemoth to another, carrying plans from the dozens of computer design stations. The nose section of a 777, its delicate aluminum skin still protected by iridescent blue coating, floated down on cables. To the rear, a wing surface was being walked into place by four machinists who gently coaxed it back and forth into a snug fit with its frame. An automatic riveting machine, two stories high and mounted on railed track, moved patiently along the wing, punching out precision stitches almost noiselessly. The "Triple Seven" had 132,000 parts, not counting the millions of rivets. The economy-class seating section inside the 747, as Boeing liked to point out, was longer than the Wright Brothers' first flight at Kitty Hawk in 1903.

In some circumstances, technology could approach the threshold of art, at least in its power to inspire exalted feelings. One could not observe the majestic functioning of an industrial site like Everett without experiencing a momentary joy at the way things actually worked. These processes fused complexity and gargantuan strength, unforgiving tolerances with the hand-held gentleness of assembly workers. The act of bringing everything together perfectly was an accomplishment that rebuked cynics and ought to confirm an industrial society's optimism about itself. This factory spoke matter-of-factly about the extraordinary dimensions of human capabilities and, in particular, about the meticulous courage of engineers.*

The Everett plant likewise demonstrated, more tangibly, the international character of advanced manufacturing. The managerial challenge was not simply to build an aircraft, but to coordinate the parts streaming in from hundreds of sources, foreign and domestic. On the shop floor, wooden crates marked Belfast, Ireland, contained nose landing-gear doors. Stacked on a metal rack were outboard wing flaps, with tags from Alenia of Italy.

The 777's entire fuselage traveled in quarter sections from Japan, shipped by Mitsubishi from Nagoya to Puget Sound, where the pieces were barged from Tacoma to the port of Everett, then hauled by railcars up the steep grade to the factory. Wingtip assembly came from Korea. Rudders from Australia. Dorsal fins from Brazil. Main landing gears from Canada and France. Flight computers from the United Kingdom. And so on.

"You've got to maintain the tit for tat if you expect to keep selling airplanes," a Boeing middle manager explained. Assembly parts were dispersed to the foreign producers because the market demanded it, not because these things could be made better or cheaper somewhere else.

"I don't think we have a total choice," Dean Thornton said. "This is a sexy business, everybody likes to be in it. It's not like toothpaste. And there's a huge surplus in this industry worldwide. So there are these pressures pushing you that way."

"I am scratching their itch," Lawrence W. Clarkson, Boeing's senior vice president for planning and international development, explained. "I have to create some jobs in those countries to get those markets. But what we're trying to do in the net equation is to protect the jobs here. I think I can show that happened with China or with Japan.

"But, overall, it's a tougher problem as I look down the future. Will I have a lot of U.S. suppliers or will I have more international suppliers? I don't know the answer, but it's clear that the U.S. suppliers don't bring me any market."[7]

The American marketplace for jet airliners remained the largest by far, but Boeing also lived increasingly on its overseas sales. "When the 727 was in its heyday, our market was probably 75 percent domestic," Clarkson said, "but Boeing is up around 60 percent international sales now. We are a U.S. company, almost a Puget Sound company, but can we continue to be number one structured the way we are now? We will do the things we have to do offshore because we have to do them for market access."

The "itch" was the ambition of nations to manufacture highly valued

---

* *The Everett assembly plant was open to the public and nearly 100,000 tourists viewed the spectacle of production every year.*

goods, products that require leading-edge technologies and provide the premier industrial jobs. Why should Boeing get to make most of the world's large-body airplanes when other people could also learn how to do it? Why should Americans have all the fun (and profit) when everyone, from German bankers to Korean rice farmers, now traveled by jetliner?

The question occurred first to the Europeans, who put together Airbus Industrie in the late 1960s—a government-financed consortium of German, French, British and Spanish companies (Daimler's DASA, Aérospatiale, British Aerospace and CASA of Spain). Despite Americans' initial skepticism, Airbus succeeded spectacularly in time, grabbing 30 percent of the world market, mostly at the expense of McDonnell Douglas, and was still expanding.

The Japanese manufacturers entered next, aggressively targeting this high-end sector. Now the rest of Asia was demanding a share—China, Korea and Taiwan, even less muscular players like Indonesia and Malaysia. From the perspective of these other nations, the process of market-entry bargaining was simply the means of diminishing an American monopoly—the dominance established during the postwar decades when U.S. defense budgets helped to build the industrial base of American companies.

The actual transactions occurred when Boeing was about to make a sale. It would be informed, either officially or informally, that it must "offset" some of the sales price by agreeing to share a portion of the value-added production or to buy other goods from the purchasing nation. The practice of offsets originated decades before in the realm of military sales—often to help a poorer country get the hard currency to pay for its new weapons—and military offsets continued. The commercial deals were usually less explicit because they violated the ostensible terms of trade.

"There are different players in China," Clarkson explained. "The Chinese airlines want to buy Boeing airplanes, but they tell us that we've got to keep those other guys over there happy or they won't be able to buy our planes." The other guys were China's four major aircraft manufacturers. Though ostensibly a private business transaction, the terms were ultimately determined by the central government in Beijing because it controlled the reserves of foreign currency that would be needed to buy the imported planes. The Asians did not invent this system; they were emulating long-established practices from European and American commerce.

" 'Offset' is a bad word, and it's against GATT and a whole bunch of other stuff, but it's a fact of life," Thornton said. "It used to be twenty years ago in places like Canada or the UK, it was totally explicit, down to the decimal point. 'You will buy 20 percent offset of your value.' Or 21 percent or whatever. It still is that way in military stuff. Commercially, it's not legal so it becomes less explicit." Nevertheless, Clarkson said the Chinese always demand a "written acknowledgment" of the trade-offs, "so typically what you have is a sales contract that references the [offset] commitment."

The offset terms fluctuated from deal to deal and were normally kept confidential, but Boeing has in recent years typically offloaded an estimated 20 to 23 percent in value to win sales from both developing and mature economies alike. Ron Woodard, Thornton's successor as president of commercial airplanes, said, "The correlation is clear: work placement has opened markets for us where they might otherwise not be accessible." That was what Dean Thornton meant by "100 percent of nothing." [8]

Japan was Boeing's leading example of how the work trade-offs sustained employment at home. Japan's three major airlines were the largest customer for the 747 and 767, and they also heavily ordered the new 777. "Now nowhere on paper does it say the Japanese airlines are going to do that because we have these programs with Japanese industry," Clarkson explained. "But you know enough about Japan to know that the overarching desire of Japanese culture is harmony, what the Japanese call *wa*. If those airlines went out and ordered competing airplanes, instead of buying the ones their brothers were deeply involved in making, that would create *fuwa*, 'disharmony.' "

The parallel objective for Boeing was to keep Japan from deciding to produce a freestanding commercial aircraft of its own. This goal has frequently been expressed by Japanese industrialists, who were presumed to be technologically capable of doing so. "We worked hard to satisfy the itch in Japanese industry and to some extent in MITI in a way that's prevented them from launching a competitor," Clarkson said. "Perhaps the same strategy will work in China."

The Boeing-Japan symbiosis has become a game of "badgers and foxes," as MIT political scientist Richard J. Samuels described it. A Japanese industrial official told Samuels: "We cooperate because Boeing is so strong. It does not make sense to try to compete with them. But we want to be in sales and marketing too. We seek technological autonomy." [9]

Boeing was so eager to please its Asian customers that it reconfigured some aircraft for them in a way likely to offend American notions of comfort and safety. A few years ago, Boeing equipped several 747s for JAL and Air Nippon with grossly expanded seating capacity for commuter routes— no-frills airliners that carried 570 people instead of the normal maximum of 420. This was accomplished mainly with smaller seats jammed closer together. "It's like turning an airplane into a cattle car," a Boeing worker complained. Though the company denied it, several workers told me the planes had been flown out of the United States in the normal configuration so as not to offend government regulators, but then the extra seats were shipped later for installation overseas. This was perhaps another minor example of how global commerce may "harmonize" standards—downward.

The newest major player, China, could demand stiffer terms than others because it has become the fastest-growing aircraft market in the world. "We have a very onerous countertrade agreement in China, based on a percentage of the airplane price," Newton L. Simmons of Boeing said.

"They are asking 20 to 30 percent of the price in local purchases. That's the way the game is played."

As Boeing's partner, the Japanese manufacturers had to contribute their share of the offsets to China, too. "Mitsubishi has its own presence in China and it can support Boeing products by putting in electronics or a concrete plant or a car dealership," Simmons explained. In fact, when the yen appreciated and pushed up manufacturing costs in Japan, Mitsubishi got Boeing's permission to offload some of its fuselage work for the 777 and 767 to China and Indonesia. This was like a triple play in production swapping—aircraft jobs that had moved swiftly from Seattle to Nagoya to Shenyang.[10]

As Boeing saw competition quicken in Asia, it began to play hardball elsewhere. It started discounting prices by as much as 10 percent and stole a major customer, Sweden's SAS, from its weakening U.S. rival, McDonnell Douglas. Boeing's global strategy evidently included driving McDonnell to the wall so Boeing would become the only American producer.[11]

Boeing, meanwhile, delivered an unsubtle warning to its suppliers in the Canadian aerospace industry: if Canada didn't order more Boeing planes, it could expect to lose the Boeing subcontracts and jobs it originally secured as offsets for sales. In a speech to the Aerospace Industries Association of Canada in November 1994, Ron Woodard pointed out that Boeing purchased $800 million a year in aircraft parts from Canadian suppliers, yet its sales to Canada had dwindled to a piddling $30 million. In other countries, Woodard noted, Boeing could expect $800 million in local offset production to support $3.5 billion to $4 billion in aircraft sales. The company's aggravation was deepened when Canada's defense department chose an Airbus military transport over Boeing's. "This made a strong impression on me," he pointedly remarked.

"We are presently conducting a Canadian make/buy review to move toward the same balance between sales and procurement applied in other countries," Woodard announced. "In other words, our Canadian business placement must understandably be market based, as it is elsewhere." Boeing was telling Canada to start playing by the rules—not free-market rules but the rules of market access.

A similar alert was sent simultaneously throughout Boeing's network of domestic and foreign suppliers: prepare to cut costs and shift some of your work to China. Thus, migration of the industrial jobs seemed sure to accelerate. Northrop-Grumman, which makes the 757 tail sections for Boeing in its Texas plant, got the message and decided to share its work with Chengdu Aircraft Company in China.

"We've got suppliers that we've dealt with for fifty years and we're asking all of them to offload production to China," said Jim Whitney, Boeing's site manager at Xian Aircraft Company in China. "We're telling our suppliers: we want a fixed price with no inflation and that means offloading the work to (low-wage) China. If they don't offload, then we'll take back the work and we'll offload it."

For many years, Airbus had stood aloof from such practices, refusing to play. After all, the Airbus consortium was frankly conceived by European politicians as a "jobs program" and heavily subsidized by the governments. So it was politically awkward for Airbus factories in Hamburg or Toulouse to trade away jobs created at public expense for German or French workers. Unlike American aerospace companies, Airbus did not do mass layoffs, but managed its employment more cautiously to avoid boom-and-bust cycles.

Nevertheless, as competitive pressures escalated, Airbus began to deal, too. The Europeans were stuck with huge overcapacity of their own and they had seen how Boeing locked up Japan by putting an arm around the Japanese manufacturers. Airbus did not intend to let that happen again with China. The consortium began to disperse modest elements by sharing carbon-fiber technology for components with Shenyang Aircraft, by putting a $25 million flight training center in Beijing and by assigning some parts production to two Chinese factories. When Airbus grabbed a $3 billion China sale away from Boeing in the spring of 1996, an order for thirty-three planes, it consigned component production to Xian, Shenyang and Guizhou factories. Airbus executives, meanwhile, were all over the region, promoting ideas for an Asian-European co-production deal that might elbow aside Boeing.[12]

Boeing was, of course, working the same ground. Asia was practically papered over with the numerous versions of the "memorandum of understanding" that companies and countries sign to explore a joint venture. A small regional 100-seater to be built by Germans and Japanese with China? Or were the Americans going to win this project? A Korean-led all-Asian consortium that included China, Singapore and India? A jumbo jet with 800 seats that everyone might collaborate on?

"We've all got pieces of paper signed by China," Clarkson said. "All this means is they're conducting an auction and we have to play this very carefully." The initial agreements were not yet very meaningful, but they reflected the deeper gravitational pull.

The heavy question stalking the aircraft industry was whether the Asian nations might get together and create an Airbus consortium of their own. If that occurred, then all of the collaborative manufacturing deals Boeing had engineered to win sales might have produced a monster—a new low-wage competitor that owned access to the thriving markets and could produce the world-class quality it had learned from Seattle. In this scenario, the industrial geography of large-body aircraft might eventually resemble what had happened in consumer electronics or machine tools.

"That's hypothetically possible," Clarkson conceded, "but whether it's probable depends upon how we and Airbus play our cards. . . . For my planning purposes, I assume I'm going to have another subsidized competitor somewhere in the world and that's probably in Asia, okay? That is the sort of scenario I use to test our strategy because it could happen. On the other hand, if Boeing plays its cards right, it doesn't have to happen."

This was the knife-edge dilemma in the globalization strategy of "scratching their itch." If Boeing refused to share its work and expertise with the Asian customers, that might have the effect of encouraging Japan, China or others to go it alone and start making their own airplanes. Or did Boeing's industrial collaborations actually hasten the rise of a new competitor by enabling others to climb the ladder? "Yes, there's a risk," Thornton said. "But, hell, life is full of risk and you try to do what you can."

Boeing officials claimed that the issue of technology transfer was "sort of a red herring," as Clarkson put it, because much of the manufacturing knowledge was already widely dispersed and available. Airbus, for instance, had leapt ahead in some design features simply by applying the new technologies developed in the U.S. space program. Foreign companies, especially the Japanese, nevertheless pushed relentlessly for greater access to Boeing's know-how and were strengthened by it. Fuji Heavy Industries, chosen once as Boeing's "Supplier of the Year," turned around and provided McDonnell Douglas with fuselage subassemblies it had learned how to make at Boeing. Kawasaki developed a fuselage assembly tool for Airbus based on its experience with Boeing. The one technology Boeing did not share with anyone was its unique wing-design methodology.[13]

But the largest barrier to entry was probably not technology but the huge capital costs and the real risk of failure. In that sense, Boeing's most valuable asset was its mastery of the overall design-and-production process —the ability to bring everything together efficiently. No one else was likely to re-create another Everett assembly plant anytime soon, and Boeing regularly reminded its partners, from Taiwan to Japan, how risky it would be for them to enter the already glutted marketplace on their own. If Japan were to sink $10 billion to $20 billion into developing a new airliner that nobody else in the world wanted to buy, that could provoke considerable *fuwa* back home.

Still, given the risk of potential rivals, Boeing's strategy included one additional element of hedging: if a new government-backed "Asian Airbus" should develop in the future, Boeing intended to be part of it. That was the unspoken premise in the various discussions of a consortium to produce a 100-seater. If China or Japan decided to make their own aircraft, Boeing hoped to be its partner. The production might be centered in Asia, but Boeing could bring all of its design and management expertise to the table —the experienced team leader for what would be a truly multinational enterprise.

"It might very well make sense," Larry Clarkson mused, "to have an airplane where Boeing doesn't make a majority of it and has some relatively small percentage, but the aircraft has a large commonality with other Boeing airplanes. We'd probably be in a minority position but with what I'd call a management lead—sort of in charge."

This was only a vision at present, but already it suggested a new nightmare for the American workers. Boeing saw the 100-seater as augmenting its existing model line, not competing with it. But once such a shared transnational enterprise succeeded in collaborating on a smaller aircraft, what would prevent it from moving up the line to larger projects? Once the Asian companies had acquired the capabilities, why should they not also produce other, bigger aircraft? Boeing officials insisted this was not what they had in mind. Still, Boeing was strategically positioned to cope with any of these eventualities.

If it played its cards right, Boeing could survive and flourish as a company, regardless of how much the aircraft industrial base was dispersed to other countries. It would exist as a "virtual corporation" on a monumental scale, with its brains still in Seattle but its workforce scattered around the globe. This could work for Boeing. It was Puget Sound and the American machinists who would have some problems.

In India, when General Motors sought market entry in 1994 for its European-made Opel, the price was radiator caps. GM agreed to sell a subsidiary business to a company in Madras that would now manufacture about half of the worldwide supply of Opel radiator caps. Thus, India got a share of export business that would provide the foreign currency to help pay for the Opels. The jobs moved from Britain.[14]

In Korea, it was trains. France signed a $2.1 billion contract to sell its celebrated very fast trains, but much of the work would be done in Asia, and a few years hence Korea intended to be selling fast trains itself. In China, AT&T agreed to manufacture its advanced switching equipment there in order to wire up Chinese cities for modern telephone service. China signed similar deals with both Intel and IBM as the two companies sought entry for their competing microchips.[15]

Such transactions were commonplace across the advanced industrial sectors. Nations were demanding elements of production and technology with increasingly sophisticated terms. Australia targeted strategic research and development, demanding investments with what might be called Anglo-Saxon directness. It persuaded Motorola to locate a new product software center at Adelaide and a communications R&D center in Sydney.

"The Australians have the most explicit program in the world," Motorola's Richard Heimlich said. "It says: if your sales are above a certain threshold, you must negotiate with the government on an agreement locating R&D in Australia, and for production you must export 50 percent of whatever you import and it must have 70 percent local content. It's been very successful. They've gotten thirty-three electronics companies to accept it—Japanese, European and American."

Motorola, which has aggressively pursued market-opening campaigns in Japan, at first considered resisting the Australian requirements, but decided that a deal made more sense. "If you don't cooperate they have the statutory authority to exclude you from bidder lists or deny you regulatory permits for products," Heimlich said. "Those are the threats, but they are obviously reluctant to employ them because they would clearly be GATT vulnerable if they did."

Such market-entry tactics looked like an unsubtle form of blackmail and obviously in violation of the established trading rules, but it was not entirely clear that a legal challenge by Motorola would have prevailed. After all, the demands were described merely as "guidelines" intended to promote Australia's economic development. No one had ever filed a formal complaint against them. "How do you blow the whistle if thirty-three companies have already signed up for it?" Heimlich said. "That's why it's a very clever program. We would have a hard time challenging it when every computer company in the world is already accepting it."

The advanced industrial states, though offended by these irregular practices, were not exactly innocent themselves. The inverse of market-entry bargaining was the use of protectionist measures, practiced selectively in Europe and North America and, of course, notoriously in the "sanctuary markets" of Japan. One approach allowed market entry in exchange for acquiring new production. The other approach limited market entry in order to protect older producers from competing goods. Either way the fundamental objective was the same: regulation of the marketplace in behalf of domestic interests, companies and workers.

Many Americans and some Europeans probably had difficulty recognizing this similarity because their own national political dialogues were devoted mostly to preachments on free trade and complaints about other violators. Asians and Eastern Europeans were perhaps less naive about market-access realities since it was their producers who encountered the Western hypocrisies.

In the European Union, supposedly liberalized by unifying fifteen national markets, the countries had more than seven hundred national restrictions on import quantities, many of which were being converted to so-called voluntary restraints. The UK's Society of Motor Manufacturers and Traders maintained a long-standing "gentlemen's agreement" with the Japanese Automobile Manufacturers Association that effectively limited Japanese cars to 11 percent of the British market. France and Italy had tougher restrictions. The EU periodically proclaimed its intention to eliminate such informal barriers but, meanwhile, it was tightening them. During the recessionary conditions in late 1993, Japanese auto imports to Europe were arbitrarily reduced by 18 percent.

Europe, moreover, imposed elaborate local-content rules on various products and on foreign investment—all designed to insulate European enterprises from glutted global markets. Texas Instruments complained that it was forced to shift some circuit-board work from its U.S. plants in order to qualify the end product as European-produced. When the European Community wished to foster a European VCR industry, it set an explicit quota on Japanese sales covering not only VCRs imported from Japan but also those actually made in Europe at Japanese factories. For quota purposes, Europe's trade rulings treated Japanese electronics made in Japanese-owned factories in the United States not as American goods, but as Japanese.[16]

The United States was, by far, the most open marketplace in the world and the leading advocate for opening other markets. Nevertheless, when influential sectors demanded it, the U.S. government also managed trade in behalf of domestic interests. During the Reagan presidency the free-market conservatives promoting economic deregulation also worked out import-limiting agreements covering autos, steel, textiles, semiconductors, machine tools and some others. These were usually said to be "voluntary," a convenient hypocrisy that may have misled some Americans but not the foreign producers.

During the Clinton administration, while the President celebrated the cause of free trade and frequently criticized Japan's market barriers, his administration also collaborated in the creation of a worldwide cartel that curtailed aluminum production and propped up prices. In late 1993, aluminum prices were collapsing, from above 90 cents a pound to below 50 cents, because the former Soviet republics had entered the global market with massive and cheap supplies; American companies were devastated and asked the White House to help work out a production-limiting agreement. It appeared to work: a year later prices were rising smartly, and aluminum was back up close to 90 cents. "As a political matter, you can't destroy our industry with Russian aluminum," one highly ranked administration official explained. "You're just not going to do it." [17]

In sum, despite the reigning pieties, the global system could not properly be called a free-trade regime. When all of the contradictions, exceptions and purposeful evasions were taken into account, most of the world's trade was not a free exchange based on market prices. One way or the other, trade was massaged and regulated, managed explicitly by governments or internally by the multinational corporations or often by both in discreet collaboration.

Lawrence B. Krause, international relations professor at the University of California at San Diego, aggregated all of the different ways in which trade was managed—openly and covertly—and concluded that only about 15 percent of global trade was genuinely conducted in free-market circumstances. Other scholars have calculated that governments directly managed 25 to 30 percent of trade through their various nontariff barriers. Multinational corporations themselves managed about 40 percent of global trade through the intrafirm trade among their own subsidiaries. Further, Krause noted that the top ten trade sectors, from aircraft to petroleum, were managed by governments or concentrated firms, with the single exception of paper. These accounted for 22 percent of world trade.[18]

Managing trade did not mean that there was no competition—the competition was fierce and potentially fatal to some. What it meant was that the global contests among enterprises were governed by self-interested imperatives far more complex, political and arbitrary than a disinterested marketplace ruled by prices and costs. This was not a secret to the businesses nor to many scholars who had studied the matter. Yet the conventional political discourse, especially in the United States, insisted on ignoring the reality and portraying the world as marching progressively toward a more and more liberalized system. Any U.S. politician who challenged this orthodoxy would likely be labeled a backward protectionist in the press commentaries.

"Academics and policy makers clung tightly to the old, comforting rhetoric of free trade and the pillars on which it was built because, despite occasional dips, global commerce continued to grow," American political scientists Peter F. Cowhey and Jonathan D. Aronson observed in their book, *Managing the World Economy*. ". . . They failed to appreciate that a market-access regime was emerging—not because it was planned but as a result of market developments and corporate strategies."

The more that firms globalized, Cowhey and Aronson pointed out, the more likely their sectors would become more managed—more subject to overt bargaining, not less. Aircraft offered a leading example of this trend. The market-access bargaining had become standard behavior because the stakes were so high for both parties, companies and nations, sellers and buyers. And both sides expected to benefit from the bargaining, both as partners and rivals. Once such political relationships were established in a sector, the likely loser was the firm that refused to play. In those circumstances, most firms decided to play.

Yet, if this was the reality, what was the point of GATT and the other free-trade agreements? If their terms were so widely ignored, why did governments and corporations devote so much energy (and self-congratulations) to negotiating them? And why did major companies like Boeing or Motorola portray themselves as ardent free traders and then, with a wink, engage in the market-access deals that blatantly violated the rules?

"Well, what are the rules?" Clarkson asked. "Part of the problem is that, to some degree, the rules are mythology."

Indeed, as enforceable law, GATT was largely fictional, even though trade lawyers always pored over the negotiating texts adding "wiggle words." GATT made more sense if it was understood as an important bargaining tool for players in the market-access trading system—"rules of the road" that discouraged certain practices but, in reality, left them open to negotiation. When I asked Dean Thornton of Boeing to reconcile the contradiction, he compared the trade rules to the speed limit on highways —a good thing to have in place, even if many drivers violated it.

The speed-limit metaphor made clear what was missing from the global system: a highway cop. There was no neutral authority with the power to enforce the rules, to make nations and firms observe them, regardless of the economic consequences. In fact, enforcement was largely left to the drivers themselves. They would decide if it was in their interest to make a complaint. Sometimes, they did. More often, they winked and bargained.

That was always Boeing's response, for instance. The company had frequently complained that the European governments violated free-trade rules by subsidizing creation of the rival Airbus consortium. Yet, on several occasions when the U.S. government was prepared to bring a formal complaint against Airbus, Boeing or McDonnell Douglas told the government to back off. Why? Because pressing the issue might have been bad for business.[19]

"Over the years," Larry Clarkson acknowledged, "the problem with the Airbus subsidies was that every time we made a big fuss about it, we'd get a call from our European customers, telling us to shut up." Boeing did shut up and told the U.S. trade representatives to do the same. "You don't do what you ought to do because of short-term customer pressures and so on," Thornton explained.

The demands for production offsets from the developing nations contained the same dilemma: the demands usually came from the customers. "The practical problem is that the [offset] requirement is usually put to you through the airline that you're trying to sell to in a competition," Clarkson said. "So your ability to effectively fight it is not very good because obviously it would put you in a competitive disadvantage."

The latest version of GATT, the so-called Uruguay Round approved in 1994, attempted to overcome the gap in enforcement by creating the World Trade Organization, an international secretariat empowered to hand out penalty rulings. Its future power was dubious. Nations were not about to cede economic self-interest to the rule of an international body of 121 governments, each with diverse ambitions of its own. Indeed, when American critics complained that the new GATT agreement usurped national sovereignty, the Clinton administration and corporate lobbyists reassured Congress by pointing out that GATT lacked the force of law. If the WTO should ever intrude on America's sovereign decision-making, the U.S. government promised to withdraw—effectively destroying the organization.

Trade rules mattered mainly as an additional form of leverage for corporations and governments in the market-access bargaining—terms enabling the threat of a formal complaint or defining the concessions that could be traded away. Indeed, the international trade negotiations were essentially the loftiest plateau for the market-access bargaining. That is why the proceedings were lobbied so intensely by the various sectors, why governments pursued the trade agendas of their own "national champions."

The trade texts set out to establish broad principles but were, in fact, densely woven with lawyerly distinctions and exceptions, most of them put there at the behest of specific corporate interests. Some major sectors were left out entirely because the multinational competitors could not reach agreement among themselves. Some nations won status as "developing" economies that allowed them to keep doing things that were generally prohibited. Japan had been a GATT signatory for three decades. Yet, the U.S. government was still complaining loudly about Japan's closed markets.

The 1994 GATT agreement did not affect the aircraft industry because it was left out. Boeing and Airbus had united in supporting a new aircraft code designed to discourage the emergence of additional government-subsidized producers—a firewall aimed at China and Russia. But major engine producers, Pratt & Whitney and Rolls-Royce, blocked it for their own reasons. Even if such a code were adopted, enforcement would be difficult since neither Russia nor China was a GATT member. Though China campaigned for entry, it was not likely to abandon its industrial ambitions as the price of admission. If China, for instance, refused to play by the rules, would Boeing and Airbus refuse to sell aircraft to China? Not very likely, unless perhaps their governments compelled them to do so.

The Chinese and others could look across the course of industrial history and argue that they were simply following a well-traveled route: they were using the leverage of their home market to acquire a stronger industrial base. Market leverage, in its usual application, provides domestic enterprises with greater economies of scale, allowing them to produce for their sheltered home market, then sell surplus production into the other guy's market, often at competitive discounts. Japan had used market leverage to brilliant advantage, relentlessly capturing market share and sometimes entire sectors, from automobiles to consumer electronics.

In its own way, however, the United States has also used market leverage to gain global advantage. In the decades after World War II, when competing industrial nations were in ruin and the U.S. domestic economy was booming, American multinationals had used their domestic market base as the platform from which to penetrate and dominate other markets in Europe and Asia. To be sure, the U.S. market was legally open to foreign competitors, but practically speaking, the foreign competition seemed insignificant. American firms pioneered the multinational structures that others eventually emulated.

Japan rose from the ashes of war by applying its own complex version of market leverage—a mix of government supervision and subsidies, cartelized home markets shared by domestic companies and sheltered from foreign producers—allowing its infant industries to develop at home and eventually capture export markets. In the United States, considerable scholarship has been devoted to explaining how Japan's feudal history and distinctive culture led to such a system. In Japan, one heard a simpler explanation: Japan was merely following the outlines of American industrial history. The Japanese model was at least partly derived from the aggressive economic doctrine the United States had itself employed in the nineteenth century, the so-called American system that helped foster U.S. ascendance as an industrial power.[20]

European governments, while ideologically committed to the free-trade ideal, were trying through the EU to perfect their own version of the Japanese model—a purposeful system of selective protection and subsidy that relied on market leverage, too. The original notion of a "common market" uniting Europe was that it would create economies of scale for the European producers (though this objective was diluted when U.S. multinationals, among others, smartly repositioned themselves to qualify as "European," too). When Europeans wanted their own commercial aircraft industry (or computers or VCRs), they went out and created one, pursuing strategies that ensured a domestic market base to absorb the new production.

China and other major developing economies were, in a sense, using market leverage in reverse fashion, granting controlled access to their home markets in order to leverage for themselves a share of the world's advanced industrial base. If these efforts succeeded, they might someday be at a stage where they too could export surplus production into other, unprotected markets. Their strategy offended free-trade principle but was not morally distinguishable from what advanced nations had often done themselves.

The fundamental dysfunction between trade law and reality was that nations and corporations were pursuing an objective that the trade agreements ignored—the global contest for a share of the industrial base. Clyde V. Prestowitz Jr., president of the Economic Strategy Institute, which is supported by U.S. multinationals, described the contradiction: "The heart of the problem is this: all of the trade agreements are based on the premise of comparative advantage and pretend that what you make and the structure of global production doesn't matter. So if the Europeans want to subsidize Airbus, it doesn't matter. It is looked upon as a gift to our consumers —cheaper airplanes. Therefore, under GATT, industrial policy, cartels, the location and structure of industries—none of this matters.

"In the real world, it does matter. Other nations understand that. That's why they are willing to subsidize or demand a share of production in order to shift the structure of global industries. So the national industries proliferate, and once they are established they do have a lot of employment and so they can't lay off people—while the U.S. companies can. The implicit notion is that the Americans will adjust by reducing their capacity and employment. That's what usually happens."

Americans, schooled in the rhetorical idealism of free trade, frequently expressed righteous indignation at the irregular practices of others, but the outrage was mostly sustained by ignorance. Their belief system was unable to incorporate the new facts of global commerce. Or even the historic truth that nations and enterprises, if they have the power, will do what they need to do in pursuit of their self-interest. Some of them would be mistaken and fail, but in the end their actions would be judged by the tangible results, not according to the abstract moral pretensions of free-market economics.

Perhaps it was Americans who were confused about this, at least American opinion leaders. Many ambitious nations have pondered the American model and then chosen to follow the Japanese model, mainly because it seemed to work. Roger Bertelson, Motorola's country manager in Malaysia, lamented Americans' weak grasp of the global reality, a frustration I heard expressed many times by business people. "Americans," Bertelson said, "don't have the foggiest understanding of what's happening to them and why."

In any case, it was a bit late in history to be lecturing poor nations on the proper way to get rich. They could see for themselves how others had done it.

The foreboding and anger felt by the Boeing machinists in Seattle boiled up into a strike against the company in fall 1995 that shut down all of its production lines for two months. The strike issue was not about wages but about job security and Boeing's accelerating strategy of outsourcing production work to other nations. A similar strike followed in June 1996 against McDonnell Douglas in St. Louis. The United Auto Workers staged a showdown with General Motors on the same question.

The machinists union did win new contract language from Boeing, a stronger guarantee of future job security, but no one in the union leadership had any illusions that the problem had been solved. The best jobs would continue to be shipped out of America by leading multinationals, IAM's president, George Kourpias, warned, until the federal government itself took a stand against the erosion. That would require Washington to confront America's own multinationals and ask hard questions about their globalizing strategies. The Clinton administraton, like others before it, was unwilling to do this.

Kourpias proposed a bolder plan for counterattack—a united diplomatic front between Airbus and Boeing, between European and American governments, that would confront the Asian nations and call their bluff. If Asians want to make their own aircraft, they can do so, of course—but not by siphoning off American or European employment, not by blackmailing the sellers to swap jobs for new orders. Neither Washington nor Paris and Berlin was as yet willing to take up his challenge.

"We're not arguing that we aren't willing to share jobs around the world—we are," Kourpias said. "But do we have to destroy ourselves in doing so? The answer is no."

In a narrow river valley in Shaanxi Province, the village of Sanyuan was a settlement of worn, brown-brick dwellings compactly set against the valley wall. A steep ridge rising behind the village was gullied and desiccated, starkly terraced by erosion. The pale village walls had the same tired, washed-out look. Most of the small houses were organized in common clusters, with dark tile or thatched roofs, though several newer ones stood apart, decorated with dramatic floral designs by their doorways. Behind the courtyard wall at one home, the family's possessions were scattered about on the hard-baked ground: a two-wheeled farm cart, bicycle and tools, jumbled rows of unused bricks, mounds of darkening cornstalks saved for fuel or livestock, a tethered cow, two white goats on the loose. The cow was for plowing, the goats for milk.

I came to this place at the suggestion of a Boeing manager in order to see the other end of the global aircraft industry. Sanyuan was doubtless like ten thousand other country villages in China—poor and primitive, remote to the world—the places called underdeveloped in the global context. In its own circumstances, it is thriving. This particular farm village is also home to the Hongyuan Aviation Forging & Casting Industry Company, a state-owned enterprise that manufactured minor parts for Boeing's world-class aircraft. As the Boeing man probably anticipated, I experienced in this village the full, dizzying dimensions of the global system, the deep strangeness of humanity united by industrial revolution.[21]

At nightfall, Sanyuan seemed especially strange since there were no streetlights along the paved national road through the village, only the occasional glow of a TV set from an open doorway. People, bicycles, handcarts appeared abruptly from the thick darkness, then seemed to evaporate. The night strollers were indifferent to the speeding, honking trucks that flashed through periodically with loads of crushed stone or steel rods. Music was blaring from a midweek dance at the community hall. Because of power shortages in the province, authorities directed some villages and factories to take their weekends on Wednesday and Thursday.

Across the street at an open-air canteen, I ordered a beer that turned out to be a nasty fruit drink. Everyone laughed at this failure of communication. We tried again, several times, and finally got it right. These Chinese people, a bit like American tourists, seemed to believe that any foreigner should be able to understand their language if the words were pronounced slowly and loudly enough.

Next morning the peasant farmers had their daily market under way alongside the high brick walls at the center of the village. They squatted back on their heels, in the universal manner of plain country folk, behind abundant piles of produce—carrots, greens, cauliflower, scallions and cabbages spread out on white muslin. A young man in a blue sweater jabbered self-importantly through a small portable loudspeaker. He was selling lotus flour, a milky white powder that he packaged in clear plastic bags and weighed on a crude hand-held scale.

At the north end of town, the Hongyuan Forging plant was a collection of dingy shops and buildings surrounded by high fences, gates guarded by young soldiers in the olive green jackets of the People's Liberation Army.

Inside, shop floors were casually littered with scrap, soiled and pitted. The towering green Weingarten screw press from Germany and a few other advanced machine tools seemed out of place in the factory gloom. Four workers wrestled with a large steel plate that, elsewhere in the world, might have been handled by a heavy crane. A row of solemn young machinists, standing at their lathes, looked like a sepia photograph from an earlier industrial era.

Hongyuan Forging was itself rising from the dead past, a surviving legacy of China's own Cold War paranoia. In the 1960s, Mao became convinced that either Russia or the United States was about to launch a preemptive nuclear attack against China, so he ordered heavy industries relocated to the interior—the so-called Third Front. Factories would be hidden in obscure places like Sanyuan so that China might survive a first strike and fight on. This was a lunatic defense strategy, but it did bring industrial development to some very poor places.

To hide things at Sanyuan, scores of caves were dug in the narrow ravines of the valley wall. These broad cylindrical tunnels ran several hundred feet into the mountainside and the company placed its laboratories and most valuable technical equipment inside them. Thirty years later Hongyuan's technicians were still operating in these caves, running the high-tech machines that tested alloys or monitored quality control in the forgings. The company officials who showed me around seemed slightly embarrassed by these primitive aspects of their enterprise. The threat of American bombs was negligible.

In the village, some families were also still living in the man-made caves, quite comfortably it seemed. A farmer invited me in to inspect one of them, a cool, cluttered dwelling lit by a single lightbulb. Walls that curved into ceiling were whitewashed and decorated with colorful travel posters and his daughter's school certificates. We sat in the coolness and drank tea from glass jars. Times were good, he said. Soon he expected to build a new house aboveground. Prosperity, Chinese style.

It was a long way from Seattle, from the dazzling factories of Puget Sound and American machinists worried about their livelihoods. Yet Hongyuan Forging was a Boeing subcontractor in good standing and ambitious to become much more—a world-class producer of advanced industrial goods. The company already made precision turbine blades for Siemens of Germany and ABB of Switzerland and was pursuing business deals with General Electric. It has opened sales offices on three continents. The general manager, Kang Feng Xiao, a gray-haired engineer who had come from the city twenty-nine years before to build Mao's Third Front, seemed confident of the new vision.

"Since we have business with Boeing," Kang said, "this makes us upgrade our forgings so our technology is very close to the world standards. Also we learned the quality-control system. Our purpose is to push into the world market, mainly aerospace, steam turbines, car forgings. We intend to

Eight

"Facai zhifu shi guangrong de"*

AN EXPLOSIVE ILLUSION has taken hold in the global system, accelerating the pace of industrial revolution. It is a wishful conviction that the world's hottest new markets can somehow provide answers to the system's deepening tensions and contradictions. Multinational enterprises from every advanced nation and sector are elbowing one another to gain a footing in these emerging markets, imagining they will find relief from their persistent vulnerabilities, at least for a time. Leading governments support them in this with aggressive diplomacy.

Surging demand in these new markets promises customers for the surplus production, an opportunity for wider profit margins and the ability to arbitrage immense new pools of cheap labor in the global cost-price competition. This lucrative new terrain is seen as an antidote to the stagnation and slow growth in the much larger, matured markets of the wealthier nations. The thought of being left out quickens the corporations' anxieties. To be left out means stagnation for themselves.

Suddenly, it seems, the rich need the poor—and the poor know it. Developing countries are naturally cooperating with this imperative, but on their own terms. They do not intend to tolerate another chapter of colonialist domination, but hope instead to exploit the insecurities of the global enterprises for their own advancement. For China, India, Brazil and some others, the rush of foreign firms and capital investors represents a one-time window of opportunity to leap into the front rank of global producers. They are targeting key industries, leveraging shares of production and technology, setting stiff terms for foreign entry into their burgeoning markets.

The illusion is that everyone, rich and poor, can fulfill these ambitions without provoking a severe crisis for the global system. The logical and more likely outcome is that the system's underlying disorders, social and economic, will be seriously aggravated by this new wave of investment. In particular, the supply problem already stalking the world is sure to grow worse for many sectors as the new producers eventually develop surplus

---

* Chinese: "to get rich is glorious."

develop our company as the biggest in China, the biggest in East Asia. I think in this way—the way of the market—it won't be long before China will have great changes."

Despite the appearance of things, people were capable of great ambitions and surprising accomplishments, even in the most unpromising places. In the company showroom, I was shown the displays of wheels, joints, rings, rods and axles that went out from this small village to customers in Germany, Japan, Korea and the United States. An honored place was reserved for the American company that had shared its precious knowledge. Displayed on a blue felt drape were five of the titanium-alloy support struts that Hongyuan Forging manufactured for the engine mounts of the Boeing 747. Possibly I had seen some of these at the awesome assembly line back in Everett, without fully appreciating their place of origin.

output of their own and become exporters of advanced goods themselves. Since that is their long-term objective, the prospect for almost everyone is greater surpluses and even more difficult price competition, unless, of course, the developing countries should fail.

A new storm is forming around these events within the global system, likely to become visibly disruptive during the next ten years or so. Overall, the system will try to adjust to the consequences, just as it has in the past, by imposing more rolling shakeouts on both corporations and countries—the painful episodes when firms, factories and workers are, somewhere in the world, declared redundant and discarded from the global production base. That is how the marketplace achieves what it calls equilibrium.

But it is the prospective scale of adjustment that raises troubling portents. Can political systems in advanced nations absorb another major downdraft of industrial dislocations without provoking popular resistance? The economic question is more concretely threatening: Can the global system itself remain upright if consumer demand is weakened substantially by the further erosion of wages and jobs in the richest economies? The players are not unaware of these risks, but no one can pass up the obvious immediate benefits of plunging forward.

Because it is so large and vibrant with change, China offers the most dramatic illustration of the dilemma. The conventional expectation, frequently proclaimed by boosterish books on the Asian economic miracle, is that China's burgeoning market of new consumers will solve the global system's fundamental problem of overcapacity—mopping up the surpluses of industrial goods. This assumption, as we shall explain, is an illusion. If China succeeds in its plans, it has the capacity to become a nightmare for the global system, a dynamic cornucopia of low-cost output that wrecks other economies and destabilizes the multinational regime. If China fails, it will disappoint capital on a grand scale, but it also has the potential to disintegrate into some form of human catastrophe. The evidence exists to support either of those outcomes or even to suggest that both will occur. So diverse and contradictory, China is like a black box where both optimists and pessimists can find proof to support their expectations.

The standard view, typically shared by firms and governments, is that neither extreme is very likely and, therefore, not a concern to them. They are assuming that China will evolve with development, gradually democratize its political order and moderate its industrial ambitions in order to be accepted as a major trading partner. As economic reforms proceed and incomes rise, its centralized controls will be relaxed, the state-owned enterprises dismantled. A prospering China, it is said, will inevitably become a less brutal society, more open and free—more like the rest of us. This reassuring vision may also prove to be an illusion since it is not reflected in either the plans or actions of the Communist leadership in the People's Republic of China.

Conceivably, a successful China could manage to have it both ways in the global system: occupying both the high and low ends of the marketplace, with unique advantages. It would be an important market of affluent consumers, perhaps as many as 200 million someday, but within a huge population—1.2 billion—that remained quite poor by global standards. This would give China the domestic market base from which to export technologically advanced goods, but its manufacturers would still be drawing upon a huge supply of extremely cheap, government-controlled labor. Its reformed market system would provide robust returns for private enterprises, yet both capital and labor would remain fundamentally under state control.

That is China's goal—"market socialism with Chinese characteristics" —and also the potential nightmare. Such a hybrid form of command capitalism, once it has learned to make high-quality goods, could underbid almost everyone in the world on wages and prices. There are many fundamental reasons China may fail at this: the instability of its banking system, the history of political repression and upheaval, its technological shortcomings, the threat of environmental collapse and some others. But it seems imprudent—not to mention inhumane—to assume, as some do, that the global system will be spared its nightmare because some sort of disaster will befall the Chinese. For China, it is difficult to know not only what to expect, but also what to wish for.

The Xian Aircraft Company played a peculiar role in the globalizing industrial system: it was one of the places where the competing multinationals met face-to-face. XAC was a huge rural factory complex in the east-central interior, a state-owned enterprise that manufactured everything from aluminum windows and diving boards to medium-range jet bombers. Its hangars and assembly halls, machine shops and technical labs provided a common work site where the world's great multinationals worked alongside one another in close proximity, competing for China's favor.

Boeing was at XAC, making tail fins and stabilizers for the 737, cargo doors and trailing-edge wing parts for the 747. But so was McDonnell Douglas, with an automatic riveting machine for fuselage assembly for the MD-80. The Airbus partners—DASA and Aérospatiale—had some of their component work at Xian, as did Alenia of Italy and Canadair. XAC managers were negotiating new production deals with Daewoo Heavy Industries of South Korea and Israel Aircraft Industries. Mitsubishi and other Japanese manufacturers had also expressed interest, and Chinese aviation authorities were counting on $100 million in development loans from the Japanese government.[1]

Sweden's Volvo was invited to make tour buses at XAC for China's burgeoning tourist industry. Volvo accepted, mainly because its great European rival, Mercedes-Benz, was entering China and Volvo had decided that to remain competitive in the world, it had to go wherever Mercedes did.

When I was visiting XAC, the Xian Silver Bus Corporation had its new assembly line operating in one of the old hangar buildings and was about to roll out its very first silver bus. Volvo expected to make only 250 buses the first year, quickly expanded to 1,000 a year. XAC envisioned reaching 3,000 eventually, one third for export to other Asian nations.

It was at places like Xian—or Shanghai, Guangdong and scores of other industrial centers—where global capitalism met up with state socialism. China was the last viable remnant of communism, the only important economy in the world that, despite its market reforms, still operated on the Marxist-Leninist design. Rather than encountering deep conflict, the two economic systems seemed to be tangibly thriving in collaboration, each drawing on the other's strengths.

The capitalists brought capital and technology, the higher arts of systems management, quality control and marketing. The Communists delivered order and discipline and, above all, consumer demand—a cheap, obedient workforce that was eager to learn, a marketplace hungry for modern goods. Volvo did not doubt that it would be able to sell thousands of buses in China. The government had already decided that people would buy them.

"If you want to avoid import duties and do well in a country like China, you should have a successful and powerful partner—XAC fulfills all of those," said Thomas Appelbom, the Volvo manager who was on-site president of the Sino-Swedish venture. "In China, people know that when XAC is involved, it's stability, it's power, it's reliability. I think we are lucky to have it in this joint venture. The fact that XAC is a state enterprise means that, as the small baby in that family, we get some extra help because no government wants its ventures to fail."

The various foreign projects were so far only a minor share of the XAC production, but they promised a new future. The company was located at the country town of Yan Liang, an hour and a half by car from the ancient city of Xian, the first capital of China. The walled city of Xian had ruled for 1,100 years but was now a sooty industrial backwater in Shaanxi Province, most famous for its stunning excavation of 8,000 life-like terra-cotta warriors, a funeral army buried with the first emperor in 210 B.C. and not discovered until 1974. The city hoped to revive its ancient greatness. Boosterish banners, in English and Chinese, were hung across the boulevards: "Promote Development to Restore Splendor." "Strive for a Socialist Market Export-Oriented Development for Xian."

Xian Aircraft Company was at the core of those ambitions. It had 21,000 workers, including 1,200 engineers, many of whom shifted from one product line to another, depending on current demand. If production was idled on the B-6 bomber, the workers might go over to the aluminum molding shop and make window frames or TV satellite dishes or Olympic-class diving boards. XAC's principal purpose has been military aircraft, but it also turned out a 60-seat prop jet for regional airlines, the Y-7, that was building a market in poorer Asian nations like Cambodia, Laos and Sri Lanka. When they weren't making airplanes, XAC's metalworkers manufactured Ferris wheels.

Like 20,000 to 30,000 other military-run enterprises in China, the company effectively belonged to the People's Liberation Army. In Western sensibilities, a factory in China, especially one operated by the military, summoned up grim images of enslavement—sweatshop toy assembly or dangerous garment-factory barracks housing teenage workers, the police-state exploitation of prison labor. In one form or another, those brutalities and others did exist abundantly in China. But XAC was utterly different. As an industrial center, it looked idyllic. Compared to the other options available to ordinary Chinese, it perhaps was.

At an early hour, with morning mist still clinging to the playing fields and shrubbery, a cheerful music played over loudspeakers on the company grounds. Soon, gentle waves of workers in blue denim jackets were gliding on their bicycles along the main boulevard toward the factory gates. The avenue was lined with a splendid allée of spreading plane trees and a soft morning light filtered through the autumn brown leaves, illuminating the arcade with a golden haze. The blue figures on bicycles, sweeping silently along the glowing avenue, had the soft-edged grace of an old romantic painting. In this setting, the daily ritual of industrial life—going to work in the morning—seemed serene, even beautiful.

The company provided its workers with everything important to their lives—the neat rows of apartment housing, two high schools, three primary schools and a technical college, a 500-bed hospital, a modern sports complex and fitness center, a huge entertainment hall that flashed at night with red-and-white neon stripes. One evening Zhao Renwei, the company translator, took me to the company's karaoke bar for a beer, and we watched some of the younger workers as they sang saccharine love ballads, accompanied by laser-disc videos playing on large TV screens. Next door, amid whirling strobe lights in the dance hall, couples performed what looked like a Texas two-step with Chinese characteristics.

Zhao had been to America—Cedar Rapids, Iowa—where he studied English aviation terminology and also learned some favorite Americanisms. "Iowa is awesome," he told me, *"bang jile"* in Chinese. XAC is *bang jile* itself, I observed. It was the model of a smartly organized, self-contained industrial town, a handsome place with its own independent social life and infrastructure, newspaper and cultural magazine, cable TV and broadcasting system. Wages were pitifully low in global terms, but in the Chinese context the living conditions were superior. Western reformers who wished to liberate these workers from the "dictatorship of the proletariat" would have to offer something more than material comforts.

In fact, XAC resembled the model company towns that some U.S. corporations had built for their workers back around 1900, when American manufacturing was ascendant. Those planned industrial communities in

America also provided every comfort, from landscaped row houses and stores to parks and libraries. The American version of corporate paternalism eventually soured and broke down, mainly because the workers began to speak for themselves, demanding more control over their own lives, their work and wages.

Conceivably, the workers at XAC had not yet reached that stage of self-determination, though it was, of course, impossible for an outsider to tell. At the karaoke bar, we chatted with a few workers, who expressed, through the company translator, their enthusiasm for XAC and its goals. "We are climbing up the mountain," said Liu Giang Gie, a thirty-one-year-old inspector on the B-6 assembly line. "We're a developing country and we have much to do." After a dozen years working at XAC, Liu earned 500 yuan a month—that is, about $50 a month.

At the factory grounds, workers entered through a stylized Ming gate crowned with a fanciful aerospace symbol and the company slogan: "Quality Is First, Quality Is Life." The assembly hall where much of the foreign production was located looked quite austere and uncomplicated compared to the Boeing works in Seattle. It consisted of a vast barn divided into five large bays, with whitewashed walls and gray girders, a single orange crane overhead. The lifting and riveting were still done mostly by human hands.

In the Boeing section, three young women in gray smocks moved along the skeletal green frame of a 737 vertical tail fin, punching holes with electric hand drills, then measuring the fittings. Overall, about half of the machinists working on the overseas production were young women. Nearby, a young man in a sweater bent intently over a section of the horizon stabilizer, rubbing and polishing its edge. Around a red tabletop seven engineers in coats and neckties debated particulars over their spread-out blueprints. Across the street the new brick hangar building under construction would house the additional fuselage work that Boeing and McDonnell Douglas have subcontracted to XAC.

The assembly hangar down the road was guarded by PLA soldiers because it contained the military production—the yellow-drab cargo planes and bombers with red-star insignia. Each year XAC turned out only a handful of B-6 bombers, clunky Soviet knockoffs from the seventies that no other nation wanted to buy when advanced warplanes were available from the Americans and Europeans. In the tumultuous evolution of its modern industry, China had relied first on the Long Marchers, aging stalwarts from Mao's revolution, next on Soviet engineers who designed heavy, simple, low-cost goods. Now China was listening to Germans, Americans, Japanese and Swedes who were schooled in the open marketplace.

At the flight test field, where more than a dozen XAC planes were lined up on the tarmac, a Y-7 regional 60-seater was being prepped for Royal Air Cambodge. The plane looked decidedly low-budget in its shabby interior appointments, but it was also bargain-priced for the poorer nations—one quarter to one third below the international market. XAC was upgrading the Y-7's quality and expected it to win airworthiness certification from the U.S. Federal Aviation Administration—a mark of distinction that should boost the marketing. If China and potential partners like Boeing went forward with their consortium to build a 100-seat jet aircraft, XAC expected to build it (but then so did Shanghai Aviation and some other state-owned rivals).

"Our strategic target," Guo Chenglin, XAC's director of propaganda and culture, declared, "is to become the high-tech and foreign-oriented enterprise, high profit and high civilization, material civilization and spiritual civilization. We want to be the first-class, successful enterprise. All the employees of XAC are marching to this goal."

Xian Aircraft illustrated an important reality in China's plans. Despite obvious inefficiencies Chinese authorities were not planning to dismantle this state-owned company or privatize it. They were enlarging it, strengthening its capabilities. Like other state enterprises, XAC carried a heavy load of surplus labor—perhaps more than a quarter of its workforce was not really needed—but it did not intend to shed these workers or reduce their socialized standard of living. It was improving housing and other aspects of life in the company town.

Guo seemed slightly baffled by my questions about privatization. "There is a policy in China that we insist on—public ownership, not private," he explained. "This policy will not change, this will remain forever." Like other large government companies, XAC was talking about selling nonvoting "B" shares to private investors, but this was intended to raise more foreign capital, not to dilute the state's control.

China's state sector was growing, not shrinking, despite the repeated stories in *The Wall Street Journal* predicting its demise. Guo's claim might be dismissed as public relations puffery except that it was consistent with the broad facts of China's development, more consistent than the reformers' repeated pleas for privatization or outsiders' wishful assumption that China will discard its state-owned enterprises. Among some 103,000 larger state-owned enterprises, employment grew from 31 million in 1978, when reform began, to 45 million in 1992. Their collective output declined dramatically as a share of China's overall production because of the robust growth of the private ventures fostered by market-opening reforms. But the state sector's exports were growing at the rate of 20 percent a year.

Furthermore, 70 percent of new investment capital in China was going into the state-owned factories, and their claim on the new capital rose sharply during the investment boom of the 1990s. An American specialist on China's economy, Nicholas R. Lardy of the University of Washington, concluded: "State-owned enterprise reform in China has become the ever-receding horizon."[2]

XAC's central ambition was not a secret—it wanted to build its own large-body commercial aircraft and sell it to the world. "The reason we cooperate with Boeing," said Huang Hang, director of the overseas production, "is so we can increase our design and manufacturing level. Boeing will force us to improve our equipment and tooling and the skill levels of employees all the time. Of course, we say Boeing is the best aircraft company in the world. But we may also say that everything we have done has satisfied the Boeing management."

XAC officials granted that they were not yet able to achieve their goal, but they were closer than people thought. "In general, our manufacturing level is still very backward compared to the Boeing Company," Guo acknowledged, "but XAC already has almost the manufacturing level to produce one whole aircraft of the level of the 737. That means we can produce a similar aircraft by ourselves. As an independent country, we still want to develop our own aircraft. Although there are still some difficulties, I am sure we will soon put this kind of aircraft in the sky on our own."

At present, the claim sounded a bit grandiose, but in time it would be quite plausible. A Boeing executive with long experience in Asia told an American labor official that China in the mid-1990s reminded him of Japan twenty-five years ago or South Korea fifteen years ago. If that assessment was accurate, then China was perhaps a decade away from serious entry into global markets with its own advanced production. American manufacturers who, two decades before, had belittled the threat of competition from Japan or Korea were less inclined to do the same with China.

"The capability of China," said Jim Whitney, Boeing's on-site manager at XAC, "as long as you oversee them, help them shape their management, is that they are the next frontier. Their ambition is to build the whole airplane, whether it's the commuter plane or the 737. They can build any part of it as good or better than anyone in North America. It's their management system that won't allow them to build the whole airplane at this point."

As a roving overseas manager, Jim Whitney was like a lonely American cowboy roaming the new frontier—a stocky man with a drooping moustache and blunt, easy manner, dressed for work in leather jacket and jeans. He was both bemused by this strange place and impressed by Chinese true grit. Whitney was fifty and a Navy veteran of Vietnam who had started at Boeing as a rivet bucker, moved up to riveter, mechanic, supervisor, then a series of overseas assignments that took him back to Asia.

It was a spare, lonely life, he said. Managers from the various foreign multinationals all lived at the same dreary company hotel and sometimes exchanged war stories at night. On the weekends (actually Wednesday and Thursday), Whitney went into Xian, got a room at the Golden Flower Hotel, had a few drinks and watched a lot of CNN. He and his pals sometimes found amusement watching the action at a small four-lane bowling alley they called Flintstone Alley.

"The Chinese are the best to work with because they want to learn," he said. "They don't have any pretense of being a world-class manufacturing concern. The Chinese work better, for instance, than the Indonesians. The

Japanese work the best of all, of course. The Koreans can do the job. Chinese workers have their setbacks, sometimes you have to go back over it again. They can turn you off. But the progress here is astounding. I've seen them accomplish a lot when they had very little to work with. You have to remember they are still very poor, just people trying to get by in real hard circumstances."

Boeing, he said, was trying to convince XAC to forgo any ambitions for a freestanding aircraft because it made no sense in the global marketplace. "Every company in China wants to build the whole thing," Whitney went on. "What we're trying to tell China is that everyone loses if all your manufacturing facilities are identical. There isn't enough demand in the world to take all of what you have right now—plus what we have in the U.S. and what they have in Europe."

In the meantime, greater sharing of production work would give the Chinese a rising percentage of total content and ought to satisfy their ambitions, at least for now. Volvo's bus venture reflected the trend more concretely. At the outset, Appelbom explained, nearly all of the components were shipped from Sweden in a knockdown assembly kit that XAC workers put together. But local content swiftly increased to 50 percent of the body, and by 1997, 90 percent of the bus would be made in China, though engines and axles would still come from Sweden.

"If we build an engine plant here," Appelbom mused, "maybe it will become one of the suppliers worldwide. With the savings on labor, we would have a low price for the competition."

The extremely low wages did matter, especially for the long run. While cheap labor was not the primary motivation that drew the high-end manufacturers to China, it was sure to become a central factor as the Chinese companies developed greater capacity for high-quality output. As manufacturers offloaded shares of their production work, they benefited immediately in cost reduction.

"Wages are a big part of it," Jim Whitney said, "because you're paying a guy here $40 a month and you pay somebody $4,000 a month in Seattle. As you move up in technology skills here, you still only add maybe $10 or $20 a step. So you might have an engineer making $60 a month. Of course, as China gets prosperous, their wages will rise eventually and they will lose the advantage, but that will take at least fifteen or twenty years."

This reality described the potential catastrophe for high-wage industrial workers in the advanced nations—another powerful downdraft was gathering force to depress their wages further and claim more manufacturing jobs. Multinationals could adjust comfortably enough by shifting more and more of their component work to China, enhancing their own competitive price positions in the process. This next wave was already underway in autos, aircraft, electronics and some other advanced sectors, but had not yet reached a scale where the dramatic dislocations were visible.

Xian Aircraft provided concrete illustration of why the alluring illusion about China—that its millions of new consumers will rescue the global system from its oversupply problems—was wishfully mistaken. The success of XAC, even if less grand than its managers imagined, would compound the global problem, both by undermining the existing consumer power and by adding more supply to the market.

First, when new production work was moved to Xian from places like the United States, the global system was, in effect, swapping highly paid industrial workers for very cheap ones. To put the point more crudely, Boeing was exchanging a $50,000 American machinist for a Chinese machinist who earned $600 or $700 a year. Which one could buy the world's goods? Thus, even though incomes and purchasing power were expanding robustly among the new consumers of China, the overall effect was erosion of the world's potential purchasing power. If one multiplied the Xian example across many factories and industrial sectors, as well as other aspiring countries, one could begin to visualize why global consumption was unable to keep up with global production.

Second, Xian Aircraft proposed to become a major producer and exporter of world-quality airplanes itself. Certainly China was buying scores of Boeing aircraft for now and would continue to do so for many years. But the long-term economic consequence would be a new source of supply—with or without Boeing as a partner—that would begin to compete for the available buyers of airplanes in the global market. This was not just the case for aircraft production at Xian, of course, but applied to autos, advanced electronics, chemicals and many other sectors. For these two fundamental reasons, China was not going to solve the supply-demand imbalances for the other trading nations; it was going to make them much worse.

Besides the vast supply of cheap, willing workers, companies like XAC had an additional advantage: complete control over their labor force. The labor market was quite "flexible" in the sense that workers obediently accepted shifts from one job to another or punitive pay cuts or worse. Boeing's workers at XAC were not free. Nor were McDonnell Douglas's or Airbus's or any of the others. The price of self-expression or disobedience could be quite high: losing everything—job, home, health care, perhaps even one's life. That was the exchange required by the dictatorship of the proletariat —free housing and health care, playing fields and a karaoke bar, in lieu of free speech, freedom of assembly, individual autonomy.

The labor union at XAC, like all unions in China, was a creature of the Communist Party. Every XAC shop had its own CP cadre. *The Wall Street Journal,* notwithstanding its pious anti-communism, saw a positive side to this arrangement. In a special section for business executives exploring China's market potential, the newspaper explained: "In some factories, the party chief is a big help: he might act like a cooperative labor-union president who will pressure you for better wages and housing, but will intervene with great authority when workers are causing problems for you." [3]

That was the case at XAC, according to Jim Whitney. "The union is really based on the party, and the party does have power on almost anything," he said. "It's a reporting system really more than a functional union. If you want something done, you go to the party member and it's done— like that. These guys are as capitalist as we are. The party is there, but everybody's cutting deals up and down the line. I won't say it's a corrupt society, but everything is done *guanxi*—favors, gifts, help someone out and they take care of you."

Boeing workers who failed to perform were criticized and punished by this apparatus, their names posted on a bulletin board in the assembly hall. Exemplary workers were listed in red characters, the scolded ones in green. As Guo Chenglin boasted to me, the model workers selected at XAC each year were nearly always Communist Party members.

Jim Whitney explained the shop-floor discipline: "There's a bonus system, but it also works the other way. They are actually fined when they do things wrong. They get paid in cash, and if a worker does bad work the first thing that happens is they take away some of their money."

Whitney noted my reaction and laughed.

"It's better than shooting them," he said. "They used to shoot them."

I expressed disbelief, but Whitney was serious.

"They used to, they used to shoot them," he insisted. "When I got here I was told this had happened awhile before in the refrigeration section. The work was bad. So they took ten guys out and lined them up against the wall and shot them. Now, they shoot them for graft."

Indeed, they did. Each year on May Day, the traditional anniversary of international labor, the local authorities in Yan Liang rounded up prisoners and drove them in an open truck through the country villages surrounding XAC. At a river bridge on the outskirts of town, the prisoners were unloaded and executed, their bodies cast into the gorge below, a cautionary message to the peasantry. A Boeing executive matter-of-factly described the May Day ritual to an American labor official as they drove over the bridge on their way to tour XAC.

In these and other ways, the People's Republic instructed its citizens on the importance of discipline and quality. The great multinationals, in their eagerness for new markets, looked the other way, pretending that the brutality of their new partners was not their business.

The core of what drew global capital to China (or India, Brazil and some other emerging markets) was a straightforward supply-and-demand function: When rising demand significantly exceeded a market's capacity for supply, it allowed producers to raise prices and widen their profit margins. That was what distinguished the hot new markets from the larger, settled economies, where demand rose slowly and productive capacity was in gross oversupply. A very poor nation, China offered global capital a way to increase rates of return.

"China can act like a kind of black hole," Yasunori Kirihara of Sony said a bit wistfully. "Everyone can rely on China to find some solution for everything—markets, sources of profit, everything. But I don't know. China can also be a threat to all of the industries."

When Deng Xiaoping launched his market-opening reforms in 1978, he provided a new slogan to guide the Communist nation: *"Facai zhifu shi guangrong de"*—"To Get Rich Is Glorious." People did not pause to examine the ideological contradictions; they rushed gloriously into fulfilling Deng's new dictum. Commerce became an island of freedom within a land of stern social control and suppressed politics. Human aspirations found expression in an explosion of private enterprise.

Fifteen years later China's economy was expanding at 12 or 13 percent a year and swelling with new projects. Shanghai, the old citadel of commerce, became a noisy forest of construction cranes. In Beijing, gleaming multistoried shopping malls have eclipsed the old-fashioned goods at the Friendship Stores the government still operated for foreigners. In a coastal province far to the south, a modern city of three million arose virtually overnight from a dusty country town at Shenzhen, booming on the sea of new assembly factories that surrounded it.

China was undertaking a staggering agenda of $155 billion or more in infrastructure projects by 2000—twenty major power plants, 280 million new telephone lines and digital switching equipment for nine provinces and cities, new airports at Guangzhou and Beijing, an express train Siemens planned to build from Shanghai to Beijing. AT&T set up a branch of Bell Laboratories in Shanghai and vied with Nynex, HK Telecom, Canada's Northern Telecom and others for the privilege of wiring China—a $90 billion market potential in the coming decade.

In consumer goods, the stakes were just as high. Motorola bumped against Intel and IBM, not to mention NEC and Fujitsu and Toshiba. Ford and General Motors, Toyota and Nissan, Mercedes and Volvo scrambled to catch up with Volkswagen, which already made cars at two factories in China. China traveled mainly by rail and river and air. Roads were scarce outside the cities, and a nation of 1.2 billion people had fewer than 8 million motor vehicles, only 100,000 or so cars in private hands. But China planned to have 22 million family cars within fifteen years, including a new low-budget "people's car."[4]

The country's theoretical potential for mass consumption—as opposed to the actual existing purchasing power of Chinese consumers—provided an intoxicating vision for multinational producers burdened elsewhere with surplus capacity. Some simple statistics suggested the epic dimensions: In America, there was one car for every 1.7 persons, compared to one for every 680 people in China. Telephones and TV sets existed in an almost one-to-one ratio with people in the United States. China had 100 people per TV, 149 people per telephone.[5]

Of course, these comparisons exaggerated the potential because everyone was not going to get rich enough for cars or telephones. In China, the new affluence was highly concentrated in major cities and the coastal provinces, where millions of new consumers were already able to buy roughly the same luxurious abundance that Americans enjoyed. China's economy had grown five times larger since Deng's 1978 reforms, but per capita income was rising much more slowly. As Malaysia's Prime Minister Mahathir warned the leaders in Beijing: "Spreading wealth evenly in a market economy is far more difficult than spreading poverty evenly in a command economy."[6]

Nonetheless, China's vigorous demand curve went straight to the bottom line for the multinationals, whether they were importing their goods from foreign factories or opening new production in China or, like most major firms, doing both. The fierce price competition that stalked the global system was, in a sense, suspended in these circumstances.

Wynn Van Bussman, chief corporate economist for Chrysler, explained: "If you're in a rapidly growing market anywhere in the world, you can generally earn a higher rate of return than you can in a mature market because demand is growing a lot faster than the supply capacity or the existing demand is only beginning to be met. So you get lots of pricing opportunities. So your profit margins ought to be pretty good in a rapidly expanding market. You're meeting latent demand and getting higher profits. That's why everyone wants to go to China."

The globalization of industry—creating regionalized structures of production around the world—was intended to maximize these profit opportunities when they appeared. It would simultaneously insulate firms from the fluctuating business cycles in different economies and regions. If demand was slowing in Europe or the United States, shift output to booming China. If China crashed, shift it elsewhere. "If you diversify your sources of supply, you're insulated against these conditions," Van Bussman said. "So you design smaller plants with lower cost curves. The world is moving toward that because it allows the flexibility to be very efficient."

In price-competitive sectors, Professor Lawrence B. Krause has observed, a firm "will maximize its profits by using its market power to differentiate its price for different markets. It will offer low prices where there are efficient competitors and/or demand is elastic, and higher prices where the competition is less capable and/or demand is inelastic."[7]

Motorola, a smart step ahead of its rivals, began seeding China's market potential in the late 1980s and by 1993 was already operating a $100 million plant with four thousand to five thousand workers, making pagers, cellular phones, semiconductors and communications components. "It's like catching a perfect wave," said Motorola's Richard Heimlich. "We sold them a concept that they could be world-class, and when the market opened up we were ready. When the wave took off, we rode it. Only one of those comes along in your lifetime and you want to be riding it rather than sitting in the water watching it."

In late 1995, Motorola agreed to build a new $720 million semiconductor factory in northeast China—a plant that might have been located most anywhere in the world, including the United States, except that China wanted it. Wu Jichuan, the minister of telecommunications, explained: "Motorola has earned a lot of money in the mobile telephone market in China. It's high time for them to transfer some technology."[8]

Oscar B. Marx III, architect for Ford's strategy to develop China's auto-components industry, remarked that Chinese managers did not seem to grasp the relationships between supply, demand and profit. "We in the U.S. are much more driven by rate of return," Marx said. "The Chinese don't even know what that concept is. There was a big desire on the part of the Chinese to put in a lot of capacity up front and we had to explain to them that we can't do that. It means you're doing a lot of investing but not selling all of your output—so no profit. At least, the Chinese are better than the Russians. In Russia, I met managers who thought profit was measured by the sales volume of their plant."

Corporations would typically expect a payback on capital investment within four or five years or at least a rate of return that was comfortably above their interest-rate cost for borrowed capital, perhaps 13 to 15 percent. China's marketplace could deliver corporate returns above 20 percent. The Chinese government became so disturbed by the soaring profits foreigners were making on new power plants that in 1994 it decreed a new profit ceiling of 12 percent on future projects. The capital investors responded by holding back new investments, a stalemate intended to make the government relent. The faster payback was justified, investors argued, because of the long-term political uncertainties. Once a power plant was built, the owners couldn't pick it up and walk away.

Truly extraordinary returns were available to venture capital that invested directly in selected projects, from concrete factories to medical-supply outlets. The returns on direct investments typically ranged around 25 to 30 percent—a payback in three or four years—but such projects often yielded returns as high as 40 percent, sometimes 80 to 100 percent. That was what inspired the great rush of capital to the "emerging markets" in the 1990s and put upward price pressure on the government bonds and other more conservative financial assets in the advanced economies.

Robert Dugger, an official of the Tudor Investment Fund, a major global pool of capital, observed: "If the return on capital is 30 or 40 percent in China and 7 percent in the United States, guess where the capital is going."

The action was chaotic and giddy, reckless with energy. By 1994, China had 165,000 joint ventures under way with foreign firms and investors, more pouring in every month. "It's like the Wild West," said Jane Zhang Hong, a business consultant whose Sino-American Development Corporation helped U.S. firms find well-connected Chinese partners. "China right now is a free-for-all. I think we are more capitalist than you are. The government says: you recognize my authority, I let you be rich. How can you argue with that?"[9]

It was a classic development boom. Leaving aside the awkward fact that a Communist government was in charge, the action resembled the raw, reckless energies of America's great era of expansion under Andrew Jackson in the 1830s, when roads and canals and important cities were being built by freewheeling developers and speculators, entrepreneurs getting rich and going broke, using and often losing the borrowed capital from Europe. That era laid the predicate for America's subsequent emergence as the world's most muscular manufacturer.

Like the Jacksonian boom, China's was driven by an unstable monetary system of wildly generous credit creation—easy money that fueled inflation rates as high as 30 percent but also allowed the vigorous expansion. The Chinese banking system is state-owned and ostensibly controlled by a central bank, but loans were dispensed to state-owned firms and by local governments, virtually by political quota and regional pressure. The easy credit amounted to state subsidies covering the losses of unprofitable enterprises —nonperforming loans that would never be repaid.

"China's state-owned banking system is for all practical purposes bankrupt," Professor Lardy wrote. China's new millionaires understood this well enough and protected their wealth by shipping it overseas, buying condominiums in New York, subdivisions in Australia and gold. Massive amounts of Chinese capital, variously estimated from $9 billion to $30 billion, moved offshore to safe havens, even as the foreign investors flocked in.[10]

As a financial system, China was probably headed for a crash—just as Andrew Jackson's frontier economy boomed for a decade and eventually crashed in depression. While that event could produce great suffering and possibly political upheaval, it was not necessarily the end of the story. The booming Jacksonian expansion had produced a permanent infrastructure for America's economic future. After China crashed it would probably boom again. The new power plants, airports and telephone systems were not going to walk away.

The historic comparison was exhilarating but also frightening in its implications for others. When business managers paused to consider the future, they acknowledged that China's success would profoundly disturb the global balance of commercial power, not immediately but eventually for sure. "We'll see a lot of creative destruction," Oscar Marx mused. "The government leaders are clearly looking past the domestic market and intend to develop world-class quality that can compete with everyone—U.S., European, Japanese—not just in Asia but worldwide."

American firms considered themselves less threatened by this prospect, at least initially, because the Chinese would first target their exports at the other Asian markets now dominated by Japan. The Japanese auto industry, for instance, already compelled to reduce its gross overcapacity, might have to cut back much more severely if China became a major exporter of cars.

"Japan is worried," Marx said. "The Chinese are planning to be a real force in Asia and there's going to be a real confrontation with the Japanese. The Japanese have a bunch of capacity they've got to destroy."

In Beijing, an auto executive from one of Japan's leading companies, while insisting on anonymity, gloomily agreed. "We are now in the same position that European or American auto companies were in when we entered their markets fifteen years ago," the Japanese executive said. "We now know how they felt. Now it is the Koreans and eventually the Chinese who will do the same to us. Or maybe the Koreans and the Chinese making cars together. And they are not likely to back off."

In the global system, this wave of new low-cost production would not stop with Japanese autos. Eventually, it would sweep over other sectors, threatening profit and employment in every producing nation that could not match China's prices. In theory, this process was supposed to yield a net plus for everyone in the trading system since China would also provide a rich new market of consumers, buying goods from others. In practical reality, however, this happy balancing of accounts did not occur, just as it had not occurred when Japan or South Korea emerged as major producers.

Once again, it was the world's largest market, the United States, that was absorbing the deficit. Japanese companies might be the first to be threatened by China's entry into advanced sectors, but it was the United States that was already suffering the economic impact from China's boom. China's low-end production exported to the American market—shoes, clothing, toys and some electronics—dwarfed what American companies like Boeing, Motorola and AT&T were selling to the Chinese. China supplied half of the U.S. doll imports, one third of imported shoes and leather goods, and 17 percent of apparel imports.

As a result, the U.S. trade deficit with China soared from $6 billion in 1989 to $30 billion in 1994, and $34 billion in goods a year later. Unlike Japan, China was not running a swollen trade surplus overall and its own foreign debts were accumulating rapidly. But its booming exports to the United States were on a trajectory to replace Japan before the end of the decade as the leading source of America's huge and persistent trade deficits.

The American political leaders who celebrated Boeing's aircraft sales or the multinationals' various deals with China neglected to mention this countervailing reality. When Japan first accumulated its huge trade imbalances with the United States, this was blamed on the uncompetitive performance of American workers and firms. That argument sounded a bit hollow now that the new source of growing U.S. trade deficits was an underdeveloped nation of primitive industrial capability.[11]

And, next, China intended to become a global producer of aircraft, cars, steel and more advanced electronics products. If nothing changed in this unfolding scenario, the trading system was headed for a destabilizing crisis—not just for the United States or Japan but for others, too.

In Tokyo, a Keio University economist and advisor to MITI, Professor

Harou Shimada, described the portents in the starkest terms. "China is a horror story for the rest of the world if it simply grows as an exporting nation," Shimada said. "Overcapacity will have to be squeezed down. It will be increasingly unprofitable for companies to build new capacity in advanced nations. If the Chinese develop the technology and become productive without wages rising, then they will be a tremendous competitive menace against the rest of the world. If you bring in 1.2 billion workers at those wages, that can destroy the global trading system."

None of the many business managers whom I interviewed provided plausible explanations of how this "horror story" was to be averted. They simply expressed the conviction that the rest of the world would not let it happen. Or they speculated that China might break down along the way, that it would somehow fail to realize its ambitious plans.

The Chinese Communist state was a more capable governing system than its reputation suggested. At least the Chinese people were more capable. Through all of the upheavals, repressions and disastrous experiments of the last forty years, the Chinese were eating better and living much longer; the specter of absolute deprivation receded as material life improved. Life expectancy had lengthened since the 1950s from forty years to beyond seventy years, longer than Russia or Mexico, not far behind Argentina or Ireland. The infant mortality rate declined by nearly half since 1970. The real output of manufacturing workers tripled. The last great famine was in the early 1960s, when 30 million people died.

Yet China's political order was also quite fragile. Given the vast size and diversity, not to mention the pent-up pressures from suppressed political freedoms, the regime always seemed to be flirting with disastrous outcomes, the possibility that the center would not hold. The labor ministry reported in 1994 that notwithstanding the industrial boom, the nation would have 268 million unemployed by 2000, most of them in the underdeveloped countryside. Something like 100 million surplus workers were already adrift in rural areas, many trying to get to the cities in search of wage jobs.

Stunning advancements were surrounded still by the primitive. Higher education was expanded dramatically in the 1980s, yet, according to Canadian scientist Vaclav Smil, China would have to double or triple its pace just to catch up with the university-educated citizens of India or even Indonesia. Most urban homes now had electricity, but three fifths of them still lacked indoor toilets. China's railroad system was approximately the size of America's in 1863. These realities persuaded many that China could not plausibly become a world-class competitor in less than a generation.[12]

Certainly, every economic plan was bounded by such contradictions and anomalies. Where would China get the engineers needed to operate advanced industrial systems? Tens of thousands of them were training at U.S. universities, but China's industrial progress would still wait upon education as much as capital. Why was China trying to make cars when its rail system was still so primitive? Because an auto industry would generate the multiplying core of stable employment. How could the government possibly keep up with the passions for consumption that Deng had unleashed? It would try, experimenting in different directions, following what worked.

"China is China," said an American stationed in Beijing. "You can try anything, but you can only screw up once."

Experimentation and control—the Chinese government was trying to have both of those at once. It was not self-evident that this would be possible, but the industrial policies enunciated by the government and its subsidiary bureaus were all attempts to reconcile that tension. China wanted to move swiftly up the ladder of industrial sophistication but without sacrificing the centralized control of its Communist Party mandarins. The extremes that existed within China, from booming coastal provinces to the impoverished interior, were as volatile as any conflicts between rich and poor nations in the global system.

The prospect of staggering unemployment, more than the ideology, explained why the state-owned enterprises were not withering away, as outsiders imagined, but instead growing. The state sector's surplus employment and socialized living circumstances provided an important cushion of social stability at the core of economic change. Redundant industrial workers were potential political dissidents and China abhorred dissent.

"If you want to reform anything, there's a lot of resistance," said Fan Gang, a Harvard-trained economist at the Academy of Social Sciences in Beijing. "The problem is the government itself still wants to strengthen the state sector, on the one hand. On the other hand, it wants to phase them out. That's the dilemma. Maybe the mass privatization will never happen, but there will always be gradualism, moving a little bit forward, lots of compromises. That's my prediction. People will call for radical steps, but nobody will have the political will to do it. But then no one will have the political strength to stop the gradual movement forward either. Maybe that's the solution."

In this political context, every deal with foreign firms was subject to change or cancellation since it was filtered through the submerged influences of party politics and regional rivalries, the Shanghai clique versus Beijing, Guangzhou, Changchun or Tianjin. "Negotiations are hell with the Chinese," said Bengt Jakobsson, a Swedish metalworkers official who served on supervisory boards of Swedish multinationals. "In the end, the Communist Party decides what the interpretations of the negotiations will be. We need good lawyers, but that's not enough. We should have authorities on Marxist-Leninist doctrine."

While these uncertainties ruled everything, the Chinese were quite explicit about what they wanted to do. The government identified four "pillar industries" for development—autos, telecommunications, petrochemicals and computers—though aircraft and steel were also often described in those terms. From the state sector, "100 model enterprises" would be designated to lead the way. In the meantime, the government was sponsoring spirited competitions among the foreign multinationals for the privilege of becoming partners in these initiatives.

The "Automotive Industry Industrial Policy," issued by the State Planning Commission in February 1994, decreed that scores of small state companies would be merged to form six or seven car-making conglomerates as "national backbone enterprises." These, in turn, were to be eventually merged again by 2000 into three or four major auto companies with the efficiencies of scale to each produce five million vehicles a year—output that "shall meet more than 90 percent of the domestic market." The policy further announced: "The state encourages automotive industry enterprises to expand exports and compete on the international market."

Though supposedly a centralized economy, the ironic reality was that China's necessary first task was to try to consolidate many small and scattered industrial parts—hoping to mimic the vertical integration of American car companies or perhaps the Japanese *keiretsu* system of allied firms. Simultaneously, it envisioned an extraordinarily rapid expansion of output that, roughly speaking, would create the girth of the North American auto industry within a decade or so. Even if these grand plans proved to be half wrong, it would still be stunning.

The pace, however, would be governed ultimately not by official plans, but by the market demand at home. If that demand grew robustly, China intended to accomplish what Japan had done before it, using its secure base of domestic consumers as the guinea pigs who would eagerly buy whatever was produced, while its companies developed the technological competence to make world-class quality for export. In that regard, China's poverty, its growing pool of hungry consumers, could be a real asset for ratcheting up production systems. Whether it was cars or computers, second-rate goods produced by Chinese factories could be sold at home, while the first-class output was shipped abroad.

Meanwhile, foreign goods would enter China under strict rules. The national auto policy permitted foreign car imports to grow, but the quantities were being regulated by high tariffs and fluctuating taxes in order to shield the domestic market for the home producers. Foreign auto companies that formed partnerships with the state "backbone enterprises" were told they must start out with 50 percent Chinese content in their production. Tax incentives were designed to push the local content as high as 90 percent.

The foreigners were given explicit instructions for investment: "A technology research institute shall be set up within the enterprise. This institute shall have the main capability to develop the next generation product. The enterprise shall manufacture products at the international technology level of the 1990s. The enterprise shall solve the problem of balancing foreign exchange on its own, relying mainly on the export of its own products."[13]

In other words, if China made these terms stick, it did not leave much room for imports—or any long-term prospect that China's new consumers were going to mop up world surpluses in auto capacity. At the outset, the foreign companies were sure to enjoy booming exports to China, but as local content and assembly rose rapidly, the national goal was self-sufficiency and exporting capacity. "China is playing hardball with all these companies, saying to them: if you're not a good boy, you won't get a contract," Fan Gang remarked. "In developing countries, people are working on how we can survive this competition."

The American Automobile Manufacturers Association protested the rules and asked the U.S. government to object, but this was a limp gesture alongside the enthusiasm of U.S. auto companies to get in on the action. Despite skepticism about China's industrial capabilities, no major auto company in the world wanted to miss the next wave.

GM and Toyota both opened technical centers and sent engineers. Ford concentrated on developing components plants—glass, plastics, instrument panels, heaters, air conditioning for taxis and vans. Mercedes went head-to-head with Ford and Chrysler to build a new minivan and apparently won the $1 billion project, though Chrysler had been making Jeeps in Beijing for a decade.* Nissan was told to produce major components, engines and transmissions, before it would be permitted to build cars. VW was trying to defend its head start and grandiosely assured the Chinese that VWs from Shanghai would someday be sold in Japan.[14]

Korea had certain geopolitical advantages in the auto auction. Companies like Daewoo were after the "people's car" project and proposing to build engines and transmissions in China, then ship them back to Korea for low-cost cars that could take on Japan head-to-head across Asian markets. "China may use the Korean card to keep out Japanese or American companies," a Japanese auto executive in Beijing speculated. "In terms of cost, nobody else can match Korea and China together."

In late 1995, General Motors and Mercedes won the first round of the car competition. GM was authorized to launch a $1 billion project to build sedans with the Shanghai Automotive Industry Corporation, where VW was already making cars and would continue its ten-year-old production. Mercedes would build minivans in south China. Ford, Chrysler and Toyota were the big losers, at least for now.

Some managers consoled themselves with the thought that even if their companies lost out, China was not really ready to absorb all of this develop-

---

* *China often used its business deals for larger diplomatic effect, punishing one country or rewarding another. Daimler-Benz announced in July 1995 that it had won "basic agreement" for Mercedes to build the minivan, but, like all such agreements, this one would not be final until all terms were fully negotiated. The timing of the announcement was most likely intended to admonish the U.S. government for its friendly gesture to Taiwan, which China regards as a renegade province. The Clinton administration had permitted Taiwan's president to enter the United States that summer to attend his college reunion at Cornell.*

ment anyway. "The Chinese have this plan, though Japanese and U.S. engineers doubt it," the Japanese auto executive said. "But you have to play the game, so you don't say that to them. They're very good merchants. I think they can do it in the long run, but not before 2010."

Likewise, Oscar Marx, the former Ford vice president and now CEO of an allied supplier company, was confident it would be a long time before the Chinese can make a car of the quality and sophistication needed for sales in Japan or Europe or the United States.

"But I don't say forever," Marx added. "There will come the day when we will produce a Ford Taurus in China. And we will meet the same standards of quality and performance." That thought was sure to chill American auto workers, who were already undergoing another major round of job erosion as U.S. components producers fled unionized wages and moved more output overseas.

On the plane ride home from Shanghai, I sat next to a middle manager from Ford who was engaged in starting up an auto-glass factory in one of Shanghai's huge industrial zones. Starting small, he said, but going to get much bigger. Components production was bound to migrate, given American wages, he explained.

"The UAW doesn't want to hear that, but it's inevitable," he said. "The good times aren't coming back. A lot of Americans still think the good times are coming back, but I don't see how that can happen, not in our lifetime. The developing countries are going to do the manufacturing. We will have to do something else." What would that be? I asked. The man from Ford shrugged. "Services or something," he said, "whatever that means."

The prospect ought to disturb the sleep of political leaders and business executives. The trading system was headed—sooner or later, China hoped sooner—for a new wave of industrial dislocations, another more fierce dimension to the price competition. The logic of the global system led naturally to those results. No one in authority has yet found the nerve to challenge that logic.

China is an unstable crucible for the global industrial revolution, testing its limits, threatening to wreck the reigning orthodoxy advanced by multinational enterprise and accepted by leading governments. Other major new markets like India add important and different dimensions to the challenge, but if the global system cannot come to terms with China's implications, it is not likely to sustain itself. Is it possible to wish for the success of the Chinese people without also assuming disaster for others? Or is the system itself bound to crash on its own internal contradictions? There is no easy way out of those questions, certainly no answers that do not require wrenching political conflict and a fundamental reordering of how the global system functions.

The various rationalizations offered by authorities and experts usually depended upon some sort of *deus ex machina* to sweep away the problem —a miraculous event or intervention that averts the logical consequences of what is unfolding. The U.S. trade representatives supposed, for instance, that they could persuade China to abandon its state industrial plans for autos, aircraft and the other sectors. China would do this, it was said, in order to join the new World Trade Organization since its industrial plans are clearly illegal under the trade rules.

That notion seemed quite fanciful, alongside what was actually happening in China. If China refused to abandon its intentions and remained outside GATT's rules, would the multinational corporations refuse to sell or invest there? Not very likely since the firms were begging to be partners in China's industrial plans. And which national government would step forward to stop them?

Or business executives like Oscar Marx believed that, one way or another, the threat would be averted because government would intervene. "I don't think this is a zero-sum game," Marx explained, "although the Japanese have played it as a zero-sum game and the Chinese will be quite content to do the same if we let them." But Americans would not tolerate that again, he assumed. "I don't see big boatloads of cars coming from China the way they did from Japan," Marx said. "I don't think the U.S. will permit another Asian country to do to it what Japan did to it. Our people won't stand for it, our policy makers won't let it happen."

Thus, while the multinationals participated in developing a major new low-wage industrial base that like Japan intended to compete from a protected domestic market base, they could tell themselves: somebody will stop this before it goes too far. But counting on timely political intervention sounded a bit wishful, too, since governments were caught up in the same illusion as the multinationals, pleading for China's favor, offering assistance.

Or there was Harou Shimada, the Keio University economist, who offered a different, more mischievous strategy: "Our objective must be to make them rich as soon as possible—give them the capital to become consumers as rapidly as they can so they will be as rich and rotten as the rest of us," Shimada said with a grin. This approach sounded approximately like what was already under way, but Shimada did not envision prosperity for all of China, only part of it. "The horror story is if the whole of China becomes involved in this, then it's a disaster," he explained. "It has to be just the coastal provinces, not the vast interior. Coastal China has 300 million people—make them as rich as Japan and we will be okay."

But wouldn't such diverging fortunes within China lead to a political rupturing, perhaps even civil war?

"Yes, the Chinese will break up by themselves," Shimada predicted. "The political system cannot sustain that kind of gap in incomes. I'd like to propel that. They're too big for the rest of the world. They have to break apart. Otherwise, they will wreck the global economy."

China will disintegrate. Or abandon its political order. Or somehow be contained before it becomes too strong. None of these scenarios sounded very reassuring. In fact, it seemed more plausible to assume that nothing much will occur to deflect events from their present trajectory. Given the fractured nature of competing nations' economic interests and the power of the prevailing orthodoxy, the global system more likely will be allowed to hurtle forward energetically to its own resolution.

If so, a few years hence, everyone will find out whether these dire portents I have described were right or not. The historical experience suggests that politicians and statesmen will not feel compelled to reexamine the logic of the global commerce and reclaim control over it until they are confronted with a full-blown crisis. In history, the revolutionary episodes did not usually end gracefully.

Nonetheless, the present challenge is to rethink the global revolution, searching for ways to reconcile the positive and negative aspects of what is happening in places like China. Getting rich is surely glorious, as Deng Xiaoping said, but accumulation is not the only human aspiration. Commerce is linking disparate cultures and political systems, but the economic consequences threaten to destroy other public values and even the social order itself. An economic system that requires people and nations to disregard their own sense of moral values will, in time, be understood as a craven retreat from conscience.

China offers the most acute—and most difficult—case in which the economic self-interest of other nations may be palpably merging with an altruistic regard for other human beings. Challenging the repression is not simply a moral act but a way to help rescue the global system from its own economic contradictions. Bringing the bottom up—that is, raising wage incomes at the bottom as rapidly as possible—offers a dual benefit to the overall system: increased consumer demand for the global surpluses and also, necessarily, a slower pace of new development and industrial migration. But the necessary ingredient for accomplishing this outcome is human freedom.

In the long run, eviscerating work and wages in the wealthier nations is not going to be a sustainable solution for the poor. As Oscar Marx remarked, people won't stand for it. Until that is faced, governments in the advanced democracies will remain in political crisis, facing dispirited, hostile electorates. Meanwhile, there is the palpable danger that these global pressures will be resolved in reactionary ways, with narrow, nationalistic protectionism based on racial and cultural nativism. The challenge is whether a moderate course can be developed between the extremes—governing interventions that temper the revolutionary action but without cutting adrift those aspiring nations that seek to escape their poverty.

This approach, if it is possible at all, would necessarily require hard conflict on both ends of the system. In a nation like China, it means commerce and capital could not proceed oblivious to the governing system—in particular, its methodical suppression of human freedoms. The rights of workers to assemble and organize, to speak freely in their own behalf, are the core issue that unites economics with social morality. In moral terms, companies and consumers in the rich nations are literally riding free on the dictatorship of the proletariat and its abusive practices. In economic terms, the key to rising wages and increased purchasing power in poorer nations is the existence of free labor, workers able to form their own trade unions and bargain in their own interests.

China, like many other poor nations, naturally reacted to such ideas with sovereign anger and deep suspicion. They sounded like a high-minded way to cut it out of the action, just as it was getting the traction to climb the ladder. It was right to be skeptical of motives, but other nations could impose new values on the global system—challenging China's dictatorial control of labor—without shutting down trade and investment in the poor nations.

A system of "social tariffs" or other penalties aimed at repressive regimes would, in effect, create new terms of trade—human values alongside price and profit. Such a system would create new incentives for political reforms and economic policies that pulled up the bottom, rewarding gradual progress and penalizing tyrants. Even so, this reform would at most only moderate the course of industrial revolution. It would certainly not cripple its creative energies or, for that matter, solve all of the disorders. All it offers is a progressive beginning, a path that is more promising than the reactionary alternatives.

The Chinese government, without doubt, would refuse to participate in such a system, more fearful of the domestic political implications of free expression than any economic consequences. That would be China's sovereign choice, just as other nations could choose to restrict the free entry of Chinese goods produced and priced on the basis of cheap, captive labor. Reform, however, would invite other developing nations to join in a new kind of global competition—access to trade based on positive social values —and many countries would find real economic advantage for themselves and their citizens in such a system. This broad leverage could reverse the flow of the global system, ratcheting upward instead of downward.

A regime like China would then face a hard new choice: Should it abandon the industrial dreams and withdraw from the global system or moderate its plans and relax the political repression? The pragmatism of Chinese leaders might, in time, compel them to reconsider—goaded by the positive energies of their own entrepreneurs. After all, new global trading standards would not destroy the natural wage advantage of China's massive labor pool, but merely moderate its impact and stimulate new purchasing power. Precisely because it has chosen to join world commerce and encourage mass consumption at home, China's social stability has become greatly dependent upon its trading partners, especially the United States. If the United States declined to absorb China's $34 billion trade surplus, what other nation would buy all the shirts and shoes and electronics? Certainly not Japan or Germany. Behind its gruff exterior, China is highly vulnerable to economic persuasion.

Multinational corporations and finance would, of course, resist any reform of this sort, as fiercely as the poor nations like China. Global enterprises fleeing high wages are naturally appalled by the suggestion that questions of free labor and wages should be introduced into trade and investment standards. They are now free to deploy production to the hot markets on their own terms, capturing the new profit opportunities while also reducing their labor costs. Reform would wreck those globalizing strategies and impose new responsibilities on them.

The great multinationals are unwilling to face the moral and economic contradictions of their own behavior—producing in low-wage dictatorships and selling to high-wage democracies. Indeed, the striking quality about global enterprises is how easily free-market capitalism puts aside its supposed values in order to do business. The conditions of human freedom do not matter to them so long as the market demand is robust. The absence of freedom, if anything, lends order and efficiency to their operations. None of the great companies is inclined to complain or forgo the advantages. The Communist leaders of China understand this about their new capitalist partners and are making good use of the knowledge.

Nine

Cooperative Capitalism

WEARY OF THE HARSH and accelerating competition, major multinationals naturally searched for shelter from the storm. Every industrial sector is engaged by the fierce contests over price and technological advantage. Most are burdened with the recurring surpluses that dampen rates of return. Many sectors, especially those on the leading edge of invention, also face a staggering escalation in capital costs—the new investment money needed just to stay in the game, never mind winning. In these circumstances, global firms have decided, one by one, to cooperate with the enemy and are fashioning limited truces with major rivals.

Manly rhetoric notwithstanding, most of the world's leading multinational corporations have entered into pragmatic partnerships with competitors or are actively exploring the potential for cooperative alliances. In these deals, companies share certain commercial assets with each other, pooling capital and research capabilities, trading technological knowledge or financial support, even collaborating in the production of goods meant to compete for buyers in the marketplace. The idea is to find at least temporary relief from their mutual vulnerabilities.

These arrangements are known in business and academic circles as "international strategic alliances," and thousands of them have appeared during the last decade or so, as even the largest multinationals reluctantly recognize limits to their own corporate sovereignty. The objectives are usually described in limited terms—designing a new product together or swapping technology, financing major projects with "risk sharing" partnerships or, more crudely, buying entry into a protected foreign market. The core problem that appears in nearly all of these deals is capital. Fundamentally, alliance is a way to spread the escalating cost of new investment among many players.

The proliferation of multinational collaborations can be read as rough confirmation of the systemic instabilities depicted in previous chapters—the desperate edge of endless technological combat and enduring overcapacity problems. Rival corporations are driven together, not by arrogance, but by mutual fear. Global capitalism has entered a crucial new stage in the industrial revolution—the search for more rational organizational structures that will reduce uncertainties, enhance profit and deliver some stability for the long term. The action is so far tentative and exploratory, but it leads inevitably to the collaborative exercise of commerce. Eventually, it may create a new hierarchy of concentrated economic power. In some ways, this search represents the most important imperative now at work in the global system because it has the potential to define the superstructure of global commerce for the next century—organizational realities that will govern the economic and political life of every nation, rich and poor alike.

Corporate alliances are, of course, the antithesis of free-market dogma and the supposed liberalization of global trade. On the one hand, multinationals preach free-market competition and aggressively promote the dismantling of governments' legal controls over commerce and finance. On the other hand, the same firms are busily forging territorial compacts with each other—collaborative mechanisms that may be used to manage trade privately, on their own terms, above and beyond the reach of national governments.

The contradiction is an abiding paradox of capitalism, first noted by Adam Smith: the more intense the competition becomes in the marketplace, the more actively enterprises will seek escape from its perils. Business leaders do not, of course, see any contradiction in this development, only the necessity to cope with adversity and survive. Still, if these corporate alliances should evolve into permanent centers for shared decision-making, market competition may not disappear, but it will be guided by a new invisible hand.

Multinational firms would object that my observations exaggerate the implications of the alliances or are, at the very least, premature. The emerging partnerships, they point out, are nearly always limited to specific business problems, not grand structural objectives. Furthermore, alliances often founder and are abandoned when the rivals discover that their individual objectives are not really compatible. In any case, the global firms scoff at the suggestion that these ad hoc arrangements might somehow harness the larger competitive forces driving the global marketplace. Their response sounds reasonable in terms of the present facts. It does not necessarily reflect the future.

To appreciate the significance of this new stage in the revolution, it helps to recognize the powerful parallel from history: the era of corporate consolidations that unfolded a hundred years ago when ascendant manufacturing corporations in the United States and Europe struggled with the same fundamentals of industrial revolution—rapid technological changes and rising capital costs, oversupply of production, downward pressures on prices and profits, intense competition for foreign markets. Starting in the last decades of the nineteenth century, these corporations also searched for collaborative remedies designed to reduce the harsher aspects of freewheeling competition.

Industrial firms in steel, electrical generation, automobiles, oil, chemicals, telephones, railroads and other sectors were merged or entered in cooperative alliances intended to achieve the scope and scale needed to dominate national markets and to stabilize them. That historic drive to rationalize production took many forms—mergers and trusts, cartels and market-sharing agreements—many of which failed or were declared to be illegal monopolies. The ultimate result, however, was creation of the corporate groupings that dominated industrial life through the twentieth century —well-known names like du Pont and BASF, General Motors and Daimler-Benz, Siemens and GE.

The global system is now reaching a similar juncture, though spread across a vastly larger landscape. Multinational firms have entered the opening stages of a similar period of sorting out—organizing experiments sure to continue because the enterprises are driven by the same fundamental pressures. As the capital stakes get bigger and the risks more threatening, the desire to hedge one's bets naturally grows stronger. The global arrangements that eventually emerge may be quite different from the American conception of free enterprise.

While this trend raises large concerns for every sovereign nation, the economic implications seem especially threatening to the poorer nations trying to climb the ladder of industrial development. If cooperative modes of organization should emerge among technologically advanced producers from the so-called Triad—Europe, Japan and the United States—the resulting power alignments could consign lesser nations to a subordinate role for many generations. Some developing nations seem to grasp that this is how the revolution might end. That is why they push so hard for technology transfers from global firms entering their markets.

Yet the future also looks perilous to the multinationals themselves, especially those in advanced sectors, because they are confronted by twin curves that are both rising steeply. One is the explosive upward curve of technological innovation. The other is the escalating curve of capital required to keep up with the new technology. The new power source that launched this industrial revolution nearly forty years ago—the computer chip—continues to expand exponentially, quadrupling its power every three years. As a result, revolution has become too expensive, even for some celebrated revolutionaries.

In the spirit of multicultural cooperation, the three electronics giants described their technological breakthrough in literary terms familiar to Americans, Germans and Japanese. IBM, Siemens and Toshiba, three of the world's largest manufacturers, disclosed in June 1995 that their consortium of design engineers, working together at IBM's labs in East Fishkill, New York, had succeeded in fashioning a new computer chip that was faster, smaller and more powerful than anything ever developed before. The new chip, they explained, could store the complete works of Shakespeare, plus the complete works of Goethe, plus the *Manyoshu,* the *Kokinshu* and the *Tale of Genji,* with enough space left for a copy of the *International Herald Tribune.*

The new device was a submicronic labyrinth of transistors etched on silicon—smaller than a man's thumbnail—and formally described as the 256-megabit DRAM—that is, a Dynamic Random Access Memory chip that could store 256,000,000 databits, the equivalent of 25,000 pages of typed text. The three corporations, despite bitter rivalries in the past, were working together because each had concluded they could no longer go it alone. Jack Kuehler, the former president and chief technologist of IBM, had fashioned the research alliance and exclaimed at the results. "The 256 development will blow the world apart in terms of technological leadership," he said.

DRAMs are the core commodity of the information age, as oil was to a previous era of industrial revolution, but with this great difference: unlike oil, the intrinsic power of DRAMs kept multiplying fantastically year after year, opening up vast new vistas for further invention and practical application. In 1980, the leading edge of semiconductor production was a "D-ram" with the capacity to store 64,000 databits—64 kilobit, or 64k, in computer-industry argot. The boom in personal computers began at that stage. During the 1980s designers quadrupled the power of the memory chips three times —from 64k to 256k to 1 megabit to 4 megabit by 1990. Each new generation of DRAMs multiplied, in turn, the speed and complexity of what the machines could do.

The exponential expansion of this power source proceeded at the same dazzling pace through the 1990s. By 1995, IBM and Siemens were already jointly producing a 16-megabit chip at a factory in France, while Toshiba and IBM agreed to build a joint fabrication plant in Virginia to manufacture the 64m. By the time the 256 comes on the market in the late 1990s, design engineers will already be working in the realm of gigabits—a next generation of memory chips with a capacity of 1 billion databits. If the technology curve continued along its established arc, by the year 2010 a standard DRAM would be available that stores 64 billion databits—that is, more than six million pages of text on a single silicon chip.

In that sense, the IBM-Siemens-Toshiba announcement was not exactly a surprise. For roughly thirty years the semiconductor industry has been riding the same curve—quadrupling the chip's capacity every three years, through a dozen generations—so no one ever doubted that the 256 was achievable. Semiconductor development was faithfully following Moore's Law—an informal rule of thumb first articulated in 1965 by Gordon E. Moore, an industry pioneer and chairman of Intel. Moore had predicted that the foreseeable technological applications would allow a continuous miniaturization of the semiconductor circuitry and, thus, the exponential expansion of computing power: more and more transistors packed into a smaller and smaller space.*

Moore's Law could not go on forever, as everyone knew. Sooner or later, the laws of physics would intervene and block further innovation or at least slow it down, as the submicronic circuit lines became simply too small to delineate reliably or the chip's internal architecture became too dense to function. But no one was certain just when the technology curve would level off. Some thought the moment was close at hand; others argued that the curve could continue rising on course for another fifteen years, perhaps longer. The question was a running controversy among industry scientists who were exploring X-ray lithography as a new method for printing the chip circuitry or the uses of more fluid materials to replace silicon. But the future of Moore's Law influenced much larger social and economic questions.[1]

Semiconductor technology was the enabling core of the industrial revolution, and so long as it continued to expand the power source in this exponential manner, the upheaval of revolutionary economic change would likely continue, for better and for worse. This was true because each new generation of semiconductor chips unleashed another glorious shock wave of invention—new design possibilities that ripple through nearly every kind of machine, through the daily conveniences of modern life and the complex processes of industrial production. The continuing newness of things guaranteed, of course, a continuing obsolescence for what had gone before.

The amplification of semiconductor power was why ordinary home computers could now speak to their owners, play music and moving pictures or retrieve arcane materials from around the world. It was why, in a few years, owners might be speaking back to their computers, commanding them by voice. The miniaturizing power source explained why every modern household now contained dozens of narrow-gauge computers doing routine chores, the chips embedded in clocks, coffeepots, radios and washers, telephones and cars. Gadgets that had begun as clunky novelties were now small, portable, quick and reliable.

The same wave of invention also, of course, continued to sweep through the mechanisms of industry and finance, elaborating new powers of control and quality, enabling new systems of management and production, displacing more human labor. Thus, technological innovations would continue to quicken the commercial contests in myriad ways, driving the strategies of firms and nations, sowing larger economic consequences for labor

* For the sake of simplicity, I have confined this account to the DRAM memory chips, but the same technological fundamentals apply as well to other forms of semiconductors like the microprocessors that execute and control computer functions. The technology that advances miniaturization in one format will be adapted to others so all types roughly follow the same curve, though microprocessors have multiplied in power even faster than memory chips.

and capital. So long as Moore's Law held up, the wondrous machine of industrial revolution was likely to keep hurtling forward, creating and destroying, headed toward some sort of critical collision with political and economic contradictions.

The technological curve drove the marketplace for this fundamental reason: it drastically reduced manufacturing costs and thus the functional computing costs for the users. Each time the semiconductor industry produced a new generation of chips, other manufacturers rushed to incorporate the devices in their own products and processes, not simply to be fashionable, but because they could exploit the dramatically cheaper computing costs—machines that do more for less. Competing on price and quality, slow-footed firms would lose out in both dimensions.

Roughly speaking, each time the power of memory chips was quadrupled, the cost fell by more than half. For instance, the 64k memory chip of the early 1980s involved a manufacturing cost of about two cents per 1,000 databits. Five generations later in 1995, the 64-megabit chip cost only .017 of a penny for the same computing power. Once in use, the 256-megabit would reduce the cost per 1,000 bits to only .007 cents. If the 64-gigabit chip appeared as envisioned in 2010, the cost would seem quite trivial—.0002 of a penny.[2]

For the semiconductor industry itself, these dynamics fueled a roller coaster of burgeoning expansion—a worldwide market that reached $110 billion by 1994, growing so fast it might double by the end of the decade—except the industry was also haunted by its own history of booms and busts and harrowing shakeouts. Typically, the company that got to market first with the next generation of memory chips enjoyed a fabulous run-up of sales and profits—a market exploding with new demand and insufficient production to supply it. Being first promised huge dividends, like the surfer who catches the next big wave. And, in this industry, a new wave came along every three years.

But, inevitably, other companies scrambled to mimic the leader and catch up, building new production of their own and joining in the boom. In time, the available supply of chips caught up with the market demand and usually overshot it. At that point, the prices leveled off—and sometimes collapsed. A fierce contest of price-cutting would ensue, a struggle to hold market shares that winnowed out weaker, smaller players. In the mid-1980s, the Japanese companies had used their market power in DRAMs to drive American producers from the field—a purposeful bloodletting that was stanched only by a formal agreement between the two governments. As the technology curve kept climbing, it left fewer and fewer firms strong enough to ride its edge.

"The next generation of memory kills the last generation of memory and everyone knows that," Jack Kuehler explained. "Some smaller firms are riding on the big boys, riding on someone else's R&D, but over time that gross profit will be eroded. . . . The only way you make money in memory is to be a leader."

But here was the dilemma that drove competitors into one another's arms: being the leader had become extraordinarily expensive. It meant keeping up with the rising curve of needed capital. As the power of memory chips multiplied, so did the capital required to design and manufacture the next generation. The factory that turned out 64k chips in 1980 cost $100 million to build, but the 256k factory that followed three years later cost $200 million. And the investment costs kept escalating in that fashion with each subsequent generation. By 1995, the new factory for the 64-megabit chip would cost $1.2 billion. When the 256 comes into production, its plant might consume more than $2 billion in capital.

The roller coaster in the semiconductor market thus played perverse games with a company's bottom line: just as one wave was subsiding, with prices and profits diminished, companies had to accumulate the financing for a new round of development that would be much more expensive than the previous one—designing a new product and machine tools for a new factory that were bound to become obsolete themselves.

"Your prices are down and, at the same time, your investment costs have to increase, so your profits lose," Kuehler said. "That's why these alliances are not just fun things to do—they're essential to survive."

Toshiba and Siemens, for their own reasons, came to the same conclusion. "The objective is to share the costs and the risks," Toshiba spokesman Ken Ishihara said, "because the development of the next generation of semiconductors requires huge costs—huge costs—and it is very difficult for any one company to do it alone."

Walter Kunerth, executive vice president of Siemens, described similar motivations in an interview with the *Financial Times:* "To set up a new technology costs a lot of money. To justify that expense, you have to build big capacity. Then you need volume to justify the capacity." Once in, he added, it was very difficult to get out. "The barrier to exit in this game is a high invested cost," Kunerth said. "If you're in it on a global basis, the sunk cost is huge."[3]

In 1992, the three companies agreed to pool their assets on development of the 256 chip and left open the question of whether they would form another consortium later to do the production together. A team of more than a hundred engineers and scientists was assembled from the three nations to collaborate at IBM's Advanced Microelectronics Research Center at East Fishkill on the Hudson. English served as the common language. They encountered predictable cultural conflicts but, as Kuehler said, "these things do not work unless all sides realize that, without this, they will each fail."[4]

Siemens, a proud and strong electronics producer with its own legacy of invention, had fallen a step behind in semiconductor technology during the 1980s, so buying into the consortium provided a way to hook up with the market leaders. IBM, though technologically superior, was suffering from an earnings crisis that hammered its stock price and credit rating, making it much harder to raise capital on its own. Toshiba, the world's third largest semiconductor merchant, brought its cash and manufacturing excellence but got to share in IBM's superb technological resources.

Each of the companies had already collaborated with one another in previous smaller alliances, though, as Walter Kunerth told the *Financial Times,* "If you have been hitting someone on the head for years, cooperation is very difficult." Nevertheless, R&D costs were escalating along their own curve, almost as steep as the factory costs. The companies did not disclose the consortium's budget, but it was said to be $1 billion.

The capital risks would be magnified if engineers made overlapping design decisions in order to speed up the cycle. "You can shorten the process by gambling on some big bets," Kuehler explained. "By designing the machine before you have the working chip, by starting to design the factory before you have the machine."

In such circumstances, Germans, Japanese and Americans learned to get along and share their expertise. "It is very clear: the process becomes unaffordable at some point," Kuehler said. "You can't be sure when, but you can count on that happening. So what do you do about that? You don't just put down your tools and go away. One of the possible solutions is an alliance—because your competitors have the very same problem. First, it's the money. Second, they will broaden the gene pool of knowledge."

The same logic argued strongly for joint production: each new generation of memory-chip production was a necessary platform to reach the next stage, and unless one decided to drop out and swallow the investment losses, the future cost of staying in the game was going to become steeper and steeper.[5] If the 256 plant cost $2 billion, would the first gigabit factory cost $3 billion and even more? The capital curve was headed in that direction.*

"The development cost alone runs into billions," Siemens' Kunerth said. "Then you have to decide to set up a factory. To get the pay-off on your R&D, the factory has to sell high quantities, which can only be done worldwide. I don't know where the factory will be, but there will be only one to supply the world market."

Though nothing had been decided, Jack Kuehler foresaw the same outcome. "I think the world is going to a common factory owned by the players, sharing everything," he said. "My guess is you'll find Siemens-IBM-Toshiba getting together to share the output."

If the industry reached that plateau, it should be possible for almost everyone to glimpse the troubling implications of cooperative capitalism: the potential for cartelized markets and global prices administered by an

* For a more detailed description of the technology-capital curves, see endnote 5.

oligopoly of a few dominant firms. That seemed far-fetched to industry leaders, given the chaotic and intensely competitive structure of the industry at present. But it did not require a dark imagination to envision what may evolve as companies perfected their alliances. Nor did one need question the sincerity of corporate intentions. Their convergence was driven not by conspiracy, but by economics.

Imagine a one-world factory, jointly owned and managed by the surviving competitors, manufacturing the basic commodity that was an essential ingredient for industrial systems and consumer products. The many would depend on the few. Yet, given the extraordinary barriers to entry of technology and capital costs, it would be most difficult—and risky—for new competitors to enter the field.

A production alliance among the three giants would also build a bulwark against another roller coaster of oversupply and collapsing prices. "Significant cost advantages on the part of the three partners should support an aggressive campaign to add capacity," the Office of Technology Assessment observed. "This should reduce the incentive for competitors to add capacity ahead of demand and to initiate price warfare to gain market share. Any increase in market discipline which resulted would further enhance the coalition's joint profitability in the product."[6]

In plain English, the three big boys could wipe out anyone who tried to undercut them. The partners in this consortium might still compete with one another for sales, but they would share an obvious market incentive: controlling the output of their factory so as not to produce the ruinous surpluses that depress prices and profits. This was always the goal of cartels or other market-sharing agreements—controlling supply in order to maintain profitable price levels. In the twenty-first century, could advanced semiconductors come to resemble crude oil, after all?

"No, that will never happen," Jack Kuehler replied. "History has taught us there are going to be multiple players. Because it's such a marvelous way to bring your nation into the forefront of nations. It's clean, it capitalizes on education and knowledge and low-cost labor. You saw Japan get into it. You saw Korea. Taiwan wants to get in it. There's a wonderful economic incentive for nations to participate."

Certainly, that seemed true so far. The global semiconductor industry was a bewildering galaxy of large and small companies, winning and losing, entering and exiting. The largest merchant in the world, Intel, held a commanding position in microprocessor chips, but its share of the overall global semiconductor market was only 9 percent. Toshiba had 6.8 percent. IBM, which had traditionally produced memory chips only for internal use in its own computers, was now selling DRAMs to others. It held a mere 3 percent of the worldwide market in 1994, though driving aggressively to double its share. In those terms, the big boys did not seem very big.

Still, many of the successful U.S. companies that had emerged in recent years were what the industry called "fabless merchants"—small firms that

designed and marketed specialized semiconductors but consigned their actual manufacture to the major producers, frequently in Japan, companies
with the capital to sustain the expensive factories. Market entry, in that
sense, depended mainly on brainpower, but it also required complex webs
of agreements linking them to the market leaders.

Even among the leaders, Professor John Kanz observes, "the extent of
horizontal linkages, though difficult to accurately measure, is startling."
Texas Instruments was more aggressive than others in hooking up with
foreign producers for research and manufacture. In recent years, it had
forged strategic alliances with companies and governments in Taiwan, Italy,
Japan and Singapore as well as other U.S. firms. Scores of similar deals
linked the biggest names in semiconductors.[7]

The prospects for consolidating market power were most visible, however, on the leading edge of development in a field like advanced memory
chips. Only two other viable competitors in the world might plausibly
match or beat the IBM-Siemens-Toshiba consortium at the level of the
256-megabit DRAM. Both of them were international strategic alliances
among major multinationals. One was a research alliance between Texas
Instruments and Hitachi, Number 6 and Number 5, respectively, in global
semiconductor sales. The other was an alliance that NEC, Japan's largest
producer and Number 2 in the world, had entered with Samsung of Korea,
Number 7 in global sales.

With directed capital, the Korean industry had brilliantly caught up
with both American and Japanese companies and was now threatening
Japan's market share in memory chips, just as Japan had done to the U.S.
industry a decade earlier. "They're giving the Japanese fits," reported one
U.S. manager. "It's one of the reasons why the Japanese decided to do
alliances." Samsung was said to have developed its own lab prototype for
the 256. NEC, despite its dominant position, decided it was time to do a
deal with the Koreans. NEC and Samsung agreed to exchange technology
on the 256 and, meanwhile, combine production assets in Scotland and
Portugal to supply DRAMs to the European market.[8]

The competing clubs, meanwhile, took on some new members who
were major players in their own right. Motorola joined the IBM-Siemens-
Toshiba consortium to explore the next plateau of semiconductor technology—development of the 1-gigabit memory chip. And the Koreans and
Japanese made room on their team for an American firm, AT&T, which
agreed to help Toshiba and Samsung in the race to capture the 256m market.[9]

No one, of course, could say exactly how these tangled relationships
would eventually sort out. As Jack Kuehler said, the rapid rise of the Korean
producers argued that it would be impossible for the largest companies to
gain monopolized control over the market. Anyone with enough capital
and determination might still come in and bust up their arrangement. Furthermore, if a consortium like IBM's got to the market first with the 256,
that would not end the contest since the others might still leap ahead on the

next round. These and other uncertainties promised that the sorting out would not produce certain outcomes for some time.

Nevertheless, the fundamentals of technology and capital drove the pinnacle of the pyramid steadily higher—and harder for others to reach. Those eventually left standing on the commanding heights will have accumulated enormous economic power, spanning the global market. In terms of the broader economic definition, the strategic alliances already could be described as cartels, though not in the narrower legal terms defined by anti-trust laws, because the combines brought together competing firms in order to increase their individual profits mutually. The alliances did not, as yet, appear to have the capacity to prop up market prices or inflict predatory damage on other firms that were not participants.

Eventually, they may acquire that kind of market power. One could get a crude idea of the possibilities by considering the dimensions of the three corporate alliances now competing for the lead in DRAM technology. One by one, none of those seven companies had overwhelming girth. But if their market shares were added up together, collectively they already held 35 percent of global semiconductor sales and their share was growing.[10]

These few firms already had the power to decide whether the next generation of DRAMs was technically feasible—and whether it was worth the price in new capital investment. Conceivably, they may someday determine that the drive for further innovation was essentially wasteful, consuming too much scarce capital and undercutting their established products and profits. When Moore's Law eventually exhausts its exponential pace and the technology curve levels off, it may be business economics, not physics, that derails it.

The rush to establish cooperative alliances across regions and national borders sometimes took on a comical flavor of musical chairs. In 1990, the news that Daimler-Benz executives were meeting with Mitsubishi's to discuss collaboration provoked a nervous flutter among U.S. industrialists. The vision of corporate synergy between the two giants was quite alarming. Together, the German and Japanese firms could make aircraft, electronics and electrical machinery, automobiles and much more.

Their talks produced no tangible projects, but unsettled American corporate planners who thought they were Mitsubishi's partners. After all, Boeing had worked closely with Mitsubishi Heavy Industries for years and made it a full partner in the new 777 airliner. So had McDonnell Douglas, Pratt & Whitney and General Dynamics. Mitsubishi had co-produced U.S. fighter planes for the world market and licensed various aerospace and electronics systems from Hughes, Magnavox, Rockwell, Texas Instruments, Goodyear, Lockheed, Loral, Teledyne and TRW. Chrysler was a partner and bought some of its engines from Mitsubishi. AT&T had a semiconductor production deal with Mitsubishi. Anheuser-Busch bought a stake in Mitsubishi's Kirin beer.

On the other hand, the rival U.S. engine manufacturers, General Electric and Pratt & Whitney, had both teamed up in an alliance with Daimler-Benz, a venture that would build small jet engines to counter another partnership formed by Rolls-Royce and BMW. For that matter, the largest aerospace companies from Europe, Japan and America had actively explored a consortium that would include all of them—a mega-alliance to build a new supersonic commercial aircraft. When the music stopped, who would get a chair? No one wished to be left standing alone.[11]

Collaboration in the auto industry was even more tangled. General Motors manufactured small cars with Toyota and owned one third of Isuzu, with which it made vans in Britain, while GM also held a small stake in Suzuki, which supplied it with small cars. Ford did joint production with Nissan and was one-quarter owner of Mazda and intended to co-manufacture a new Mazda model for Europe. Chrysler had a joint sales system with Honda and from Mitsubishi it got small cars, commercial vehicles and engines. The two German rivals, VW and Mercedes-Benz, collaborated with one another, developing a new light commercial van.[12]

The electronics industry was, likewise, quilted over with international cooperation. Advanced Micro Devices of Sunnyvale, California, entered a joint venture with Fujitsu to make its flash-memory chips in Japan and made a separate deal with Siemens. Intel, though it usually stood alone, fashioned a similar compact with Sharp. Motorola had co-production deals with Toshiba and Philips, not to mention IBM and Apple. Hewlett-Packard consigned switching systems for its new telecommunication networks to Fujitsu. Hitachi would make the engines for IBM printers and GoldStar of Korea would make DRAMs for Hitachi. NEC and IBM both owned an equity stake in Bull, the French computer company, which owned a majority of Honeywell, and Honeywell was in alliance with NEC, which, of course, competed with IBM.[13]

Telecommunications firms were engaged in the most visible and dramatic drive for corporate alliance and consolidation. AT&T, Time Warner, TCI, MCI, Ameritech and Nynex, CBS, ABC, Disney and many others—the overlapping deals were stunning as U.S. firms rushed to unite market power and technological assets in cable and telephone systems, broadcasting, film-making, publishing and other media, while simultaneously forging telecom partnerships abroad. U.S. consumers would provide the capital for these huge new conglomerates through the deregulated rates they paid to cable and telephone companies. The winners, it was clear, would be a handful of broad and powerful media combines, as dominant as the railroad and oil trusts were in the 1890s.

The list of interlocking producers ran on bewilderingly, especially in computers and telecommunications, autos, aircraft, electrical equipment and biotechnology. Their meaning was not subject to simple generalization, but many of them, if not most, were driven by the same capital squeeze that had motivated the IBM-Siemens-Toshiba consortium. Alliance propped up weakened profits by spreading the fixed costs among many firms.

The relentless pressure on profits was a recurring lament among multinational managers and a central paradox of the industrial revolution. In an era of declining labor wages, proliferating billionaires and awesome global enterprises, many people would intuitively reject the complaint as fraudulent. Nevertheless, the corporate anxieties were quite real, especially for manufacturing firms. The basic dynamics of technological innovation—more from less—had the perverse effect of depressing returns per unit of production while simultaneously increasing the new capital required to invest in the next round of innovation. This squeeze left even the largest companies exposed to the threat of weak profits and capital shortages.

Across the last thirty years of globalization and technological change, corporate profits in the United States suffered almost in direct relation to the pace of revolution. In the booming 1960s, profits were typically 11 or 12 percent of U.S. national income and peaked at 14 percent. By the 1980s and early 1990s, they had declined to around 8 or 9 percent and fell as low as 6 percent. Manufacturing, in particular, used to be much more profitable than service industries, but was now less so. The wave of corporate restructurings that shed workers and factories in the first half of the 1990s succeeded in reversing the trend—after-tax profit rates were booming again and reached a twenty-five-year peak in 1994—but it was not yet clear if this turnaround was permanent.[14]

The capital insecurities, however, were deeply embedded in corporate balance sheets: U.S. companies had become much more dependent as borrowers. The retained earnings that corporations traditionally held for future capital investments had declined drastically as a percentage of profits since the 1970s. Corporate profits were 34 percent of corporate debt in 1960; by 1990, profits were only 15 percent of debt. In that sense, the corporate managers had lost real power—the power to make capital decisions on their own, independent of the discipline from financial markets.[15]

"The company share of capital is smaller," Dean Baker of the Economic Policy Institute explained. "Debt has grown enormously and a much higher share of profit has to be paid out in interest on the debt. So they feel under tremendous pressure to maintain their profit levels in order to make new investments and stay productive. From their standpoint, there is very little room to spare, which is one reason why they keep trying to reduce labor costs." *

---

* *The paradox of corporate profits begs an obvious question: If labor lost wage incomes and corporations lost profitability, who got the money? The answer, roughly speaking, is the owners of financial capital, the people and institutions who lend money to companies, governments and consumers. Their role in the global system will be examined in Part Three.*

American corporations, pursuing short-term returns in order to satisfy financial investors, were often eclipsed by Japanese rivals because Japan's financial system was structured to provide cheaper and less demanding capital. Investors in Japan accepted lower returns in the interest of fostering greater capital investments in advanced manufacturing—the edge of efficiency and quality that would win larger market shares in the long run and create a larger, lasting industrial structure. The so-called patient capital of the Japanese and European banking systems was an important advantage, though differences in the capital costs had diminished greatly by the 1990s. Japanese companies continued to bring capital to the "risk-sharing" partnerships and usually took home American technology.

Not all of the alliances were driven by capital, of course. Some were simply devices to gain entry into hostile markets. Motorola, like Boeing, had figured out that the easiest way to sell more goods in Japan was to find an important Japanese partner and let it do much of the manufacturing. In fact, many U.S. companies have tacitly conceded the superior quality of Japanese manufacturing firms and consigned production to them, despite the higher labor costs in Japan. Some firms, especially the Europeans, joined alliances to overcome their own technological weaknesses.

But another potent motivation ran parallel to all of these: the desire to stabilize markets and escape persistent problems of oversupply. Sharing production was a means of rationalizing the output among rivals, spreading the risks and possibly reducing the harrowing price pressures that resulted when too many goods were chasing too few buyers.

"Capitalism everywhere is turning out to be too damn productive," observed William W. Keller, director of the Office of Technology Assessment's study of multinationals. "Superior forms of capitalism will benefit for a time, but ultimately what you will have is a greater consolidation of firms—with fewer workers, fewer suppliers, more cartels. Strategic alliances are the answer to the fierce competition."

The history of capitalism suggested that this was an inevitable stage of industrial revolution—an explosive run-up of new technology and production, then intense competition and the emergence of vibrant new enterprises, followed by their collective struggle to establish order and a more settled business environment. Alfred D. Chandler Jr., economic historian at the Harvard Business School, in his monumental work *Scale and Scope: The Dynamics of Industrial Capitalism,* described the rise of the great modern corporations a hundred years ago in words that seemed uncannily appropriate to conditions in the late twentieth century.*

* *Professor Chandler refers to the present upheaval as the Third Industrial Revolution. In his framework the Second Industrial Revolution of the 1890s revolved around oil and electricity, and the First, in the early 1800s, centered on steam power and mechanical production. Across the full sweep of human history, historians have actually counted eleven or twelve such episodes when inventions abruptly improved the processes of agriculture and industry and set off revolutionary economic change.*

"Increasing output and over-capacity intensified competition and drove down prices," Chandler wrote. "Indeed, the resulting decline of prices in manufactured goods characterized the economies of the United States and the nations of western Europe from the mid-1870's to the end of the century. On both continents the standard response by manufacturers to intensified competition and the resulting price decline was, first, to reach informal agreements as to price and output, and then to make more formal agreements (enforced by trade associations) to reduce output, set prices and allocate regional markets. . . . The incentive to form such associations was particularly strong in the new capital- and energy-intensive industries where several entrepreneurs had simultaneously adopted innovative technologies of production." [16]

The emerging cartels were unstable, however, because they lacked the ability to enforce price-output agreements and keep individual producers from cheating by undercutting the price levels (OPEC's oil cartel struggles constantly with the same problem). Cartels led producers to other variants —mergers and trusts, holding companies, industrial groupings that shared assets or managed markets more systematically. "The predominant motive behind the majority of mergers was to achieve or maintain market power by transforming existing trade associations into holding companies or by uniting unassociated competitors under a single corporate roof," Chandler explained.

Early on, American corporate development diverged from the German experience because the U.S. Congress, mainly at the behest of small businesses, began enacting anti-trust laws to protect localized firms from the new behemoths. The German industrial groups, on the other hand, continued to flourish through cooperative fraternities that regulated output and price, allocating market shares among competing firms. The Japanese industrial system, starting from a weaker base, followed a similar pattern and, over time, developed a more sophisticated structure: government supervision of industrial strategies and sectoral cartels that discreetly share markets, coordinate capital investments and target export opportunities.

At the dawn of the twentieth century, notwithstanding the anti-trust laws, the ascendant U.S. enterprises entered a climactic era of corporate consolidations that, ironically, created industrial organizations that were much larger than their cartelized European counterparts—well-known names like du Pont, General Electric, General Motors, U.S. Steel, Goodyear, Standard Oil. Britain, in Chandler's telling, lost its manufacturing supremacy during this period mainly because its corporate owners clung to "personal capitalism" while U.S. and German corporations were developing their broad ranks of managerial expertise.

Market power and profit protection were the main goals, but the reorganizations were also designed to create "scale and scope"—the economies of scale needed for efficient mass production and the centralized managements with the scope to rationalize far-flung systems of output and marketing. As astute firms discovered, monopoly was less valuable than securing an overwhelming market position and the capacity to undercut prices.

"If we could by any measure buy out all competition and have an absolute monopoly in the field, it would not pay us," a du Pont executive wrote privately in 1903. ". . . If we owned all, therefore when slack times came, we would have to curtail product to the extent of diminished demands. If on the other hand we control only 60 percent of it all and made the 60 percent cheaper than others, when slack times came we could still keep our capital employed to the full and our product to the maximum by taking from the other 40 percent. . . ."

The du Pont corporation followed this advice and so did many others. A century later the logic remained fully relevant to the scope and scale of industrial organizations, only now the marketplace was globalized, far larger and more porous and more difficult to dominate. Alongside the nineteenth-century history, one might say global firms have now reached a stage equivalent to about 1880—beginning to experiment with cooperative forms, searching for more rational arrangements.

Anti-trust law in the United States retreated meekly before these forces and was virtually silent on the question of "international strategic alliances." Indeed, Congress had relaxed the law in 1984, allowing U.S. companies to enter research and development alliances with both foreign and domestic competitors and encouraging them to do so in the name of competitiveness. Some American managers still believed, nevertheless, that it was safer in legal terms to form partnerships with foreign firms than at home.

"Here is the crazy situation companies are in," said Clyde Prestowitz, president of the Economic Strategy Institute. "The U.S. government doesn't mind if GM and Toyota get together to make cars, but not GM and Ford. It's okay for Texas Instruments and Hitachi, but not Texas Instruments and Motorola."

The historical parallel with the 1890s had a political dimension: cooperative capitalism on a global scale eclipsed the power of national governments, just as the nineteenth century's nationalizing trusts were a way to escape the state laws that then regulated commerce. The Justice Department did not challenge the modern wave of globalizing alliances, just as the federal government had not objected to the Standard Oil Trust that John D. Rockefeller created in 1882. Political controversy developed only after the fact, once people could see the powerful consequences of the new corporate organizations.

The contemporary international alliance, Cornell political scientist Theodore J. Lowi predicted, represents "a tremendous opportunity for corruption and collusion . . . in which a given MNC [multinational corporation] might hope to escape from its own domestic laws and, beyond that, an opportunity to operate outside law altogether or within the law made by the international alliance itself." The first step toward confronting this reality, Lowi said, was for national governments to acknowledge frankly that their old rules were obsolete. Then they must begin collectively to construct new laws.

If the largest and most powerful nation-state was impotent in this regard, then who would govern these new creatures? More importantly, if leading governments did decide to act in concert, whose national values would be imposed on multinational commerce? Other nations may not choose America's.

As the organizational structures of global industrial firms gradually converge, a profound debate is forming between two competing capitalist systems: the American model of independent, profit-maximizing enterprises versus the cooperative and state-administered version in Japan. One promotes Anglo-Saxon legal rules to ensure freewheeling competition. The other constructs webs of business relationships and social obligations among many firms. One preaches a laissez-faire approach to managing the overall economy. The other plans national strategies for industrial development and actively supervises competitors in the marketplace. One thrives on individualism, the other on loyalty.

In functional reality, the two systems are probably less different than the competing theories and ideologies presume. That is, there is more corporate collusion and direct government subsidy and supervision in American capitalism than is acknowledged, more cutthroat competition, piracy and personal greed in Japan's cooperative system than is admitted. The American system has been more creative in fostering new invention, not to mention entrepreneurial freedom, while the Japanese model has clearly generated greater economic equality and social cohesion, as well as efficiency and quality. My purpose here is not to resolve the debate between the two systems, but to encourage people to begin considering seriously their competing virtues and flaws. The choice is upon us, like it or not.

For better or worse, there might not be much of a public debate on this large question since the gravitational pull of world commerce is already perceptibly toward the Japanese model. This drift of events is difficult for people to see, especially Americans, because the politics and propaganda of global trade are still suffused in the Anglo-American language of liberalization—removing governments from commerce—while the vital substructure of commerce moves in an opposite direction.

American leaders (and most citizens) start from an egocentric presumption that everyone else in the world wants to be like them, so they assume the task of "reforming" Japan and other nations—that is, persuading them to abandon an economic approach that has been vividly successful in terms of their own national interests. For their part, the Japanese and others have no incentive to provoke American opinion by declaring that the American system is obsolete, though that is what many of them believe.[17]

In Europe, as national governments attempt to fashion a viable economic union, they are actively emulating elements of the strategic industrial coordination perfected in the Japanese system. Industrial cooperation has proved difficult to do across national borders, but the EU has encouraged strategic subsidies and corporate collaborations to achieve scale and scope in targeted industries, often shielded from foreign competitors. Airbus is the most successful example, though similar efforts in electronics have so far disappointed the sponsoring nations.

In Frankfurt, a German labor leader told me: "If you look at the way Japan conquered markets with MITI, there are such discussions in progress in Germany and the EU. It is already working to a certain extent if you look at R&D. We are doing it here by mandating subsidies and financial incentives."

Europe's own tradition of cartels and state-owned enterprises was consistent with such efforts. Indeed, the major European and Japanese producers have been accused of forming a functioning global cartel in steel that limits exports into each other's territory and agrees on prices in third countries. The allegation from U.S. steel companies was substantially confirmed in the *Nikkei Weekly* of Tokyo, which reported that cartel members split the world market into East and West, with Myanmar as the dividing line. Former top executives of NKK and Kawasaki acknowledged a secret compact that "arranged prices and divided export markets in India, South America and elsewhere." Japanese industry officials dismissed this as merely a "voluntary export agreement." [18]

In the United States, when leading multinationals forge alliances with Japanese rivals, it is often an implicit acknowledgment: if you can't beat 'em, join 'em. Companies injured by Japan's cartelized sectors conclude that the only way to compete against their advantages is to arrange a friendly truce and share in their assets, the secure markets and abundant capital. These firms do not renounce their American values, of course, but they do lower their voices. The alliances with Japan "tend to neutralize U.S. companies politically on the trade issues," Clyde Prestowitz observed. "Once a company has got a deal with Hitachi, they become silent on these issues. Why attack your partner?"

Among the poor but fast-developing nations of Asia, there is no debate whatever about which economic system seems more promising for them. In varying degrees, all are mimicking Japan's administered strategies and structures, often with direct tutelage, development aid and capital from Japan. South Korea's *chaebol* are a close equivalent of Japan's *keiretsu*, intimate industrial groupings that operate on interfirm loyalties and national industrial strategies. Korea's success has produced multinationals of its own, large enough to play with the big boys, and other governments like Taiwan strive to do the same.

In this new world, developing nations that lack multinational corporations of their own may become the new equivalent of colonies, assigned to subordinate roles in the global production system. These countries may enjoy rising prosperity as they industrialize, but their economic sovereignty will remain hostage to decisions by the webs of global alliances. Subordination, of course, is not a new condition for Third World nations, and they understand who runs the global system. Since 1980 the advanced economies actually expanded their share of global exports, from 63 percent to more than 72 percent, while most regions lost ground. The exception was Asia, which increased its share of world trade from 9 to 15 percent. These prospects explain why poorer economies target advanced-technology sectors in their nation-building strategies. It will determine their ultimate place on the ladder.[19]

In broader terms, the Japanese approach offers an alluring possibility to weary combatants in the global system—the chance to rationalize output among major producers and perhaps stabilize markets, freeing them of persistent surpluses and roller-coaster prices. According to one scholarly study, Japanese officials have quietly advanced numerous "trial balloons" in recent years, proposing various schemes for global market-sharing and coordinated planning of capital investment in new production. None of these suggestions has gone anywhere as yet, but the temptation is clearly present.

"Japan and other Asian countries are openly discussing the creation of global blueprints for the international division of labor—an idea that is anathema to the traditional notion of national comparative advantage," Peter F. Cowhey and Jonathan D. Aronson reported in *Managing the World Economy*. "Japanese policymakers suggest that it is foolhardy for countries to randomly seek new industrial niches. . . . If countries agree to allocate segments of an industry among themselves according to a consensual blueprint, they can encourage complementary investments." In this approach, the developing countries would be assured a piece of the action and Japan would be assured of dominance.[20]

American firms and the U.S. government have always rebuffed such ideas, at least so far as is known. More specifically, when the United States and Japan were renewing their 1986 semiconductor agreement in 1991, American negotiators dismissed the "Japanese hints that there could be more global planning about production capacity, demand forecasting and investment plans," according to Cowhey and Aronson. At that stage, when U.S. producers had lost so much ground, cooperative industrial planning might have simply ratified Japanese hegemony.

But the semiconductor agreement was itself a form of global market-sharing designed to cope with the problem of surplus production—a negotiated settlement between two governments that protected U.S. companies against Japanese price-cutting and promised them a stable 20 percent share of Japan's market. In fact, the agreement also covered semiconductor sales to third countries. To prevent Japanese dumping in other markets, their government explicitly promised to "monitor, as appropriate, costs and export prices on the products exported by Japanese semiconductor firms from

Japan." If this deal did not constitute a government-fashioned cartel, it seemed to come rather close.

Afterwards, American semiconductor firms staged a much-celebrated rebound in market share, but some critics claimed the "American victory" was largely illusory since much of the U.S. industry's sales growth actually came from its overseas production, including its factories in Japan itself. It is perhaps significant that following the 1986 agreement, new corporate alliances with Japan proliferated in the electronics sector, as though both sides were tacitly accepting new ground rules for cooperative competition.

When the semiconductor deal came up for renewal again in 1996, Japan at first resisted, arguing that any new market understanding should be worked out among the companies, not the governments. The U.S. industry pushed for another formal agreement between the two governments to maintain the explicit quotas for its share of the Japanese market. But Japan's proposal might become a meaningful precedent. When the market competition gets too bloody in a particular sector, the governments step in and negotiate a truce, allocating market shares. Then, the governments turn the deal over to the multinationals to refine and administer.

Indeed, supported by MITI and the European Union, the leading Japanese companies decided to organize a new global council of semiconductor producers—including the Europeans and perhaps also Korea·and Taiwan. In June 1996, meeting in Tokyo, representatives from NEC and Toshiba, Siemens of Germany, Philips of the Netherlands and SGS-Thomson from Italy and France agreed to organize the council and invite the Americans to participate. They denied, of course, any intention of allocating market shares or fixing prices. "European Union officials denied that closer industry cooperation risked creating a global cartel which would work against the interests of chip consumers," the *Financial Times* reported. Ultimately, the U.S.-Japan agreement was renewed, but on Japan's terms—without explicit numbers on market shares.[21]

In Tokyo, when I interviewed an influential economist, Makoto Utsumi, a former vice minister of Japan's powerful Ministry of Finance, he was surprisingly direct about the prospect of more explicit collaborations among major competitors. "Yes, there might be such a tendency," he said. "I don't know whether the U.S. agencies would regard this as an antimonopoly case or not, but the need for huge amounts of capital for capital investments might bring this kind of corporate partnership into existence." The difficulty, he went on, is that U.S. officials usually insist on formal, public discussions of these matters. "To my view, this is an important process if we keep it quiet and do not make it a political argument," he noted.

Was the global system in the process of perhaps constructing new organizational alignments that may eventually resemble the great oil and railroad trusts of the 1890s? "I think so, yes," Utsumi responded. "The borderless society is much more advanced than the relations among nations.

Business goes much beyond the frontiers of each nation and each government to shape things for the future."

Explorations in this realm will doubtless continue—discreetly offscreen from the public debate—but corporate convergence contains the seeds of a great political crisis. Sooner or later, as the global system progresses along these lines, people will begin to grasp that enormous economic power is becoming concentrated in a very few hands and on a plane beyond national systems of accountability.

Furthermore, convergence requires marriages of convenience between vastly different systems of enterprise—some firms that are freestanding and mainly accountable to shareholders, others that function as members of broad business networks and are intimately supervised by their governments. What if someday the People's Republic of China has the industrial girth to demand a partnership? Or some of the ambidextrous transnational conglomerates formed by ethnic Chinese families from Asian nations? U.S. multinationals would find themselves negotiating market share with foreign governments. But, of course, if one government is at the table representing its own global producers, then all governments must be there, doing the same for their companies.

If that becomes the mode for organizing and rationalizing global commerce, it does not require a gloomy imagination to see the grave implications for democracy. A hybridized system, evolving from necessity, may encourage the corporate state as the principal mechanism of governance—a governance in which public and private distinctions lose their meaning and the separate sources of economic and political power are coalesced. That form of capitalism would profoundly violate democratic values and deprive individuals everywhere of a right to self-determination. Americans who are appalled by the prospect should note that many successful trading nations already have similar arrangements.

Against the present reality of intense and freewheeling competition, my observations on the future perhaps sound far-fetched. One can reasonably doubt whether such a system could ever be successfully put together or that it would function reliably, given the diverse multitude of competing interests. Still, it is troubling enough to observe that the architecture is already partially visible and, in some quarters, a subject of active discussion.

Back in the 1890s, most Americans would not have believed that only a few hundred corporations would someday dominate the nation's commercial life or that five hundred global firms could rule the world's. They would have been quite skeptical and amused by the suggestion that someday their local banks and businesses would be owned and managed from New York or London, Frankfurt or Tokyo. The future often seems improbable until it happens.

Ten

The Buyer of Last Resort

THE TRUE DIMENSIONS of underlying disorders in the global system are masked—and prevented from reaching critical mass—by the benevolent role played by the wealthy progenitor of revolution, the United States of America. In various fundamental ways, the United States promotes and props up the global trading system, allowing it to evade many of its gathering contradictions and instabilities. An economic crisis will likely be joined when the United States is no longer able to do this—a climactic moment that is fast approaching.

For roughly fifty years, the U.S. government has served as the tolerant and broad-shouldered leader that articulates the global system's putative rules and values and scolds (or sometimes punishes) those nations that fail to observe them. American policy permits the liberal dispersal of its own advanced technologies. It encourages and subsidizes U.S. multinationals globalizing their production. It provides financial support for foreign development and for the global institutions that supervise international finance and developing economies. It generously guarantees the military security of its economic competitors. It educates engineers and scientists for the world.

But the U.S. economy provides support for the global system of a more crucial nature: the American market serves as buyer of last resort for the world, the only major economy that is willing year after year to absorb gross surpluses of production from other nations. Furthermore, with the government's blessing, American enterprise facilitates the global adjustments to continuing overcapacity and other market tensions by gradually abandoning elements of its home base of production. The U.S. manufacturing structure adjusts more readily than others, dispersing or shutting down, and thus allows the world's industrial base to migrate. In these and other ways, the great wealth of American economic life serves as a kind of safety valve for the global marketplace, reducing conflicts, keeping it afloat.

This role cannot continue indefinitely and may soon come to an end. As America's economic dominance has steadily weakened, the nation takes on an increasing volume of foreign indebtedness through its large and persistent trade deficits—the losses sustained every year by buying more goods from other economies than they are willing to buy from the United States. At the same time, the nation's broad capacity for mass consumption is being slowly eroded by declining wages and the loss of high-income employment, whether from technological reform or the migration of manufacturing sectors. Thus, the nation's economic resilience is weakening as its debt obligations accumulate.

A very rich nation can manage to do this for quite a long time. But not forever. Sooner or later, like any other kind of debtor, the United States will be tapped out—no longer able to afford its role as buyer of last resort. As the enormous U.S. trade debts accumulate, the dollar declines steadily in foreign-exchange value, reflecting the country's diminishing strength. At some point, the nation's devalued purchasing power in global markets will, literally, price it out of buying so much from others. Like Britain's before it and for roughly the same reasons, American hegemony will be ended.

This reality may surface as a dramatic thunderclap or simply emerge from the slow, bleeding process that is already in progress. Either way, the moment of recognition promises crisis, not only for the United States, but also for the global economy at large. For Americans, the meaning is already being felt: a lower standard of living for most people, perhaps abruptly lowered if a sudden financial markdown of America's economic worth occurs. That by itself does not constitute a global crisis, given the luxurious and often wasteful nature of American consumption, and might even be therapeutic for Americans themselves in the long run. But it is sure to trigger a grave moment in U.S. politics and a deep psychic wound to the national self-confidence.

For the rest of the world, American eclipse begs an economic question: Who will buy the surpluses when the United States cannot? Will Japan simply stop exporting so many cars? Will Germany or France agree to absorb China's huge and growing outflows of manufactured goods? And which nations will volunteer to phase out major industrial sectors or let them migrate freely to the developing economies? In short, when America taps out, the systemic contradictions should become fully visible to all.

At a minimum, the revolution is entering an unstable interregnum in which the hegemonic power gradually loses its capacity to lead and lubricate the global marketplace, while no one else is yet willing to assume those burdens. Japan is well aware of the potential vacuum, and much more than Americans may understand, it has been quietly propping up the world leader—mainly by lending it lots of money—just as the United States tried to keep Great Britain upright during its final years of declining power in the 1920s.

The solemn, unexpressed hope of statesmen is that these great shifts of power will evolve gradually, without provoking a bloody breakdown. In the worst case, if many nations are abruptly unable to sell all their output and compelled to produce much less, it will trigger a worldwide implosion of commerce, that is, global depression. This is more or less how the last industrial revolution ended in the 1930s—in an abyss of mass suffering and conflict. It happened because neither governments nor enterprise was willing to pull back from the same economic imperatives that were driving them toward a disastrous climax.

The standard response to this line of analysis is that, one way or another, things will work out—nations will adjust and the American imbalances will dissipate. Japan, it is said, will evolve into a mass consumption economy that eventually buys much more from the United States. Or American trade negotiators will win new market-opening agreements from Japan, China and others that gradually correct the negative trend line. Or the emerging economies of Asia will produce the affluent consumers to mop up the global surpluses. In theory, this is possible. In practical reality, these reassuring assumptions have failed to materialize for twenty years.

The concrete evidence from the last two decades points in the opposite direction: the U.S. trade debt worsens steadily despite the American government's supposed success at fashioning liberalized trade agreements and more open markets, despite the much-celebrated revival of American competitiveness, despite the emergence of hot new markets with rising consumer demand, despite the declining dollar that has made U.S. goods cheaper in overseas markets. Given these facts, one would think it is time to reconsider the prevailing theory. Instead, American elites have become even more dogmatic in their attachment to it.

In the broader sweep of human history, the prospect of Americans becoming relatively less rich and powerful is neither tragic nor unjust, but a positive development for the world as a whole. Certainly, people in China or Japan, even Western Europe, will not mourn the end of American imperium, any more than Americans lamented the decline of the British Empire. Many may even look forward to it.

Conceivably, this event could also renew American society if it prompts citizens to reevaluate their own social arrangements, to confront the harsh inequalities generated by the U.S. economic system and the gross wastefulness embedded in American material life. The loss of global hegemony need not be tragic but could offer a new opening if it leads Americans to new understandings about themselves and their country.

America's dilemma, however, is really a principal symptom of the global system's much larger disorder: the imperatives of industrial revolution create more supply faster than new demand and the expanding productive capacity overruns the available market of consumers. Together and separately, no one in the global system—not governments or enterprises—is willing to face the gathering crisis of inadequate demand and to reverse the flows of incomes between capital and labor. If America taps out financially or retreats into a thicket of reactionary politics, the world's producers will find themselves looking frantically for buyers.

○

In Washington, Bill Clinton spoke for the old order. Despite his youth and energetic style, Clinton's presidency has been conventionally devoted to the same economic premises that have guided American governments since World War II. Free trade and liberalized markets for business and finance, the active promotion of American multinationals and globalized production, a tolerant stewardship of the world trading system, a vast military infrastructure committed to ensuring world order for others—Clinton inherited these commitments and optimistically elaborated on them. It became the central weakness of his presidency because the old order was no longer working to the benefit of most Americans.

Since he liked to emulate his boyhood hero, John F. Kennedy, Clinton went to American University early in his term to deliver an important foreign policy address, just as JFK had done thirty years before. The Cold War was ended, Clinton told the young audience, but some things have not changed: America was still "the engine of global growth."

"The truth of our age is this and must be this: open and competitive commerce will enrich us as a nation," he declared. "It spurs us to innovate. It forces us to compete, it connects us with new customers. It promotes global growth without which no rich country can hope to grow wealthy. It enables our producers, who are themselves consumers of services and raw materials, to prosper. And so I say to you in the face of all the pressures to do the reverse, we must compete, not retreat." [1]

In that spirit, Clinton embraced the unfinished work of his Republican predecessors and pushed new liberalizing trade agreements to completion, the North American Free Trade Agreement (NAFTA) that put the United States in a common market with Canada and Mexico and the new worldwide GATT agreement that further lowered nations' tariffs and created the World Trade Organization. Each time, the President surrounded himself with a bipartisan elite—former Republican presidents and cabinet officers, corporate CEOs and important Wall Street bankers—to push these measures over opposition from some of his own constituents, organized labor and anxious working people.

He prevailed in this, but at great price because, in order to argue for the orthodox free-trade agenda in the 1990s, Clinton was required to advance some spurious claims—promises that were not borne out by subsequent reality. NAFTA, he declared in late 1993, would generate 200,000 good, new jobs for Americans by boosting U.S. exports to the vibrant Mexican economy. Two years later Mexico was mired in depression, and just as NAFTA's critics had predicted, it was being used by U.S. and foreign multinationals as a convenient low-wage export platform into the rich American market.

America's merchandise trade deficit with Mexico soared, reaching $15 billion by 1995, a major new source of the U.S. trade debt. If one relied on the Clinton administration's own dubious formula for trade's relation to employment, the negative flow with Mexico translated immediately into 200,000 lost jobs for Americans.

When Clinton launched the bipartisan campaign to win congressional approval for the new GATT agreement, he offered an attractive rationale for supporting it. "We have a golden opportunity here," he declared, "to add $1,700 in income to the average family's income in this country over the next few years, to create hundreds of thousands of high-wage jobs, to have the biggest global tax cut in history and to fulfill our two responsibilities: our responsibility to lead and remain engaged in the world and our responsibility to try to help the people here at home to get ahead." [2]

Most American families would not get the $1,700 a year that the President proffered or perhaps any added income at all. Their incomes were stagnant or shrinking. Clinton's number was a mythical average, based upon economists' assumptions about how liberalized trading rules would increase overall efficiency and, therefore, stimulate greater U.S. economic growth. The statistic came from a study done in 1990 by George Bush's advisors.

Clinton's promise ignored the contemporary reality of American economic life: The gains from growth in the Gross Domestic Product were being distributed most unevenly among citizens, heavily skewed toward those already in the upper brackets of wealth and income. In 1994, when the economy was expanding at a vibrant pace, labor wages and benefits were virtually flat, behaving as though the economy was still in recession. The $1,700 statistic was like asking people to assume that if their next-door neighbor wins the lottery, everyone on the block will get richer. [3]

More to the point, the theoretical assumption supporting Clinton's claim—that greater global trade leads automatically to greater U.S. economic growth—is itself highly suspect. During the previous twenty years, when global trade and investment entered into dramatic expansion, the United States experienced the opposite: much slower economic growth. This might be attributed to the peculiar problems of the American economy except that the same thing was happening to nearly all of the most advanced economies in the world. Since the early 1970s the overall growth rate of the nations belonging to the Organization for Economic Cooperation and Development was cut roughly in half from prior decades—from 4 to 5 percent to 2 to 2.5 percent. [4]

In any case, no matter what Clinton told the public, the governing authorities in Washington did not really want faster economic growth since they regarded it as inflationary. If faster growth occurred, the government would step in and stop it. With Clinton's concurrence, that was exactly what happened in 1994. When GNP growth briefly exceeded 4 percent, the Federal Reserve depressed the economy by raising interest rates and the growth rate quickly subsided to below 2 percent. The White House supported the Fed's intervention, without ever explaining how those average families were supposed to collect their $1,700 when government policy was committed to preventing the faster growth that Clinton had promised.*

Contradictions accumulated for the President. For instance, a Census Bureau survey reported that American workers who had lost their jobs in the recessionary years of 1990–92 suffered a 23 percent drop in wages, on average, when they found full-time work again. The news that corporate profits reached a twenty-five-year high in 1994 and the stock market regularly achieved new price peaks was not especially comforting to most wage earners. Among male workers, 80 percent saw their wages stagnate or decline. For the median wage earner, pay had shrunk in real terms, by one percent a year, every year from 1989 through 1994.

As U.S. multinationals restructured their managements and stripped away hundreds of thousands of white-collar jobs, a rising sense of insecurity was palpable across the country. *Fortune* magazine reported that since 1982 the number of people who felt confident about their job security had plummeted from 79 to 55 percent. That was among the managers, not workers.[5]

For these and other reasons, Bill Clinton was powerfully repudiated at midterm. In the fall of 1994, voters elected a Republican majority in Congress for the first time in forty-two years. Afterwards, the President's tone and rhetoric changed considerably. He began to lament what was happening to Americans and enthused less on the success of his own economic policies. In speech after speech he delivered soulful meditations on the painful losses that people were absorbing as a consequence of the globalization he had previously celebrated.

"I came to this job committed to restoring the middle class and I did everything I knew to do," Clinton told a conference of community leaders in July 1995. "We lowered the deficit. We increased investment in education, in technology, in research and development. We expanded trade frontiers. We have seven million more jobs. We have a record number of millionaires. We have an all-time high stock market. We have more new businesses than ever before. . . . And most people are still working harder for lower pay than they were making the day I was sworn in as President."[6]

This was a devastating admission for a sitting president since, as he presumably understood, the iron law of American presidential politics holds that an incumbent party wins reelection on rising prosperity and loses when it is generally absent. Unlike previous presidents, Clinton was also candid in identifying the main source of the economic distress: the great economic transformations under way in the world. "How did this happen? We're moving into a global economy, an information society," he would explain.

"These income trends are huge, huge trends, huge, sweeping over two decades, fast international forces behind them, trillions of dollars of money

---

* The role of central banks and monetary policy in governing the global system is examined directly in Chapter 13.

moving across international borders working to find the lowest labor cost and pressing down, untold improvements in automation," Clinton enumerated for Georgetown University students. "So fast that you can't create enough high-wage jobs to overcome the ones that are being depressed in some sectors of the economy."[7]

Yet, despite his frankness, the President did not rethink his assumptions or alter his fundamental approach in any important way. His sympathies might have been with the many people who were losing, but his intellect and policies were still fully committed to promoting the global system—fashioning still more trade agreements, playing salesman for U.S. multinationals abroad, trying to lead the world much as American presidents have done for fifty years.

The disconnect in his thinking was obvious in many of his speeches. Clinton would deliver eloquent soliloquies on what the global economy was doing to American families, but when he turned to describe remedies his proposals seemed trivial or irrelevant to the problem. Protect kids from TV violence. Enforce child-support payments from wayward fathers. Improve Head Start and adult education. Control guns, curb teenage smoking. Against the economic reality, social palliatives sounded like evasion.[8]

Bill Clinton's dilemma was, in fact, the American establishment's dilemma. While his rivals may have enjoyed the President's discomfort, most politicians in both parties shared the same contradictions and indulged in social evasions of their own. As the negative evidence accumulated, it was not just Clinton who clung to the faltering old order, but the entire spectrum of important opinion leaders and powerful actors—business executives and financiers, academic and military leaders, editorial writers and politicians, Republicans and Democrats alike. Beyond sympathetic gestures and renewed expressions of faith in the system, none of them offered meaningful answers to the popular distress.

As a whole, the establishment was still in denial. Some opinion leaders, supported by orthodox economists, smugly declared that nothing much had actually changed in American economic life. Overall consumption continued to rise (despite the wage erosion and maldistribution of incomes). They frequently asserted (inaccurately) that U.S. manufacturing output had not actually declined at all, but was simply restructured and modernized (albeit with many fewer employees as a result). Other authorities, like Clinton, acknowledged that large segments of the population were suffering, but insisted this was simply a period of painful transition toward a much brighter, more prosperous future. If anything, the Republicans' 1996 presidential candidate, Bob Dole, was even more orthodox than Clinton, since his party was traditionally more closely aligned with business interests, more opposed on principle to government intervention in market affairs.

When eccentric figures rose on the political margins to attack the status quo, these new voices were derided as reactionaries (indeed, some were), but "responsible opinion" was no longer fully persuasive itself. The ascendant

Republicans' answer was to launch a zealous "revolution" to strip the federal government of size and power, discarding social programs and regulatory rules, awarding additional tax benefits to capital, in sum, relying on the unfettered marketplace to restore prosperity.

The center was not holding. The destabilized condition of American politics was similar in fundamentals to what was happening in many other leading economies—distraught and volatile electorates, weak and unstable leadership—but America was distinctive because it was the established center for global politics. The United States had led the capitalist world through four decades of Cold War confrontations, and in the end the Communist alternative collapsed. Without its old adversary, the triumphant leader suddenly faced a vacuum of its own.

As empires go, the American hegemony was quite benign compared to most of history's imperial regimes and, despite its violent aspects, even liberating for many subordinate nations. These qualities were not always evident to foreign peoples who encountered the heavy hand of American self-interest, but, in hindsight, it seemed indisputable that American power had shared its assets broadly and without the systematic racial brutality of British colonialism or the French, German and Japanese attempts at empire.

It was U.S. military procurement that provided the market demand enabling Japan to rapidly rebuild its manufacturing industries after World War II. U.S. defense spending and other aid ignited industrial development in South Korea, Taiwan and Thailand and, of course, renewal in Western Europe, too. It was American anti-trust law that required the largest U.S. multinationals to share their technological inventions abroad by granting licenses to potential competitors (a generous legal doctrine that Japanese firms used to great advantage).[9]

From Bangkok to Berlin, America's expressive colloquial English and its free-spirited popular culture have become ubiquitous—a loose, new Latin for the world. From central Europe to Korea and even Japan, American troops were still stationed in defense of others, even major economic rivals (though Japan now reimbursed some of the U.S. expense). It was American firms that pioneered the globalizing of production and American policy architects who designed the international rules and structures to govern Wendell Willkie's "one world."

The most valuable sharing, though less celebrated, was probably education. America held open the door of its superb system of higher education and has trained hundreds of thousands of engineers, scientists and future leaders from poorer nations. From Taiwan to Iran, new elites were exposed to America's own politics of democracy and its liberating social values. This did not make dictators into instant democrats, but it advanced the idea of individual rights in a profound manner.

Despite their good deeds empires do not last forever. For many years, America's weakening economic position was concealed by the continuing saga of the Cold War, which provided a unifying cause for the nation and also an important prop for its domestic economy. The paradox of America's postwar prosperity was that, notwithstanding the exotic new technologies and emphasis on global trade, the vital core of the U.S. economy was always dependent on three more prosaic pillars at home: military production, housing and the mass consumption of goods like cars and appliances—spending fueled by the broadly rising wages, profits and productivity (the "virtuous circle" described in Chapter 4).[10]

All three of these domestic pillars have been gravely weakened by events, deterioration that is directly or obliquely traceable to the globalization of business and finance. After the false boom of the 1980s, defense industries were shrinking and destined to shrink much more. Politicians were reluctant to cut defense spending more rapidly and shift national resources to other, more promising investments because that might only exacerbate the job losses. Besides, they could not see any convincing alternatives to building more bombers and submarines.

The housing sector was permanently damaged by financial deregulation and elimination of the federal interest-rate controls that for forty years had discreetly subsidized home ownership by providing cheaper credit to families of modest means. Home building remained a vital industry, but its last peak was in 1986, a year that itself was well below the records set in the 1970s. Home ownership had declined unevenly since 1980, but most dramatically among younger families.

The domestic-goods-producing sectors like autos suffered on two fronts: the imports that penetrated their home markets and the stagnating incomes that eroded the U.S. potential for mass consumption. In 1995, economists at Chrysler took the unusual step of downgrading the U.S. market's potential—revising its basic forecasting model to acknowledge that in a normal year Americans would buy 3.3 percent fewer cars and trucks than previously assumed. Other auto companies were expected to follow, along with the wide array of related firms that depended on this core industry.[11]

The striking quality about American economic debate in the 1990s was that none of these old domestic pillars got much discussion, aside from the downsizing problems of military production. A subject like housing seemed passé to policy thinkers absorbed by the global action—the spectacular emerging markets or contests over corporate competitiveness. Domestic America was regarded as a "mature market," less interesting because it was bound to grow but slowly.

Furthermore, an ominous shift of values occurred among American political and business elites during the last twenty years—ominous because it resembled the same shift in influence among British elites during their country's fateful decades of decline. The old-fashioned, parochial concerns of domestic manufacturing and labor were eclipsed as elite opinion in the United States gravitated to the global perspective of financiers and financial markets. In the 1920s, Britain's leadership had undergone a similar transformation as the City of London's urbane bankers displaced the industrialists. British policy was ruled, thereafter, by a "gentlemanly capitalism" that fixated on financial values over the more mundane questions of production or employment.[12] Now it was American politicians, Clinton and Republicans alike, who deferred to the abstract judgments of the bond market.*

In human terms, it was easy enough to understand why influential leaders in government, academia, media or business were unable to step back from their inherited orthodoxy and reconsider the new realities. This was what they knew, what had worked in the past. America's preeminent role—and the economic assumptions that accompanied it—constituted the natural order of things across two generations, the big idea embedded in public consciousness and everyone's working experience. People had attained position and power by subscribing to those ideas. The leading institutions were all deeply committed to supporting them, from government agencies to research universities to newspaper editorial boards.

But governing elites had a more substantial reason not to challenge the old order: To do so would threaten America's glorious role as leader in the global system. Reexamining the premises might well lead to the awkward conclusion that, for its own good, the United States must yield the prerogatives of benevolent steward, the generous nation that held things together for others, and instead attend more directly to national self-interest. Leaders were accustomed to leading. Those who participated in exercising America's global authority were naturally reluctant to abandon it. Ready or not, the possibility was bearing down on them.

The United States crossed a critical threshold in its national worth during Bill Clinton's presidency, though no one blamed him and, indeed, few Americans seemed even to notice. In the fourth quarter of 1993, for the first time in nearly a century, the outflow of financial returns paid to foreign investors on the assets they held in America exceeded all of the profits, dividends and interest payments that American firms and investors collected from their investments abroad. The following year, 1994, the annual outflow was negative for the first time since 1914.

The initial loss seemed trivial, less than $30 billion, but the bleeding was now visible and sure to accelerate—even compound and hemorrhage —if nothing fundamental was changed in America's position. The outflow of these so-called factor incomes reflected the nation's true balance sheet in the global economy. They were the net sum of earnings on assets going both ways—the profits and interest payments foreigners got from what they had lent or bought in the United States minus what Americans got from their assets overseas. The outflow covered every form of public and private in-

---

* The triumph of the bondholders' values in American politics was chronicled in my book Secrets of the Temple: How the Federal Reserve Runs the Country (New York: Simon & Schuster, 1987).

vestment, from real estate and corporate stock shares and venture capital to the government and corporate bond borrowings and commercial bank loans.

Bottom line: while U.S. multinationals were finding robust new markets abroad and adventurous financiers realized amazing rates of return on their capital, the global economy was now a losing transaction for the nation as a whole. As recently as 1980 the United States enjoyed a net surplus in "factor incomes" every year of $35 billion or so, equal then to 1.5 percent of the national income. The inflows had exceeded outflows by nearly 2 to 1. The money repatriated from abroad was like an annual bonus to the national economy, the returns from decades of previous investments around the world.

Now it was like a bill for interest due on previous borrowings. The negative flow was certain to continue and increase because it was based on the underlying debts and obligations that have been accumulating for twenty years, primarily from America's annual trade deficits with other nations. Cumulatively, since 1980, Americans have bought $1.5 trillion more than they sold in their merchandise trade with foreign nations. The trade deficits started modestly in 1975, exploded during the 1980s and, despite ebbs and surges, set a dollar-volume record of $180 billion in 1995.

Like any other sort of debt, these foreign obligations had to be covered every year. Collectively, the U.S. economy either borrowed the money from abroad in the form of government bonds and private borrowings or foreign capitalists came to the United States and bought things—income-producing assets like office buildings in Los Angeles and New York or new auto factories in Kentucky and Ohio or whole companies like Honeywell or Columbia studios.

Year by year, as it added up, the cumulative process has produced an epochal shift of wealth, probably unmatched in human history for its size and speed, as the richest nation on earth swiftly redistributed wealth to others. As Economics Professor Wynne Godley at Bard College's Jerome Levy Economics Institute has described, the United States went from holding a net surplus of foreign assets equal to 30 percent of its own annual economic output in 1970 to a debtor position by 1994 of −8.5 percent. That is, foreign interests now owned the net surplus of assets—equal to 8.5 percent of the U.S. annual Gross Domestic Product. That was why the flow of profits and interest turned negative.[13]

As Godley observed, it might have been worse—and occurred sooner —if the foreigners had been smarter investors. The Japanese bought lots of California real estate in the 1980s at its peak—just before prices collapsed —and took a bath on many other U.S. investments as well. Americans were amused or reassured by this only if they did not understand what was actually happening.

Given these events, historians of the future may well decide that 1994 marked the end point of America's economic dominance. If so, the American century will have lasted eighty years, a bit shorter than the reign of British imperialism, which first displaced Amsterdam in 1814 and led capitalism until World War I, when it fell into similar financial straits. Of course, it took the British several decades—two world wars and a great depression —before they could bring themselves to acknowledge that the empire was over. Americans have entered their own twilight of self-delusion. Economic reality nearly always runs ahead of political understanding.

The ominous truth, though widely ignored and often denied in American political debate, was this: Given the immutable laws of credit and compounding interest, America's debt position was going to rapidly deteriorate further in the immediate future as interest payments mounted on an outstanding balance that was itself still growing, as the negative outflow of annual returns to foreign investors grew larger, too. Each year the American economy was taking on new balance-of-payment deficits equal to 2 to 2.5 percent of its total economic output. And the nation was borrowing to cover this shortfall at real interest rates between 3.5 and 4 percent. When interest payments and the negative flow of "factor incomes" were added, it meant the nation's foreign debt obligations were growing at a much faster pace than the underlying economy that would have to pay them.

That equation, if continued, defined the classic debtor's trap, familiar to any household that tried to live on its credit cards and had to keep borrowing more each month to pay for last month's spending. Eventually, the gap between debt payments and income became too great to sustain. Creditors stopped lending. The spendthrift family was tapped out. Roughly the same thing happened occasionally to nations, though usually the poor nations, not the rich.

This deterioration was already under way—that was the meaning of the negative outflow of returns that began in 1994—but would compound much faster than complacent political opinion seemed to grasp. Given present trade trends and the elevated level of global interest rates, Godley estimated that America's debt position in net foreign assets—now around 9 percent—would roughly double in five or six years, reaching 20 percent of the U.S. GDP by 2000. Then, by 2005, it would reach 30 percent and, five years later, more than 40 percent. As dire as these estimates sounded, they merely extended the present trajectory to its ruinous conclusion.

"If the deficit continues for a few more years," the economist wrote, "the U.S.'s foreign debt and payments of interest on it will rise to an unacceptable level and may begin to explode, imperatively demanding correction at some stage."

Professor Godley is British and perhaps that is why he was able to observe clearly—and say aloud—what so many Americans no longer seemed able to see: the emperor was not yet naked, but his pants were sliding down around his ankles. In fairness to American economists, some of them had sounded the same alarm a decade earlier when the United States was first sliding into heavy trade debts during the 1980s. Their warnings were largely ignored—at least nothing fundamental was changed in response to their outcry—so many of them fell back in silent resignation. Besides, they were accused of "crying wolf" since nothing grave seemed to happen as a result.*

As the nation failed to confront this new condition, various evasive rationales took hold instead. The annual trade deficit reached a peak in 1986 of nearly 4 percent of the overall economy and by that measure subsided in subsequent years, so it was possible to claim that this problem would eventually correct itself. Or, as many argued, the declining value of the dollar in foreign exchange would solve the problem by reducing the global prices of U.S. exports. Ten years later the dollar had declined from 250 to around 90 yen. The trade deficits endured.†

A popular argument also arose that this imbalance actually represented a healthy exchange for the U.S. economy: it meant Japanese, German and other investors were building new factories in the United States, creating jobs and productive investments for Americans. That was certainly true, but left out the troublesome matter of who would collect the profits and other returns on these investments—the "factor incomes" that had not yet turned negative when this morale-boosting rationale was offered.

Another familiar evasion, embraced by the Clinton administration, was the observation that U.S. service sectors—banking, insurance, engineering and some others—were producing a growing surplus in global trade, and, it was said, this would eventually offset the nation's deteriorating trade in manufactured goods. Service exports were indeed in surplus and growing, but this was a fanciful remedy. By 1995, the service sectors would have to quadruple their annual trade volume—right now—in order to reverse the trade deficits in real goods. This was not just unlikely, it was impossible.

In time, political discussions of the trade deficits subsided in exhaustion and elite opinion settled instead on a simpler explanation for the problem: it was Americans' profligate consumption habits—free spending and low savings and heavy indebtedness, especially the government's fiscal deficits— that explained why the United States was out of balance with the rest of the world. America was living beyond its means and an obvious solution was

---

* In the mid-1980s, the United States began borrowing more each year from over-seas than it was lending out, and this led to the general understanding that America had become a debtor nation. This was technically incorrect at the time—or at least premature—since the United States still held a positive balance of foreign assets. The United States, according to Godley, did not reach a negative net-asset posi-tion until 1988 or 1989. In any case, technical quibbles did not change the larger meaning.

† Oil imports were another major component of the trade deficits and posed another kind of threat, but since oil was traded in U.S. dollars its true price to Americans actually declined as the dollar lost foreign-exchange value. Eventually, however, oil will likely experience another price run-up and financial crisis when the producing nations try to recover the lost value of their asset.

to stop doing so. As a bookkeeping proposition, this seemed to make sense: anyone who saves more will have to borrow less.

Foreign governments regularly lectured the United States about its low savings, scolding Americans for this character weakness, and most American leaders accepted the diagnosis. The way out of the foreign-trade debt swamp was to eliminate the bloated deficits in the federal budget and encourage a higher savings rate in the private sector among both firms and families. It sounded like an accounting problem.

The problem was that reality did not cooperate with this theoretical assumption. If the theory was correct, then the trade deficits should have shrunk visibly during Bill Clinton's term since savings rose as he took early, dramatic action that substantially reduced the size of the federal deficits. Instead of subsiding, the trade deficits soared. Why? Because the American economy was growing again, coming out of the worldwide recession a bit ahead of other major economies and pulling in more imports from them. All of Clinton's celebrated activism on trade, challenging import barriers in Japan and China, promoting new trade agreements, did not alter this trend in the slightest.

The awkward fact was that across the last twenty-five years, real-world experience has revealed only one sure way to reduce the U.S. trade deficits: put the U.S. economy in recession. That perverse relationship has materialized four times since 1970: Each U.S. recession temporarily produced a surplus in its trade balance or at least sharply reduced the deficit. Each time, when the economy came out of recession, the trade deficits resumed and grew steadily, right along with the American economy. This pattern occurred in the 1970, 1974–76, 1980–82 and 1990–92 recessions. During the last down cycle in 1991 the United States created a brief, artificial current-accounts surplus by conducting a war in the Persian Gulf and persuading allies to pay for it.

Obviously, recession did not offer a satisfying solution (or a viable one unless politicians could persuade Americans to accept permanent conditions of stagnation). More to the point, the recurring pattern suggested there was a deeper structural explanation for the persistent U.S. deficits: the unbalanced behavior of trading nations themselves. If conservatives persevered in their campaign to balance the federal budget, they would encounter the same disappointment as previous strategies.

Eliminating the federal government's deficits—virtuous as that goal seemed to people—would remove several hundred billion dollars a year from aggregate demand, and that, without doubt, would also shrink the nation's trade deficit. It would also deflate the national economy—spending, incomes and profits. If Congress ever actually balanced the budget, the evasions might at last be exhausted because the trade deficits would resume just as soon as the economy recovered. People would then have to face the real source of America's growing indebtedness: its willingness to serve as the world's buyer of last resort.

Character flaws aside, the economic fact was that the United States kept the global trading system afloat by mopping up a generous share of the excess production every year. In 1980, the United States absorbed 27 percent of world vehicle exports, more than 41 percent in 1989 and then back to 23 percent by 1993. Germany, by contrast, absorbed only 8 percent and Japan, of course, a trivial share. The United States took 15 percent of world exports in office machine and telecommunications equipment in 1980 and 23 percent in 1993. It absorbed 10 percent of all steel exports, 18 percent of heavy machinery, 9 percent of chemicals.

Across the entire spectrum of production, America's trade deficits during the last decade accounted annually for 4 to 8 percent of all the merchandise exported from other nations (except during the 1990 recession, when it dipped below 3 percent). For a global marketplace burdened by oversupply, this absorption provided an essential lubricant on the margins. It relieved the tensions of market-access disputes in other countries that did not freely accept imports and it probably kept the downward pressures on prices from becoming even more severe.

To appreciate the significance, imagine that this U.S. override on global sales was eliminated abruptly. Where would foreign producers sell all those cars if the United States was unable to buy them? Or the electronics equipment? Or clothes and shoes, machine tools and chemicals?

"We are the market of last resort," said Clyde Prestowitz of the Economic Strategy Institute. "You got excess capacity and you can't sell it anyplace else? Sell it to the Americans. We are also the market that props up development. If you are China or Indonesia, Thailand or Korea, you achieve rapid economic growth by supplying the Americans. You run a trade surplus with the U.S. and that's how you earn the capital to finance the rapid growth."

Despite the many sermons about making U.S. exports more competitive in the world, the real abnormality in global trade was centered on U.S. imports—the foreign goods that freely penetrated and, in some sectors, took over America's domestic market. U.S. imports of goods accounted for 15 to 19 percent of the world's total trade (while its exports ran around 11 to 12 percent). If America's trading position had held constant since 1980, the level of its exports would not be much different fifteen years later, but the volume of its imports should have been two thirds smaller.

The heart of this abnormality was manufacturing. According to Godley, America's imports of manufactured goods (a slightly narrower definition than merchandise trade) rose from 14 percent of total U.S. manufacturing output in 1977 to 36 percent in 1993. The annual trade deficit in manufactured goods was by itself equivalent to 2.2 percent of the nation's total GDP—virtually accounting for the entire problem. Those commentators who claimed that nothing much had changed in American manufacturing were pretending that this great shift in market shares did not matter to U.S. employment and incomes, sales and profits and, ultimately, to the national balance sheet.

In the real world, it did matter. Across five centuries of capitalism, manufactured goods have always been the vital center of trade among nations. That was why poor nations struggled to attain manufacturing sectors and why developing countries protected their infant industries by refusing to buy imported goods from others. Or why the U.S. government itself subsidized technological research and overseas sales. It was also how postwar Japan went from poverty to great wealth, as other nations hoped to do themselves.

Japan was the principal source of the global system's trading imbalance, growing from its surplus of $5 billion in 1980 to $135 billion in 1995, equal to about 3 percent of its own Gross National Product. Most of that surplus—about $70 billion—was assumed by one country. A hoary joke among international economists went like this: "The trouble with the Japanese economy is that it depends on outsiders. It depends on Korea for labor, on Saudi Arabia for oil and on the United States for consumer demand."

But many other Asian nations, led by China, were following the same track, enjoying a lopsided trading relationship with America. China, as previously described, was on a path to surpass Japan in five to seven years as the leading source of U.S. trade deficits. Overall, the Asian rim's surplus with America exceeded $108 billion in 1995, yet the U.S. export market share in those countries was generally flat or falling—and far below Japan's or even Germany's.[14]

This contradiction inspired the Clinton administration to launch its aggressive salesmanship in the so-called big emerging markets, promoting U.S. companies in the developing nations that participate in the Asia-Pacific Economic Cooperation organization, or APEC. Behind the headlines, the frustrating reality was that APEC was the main problem. Following Japan's model, the APEC economies restricted imports one way or another and exported aggressively, relying mainly on U.S. buyers.

When President Clinton traveled to Indonesia for the APEC conference in the fall of 1994, he announced a grand diplomatic breakthrough: the APEC governments agreed to follow America's lead and abolish their trade barriers, fully opening up their economies. But when? Actually not for another twenty-five years. On its present course, the United States would be tapped out long before 2020, the year APEC partners have promised to adopt free trade.

As Japan dispersed its own manufacturing base across other Asian nations in order to offset the rising yen's impact on the price of its goods, the Asian trade flows became increasingly difficult to identify by national origin. Was Malaysia's growing surplus with the United States really Japan's offshore production? Did China's surge actually reflect the rush of investments from Hong Kong, Taiwan and Korea? From the American standpoint, it hardly mattered, except it was no longer sufficient to blame the Japanese for U.S. trade problems.

"It's hard to imagine the Asian nations changing their strategies when those strategies are working for them," said Robert A. Johnson, a global financier in New York. "You can't make governments switch to consumer-led economies when they have built their strength on the opposite—export-led production. Clinton hammers on the Japanese, and they keep promising to open up, but it's going to take twenty years to pull it off. Does the U.S. have twenty years? Not at its current rate of indebtedness."

Some Japanese authorities would claim I have described things upside down: It was Japanese generosity that propped up the system. Japan's surplus wealth from trade, they would say, enabled it to lend hundreds of billions back to the United States every year and keep the indebted leader upright. Certainly, if Japan and others stopped lending so heavily, the United States would abruptly be in crisis: U.S. interest rates would rise sharply and collapse the domestic economy. But America was borrowing and buying from the same people, a negative recycling of wealth that left the United States with the debts as well as the Japanese products.

Japan's perspective on this was expressed directly by its Ministry of Finance during the Bush administration when the MOF's vice minister, Makoto Utsumi, proposed a kind of truce. Japan, he suggested, would agree to hold its annual trade surplus to 2 percent of its GNP and the United States would stop complaining about Japan's closed markets. To the Americans, Utsumi's suggestion sounded like terms of surrender and they reacted angrily. But it was a revealing moment: Japan's financial leverage was enormous and growing.[15]

The peril was mutual, however. If Japan pulled the plug, then it and other trading nations would be stuck with their own problem: Where would they sell the surpluses if not to Americans? Japanese officials were not insensitive to these downside risks, and Utsumi's proposal revealed how much control they could actually exercise over their trade flows if they wished to do so. Japan understood that it must not provoke a crisis, not while America was still its most important export market.

Richard Medley, a Yale political scientist and authority on global finance and politics, explained: "One of the Japanese strategies is to keep us from doing anything rash for the next decade and a half—until they have become self-sufficient in Asia and can go on along without us."

The visible indicator of the coming crisis was the dollar's historic decline in value. The dollar could also be the mechanism that triggers it. As the United States took on billions in new foreign debt each year, the dollar's ebbing value reflected the waning relative strength of the national economy behind it. In the short term, currency values reacted to political tempests, interest rates and other transient influences, but the deeper trend was unmistakably downward. America's global purchasing power was declining with it.

Sooner or later, the dollar's value would become so diluted that foreign investors would either refuse to buy more U.S. bonds and other debt paper or else they would demand punishing interest rates in exchange. Conceivably, the dollar would also become so cheapened in foreign exchange that as this made foreign products more expensive, U.S. consumers would literally be unable to afford to buy so much from others. Either way, the consequence was the same: a flattened economy and lowering standards of living. Some economists even blandly assumed that America's coming devaluation will provide the natural resolution for the trade imbalances (though Americans were not likely to see this event as therapeutic).

But if the United States stopped buying the world's surpluses, that would not really correct the global system's underlying problem, but simply make it visible and inescapable. As exporting nations suddenly scrambled for buyers, cutting production and prices and erecting protective barriers, the shrinking marketplace could trigger a collapse of commerce.

"The trade deficits will provoke a moment when you have to say stop," Prestowitz predicted. "Nobody knows when that moment is, but the longer you postpone it, the more indebted we become. Sooner or later, we are going to have to stop importing. But the other countries are still refusing to import more. That's the point of breakdown. Sometime in the next five or ten years, we are looking at some kind of crisis."

To prevent this eventuality, the United States would have to do something "rash," both to save itself and the system. The U.S. government was not as defenseless as it appeared, but in order to act, the political order would have to acknowledge the nation's dilemma frankly and resign from the role of apostle and guarantor for the global system. In fact, American statesmen would have to invoke a forbidden word in American politics— tariffs—and be prepared to use them in the national interest.

An emergency tariff of 10 or 15 percent, designed to reduce the trade deficits over several years, would bring the abnormalities to an immediate confrontation with other trading nations and, of course, greatly upset them. But, as Professor Godley noted, import-control measures intended to correct a country's grave financial imbalances were not prohibited by GATT's international rules. Other nations have employed them. Further, if the exporting countries tried to retaliate, it was the deficit nation that would have the high ground in such a fight, as the others understood.

Only in America, and especially among the proud American establishment, the obvious remedy was regarded as unthinkable.

Bill Clinton's essential trade strategy was a hearty brand of patriotic mercantilism, dedicated to advancing the particular fortunes of America's multinational corporations by winning new markets for them. He dispatched cabinet officers to China, India, Indonesia, Malaysia and elsewhere, often accompanied by corporate CEOs, to help sell their goods. The President personally celebrated when they came home with new contracts. His trade negotiators provoked a series of dramatic showdowns with other governments, demanding that the Japanese, Chinese or others open the door to various American products.

American presidents have been doing much the same for years, albeit with less fanfare and self-congratulations. Despite its free-market ideology Ronald Reagan's administration was actually more aggressive (and successful) in defense of U.S. industrial sectors, fashioning temporary market agreements to help steel, textiles, autos, semiconductors and some others. Republicans and Democrats alike, the government took its cues in this from the major multinationals. "In our system," Commerce Undersecretary Jeffrey E. Garten confided, "the fact is, trade policy is driven by private interests."

But a provocative question was never asked: Did all this globe-trotting activity in behalf of private interests actually benefit the broader national interest? The government's salesmanship would surely be good for the companies, but was America's openhanded approach to the global system actually good for the nation and most of its citizens? In broad terms, the accumulated evidence appeared to be negative: the general stagnation of incomes and loss of high-wage jobs, the slower U.S. economic growth, the widening extremes of wealth and poverty, the nation's staggering foreign indebtedness, the general sense of insecurity and social stress. From these facts alone, it would be most difficult to demonstrate that over the last two decades globalization improved economic well-being for most Americans.

At a minimum, the facts demanded that the fundamental question be asked and the reigning assumptions reconsidered. Having launched a great industrial revolution, the United States did not have the option of withdrawing from it. These freewheeling economic forces existed independent of the progenitor, creating and destroying in wondrous ways around the world. The real question was how the United States could best cope with what it has wrought, confronting these forces in behalf of its own citizens.

The old order assumed that the fortunes of multinational firms were roughly synonymous with the nation's self-interest. Since the New Deal's liberal activism, a universal premise was implanted in American politics, shared by most conservatives, too, that government's active support for business would be an undiluted good thing for all. If enterprise prospered, the benefits flowed widely, if not uniformly, throughout the society. Clinton reiterated this premise every time he celebrated a new trade deal: exports meant more jobs for Americans, new markets meant more exports. Company by company, that was usually true, though not true when the company intended to do its production elsewhere.

The narrow logic of export promotion, however, left out the vast collateral consequences of the global system and the other offsetting losses absorbed at large, given America's passive acceptance of the imperatives to globalize. For instance, Clinton's frequent job claims were based on a crude rule of thumb about how many new jobs were created for every $1 billion in exports. But the government's own estimate kept shrinking as U.S. firms globalized their production. The Commerce Department used to claim that $1 billion of exports produced 20,000 jobs, but it had to adjust that downward as the actual American labor content in "American exports" was displaced. In Clinton's first year, Commerce officials put the number at 19,000 jobs. By 1996, it was only 14,200 jobs. If that was correct (and it probably wasn't), then one must conclude that global trade was costing Americans a net loss of two to three million jobs a year. As the frustrated President conceded, the global economy seemed to be destroying good jobs faster than he could create them.

But the economic loss was more fundamental than that. Many of the very export deals that Clinton celebrated actually required the transfer of American jobs to foreign economies—elements of the production base that were permanently ceded to other nations in order to win their sales. The government did not object to this or inquire into the long-term implications. It good-naturedly accepted the industrial migration as a positive aspect of the globalization.

Alongside the perennial trade deficits, this represented the other great force steadily weakening the American economic hegemony. The United States was not only buyer of last resort, but also the most flexible industrial economy in terms of its willingness to shut down or offload its manufacturing production. The American attitude was unique. Other nations, rich and poor, targeted manufacturing sectors and did whatever they thought necessary to develop them or hold on to them. The U.S. perspective was more global, as though it did not matter where basic industries were located so long as the corporations were competitive and prospering and exports were expanding.

In this way, America provided another crucial form of support for the global system. As other nations built new industries and overcapacity inevitably developed in those sectors, the United States took the adjustments. Not right away, of course, but over time, U.S. firms either closed out production in the face of foreign imports or began to share their production base with foreign customers and competitors. The trend was so diffuse it was difficult to see, but its importance to the system would become obvious if the United States were ever to decide it would no longer tolerate the erosion.

Notwithstanding the usual reassurances, American manufacturing was shrinking as the vital core of the U.S. economy. In 1977, its output was 20.2 percent of Gross Domestic Product; by 1993, it was 18.7 percent. If that shrinkage seemed statistically trivial, it represented millions of high-wage jobs, and, of course, manufacturing's share of output continued to fall as the U.S. defense industry was downsized. More important, as Godley pointed out, it did not reflect what America's manufacturing output might have been if the country were still relying mainly on domestically produced goods. In those terms, the United States had ceded about one third of its domestic market to foreign manufacturers over the last twenty-five years.

American firms often resisted the domestic erosion, of course, but they had the latitude for adjustment that other nations did not permit their national firms. U.S. organized labor was much weaker, as were the labor laws that, in other countries, put a high price on discarding workers by requiring companies to pay significant redundancy benefits and other social costs. Aside from the defense industry and assorted high-tech subsidies, the U.S. government was mostly indifferent to the question of industrial structure. Its occasional efforts to negotiate so-called voluntary agreements curbing imports helped to defend U.S. producers, but usually only temporarily, giving the U.S. firms time to downsize or relocate production elsewhere.

Clyde Prestowitz, whose Economic Strategy Institute speaks for U.S. multinational manufacturers, explained how these transitions typically unfolded: "Basic industries are big employers and have a big impact on trade figures so every government thinks it has to have them. So there is a proliferation of national industries and excess capacity. Once these new industries are established, they do have a lot of employment and so they can't easily lay off people—while the U.S. companies can. The voluntary import agreements are certainly ways to cope with excess capacity, but tend not to work very well because we tend not to enforce them very well.

"The implicit notion is that the Americans will adjust and so the agreements give the American companies a few years to reduce their employment. That's what usually happens."

In the world at large, the great contest among nations was for permanent shares of the emerging global industrial base. In the United States, this contest was regarded as illegitimate, offensive to the doctrine of free trade and detracting from the efficiency of the marketplace. No wonder the United States was losing its hegemony: it was targeting free trade and export growth, while the rest of the world targeted industrial base.

Against this background, the trade activism of Clinton and his predecessors seemed quite limp and sometimes even counterproductive. It assumed that sales by American multinationals would, one way or another, translate into a general benefit for the nation, but the steady globalization of the U.S. firms had created awkward contradictions and tangled national identities. What exactly was "American" now that American companies were producing in factories all over the world, often in partnership with their competitors? If free trade was a good thing, one now had to ask more precisely: good for whom?

When President Clinton promoted Boeing's aircraft sales abroad, for instance, he did not mention that, in effect, he was also championing Mitsubishi, Kawasaki and Fuji, the Japanese heavies that manufactured a substantial portion of Boeing's planes. Or that Boeing was offloading jobs from Seattle and Wichita to China as part of the deal. When U.S. Trade Representative Mickey Kantor staged a press conference to protest against Japan's closed telecommunications market, his staff had to make certain the Motorola cellular phone Kantor held aloft did not come out of one of Motorola's factories overseas.

At the auto industry's behest, the Clinton White House launched a fractious dispute with Japan over opening its domestic auto-parts market and threatened to impose selective tariffs. The logical target for tariffs was Japanese-made auto parts. But when officials suggested this, Chrysler and the other U.S. companies objected strenuously. They bought a lot of Japanese auto parts themselves. A relatively innocuous target, luxury cars, was selected instead (including Toyota's Lexus 400, made at the Tahara plant described in Chapter 6). The United States was promised a larger share of Japan's market, but no one expected much benefit to U.S. employment since the U.S. auto-parts producers were themselves already on the move to Asia —both to low-wage China and high-wage Japan.[16]

In early 1995, Clinton claimed an important victory for the "intellectual property rights" of capital when the Chinese government agreed to shut down the notorious knockoff factories that churned out millions of illicit compact discs, pirated from the American music and film industries. Jack Valenti, president of the Motion Picture Association, promptly announced that American companies would probably buy some of the outlaw factories and start producing CDs in China themselves. Japan's Mitsubishi became the first company to do that. Thus, a new opening for capital had little meaning for American labor. In any case, the Chinese did not enforce the agreement, the pirate plants kept operating and, a year later, the U.S. government had to threaten again to impose penalty tariffs.[17]

The Clinton administration was faced with a more excruciating question of loyalties in the contest among telecommunications giants to win the phone franchise in China's burgeoning market. Northern Telecom, a Canadian firm, sought U.S. support for its bid and promised to manufacture the hardware in its U.S. factories. AT&T would make no such promise, but it was an American company (and, unlike Northern Telecom, had a unionized workforce). The U.S. government backed AT&T as the American entry, but AT&T won by agreeing to build two new factories for advanced switching equipment, a semiconductor plant and a branch of Bell Laboratories— all in China.[18]

The question of "American-made" has become ludicrously complicated and subject to endless manipulation. To avoid federal fuel-efficiency standards, Ford twice switched the "citizenship" of its Crown Victoria and Mercury Grand Marquis models back and forth between Canada and the United States by shifting component production, including to an axle plant in Mexico. One year the cars were "domestic" and the next year they were "imports." The Commerce Department issued a NAFTA advisory bulletin that, among other things, instructed firms on how to swap internal parts of a hair dryer to qualify it as duty-free "North American"—that is, 50 percent made in Canada, Mexico or the United States.

In the U.S. multinational perspective, questions of "local content" were regarded as remnants of a narrow-minded nationalism—impediments thrown in the path of a modernizing world by retrograde politicians. At the U.S. Export-Import Bank, an agency that underwrites billions of dollars of export deals with its subsidized financing, major multinationals launched an insider campaign to loosen—or, better yet, abolish—the "local content" requirements on the bank's loans and guarantees. If General Electric, IBM, Caterpillar or AT&T needed cheap, taxpayer-financed loans to compete successfully for global sales, why should they be hampered by petty inquiries about where their products were made?

The original idea of the Ex-Im Bank when it was created in 1934 was, of course, to promote domestic employment, and for many years the government's cheaper credit was available only for exports that were 100 percent made in America. In 1987, under pressure from the "exporting community," the Ex-Im Bank agreed to permit 15 percent foreign content in the products and adopted a sliding scale that permitted some government subsidy up to 50 percent foreign-made. In 1995, the major multinationals came back, demanding even more latitude to produce their goods overseas, while still relying on U.S. taxpayers to finance their sales.[19]

A revealing exchange occurred when the Ex-Im Bank convened an advisory committee in July 1995 to examine the question. A representative from ABB, a Swiss multinational that manufactures power turbines at its U.S. subsidiary, urged that greater foreign content be allowed since the company had to get components from the cheapest sources worldwide to win contracts. General Electric agreed. Caterpillar said the United States was only hurting itself since other nations like Japan had more flexible rules. An AT&T manager argued that the bank's concerns about domestic content were obsolete. The United States was in a transitional stage, he explained, deindustrializing and becoming a service economy, so American companies naturally had to rely on foreign producers.

But the labor representatives at the table asked: How was this change supposed to support American jobs? And wouldn't relaxing U.S. content rules make it more inviting for the companies to shift their production offshore? In fact, if the multinationals chose to manufacture their U.S. "exports" in other countries, why should American taxpayers help them at all? The response that globalization and deindustrialization were inevitable was not much of an answer.

In the global perspective, the very idea of national "exports" and "imports" was regarded as antiquated. After all, 40 percent or more of global trade was conducted intrafirm, not in open markets among nations. Indeed, it was even argued by some economists and corporate leaders that the "national" trade deficits no longer mattered either. This line of reasoning was especially popular among forward thinkers in Japan, though they did not explain why Japan insisted on running huge "national" trade surpluses if these no longer mattered to anyone.

For instance, Kenichi Ohmae, author of *The Borderless World* and a celebrated consultant to multinationals with McKinsey & Company, wrote in the *Japan Times:* "In the borderless world, trade statistics are very misleading. Successful American companies are all over Asia, and they don't care if they make products in the U.S. and export to Japan. They *are* in Japan, either producing in Japan and/or Asia, or licensing their partners to do so there. . . . Trade negotiations are being pushed by special interest groups and political campaign managers." [20]

From the point of view of the U.S. multinationals, America's trade deficits really didn't matter. A sale was a sale, regardless, whether it came from a domestic or foreign factory, whether it was booked as an export or an import. If one accepted their perspective, then the United States looked much stronger since American firms were more widely dispersed than foreign firms. Walter Wriston, former CEO of Citibank, pointed out that 1,300 American and European companies operated in Japan, with sales totaling almost 11 percent of Japan's GNP, only this production did not appear in trade statistics. A British economist, DeAnne Julius of Royal Dutch Shell, argued that, if trade accounting was done according to the commercial flows of the globalized firms instead of the country, then America actually enjoyed a huge surplus "on an ownership basis." [21]

But which Americans were the owners? The logic seemed suspect as soon as one asked that question (the argument was nonetheless being popularized among American elites by such influential voices as the *Wall Street Journal*). The foreign trade indebtedness that the United States has accumulated would not be paid by the stockholders of Boeing or General Electric or IBM, but by Americans generally. In another sense, it was already being paid by American workers who experienced lost jobs or shrunken wages. Global firms might escape from the national borders, but debtors and workers would not.

A divisive political question was embedded in the facile argument about national trade—the same threatening question that lurked, more broadly, in the U.S. government's posture toward the global system. Whose interests was the government defending? Julius acknowledged the dilemma when she wrote: "In any fundamental sense, only people have nationalities." To resolve the question, she suggested, policy makers would have to define the nationality of global firms in terms of who benefited from their success. Was their nationality defined by their stockholders or their employees? Was it the country where the firm was chartered or the nation where it produced most of its goods, sales and profit?

"An Anglo-Saxon economist would choose the nationality of its shareholders as the best criterion," Julius observed. "A German or Japanese economist—and most politicians—would prefer the nationality of its workforce."

Crudely stated, the globalizing of production subverted the comfortable assumptions of the old order and asked the U.S. government to choose: Was it defending workers or stockholders, wage incomes or profits? Any government, of course, would insist it was doing both—and must do both for prosperity's sake—but the question of priorities was crucial because it would define what a nation expected of its global firms. The American government simply ducked the question, pretending that this divergence of economic interests had not occurred.

Elsewhere in the world, the question was always asked. From Germany and Sweden to Japan, the assumption in most advanced economies was that their multinationals would do their best to protect the home base of employment, even if they had to disperse some production. The social confidence in those other countries was weakening visibly as global pressures increased on their firms, but their political bonds governing corporate obligations were still much stronger; so was the vigorous oversight by government and organized labor. Public confidence in America's multinationals eroded dramatically as major firms briskly dismissed home loyalty as an outmoded concept.

General Electric tripled its revenues and profits during the last fifteen years, while it shrank its worldwide workforce from 435,000 to 220,000. In the last decade, its U.S. employment fell from 243,000 to 150,000, while offshore it expanded modestly. GE not only became smaller and more profitable, but as Executive Vice President Frank P. Doyle bluntly acknowledged: "We did a lot of violence to the expectations of the American workforce." Other firms followed GE's stern example and "did violence" of their own to the social fabric. When IBM invoked the cost-cutting imperatives as the reason for discarding 75,000 or more U.S. employees, it did not mention that it was simultaneously increasing its employment in Japan, despite the higher wage levels there.[22]

The hard, plain truth was that America's multinationals were not going to save the American economy, and neither were exports. U.S. exporting was, in fact, highly concentrated among relatively few firms—about half of the volume came from only 100 companies, 80 percent from some 250 firms. The top 15 exporting firms—names like GE, GM, Boeing, IBM—were in a class by themselves and accounted for nearly one quarter of all U.S. manufacturing exports. It was those same top firms, with a handful of exceptions, who were doing the most "violence" to U.S. employment. General Motors, the Number One U.S. exporter, shrank from 559,000 to 314,000 American employees during the last decade. Boeing, despite its great success selling airliners to Asia, downsized its workforce by one third —60,000 jobs since 1989. IBM eliminated 132,000 people, more than half of its American workforce, and by 1995 was a truly global firm, with more employees overseas than at home.

During my travels I encountered many American managers and executives, most of whom were smart, engaging, helpful people. Without badgering them, I usually asked how they felt about what was happening to the workforce back home. A few expressed genuine anguish and worried aloud about the future of America's middle class, given the lost jobs and deteriorating incomes. Most of them, I have to report, did not seem especially concerned or sympathetic. They shrugged and repeated bromides about the inevitability of the global economy or clichés about lazy, overpaid American workers and the need for job training.

Training for what? Not manufacturing, as the manager from Ford told me on the plane from Shanghai. Those jobs were going or already gone. People would have to do services, learn computers or something, he wasn't sure what. If the peasants cannot buy bread, let them eat cake. If Americans cannot make steel or cars or aircraft, let them be computer engineers.

In fairness, what sounded like crass indifference may have been only an informed fatalism. Most of these managers probably did not spend much time thinking about the larger social problem at home because, in truth, there was not much they could do about it as individuals. They were in China or Malaysia or Eastern Europe to cope with the new global realities in behalf of their own firms; they would succeed or fail as individuals based on whether their companies survived and flourished, not on what happened to the American prosperity at large. Living daily with the full force of the revolution probably made it harder to imagine alternatives or that the United States could change its course. Besides, some manufacturing sectors had tried a decade or two earlier to alert Americans and rally political support to defend American manufacturing but, for various reasons, failed. So now they were going global themselves, resigned to the consequences.

Back in Washington, the fatalism—or indifference—influenced government policy. Though it was seldom stated aloud for obvious reasons, there was a widespread, implicit acceptance of the notion that the U.S. economy will simply evolve to nonmanufacturing endeavors and that it would be futile to resist. In the bargaining strategy for GATT and other agreements, both Clinton and Bush put their real muscle behind banking and other service sectors, not manufacturing. The "information revolution," it was said, would create the good, new jobs to replace the dirty, old factory jobs. Americans needed only to get smarter and prepare themselves for this bright future.

The idea of a "postindustrial society" was appealing (the concept has been around for nearly forty years), and perhaps someday, over several generations, it would materialize. That time was not at hand. In the here and now, people still drove cars and consumed myriad other manufactured goods, and their overall economic well-being was still directly tied to where those things were made. Old-fashioned as it might sound to some, there were no societies prospering in global trade that did not rely upon manufacturing as their vital core. For good reason: 100 jobs in manufacturing sectors, on average, created another 422 jobs around them. Personal and business services created only 147. Retail trade created only 94. Despite the efficiencies of modernized production, mass employment in manufacturing was not soon going to disappear as agriculture's had a century before. But it was relocating.[23]

The illusion that the cleaner "brain work" of new high-tech ventures would somehow solve the U.S. wage and employment problems was also alluring, though quite dubious against the present facts. The "information highway" of new media interconnections created hundreds of thousands of jobs, but it was destroying old, good jobs in telecommunications at almost the same pace. The government projections that predicted millions of new jobs from these technologies were based on the same theoretical formulas that promised average families $1,700 a year from GATT.

Microsoft, the computer software producer, was celebrated by the press as a fabulously successful company (and it has made its owner fabulously rich), but Microsoft employed 15,000 people. It was smaller than Bethlehem Steel, which, of course, was a shadow of its old self. It was twenty times smaller than the Ford Motor Company, which itself had shed thousands of redundant workers. Anyway, as we have seen, Indian engineers can design computer software about as well as Americans; so can Malaysians, Chinese and many other peoples. That is the wonder of this revolution and also its dreadfulness.

If America expects to lead the world into the future, it will have to get its own accounts straightened out first. The largest political burden— reordering domestic economic priorities and restoring greater equity among citizens—does not really involve the rest of the world (though, as we explore later on, Americans could learn useful insights by examining the social understandings in other nations). The instability of U.S. politics revolves around many stressful questions, but the central one is at present unfashionable: economic inequality. Until American politics confronts that subject again, the various forms of social deterioration and conflict are sure to continue.

In the global system, the United States faces two essential tasks: First, it must bring a halt to the unbalanced trade that is draining national wealth. Second, the government must shift its primary focus to defending the U.S. industrial structure and employment, not the U.S. multinationals themselves. On both fronts, the status quo is not sustainable. Yet both of these goals can be mutually reinforcing: confronting the persistent trade imbalances would enhance domestic employment as well as U.S. producers, and at the same time it could turn the global system in positive directions— away from the approaching cliff.

U.S. multinationals may appear powerful and arrogant, but as I have tried to demonstrate, they are merely responding to the real imperatives of the present system, doing what they think is necessary to survive. Thus, their behavior is not likely to change unless the risks and incentives are altered for them in the system itself. Foreign producers, likewise, are pursuing their own self-interested strategies within the context of what the present system allows trading nations to do. Neither firms nor foreign nations are going to behave much differently until the United States confronts the weaknesses in its own dogma.

If the U.S. government were to decide that, rhetoric aside, its economic strategies really will be focused first on domestic employment and the industrial base, then it must work out a new, more reliable relationship with its own global firms as well as foreign ones. This would mean imposing domestic obligations on business enterprise, commitments that are now so easily evaded. The U.S. government would ask questions about the balance of their capital investments at home and abroad. It would intervene when portions of the U.S. industrial structure are simply traded away for exports sales.

A purposeful politics would focus less on the fortunes of the multinationals and more on reconstructing the domestic economic pillars for work and wages. As that implies, a reexamination of corporate subsidies and the tax code is the place to start. It makes no sense for American taxpayers to subsidize the dismantling of their own industrial base or to provide various tax breaks to support the balance sheets of companies determined to globalize their employment base. If the multinational firms feel they are unable to make concrete commitments to the country, then they should also be freed of the generous financial support they draw from the government and taxpayers. If the Export-Import Bank cannot learn to uphold this distinction, then it ought to be abolished.

In the American context, these ideas sound quite radical and business would naturally mobilize fierce political resistance to them.* Yet I am confident that if such domestic requirements existed, U.S. multinationals would quickly adapt to them. Why do I think that? Because this is what the companies already do elsewhere in the world in order to do business. What I have sketched in crude outline are merely the operating social principles that, directly or implicitly, govern commerce in other trading nations, rich and poor. One way or another, nations impose these domestic economic requirements directly and global companies comply with them—indeed, even claim it would be wrong for them to resist the local practices. Only in America is this regarded as forbidden.

In the real world, business enterprise is relentlessly practical, more realist than ideological. If Malaysia wants ethnic balance in Motorola's

---

* I enumerate these ideas because I think they are right, not because I have any illusions about the political order's willingness to address them. These measures all lie beyond the realm of conventional thinking, and even if most Americans accepted them as plausible they would still face the concentrated political power of major corporations and finance. The multinationals, I believe, have made themselves quite vulnerable to popular political assault by their disregard for domestic obligations, but they still dominate America's decayed democracy. See my previous book, Who Will Tell the People (New York: Simon & Schuster, 1992).

workforce, then Motorola does affirmative action. If Germany expects General Motors to deal with elected representatives from its labor force, then GM accepts a works council. If China wants to make world-class aircraft, then Boeing gives it a piece of the action. Political demands, not market forces, produce these concessions. If American companies are willing to operate factories where their workers are policed by Communist cadres, if they accede to foreign demands for certain levels of investment, employment and output, then they can surely learn to deal fairly with their own native land. Patriotism aside, the U.S. remains, despite its troubles, the richest, largest market in the world. Every global producer understands that, but U.S. firms seem to take it for granted.

These measures would not derail the revolution, though they might help to stabilize it. Nor would this approach solve all of America's underlying economic problems. The shifting of wealth and other great transformations under way are profound historic forces and, as I have said, should be generally positive for the world at large. But for the United States, even if one accepts the most optimistic understanding of where the revolution is headed, the future means one generation and, more likely, two generations in which masses of Americans face faltering incomes and insecure employment opportunities. To prevent this "transition" from turning into ugly class conflicts and political upheaval, the society will have to embrace active measures to create employment and support wages.

More important, America will have to start thinking more concretely about what it wants the distant future to look like. If the nation decided, for instance, that its goal was restoring domestic economic pillars, it could quickly set about developing the priorities and projects to achieve that. Beyond the present, it could experiment inventively with the long-term social possibilities offered by new technologies, exploring beyond the conventional ideas that define work and consumption. What is missing is not so much plans, but a serious vision. America needs what so many struggling poor nations have developed—its own *"Wawasan 2020."*

American prospects aside, if I am right about the underlying imperatives, our wondrous machine of global industrial revolution is, indeed, headed toward some kind of abyss. The paradox is that, by helping itself, the United States might actually help the global system avert disaster. Of course, other nations will not see it that way, at least not initially. Imposing emergency tariffs to staunch the U.S. trade deficits would be extremely upsetting to them, but also greatly disruptive for the U.S. economy, since American production and consumption are now so dependent on imports. Immediate sacrifices would be felt by all. The only justification for taking such an extreme step is the consequences of doing nothing.

The global system is astride a great fault line: The wondrous new technologies and globalizing strategies are able to produce an abundance of goods, but fail to generate the consumer incomes sufficient to buy them. This is true with or without America's role as the buyer-debtor, but it becomes even more critical as America's consumption power erodes further. Shipping high-wage jobs to low-wage economies has obvious, immediate economic benefits. But, roughly speaking, it also replaces high-wage consumers with low-wage ones. That exchange is debilitating for the entire system.

Automobiles, once again, provide a simple illustration of the general problem. When U.S. auto companies downgraded their expectations for the U.S. market, they were acknowledging that the industry's oversupply problem was even larger than they had thought—a fact that will ripple through every economy that produces cars. If Americans must consume fewer cars and trucks, what happens to the 4.5 million vehicles that German, Japanese, Swedish and Korean producers have targeted for the U.S. market? They can cut production or prices and perhaps hang on to U.S. sales, but someone somewhere has to lose out.

America's wage problem, in other words, translates eventually into its export problem and the global system's problem of excess supply, inadequate demand. The same erosion of consumer demand is under way less dramatically in other advanced economies, whether it is revealed as declining wages or permanent mass unemployment. Amid the exciting news of global ventures and new markets, it is difficult for many informed people to take this crisis seriously, just as smart people blithely dismissed the same reality during the 1920s. After 1929 they began to understand it better.

"We are headed for an implosion," Christopher Whalen, a conservative financial economist in Washington, predicted. "If you keep lowering and lowering wages in advanced countries, who's going to buy all this stuff? You look around and all you can see is surplus labor and surplus goods. What we don't have is enough incomes. But the only way people find out there are too many factories is when they wake up one morning and their orders are falling. If this keeps up, we're going to face a lack of demand that's worse than the 1930s."

American intervention with emergency tariffs would compel other producing nations to face this reality and begin adjusting—before an implosion is upon them. As Godley has estimated, a 10 percent general tariff would yield $50 billion to $60 billion in new revenue that the government could devote to reducing taxes or increasing spending, either way stimulating the economy instead of depressing it. If the United States wished to establish its higher motives, it could even rebate much of the tariff revenue back to poorer nations, demonstrating America's continuing commitment to their development while it also curbs the egregious trading practices.

An alternative approach, proposed in the 1980s by the late Eliot Janeway, would target the tariffs on specific sectors and those foreign producers whose imports exceed 25 percent of the domestic production. This would send a more focused message—the United States intends to defend its manufacturing sectors against predatory imports—and it would also penalize the right parties (though it would also probably violate GATT rules). "The practicalities suggest that America need only set equitable terms for buying access to sell goods in her market and the world will willingly meet them," Janeway wrote.[24]

Expressed in political terms, the great fault line in the global system is the collision between two different kinds of capitalism—the American model and the Japanese model. Leaving aside ideological objections, the central flaw in the Japanese approach to global trade is that it can function brilliantly for one nation and even for many smaller nations that copy it, but it cannot work if everyone tries to do the same thing. It does not take anything away from Japan's manufacturing excellence to observe that its economic strategy requires a loser somewhere—wealthy, willing buyers who absorb its surpluses year after year, without being able to sell equivalent goods in return.

As a simple matter of logic, a few can play this zero-sum game quite successfully, but if every nation tries to play, the whole game stops. The negative logic in the present system will become transparent once the United States forcefully asserts itself. Many Japanese are no doubt sympathetic and sincerely believe that their economy should become a greater consumer of the world's goods, but the problem is now much larger than Japan. Other Asian nations, led by China and Korea, follow the same strategy, and as their production expands, the abnormal flows will intensify, not just for the United States but for Europe as well. Someday even Japan may experience the deleterious effects of allowing unbalanced trade.

"It is a well-kept secret," Godley wrote, "that the theory of international trade—the entire story about the benefits every country can gain by exchanging its goods with other countries—depends upon the assumptions: a) that trade between countries is balanced and b) that trade does not alter the level of employment or unemployment. . . . International trade, if it is endemically unbalanced, threatens to impart a disinflationary shock to the U.S. economy which would cause severe unemployment and the shock would then be transmitted to the rest of the world."

Thus, by defending itself, the United States would be defending its own basic conviction that the global system is supposed to work to everyone's benefit. That is the American model, but it can be made to work only if everyone buys in on more or less the same terms. Once nations are persuaded to cross that bridge, then they might be able to address together the underlying problem of inadequate demand.

A shift in thinking to the problem of demand would require a great array of different policies, but starts with the understanding that wages and employment, on both ends of the global economy, are central to the system's long-term health. Excess supply can be controlled in different ways, but that is the negative method of achieving a balance, essentially by shutting down production. The much more positive approach is to bolster worldwide demand.

To promote greater consumption, advanced economies would have to return to some old questions (and unfashionable doctrines) about how to foster greater growth and distribute incomes across a broader front. In the developing economies, this means "bringing the bottom up" as rapidly as possible, more systematically than commerce or capital would like. Among other things, it means freeing workers to demand a larger share of the returns from their burgeoning economies. In broader terms, it is the imbalance of returns between capital and labor that has to be redressed everywhere, among rich and poor nations.

To state the matter clearly makes plain the formidable reasons the problem is not addressed: it would require governments to confront the free-running industrial revolution and try to moderate its course. No nation, including the United States, yet has the will to stake out such a provocative position. In the midst of the storm, governments, like people and enterprises, hunker down and hope that it passes.

But another imposing barrier also stands in the way: finance capital itself. Neither the United States nor others could undertake the actions I have described unless they are also prepared simultaneously to reassert control over unregulated global capital. The industrial multinationals are the main engines of the revolution, but they themselves are supervised and buffeted by a higher order of power, finance and financial markets. In the next section, we examine the realm of finance capital, where the global revolution finds its purest expression.

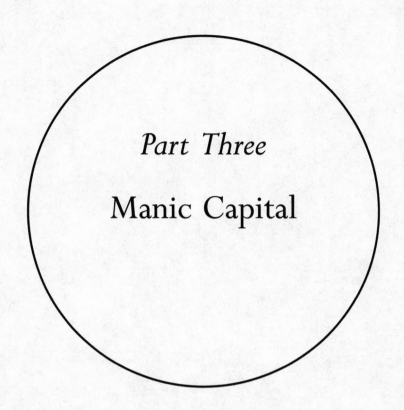

Part Three

Manic Capital

Eleven

The Alchemists

IN THE HISTORY of capitalism's long expansionary cycles, it is finance capital that usually rules in the final stage, displacing the inventors and industrialists who launched the era, eclipsing the power of governments to manage the course of economic events. As capital owners and financial markets accumulate greater girth and a dominating influence, their search for higher returns becomes increasingly purified in purpose—detached from social concerns and abstracted from the practical realities of commerce. In this atmosphere, investors develop rising expectations of what their invested savings ought to earn and the rising prices in financial markets gradually diverge from the underlying economic reality. Since returns on capital are rising faster than the productive output that must pay them, the process imposes greater and greater burdens on commerce and societies—debt obligations that cannot possibly be fulfilled by the future and, sooner or later, must be liquidated, written off or forgiven.

Amid the glow of personal accumulation, this divergence is difficult for individual investors to see. Instead, they plunge forward optimistically, embracing new and more speculative opportunities despite occasional evidence that something may be awry. A period of manic investing typically unfolds at this point, as masses of investors, large and small, rush this way and that in their search. Their enthusiasm is interrupted now and then by sudden disappointments that set off panics and collapsing financial prices, but the sheer energy of amassed wealth pushes forward, nonetheless. And finance becomes further unhinged from reality.

Across many centuries, this story of finance capital's capacity to become deranged in pursuit of higher returns has played out again and again in different forms of manias and crashes. Eventually, as history informs us, the disorders may be corrected in a grim, violent manner—a great war or economic depression. Those events will destroy financial capital on a massive scale and thereby restore a balance between the demands of old wealth and the needs of new productive enterprise. This sort of resolution produces vast human suffering and political upheavals, of course, but also clears the way for capitalism's next expansive era.

The present industrial revolution of "one world" has now reached this pathological stage. The divergence between financial values and real economic activity is visible and growing. It invites another disastrous climax, though it does not necessarily guarantee that this will occur. The symptoms of disorder can be glimpsed in the recurring dramas of financial-market "disturbances," in the spectacular debt failures and in the continuing gyrations of money values that regularly destabilize global commerce and national economies.

These events produce temporary alarms, but are seldom perceived as an ominous pattern. The power shift to finance capital and the financial markets' divergence from reality are masked by complexity, but also by a popular conviction that the occasional calamities can be explained away as the individual "errors" of investors or governments. This explanation becomes more tenuous as the pattern of financial shocks extends and accelerates. The flavor of this systemic instability is suggested by simply listing some of the better-known events:

In 1982, Mexico, Argentina, Brazil and more than a dozen other developing nations virtually defaulted on their massive debts to foreign banks. Yet, a decade later, the external indebtedness of all developing nations had more than doubled. In 1987, the American stock market crashed from a peak of 2,700 in the Dow-Jones industrial average to a low of 1,700, and European exchanges crashed with it. The Dow-Jones was back up at new record levels, around 4,800, by late 1995, then surged within a year to reach 6,000. This implied that, in the judgment of investors, the value of these American companies more than tripled in less than a decade.

In 1989, Japan's fabulous "bubble economy" of inflated financial values collapsed. In their freewheeling borrowing and lending, investors had valued Japanese real estate as worth more than all of North America. Simultaneously, the U.S. government began expending $150 billion to liquidate the failed investments generated by the savings and loan industry, plus many billions more to clean up the failures of major commercial banks. In 1992, the cumulative power of financial-market speculators successfully attacked the British pound and Italian lira, forcing the governments to devalue their currencies. The following year a similar assault on the French franc and other currencies blew apart Europe's currency-exchange system, the supposed foundation for European economic union.

Early in 1994, an abrupt worldwide sell-off of government bonds, the debt paper issued by the United States and other major nations, produced a global crash in bond prices and the equivalent surge in long-term interest rates. In early 1995, Mexico failed again and its new financial collapse touched off a worldwide panic of investors, rushing to get their money out of other emerging markets. Meanwhile, the world's new financial citadel, Japan, was ensnared in a far graver crisis of deflation—falling prices and failing debt on a massive scale. Some of the world's largest banks struggled to contain an accumulation of bad loans, conservatively estimated at $400 billion to $500 billion.

These scattered crises, though each did involve its own peculiar errors and misapprehensions, are all expressions of the deeper disorder, but not its cause. This section on finance capital sets out to examine some of these episodes and explain the implications. Our focus shifts from industrial enterprise to the commanding heights of global finance, the revolutionary dynamics that both drive the globalization and discipline the global system. While great new fortunes are being amassed, free-running capital is in the process of destabilizing its own revolution.

This chapter delineates the shift of power from government to finance and explains how deregulated financial markets have produced a restless core in the world's economic instabilities—the unreliability of money itself. Chapter 12 explores how global finance governs developing nations and asks whether unregulated capital enables poorer nations to become less poor or may actually prevent them from doing so. The following chapter explains the critical financial dilemma confronting the advanced economies, including the United States, as they become increasingly indebted, yet are blocked by financial markets from achieving the faster economic growth that might allow them to dig out. As their predicament deepens, it could well become the trigger for financial reckoning. The concluding chapter of this section offers a panoramic vision of how timely reforms by leading governments—the recontrol of capital—could avert disaster and redirect the global industrial system toward a more positive path.

First, to understand what is unfolding, it helps to put aside intuitive reactions such as blaming the greed of financiers or rich people. Greed is abundantly present in financial markets, certainly; so is the "money fever" that grips some young traders and leads to the ruinous speculations that can wreck venerable financial institutions. The personal dramas of reckless investors, employing phony accounting or exotic financial instruments like derivatives to temporarily defy gravity, do reflect the frenzy of money-seeking that is tolerated, even admired, in the deregulated financial system. But these stories are essentially the froth on top of more fundamental problems.

Furthermore, it is essential to start with a clear understanding of what capital is and how it interacts with financial markets. Technical distinctions aside, capital is basically the money accumulated from past enterprise, savings from profits or wages, the stored wealth that is available to finance new enterprise. Physical capital exists as factories and machines; finance capital exists as wealth invested in enterprise through loans or stock shares or other financial instruments. This exchange—the past lending to the future, old money investing in new ventures—is the energy core of capitalism, the transaction across time that enables the creation of multiplying new wealth. Karl Marx described capital derisively as the "accumulated labor" owned by the bourgeoisie, as opposed to the more virtuous "living labor" of the working class. The distinction still has economic meaning, but by the late twentieth century, social categories have become a bit scrambled. Capital owners and labor, finance and industry have competing interests, but, in many instances, the same people can be found on both sides of these divisions. Industry, for instance, is a major participant in finance capital, though it also undergoes the financial markets' scrutiny and discipline.

Aggregate wealth remains dramatically concentrated among relatively few people, especially in the United States, where the distribution of wealth is becoming even more lopsided. Still, it is also true that even the working class might hold a small stake in capitalist enterprise if the family has acquired net savings or a pension. Either of those will draw income from the same exchange that wealthy capitalists undertake on a monumental scale.

In fact, one ominous symptom of the present disorder is that the small holders are now also heavily committed to the global search for higher returns. Millions of Americans, by taking family savings out of government-insured bank deposits and consigning their money to mutual funds, are able to share in the fantastic returns from emerging markets. The middle class now has hundreds of billions of its savings roaming the world, too, perhaps without fully appreciating the risk exposure. Mutual funds, unlike commercial banks, are not federally insured; the losses will be fully absorbed by the investors themselves, not the financial intermediary. In financial-market history, when people of modest means become swept up in the speculation, it usually means that a climax is approaching.

Financial assets, whether they are corporate stocks or government bonds or more esoteric instruments, are all essentially claims on the future —literally pieces of paper invested with value because they promise income from future economic activity, either interest payments on loans or dividends from business or, better still, an appreciated price when the assets are sold. Financial markets, in effect, reprice the value of these assets every day as they trade them in huge volumes among buyers and sellers.

Thus, the assumed value of the capital regularly changes once it is invested in finance—expands or shrinks as the marketplace determines new prices for financial assets, the bonds or stocks. Rising financial prices are a crude expression of investors' rising optimism about the future's economic activity, though subject to reversal the next day if the news turns bad. An investor may determine each day how much his holdings are worth from the market prices, but this wealth exists more as potential than reality.

It is this basic elasticity in the value of financial assets that allows financial markets, in extreme circumstances, to become unhinged from the tangible realities of commerce. To offer a simple example of how this can happen, imagine a banker who lends a real estate developer several million dollars to build a shopping center at a busy crossroads. The center thrives and another banker and developer decide to do the same, then another and another. Soon, there are too many stores at the same location and some of them are empty and all of the shopping centers are suffering depressed sales—including the original one. As the revenues disappoint the original projections, some of the enterprises are unable to keep up with their loan payments and some perhaps default. At that point, the market value of the original bank loans has to be marked down, perhaps even written off as a dead loss.

The same dynamic applies, more complexly, to the finance capital invested in corporations, either through the purchase of equity shares of ownership or through lending in the form of bonds and other kinds of credit. False assumptions about the future may look right to investors in the moment, or even for many months and years; their projections may also be confirmed for a time by the financial markets that price these financial assets in the daily buying and selling. But sooner or later wrong assumptions will have to confront the concrete reality—if the enterprises do not yield the expected profits or the debtors fail.

When that occurs, the asset prices fall and the inflated financial value of the invested capital simply evaporates. Judgments are reversed and prices are marked down, deflated—perhaps suddenly and violently if the new realism shatters an entire market's confidence. The physical property—factories or office buildings and shopping centers—continues to exist, of course, but its supposed future worth as an income-producing asset is gone. A market crash, in other words, is the abrupt deflation of prices and of misplaced hopes.

If financial prices are really estimates of the future, then, of course, they can never be fully rational or scientific despite the dense analytical techniques of investors, traders and economists. The financial markets that make these estimates, in fact, behave like crowds—sometimes even like mobs—since the participants must always necessarily react to each other as well as to the economic facts. The herd of investors drives the price changes, and even if a smart trader knows the herd is mistaken, he must still respect its behavior since its actions will alter the presumed value of his assets, too.

This ancient truth about financial markets—they are moody crowds, not scientists—has been well chronicled by economic historians describing history's great manias and crashes, and is fully understood by astute market players. Yet it is strangely neglected by the economic orthodoxy of free markets. Academic economists who exalt the marketplace as rational are typically enthralled by the mathematical beauty of the intricate financial flows and the abstract perfection they see in the market's price-setting mechanism (perhaps because these functions fit so neatly with the algebraic methodologies that dominate their discipline). Financial markets, meanwhile, still behave like crowds and still get things wrong about the future, sometimes disastrously wrong if they are misled by the force of their own shared enthusiasms.[1]

The crucial fact about present conditions is that these crowds have become much more powerful in economic life. The aggregate force of global financial markets has expanded enormously during the last generation, as major governments removed national controls on finance capital. But finance gathered strength for a more fundamental reason: financial assets are growing in value much faster than everything else—explosively faster. According to one estimate by McKinsey & Company, a global consulting firm to multinational banks and businesses, the total stock of financial assets from advanced nations expanded in value by 6 percent a year from 1980 to 1992, more than twice as fast as the underlying economies were growing.

Finance has become more dominant in the economic sphere simply because it grew larger in size relative to everything else. By 1992, financial assets from the advanced nations of the Organization for Economic Cooperation and Development totaled $35 trillion, double the economic output of those countries. McKinsey bullishly predicts that the total financial stock will reach $53 trillion, in constant dollars, by the year 2000—that is, triple the economic output of those economies. By McKinsey's estimate, financial assets that are now thirteen times the size of these nations' exports will soon become nineteen times larger.[2]

These statistics suggest the great divergence that is under way in the global system. Financial prices, whether one thinks they are sound or illusory, are rising much faster than the collective economic activity upon which they are presumably based. To put it another way, finance appears to be extremely optimistic about the future, judging from the trend lines of financial prices. At least, it thinks its own invested hopes will be realized.

Rising prices are only part of the explanation for the growing girth of financial assets. A basic law of physics is also asserting itself in capitalism, as it has before in history: the longer an expansionary era continues without the disastrous interruptions of war or depression, the larger the gross pool of accumulated savings will become in relation to the productive economy. In other words, a period of long-running peace and prosperity inevitably feeds the imbalance by piling up a greater and greater store of "accumulated labor." This should be cause for celebration, not gloom.

Yet, as the savings from past enterprise accumulate and flow into new financial assets, the rate of new capital investments in those same advanced economies—new factories and other productive projects—has actually declined somewhat. Those same nations, meanwhile, are confronted with their own growing indebtedness. At a minimum, the optimism expressed in the financial values has not as yet been realized by others. In fact, in contrast to the financial optimism, the overall performance in the real economies of productive commerce has been persistently disappointing—expanding much more slowly in the advanced nations. That does not by itself prove the optimism is mistaken about the future, but it ought to invite doubts.

The fastest and largest component in the growth of global financial assets is debt, especially government debt. Capital is lending to enterprise and national governments of nearly every major economy to finance their deepening indebtedness. Across the OECD countries the stock of government debt grew at 9 percent a year from 1980 to 1992—more than three times faster than their economic output. As slower growth persists, tax revenues repeatedly fail to match the governments' spending commitments so they borrow to cover their deficits. The process of compounding debt is by now quite familiar to Americans, though they perhaps do not realize the same thing is occurring in all of the major industrial nations, even now Japan.

Something has to give: any nation (or individual or firm) that borrows faster than it creates the new productive base to pay for the loans is in trouble. When many wealthy nations are doing this at once, the system is in trouble. Chapter 13 returns to this aspect of financial disorder and explains why the obvious challenge of cutting budget deficits does not promise a genuine solution to the larger economic problem. For now, the point is this: somebody's expectations about the future are wrong and bound to be disappointed.

The evidence of recent years—the recurring bubbles of private and public debt that go bad and abruptly collapse—strongly suggests that it is finance capital that is overreaching reality. In the previous section, we identified some fundamental explanations for this: The central one is the global revolution's inclination to create new productive supply faster than the available demand can consume the goods. Too many auto factories chasing too few car buyers. The growing imbalance of industrial overcapacity ultimately means that the capital investors must be disappointed too, since they are busy investing in more factories than the world really needs. Sooner or later the marketplace will discard many of those surplus factories. When that happens, the capital invested in them fails, too.

This destructive supply imbalance, as we described, is building across nearly every major sector, but difficult for investors to take seriously when they see industrial booms with soaring returns under way in so many places. Dispersal of industrial production aggravates the supply imbalances, but the underlying problem is ultimately rooted in incomes—the faltering ability of the world's consumers to keep up with the new production capacities that are being created. The rising return on financial assets exacerbates this problem because, on the whole, it shifts income toward those who are already quite wealthy. The pensioner and small saver may enjoy a small piece of the action, but the aggregate income flows from finance capital are not recycled to the ranks of ordinary consumers.

Globalization has further enhanced the power of finance by quickening the competition for capital. Liberated from the old controls that once largely confined capital to home markets, the world's investors can now roam freely across three great auctions, each one bidding for use of their money. One auction is the Old World debt of Europe and America, rapidly growing and requiring more lending. Another is the energetic industrialization of the emerging markets in Asia and some Latin American nations— the new factories, power plants and highways that require financing and promise robust returns. The third auction is less distinct but also quite voracious: the rising volume of capital that multinational firms need to keep up with the technological contests in advanced sectors.[3]

This description, of course, greatly simplifies the extraordinary complexity of how global finance is organized and functions. The three auctions actually exist in myriad forms and places—stock and bond markets around the world, investment and commercial banks, hedge funds, private venture-capital firms and some others. With one financial device or another, all these agents generate and manage the flows of capital across borders, now in staggering volumes. For instance, the daily trading of national currencies expands ferociously and now exceeds $1.2 trillion a day—foreign-exchange trading that in four or five days equals the annual output of the U.S. economy. Britain has become a low-wage assembly outpost for industry in Europe, but the City of London remains the world capital of foreign-exchange traders, with daily volume of $460 billion, nearly twice Wall Street's.[4]

The most alarming aspect of globalized capital is not the speed or volume, however. It is the price. As national financial markets gradually converge in globalized trading, the price demanded by capital has risen to a higher plateau—in effect, claiming a larger share for lenders or investors from the overall returns of economic enterprise. Starting in the 1980s, this shift has been reflected in the historically high levels of real interest rates (the nominal interest rate discounted by inflation).

While this new burden is not uniformly felt across the global system, it means that in most places both debtor governments and private enterprise must devote an increasing share of their revenues or profits to the capital owners. In the United States, for instance, the real interest rate on long-term borrowing runs consistently between 4 and 5 percent—twice the average rate of U.S. economic growth and nearly twice the historic average for interest rates. A recent study of the ten largest economies found that real interest rates were at 4 percent, having crept up a full percentage point in recent decades.[5]

The effect of abnormally high interest rates is like a vise, slowly squeezing more out of the economic system, requiring it to run faster just to keep up with its old obligations. The condition becomes pathological when the interest-rate cost persistently grows faster than economic activity expands, a malignant relationship present in nearly all of the spectacular collapses of debt. The arithmetic is straightforward: A family (or a nation) taking on new debt at 4 percent interest while its income is flat or growing more slowly has to make up that gap somehow, either by discontinuing other kinds of spending or by borrowing more to pay the mounting interest. As the debt principal accumulates, the impact compounds.

Why did capital become more expensive? The conventional explanation is that capital is scarce. Interest rates have become stuck at elevated levels, it is widely assumed, because the demand for capital exceeds the supply and so the price of capital is naturally set higher (just as the price of labor or manufactured goods falls because both are in surplus). The supply-demand explanation may satisfy the orthodox faith in markets, but it does not match the reality, and, indeed, many astute market players dismiss the "capital scarcity" argument as irrelevant cant.

Capital, as the McKinsey study suggested, is becoming more abundant in relation to its universe of users, not more scarce. Yet its price—global interest rates—remains stuck at a historically high plateau. Three factors help explain this supposed anomaly: the heightened risks present in the global system, the upward pull of competing returns available to investors and governments' abolition of interest-rate ceilings.

The first and perhaps most important factor is risk: Investors may look wildly optimistic as they bid up stock prices, but they can also read ominous portents in the debtors' increasingly precarious positions, including the risk that governments may someday try to inflate their way out of their growing debt burdens. So financial investors demand "risk premiums" on their lending, especially from the sovereign governments traditionally regarded as the safest borrowers. As a German banker explained to me: "The problem lies in a lack of good debtors rather than a scarcity of capital."

Second, free-roaming capital now enjoys a much wider range of choices —so that staid old investments like U.S. Treasuries or the financing of a new American factory must compete with high-flying possibilities overseas. The stock market in Hong Kong has generated a twenty-year average annual return of 21 percent; India's yield was 18 percent, Argentina's 28 percent, compared to 11 percent in the U.S. stock market or Germany's. The risks and price volatility are much greater in the emerging markets, but their higher yields exert an upward pull on the returns offered by other, more traditional forms of investment.[6]

Finally, when the United States and some other nations deregulated their domestic financial systems and abolished the ceilings on bank-deposit interest rates, huge volumes of savings were, in effect, freed to chase the higher market returns. This might be regarded as a just outcome for the virtuous small savers, but it effectively abolished the credit subsidy implicit in the old controls that benefited borrowers, large and small.

Taken together, these three factors all flow from the free-market reforms of financial systems and give capital more leeway and leverage to bid up the price. The inflated return for capital, whatever the cause, sets up a basic economic collision within the global system: if the price of capital does not decline or if economic growth does not accelerate smartly, the vise will continue to tighten on borrowers across many sectors and nations. The logic is inescapable and predicts more ruined debtors, more panics and crashes.

"The scale of financial wealth in relation to the underlying economy has become much larger and the reactions of this stock of financial wealth can be absolutely violent, compared to quite small adjustments in the real economy that it is reacting to," said Robert A. Johnson, a financial economist who studies the larger currents of global finance and has also experienced the volatile action as a leading trader himself. "The pendulum is oscillating more rapidly and at the same time its fulcrum is drifting. You have real changes on planet earth, moving glacially, as the Old World debt grows and Asia stores up enormous wealth. Then you have the beehive of speculators rolling over each other, pushing things to extremes. The general uncertainties make everyone demand a risk premium because, in general, it feels more like we're heading toward destruction rather than stability."

The one great bulwark against a disastrous climax is, ironically, government—ironic because the apostles of "one world" finance disparage national governments as archaic and urge them to cede their powers completely to the globalizing marketplace of capital. Yet it is the national governments that, again and again, have had to step in to manage the occasional financial crises and staunch deflationary collapses before they turned into a general depression. In one episode after another, from the Third World debt defaults of 1982 to Japan's banking crisis in 1995, government managers have intervened—successfully so far—to prevent the full catastrophe. In many instances, of course, governments had helped foster these debacles by their own derelict policies.

The existence of government intervention is the one crucial fundamental that separates the present situation from the celebrated financial crashes in capitalism's history. Mainly because of those previous disasters, major governments now possess the administrative capabilities to intervene with emergency subsidy, bailouts and market controls when debt or financial prices suddenly crash on a massive scale—measures that can allow an orderly liquidation instead of a bloody unraveling. For fifteen years, together and individually, the major governments and their central banks have been playing the role of fireman for global finance's misplaced enthusiasms. Their timely actions have ameliorated losses from the periodic deflations and cauterized the broader impact on the productive economy.

Based on this performance, many people plausibly assume that governments will continue to succeed in this role, thereby averting the kind of general catastrophe that the underlying disorder seems to predict. Many well-informed people believe this, and I am not prepared to claim they are necessarily wrong. But what I do suggest is that there are two large contradictions pulling in the opposite direction—forces that refute the general confidence and may undermine the governing system's capacity to prevent a general collapse.

The first contradiction is that, in most cases, governments have successfully managed the recurring debt deflations largely by shifting the bad debts from private holders to the public—"socializing the costs," as financial economists would put it. After the debt crisis of 1982, the government-supervised workout plans for the Third World's failed debt required vast new lending from publicly supported institutions—the World Bank and International Monetary Fund—so that the endangered commercial banks could gradually reduce their exposure. A similar remedy occurred in the different circumstances of Mexico's 1995 collapse: an emergency $50 billion credit line from the U.S. and other governments stabilized Mexican finance, at least for a time, and calmed the panicky investors. America's various banking debacles in the 1980s invoked the same approach. So has the Japanese strategy for containing its deflationary banking crisis.[7]

A kind of remnant socialism still exists in behalf of financial institutions and investors, who are rescued from their own mistakes by governments that discreetly spread the costs among other citizens. This is politically unfair obviously, but it also encourages irresponsibility. Finance capital is free to seek its own rewards around the world, but when ill-founded hopes evaporate, global financiers rush back to their home governments (and home taxpayers) for rescue and relief. National taxpayers, if they ever manage to grasp how this works, are unlikely to endorse such an open-ended commitment to support global capital, especially since they have been told that capital no longer has any obligations to them.

Inequities aside, the process works mainly by transferring the losses from private balance sheets to the public's—when the public treasuries are already heavily indebted. Even if taxpayers were willing, this approach has the deleterious consequence of cumulatively deepening the governments' own financial predicament. Thus, the reckoning with bad debt is not really resolved so much as it is pushed off into the future—where tomorrow's citizens will be expected to pay for it.

The second contradiction is that finance capital now has the power to sometimes overwhelm the governments themselves. The steady accumulation of financial girth has altered the balance, not only between capital and industry or capital and labor, but also between capital and government. Managers in national governments are supposedly responsible for overseeing a larger and larger global system of private finance and protecting it from disastrous error. Yet the finance system now has the ability to turn around and punish governments themselves. The steady weakening of government authority, alongside its rising debts, suggests an abnormal arrangement that is not sustainable.

To illuminate these unstable relationships more concretely, we will first explore the starkest example of how finance capital has captured greater power—the furious global market in currencies. Maintaining reliable money is government's most important function, aside from war-making, because many innocent parties are randomly injured, including entire national economies, when money values gyrate wildly. Yet governments have lost control of this function to the global financial markets. Or, at least, they must now share responsibility with a shrewd private partner who can become quite fickle and overbearing. The result is not the stability and efficiency that market theorists predict. Instead, national currencies have become one more commodity in global trade—erratic and undependable, but very profitable for smart traders.

○

Late one afternoon in July 1993, I happened by chance to telephone an old friend in New York, Robert A. Johnson, just as he was in the middle of another storm of global finance. Rob Johnson was a Ph.D. economist educated at MIT and Princeton, an alumnus of the Federal Reserve's research staff and the Senate's budget and banking committees. He was then working in the highest ranks of global financial traders, as a partner of George Soros, whose strategic speculations were famed and feared across continents.

When he came on the phone, Rob's voice was supercharged with adrenaline, fairly crackling with electric intensity as he spoke in a rapid rush of words.

"What a day!" he said. "I bought more bonds today than in any other single day I've worked with Soros. We probably bought $4 billion in bonds today—government bonds from France, Denmark, Portugal, Spain, everywhere we could. Europe just stood there while we shoveled in bonds. We probably did another billion and a half in equities.

"We were paying ten basis points [a tenth of one percent] over the market price when, usually, if you pay two or three points premium, people think they are really cleaning up on you. This time, if we were going to nickel and dime it, we wouldn't be able to get all the bonds we wanted. So we went for it.

"People on the other end couldn't figure out what we were doing, but the price was so good they sold to us. Sometimes, I wonder why these people take such a short-term view. They might figure: if Soros wants these bonds so badly, maybe I ought to hold on to them. The smart ones do."

None of this made much sense to me until Johnson explained the play: George Soros was staking out another bold market position, two steps ahead of other traders but also ahead of governments and central banks. A new currency crisis had been triggered in Europe that morning when the Bundesbank, Germany's central bank, failed to cut German interest rates, as others had hoped. That nonevent inspired major market players to launch a heavy speculation against the French franc and other weakening currencies in Europe, betting that they would fall in value.

The Soros partners decided to play for the second-day bounce: instead of shorting the currencies, they bought bonds and stocks from across Europe, financial assets that should surge in value once the governments surrendered to the speculators, cut interest rates and devalued their currencies. The logic was like a three-cushion shot in billiards.*

Either way the financial traders were playing off the political crisis

---

* *"Shorting" a currency (or bonds, stocks and any other commodity) is the trader's technique of borrowing the asset from another holder and selling it at the current price—gambling that the price will fall and the asset can be bought back later for less. The trader satisfies the loan and pockets the price difference. In massive volumes, shorting itself helps drive down the price.*

ignited by the Bundesbank's inaction that morning in Frankfurt. From the Spanish peseta to the Dutch guilder, the continent's major currencies were all linked to Germany's deutschemark through Europe's Exchange Rate Mechanism—a formal commitment to maintain currency values within a fixed band of relationships. Since the D-mark was the strongest currency and the anchor for this system, the Bundesbank essentially set monetary policy for all of Europe. When the Bundesbank raised interest rates or persisted in holding rates at a high level, the others had no choice but to follow. Otherwise, their currencies would be rapidly sold off by investors, depreciate in value—and fall below the ERM's required floor.

The French franc and several others were already trading quite close to the ERM margins. But their governments were also desperate for relief from high interest rates because every nation was stuck in recession, with unemployment rates running at 10 to 13 percent. Another interest-rate increase would only flatten their economies further. Should the governments hang tough and stay in step with the D-mark, even raising interest rates to do so? Or would they accept the humiliation of dropping out of the exchange-rate system in order to reduce domestic economic pain? If the ERM broke up, that would postpone—if not destroy—Europe's vision of achieving a unified currency and economic union by 1997. Soros and the other speculators were betting, in different ways, that the governments would fold.

"The French have to cut rates," Rob Johnson predicted. "Realistically, French interest rates should be about four percent on long bonds and they are at seven percent. If they break out of the system, their interest rates will collapse and you'll get a huge bond rally and a huge equity rally. When the Bundesbank refused to cut rates, it creates a French political crisis. The French put all their faith in the Germans and the Germans stuck a boot in their face today. France sticks with the Germans to show its faith in a unified Europe—they envision the EC as run by a French-German alliance at the core of Europe. Now they are getting screwed."

From New York and London, Singapore and Zurich, the world's major currency traders ganged up on the French and Belgian francs, the Danish krone, the Portuguese escudo, the Spanish peseta—selling them short in heavy volume and driving their value lower, closer and closer to the ERM's breaking point.

Europe's central banks fought back vigorously, collectively defending the weak currencies by buying up huge quantities of francs, pesetas and the others with the D-marks stored in their own foreign-exchange reserves. By selling more deutschemarks into the market, the central bankers softened the D-mark's value while simultaneously boosting the prices of weaker currencies by mopping up the market's supply of them. That was the intention, anyway. In a few hours, the central banks expended 15 billion D-marks (about $8.7 billion) to defeat the speculators.

The central banks lost. The Bundesbank stood its ground against the market pressures and did not cut rates, but the ERM blew apart. Four days later the governments sheepishly announced that they were adopting a new, much wider band of currency relationships for the ERM—a de facto surrender that allowed the weak currencies to decline and their interest rates to subside. The crisis was resolved, papered over with stout declarations that the ERM had survived and European union would not be derailed. But every party understood the real meaning: finance capital had once again bested major governments, forced them to retreat from their own economic policies. A heavy shadow was cast over Europe's vision of unification.[8]

George Soros—urbane, brilliant, fabulously wealthy—was the arrogant symbol of this worldly power. An American born in Hungary and educated in London, a Jewish émigré from World War II's fascism, Soros had amassed a great fortune from his strategic sense of finance. After three decades his Quantum Fund was worth about $11 billion, of which he was the principal owner. This time his play was actually a bit disappointing—wrong about the Bundesbank, though right about the other governments. While he made many millions, the crisis did not lead to the explosive rallies he had anticipated, price surges that could have yielded hundreds of millions in overnight profit.

Soros was attacked, nonetheless. French politicians and press assailed the "Anglo-Saxon speculators" profiting on international discord, undermining European community. Jacques Delors, the French president of the European Commission, denounced them as "golden boys." Some of the disparaging remarks suggested a whiff of old-fashioned European anti-semitism. Soros was widely disbelieved when he explained that he himself had not speculated against the franc, and, in fact, he supported a unified European currency as a great historic project. In Eastern Europe, where Soros has devoted hundreds of millions of his wealth to supporting new democratic institutions, the anti-semitic barbs were less subtle.[9]

"George Soros calls the bluff of governments," Rob Johnson explained. "Their job is to pretend that they're in control and he represents a force that blows away that illusion. The ritual of a very rich man who has the power to ridicule governments is frightening. That's what bugs people. But George Soros isn't dangerous if your country is doing sound economic policy."

Ten months earlier Soros's fund had earned $950 million in one brief exercise by demonstrating that the British government was defending "unsound" policy. The British press called it Black Wednesday and dubbed Soros "the man who broke the Bank of England." In September 1992, the pound sterling was trading around 2.85 pounds to the D-mark, perilously close to the bottom of the ERM band of 2.77. To stay in the band, the venerable central bank had to keep raising interest rates despite the recessionary conditions at home, in order to attract foreign money to its currency. Soros, meanwhile, sold sterling short massively, betting $10 billion Britain could not stay the course.

At noon on Black Wednesday, the Chancellor of the Exchequer, Norman Lamont, bravely announced that Britain would never yield and raised interest rates by an additional 2 percent. The government, he said, intended to borrow $15 billion to defend sterling. "We were amused," Soros wrote afterwards, "because that was about how much we wanted to sell." By nightfall, the UK government caved and dropped the pound out of the exchange-rate system. Italy had already given up the fight for the lira. Soros, counting other coordinated currency plays, figured he realized a $2 billion profit from about two weeks of investing.[10]

What did George Soros know to be so bold? As he has repeatedly explained over the years, his basic investment strategy involved identifying the fundamental misalignments in market perceptions—prices or political judgments that were way out of line with the underlying realities of economics and politics, that would be sharply reversed once markets or governments were compelled to recognize them. Soros's basic play was to stake out a position in advance of that moment, then wait for others to see the light. Sometimes, this was a matter of hours or days; more often his positions were based on deeper fundamentals that might take weeks or months to materialize.

In this instance, Soros had concluded not only that the British pound was overvalued against the real output of the British economy, but also that the government could not possibly defend its position for domestic political reasons. Britain's financial system relied heavily on variable-rate mortgages and other debt instruments whose monthly payments fluctuated with the market interest rates. Thus, as the Bank of England raised rates to defend sterling, it was putting an unbearable squeeze on British homeowners and businesses. The alternative to raising rates—buying pounds in the financial markets—would exhaust the government's resources, Soros figured, before it exhausted the speculators. In the end, the Bank of England wasted $20 billion in the struggle, some of which wound up at Soros's Quantum Fund.

In fact, when the official embarrassment had subsided, some people in Britain began to grasp that George Soros had actually produced a White Wednesday for their national economy. While egregiously enriching himself, Soros also liberated Britain from its own government's wrongheaded and punishing monetary policy. Once the humiliated officials dropped out of the European monetary system, Britain's interest rates plummeted, its economic growth recovered and its unemployment declined. No one mistook Soros's motives, but the actual effect of his assault was broadly beneficial for the British public.

The distinctive quality behind his boldness was Soros's intellectual disdain for the orthodoxies of economics. Economic theory, he had explained in a book many years before, begins with an assumption of rational choices by informed individuals. "The result is a theoretical construction of great elegance that resembles natural science but does not resemble reality," Soros wrote. "It relates to an ideal world. . . . It has little relevance to the real world in which people act on the basis of imperfect understanding and equilibrium is beyond reach."

In the economists' perspective, markets are right and rational and market prices accurately reflect the future by discounting the various risks. "I start with the opposite point of view," Soros declared. "I believe that market prices are always wrong, in the sense that they present a biased view of the future." Furthermore, he explained, the misperceptions by financial markets also influence future events—driving prices even further off course from reality by seeming to confirm investors' original misjudgments. This continuous interaction between misperceptions and market actions created the landscape where Soros operated—identifying the fundamental gaps between prices and reality that would offer great opportunities for profit.

Soros's methods were first articulated in his 1987 book, *The Alchemy of Finance*. His own investing, he acknowledged, was also driven by emotional biases. "I had a very low regard for the sagacity of professional investors and the more influential their position the less I considered them capable of making the right decisions," he wrote. "My partner and I took a malicious pleasure in making money by selling short stocks that were institutional favorites." Soros has since become an esteemed alchemist of global finance himself, though he still cheerfully acknowledged he gets things wrong, too.[11]

Personal brilliance aside, currency speculators like Soros all operate on a fundamental insight about the great political disjunction present in the global system: the national governments expected to guarantee stability were trapped between two worlds—their obligations to domestic economies and the new force of the global market. Central banks and elected governments were regularly compelled to choose between the two: either defending their home economy or yielding to the quick, disinterested judgments from the global traders. This was often a "no win" choice for political leaders since yielding to the markets' idea of "sound economic policy" frequently required them to depress their own economies, increasing unemployment or cutting social spending. Satisfying finance capital could be a formula for losing the next election.

Traders like Soros and Johnson, when they formed opinions about the fundamentals, were actually making sophisticated estimates about politics as much as economics. In the real world, as opposed to market theory, the two realms were inseparable, as every trader understood and the various currency crises illustrated. The British government could squeeze the homefront borrowers in defense of sterling only so much before it had to relent. For deep historical reasons, France wanted to stay closely aligned with Germany and accepted the pain of higher unemployment as the price of that political goal. The Germans, for their own political reasons, kept setting the pain threshold higher.

Soros thought he understood why. Germany was ostensibly committed to Europe's unification, but the Bundesbank would lose its dominant position if a single currency ever actually came into existence since monetary policy would then be managed by a new European central bank. By holding rates high and deepening the crisis for other economies, the German central bank was defending Germany first against inflation. But it was also slyly subverting the goal of a unified Europe.

During the sterling crisis Soros got a hint of this realpolitik in a conversation with Bundesbank President Helmut Schlesinger, who remarked that he liked the concept of a single currency for Europe, but would prefer that it be called the mark. For Soros, the quip was a signal that the Bundesbank was not going to sacrifice its own national priorities in order to hold the ERM system together. His speculative attack followed.[12]

The same sort of political-economic dilemmas regularly confronted the Federal Reserve and the Bank of Japan as those dominant central banks also attempted to manage the competing imperatives of domestic interest rates and international capital flows. Milton Friedman, the American apostle of free markets, had argued twenty years before that if governments would allow the global marketplace to determine currency values with a system of "floating exchange rates," then the central banks would be free to concentrate on their main function of controlling the money supply and domestic inflation. Roughly the opposite of Friedman's prediction has occurred, as global markets repeatedly trumped the domestic policy decisions of central banks—sometimes deliberately, sometimes randomly.

This disjunction—national governments caught between cross-purposes—was perhaps inevitable once governments accepted the deregulation of global finance and allowed capital to roam freely across borders. The consequences have been most dramatic in the realm of currencies because currency was the first financial asset to be fully liberated, starting in 1973 when the old Bretton Woods system of fixed exchange rates for currencies was abandoned. In those days the foreign-exchange market existed mainly to facilitate commercial trade and its size was trivial—a turnover of $10 billion to $20 billion a day, compared to $1,200 billion a day two decades later.[13]

From World War II until 1973 the U.S. dollar had been the stabilizing anchor for the world's currencies, and the United States guaranteed the fixed exchange-rate system with its own gold reserves. An ounce of gold was worth $35, and other nations could cash in dollars for gold, if they wished. This imposed financial discipline on every government, including America's. But as dollar inflation increased in the late 1960s and the U.S. gold reserves were drained, it could no longer sustain the guarantee. Richard Nixon's government first devalued the dollar in 1971—that is, diluted its exchange ratio with other currencies—then two years later "closed the gold window" permanently, unilaterally canceling the Bretton Woods commitment.

Money was now free to seek its proper level in the marketplace. Two decades later it was still searching—and oscillating in wide arcs. One crude measure of what has followed since Bretton Woods was that, by 1995, gold was worth $380 an ounce. But the gold price could also swing widely with transient market currents of political unrest or economic fears. When Soros disclosed in the spring of 1993 that he was buying gold, the price soared $50 an ounce, then receded again. The surge was attributed to China's new millionaires who, with their offshore hoards of wealth, rushed to follow the savvy American's play.

The acceleration in trading has spread to other financial markets besides currencies—bonds, stocks, commercial notes, even bundles of home mortgages—as major governments gradually repealed their controls on capital inflows and outflows, as national markets were opened step-by-step to foreign firms and money. Germany withdrew its controls on cross-border capital flows in 1981; Japan has liberalized its system more slowly and was still eliminating barriers in the early 1990s. As a result, global bond trading grew during the 1980s from $30 billion daily to more than $500 billion, according to McKinsey.

National stock markets were converging much more slowly, but equity trading grew at a compounded rate of 17 percent a year from 1980 to 1992 —seven times faster than the economic growth rate in the OECD nations. The scope of trading widened still further with the so-called securitization of commercial-bank loans—the bundling together of loans like home mortgages in one security instrument that could be sold and traded in markets.

To reduce the risks in all of these, complex derivatives were popularized as hedging devices, intended to protect investors against sudden swings in national interest rates, currencies and other variables. Derivatives became, in turn, a source of volatile play and huge risk themselves.

In sum, the process of financial globalization was still rolling forward and not yet complete. Whatever its merits, the "one world" convergence of capital promised more violent oscillations ahead, more sudden surprises and cross-border panics, because the impulses of investors were transmitted almost instantly as abrupt shocks throughout the global system. "Investors are like fluid mechanics," Rob Johnson observed. "They will flow toward the higher return and most profitable enterprise. Sometimes, everybody runs to portside, then to starboard, trying to adjust. There's a continuous, boiling reallocation process so you never reach equilibrium."

The occasional crisis made this temporarily visible, but it was the cumulative force of finance capital that carried the power. "The real story," Johnson said, "is the deeper flows of equity as capital moves toward the best value available anywhere. That's a complex, slow-moving process. But it builds up pressures—like water against a wall. When the force of the water breaks through the wall, the British pound collapses or the European monetary system breaks apart, but the real drama is the buildup of hydraulic forces."

In this drama, the major governments were quite weak, having largely surrendered their national claims on capital. As finance swelled in size and strength, it was literally able to outgun the governors who tried to stabilize financial flows or influence their direction. Though Soros occasionally boasted about a market triumph, he more often professed humility. In the sterling crisis, he noted, "I was just a member of the crowd—maybe larger and more successful than most—but still one of many. Even now, my influence is largely illusory."

This was not false modesty: despite his reputation George Soros could not single-handedly overwhelm governments. He was powerful only if many others were on board with him. Roughly speaking, that is what occurred. His fellow speculators were not simply rogue investors or other hedge funds, but the largest financial institutions from several continents. "The big banks, commercial and investment banks, surf on Soros—trading behind Soros's trades and multiplying the amplitude," Johnson explained.

David Smick, consultant to multinational banks and editor of *International Economy* magazine, described the uneven contest of the market versus governments. "The process of resisting the market is mostly theatrics because the central banks' reserves are so small by comparison. They are tiny. The elephants come charging over the hill and the natives are trying to stop them with peashooters. The elephants are the guys with the money. They can topple currencies and the central banks can't stop them."

This epic shift of power was delineated in numbers from the McKinsey report on global capital: In 1983, five major central banks (the United States, Germany, Japan, Britain and Switzerland) held $139 billion in foreign-exchange reserves versus an average daily turnover of $39 billion in the major foreign-exchange markets. In other words, the central bankers' combined firepower dwarfed the marketplace by more than 3 to 1. By 1986, the two were about even in size. By 1992, the balance of power was reversed: These major central banks had $278 billion in reserves against $623 billion in daily trading activity. The market traders now had the size advantage by more than 2 to 1.

"Surfing" on the same wave was a natural element of the global system since, around the world, twenty-four hours a day, every major trader was linked electronically to the same reality—the shifting market prices, political bulletins, traders' gossip. Soros occasionally expressed regret that he had become a world-famous "guru" others followed, but this was rather disingenuous since, when it suited him, Soros virtually announced his market positions to the press, inviting others to join his crowd.

Even when he did not do this, Soros's major plays would not remain secret for very long since every time his traders placed a buy-or-sell order, their transactions were executed by major banks and brokerages in New York and Chicago, Europe and Asia. Their trading desks would swiftly pass along the news of what Soros was up to, and if it sounded promising, the firms would duplicate his play themselves. The impact of Soros's money was thus amplified. The new communications technology has created a small, elite community of international finance—perhaps no more than

200,000 traders around the world who all speak the same language and recognize a mutuality of interests despite their rivalries.

One quiet morning in 1994, I sat alongside Rob Johnson at the Soros Fund Management offices on Seventh Avenue in New York and watched how it worked. Through the morning Johnson chatted with London, Sydney, Zurich, Chicago and other U.S. firms, while making light trades here and there. Buy $50 million Australian dollars in Sydney. Dump a $100 million position in the Standard & Poors stock index. Buy thousands of contracts for German bunds in London and Zurich. Liquidate a $10 million silver position.

"This is nickel and dime stuff," Johnson explained. "I'm just playing around. But when you play around, you get a feeling for the tone of the market." The market was waiting that morning for another interest-rate increase from the Federal Reserve, expecting a bond rally when it occurred because it was assumed to be the last one in a series. In the meantime, the traders exchanged local market intelligence or theorized about the next big play or fumed about the Fed's inaction.

The Quantum Fund did not actually exist in New York City; only its managers worked there (and paid U.S. taxes on their personal incomes). The capital itself was officially banked at Curaçao in the Netherlands Antilles, where it was exempt from the U.S. securities laws and their limits on risk-taking. Except for managing partners, Soros's funds were open only to non-American investors who presumably paid taxes in home countries, if and when their profits were repatriated. Soros is reported to have paid more than $100 million in U.S. taxes in the banner year of 1993 and would have paid much more if he hadn't given away $400 million that year to various philanthropies.

Johnson sat before a broad panel of three computer screens: the Reuters data feed on every financial market in the world whose green numbers flashed red when a quotation changed, a news wire of political bulletins and major market indexes, a personal communications screen that flashed E-mail messages from allied dealers and bankers worldwide. Union Bank of Switzerland in Zurich chimed in: "Think deutschemark/yen the play of the moment." Bankers Trust's bond desk in London: "Panic selling here from corporates." A Chicago trader: "I swear to God, if those guys raise rates today, this thing's going to rally."

"It's like a video game—the greatest video game in the world," Johnson mused. "The fundamentals really work in the medium and long term, but what matters in between is what other people think." By 2 P.M., the Fed's failure to raise rates had demoralized the traders. The dollar declined, U.S. bonds were off 1.4 points, the Dow-Jones was down 40. "God, this is really ugly," Johnson said and bought more German bunds. A few days later he summarized the action: "I lost money in currencies big time because they all blew against me, but I made a lot of money on bonds, so we came out all right."

Global trading required a kind of split vision—studying the individual balance sheets of nations and companies, but simultaneously seeing the world as one market. When equity analysts at Quantum Fund examined the paper and pulp industry, for example, they scanned the conditions in Indonesia, Sweden, Oregon, Finland and other scattered subsectors in a unified industry. "We used to have a thing called the German economy or the Swedish economy or the American economy, but now we have the whole planet sitting in one stadium," Johnson said.

Winning at the "video game" also required a flinty intellectual detachment. "The best and smartest people in this business," Johnson said, "are the ones who can hang in there with the pain and contradictions and see what the reality is without drawing back from it, without letting ideology or emotions get in the way of what they see happening. It's a little like a good surgeon who knows he's working on a human body, but to perform well he has to disengage from those emotions."

Financiers, large and small, multiplied their own investing power by using the leverage of borrowed money—buying stocks or bonds "on margin." With $1 million of his own cash, Soros could buy $2 million in stocks or as much as $50 million in bonds. The various derivative instruments multiplied the investors' potential play even further, though Soros has testified that he seldom used derivatives himself.[14]

Robert Dugger, a financial economist and political analyst at Tudor Investment Fund, another leading hedge fund, explained that the important banks "surfing" on Soros actually dwarfed him and other celebrated players. "The largest global banks and investment houses have hedge funds inside them whose resources are many times larger than the hedge funds like Soros. In the early 1990s, these institutions fully leveraged could move $500 billion through a market while the largest hedge funds could reach maybe $100 billion."

Indeed, the combined activities of currency trading and selling various derivative devices to investors and multinational firms have become a major profit center for the largest commercial banks, especially in America. Citicorp reported a profit of $829 million in the first quarter of 1995—$324 million of it from foreign-exchange dealings. Bankers Trust of New York was the aggressive leader in this realm, issuing $1.9 trillion in off-balance-sheet contracts during 1993 while its regular loan portfolio was a mere $92 billion. Other major players were J. P. Morgan, Goldman Sachs, Salomon Brothers and Merrill Lynch. Overall, the nominal value of these various risk-swapping contracts mushroomed from less than $3 trillion in 1986 to more than $17 trillion by 1991.[15]

The inherent risks became apparent during the global bond crash in 1994 when one major investor after another suffered huge sudden losses from holding derivatives. To name a few losers: Procter & Gamble, $157 million; Metallgesellschaft of Germany, $1 billion; Glaxo of Britain, $160 million; Orange County, California, $1.7 billion; Bank Negara, Malaysia's central bank, $4 billion. Procter & Gamble, among other losers, sued Bankers Trust, accusing the old Morgan bank of misleading it on the risks of derivatives. The bank settled out of court for $150 million.

The losses revealed that corporate treasurers—even some government treasurers—had joined in the speculation, profitably playing the market swings and getting burned. The larger systemic risk of all this unregulated action was unknown, but it might wind up as a public liability someday if there was a general failure, since government-regulated banks were among the major purveyors. In a crisis, governments rescued the major banking institutions from their recklessness in the name of defending the system.[16]

George Soros was himself capable of losing money on the grand scale. In early 1994, he lost $600 million in a wink when he and other speculators were caught wrong-footed on bonds and currencies. He was betting that Japan would yield in its trade dispute with the United States and that this would cause the dollar to rally. Instead, Japan stood its ground, the dollar fell and the global market panicked. Everyone began dumping bonds at once—worldwide—driving bond prices down and causing interest rates to surge in Europe, the United States and some Asian nations. "We got tattooed," Johnson said. "When one group starts selling, other groups lose value in their holdings and so they start selling and the whole thing unravels around the world."

George Soros had a terrible year: Quantum Fund was up only 3 percent in 1994, compared to 60 percent in 1993, and some of his subsidiary funds actually lost money, as much as 9 percent. This performance was far better than most other hedge funds that shrank that year by 10 to 25 percent or, in a few cases, failed completely. Soros was doing much better in 1995 and finished the year up by 39 percent, but he and others became temporarily less aggressive.

The system's roiling events—the bond crash, the Mexican collapse, Japan's deflation crisis or perhaps his own streak of bad plays—seemed to put Soros in a darker mood. The chief alchemist began to ruminate gloomily in his public comments about the dangers he foresaw of a general breakdown—the collapse of the global financial system and the trading system with it. The markets liked to surf on Soros's currency plays, but his insights on the larger historical reality were strangely ignored.

"I cannot see the global system surviving," Soros mused in a new book. "Political instability and financial instability are going to feed off each other in a self-reinforcing fashion. In my opinion, we have entered a period of global disintegration only we are not yet aware of it."[17]

The fundamental misalignments that George Soros liked to identify as profit opportunities now looked to him like portents of impending tragedy.

The arcane gyrations of currency markets and other excesses of global capital would hardly matter if the only consequences were to produce fabulous fortunes for some individuals and occasional embarrassment for central bankers. The evidence, however, was that the system of liberated finance has severely and aimlessly damaged commerce and national economies by destabilizing the very core of capitalism: the value of money itself. Firms and workers, sales and profit, jobs and incomes—all were held hostage by the gross price swings of this unpredictable commodity called money.

The dollar, the deutschemark and the yen, in descending order of importance, were the three main reserve currencies that served as anchors for global trade, but each was subject to its own continuing uncertainty and dramatic volatility. The monthly swings in exchange value between the dollar and the deutschemark, for instance, typically ran around 5 percent a month and frequently greater than 10 percent. In 1995, the dollar lost 20 percent of its value against the yen in three months. Then, as the three leading governments intervened to staunch the decline, the dollar lurched back upward and, three months later, was 20 percent stronger. How could the market be right about money values when it was always changing its mind?[18]

Across several years the market shifts in currency values were so extreme and contradictory they might be described as irrational. The dollar, for example, was said to be worth 260 yen in 1985, then marked down to 130 yen by 1987, then up to 160 yen in 1990, down again to 80 yen in early 1995, then up to 100 yen a few months later. Nothing in the economic reality corresponded to those violent swings in financial numbers. The United States did not suddenly become half as strong, then suddenly much more productive. Nor did Japan's underlying value as a national economy abruptly weaken, then surge. As Rob Johnson said, everyone runs to portside, then to starboard, but the boiling process of reallocations never achieves equilibrium.

The long-term decline of the dollar's value was driven, to be sure, by the deeper economic forces, including especially the U.S. trade indebtedness described in Chapter 10. But people and enterprises did not live in the long term. In the here and now, the effects of the money misalignments were devastating. Multinational firms had to protect themselves against global price shocks, just as consumers tried to protect themselves against domestic inflation.

"A sharp appreciation of the home currency throws tradable industries into disarray," Kenichi Ohno, a financial authority at Tsukuba University, wrote. "A sudden loss of international price competitiveness, amounting to 10–40 percent in real terms, is much larger than typical profit margins in these industries. . . . To survive, these industries are forced to make costly downsizing adjustments. These include operating below capacity, implementing cost-cutting measures, scaling down investment plans and even scrapping existing facilities, laying off workers . . . outsourcing, shifting manufacturing bases abroad, joint ventures with foreigners, and so on."[19]

The instability of money, in other words, was itself a major force driving the globalization of industrial production, alongside the other imperatives like cheap labor, robust demand in foreign markets or government industrial policies that demanded technology and jobs in exchange for sales. Firms were literally driven offshore by the competitive disadvantages induced by their own home currency. American manufacturing took a devastating hit from the overvalued dollar in the first half of the 1980s; then it was Japan's turn to suffer the stronger yen. Companies systematically dispersed their production base to many different countries and regions in order to create a straddle that would insulate them from the recurring price shocks of "floating exchange rates." Most multinationals have learned to live with this reality, but at an incalculable cost to the general prosperity.

When economists celebrated the globalization of finance, they assumed general economic benefits would flow from the more efficient "allocation of resources"—that is, capital deployed to its best use, rather than diverted by political barriers into other, less valuable activities. "Best use" was measured, however, in the narrow terms of the higher returns that capital could earn, once it was freed of political regulation. In this logic, globalized markets were more efficient—able to attain the highest possible return—precisely because they were free to ignore the other consequences.

Given their narrow premise, market economists never attempted to calculate all of the collateral damage that could also be attributed to the liberalization of finance—the capital investments destroyed when viable factories were abruptly abandoned, the economic output lost when economies grew more slowly, the public welfare costs from rising unemployment or declining wages, the instability for companies and nations caused by the shifting money values.

If that measure were ever taken, it would likely reveal that the era of "floating exchange rates" has brought far more damage to societies than benefits (though, of course, some members of those societies benefited mightily). One authoritative judgment along these lines came from a private assembly of forty-seven international financial experts called the Bretton Woods Commission, whose chairman was Paul Volcker, the much-admired former chairman of the Federal Reserve. In 1994, this group reported its conclusions on the impact of unregulated currency markets: "Since the early 1970's, long-term growth in the major industrial countries has been cut in half, from about 5 percent a year to about 2.5 percent a year. Although many factors contributed to this decline in different countries at different times, low growth has been an international problem, and the loss of exchange rate discipline has played a part."

As the report observed, the era of liberated finance and expanding trade has led to other disappointing results: unemployment in the G-7 nations rose from 2 to 3 percent on average in prior years to between 5 to 6 percent and averaged 8 percent across the OECD economies in 1994. Capital investment in the wealthiest nations also declined. It peaked at 24 percent of GDP in 1973 and fell below 20 percent in subsequent years. "Since a good deal of this investment is needed to replace old capital, a fall of 4 percent is a significant drop—between a quarter and a half in the 'new capital' available for growth," the commission reported. In other words, the new freedom increased the "efficiency" of capital by allowing it to escape old obligations like reinvesting in economic growth at home. Given their slower growth rates, these major governments also began running larger budget deficits and borrowing heavily to finance them.

"When current exchange rates are misaligned, resources are misallocated; when exchange rates are unduly volatile, it creates uncertainty and productive investments are inhibited," the commission report continued. "Exchange rate misalignment adds to protectionist pressures from vulnerable industries in one major country after another as their international competitiveness waxes and wanes."

This provocative analysis would doubtless be ignored if it came from left-wing labor critics or the nationalist right, but the Bretton Woods Commission represented the establishment of global finance. Its blue-ribbon members were leading bankers and economists from America, Europe and Asia. Its sponsors included twenty-two of the world's most powerful financial institutions, some of the very banks that played and profited in the currency markets, from Deutsche Bank to Crédit Suisse, from Salomon Brothers to J. P. Morgan, from Daiwa Bank to Nomura Securities. They urged governments to construct a new international system of stable relationships between major currencies. Despite its formalistic prose the report sounded a bit like an anxious plea for help: stop these insane currency games before we do more destruction.

The essential cause of money's instability was not the excesses of currency speculators or the occasional errors of national governments—it was the fundamental disjunction between the two realms. The world, in a sense, was stuck halfway between the nation-state and a fully integrated global market. These two centers of power tugged against each other's values and priorities, producing constant friction and conflict, yet they were unable to disengage or to evolve to the next stage.

How this stalemate between government and markets was characterized depended mainly on whose perspective was defining it. Market players, Rob Johnson observed, typically described the conflict as "sclerosis versus dynamism"—the outmoded governments impeding the creative marketplace. Social critics or traditional central bankers, for that matter, would portray the power struggle as "order versus chaos"—governments trying to maintain order despite the chaotic markets. "At some level," Johnson said, "the trade-off is between which kinds of human errors seem worse—errors by governments or by private speculators. What bothers me is that I sometimes think the trade-off is sclerosis versus chaos."

Instability, in other words, flowed from the fracturing of power and responsibility that globalization has produced. The immediate force behind the more dramatic swings in currency exchange values was, after all, the monetary policy of the three major central banks, setting interest rates and controlling national money supplies. But the currency traders played off those actions, kibitzing and speculating like theater critics, occasionally vetoing the governments' policy decisions by ganging up and attacking them. And each of the central banks was itself trapped between its own conflicting obligations—the domestic economy versus the global money system.

In effect, the Federal Reserve, Bundesbank and Bank of Japan were trying, collectively but independently, to manage the world's money supply —providing or withdrawing the global liquidity that would either stimulate or depress global economic activity—while they also regulated their domestic prices and output. Despite various formats for coordination and the occasional cooperative exercises, their separate policies were inevitably driven by what was happening in their home countries. As a result, the world's three main currencies frequently caromed off each other in foreign exchange—creating perverse, disastrous side effects for commerce and for nations.

The story of how this interaction occurs was spread across many years and buried in the daunting complexities of how monetary policy influenced real economies. To understand it, one could follow a meandering chain of events that began in the early 1980s, when the Federal Reserve under Paul Volcker launched its stern campaign to subdue the virulent U.S. price inflation of the 1970s. To accomplish this goal, the Fed kept domestic interest rates at historically high levels for more than five years. But one collateral consequence of the higher rates was the relentless appreciation of the dollar's exchange value, as foreign money poured into U.S. financial assets to enjoy the higher returns. In a few years, the dollar rose by 50 percent against all other major currencies, from a low of 190 yen to a peak of 260 yen.

As a result, American-made goods were priced out of foreign markets by the mid-1980s and U.S. manufacturing was compelled to relocate production offshore to escape the artificial penalty of a strong currency. For the same reason, the U.S. trade deficits soared as foreign imports became much cheaper for American consumers and Japanese firms gained market share in the United States.

Next it was Japan's turn to feel the consequences. In 1985, reacting to the destructive imbalance in their currencies, the two governments agreed in the so-called Plaza Accord that they must take steps to reverse the gross misalignment (the Bundesbank participated, too, though its own management of the D-mark has largely avoided the extreme swings of the yen-dollar relationship). The Fed and the Bank of Japan shifted their monetary policies in late 1985 and the dollar began a rapid slide in value while the yen appreciated steadily. This started the hollowing-out process the Japanese called *kudoka,* as their manufacturers offloaded production to Taiwan, Singapore and other low-wage Asian neighbors to escape the price disadvantages caused by the strengthening yen. Their move was admired at the time but regretted a few years later when Japanese manufacturers found they had to move some factories again, this time to Thailand or Indonesia.

"While shifting the manufacturing base to overseas may be a long-term trend for Japan," Ohno wrote in the Bretton Woods report, "the yen appreciation unnecessarily accelerated it. . . . Costly adjustments to exchange fluctuations serve no useful purpose and substantial real resources will be wasted along the way."

The yen-dollar distortions fed right back into Japanese finance and produced further damage of even greater consequence. Trying to keep the yen from appreciating further, the Bank of Japan shifted in the latter 1980s to an easy-money policy of low interest rates and generous increases in its money supply. This excess liquidity in yen encouraged the increased Japanese lending to the United States—buying Treasury bonds and other assets to keep the debtor nation afloat—but it also fueled Japan's "bubble economy" of inflated financial prices, the frenzy of optimistic lending that eventually collapsed. Americans who clucked over Japan's financial profligacy perhaps did not understand that its easy money was also propping up the United States.

Japanese investors lost heavily on both ends. They lost hundreds of billions by investing in U.S. bonds because the dollar kept depreciating in exchange value, so their financial wealth invested in U.S. assets shrank dramatically. A U.S. bond they bought when the dollar was worth 200 yen was worth only 140 yen when the bond was sold and the wealth converted back into yen. But Japanese investors were burned again, even more severely, by their own collapsing stock market and the hundreds of billions in failed real-estate debt.

That sobering experience, in turn, led to further currency misalignment and industrial damage in the 1990s. Trying to clean up the excesses, the Bank of Japan tightened monetary policy, and a long-running recession followed. Chastened by their losses, Japan's major financial institutions and investors turned cautious and for a time virtually stopped the recycling of their wealth—the money they accumulated from trade surpluses and sent back to the United States in the form of loans or investments. Keeping the money at home, rather than shipping it back to America, had the unintended consequence of pushing the yen still higher in value against the weakening dollar. The stronger yen, in turn, renewed the price pressures on Japanese producers, and that set off another, more substantial round of *kudoka*.

For Japan, which had built its economic strength on export manufacturing, the impact of these money disorders seemed especially perverse. "If the strong yen continues, our best industries in Japan will be wiped out," Richard Koo, an economist at Nomura Securities, lamented in early 1994. "This is a cruel trend because it punishes Japan's best industries and doesn't hurt our worst."[20]

In midsummer of 1995, though the details remained secret, some sort of mutual assistance pact was engineered between the U.S. Treasury and Japan's Ministry of Finance to ease the crisis. The United States backed off its trade dispute over auto parts and settled for a fig-leaf agreement. Japanese institutions started buying more U.S. bonds again. Joined by the Bundesbank, the Fed and the Bank of Japan staged dramatic interventions in currency markets to push up the dollar and pull down the yen. Japan cut interest rates to stimulate its weak economy. Its administrators launched a major campaign to liquidate the mountain of failed loans and bail out major banks. The Federal Reserve agreed to supply emergency liquidity to the Japanese banking system if their crisis worsened.

The world was, in fact, flirting with a large, historic crisis—the threat of a general deflation like the 1930s—and major governments were more nervous than they revealed. If Japanese banking collapsed, it would likely bring down the world system. The government managers were, once again, at battle stations, trying to avert the full catastrophe.[21]

Recounting this complicated history, albeit in simplified outline, demonstrates, in any case, how caroming interactions of unstable currencies compound the damage and spread it around. Innocent victims accumulated on all sides from these egregious swings in money values—the companies, workers, economies that suffered in both Japan and the United States, but also in other nations that, one way or another, had to adjust to the yen-dollar gyrations. Governments tried to manage the swings, but their policy decisions often merely started the oscillations in a new direction, with new ripples of unintended destruction.

The winners presumably included countries where new factories were relocated and the largest, strongest firms that took advantage of the adverse conditions to grab market share from weaker competitors. The winners were also, of course, the currency markets that played off every stage of instability. A smart global trader made money both on the upside and the downside, regardless of what the market movements did to mere nations.

Could Humpty Dumpty ever be put back together again? Possibly not, given the weakness of political leaders and parties in major countries since they are the ones who would have to reconstruct a stable currency system. Conscientious financiers and economists still felt the world must try, both to halt the aimless destruction and to avert the possibility of a larger calamity. That fear was an unspoken premise behind the Bretton Woods Commission report. Like other similar studies, it proposed a new system of international governance to stabilize money: major nations would commit to a flexible band of exchange relationships among their currencies, policed by the International Monetary Fund, which would be empowered to oversee the domestic economic policies of national governments.

In theory, the scheme seems plausible, but the real-world facts argue against its viability. After all, what Volcker and his colleagues proposed was a global system quite similar to the European Exchange Rate Mechanism that had just been blown apart by the currency speculators. In the right circumstances, the speculators would do the same to a worldwide currency mechanism, searching for contradictions and attacking the weaker currencies until they were driven out or the system itself buckled.

The fundamental problem is that the world at present has no reliable anchor for setting up such a system, certainly not the U.S. dollar, the rock upon which the Bretton Woods system was founded after World War II. For twenty years, the Bretton Woods system of fixed exchange rates worked so long as the dollar itself was dependable. It broke down once the dollar was not. Since 1971 the dollar has undergone four major devaluations, and its value is sure to decline much further if the United States does nothing to correct its trade deficits and mounting foreign debt.

Eventually, one might imagine a troika arrangement among the three leading currencies that could provide a stable base, but that possibility does not seem at hand. Among all the currency reserves held by nations, 56 percent are still held in dollars, only 17 percent in deutschemarks and 10 percent in yen. As the dollar continues to lose value, more reserves and transactions will shift to the yen and D-mark, but for political and historical reasons, the global system still relies mainly on the dollar—a rock that is eroding swiftly.[22]

A declining currency would, of course, stimulate a country's exports and dampen foreign imports by shifting the price of both in trade. Many in America persisted in believing that the declining dollar would thus eventually restore general prosperity. This widely held view misunderstood the dynamics of global investment and wealth: a declining currency meant a nation and its enterprises were losing wealth relative to others. A U.S. multinational, for instance, calculated its stock price combined with the value of the U.S. currency as the expression of its own buying power for foreign investments, since it could pay for them by issuing new stock shares. If the dollar declined, a company gained a short-term edge in prices but lost long-term capacity to acquire new assets for the globalizing contests.

As this suggests, the long-term underlying cause of confused money values is the great shift of wealth that is under way in the world through global commerce and the relocation of its industrial base—a wealth shift from older economies, especially America's, to the most successful developing nations. Just as this shift is reflected in the U.S. trade deficits described in Chapter 10, it is also reflected in the financial balances. In rough terms, the newly prosperous Asian economies are storing up new wealth from their trading surpluses, lending and investing it, while the U.S. and European economies are borrowing capital to cover their own deficits.

A snapshot of this shifting wealth can be seen in the foreign-currency reserves held by the various governments. In 1995, the United States had $80 billion in foreign reserves and Germany about the same. Japan held $240 billion. Leaving out Japan, the other fast-prospering Asian nations collectively held an awesome total of more than $400 billion in foreign reserves. That vast store of wealth represents a new center of power in the global system, not yet fully appreciated by the Old World capitals. This new power will sooner or later assert itself on such fundamental matters as reforming the world's currency system and may someday be bold enough to instruct the United States and Europe on what is sound economic policy. After all, the richer one gets, the greater one's stake in maintaining stable money.[23]

Economic difficulties are immense, but the real question involved in stabilizing the globalized financial system is about political power: Who shall govern these important matters, governments or private markets? Finance capital wants government to get out of the way and let the markets rule, but global capital needs old-fashioned national governments much more than it acknowledges. If the nation-state loses its authority to govern, who will protect the sanctity of property rights or rescue capital owners in a market crisis? Without trustworthy national governments, who will issue money that people can trust?

The apostles of free markets continue to argue that if the governments will yield their role, the global marketplace will converge fully and produce greater stability for all. That claim looks increasingly far-fetched against the last twenty-five years of instability and the recurring crises. Indeed, as global finance has acquired more freedom and power, the ideological contradictions have deepened. With increasing frequency, capital calls on government to manage the disruptions and expects societies to pay for the debt liquidations. Someday in the far distant future, the nation-state might evolve into some sort of globalized governing system, but right now that visionary solution remains a mere vision.

The Bretton Woods Commission's proposal represented the establishment's idea of an interim step toward the vision of eventual "one world" governance. Though the report does not say so, its reforms implicitly assume national governments will cede control over their domestic economic policies—budgets and interest rates, growth and unemployment—to international supervision. In some vague manner, the IMF would be authorized to discipline governments in the advanced economies, more or less as it already does with the poorer developing nations.

This arrangement would satisfy the anxieties of the international financial community since the IMF is closely aligned with the world's bankers in political purpose and economic orthodoxy. If the IMF imposed "sound economic policy" on elected governments, those policies would not look much different from what global finance tries to impose. But this shift in governing power is a hard sell with citizens.

Which government would dare to propose this surrender of sovereignty to its own electorate? Certainly not American political leaders, already faced with rising anger among voters. The IMF may bully poor nations into adopting austerity budgets, cutting wages and social spending, but would

citizens in rich nations stand for this? Financiers may be ready for "one world," especially if they get to supervise it, but most people are not.

Political impasse is fused with the economic disjunction. The global system seems trapped between two stages of history as it stumbles toward some sort of disastrous event that will smash confidence and force governments to resolve the contradictions.

A plausible alternative to catastrophe is for nation-states to reclaim power and responsibility from manic investors in the marketplace—that is, to restore political controls over capital and finance. National governance and broader social priorities could be swiftly reasserted over capital and its movements in the old-fashioned way: by taxing it. Renewing regulatory controls would impose explicit obligations on capital in exchange for the protections societies provide to capital owners. This political reversal would not foreclose a future of globalized finance and trade, but might instead save it from a terminating crisis.

If "global disintegration" is under way, as George Soros warns, the responsible imperative of history is for governments to find the courage to intervene before it is too late. The steady retreat by governments from their own obligations has helped to foster the irresponsibility of unfettered global capital and led to the recurring crises that governments must in turn clean up. This bizarre arrangement has so far succeeded in averting a global breakdown. When it fails, it will ignite an explosive counterrevolution against the global system.

The first and simplest reform governments could undertake is a measure proposed more than fifteen years ago by Yale economist James Tobin: impose a very slight transactions tax on all cross-border flows of capital. Applied at major foreign-exchange centers, a small exit-and-entry toll would slow down the furious pace of global finance by taking a nick out of the quick profits (at present volumes, an infinitesimal levy on capital's cross-border movements would yield hundreds of billions in new revenue). Capital controls of a more focused nature could follow. This would not destroy globalized markets, but should greatly reduce the unproductive daily turnovers in currencies and other assets, thus increasing stability in money values. Traders imagine they could always evade such measures, but not if leading governments were serious about employing them.

Indeed, given its centrality to global money and markets, even the financially weakened United States might still impose controls unilaterally, both on foreign and domestic capital, encouraging other governments to do the same. After the initial anger and disruptions subsided, foreign investors would discover that they, too, need the American market. American investors would discover that they must respect U.S. rules if they wish to rely on U.S. protection. The Federal Reserve, for instance, could eliminate the leakage from offshore banking centers in an instant, if it wished, simply by declaring that U.S. banks cannot accept transfers from them. In any fundamental power struggle with private capital, governments will prevail.

Once global finance was recontrolled in this manner, then major governments would have a better basis for addressing the deeper problems of how to coordinate the management of the world's money supplies and economic cycles, thereby reducing the wider misalignments in currencies. Of course, the emerging Asian powers must have a seat at the table for this discussion. The particular methodologies are less important, I think, than the question of political priorities. Reforms that simply stabilize the present system by reducing the most visible risks are an insufficient answer to the general economic upheavals and distress. Indeed, if a new currency system worked simply for the interests of finance, it might merely compel governments to adjust their balance sheets by lowering domestic standards of living more swiftly. In that case, if speculators did not blow the system apart, political reactions would.

People everywhere ought not to be expected to accept a new international order if it holds no promise of benefit to their own economic conditions, if it does nothing to ameliorate their insecurities and losses. To address that, governments would be compelled to confront the deeper disorders in the real economy of global commerce—the unbalanced trade, the underlying disorders of supply and demand, the broader questions about wages and labor rights and how to bring up the bottom of the wage ladder. Naturally, free capital is opposed to all of these propositions.

Given the momentum of events and the weakness of political leaders, none of these steps seems likely to occur. The very idea of government intervention sounds radical to Americans imbued with the theory and propaganda of free-market virtues and ignorant of the fact that many other governments still do exercise control over capital, formally or informally. These other nations might be more willing to discuss a new economic agenda for the global system if they thought the global leader was prepared to consider the subject seriously.

A genuine debate on these questions in America is most unlikely, however. Alternatives to further deregulation of global finance are seldom discussed in the U.S. press or politics and are automatically derided by influential economists and bankers. The orthodoxy reigns confidently despite gathering signs of systemic stress. The system hurtles forward on its present course despite the contradictions. The future will eventually reveal whether dire warnings such as mine are justified, whether the optimism of finance capital is well founded or another tragic episode of manic, misplaced hopes.

Twelve

El Barzón[*]

THE POWER of global finance includes an extraordinary ability to create its own version of reality and persuade others to believe in it. When investment analysts determine the financial outlook for a company or a nation, their portraiture is based on statistical indicators, market trends and political intelligence—an analysis cleanly abstracted from the messy facts of daily life. The financial data seem so concrete and logical, so consistent with orthodox principles of economics, that others are regularly seduced by the market's self-confident assumptions. Governments, press and politicians typically embrace these financial projections and amplify them into a general metaphor of economic progress. When the messy truth intervenes, the duped ones are often reluctant to accept it.

The case of Mexico is the most vivid—and tragic—example, among many others in recent years, of how supposedly learned people can be swept up in the enthusiasms of financial investors and led to accept a quite fanciful version of what another country is really like, what is happening there. President Clinton and his senior advisors (as well as their Republican predecessors) were taken into finance's reality warp and they zealously promoted the mythology of a newly modernized Mexico. But then so did leading figures from business, finance and academic economics. Their illusions were faithfully rebroadcast by the establishment media, the leading newspapers and commentators, while dissenters were dismissed as reactionary.

Mexico, it was said, was about to enter the front ranks of trading nations, reforming and modernizing its industrial system, dismantling an outmoded nationalist economic structure and the political corruption endemic in its state-controlled enterprises. The educated middle class, its confidence and incomes growing, demanded political reform and provided a dynamic market of consumers, and Mexico was enjoying a fabulous investment boom. Instead of the ruling party's old power cliques, the nation was now led by reform-minded technocrats—men educated at Harvard, Yale

Spanish: "the yoke" or, more literally, the leather strap that connects a wooden yoke to oxen. In popular usage in Mexico, el barzón refers to the yoke of debt.

and Stanford—who understood that Mexico must embrace global integration if it wished to prosper.

In the United States as well as Mexico, these progressive assumptions were articulated as the common understanding of the Mexican reality, the context in which Clinton and bipartisan elites promoted the North American Free Trade Agreement between the two countries in 1993. Despite the supporting data, almost none of it turned out to be true.

Two years later Mexico was in ruin, its economy contracting by a devastating 7 percent, its domestic commerce frozen by a banking crisis that was devouring both financial institutions and industrial firms. At least one million jobs were destroyed, probably many more. Wage incomes fell in value by nearly one third. With incomes shrinking, as many as one in five Mexicans fell dangerously behind on their loans for cars, homes, businesses. More than eight thousand firms failed.[1]

The reformers turned out to be corrupt themselves. Former president Carlos Salinas de Gortari was in disgraced exile (though still serving on the board of the *Wall Street Journal*). His brother was in prison, accused of stealing hundreds of millions in state assets and of complicity in murder. For the first time since Mexico's revolutionary turbulence in the 1920s assassination was revived as a tool of political conflict. Salinas's handpicked presidential nominee was murdered; so was a young reform politician about to become the majority leader in Congress.[2]

An armed uprising in the southern state of Chiapas provoked heightened paranoia among other governors, and violent clashes occurred in the states of Guerrero, Morelos and Oaxaca in which troops or police fired murderously upon peasants marching in protest. The U.S. government, meanwhile, evidently rediscovered what its investigative agents had always known—namely, that a major sector of Mexican commerce was involved in drug trafficking protected by highly placed patrons in the PRI (Partido Revolucionario Institucional), the political party that has held an uninterrupted monopoly on power for nearly seventy years. Instead of prospering, ordinary Mexicans formed a swollen new wave of immigrants, heading north.

Reality is often quite prosaic alongside the glamorous mythmaking. In hindsight, as financiers acknowledged, the Mexican boom of the early 1990s was mainly confined to its financial sector, not its real economy of domestic production and employment. It was fed by borrowed money and selling off state assets.

Rather than political reforms, the financial boom was fundamentally driven by a single fact of global finance: the opportunity to arbitrage the differences in interest rates between the U.S. and foreign financial markets. By borrowing in New York's money market where interest rates were then comparatively low, an investor could buy Mexican stocks or short-term government notes and capture the spread between returns of 5 to 6 percent in America and 12 to 14 percent in Mexico.

As more investors were inspired to do this, the price of Mexican stocks naturally soared and the Bolsa de Valores index doubled, tripled, even quadrupled during a span of only three years. Smart investors (including major Mexican banks) reaped fabulous returns—as much as 80 to 100 percent—by borrowing in America and buying Mexican financial assets they might hold no more than a few weeks or months. Dumb investors thought it would last forever.

The Mexican bubble popped in December 1994—a harrowing collapse in financial values when the foreign investors panicked and fled en masse. The proximate trigger was the Mexican government's dwindling reserves of the foreign currencies needed to redeem the mounting short-term debt paper held by the overseas lenders. When this condition became critical, the government was compelled to devalue the peso, which for several years it had propped up at overvalued levels to attract the foreign money. The global investors felt betrayed and rushed for the door, all at once, dumping Mexican assets of every kind. Something like $25 billion flew out of the country. Instead of modest devaluation, the national currency collapsed, losing half of its purchasing power during a few frantic weeks.

In the aftermath, there were endless disputes in the press and among policy makers over how clumsily the devaluation crisis had been handled by Mexico City or why American investors, including some of Wall Street's largest brokerages, had not seen it coming. When market illusions are shattered, a search always begins to identify the human errors that might explain it.

A deeper cause of the collapse, however, was grounded in the pedestrian conditions of global finance itself: The Federal Reserve in Washington was raising U.S. interest rates throughout 1994 and thus steadily reducing the easy rewards to be gained from the financial arbitrage across borders. As this occurred, Mexico had to keep raising its own interest rates to continue its borrowing and, meanwhile, expended more and more of its scarce hard-currency reserves to cover the maturing debt paper held by foreigners. Amid the political cheerleading for NAFTA, these threatening implications were ignored by most market players, even when a few savvy observers pointed them out.

In other words, the profitable game of arbitrage that had helped generate the illusion of booming Mexico was coming to an end, regardless. Indeed, the sudden crash that unfolded in early 1995 was not confined to Mexico, but spread quickly around the world, collapsing other "emerging markets" in Latin America and Asia where global investors had also arbitraged the interest-rate spreads. Latin American markets fell 38 percent in two months; even Asia's hottest markets fell 10 to 21 percent as the global money abruptly rushed home to safe haven. This worldwide panic was widely attributed to a "Tequila Effect" and blamed on the Mexican officials, now described as hapless by the same experts who had previously touted their virtues.[3]

In Washington, Undersecretary of Treasury Lawrence Summers depicted the Mexican debacle ominously as "the first crisis of the 21st century." Michel Camdessus, managing director of the International Monetary Fund, warned that the unraveling of Mexican finance could lead to "a true global catastrophe." Thus armed with a sense of crisis, major governments stepped in to save Mexico and rescue the misguided American investors, rather than let the free market impose its own harsh punishments on them. The Clinton administration, without acknowledging any embarrassment for its own misplaced hopes, took the lead in assembling an international bailout—$50 billion in immediate credit to staunch Mexico's hemorrhage and reassure the capitalist adventurers.[4]

The bailout provoked some bitter reactions in American politics, but it ostensibly succeeded. At least the free fall of the peso's value was halted; the Mexican stock market stabilized and began rising again. U.S. officials congratulated one another on their timely action (while warning investors not to count on such assistance again in the future). In time, the American press began to report the standard reassurances: Mexico would undergo painful adjustments, but the "fundamentals" were back in place and Mexico was again on the road toward a more promising future. Official illusions, fostered by the financial indicators, diverged once again from reality on the ground.

The "fundamentals" were not in place for the country and its people. Mexico was still bleeding savagely, stumbling toward a graver crisis, both in its politics and economics. Its economy was effectively in receivership to foreign creditors (principally represented by the U.S. government) and its domestic industrial structure was gradually coming unwound, as large and small enterprises had no consumer demand for their products and, therefore, no money to pay swollen debt burdens or even sometimes their workers' wages. Amid rising street violence by desperate people, the fratricidal political assassinations also continued. While Americans looked the other way, focused on their own presidential elections in 1996, the center was not holding in Mexico.

In the face of full-blown depression, the Mexican government was pursuing a harsh remedial strategy—cutting federal spending and raising the taxes on consumption, while its central bank imposed tight credit and high interest rates—thus further depressing incomes and aggregate demand. The government executed a series of bailouts for the eighteen major banks, eight of which failed, and for some leading industrial groups, yet some failed again. The debt defaults multiplied and social disintegration spread, feeding the generalized sense of political insecurity.

This draconian approach to crisis was not exactly a sovereign decision. The strategy was imposed on Mexico by its foreign creditors and their enforcement agencies, including the U.S. Treasury and Federal Reserve. This financial discipline was known as structural adjustment—an approach that the IMF and World Bank frequently prescribed for developing countries fallen dangerously in arrears on foreign debts. The basic idea is to correct financial imbalances first and deal with the real economy later, restoring a reliable national currency so that foreign capital may safely return to lend and invest. Around the world, scores of debt-burdened nations have experienced the same stern medicine.

To secure the emergency credit from Washington, the Mexican government had to accept its terms. The alternative might have meant opting out of the global financial system, at least temporarily, by defying its dictates or admitting that Mexico was not really ready for the prime-time status promised by the NAFTA advocates. That choice was unthinkable to the technocratic reformers in power. Mexico's new president, Ernesto Zedillo Ponce de León, was a Yale graduate, schooled in the free-market orthodoxy promoted by American government and finance, the doctrine known throughout Latin America as neoliberalism.*

Another option did exist for Mexico, a strategy that could have stopped the unraveling quickly and with far less economic destruction and human suffering: government controls on capital. Once confronted by the market's panic, Mexico could have imposed emergency foreign-exchange controls on both the inflows and outflows of finance capital—stabilizing measures that would have halted or slowed down the capital flight, at least until everyone could make orderly adjustments. When some independent economists proposed this approach, Zedillo brushed it aside.

Controlling capital's movements across national borders violated the reigning assumptions of neoliberalism. The IMF and the U.S. government always opposed such market interferences on principle (though the IMF did subsequently admit that such measures may have been justified in Mexico's case). The option of challenging capital's prerogatives was the road not taken.[5]

The case of Mexico illustrates, in the most horrendous terms, that developing nations make a kind of deal with the devil when they open themselves to the animal spirits of global capital. As liquidity sloshes about in the global financial system, seeking the highest returns, a nation may find itself inundated with "hot money" from abroad that can ignite a giddy boom—or abruptly starved for credit when the foreign money decides, for whatever reason, to leave. Mexico is among scores of aspiring countries that have been taken hostage in this manner, the entry price they paid for pursuing industrial advancement in the trading system. Like Mexico, many other nations have found the promised prosperity to be quite illusory.

The question of free capital is the ultimate strategic issue for ambitious developing countries, far more important than all the other economic variables, and poorer nations are divided, one from another, by how they choose to answer the question. Will allowing global finance unfettered ac-

---

* In American political usage, "neoliberalism" would translate as libertarianism, the free-market and anti-government ideology of market reformers.

cess to the domestic economy advance a country's development strategy or cripple it? Must a government yield national destiny to capital in order to attract foreign investment or should it instead rigorously regulate the flows of finance to advance up the ladder of prosperity? For Americans imbued with free-market ideology, the answer might seem obvious. Yet the practical evidence from around the world contradicts the ideology.

The awesome paradox of free-market capitalism in this revolutionary era is that the poorer nations that have succeeded most spectacularly during the last three decades are ones that exercised stringent controls over capital. They restricted the cross-border flows of foreign capital and their own domestic wealth, either by quantity or quality. They purposefully steered capital to selected domestic industries and away from other sectors. They sought foreign investors, but kept certain of their own financial markets closed to outsiders. On the whole, it worked. At least, the fastest-rising economies in the world all followed variations on this basic economic strategy.

The original model, of course, was Japan. Its development strategy has been successfully mimicked, most notably by South Korea and Taiwan, and many other nations are now applying similar principles, most notably China, striving to develop an advanced industrial base by retaining strategic control over investors and investments. The capital question by itself does not, of course, guarantee anyone's advancement, given the many other factors of economic resources, politics, history and culture. But it does appear to be a central predicate for success.

As a crude generalization, the comparison is between East Asia and Latin America. One region followed Tokyo's example and often achieved astounding results. The other region followed Washington and Wall Street and lurched from one crisis to another. Latin America relied heavily on foreign capital (mainly from America) for loans and investment and experienced disappointing growth rates. Asians pursued economic strategies designed to generate savings at home, enough capital to finance their own indigenous industrial structures. One region has lost ground in global trade. The other nearly doubled its share.

Tokyo versus Washington. In policy circles, these strategic differences have hardened into a running intellectual debate that pits the two models against one another. American leaders, joined by World Bank and IMF officials, promote an ideology of financial deregulation and privatization they immodestly call the "Washington consensus." Japanese authorities point out, in their usual diffident manner, that there is no "consensus" on this question. Besides, they observe, the "Washington consensus" doesn't seem to work very well for poor countries.

The developing nations, whatever they may wish for, do not always have a free choice on these questions. Many are simply too weak and disorganized to set their own terms. Many are too deeply indebted from their own past failures to challenge the rules set by capital. Other nations are bound by geography and history, by their own political and cultural legacies, to one model over the other.

Americans, in general, are oblivious to this debate over free capital, just as they are largely ignorant of the diverse and wondrous people who live in the struggling nation on the southern border. Mexico brings its own tragic burden to its problem, of course, the brutal class divisions and corrupt elites, the fateful history of many past opportunities that were squandered. Still, Mexico's fate also includes geography. The familiar lament was first expressed nearly a century ago by President Porfirio Díaz: "Poor Mexico, so far from God, so close to the United States."

At the town of Uruapan in the state of Michoacán, a bereaved family brought the corpse of their dead father to their local bank and turned the bank's lobby into a funeral parlor. He was a small farmer whose avocado fields were seized when he failed on his loans. The family blamed the bankers for his death. The bank was embarrassed enough to return the land to the widow and write off the bad debts.

This occurred in early 1995 at the height of the crisis. From December to February interest rates had jumped from 15 to 80 percent, then to 130 percent. Mexicans found themselves suddenly united across traditional class lines, city and countryside, *campesinos* and landowners and even major business conglomerates, by a common condition: they were all bad debtors. The sudden interest-rate spike put nearly everyone under water, instantly, because most of the lending in Mexico was done with variable interest rates, tied to the money market's rates. When the U.S. bailout arrived and the peso stabilized, interest rates fell sharply but still remained at impossible levels around 40 percent (with the real interest rates held at a punishing 10 percent). By the spring of 1996, when I was in Mexico City, the debtors had become a popular army of protest, a movement called El Barzón, half a million strong and engaged in running conflict with the bankers.

"We have succeeded in putting a hold on the confiscations of trucks and small businesses," said Alfonso Ramírez Cuéllar, a thirty-four-year-old anthropologist and movement leader. "When we get a call from someone who's about to lose their house or their business equipment, we go there and stop it. El Barzón is the rebellion of the productive middle class in Mexico. We fight together, from the *campesinos* to the people of enterprise, the indigenous peoples and also the small and medium landowners."

In Colonia Algarin, south of downtown, El Barzón's metropolitan office was housed in a shabby two-story stucco apartment building. A large white moving truck was parked at the curb out front, equipped with computers and legal documents. Two or three times a week the truck would rush off to disrupt debtor auctions or property confiscations, carrying lawyers to provide technical advice for the people defending homes or businesses, while others physically halted the proceedings. The slogan on the truck's side declared: *"Debo, no niego/Pago lo justo."* "I owe, I don't deny/I pay what's fair."

El Barzón's offices were arranged like a service center for drowning people. One office was for small-business people, another for truckers, another for the homeowners with failed mortgages. The headquarters for the flying squads of activists was called the "White Army." Next door was the office for desperate people ensnared by usurers, underground lenders who charged 300 to 400 percent interest. A small shrine to the Virgin with two votive candles was on the wall by the stairway. The green and white posters demanded: *"No Mas Dinero a Los Bancos!"* (No More Money to the Banks!).

The organization was growing daily, more or less spontaneously, as the interest payments ground up more families and firms. On the day I visited a number of mournful-looking couples were waiting patiently to explain their problems and sign up for help. El Barzón was a term that originated in the countryside—the name for the leather strap that ties the yoke to oxen —but its meaning seemed appropriate to the national condition. The grim irony of Mexico's plight was that financial desperation bridged social chasms that Mexican politics has long neglected.

"El Barzón started as a rural movement and we have moved to the city," Ramírez said. "We were born in the agricultural sector where the problem of nonperforming loans had already reached serious proportions by 1993, before NAFTA, before the devaluation. Our first political action was to pull out the tractors and put them in the streets. In March we had a national mobilization and blocked the government offices [tax collectors and bank regulators] all over the country. When we took the economic problem out of the cabinet discussions and put it in the streets, that brought together people who were not previously allied or even sympathetic to one another."

Bankers, not surprisingly, both resented and envied the popular success of the debtors' movement. After all, the value of bank employees' wages had fallen drastically, too, and it was their institutions that were drowning in portfolios of bad loans, their capital reserves wiped out. The government, assisted by a $1 billion loan from the World Bank, had executed a series of bank bailouts, including limited relief measures for debtors, but none of these staunched the crisis. How could they when the economy was still so depressed and almost no one had any money to spend?

About 20 percent of Mexican housing mortgages were no longer being paid, according to the government, but American consulting firms estimated that more like 40 percent were nonperforming (Ramírez thought the problem was even larger). A retired engineer who owned a modest downtown apartment valued at $53,000 received a mortgage notice from the bank informing him that between the peso devaluation and the higher interest rates, he now owed more than $100,000.

Credit cards and car loans, both of which had expanded explosively during the financial boom, were nearly hopeless. A young middle-level bank manager, Juan Octavio Schietekat Ballesteros, a vice president at Bancomer, explained: "We don't repossess the cars. We just keep renegotiating with the customers to keep the loans going. If Bancomer repossessed all the car loans that are nonperforming now, we would have a huge parking lot of cars. We have 250,000 car loans and something like 30 percent of them are nonperforming."

The outlook for business debtors was not much better. "There have been many, many efforts," Schietekat said, "but what can you do when interest rates are still so high? What business will return 40 percent? Not very many. So why should people risk their money on a business when you can put it in government notes or money-market paper and get your 40 percent without risk? It's very simple. What happens in a period like this is that people with a little capital become very rich and people without capital become much poorer."

Emilio España Krauss, the owner of Usher, a small candy company with three hundred employees that produces pocket mints and cocoa products, fought back when the bank sued him. He showed me an interest-due notice he had received from Bancomer on his company's $100,000 loan for operating capital. The interest rate was calculated to be 171 percent. A bank's rate card on short-term loans in 1995 was 194 percent for seven days and 228 percent for twenty-one days. "It comes to the point where your loan comes due and your customers haven't paid you because the economy has collapsed, so you have to borrow short term again to keep going," España explained. "That's why so many companies have disappeared. Nobody can afford that and survive. That's why I started a crusade against the banks."

Yet the banks were tethered themselves—yoked to the money markets where they borrowed short-term funds in order to finance their lending. When I asked Juan Schietekat about triple-digit interest rates charged on one-week loans, the young bank vice president shrugged. "Long term in Mexico means like twenty-eight days," he said. "This was not a price the banks determine. It's determined by the money market. It's just funny money that comes and goes in minutes or days. That's what makes Mexico so vulnerable."

Despite their differences people like the business owner, the young banker and the El Barzón leader were all worried about the same thing: the steady unraveling of Mexico's social fabric. "We are coming very fast to some kind of catastrophe," España lamented. "It could be a revolutionary situation which the government would be unable to control. I'm very afraid of that."

Schietekat assumed that economic growth would revive, but he doubted that improving statistical indicators would mean much to the broad population. Instead, he expected wages and employment would continue to be depressed in most domestic sectors. "I think we will see more and more crime and violence in the streets, stuff like that," the banker predicted.

"The bottom line," Alfonso Ramírez warned, "is there will not be a recovery in Mexico if we do not address the bleeding of resources to pay the foreign debt. If Clinton and the U.S. Treasury do not make room for greater flexibility, every single Mexican will wind up in the United States by the year 2000—every one of us." He and his colleagues at El Barzón laughed at the provocative thought since they knew Mexico meant only one thing to many Americans: *mojados,* "wetbacks."

Of all the strange convergences I glimpsed during my travels, none was more bizarre than this: the United States had formed a partnership for economic integration with an aspiring neighbor it barely knew. In American consciousness, the complex realities of Mexico were reduced to crude stereotypes: either a hapless, backward place that sent illegal immigrants north to claim U.S. jobs or—equally inaccurate—a modern industrial state ready to collaborate on equal terms with the largest, richest economy on earth. Many talented Mexicans had yearned to believe in the latter myth themselves, to escape the corruption and disappointments of the past and become truly modern. Now they felt betrayed by their own naive optimism, but also by the indifference of Mexico's new trading partner.

Aside from the movement of El Barzón, the social suffering was mostly expressed incoherently, often as street crime. An opinion survey by *El Universal,* the Mexico City daily, asked citizens how many had been assaulted during the previous year. Answer: 36 percent. How many knew friends or family who were robbed or attacked? Answer: 61 percent. Only 21 percent felt secure riding buses or other public transportation. Only 14 percent felt safe walking the streets.[6]

Along the Paseo de la Reforma, a hunger strike by several dozen dismissed federal workers occupied one of the gilded fountains. At the Zócalo, the broad plaza next to the National Palace, peddlers sold tiny Salinas dolls that depicted the celebrated ex-president in prison garb, clutching a fat bag of money. The dolls of Subcomandante Marcos portrayed the rebel leader of Chiapas as a masked man on horseback. A delegation of protesting *campesinos* marched to the U.S. Embassy and dumped cow dung outside.

Mexicans of every station were pained and angered by the news from Riverside, California, where the sheriff's police had chased down a truckload of Mexican illegals and administered a savage beating that was captured on videotape. Forget NAFTA, people told one another, this is how Americans feel about us.

A week later the sense of humiliation was deepened when Mexican politicians performed the annual ritual of commemorating the death of Zapata. Emiliano Zapata, the dashing peasant general of the Mexican revolution, remained a beloved symbol of social justice; his murder by government forces in 1919 was still freshly mourned each year as a fatal wrong turn in national history. In 1996, President Zedillo traveled to Zapata's home state of Morelos, south of the capital, to make a speech declaring his government's dedication to Zapata's ideals.

A few miles away, a caravan of five hundred *campesinos* from Tepoztlán was en route to deliver a protest petition to the president when they encountered a blockade of three hundred state police. The police opened fire on the peasants, wounded thirty people and killed their aged leader. A similar clash had occurred the previous summer at Aguas Blancas in Guerrero, where seventeen peasants were massacred. In both instances, the local governors at first claimed the attacks were provoked by violent agitators—until, like the Riverside incident, videotaped evidence surfaced to set the facts straight. It wasn't just gringo police beating on poor Mexicans, but the Mexican authorities, too.[7]

Elite political opposition, though still confused and fragmented, was beginning to find its voice. Almost daily in Mexico City, business and academic leaders called upon the Zedillo government to change direction. Some of them mused privately on a possibility that the president might even be removed from office by his own party or that the PRI's long monopoly on political power would finally be smashed in the coming legislative elections. Yet everyone also understood that nothing significant was likely to change until after the U.S. elections. Perhaps then Washington would acknowledge what was happening to Mexico and address reality.

For now, Mexico seemed frozen in time. Like any tourist, I went to see the stunning nationalist murals by Rivera and Orozco—class-conscious political paintings in uncompromising colors that had seemed too romantic and antiquated, even cartoonish, when I had first seen them many years before. On walls and stairways at the National Palace and a nearby school, the two great muralists had painted the national story, the dark moments of betrayal, fallen empires, the violence of invading armies and capitalist robber barons, the enduring simple hope of modest peoples. Only now their stark caricatures of the rich feeding on the poor seemed to me perversely relevant again, as though doomed Mexico was replaying its bloody past in modern dress. Great art, conceived in the revolutionary fervor, lived on to rebuke the shallow pretensions of progress.

Mexico was broke again, yet still fabulously rich in its cultural knowledge. The bleak economic facts did not do justice to the country (and perhaps only encouraged the old stereotypes) because Mexico was more dynamic and sophisticated and entrancing than financial statistics could convey—and more haunted by history than the free-market reformers could understand. Mexico City, the most populous in the world, was afflicted with well-known problems of congestion and pollution, yet also urbane and beautiful and wonderfully animated. Its European grace notes, the broad boulevards and castles inherited from colonial eras, were splashed with wild, magical colors that could only be described as "Mexican." At the city's center were the ruins of a great civilization that had flourished before the *Mayflower* landed. Mexico's high culture began when Greece itself was young.

The popular despair was palpably present in the streets, even along the grand boulevards, where mothers and children begged in teams. Yet the antic music was still present, too. Some families of beggars dressed up as clowns or strange animals and played wooden flutes to amuse their benefactors. The country's outlandish sense of humor was mixed up with the sorrow, both well earned from national experience. People seemed to have learned something from their troubled history—a knowledge of the raw, ripe mystery in human existence—that many wealthy people to the north did not yet fully understand.

"That's our true comparative advantage," Mexican author Jorge G. Castañeda insisted. "Not oil, not tomatoes, not the Ph.D.s in our government, but the strength of our national culture."

From the American side, the pivotal event in the relationship was the approval of NAFTA in 1993. U.S. critics continued to point out the many promises accompanying the free-trade agreement that had not been fulfilled for the U.S. economy. From the Mexican perspective, however, the critical juncture with America came much earlier, back in 1986, when the debt-burdened Mexican government opted to embrace the small-state economic model that is known among policy experts as the "Washington consensus."

The decision meant a radical departure from the centralized socialist state that the PRI power structure had developed and managed since the 1930s—instituting mass privatization by selling off the state-owned industrial groups to private investors both in Mexico and abroad, deregulating financial markets and shrinking the government's subsidies and controls in commerce, relaxing the various trade barriers that protected domestic producers and signing the GATT treaty that signified full membership in the global system. For Mexicans, neoliberalism started from that moment, and the trade liberalization authorized by NAFTA merely accelerated what was already under way.

Mexico's choice was leveraged by its 1982 debt crisis and the lingering burden of failed debts that marked the failure of the old regime. As in many other Latin American nations, the self-indulgent elites of Mexican business and politics had for years participated in a malignant marriage with foreign capital—mainly leading American banks—a borrowing binge that enriched both while it lasted. When global recession brought the game crashing down in 1982, Mexico and more than a dozen other Latin nations were in effective default on their mountainous foreign debts. Mexican finance collapsed, as did growth and incomes. The U.S. government and the international agencies came to the rescue of the commercial banks, supervising a tortuous series of work-out deals underwritten by massive public lending from the IMF and World Bank.

For Mexico, the economic dilemma was how to get out from under and jump-start a recovery. The appealing logic promoted by Salinas and the other advocates was that neoliberalism offered a clean break with the past —an opening to the global system that would drive Mexico's industrial modernization and escape the deep corruption and complacent inefficiencies embedded in its major enterprises. Besides, the American government was pushing all the Latin debtors to do the same—the implicit price for resolving their debt problems and regaining credibility with global capital.

"The attraction of the neoliberal model resided in its novelty," Jorge Castañeda, an economist and political critic at the National Autonomous University of Mexico, wrote. "Since nothing done before had worked, maybe this experiment would. It didn't, in the sense that the underlying problems remained without a solution or an answer. The combination of growth and equity seemed as distant as before." [8]

By 1989, Mexico was a member of GATT and Carlos Salinas was the newly inaugurated reform president (though his victory was generally understood to have been stolen by the PRI's gross election fraud). Privatization and financial deregulation were under way and foreign capital began pouring in again. Economic expansion resumed modestly and wage levels that had been depressed since the 1982 debt crisis turned upward. The neoliberal shock effect seemed to be working. At least American multinationals and financial investors were convinced, and both focused on the opportunities in this hot, new emerging market so close to home.

From that point forward the Mexican condition diverged into two conflicting stories—two starkly different economic realities that effectively pitted Mexicans against themselves. One was the energetic investment boom, the story Americans saw heralded frequently in the news and that provided the optimistic premise for NAFTA's approval. The other reality was more visible to ordinary Mexicans—the swift, steady erosion of the domestic producers in manufacturing and agriculture who were ill equipped to compete in the global system. As the protective mantle of government was rolled away, many of them were decimated.

The toy industry and garment manufacturing fell to Asia, the low-wage imports from China, Taiwan and elsewhere. To staunch the flood of cheaper goods, the Mexican government was compelled, despite its free-market principles, to impose 500 percent tariffs on Chinese imports. Paper products and the candy industry went down before the much larger and more efficient American companies that captured market share by underpricing Mexican producers. After NAFTA reduced barriers further, retailing was targeted by the major American discounters (though the retailers' invasion stalled out with the subsequent economic collapse). Across many other product sectors, domestic firms were squeezed by the new price-cost pressures of globalization.

"The old model in Mexico was complete protectionism, very paternalistic and inefficient," Juan Schietekat explained. "In that economy, you could afford not to invest in your products and you would still sell because you had no competition. Then all of a sudden they open the economy and say: you have two years to modernize. Most enterprises couldn't do that. So they couldn't stand the competition and they went down. If you want to play a role in the global economy, you cannot take a country that's been protected for forty years into the global market overnight. The economy will go down."

Mexican agriculture, including the vast fabric of peasant farmers who worked millions of small plots organized as communal lands, underwent a similar upheaval. Price controls and direct subsidies were being withdrawn while markets were opened to cheaper foreign imports, especially American corn. By 1995, Mexico was importing more than nine million tons of basic grains—one third of its domestic consumption—while the price supports for tortilla producers were steadily reduced. A country of small farmers that had once been a net exporter of foodstuffs was becoming dependent on the large-scale, capital-intensive agriculture to the north.

"This may sound romantic, but the way land is farmed in Mexico is integral to how the communities function," said Carlos Heredia, a former government economist working for Equipo Pueblo, a civic development organization. "Salinas said: let's bring private money into the countryside, let's privatize. The idea was we can transform a depressed agriculture by modernizing—capitalize the peasant economy—and we will prosper by catering to the U.S. market, shifting to cash crops for export. The tragedy is that after they privatized, nothing happened. Instead of creating jobs in the local community and rooting people there, there has been a massive process of disintegration driven by the massive imports of cheaper grain, mainly from the U.S. Midwest."

These economic disruptions helped explain why the streams of Mexican immigrants to the United States were swollen, even in the years before the financial crash. Mexican incomes had been deflated through the 1980s, but when the Salinas boom started it undermined the fragile security for millions more. Many of them naturally headed north.

Mexicans understood the functional reality of immigration in terms that were never frankly discussed in American politics. "Immigration is the safety valve for economic crisis in Mexico and now U.S. policy is moving toward closing it down," Castañeda observed in a Mexico City lecture. "We know that the best young people, usually those with at least a high school education, are the ones who migrate to the U.S.—the ambitious and responsible people in search of jobs, trying to support their families. Mexican taxpayers cultivate the lamb and the U.S. reaps the harvest: cheap labor that is relatively well educated."

Despite these massive dislocations on the downside, the reformers had remained confident their economic model was working. Losers were to be expected in a vast economic transformation, but the new capital was indeed coming into Mexico—building steel mills, auto factories, chemical plants and other kinds of new productive capacity. For twenty years American multinationals had been producing various components at more than a thousand factories in Mexico's duty-free *maquiladora* zone along the U.S. border—a cheap-labor export platform for the major manufacturers. Now, in effect, they were offered the same globalizing advantage for the entire country.

For a brief time NAFTA advocates on both sides of the border could claim that the trade alliance truly was a win-win proposition. Mexico, to be sure, was borrowing heavily and running a huge trade deficit, $18 billion to $20 billion a year, but the inflow of American exports included capital goods—the machines and equipment needed to create the new factories for industrial advancement. If some U.S. jobs were relocated in the process, the growth in U.S. exports proved the overall impact was still positive for America, too.

After the financial collapse, the advocates stopped using those arguments because the investment in capital goods fell sharply and, more importantly, the trade flows were reversed. Mexico was suddenly running a trade surplus with the United States of $15 billion in goods, serving as a convenient low-wage export zone for entering the American market, just as opponents of NAFTA had predicted.

In theory (but only in theory) this trade surplus should have at least generated new jobs and rising prosperity for Mexicans. Yet it didn't seem to help. "You have quite a paradox," Heredia said. "Our total exports went up 23 percent in 1995, while Mexico's total output went down 7 percent." Apologists could argue that the depression would have been even worse without the export growth, but the paradoxical statistics indicated how violently the structure of the Mexican economy had been altered. Mexico was entering the big leagues of exporting nations. Yet its domestic economy was in ruin.

"We're actually undergoing a massive dismantling of Mexico's productive capacity," Heredia said. "Let me explain: if the economy concentrates on export industries, that means only three hundred companies that account for 85 percent of total exports. Out of those three hundred companies, a good chunk of them are subsidiaries of the U.S. multinationals. So what you have is intrafirm trade that's not really integrated with the domestic economy. It's General Motors exporting auto parts from its Mexico subsidiary to Ohio or Michigan. Since NAFTA the proportion of exports that is intrafirm trade has grown from 40 percent to 55 percent.

"At the same time, the rest of Mexican manufacturing that is not geared to exporting cannot cope with the opening of the border. Even after the devaluation reduced wages, they can't survive the competition or the high interest rates."

The investment boom, while it had lasted, was not as creative as many supposed. Most of the capital inflows went to the financial markets—buying stocks and debt paper, rather than building new factories. "Mexico did enhance its productive capacity, but this was not linked to the domestic economic structure because most of it went into the *maquiladoras* or to buy assets the state was selling off," Heredia said. "And only one fourth of the capital inflows actually went to direct investment in plants—while three fourths went into financial markets and speculation."

The "structural adjustment" policies imposed after the peso collapse effectively pushed priorities even further out of balance. The first objective was stabilizing the currency to reassure capital—getting the financial accounts straight—as the assumed precondition for restoring growth. Thus, the debt problems of domestic firms and families were hostage to the globalization strategy. So were Mexican workers since their wages were effectively depressed by the strategy, too.

"The IMF and the World Bank don't explicitly say you have to follow a low-wage policy, but the overall policy framework leads to a strategy of deliberately depressing wages," Heredia explained. "The model is geared to exports and puts pressure on wages by telling countries: we won't invest in your country's export industries if you don't give us a competitive advantage —low wages. Since the rest of the economy always lags behind the export sector, if you hold down wages to encourage investment in exports, you hold down the rest of the economy, too. Everyone else subsidizes the export sector."

So long as the Mexican government followed the neoliberal script, the imbalance between external and internal obligations would likely continue to chew up domestic enterprise even when economic growth was restored. Enrique Quintana, a financial editor and commentator at *La Reforma*, perhaps Mexico's most respected newspaper, explained why he and many others saw a deepening crisis ahead: "We will have growth, but it will be very, very unbalanced because the exporting sector will continue to grow and some segments of the internal economy, but the main part of the population will not benefit. This means additional social unrest and very probably the electoral defeat of the PRI in the coming elections. The government of Zedillo is seen by most of the population as widely discredited and so there will be a very high level of opposition. . . . The worst scenario is one in which the social unrest explodes and we have disorders in the countryside."

Beyond the political instability, the banking crisis would continue to claim more victims too, so long as the government did not alter its course. "At this point, we haven't gotten yet to the bottom of the banking crisis," Quintana predicted. "It is calculated that the bad loans will increase by 80 percent next year [when Mexico was scheduled to adopt the U.S. bank accounting rules on nonperforming loans]. The prospect is there will be no increase in incomes to service the debts and so it's very probable we will see a new peak in the banking crisis, followed by more fiscal cuts and bank sales to foreign interests."

Given the government's preoccupation with global capital, Mexico was in a kind of economic trap: it could balance its financial books by suppressing domestic demand and stimulating exports. But if a general expansion did resume, that would likely lead the economy back into the same problems—a stronger peso, rising imports and overpriced exports, increased foreign borrowing and renewed vulnerability to the random shocks from global finance. Ironically, if there had been no bailout from Washington in 1995, Mexico might have escaped the trap—compelled either to default or to renegotiate the terms on debt and trade with its creditors and its major trading partner, the United States.

"The greatest paradox," Heredia said, "is that since 1982 we've followed free-market policies that failed and we had to be bailed out twice, not by the Mexican government, but by a foreign government."

For all these reasons, leading figures from business, politics and academia were trying to formulate alternatives that might avert the deeper unraveling they foresaw—a quick write-down of domestic debts or renegotiation of NAFTA's trading terms or a strategic shift in economic policy that refocused on building domestic demand and industry rather than exports.

These and other ideas were floated almost daily in the public commentaries in Mexico's capital, though utterly ignored in Washington. Aside from the campaign promises to repel illegal immigrants, Mexico was a nonsubject in the U.S. political season. Aside from official embarrassment, another Mexican crisis would not greatly injure American interests, unless, of course, the United States had to bail it out again.

Rogelio Ramirez de la O, an influential financial consultant who advised American hedge-fund investors like George Soros and many U.S. multinationals, was among those trying to persuade the elite opinion leaders that Mexicans couldn't wait on Washington but must mobilize change themselves. "Consensus: things are terrible and won't get better on this present course," he said. "The longer it takes for this consensus to develop, the greater the risk of divisions and crazy responses and the more chance that it never gets back to normal."

Ramirez proposed a different sort of shock therapy: a one-time writedown of all the failed domestic debts held by Mexican banks—forgiveness of bad loans amounting to 30 percent of their book value. This would free up cash for both producers and consumers—the stimulus needed to restart the economy. The banks would lose in nominal terms, but they were never going to collect on these loans anyway.

If something like that did not happen, Ramirez thought, Mexico would find itself back in another crisis of foreign debt eventually. Total external debt was at $173 billion and rising, less ominous than Mexico's position in 1982, but sure to worsen as the stagnation continued. The annual interest payments on foreign loans amounted to 10 percent of Gross Domestic Product. *El Financiero*, Mexico's leading newspaper of finance, concluded: "Foreign debt will continue to strangle the productive operations [of the economy] and make it deepen in the median term."[9]

Debt forgiveness among Mexican banks and borrowers, Ramirez reasoned, could reverse that trend. "The important thing is to give the subsidies to the producers, not the banks," he said. "Write down the debt of the producers. The only way to get out of this is a great shock." His program did not sound so different from what El Barzón, the debtors' movement, had proposed. The essential point was that the financial system could not be saved from its downward spiral until the real economy was rescued.

Some voices called for more dramatic action—reversing or modifying Mexico's commitment to global economic integration, recontrolling the capital flows to reclaim the national destiny, devising a national industrial strategy more like East Asia's. "The only way in which Mexico will recover," said the factory owner Emilio España, "is when the U.S. won't lend any more money. Shut down the U.S. lending to Mexico. Then the banks won't be able to get any more loans and they won't be able to continue these practices."

Almost everywhere the anger and anxiety were mixed with a residual embarrassment, for many people had wanted to believe that Salinas's vision of modern Mexico had arrived. "I admit, if you'd asked me two or three years ago, I would have said I believed in it myself," said the banker Juan Schietekat. "But the truth is we weren't ready for this. We are forty years behind where Japan was and thirty years behind Korea and the others."

Rogelio Ramirez mused: "People say: why did Salinas fool us? It was not just Salinas. It was Salomon Brothers and Goldman Sachs and the U.S. government."

In the fog of American political debate, the real policy questions surrounding global capital and developing countries are seldom even mentioned, so most Americans are perhaps unaware that Washington's orthodoxy is widely challenged around the world or that alternatives exist that flatly contradict its principles. But when the World Bank's annual development report in 1991 consecrated neoliberalism as "the Washington consensus," the government of Japan issued a polite dissent. Look at the "Asian tigers," the Japanese said, look at us.

The global system's greatest success stories did not follow the "market-friendly" strategies that the World Bank and International Monetary Fund regularly prescribe for poor countries. Instead, they practiced a purposeful medley of state intervention—government policies that steered and subsidized enterprise, that suppressed domestic interest rates and controlled foreign capital, that protected their infant industries from the raw market forces, that set artificial prices for export goods, domestic food production and even national currencies, that provided socialistic assistance to their general populations.

Led by Japan's example, seven other Asian nations, from South Korea to Thailand, have followed this strategic approach. They are at vastly different stages of advance, but since 1960 these eight economies have collectively grown twice as fast as the rest of Asia, three times faster than Latin America, twenty-five times faster than sub-Saharan Africa. Indeed, the strategy has worked so well at stimulating growth and storing up new wealth that the great political challenge facing the global system now is how to persuade the newly rich nations to back off their successful strategies, to open up their economies and become responsible consumers in the glutted trading system.[10]

In rebuttal to the World Bank, Japan's Overseas Economic Cooperation Fund issued a white paper that gently questioned the standard "structural adjustment" plans that the international lending agencies imposed on developing countries:

Point: "If imports are liberalized too quickly, is it possible to develop industries which will play leading roles in the next stage of economic development? If not, isn't it necessary to protect the domestic industry to some extent for a certain period of time in order to allow a viable export industry to develop?"

Point: "We are afraid that the financial-sector policy of the World Bank is too much stressing market mechanism. Isn't it indispensable to have development finance institutions lending with subsidized interest rates, under some circumstances, in order to maximize the social welfare?"

Point: "It is too optimistic to expect that industries to sustain the economy of the next generation will come up automatically through the activities of the private sector. Some measures for fostering industry are required. . . . The structural adjustment approach seems to lack the long-term viewpoint of how to develop such industries, perhaps because it assumes that activities of the private sector will attain this goal. This lack is very regrettable."

Point: "It is impossible to achieve optimum allocation of resources solely through market principle, regardless of the level of development. . . . Where market interest rate cannot handle some problem, the introduction of subsidized interest rate becomes indispensable."

Point: "Most developing countries have had bitter experience with colonialism. The idea of transferring the basic industries to foreign capital is a serious political and social issue in view of their history. Moreover, even from an economic standpoint, we must also consider that monopoly of foreign capital will lead to the repatriation of rents."[11]

Tokyo's white paper provided an implicit summary of how Japan itself had gotten wealthy across thirty-five years and, for that matter, a checklist of what went wrong in countries like Mexico. The Japanese economic perspective includes a crucial social subtext: a poor country aspiring to industrialize, Japan argues, must do so in ways that share the economic benefits widely among its citizens, both to maintain political stability and to justify the subsidies and special treatment accorded certain sectors.

"Although efficiency and fairness are the major objectives to be pursued in economic policy," the OECF paper stated, "there is sometimes trade-off between the two. In the 1980's, economic theory as well as economic policy were heavily oriented toward the pursuit of efficiency. . . . What is now needed is a policy well balanced between efficiency and fairness, in order to improve the welfare of the entire society."

With prodding (and financial contribution) from Japan, now a major patron of the Bretton Woods institutions, the World Bank agreed to reconsider the strategic questions. In 1993, the bank produced *The East Asian Miracle,* a book that grudgingly acknowledged that Japan and the others had departed from the neoclassical model with spectacular results. The bank's economists conceded that the rapid growth in Asia "has at times benefited from careful policy interventions." Still, they were unsure of the precise cause and effect and insisted that to succeed, nations must still get "the fundamentals" right.

The Japanese critique of "structural adjustment" seems to have had very little actual impact on the World Bank and IMF. The Mexican bailout of 1995 still adhered to the old orthodoxy and so have the loan programs in Eastern Europe (where voters responded by electing ex-Communists to power). The harsh medicine of "structural adjustment" was not visibly diluted in Africa or elsewhere. The World Bank's study affected a condescending tone of bemused tolerance, as though the economists were impressed by the facts of Asia but still not convinced, since they could find no theoretical basis for explaining why the Asian approach should have worked.

Elsewhere in the world, opinion was less ambiguous about the effectiveness of the Japanese model. Professor Lal Jayawardena of Cambridge University, in a background paper for the Bretton Woods Commission's 1994 report, observed that "the uncertainty of success of the Washington consensus, especially in the big-bang format, and the substantial social costs incurred in the process have drawn attention to the alternative model."

Economist Lance Taylor of New York's New School for Social Research put it more bluntly: "Because Mexico (not to mention other unhappy countries such as Turkey, Russia, Bangladesh and most of sub-Saharan Africa) has been hewing to liberalization now for a long time with meager success, the theoretical arguments in favor of this policy inclination are losing their force. The assumptions underlying neoclassical economic theorems about the benefits of liberalization are revealing themselves as so peculiar that they don't work out in practical terms." [12]

The central elements of the Asian model ignored the theorems and instead merged the market's energies with a nationalist understanding of historical development. First, instead of promoting the strong currency expected by global capital, an Asian tiger deliberately undervalued its currency, thus keeping its export prices artificially low while discouraging imports by keeping them overpriced. The infant industries designated to become major exporters were targeted, protected and subsidized in multiple ways. Foreign multinationals were invited to participate in the industrial development, but on terms that fit the national plan, requiring the transfer of technology and jobs as well as market-sharing agreements.

Instead of giving free run to investors, the governments practiced what the World Bank economists called "financial repression." Some financial assets like bonds were kept off limits to outsiders; foreign capital was allowed to build new factories but as joint-venture partners, not absentee owners. Real interest rates on industrial loans were held low, even with negative returns to the lenders—a discreet subsidy from the savers to the producers, from households to manufacturers, from the financial system to industrial sectors. Consumer credit, meanwhile, was implicitly rationed by stringent controls and high interest rates on consumer loans.

By classical theory, this regime ought to have severely undermined national savings rates, but, in fact, of course, East Asia's savings soared. As manufacturing exports grew, enormous investment capital was being stored up within the firms and also by the governments. In many cases, citizens were forced to save—and subsidize the development—because, as the workers enjoyed rising incomes, portions of their wages were consigned to compulsory savings programs that paid low interest rates on the deposits. Besides, consumers were limited in their choices and effectively constrained to "Buy Japanese" or "Buy Korean."

The most critical dimension of the strategy, however, may be the social context: How can people be persuaded to accept such rigorous terms of shared sacrifice? Partly by force. In varying degrees, most of these governments started from an authoritarian power base—supported by both military and major business interests—and many of them still relied on suppression of political dissent and free labor organizations. The political repression was often quite brutal, though anti-democratic practices were eventually relaxed or abandoned by the most advanced economies—usually after explosive popular uprisings.*

What was less well understood, however, was that the most advanced Asian economies also established a concrete economic basis for social consent—a convincing commitment to equity. In contrast to Mexico's upheaval in the countryside, Japan, Korea and Taiwan all began their development by supporting the rural population in agriculture—propping up rice prices and protecting small growers from cheaper imports. Land reform programs distributed the nation's basic assets among many small holders. Thus, as urban industrial incomes rose, the farmers gained, too. Instead of generating sharply divisive outcomes, the strategy encouraged unity.

Various social-welfare programs ensured a basic floor under living standards and often jobs. Singapore and Malaysia financed massive public hous-

---

* *The economic consequences of political repression remain vastly different among these Asian nations and do not conform to the facile assumptions that democracy evolves, more or less naturally, after rapid economic growth. These social implications are addressed directly in the concluding section.*

ing. Japan sacrificed efficiency to ensure permanent full employment. These and many other measures created the social basis for rapid economic growth: nobody was to be left behind.

Even the World Bank expressed its admiration: "To establish their legitimacy and win the support of the society at large, East Asian leaders established the principle of shared growth, promising that, as the economy expanded, all groups would benefit. . . . They had to persuade the elites to share the benefits of growth with the middle class and the poor. Finally, to win the cooperation of the middle class and the poor, the leaders had to show them that they would indeed benefit from future growth."

This brief summary, of course, leaves out the complexity and conflict that have accompanied the Asian strategy, but it does describe the stark contrast with how governing elites in Mexico and the rest of Latin America have dealt with the question of equity and, for that matter, how the Washington model ignores the social consequences of its free-market principles. One might argue that a Mexico or Brazil, given cultural differences and a history of severe class divisions and self-dealing elites, could never manage such an approach successfully. Certainly, after all that has occurred, it would be very difficult to shift to the Asian model now.

Still, one should recall that two generations ago, Japan (not to mention South Korea and others) was widely regarded as a hopeless case for approximately the same reasons—a nation ruled by harsh, feudalistic elites incapable of modern industrialization. Furthermore, the one major exception in Latin America, Chile, has managed in the last decade to achieve rapid economic growth by abandoning the pure free-market theory taught by American economists and emulating major elements of the Asian strategy, including forced savings and the purposeful control of capital. The Chilean government tells foreign investors where they may invest, keeps them out of certain financial assets and prohibits them from withdrawing their capital rapidly. For other Latin nations to do the same, they would have to develop a sense of shared purpose that does not now exist in their politics. They would also have to find the courage to break with Washington and risk losing favor with global capital.[13]

In the long run, the conflict between Tokyo and Washington poses a far more profound crisis for the global system as a whole. If more poor nations embrace the East Asian model because it appears to work better than Washington's, the larger problem of global surpluses will be made even worse. Asian savings, after all, are accumulated by selling in surplus to the other trading nations, especially the United States, and the Japanese model encourages the creation of excess productive capacity for export, further aggravating the glut of goods that threatens the trading system. The collision between these two models could, in theory, by resolved by moderate compromises—terms of trade that give poor nations the protective space to develop, but also obligations to support the trading system and contribute to balancing supply and demand.

This sort of compromise is impossible, however, in a regime ruled by free capital. Pursuing the goal of a "one world" financial market leads the major governments, the IMF and World Bank to oppose national controls over capital, even in the poorest countries, even when these flows of capital regularly disrupt or destroy a poor nation's economic progress. To find the grounds for compromise, in other words, the advanced nations would have to accept that the theory of unfettered global capital is the wrong dream for the world, at least in the present era, that the "Washington consensus" feeds instability rather than rising prosperity.

Unless the major governments are prepared to impose some restraints (and tangible penalties) on adventurous capital investors, developing nations are bound to be skeptical of any calls for reforming the system. Many poor nations will instead choose to follow Tokyo's example, if they can, and let someone else worry about saving the system.

When the World Bank celebrated the fiftieth anniversary of its founding in 1944 at the historic Bretton Woods Conference, a lively network of critics organized itself around the world with a provocative counterslogan: "Fifty years is enough." The bank was created as an internationally financed development program for the poor nations, but, the critics charged, it now did grave harm to the very people it was supposed to help. Shut it down. These critics were not right-wing libertarians but activists from the nongovernmental organizations committed to social and environmental justice in the developing world. The bank listened politely, promised to consider their complaints and then went on with business in the usual manner.

The Bretton Woods institutions, whatever they contributed in their earlier decades, have by now failed spectacularly in the fulfillment of their original purposes. The International Monetary Fund was created to assist in maintaining stable exchange rates among trading nations, but, as the previous chapter described, even the major currencies now routinely fluctuate by wild margins. The World Bank's loans have built a vast store of modernizing infrastructure for the poor—dams, roads, power plants—but the gap between rich and poor has not narrowed. With the important exception of Asia and a few other scattered countries, the overall gap in incomes and wealth has grown much wider. Scores of nations around the world are now concretely in worse shape than they were twenty years ago.

In the transformations wrought by global industrial revolution, both the IMF and World Bank have gravitated to a different purpose: advancing the revolution, fostering conditions necessary for the "one world" market envisioned by finance capital. In various collateral ways, both institutions now serve as the paternalistic agents of global capital—enforcing debt collection, supervising the financial accounts of poor nations, promoting wage suppression and other policy nostrums, preparing the poorer countries for eventual acceptance by the global trading system. The two agencies behave like righteous gatekeepers, instructing and scolding aspirants on the principles of neoclassical economics. If a nation learns well, it may become eligible for loans and projects. If it refuses to conform, it will continue to dwell in the outer circles of backward poverty.

Two leading critics, Susan George and Fabrizio Sabelli, have likened the World Bank to a powerful medieval church that proselytizes for a fundamentalist theology. "The missionary," they wrote, "is replaced by the neoclassical economist, the development expert mediates between the developed and undeveloped worlds as the priest mediates between the divine and the secular ones, helping the underdeveloped to tread the long road to salvation. The way is hard and steep; it is not for the faint-hearted." [14]

This religion has clearly failed to save the sinners from their poverty, but it is also doubtful that it serves the interests of the established parishioners. If the success of finance capital and multinational enterprise is assumed to be synonymous with the interests of citizens in patron nations like the United States, then clearly the World Bank does good works in their behalf. But, of course, finance capital does not constitute the broad national interest in America or in any other nation that provides the funding for World Bank loans.

In fact, if Americans ever examined the matter, they would discover they are financing an agency that directly contributes to the downward pressures on their own wages. The World Bank and IMF preach a supply-side doctrine that suppresses the wages in poor countries when the self-interest of ordinary American wage earners runs in the opposite direction. These organizations' programs suppress aggregate demand for the global trading system and help create more productive capacity for already glutted markets, further undercutting the viability of established factories and jobs.

National self-interests aside, this regime is headed for another great crisis, toward another collapse of debtors. The global financial regulators are sowing this crisis with their own lending policies because, with some exceptions, the poor of the world are steadily sinking deeper and deeper in debt. They are not going to get out from under this, not without a miracle. Indeed, many nations, especially in Africa, now borrow more each year from the World Bank simply to make nominal payments against their old accumulated debts. In 1974, the total external debt of all developing nations was $135 billion. By 1981, it reached $751 billion. By the early 1990s, it was estimated to be $1,945 billion. [15]

In time, when people of future generations are able to look back on this system with clear eyes, they may recognize its true ugliness: the rich nations of the world are acting like ancient usurers, lending money to the desperate poor on terms that cannot possibly be met and, thus, steadily acquiring more and more control over the lives and assets of the poor. This is done mainly by commercial banks and private capital, but amplified and policed by the public lending institutions. Citizens on the wealthy end of the global system may claim to be innocent of these practices, but their ignorance and indifference make them complicit, too.

The facts would seem ludicrous if they were not so tragic for people. By 1993, the foreign debt of all developing nations had reached 40 percent of their total GDP, the highest level ever by that measure. Sub-Saharan Africa's debt nearly doubled in less than a decade, from $210 billion in 1984 to $352 billion by 1991. In fact, after the last global debt crisis in 1982, the flow of capital transfers between rich and poor reversed, as new lending dried up and indebted nations struggled to keep up with their interest payments. Ashwini Deshpande of India's Delhi School of Economics has estimated that the net negative outflow of capital from developing countries to wealthy countries totaled $163 billion between 1984 and 1988. The picture improved subsequently as foreign investing revived and old loans were written off, but many poor nations continue to suffer a negative cash flow with their wealthy creditors.

The obvious imperative, the remedy always required to end usurious relationships, is debt forgiveness. The alternative is eventual default anyway, since much of this accumulated lending will never be repaid. The debt obligations now serve mainly as a way to bleed the poor further, depriving them of scarce cash and purchasing power. At a minimum, the publicly held loans issued by the World Bank and IMF could be drastically reduced without financial shock. Commercial banks would suffer major capital losses in a write-down and thus pose a more difficult obstacle. But the banks' global lending behavior must at the least be restrained by new regulations to prevent these recurring run-ups in impossible debt burdens. Alternatively, if the commercial banks resist controls, they should be cut loose from the government support systems that bail them out of their own recklessness at taxpayer expense.

Government officials in the poor nations are, of course, complicit with their bankers in the folly and error of borrowing. "But the brunt of the burden does not fall on them," William F. Darity Jr., a University of North Carolina economist, has observed. "Rather, it falls on the masses of their relatively impoverished fellow citizens who must endure a litany of policies that frequently spell recession in the name of expanded export earnings, coupled with the clubbed hand of the IMF." [16]

The imperative of debt liquidation is so compelling that even the World Bank's new president, New York financier James Wolfensohn, has proposed a small step in that direction—a modest fund of $6 billion to $8 billion to ease the debts of the world's forty poorest countries. Even so, Wolfensohn encountered muttered complaints from private finance and some resistance from the IMF. The logic of Wolfensohn's proposal, they perhaps recognized, may lead to more significant demands for debt relief. [17]

William Darity is among the experts on global finance who urge a major write-off of the developing countries' debts, not simply to alleviate the social suffering, but as the necessary predicate for global growth, restoring a shared prosperity around the world. "Then the world could get back on the path toward a condition where the developed countries could sell their exports to the debtor countries without endangering the latter's capacity to repay the debt," Darity wrote. "The debtors would not all be scrambling against one another for market shares merely to earn foreign exchange to meet debt obligations. Trade and growth could proceed with a certain cosmopolitanism lacking on the debt-driven scene prevailing today."

Like other great questions in the global system, this one requires a larger perspective from citizens if they wish to see their own self-interest clearly. Americans who nurse provincial resentments against "foreign aid" may be surprised to hear a Mexican business owner urge that U.S. lending to his country be shut off or to learn that social activists from poor countries are demanding abolition of the World Bank. The self-interests of different peoples are more convergent than Americans recognize.

The imperative that unites rich and poor, of course, is the need for global economic growth at a faster pace—more demand for the products that everyone makes. Debt relief on a significant scale would be a powerful stimulant for that, freeing up cash for global consumption and opening greater opportunities for domestic enterprises. By itself, that would not guarantee any poor nation's successful development or the reversal of fortunes for wage earners in wealthy nations. But it would reverse the flows in a positive direction. It would give the aspiring nations more space to work out their own destinies, with or without the aid of global capital.

The Bretton Woods institutions are technically equipped to lead this resurgence, but it would require them to embrace the heresy, to throw off their orthodoxy and help invent a new doctrine that relies less on financial accounting and more upon economic reality and social equity. Despite the presence of substantial critics, these institutions are unlikely to change themselves, dependent as they are on the political power of capital. If the World Bank cannot reform itself, then the critics are right: fifty years is enough, shut it down.

Thirteen

The Rentiers' Regime[*]

THE REVOLUTION has turned upon its original sponsors and ensnared them in a circle of bad choices, trapped between the old politics of the twentieth century and the new economics of globalized finance. The wealthiest industrial societies, the very ones that first promoted the globalization of commerce, find themselves governed now by unforgiving imperatives from the capital market—a commandment to undertake a forced march to reduce living standards for their own citizens, discard old political commitments to social equity and reduce benefit systems for pensions, health care, income support and various forms of ameliorative aid.

If governments resist, they face recurring financial crisis. If governments comply, the social aggravations will be deepened and an era of divisive, reactionary politics is likely to flourish. One way or another, the societies that fostered the global revolution are going to be punished for their great and grandiose ambitions.

The visible expression of the dilemma is debt: Every major economy, except perhaps Japan, is caught in a deepening mire of government deficits and accumulating debt payments. The United States has the largest burden —U.S. federal debt grew from 35 to 70 percent of GDP in less than twenty years—but many other nations are actually in worse condition. Italy's gross debt is 124 percent of its economic output, Belgium's is 132 percent and Sweden's is 95 percent. Even in prudent Germany, the debt burden has doubled since the 1970s and now approaches 60 percent of Germany's economic output. Across the older industrial nations, every government runs swollen operating deficits, taking on new debt each year much faster than its economic growth.[1]

The neutral accounting explanation is straightforward: tax revenues in these countries are no longer growing fast enough to sustain the social commitments and other spending obligations that these wealthy societies

---

* Like "laissez-faire," the French words carry the same meaning in English: "a governing system by and for the rentiers, wealth holders who derive their incomes from returns on capital."

assumed more than a generation ago when their economies were expanding much faster. The ideological debate begins with the question of what constitutes the cause and the remedy: Should governments pursue faster economic growth and other measures that might restore their revenue base? Or must they instead undertake a general retrenchment of the welfare state and other spending to balance their accounts? The prevailing orthodoxy of laissez-faire economics naturally agrees upon the latter course, and this objective is being enforced by the powerful hand of financial markets.

Though politicians are typically reluctant to impose austerity on voters, governments that resist may be subjected to the harsh discipline of a "capitalist strike"—the sudden withdrawal of lenders willing to finance the deficits, followed by an upward spike in interest rates that collapses economic activity. This dramatic form of market pressure has already been imposed on Sweden, Italy and several other peripheral economies in Europe, but the mere threat also intimidates policy makers in the most powerful nations, including the United States. In the meantime, since financial investors regard the general buildup of debt as dangerously unsustainable, they are demanding a "risk premium" when they lend to these governments—higher interest rates that, of course, magnify debt burdens for the borrowers.

In the worst-case scenario, as their aging populations add to public welfare costs and their economic growth continues to falter, the Old World nations of Europe and North America might eventually hit the wall—a general debt crisis resembling the collapse of Latin America's creditworthiness in the early 1980s. What is more likely, however, is a series of individual crises as nations encounter financial-market discipline and are, one by one, compelled to retreat. "Governments in Europe," as one financier put it, "must confront their deficits—and throw more people over the side—but they really can't do that because they get de-elected if they do."

Resolution of this deep conflict will play across the next decade, probably in ugly, sporadic rebellions arising from either markets or voters. McKinsey & Company, the multinational consulting firm, urges governments to cooperate with finance capital and contain their debts, but the firm adds: "It may well be necessary for some nations to experience a series of financial crises before they are prepared to change. If they resist too much, for too long, however, the consequences to the individual nation could be severe. And, if too many nations resist for too long, the consequences to the world's economy could be disastrous." [2]

The orthodox economic theory promises that by balancing national accounts and "liberating" the private economy from the burdens of government spending, the rich nations can return to the halcyon days of thirty or forty years ago when their economies were stable and growing much faster, when productivity and wages rose together, when inflation was low and government deficits quite modest. The soundness of this theory will be tested if governments actually try to follow it, since it requires them to withdraw hundreds of billions of dollars from the demand side of their economies—the loss of more consumption in a world market where consumer demand is already inadequate.

To offset the loss in spending, there is only the vague promise that financial markets and central banks will reward responsible governments by lowering their interest rates. The trouble with that promise is that it has usually proved illusory in the past. The United States, for instance, has not enjoyed lower interest rates, though it has undergone significant deficit reduction. One reason for this is that finance is increasingly globalized and responds to the supply and demand for capital across a much broader marketplace. Interest rates on government bonds now appear to be converging across the major nations, responding to global financial events and myriad investment opportunities, not simply to the fiscal accounts of individual nations. What if a government balanced its budget and the interest rates did not fall? It would have opted for stable austerity.

Nonetheless, the ascendant Republicans in the United States, ahead of most European politicians, fully embraced the orthodox premise (belatedly joined by President Clinton) in their commitment to balance the federal budget within seven years. Despite the vigorous beginning, it was not clear they could sustain this agenda through seven years, since the program would have to survive the political test of three congressional elections (and started with the easier task of cutting aid for the poor first). One recalls that Ronald Reagan launched a similar campaign in 1981, promising to balance the federal budget in three years. The spending controls Congress enacted in 1985, known as the Gramm-Rudman-Hollings amendment, promised a balanced budget within five years. As the deficits endure, the timetable for correcting them lengthens.

The logic of the balanced-budget solution is oddly nostalgic and inward-looking, in any case, since it assumes that a nation's economic life is still governed by its own national balance sheet, not by the vast and random flows of international capital or the other great transformations that have occurred. The notion that balanced budgets will restore a stable prosperity ignores what globalization has wrought since the 1950s and 1960s—the great shifts in trade and wealth, the dispersal of technology and industrial production, the debilitating impact of wage arbitrage and other influences on domestic economies. The United States and its industrial allies changed the landscape of global commerce; now they are living with the consequences.

"The Bretton Woods era was a dream—an arrogant dream," Christopher Whalen, an international financial consultant in Washington, asserted. "The notion that we could rebuild the world and develop the industrial capacity of poor countries and think that we would not someday have to compete with them and their low-wage labor—that was arrogant. What we are now essentially doing is redistributing capital to certain poor countries at the expense of industrial workers in the advanced world. So we have to lower our standards of living for the middle class. All of the industrial economies are going through their own versions of successive deflation and deindustrialization as this transfer of capital proceeds."

A balanced budget cannot undo this new reality and conceivably would make conditions worse, especially in the social realm. In the longer sweep of human history, the shift of wealth from rich nations to poor may be recognized as a positive breakthrough, but making that observation does not answer the financial dilemma facing the wealthier countries. In fact, as this wealth shift has gathered momentum across the last twenty-five years, the organic political response in the advanced nations has been to pretend it was not happening or to lurch into a series of grand evasions—economic episodes that temporarily glossed over the contradiction of their weakening economic base.

In these terms, the first great evasion was the runaway inflation of the 1970s, a lubricant that masked the deeper structural changes for a time and also provided a ready explanation for what had gone wrong. Rapidly inflating prices and wages made it harder for people to recognize that their economies were no longer producing enough output to satisfy everyone's expectations. Someone had to lose shares, but societies were naturally reluctant to choose whom. Once central banks mobilized to curb the inflation, another form of evasion surfaced—debt—in the massive buildup of public and private debts during the 1980s. Both of these financial excesses were implicit expressions of underlying economic disorder, futile attempts to paper over what was happening. The renewed preoccupation with balanced budgets may be understood, similarly, as the latest form of denial.

The conservative orthodoxy that has taken charge—finance capital's demand for balanced budgets and stern monetary policies to harden money values and protect against inflation—will endure at least until societies recognize that this does not represent a solution either. Or until the system cracks apart from the stresses that this regime imposes upon it. The pressures will inevitably build on these economies because, in addition to the punishing level of interest rates, the central premise of the new regime is a conviction that these domestic economies must be restrained—limited to modest or even tepid levels of growth—in order to restore stability. This commitment to slow growth does protect the value of money and financial assets, but it is like a noose thrown around the advanced economies, sure to deepen their imbalances in production and employment. Indeed, it closes off the only possible exit from the debtor's trap.

Until voters and politicians grasp the meaning and revolt, the leading nations are being governed by a hybrid system of private markets and central banks, imposing in tandem their conservative ideological values on economic life. French economist Alain Parguez has called this arrangement "the international rentier economy," or "the rentier welfare state"—a regime that places the concerns of wealth holders ahead of other economic interests.

The rentier regime's abstract accounting values create a circular flow of wealth that, as Parguez observed, becomes malignant. "Governments," he wrote, "are entering into debt and borrowing heavily from individuals or financial institutions just to pay interest income to what is largely the same class of high income earners or rentiers at usurious rates set by another arm of government—the respective countries' central banks." [3]

The rentier system of governance is profoundly anti-democratic, of course, but it also deranges the conventional political debate since, from left to right, economic growth is the standard rationale behind every important proposition in the modern nation-state. If elected governments are made impotent on the crucial question of growth, so are politicians and elections. When this logic triumphs, it is the marketplace that rules.

Describing this deep conflict in broad outline, as I have done, makes the reality seem more orderly—and less irrational—than it actually is. In fact, global financial markets are subject to their own occasional frenzies and are, therefore, not reliable masters. Governments that defer to the wisdom of finance capital are frequently jarred by the results, since financial markets react to other influences, including their own random follies.

Global finance passes judgment on a nation's balance sheet, but it is also driven by its own market forces, random ebbs and flows of capital across borders that can produce contradictory results for the governed. In those circumstances, the confident theorems on the benefits of fiscal order become meaningless. As Bill Clinton learned, a government that does the "right thing" to satisfy the rentier regime may be punished anyway.

The President's economic advisors were understandably pleased with themselves. During the first year of a new Democratic administration, instead of adding expensive new programs as Democrats were expected to do, Bill Clinton was persuaded to abandon his own campaign promises and turn in the opposite direction: his first budget was devoted to deficit reduction and the deficit actually fell by $72 billion. Moreover, Clinton had set future deficits to run at less than 3 percent of GDP, still a bit faster than average economic growth, but much improved from the 4 percent ratio during the previous decade of Republican administrations.

Yet the White House economists were also justifiably puzzled. Thanks to Clinton's policy, a fiscal contraction was under way, shrinking the proportions of government spending and borrowing, and inflation was subsiding. Yet long-term interest rates were rising in the bond market—rising dramatically. Economic theory predicted the opposite: market interest rates were supposed to decline as the deficits shrank since that reduced the demand for capital. Bill Clinton had been persuaded to embark on this course by assurances that the economy would be rewarded with lower interest rates. Instead, after falling to a low of 5.78 percent in October 1993, the thirty-year bond rate soared, hitting a peak of 8.16 percent by November 1994.

For some reason, despite the President's virtuous behavior, bondholders were demanding and getting a much higher return on the capital they lent to the government—about one third higher. Moreover, this was not just happening to the United States but to the major governments of Europe and Asia as well. The other G-7 nations (Japan, Germany, France, Italy, Canada and Britain) suffered the same sudden run-up in borrowing costs—as much as two percentage points. Clinton's Council of Economic Advisers pored over various dense formulas, trying to explain their "prediction error." The anomaly, they agreed, could not very well be attributed to market anxiety over inflation since inflation rates were flat or falling in all those nations. In their annual report, Clinton's advisors speculated on various answers and, basically, threw up their hands.[4]

If the economists had put aside the statistical models and simply talked to a few market players, they might have discovered practical explanations for why theory was disappointed. The bond market trashed Bill Clinton's economic program for reasons that had very little to do with him or the U.S. budget. Bondholders, in fact, were caught up in their own bubble of rising expectations in 1993—buying bonds on credit in huge volumes, running up the prices and betting that the bond market rally would keep going higher.

When that hope faltered, panic set in, the borrowers had to dump bonds and the market crashed. In the bond market, when the price of these financial assets falls, the market interest rate rises inversely. The run-up of long-term rates was essentially driven by the market's own internal turmoil, not by anything Washington had done. And the striking aspect of this episode was that it occurred almost everywhere at once—from New York to London, from Frankfurt to Tokyo—a global binge of speculation in government bonds, followed by a global crash in prices.

This financial event was seminal to the Clinton presidency, yet it barely registered on the political consciousness of Washington, consumed as it was with the partisan debates over federal spending, health-care reform and other issues. If American politicians knew about the bond collapse at all, it was an oddity of the financial pages, and very few saw any connection with their own affairs. Yet during my travels the bond crash was the riveting political event that financiers always talked about first. In Frankfurt, the citadel of German finance, I encountered lucid and candid explanations of what the markets had done to the American president's plans.

At the headquarters of Deutsche Bank, the pillar of the German financial system, the chief economist expressed great misgivings. "The financial markets totally discarded the Clinton administration for, in my view, not very sound reasons," Norbert Walter said. "Clinton did make mistakes, but they are minor to what the markets assessed."

"Financial markets were getting carried away and by a certain self-delusion," explained Thomas Mayer, an authority on German finance who was chief economist at the Goldman Sachs office in Frankfurt. "It's a kind of merry-go-round. They were betting that the bond price would go up and keep going up, as long as the next buyer could get the credit to keep buying. You bet that the next person will do what you've just done."

Modern Germany has acquired a well-earned reputation for financial prudence and patience—with a central bank that controlled inflation more zealously than others, a concentrated banking system closely aligned with industrial capital and committed to long-term prospects rather than overnight profit. Yet conservative German financiers were caught up in the bond frenzy, too, behaving more or less like Americans. Global convergence has united the separate crowds of national financial markets into one restless, multinational herd.

"The financial markets are crazy," the Deutsche Bank economist lamented. "Many people in the markets are very young, too young to understand that they can be killed out there. Some of them are going to be fired when they lose fortunes. In Japan, capital has become obsolete. They have to close down the most modern production facilities in the world because of the exchange rate. It's crazy." The world did seem upside down. U.S. and European financial markets acted as though capital was scarce, justifying higher interest rates, while Japan's best capital assets—its efficient factories —were being taken out of production.

The explosive shift in the bond market's behavior, Mayer observed, "is certainly a consequence of the herd mentality. Once you have established a herd, it's possible to create a stampede. Once it goes completely crazy, you have to kill it. This has the ability to destabilize the real economy and it did."

As astute financiers around the world understood, the bond stampede actually originated—inadvertently—from the august central banks of Germany and America, the Bundesbank and the Federal Reserve. Despite their stern reputations both of these monetary institutions supplied the easy credit upon which the bond speculators ran up their bubble of borrowing and buying. The Fed and Bundesbank frequently scolded elected governments for their deficit spending or disciplined labor and industry for excessive wage demands and price increases. But the central banks were far less resolute about policing the runaway inflations of financial prices.

The fluid mechanics that connected the central banks to the bond speculation involved their function as regulators of their national money supply and credit expansion. In theory, a nation's gross supply of money and available credit is supposed to grow in step with its expanding real economy, providing the necessary liquidity and lending to conduct commerce. For different reasons, both the Fed and the Bundesbank allowed overly generous money and credit growth during several years in the early 1990s, expanding the supply of credit beyond commerce's need for it, since the real economies of both nations were flat or in recession. In that situation, a very old monetary phenomenon takes hold: The excess liquidity flows into financial markets. Banks have more capacity to lend than producers and consumers can usefully borrow, so the excess lending is used by financial investors to do the leveraged investing that drives up the prices.

Though it was not much understood by the American public at the time, the Federal Reserve was actually supplying easy credit as an indirect way to bail out the troubled commercial banks. After the debt binge of the 1980s, many of the largest U.S. banks were threatened by their own crisis of failed loans, similar to the savings and loan disaster though smaller in size. Rather than bail them out directly or close them down, the Fed discreetly helped them "get well" by holding down short-term interest rates around 3 percent. The easy credit conditions enabled the banks to profitably borrow short and buy long—borrowing at 3 percent to acquire huge volumes of long-term bonds that yielded 6 or 7 percent and replenishing their balance sheets by capturing the spread between the two. The problem with this sort of "silent bailout" was that it also stimulated an artificial inflation of financial prices—and not just in the United States.

"The run-up of the American bond and stock markets was fueled by the rapid run-up of liquidity from the Fed," Robert Dugger of the Tudor Fund explained. "The low U.S. interest rates were used to finance market rallies all around the world. You borrow at 3 percent in the U.S. and buy bonds in the Philippines or Hong Kong or wherever at 10 percent." This was the same arbitrage opportunity that had fueled Mexico's false boom.

In Germany, the same phenomenon was under way, though the Bundesbank was motivated by an entirely different domestic situation. The reunification of East and West Germany in 1990 produced a one-time magnification of the German money supply—when the nearly worthless marks of East Germany were exchanged at one-for-one value for West German deutschemarks. The swollen money supply promised an inflationary stimulus to the economy that the Bundesbank was determined to check. The central bank raised interest rates to very high levels, pushing Germany and all of Europe into deep recession, and it held them there. Yet the money-supply growth still remained far above its own policy targets. Since economic output was contracting, the excess lending went into finance.

"Central banks are not quite without blame in this game because they provided a fairly generous supply of money during 1991–92–93, in the U.S. but also in Germany," Mayer explained. "That obviously prepares the ground for a liquidity-driven bond rally that is magnified by the hedge funds and the leverage they use. What is more amazing is that most of this foreign purchasing of bonds was done on short-term credit from German banks. We lent the money to them so they can buy the bonds which they then give back to us as collateral."

Given the deregulation of cross-border finance, the excesses of one nation's monetary system spilled over easily into the others. When two of the world's dominant central banks were providing excess fuel for borrowing, then every market would experience the same speculative ride. Japan's monetary policy was less involved since it was struggling to contain its own accumulation of bad debts, though the Bank of Japan was also lowering interest rates. Hedge funds like Tudor and George Soros's Quantum Fund were widely blamed for the bond spree, but in reality the largest commercial and investment banks were the major players.

While the U.S. economy remained flat, American banks were using the excess liquidity to repair their own balance sheets, pleased by the rising value of their bond portfolios. A basic contradiction in modern financial systems was that easy borrowing terms were granted to financial players, as opposed to the more rigorous credit standards imposed on business or consumers. A bond buyer could multiply his play by fifty by borrowing "on margin." This easy leverage—borrowing to invest—drove the action.

"Let's say I'm a Bermuda-based hedge fund," Mayer explained. "I call Goldman Sachs and say, I want to buy 100 million D-mark government bonds. They would put down 10 million D-mark from their own money and ask us to finance the other 90 million. As collateral for the loan, they would give us the bonds to hold. As long as the bonds are not falling in value, we're happy."

Unlike the U.S. situation, the bond buyers in Germany had to borrow at a much higher rate since German short-term rates were above 7 percent, above the 6 percent yield paid on the German government bonds. "They obviously had a negative carry—paying more to borrow than they received from the bonds," Mayer said. "But this was not a major problem for them because they expected to make much more as the bond prices keep rising. They are betting that interest rates fall and people can keep buying, so bond prices rise and, therefore, a major capital gain."

Instead, the merry-go-round suddenly stopped. By the fall of 1993, the Federal Reserve had begun to express vague concerns about the signs of accelerating U.S. economic growth—the good news President Clinton had been promised when he agreed to confront the budget deficits. Only now the Fed's chairman, Alan Greenspan, claimed to be worried by portents of inflation. In the financial markets, his statements were understood as a warning signal: the low interest rates and easy credit were about to end. In Germany, meanwhile, despite Europe's devastating unemployment, the Bundesbank was reluctant to reduce interest rates faster—perhaps fearful that it would simply add fuel to the merry-go-round. The bond traders kept predicting German interest-rate cuts and the Bundesbank kept disappointing them.

Taken together, these events began to sow doubts. "When the Fed starts to talk about raising rates, people begin edging toward the door," Rob Dugger said. "When you see the market going up at a rate that is unsustainable, that's when you have to get out." Most bond traders were not so wise. They did not quit the game gracefully but clung, instead, to their hopes for more quick profit. The bubble of inflated prices continued for several more months, until it collapsed suddenly early in 1994.

Two events popped the bubble. The major hedge funds, led by Soros, got burned badly on currency speculation when they guessed wrong on how U.S.-Japanese trade politics would affect the dollar-yen relationship. The losses compelled them to sell off bonds rapidly. Simultaneously, the Federal Reserve finally did what it had been threatening for months: it raised short-term interest rates. The Fed's increase in February 1994 was slight—only a quarter of one percent—but it destroyed the psychology of hope in the bond markets. A violent cascade of selling swept the world.

"The merry-go-round went into reverse," Mayer of Goldman Sachs explained. "The bonds that originally were worth 100 million deutsche-mark and were collateral for 90 million in credit are all of a sudden worth only 80 million. We call the counterparty and ask him for the 10 million. He doesn't have this money so he has to sell some of his investments. Then the whole game circles downward. As he sells, the price of bonds falls further and the whole thing unwinds, as others have to do the same."

Mayer thought the margin calls and panic selling started in the United States and spread to Germany. Others thought it started in Europe and spread around the world. Regardless, the world's bond markets were behaving as one—suddenly selling huge volumes of European bonds, Asian bonds, American bonds. The reward Bill Clinton had anticipated for good behavior was abruptly withdrawn: long-term interest rates rose sharply and remained high—higher than the day Clinton took office. In addition to discouraging growth, this "market disturbance" added many billions more in higher interest payments to the U.S. budget deficits that Clinton had labored to reduce.

The impact on the real economies of Europe and the United States was deleterious, though impossible to gauge. Long-term rates did subside again through 1995 but not until economic growth was also weakening in those nations. Even then, the bond rates remained stuck at a higher plateau—and rose again in 1996 when investors again feared reviving growth. Aside from its own irrational turmoil, the market's message seemed to be: interest rates can subside only if economic activity seems to be weakening, regardless of what happens to the government deficits.

The Federal Reserve's own actions in this episode were especially suspect. While Greenspan publicly claimed to be responding to the threat of price inflation from the real economy, some financial-market participants regarded this explanation as bogus—a cover story so the Fed could raise rates in order to curb the financial speculation. The circumstantial evidence supported that observation, including Greenspan's acknowledgment that there was no visible evidence of inflation. A conclusive judgment on the central bank's true motives was unlikely, given the opaque secrecy in which it was allowed to operate. If the market players were correct, the Federal Reserve chairman had executed a grand sleight of hand on the American public, including the American president whom he had urged to tackle the deficit problem.

"The Fed knows there is no inflation problem," a Wall Street economist told me some weeks before the Fed's rate increase. "The Fed is trying to manage expectations in the financial markets. By threatening to raise interest rates, they hope to persuade people to back off a bit before the bubble bursts. Rates go up a little—perhaps a quarter of a percent—to educate investors about the risks."[5]

In Frankfurt, the chief economist at Goldman Sachs made the same diagnosis of events. "The Fed's rate hike," Mayer said, "was an attempt to correct the developments in the financial markets—to deflate the bubble before it got too dangerous. In retrospect, the surprise was that the bubble was bigger than realized—and the deflation was more painful."

In general, central banks responded to the bond market's "disturbance" by raising interest rates—in effect, punishing commerce for the folly of finance. "These central banks are almost totally misguided," Robert Johnson, the New York financier, remarked during the global bond sell-off. "The central bankers ask me: 'Gosh, we cut rates in Britain and long rates go up. Do people think we're irresponsible? This must mean inflation fears are going up among investors.' But bonds are selling off because we have a liquidity crisis—not inflation fears—so in those circumstances central banks ought to ease and bring down rates."

Governments and societies were hostage to this random power. Their individual ambitions were now circumscribed by the disinterested—and sometimes reckless—passions of global capital. At Deutsche Bank, the chief economist of that conservative institution mused solemnly on the implications for the future of the system itself—the dangers inherent in the financiers' fully leveraged investing, the weakening control that major central banks exercised over the globalizing markets.

"The idea of being fully hedged is a very questionable assumption," Norbert Walter reflected. "If the counterparty [holding the hedging obligation] is out of business, you won't find anyone to cover the position. Small players in the market will have difficulty, only the Triple-A players will survive. We are developing toward the *Titanic* solution. We only build bigger and bigger ships, but not remembering there are still icebergs."

The operating principles of the rentier state relied upon financial indicators to govern the course of economies—bond interest rates, market prices like gold, various indexes of inflation, arcane formulas of prediction. While the logic seemed internally consistent, it necessarily obscured a large anomaly: the finance economy and the real economy of commerce, as the bond crash of 1994 illustrated, were not always in synch with one another, but were sometimes pulling in contrary directions. The potential for conflict between these two realms was not new to capitalism, of course. Trying to maintain balance between their competing rhythms and desires has always been a central challenge for central banks. What was new about the rentiers' regime was that the values of finance capital have won precedence over all others.

The political triumph of the financial perspective was routinely reflected in the policy-making arguments of governments and the economic factors they deemed most important. For instance, Clinton's decision to abandon the job-creation projects he had promised as a candidate and concentrate instead on the deficits was, in essence, an act of deference to the wisdom of the bond market. Rival politicians attacked his budget proposals, but very few quarreled with the premise. A new governing consensus had evolved and hardened during the last twenty years across party and ideological lines, at least among the influential elites: financial accounting had displaced other governing priorities.

The shift in political thinking was driven partly by the large disorders —inflation and debt—that confounded and discredited the old liberal orthodoxy based on Keynesian economics, a governing doctrine focused on maintaining full employment and aggregate demand for mass consumption. The revolutionary globalization also drove the shift as commerce and finance demanded and won deregulation, as multinational enterprise constructed a new order that rivaled the power of nations.

The seminal event in this shift of influence was the dedicated campaign launched by Federal Reserve Chairman Paul Volcker in the early 1980s to successfully extinguish the runaway price inflation that had dominated the 1970s. With other major central banks collaborating in the effort, their success left an indelible and distinctly conservative message about governing power: central banks could get things done while the politicians fiddled and stalled. Notwithstanding the collateral consequences of Volcker's relentless monetary policy, financial stability was restored—or so it seemed—as the domestic value of money hardened, as the social insecurities and economic dislocations connected with inflation were eradicated.

As a result of these events, governing power shifted informally but perceptibly from elected governments to the unelected central banks. Yet, as the globalizing financial markets gained in size and strength, power was shifting again. Even central bankers were intimidated by the global market's new influence, which they readily accepted as an arbiter of sound policy, courting its approval, deferring to its signals. By nature, the monetary institutions and the major financial players were compatible in their economic values—bankers, after all, are the core political constituency of central banks—so they agreed on the basic goals while frequently clashing on the policy specifics.

The rentiers' core goal was stable money—zero inflation, if possible —and the entire intellectual framework for managing economic life was reconstructed around that premise. Everything else—sales, employment, social relations, government obligations—was considered secondary to the objective of protecting stable money, though the doctrine assumed that everyone in the society would benefit in the long run if this stability was maintained. Wealth holders, of course, benefited immediately from this regime, since it both defended the value of their stored savings and produced the higher interest rates paid to them as creditors.

This preoccupation with stable money as a reliable surrogate for the general well-being had historical precedent: A similar obsession prevailed during the last great industrial revolution at the end of the nineteenth century. In that era of economic change and upheaval, governments relied on the gold standard to maintain the fixed value of money and embraced the same conviction that financial stability was the core requirement for a stable prosperity. The populist uprisings by debtors in the 1880s and 1890s, mainly by desperate small farmers who had to pay the usurious interest rates imposed by the gold standard, were largely deflected.

Despite damaging side effects, including the periodic financial crises and depressions, the gold standard endured for many decades, until its control was blown apart by World War I and the gross indebtedness contracted by the major European governments. Even then, gold was not finally discredited and abandoned until the great financial crash of 1929 and the long worldwide depression that followed. Paul Volcker's relentless campaign for disinflation could be understood as a modern equivalent, a technocratic effort to establish through very high interest rates the old-fashioned discipline of the gold standard. The Volcker era's strict monetary control has continued and largely succeeded in its primary goal: domestic price inflation has become quiescent everywhere, flat or declining in all the major industrial economies for five years or longer. This achievement has not led to stability, not in financial markets nor in the value of money in global exchange which, as Chapter 11 described, became even more erratic and unreliable. Nor has "sound money" as yet restored the stability or general prosperity predicted for real economies—for firms, workers or governments —though a general belief in this prospect persisted.

In conventional wisdom, the "good times" were "just around the corner" and sure to return if central banks maintained their vigilance. In the meantime, the major economies experienced swelling armies of the permanently unemployed—35 million officially, but nearly twice that total if marginalized workers were also counted—and working families suffered a continuing erosion of incomes and rising insecurity. Some unconventional commentators, observing the real effects of this governing regime as opposed to its theoretical claims, have described this era as a "contained depression."[6]

The operating logic of the rentier regime virtually guaranteed this outcome. Notwithstanding the orthodoxy's promised benefits, the practical effect of finance capital's hegemony was to lock the advanced economies and their governments in a malignant spiral, restricting them to bad choices. Like bondholders in general, the new governing consensus explicitly assumed that faster economic growth was dangerous—threatening to the stable financial order—so nations were effectively blocked from measures that might reduce permanent unemployment or ameliorate the decline in wages. That orthodoxy was what spun around Bill Clinton when he took office.

The reality of slow growth, in turn, drove the governments into their deepening indebtedness, since the disappointing growth inevitably undermined tax revenues while it expanded the public welfare costs. The rentier regime repeatedly instructed governments to reform their spending priorities—that is, withdraw benefits from dependent classes of citizens—but the deficit disorders endured and even grew in many European nations. While every government rhetorically accepted the need to act, their political reluctance reflected the lack of any evidence that the withdrawn government assistance would be replaced by new jobs and income growth in the private economy.

In rough outline, these dynamics set up a vicious circle of responses that interacted like this: Bond markets, though increasingly influenced by the global flows of capital, rendered conservatively prejudiced judgments on the economic conditions of individual nations—conservative in that capital owners always felt threatened by faster economic growth and exaggerated the potential for inflation. Their anxieties were expressed in bond prices and the long-term interest rates.

Next, central banks interpreted these market signals as straightforward statements of the bondholders' "inflationary expectations" and adjusted their monetary policies in response. If long rates were rising, it must mean that bondholders, for whatever reason, perceived a growing threat of future inflation and were skeptical of the central bank's vigilance. The Fed and others sought to reassure the capital owners by raising short-term interest rates—a move that would dampen economic growth and keep markets in slack capacity, thus foreclosing any possibility that labor might be able to bid up wages or that producers could raise their prices.

Elected governments, in turn, were obliged to accept the discipline of higher unemployment as the price for preserving their status as worthy borrowers. If growth was held to a moderate or tepid pace, perhaps the bond market would be persuaded to lower its long-term rates. However, the natural consequence of slower growth was further increases in deficit spending—more borrowing.

Finally, as bond markets observed the trend of rising deficits, their anxieties were not relieved. Indeed, judging from the elevated level of real interest rates, bondholders were becoming even more alarmed despite the rentier regime's success at suppressing economic growth. After all, they could see that many nations were taking on new debt faster than their economic base was expanding—and borrowing at real interest rates that were higher than their growth rates. This abnormality described a malignant condition that, as economic history taught, would lead sooner or later to a crisis for the rentiers themselves: either a debt default by governments or an inflationary episode that devalued their bonds, because the borrowed capital would be paid back with money of cheapened value.

Therefore, in order to protect themselves, the bondholders demanded a "risk premium" on their continued lending—higher interest rates on bond borrowing by suspect nations. The rentiers' premium, of course, simply compounded the problem for the borrowing nations, deepening their deficit positions. By the mid-1990s, this process had placed nearly every major government in the suspect class.

The most serious consequence of the rentier discipline—probably more serious even than the damage done to wages and business balance sheets—was that it effectively suppressed new capital formation. Because the economy was prevented from ever achieving its peak rates of growth, the incentives for new investments were undermined too. Companies and investors tracking domestic demand and productive capacity learned to accept that, if accelerated demand did develop, the Federal Reserve and the bond market would step in and smother it—eliminating the business cycle's highs. In those circumstances, only the foolhardy would rush to build new factories —since the upward surge of demand would be swiftly extinguished by authorities. The result: the rate of productive investment declined in the United States and elsewhere; the rising productivity needed to support rising wages was slowed.

This debilitating chase to achieve the elusive goal of extinguishing the "inflationary expectations" of the bond markets has been under way for approximately fifteen years. Yet the goal kept receding further into the future as governments tried to approach it. The bondholders were not reassured by the years of slow growth or recession and continuing price stability, but were evidently as nervous as ever. Their response—demanding still higher interest on their capital—reflected rational self-interest, yet it made matters only worse. Nations were unlikely to escape from this deadly spiral so long as they accepted the rentier logic, so long as finance capital held its commanding influence over public affairs.

Their economic arguments aside, owners of capital had a compelling reason to promote their perspective: they were enjoying fabulous returns on their wealth, among the highest of the century and even greater than the riskier investments in corporate stocks. According to a study of global interest rates for the G-10 finance ministers, the real return on holding long-term U.S. debt during the 1990s was even higher than in the 1980s and second only to the decade of the 1920s. The study found a similar pattern in Britain, France and Italy. While real interest rates had declined somewhat since the 1980s, the appreciating market value of the bonds more than made up for the declining yields.

The real profit on owning U.S. bonds was 8.2 percent in the 1990s, compared to 6.7 percent in the 1980s and 8.8 percent during the Roaring Twenties, when monetary policy was also extremely restrictive. The modern triumph of the rentiers was expressed in those numbers since, across the twentieth century, the average real return on holding long-term bonds has been only 1.6 percent. In other words, creditors were at present receiving returns on their wealth five times the average while real economies functioned at subpar levels, labor wages declined and governments sank in debt.[7]

Yet rather than reconsider the premises, governing authorities rededicated themselves to the chase of reassuring the rentiers. U.S. inflation, for instance, had been subsiding for five years, but Chairman Greenspan declared in 1994 that the Federal Reserve's "job is not yet complete . . . judging from the remaining inflation premium embodied in long-term rates." The official inflation rate was running around 2.6 percent in 1995, and if one accepted Greenspan's assertion that the Consumer Price Index overstated inflation by as much as 1.5 percent, then the Federal Reserve was actually quite close to ultimate victory—a zero inflation rate. Yet when the bond market expressed displeasure with these conditions, the Federal Reserve chairman accepted its criticism and began raising interest rates.

"The test of successful monetary policy in such a business cycle phase," Greenspan testified, "is our ability to limit the upward movement of long-term rates from what it would otherwise have been with less effective policy." If that was the test, then major central banks have failed utterly since real long-term interest rates remained stuck at historically high levels. In fact, the Federal Reserve's vigilance produced perverse results: as it raised short-term rates through 1994, the bond market kept pushing long rates higher, too—the opposite of what the theory assumed should happen.[8]

The self-contained logic of the rentier system was founded on two dubious premises regularly contradicted by real events. First, bond markets were simply not as rational as authorities presumed. The bond interest rates, as every trader understood, responded to a complex set of influences —some quite random and transient, including the investors' own occasional folly—and these factors might or might not have anything to do with national economies or budget accounts. The central banks inferred unambiguous judgments about inflation from interest-rate shifts that, in the end, were driven by the global supply and demand for capital, the structure of short- and long-term interest rates and many other factors internal to the market itself.

For bondholders, this confusion hardly mattered since they would benefit from sterner monetary control regardless, whether it was right or wrong. A policy of tighter credit suppressed economic growth and amplified the value of financial wealth.

Second, the rentier system assumed that financial markets with their acute sensibilities and abstract indicators could see what no one else was able to perceive—evidence of latent inflationary forces within the real economy of production. For instance, when the Fed chairman initiated his campaign to slow down the U.S. economy, he conceded critics were correct that no tangible evidence of accelerating inflation was present, but said this was irrelevant. Markets were alarmed by the quickening economic activity—a robust but unspectacular growth rate of 4 percent during 1994—that, he said, required a preemptive strike. Given the central bank's intervention, it would be forever impossible to know whether his fear had been valid since the tighter monetary policy forced the economy to subside rapidly to a growth level around 2 percent and actual inflation declined still further. In the rentier logic, vigilance became its own self-fulfilling proof.

Meanwhile, in the real world of commerce, expectations of inflation were utterly dormant—business managers typically struggled with the opposite pressure of falling prices—though firms did have to react to the rentier discipline from financial markets. In most industrial sectors, the actual decisions on wages and prices were now circumscribed by the larger realities of global industrialization—the gross oversupply in both production and labor worldwide as well as the multinationals' ability to shift production from country to country, adjusting for the changing circumstances in local sales or costs. If U.S. labor markets were dangerously tight, as the Fed claimed, then why did wage increases remain so flat? If U.S. manufacturing was operating at close to full capacity, as the central bank's capacity-utilization index indicated, then why were the companies unable to impose price increases and make them stick?

The answer in both cases was, of course, that the global competitive forces of supply and demand and price would not allow it. Neither labor nor management any longer operated in a self-contained domestic economy, though, oddly enough, that was how the central bank still looked at it. If labor unions tried to bid up wages on the basis of a tightening labor market, they were inviting the company to move the factory elsewhere. Likewise, companies set prices to compete against imports. In autos, chemicals, computers, steel and other principal sectors, companies assumed that global capacity was the relevant measure driving the price competition, not the Federal Reserve's narrow measure of U.S. domestic capacity.

"It is nuts," said Wynn Van Bussman, Chrysler's chief economist. "The assembly capacity that the Fed looks at in the auto industry is not really meaningful. First of all, you've got to take account of North America, Canada and Mexico, while the Fed is used to auditing only U.S. capacity. But you also have to take into account our production in Graz, Austria, because we added capacity over there to make the Grand Cherokee to reduce the pressure to export from U.S. plants that were already overwhelmed. We knew we could sell more anyway than we could build here, so we didn't try to expand in the U.S. This freed up our U.S. capacity—maybe 20,000 to 30,000 units that we would have exported to Europe."

Even without rising labor costs, companies were now routinely shifting their production from one plant to another overseas, when their U.S. plants approached full capacity. As Chapter 6 described in the auto industry, the new imperative of manufacturing firms was to reposition a global base of production that could operate profitably in the presence of permanent unused capacity. Their goal was a lower break-even point that still sustained their per unit returns, even when as much as 40 percent of the firm's world-wide production capacity was idle.

Given the governing system's response to faster growth, American companies were naturally reluctant to invest in an expanded U.S. workforce to meet surging sales, since they knew the central bank was likely to intervene and dampen consumer demand. The United Auto Workers local in Flint, Michigan, called a strike against General Motors, demanding it hire five hundred more workers for an auto-parts plant running at full capacity. But GM preferred to keep its shift workers on overtime rather than assume the long-term cost of expanding its workforce. "The price of excess hiring during an upturn in this cyclical industry is a heavy financial burden when a downturn occurs," GM's president of North American operations told the *Wall Street Journal*. As the union well understood, GM was committed to the goal of a much smaller American workforce.[9]

Rentier power was directed at labor, both the organized and unorganized ranks of wage earners, because it regarded rising wages as a principal threat to the stable order. For obvious reasons, this goal was never stated very clearly, but financial markets understood the centrality of the struggle: protecting the value of their capital required the suppression of labor incomes.

When the global bond rates soared and the Fed began tightening credit again in early 1994, Merrill Lynch reported the good news for investors: "Wage restraint is the key to our forecast for another year of disinflation in 1994. Real wage growth in the U.S., Japan and Germany is near zero—the result of slack labor markets and competitive pressures from developing countries. . . . German and Japanese unemployment rates should remain near historical highs in 1994–95 as firms restructure and continue to shed labor. . . . U.S. growth is being led by productivity and that permits healthy gains in output with only minimal tightening in the labor market."[10]

Strangely enough, this market perspective has enveloped elected governments, too. On occasion, Bill Clinton's economic advisors even boasted about the weakening of wages, though his was a Democratic administration, ostensibly dedicated to addressing the wage problem. "We see a very well-behaved employee compensation index," Laura Tyson, chair of the Council of Economic Advisers, told a monetary policy forum in the fall of 1994. The rise in unit labor costs for 1993, she declared, was "among the lowest annual increases in three decades," and pay raises were running even lower in 1994. In fact, Clinton's presidency was distinctive for that fact: throughout his term, despite economic recovery, wages were flat or falling for all but the top 20 percent of the wage earners' ladder.[11]

While the President occasionally lamented the damage that declining wages inflicted on most American families, his White House did not sound very different from the conservative Republican who was chairman of the Federal Reserve. Both deferred to bond-market expectations. "We believe that fears of a large increase in the inflation rate appear at this point to be unwarranted," Tyson said. "However . . . we also recognize that the only way to reduce inflationary expectations over the long run is, in fact, to experience a period of sustained growth with modest inflation." [12]

Yet the logic of who got disciplined and who got rewarded in the rentier system was more perverse than economists like Tyson acknowledged. Just as Bill Clinton had not been rewarded for reducing the budget deficits, a nation would not necessarily be rewarded for reducing inflation either. In fact, the study of global interest rates commissioned by finance ministers from the Group of Ten nations discovered that the opposite happened in the 1990s. "In general," the G-10 economists reported, "the countries with the highest measured real interest rates in the 1990s experienced the largest declines in average inflation between the 1980s and 1990s."

In other words, those nations were penalized for their good behavior, not exactly what the theory promises. What happened to them was that their nominal interest rates on long-term debt rose along with other nations' while their inflation rates subsided, so the actual cost of borrowing for their economies—the real interest rate determined by subtracting inflation from the nominal rate—rose higher than the others, thanks to their virtuous performance. The G-10 study tried to explain this paradox by speculating that perhaps markets were still wary of these countries because of behavior in the distant past. The more logical explanation was that national performance mattered a lot less than government economists assumed. The bond rates were driven more by global pressures. The innocent were punished along with the guilty. [13]

Yet politicians, with rare exceptions, did not challenge the operating rationale of the rentier regime. The U.S. central bank, for instance, promoted a fatalistic conclusion that the economy could not expand on average faster than 2 to 2.5 percent without endangering the hard-won gains in price stability. Alan Greenspan explained his simplistic formula for determining these limits: the labor force expanded by about 1.1 percent a year and overall productivity grew by about 1.4 percent. Added together, this meant 2.5 percent growth was the economy's potential—"the maximal growth of a nation's well-being," as Greenspan put it. [14]

"Unfortunately," he conceded, "even when the economy is producing at its 'potential' many people are still unemployed. But attempts to run at lower levels of unemployment . . . would in the end do more harm than good." Actually, the Fed's logic did assume that the American labor force was already fully employed, though any citizen could observe the opposite reality: a major segment of the workforce was now confined to part-time "temporary" jobs and many millions more were no longer even counted in the unemployment statistics. Young people, even with advanced educations, found themselves accepting lower-rung jobs; older white-collar workers experienced the massive corporate restructurings. These Americans and many others were not producing at their full potential.

The true nature of unemployment was nearly double the official count. The slack labor market in America was closer to the European condition than many supposed. If this reality were incorporated in the calculation, along with the actual growth in productivity stronger than 1.4 percent, then by Greenspan's own logic it would probably double the economy's theoretical "potential."

In any case, it was the Federal Reserve itself that helped to thwart the productivity growth with its own restrictive policy. That was the fundamental consequence of monetary policy dedicated to holding economic growth to Greenspan's "maximal" rate of 2 percent to 2.5 percent. When Greenspan engineered his preemptive strikes against faster growth, it meant the business cycle lost its highs—the surges in growth that stimulated new capital formation, the new investments in expansion and modernization that were the essential core of increasing the nation's productivity. In effect, the Fed policy dictated that the economy would either motor along at a moderate hum or slip into an actual contraction. Without the peaks needed to boost wages and investment, the next valley would seem a lot lower for everyone—an observation that should become clearer to people when the next recession occurs.

Other major central banks, despite varying styles of operation, pursued a similar set of objectives. Indeed, the Federal Reserve existed in its own competitive environment—competing to demonstrate its vigilance was as steadfast as the others. The Fed was still the most important central bank in the world, but not the most conservative.

The Bundesbank was even more forceful in containing growth and more explicit about its disciplinary intentions. When German unions entered their industry-wide wage bargaining, the Bundesbank offered its own expert opinion on what would constitute an appropriate settlement. When Germany and the rest of Europe were in severe recession, the Bundesbank was accused of prolonging the contraction as a way of pushing both companies and unions to restructure—that is, to shed workers faster. Given floating exchange rates and the converging global interest rates, German sternness was swiftly transmitted to American policy.

"The tone for the entire system can be set by the central bank with the most restrictive policy, provided that it is strong enough and is determined to hold to that policy," W. R. Smyser, a Washington consultant on international economy, wrote. In the 1970s, the United States was accused of "exporting inflation" to other economies, but now the Bundesbank could be accused of "exporting deflation"—depressing U.S. and European economic growth with the weight of its own stricter control. German industrial interests benefited up to a point because the tighter policy kept the pressure on Germany's strong unions to yield to restructuring plans, but the doctrine ultimately depressed profits, too.[15]

Adhering to its own circular principles, the rentier regime was flirting visibly with catastrophe, a monetary disorder the world had not experienced in sixty years: a full-blown deflation of prices, collapsing values for both financial assets and for real goods and labor. As nations learned after 1929, once such a disastrous downward spiral of prices was under way, the contraction of economic activity was very difficult to reverse. Everyone would behave in a self-interested way—dumping stocks and bonds, closing factories and turning out workers, marking down prices to unload surplus goods—and that would simply feed the unraveling. In Japan's financial crisis, the elements for such a historic disaster were present. Anxious officials on three continents worked to avert a replay of the 1930s.

Some financial analysts occasionally expressed their concern about the deflationary implications that were present, though markets ignored these warnings and plunged forward on their own rising prices. "It looks very much like a deflationary world to us," Charles I. Clough Jr., chief investment strategist at Merrill Lynch, wrote in September 1993. "The deflation that once ravished the energy, manufacturing and real estate sectors is now focused squarely on consumer goods. . . . The shortages of the 1980's have turned into the gluts of the 1990's. . . . Retailers struggle with excess capacity and await a 1980s-type boom that will likely never reoccur. . . . The momentum behind these deflationary patterns is not easily reversed." [16]

The disjunction between the real economy of commerce and the high-flying economy of finance, created and made worse by the rentier regime's control, has incendiary potential for the world. If breakdown occurs, it would likely begin in the facts of this divergence. By 1996, for instance, the U.S. stock market was reaching again for record highs, riding another bubble of investors' exaggerated hopes, while the real economy of production and employment sputtered along at a tepid pace, accumulating more losers from the deflationary momentum.

The financial boom was, once again, driven by excess liquidity in the global money system—and stirred the same fears that the bubble might suddenly pop. This time, the easy money was provided principally by the Bank of Japan, which, trying to overcome Japan's five-year-old recession, had cut short-term interest rates nearly to zero. Investors borrowed in Tokyo and bought stocks and bonds in New York, propelling the markets higher. The Federal Reserve seemed trapped by its own logic: if it reduced interest rates further to help the real economy, that might simply fuel the speculative boom in stocks and bonds. If it raised rates to stanch the inflation of financial prices, it would likely drive the real economy into contraction.

Faced with this dilemma, the Fed did nothing and was congratulated for its achievement. The President, running for reelection, hailed the economic performance as the best in thirty years: stable growth, low unemployment and no inflation. The Republicans talked about ways to achieve faster economic growth, but they did not challenge the Federal Reserve's prerogatives or the rentiers' premises. Germany was flirting with another recession; Japan was still struggling to get out of one. Yet the rentiers' general air of self-congratulation silenced doubts.

The world economy was astride a fundamental disorder in the imbalance between production and consumption—the same conditions of surplus that had led to global depression in the 1930s—while financial markets rode a historic curve of inflated returns. The warning signs implicit in this divergence from reality were largely ignored by the confident authority of finance capital. Indeed, as these divergences widened, more and more small holders rushed to join the big money in the adventurous search for maximum returns.

"The problem," said Norbert Walter of Deutsche Bank, "lies in a lack of good debtors rather than a scarcity of capital." He meant that the elevated level of global interest rates was explained by the growing risk of lending more capital to deeply indebted governments rather than by any market pressures of supply and demand. All of Europe, not to mention the United States, was consuming more capital to cover the swollen operating deficits of governments. "Ultimately," Walter continued, "there's the question: Is there a political basis for these societies to make a U-turn in their policies? Financial markets ask this question by demanding higher spreads."

Sweden felt the market's lash in the summer of 1994 when major institutional purchasers of its bonds suddenly went on strike, announcing that they would buy no more. Long-term interest rates soared into double digits, rising a full four percentage points that year, the highest borrowing cost demanded of any advanced industrial nation except Italy. Though Sweden had elected a conservative government determined to scale back its celebrated welfare state, the annual deficit was still above 10 percent of GDP and the government's accumulated debt had grown explosively, from 44 percent of GDP in 1990 to 95 percent in 1995.[17]

To end the bondholders' boycott, Sweden's central bank was compelled to tighten credit still further and the prime minister quickly announced new plans for further spending cuts. Yet Sweden's economy—once the model of a stable, prosperous social democracy—was already deeply depressed, with staggering unemployment around 16 percent. The new measures would make things worse. At the next election, Swedish voters returned the socialists to power, though they would face the same dilemma.

"Sweden and Finland are the tip of the iceberg, they're having the worst crisis since the 1930s," Rob Johnson explained at the time. "Finland's deficit is 14 percent of GDP, yet they've got bread kitchens for the unemployed. Belgium has a huge debt of 135 percent of GDP, but its deficit is mostly interest payments and unemployment is 15 percent. Italy went bust last year when Italian bonds crashed. Investors demand a risk premium of 3 percent and Italy's interest payments are about 12 percent of its GDP now. Italian living standards have just been smashed in the last two years—taxes up, real wages down, business weak."

Given the trend lines, Johnson foresaw a major debt crisis for Europe, starting with peripheral economies and moving toward the stronger nations at the center. "I think they're all going to go the way of Italy—debt financing that will put them so much in debt they won't be able to do anything until the bond markets rebel and the technocrats get control," he said. "It has just spiraled out of control. Europe is heading toward a Latin American–style debt crisis sometime in the next seven to ten years—a sovereign rerating of debt across Europe."

Certainly, the fundamentals were in place for some sort of financial reckoning in the not-distant future. The essential collision was between global finance and the welfare state. A long political struggle was under way between the two: governments in the mature industrial societies were reluctant to sacrifice their social obligations, their deficits rose as growth faltered and creditors became increasingly edgy about the dangers Johnson described. The longer-term social consequences of the deteriorating welfare state will be examined in Chapter 16. But the economic consequences were immediate and devastating: the wealthiest nations were trapped between their own history and the decisive discipline of rentier governance.

In volume, the American deficits and debt were naturally larger than Europe's and consumed a much larger share of global lending, but the U.S. fiscal condition was actually manageable by comparison to many. Since 1993, thanks to Clinton's policies, the U.S. government's total debt had been stabilized in relation to economic output, around 70 percent of GDP. At least the U.S. debt ratio was no longer growing rapidly, as it still was in Canada, Germany, France, Britain, Sweden and Switzerland. Even Japan, given its long recession, was joining the front ranks of debtor governments, with an annual deficit/GDP ratio in 1995 nearly twice as large as America's.

Among other things, the fiscal disorders mocked the political plans for the European Union since most of Europe's governments could not qualify for admission under the very terms they had set for themselves. The Maastricht Treaty on unification required a general convergence of fiscal policies and prescribed conservative criteria for EU entry: national budgets with annual deficits no greater than 3 percent of GDP, total debt no greater than 60 percent. Among the fifteen nations expected to participate in a unified Europe, only two met both these criteria in 1995—Germany and Luxembourg—and Germany was perilously close to exceeding the debt/GDP limit. The trend line was ominous for most nations; all governments agreed they must act to reverse it. Political hesitation was not the only reason they failed to do so.[18]

The perverse reality was that global finance made it increasingly difficult for governments to make any lasting progress on their deficits because investors kept pushing the level of real rates higher and demanding larger risk premiums from the borrowers, thus depressing economic activity and further compounding the debt obligations. Nations were not rewarded for good behavior, but faced larger burdens.

Despite frequent scoldings from financiers, a number of nations, including the United States, had already put their operating budgets in balance and were actually running surpluses—except for the annual interest payments due to their bondholders. Though many Americans were perhaps unaware of the achievement, the federal goverment had moderated spending sufficiently so that the so-called primary budget was in surplus—a surplus of $68 billion in 1995 and an expected surplus of $100 billion in 1996. That is, the spending on all the government's actual programs was less than its tax revenues. It was the debt costs that wholly accounted for the annual deficits. (The U.S. primary budget first came into balance in 1989, went into deficit temporarily during the recession, then returned to balance in 1994.) Germany, Italy, the Netherlands, Britain and Belgium have achieved a similar fiscal condition, though at much different levels of indebtedness.

The U.S. primary budget was in balance as an economic fact, though not as a political reality, since the surpluses were made possible by the vast inflow of Social Security tax revenue—the billions in accumulating surpluses that were dedicated to future recipients and invested, in the meantime, in government bonds. The nation doubtless faced a future political collision over Social Security benefits, but the accounting balance was real in present-time economic terms and more relevant to the question of existing market pressures and interest rates.

Despite this budget discipline the debt costs continued to escalate. In practical reality, the U.S. government had to borrow more money every year —$200 billion or more—simply to pay the interest due on its old debt. The arithmetic was compounding: paying the rentiers has become a major function of national governments. In the United States, interest costs had swollen from $52.5 billion in 1980 to $184 billion in 1990. By 1996, debt payments would reach $257 billion—despite the deficit-reduction campaigns by Clinton and his predecessor, George Bush. U.S. spending devoted to debt was roughly equal to national defense or Medicare and Medicaid combined.[19]

The political imperative to reverse this condition not only grew stronger each year, but also became more difficult to accomplish since it posed stark implications for social division: governments were expected to withdraw more and more benefits from dependent classes of citizens—the poor and elderly and unemployed—but also in various ways from the broad middle class, in order to honor their obligations to the creditor class, the people and institutions with accumulations of wealth. There was no precedent in the history of modern industrial democracies to suggest this transfer could be achieved—not without dramatic electoral repudiations or social upheaval.

The rentiers, to be sure, were a more diverse social class than the wealthy alone, but still a much narrower group than conservative rhetoric pretended. Millions of middle-class families have acquired modest shares in the government's pool of bonds through mutual funds (which held about 6 percent of all U.S. long-term debt) or a presumed interest in pension funds (which held another 6 percent of the total). But, in reality, most families did not have a mutual-fund nest egg or even net savings of any kind. A majority of families, aside from any equity they had accumulated in their homes, were net debtors.[20]

The ownership of financial wealth, like incomes, has shifted dramatically to the top rungs of the society, further aggravating the gross inequalities of wealth that have always existed. Edward N. Wolff, an economist at New York University, found, for instance, that the share of total financial wealth held by the bottom 80 percent of American families declined during the 1980s, from 9 percent of the total to 6 percent. The top 1 percent, meanwhile, increased its share of financial assets from 43 to 48 percent.[21]

To compound this social imbalance, the globalization of finance has opened up major venues for tax avoidance by bondholders—individuals and firms—if they deploy their capital offshore. To attract foreign capital, the United States and other major governments have agreed not to report the interest income back to the investors' home countries where it would be taxed. The lost revenue from all these practices, given the rising volumes of global bond markets, probably ran in the hundreds of billions worldwide —directly adding to the deficit disorders. Yet governments did not close down the loopholes because they were fearful of offending the bond buyers.

"The whole Eurobond market is tax-avoidance money—not hot money like drugs but basically zero-tax money," said Michael McIntyre, a Wayne State University law professor and authority on international taxation. "Everyone arranges it so it's impossible to identify the home country of the owners. So no one who trades in those bonds expects that they will ever pay a nickel of taxes and there's a significant percentage of Americans using this exception—they just channel their money through foreign addresses. The United States itself also attracts foreign bond investors by not withholding or reporting to the home country. The presumption of our policy is that the foreigners are paying tax at home, but we know they're not. It's a sham."

The social inequities and political conflict embedded in the fiscal disorders were secondary, however, to the larger economic question: Politics aside, would economic prospects actually improve if governments complied with the bond markets' commandment and balanced their budgets? The rentier logic that promised renewed prosperity was based upon simple accounting distinctions that seemed plausible to people, but did not conform to the complex dynamics of how and why economies actually prospered. If governments pursued this logic to its natural conclusion, they would begin to encounter its flaws. And they would discover that the process of restoring fiscal balance effectively deepened the austerity in their societies.

In fact, the rentier logic was grounded in wrong economics—not just wrong in its operating methods or relentless demands for fiscal order, but wrong in its fundamental understanding of what is required to achieve economic growth and prosperity. The rentier reasoning focused, not surprisingly, on capital and the indisputable observation that savings were an essential element in the wealth-creating dynamic of capitalism. But the rentiers' narrow-minded (and self-interested) economic logic put the cart before the horse and somehow expected it to go forward.

The orthodoxy's accounting went like this: Government deficits caused overall national savings rates to decline, so it was assumed that reducing the public deficits would automatically increase private savings. If capital was thus made more plentiful, interest rates should fall and new investments should increase—more factories, more jobs—and economies would therefore prosper again. This reasoning misstated the fundamental relationships between savings, investment and growth. Yet it was repeated as a self-evident mantra among the economists, politicians and opinion leaders who promoted balanced budgets as the road to salvation.

The contemporary global reality provided compelling evidence that contradicted virtually all of the conventional assumptions. First, the orthodoxy assumed implicitly that capital was scarce—too many borrowers bidding for funds across the three great auctions—and this explained why interest rates remained at historically high levels. Despite many attempts economists were unable to produce any concrete proof for this assumption, but they repeated it anyway, reasoning backward from their own faith in "rational" markets: if interest rates were high, that must mean the markets faced demand for capital that exceeded the supply.

In the real world of finance, many analysts scoffed at this simple-minded description of cause and effect. Instead, they agreed with Norbert Walter of Deutsche Bank, who had remarked: the problem with high interest rates was not a "scarcity of capital" but the shakiness of the borrowers —and the increasing risk premiums demanded by the lenders. As the national debt burdens swelled, the lenders naturally became more nervous and kept ratcheting up their demands for protection.

The bond market, once the safest arena for financial investment and ostensibly a market that took the long view, has become edgy and impatient with the future. As Robert Johnson explained: "In general, it feels more like we're heading toward destruction rather than stability." The extraordinary interest rates on long-term debt could be understood as a form of political insurance—creditors indemnifying themselves in advance against the possibility of eventual revolt by the borrowers. Finance capital could glimpse a crisis coming and sought to protect itself.

In fact, enormous pools of savings have accumulated worldwide during this long-running expansionary era—reflected in the phenomenon that financial assets were growing in volume much faster than the real economic activity (as documented by the McKinsey & Company study cited in Chapter 11). What was different in this era, however, was the shifting geography of the capital accumulation—a migration of financial wealth that reflected the shifting fortunes of industrial expansion from old places to the new.

National savings rates did decline in the older, deficit-ridden industrial nations during the last twenty-five years, but soared among the fast-growing developing countries, especially in Asia. While the advanced economies' saving rates fell below 20 percent of GDP, the rate for developing economies rose from 19 percent of GDP in 1970 to 27 percent in 1994—and even higher in booming East Asia. The industrial boom under way among some poorer nations was not responsible for pushing global interest rates higher, as many supposed, since the Asian expansion was largely financed by its own growing pool of domestic capital. The net outflow of capital investment from the United States, for instance, was quite modest in size, and in net terms, mostly went to Latin America.

The Group of Ten study of global interest rates confirmed that conclusion: "Despite the growing importance of non-industrial countries in world financial markets, it does not appear that capital demands from developing and transition economies [the former Soviet Union and allied nations] have been a major source of secular upward pressure on real interest rates. . . . The marked increase in investment in developing countries over the last 25 years has been largely self-financed."

This geographical contrast in savings behavior begged the critical question: Why? Why did Asian nations and a few others begin saving so much more capital than they had in the past? And why were they saving at rates much higher than Europeans or Americans? The usual cultural explanations —frugal Asians versus the spendthrift Caucasians—were mostly nonsense and ignored the many concrete measures that Asian governments took to induce (or force) higher domestic savings. In any case, culture could not account for why the Asians themselves had changed their behavior. The economic explanation was fundamental and universal: an economy accumulated greater savings for investment when it was growing faster—not the other way around as the rentier logic supposed.

Asian savings soared for the very tangible reason that people and enterprises were experiencing rising incomes from their faster economic expansion. Savings in Europe and the United States declined for the opposite reason: their economies were growing at subsiding rates. The G-10 finance ministers gingerly reported this unconventional conclusion: "It is generally assumed that higher saving, through higher investment, raises growth. . . . The above findings, however, point to the possibility of significant reverse causality running from growth to saving. Indeed, in many Asian high-growth countries, increases in saving rates appear to have lagged behind the acceleration in growth." Thus, the report observed, higher growth could generate "a positive saving response which in turn would permit it to finance the increased investment demand and dampen the upward pressures on interest rates."

The government dilemmas of rising deficits were, likewise, driven by the same economic force: slower growth. "A declining growth rate," the G-10 study noted, "may help to explain the deterioration of public finances in industrial countries after the first oil shock [in 1973]. In the United States, rule-driven expenditure programs set up in a high-growth period began outpacing revenues when growth slowed down. Budget processes that might have tended toward surpluses began producing deficits, requiring continuous and difficult discretionary fiscal corrections."

One other factor explained the differences in savings behavior: financial deregulation. Western governments had generally removed their capital controls and domestic interest-rate ceilings, and allowed investors to roam free of national obligations, seeking the highest return. Most Asian nations, including Japan, had not. The G-10 study of global interest rates acknowledged that the deregulation of finance itself helped to induce the higher interest rates. "It is likely that the financial liberalization of the 1980s contributed to the upward shift in interest rates," the report said. Furthermore, the removal of controls contributed to the decline in savings by making it easier for everyone, including governments, to borrow more freely. "Financial liberalization has probably affected savings negatively . . ." the G-10 study concluded. "Countries which have liberalized the access to consumer credit have experienced a decrease in the aggregate saving rate."

Commonsense experience supported the report's observations: ordinary wage earners well understood that they could save more when their incomes were rising—and were tempted to borrow more when the opposite occurred. The same dynamic applied to an overall economy that was expanding robustly: the increased economic activity was throwing off more surplus wealth—both through wages and profits—more of which could be set aside as savings, after the immediate needs and desires of consumption had been satisfied. In these conditions, firms reserved more of their own profits for new capital investment, and rising consumer demand gave them the incentive to expand production and employment rather than shrink it or relocate it elsewhere. For the same reasons, governments were able to spend more—and borrow less—since the expansion also generated rising tax revenues.

In broad outline, this crucial economic relationship—rising growth leads to greater savings and new investment, not the other way around—contradicted the orderly logic of the rentiers' regime, which assumed that savings must precede growth. The G-10 report artfully attempted to side-step the obvious inference in its findings: it was faster growth that represented the genuine remedy for the budget deficits, rather than the slower growth prescribed by the rentier system.

This conclusion was politically incorrect since it sounded perilously close to the old, discredited doctrine of John Maynard Keynes, the great British economist whose demand-led theory of economic growth had displaced the classical economic orthodoxy sixty years before during the crisis of world depression. The old orthodoxy was back in power again, defending the necessity of high interest rates and restrained growth, imposing its traditional sense of accounting on the economic dynamics of commerce and societies. As a result, the older advanced economies were all caught in the same vicious circle: disappointing growth that led to lower savings and investment, accompanied by higher unemployment and eroding incomes, the weaker demand that further inhibited growth.

The evidence contradicted conventional wisdom in one other important respect: despite the higher returns available to capital, despite the supposed economic efficiency of liberating financial markets, new capital investment has actually declined in those advanced countries that fully embraced the free-market logic and their productivity growth rates declined with it.

The G-10 study observed the contradiction: "The past 35 years have witnessed deep and widespread market-based reforms in national and international markets. . . . But the growth rate of total factor productivity—which is determined by technological progress and changes in economic efficiency—has slowed in every G-10 country since the early 1970's. This slowdown in the growth of total factor productivity implies that the positive effects of liberalization, deregulation and globalization have been outweighed by slower technology growth." In other words, the older economies that had fostered technological revolution were themselves benefiting less from the process—growing more slowly and getting less of the new investment that would maintain their productive edge.

This malignant circle was not going to be reversed by balanced budgets. Indeed, the achievement of fiscal order would make things worse. Suppose, for instance, that the United States went first, as the Republican conservatives promised, and restored a balanced budget ahead of the other nations. The popular assumption that this would somehow give the United States an edge over its economic rivals rested on the dubious promise of lower interest rates. But the global reality of finance imposed higher rates on every nation, regardless of its individual fiscal condition.

The G-10 study made the point that the fiscal deficits were a shared problem: "The effects on real interest rates of changes in fiscal deficits are now spread across all countries integrated into the global financial system," the report noted. "This means that countries collectively have an interest in the soundness of fiscal policies."

Suppose, then, that all of the advanced economies somehow corrected their fiscal disorders together, more or less at once. The economic consequence would be dramatic and depressing: a gross withdrawal of aggregate demand, as governments reduced income-support benefits, cut public spending and stopped new borrowing. Fiscal order, for example, would require the United States to reduce domestic demand by more than 2 percent of its GDP, Germany by 2.5 percent, Japan by 3.7 percent, France by 5.2 percent, Italy by 7.7 percent, Britain by 4.9 percent and so forth. This event, if it ever occurred, would pose an interesting challenge for the global system: Who will replace the lost demand—the incomes, sales and profits derived from the deficit spending—when governments get their accounts in order?

The global demand for capital would abate, most certainly, but private savings would not likely increase since savings did not accumulate miraculously when economies were flattened. The consequence would instead be a general austerity—a financial accounting that looked like equilibrium in the statistics but rested upon the gross underemployment of people and economic resources, not to mention widening social distress.

Underneath the financial problems of growing debt and punitive interest rates, the real cause of these disorders was the new economic reality of "one world." The great globalization of industrial production has launched vital, new producing nations on an upward path, but also deranged the basis for the general prosperity in settled, older economies. The old political order talked about these changes endlessly, but did not yet grasp the essential meaning.

In both Europe and America, the usual political debates surrounding government were blocked by the rentiers' message: elected government is impotent, nothing it does can alter the economic outcomes. Yet American politics, from left to right, was still focused on the prize of faster economic growth, while Europe's still defended its social welfare system. One could imagine a future politics that redefines the meaning of economic growth with a different set of values measuring the public well-being. In the here and now, politicians did not campaign for office by promising a slower economy.

Even the U.S. conservatives who proposed to scale back the federal government and balance its budgets (and reduce taxes for capital owners) argued from the same premise: these measures were offered as the way to stimulate faster growth—more factories, more jobs. But how could they if central banks and the bond market were determined to block faster growth, if the rentier logic regarded a robust economy as threatening? Conventional politics was in a dangerous cul-de-sac—promising what it could not deliver, losing the public's trust—yet lacking the courage to challenge the reigning wisdom.

The overall logic of the rentier regime began to make more sense if one put aside the usual rationales for its policies and assumed, instead, that it was serving a deeper historical purpose: compelling people to accept capitalism's revolutionary transformations. Like the gold standard a hundred years before, the rigid control of growth and employment in older economies was a way of forcing people in those societies to accept the deep adjustments that were under way—the industries reorganizing and adopting globalized platforms of production, the underlying erosion of living standards, the great shifts of wealth to Asia and elsewhere that accompanied these developments. Other competing social and economic interests were bombarded by insecurity and lean circumstances, compelled to hunker down defensively, discouraged from resisting these fateful changes in their lives.

No one in authority spoke in such blunt terms, of course, and many officials were probably unaware of serving the deeper tides of capitalism. At most, politicians obliquely acknowledged the pain and insecurity for people in this awkward passage by describing the economy as "in transition" toward a brighter future. In the meantime, the rentier regime would defend capital and keep the pressure on others to yield to their fate.

Fourteen

The Economic Question

IF MY ANALYSIS is right, the global system of finance and commerce is in a reckless footrace with history, plunging toward some sort of dreadful reckoning with its own contradictions, pulling everyone else along with it. Responsible experts and opinion leaders, of course, do not generally share my sense of alarm. Nor do most political authorities, who, in any case, seem thoroughly intimidated by the economic events. Some important voices in business and finance do occasionally express similar anxieties, but multinational enterprise is preoccupied with its own imperatives, finance capital consumed by its own search for returns. Public opinion may be uneasy, even angry, but people generally are also confused and rudderless.

In sum, I do not see much likelihood for timely political action, the kind of government intervention that might avert the disastrous outcome I foresee. If nothing changes, events will reveal soon enough whether I was wrong.

The burden of my argument, though it probably sounds radical to conventional opinion, is actually for moderation. The wondrous machine of global revolution is oscillating out of control, widening the arcs of social and economic instabilities in its wake. The destructive pressures building up within the global system are leading toward an unbearable chaos that, even without a dramatic collapse, will likely provoke the harsh, reactionary politics that can shut down the system. This outcome is avoidable, I believe, if nations will put aside theory and confront what is actually occurring, if they have the courage to impose remedial changes before it is too late.

If the positive energies of the revolutionary process are to be preserved, it has to be slowed down, not stopped, and redirected on a new course of development that is more moderate and progressive, that promises broader benefits to almost everyone. The economic problem requires governments to throw off the depressive logic of the rentiers and formulate a more hopeful vision of the economic possibilities, to discard the hollow abstractions of financial accounting and begin rebuilding the tangible foundations for balanced prosperity, for work and wages and greater social equity—not only for older, wealthier nations but for the aspiring poor in the emerging "one world." It is far easier to describe some ways in which this might be achieved than to imagine that governing elites will act upon them.

The first imperative is to impose some order on the global marketplace, to make both finance and commerce more accountable for the consequences of their actions and to give hostage societies more ability to determine their own futures. The larger economic imperative is more profound: governments must alter the directional flow of the overall system itself, away from the debilitating practices that bid wages down while building up impossible surpluses and toward a regime that fosters rising growth and employment in every region. Both objectives are naturally intertwined, since it will be impossible to redirect the global system's energies toward a pro-growth strategy without also establishing new political standards for the behavior of commerce and finance.

The first priority is to reregulate finance capital. Governments will have to reimpose some of the control measures that they discarded during the last generation, both to stabilize financial markets and to make capital owners more responsive to the general needs of the producing economies. The essential goal is to restore a reasonable balance between the twin realms of finance and commerce and their competing demands. Finance capital has proved itself a capricious master of the general prosperity, occasionally irrational and not committed to the same results that almost everyone else wants and needs.

Financial reform can begin with measures like transaction taxes on foreign exchange, designed to moderate the gargantuan daily inflows and outflows of capital across national borders. By raising the cost of short-run transactions, capital controls would take some of the fun and profit out of currency trading and other speculative activities in the global market. It would not inhibit the long-term flows of capital for foreign investment and trade. The recontrol of capital will not by itself restore stable currency relationships among nations, but it is the necessary predicate for achieving that goal.

Governments, in essence, must reclaim the governing obligations of the nation-state from private markets. This would not eliminate the critical role that markets play in challenging the soundness of government policies, but it might moderate these conflicts, make them more evenly balanced and rational.

Reregulation will not necessarily foreclose a gradual evolution toward the larger global system of governance that some envision. But that evolution cannot possibly succeed on its present unstable terms. If globalization is truly to be the future, then it must serve more than capital returns or the market shares of multinational corporations. A system that randomly punishes national economies, even for good behavior, or arbitrarily denies societies reasonable prospects for growth and full employment cannot survive. Sooner or later, people will figure out what is happening to them and rebel.

To disarm the exaggerated power and random follies of the global bond market, governments can begin by tightening the terms for easy credit that are routinely extended to financial markets. That is, regulators must reign in the hedging and derivative devices that allow speculators to multiply the size of their plays many times, magnifying the subsequent financial shocks on real economies. The margin requirements for purchasing bonds and other financial instruments on borrowed money can be set higher and employed flexibly as temporary credit-control levers during conditions of market excess. The use of derivatives could be restricted to the genuine market-hedging needs of multinational commerce by requiring that the issuing banks post capital reserves to back up these contracts.

In some arenas of credit, ceilings on interest rates might also be reimposed, limitations that can curb reckless borrowers and also encourage the flow of savings into worthier, long-term investments. The old regulatory systems that limited interest-rate returns had many flaws and inflexible qualities that were eventually overwhelmed by financial modernization, but that does not prevent the invention of new systems that can effectively moderate the runaway accumulations of debt. As the G-10 economists noted, financial liberalization has contributed not only to the decline of savings in advanced economies during the last two decades, but also to the unprecedented level of global interest rates. The exaggerated level of interest rates is not likely to subside until governments, once again, compel capital owners to accept more moderate returns on their wealth.

If the major trading nations reassert such controls on their own investors and markets, they must inevitably ask themselves: Why should the world tolerate the offshore banking centers where capital hides from banking and securities laws or from national income taxes? The leading governments, if they had the will, could swiftly cripple or close down these unregulated financial outposts simply by prohibiting their own banking systems from honoring the transfers of offshore capital. Eliminating these havens for tax avoidance would not only significantly improve tax revenues for nations, but also strengthen their law enforcement.

Above all, the reregulation of finance will confront the anomalous relationship that now exists between national governments and global capital. The standard claim of the global financiers—that governments are impotent to regulate their behavior—is always quickly put aside when a large crisis like Mexico's collapse develops. Then the national governments are expected to step in and provide the funds and regulatory supervision to clean up the mess. This unnatural relationship between public authority and private interests actually encourages irresponsibility among the investors, since they assume the burden of their mistakes can be transferred to the unwitting taxpayers. Global capital that needs the protection of the nation-state needs to learn to live by its rules and obligations.

The usual argument against the reregulation of finance is that globalization and telecommunications technology have made it impossible.

Money, it is said, now flows so quickly and secretively by instant electronic transfer, no government agency can hope to monitor it, much less assert regulatory control. This argument ignores the practical reality of finance. Astute traders, as we saw earlier, share their own informal intelligence system on the daily capital flows—who is buying what from whom, hour by hour, around the world—and there is no reason government regulators could not easily duplicate this surveillance in a more systematic manner. Despite mythology there is very little real leakage in the global financial system—at least not of legal money—since virtually all of the global transactions flow through several dozen major banks and brokerages somewhere in the world. These regulated financial institutions, already under government supervision, provide the mechanism for thorough monitoring and rule-making.

But, the conventional wisdom argues further, any nation that attempts to curb the free flows of international capital will be punished severely—capital will flee, interest rates will soar. For many poorer nations, that can certainly be the case: they are hostage to foreign capital and its sudden flight, just as the deeply indebted industrial nations are vulnerable to the whipsaw of a "capitalist strike." Still, it is also true that finance capital already accepts national controls when it is compelled to do so. Among the regulatory controls I have described, almost all are in use one place or another around the world, often in the poorer nations.

Successful developing countries understand that they must regulate the foreign capital flows in order to retain control over their own development. The financial markets may complain about the controls imposed by a nation like China or Chile, but, meanwhile, capital still invests in those places because the prospects look promising. If poor countries may regulate global finance in their own self-interest, cannot wealthy nations do the same?

The power of finance capital would be disarmed swiftly if the four or five nations with the most important markets—New York, London, Frankfurt, Tokyo and Hong Kong, for instance—acted collectively to reassert controls like transaction taxes. Their joint action would effectively straddle the entire global financial system (and could severely penalize any outlier nation that refused to cooperate). Many of the poorer nations should welcome this, so long as it does not shut them out of capital markets, since it ought to reduce their own vulnerability to the random financial shocks.

But it is the major governments, of course, that are as yet unwilling to consider any measures to moderate the effects of financial liberalization. These regimes are all closely allied with the interests of global finance and enthralled by its conservative orthodoxy. The main barrier to financial reform is not technology or economics but politics—the dominating political power of finance capital.

"The lesson to be learned is that financial markets need to be supervised," George Soros wrote. "It is truly surprising that the lessons of the international debt crisis have still not been learned. The champions of unregulated competition are more vocal and influential than ever." Soros offered this observation a decade ago, following the various financial crises of the 1980s. The contradictions have since grown larger and more dangerous.[1]

The larger imperative at hand is redirecting the global system toward a pro-growth regime that overcomes the "contained depression" in advanced economies and creates a basis for rising prosperity on both ends of the global system, among both rich and poor nations. Financial reforms will assist this objective by curbing the appetites of capital for quick returns and by repudiating the governing values of the rentier system. In the end, capital does not lose in conditions of general prosperity; it gains new opportunities.

The central economic problem of our revolutionary era, not so different in nature from the previous industrial revolution, is an excess of supply —the growing, permanent surpluses of goods, labor and productive capacity inevitably generated by technological innovation and the free-running industrial globalization. The supply problem is the core of what drives the destruction and instability—the accumulation of redundant factories as new ones are simultaneously built in emerging markets, the mass unemployment and declining wages, the irregular mercantilist struggles for market entry and shares in the industrial base, the market gluts that depress prices and profits, the fierce contests that lead to cooperative cartels among competitors and other consequences.

These conditions are accepted—actually ignored—by the laissez-faire orthodoxy since it holds, first, that governments must not interfere with markets and, second, that these disorders will be naturally self-correcting. Market supply and demand will come into balance—once wages have fallen far enough, once the army of unemployed is sufficiently large and desperate, once price competition has destroyed enough productive capacity and invested capital to eliminate the overcapacity.

The doctrine, thus, requires political passivity in the presence of social brutality—the general losses and suffering that have been accumulating for a generation and are likely to continue for another generation or longer. Even if the supposed equilibrium is achieved eventually, it will not be what most people would call prosperity. The marketplace will stabilize at perpetual underemployment and unfulfilled potential. This assertion is not theoretical speculation, but describes the actual conditions generated by the prior era of free-running industrial revolution just before it ended in collapse.

The shocking lesson of economic history—experience that now seems largely forgotten—is that vast human suffering and random destruction of productive capacities are unnecessary. From the crisis and turmoil of the early twentieth century, nations painfully discovered that there is nothing inevitable about these market forces or the social convulsions they sow if societies will act to counter them. A world of wondrous new labor-saving technologies ought logically to become a world of general abundance. But this condition does not arise inevitably from the marketplace alone, not without political and social struggle. A shared prosperity emerges, as Keynes taught, only when people throw off passivity and learn to take control of their fate.

Governments can counter the disorders and ameliorate losses mainly by stimulating consumption, creating more buyers for unsold goods—the rising market demand that activates idle factories and workers. The present regime is pathological fundamentally because it broadly destroys consumer incomes while it creates the growing surfeit of goods. Many different measures, large and small, can push the global system in an opposite direction, but the underlying transaction, bluntly stated, requires shifting returns from capital to labor, reversing the maldistribution of incomes generated by the marketplace under the rentier system.

Greater social equity is consistent with and, indeed, required for a sound and expanding economy: when rising incomes are broadly distributed, it creates mass purchasing power—the rising demand that fuels a virtuous cycle of growth, savings and new investment. When incomes are narrowly distributed, as they are now, the economic system feeds upon itself, eroding its own energies for expansion, burying consumers and business, even governments, in impossible accumulations of debt. A relative few become fabulously wealthy, but a healthy economy is not sustained by manic investing. Nothing about modern technologies or the "information age" has altered these ancient fundamentals.

Governments may not find the courage to confront this malignant condition and adopt remedial measures until a full-blown crisis is upon them, but they will assuredly do so afterwards. The footrace with history is about whether modern societies can act intelligently on these large matters without the presence of visible catastrophe. Put another way, is contemporary capitalism capable of learning from its own past excesses or must it repeat the bloody errors of the twentieth century?

The great difference in the present era, of course, is that the economic question is now spread around the globe, encompassing nations that were once impoverished colonies but have acquired the skill and scale to realize their own industrial prosperity. The challenge is no longer solely about Europe and North America and Japan, or entirely in their hands. Developing nations are rightly skeptical of talk about altering the present course of development since it seems to be working for many of them. At least, they can see a historic opening in the global revolution and may resist measures to modify it. In this hour, both history and morality are on their side.

The genuine meaning of "one world" will be tested by how nations answer this question: Can the global system be turned toward a less destructive path without throwing the poor people over the side? Older economies may be tempted to revert to insular, self-protective devices, but this will destroy the promise of the globalizing revolution and could even produce its own implosion of commerce—balkanized struggles for markets that substitute political conflict for the economic disorders. The challenge of "one world" is to create the standards for a progressive system that everyone can trust, that does not leave anyone out.

To accomplish this, people have to reimagine the dimensions of their own world, to free themselves of buried cultural and racial assumptions inherited from the colonialist past. On both ends of the global economy—old and new, rich and poor—people must be able to envision an all-encompassing prosperity, a system that nourishes both realms mutually rather than exploiting each other's economic weaknesses. The dynamic spirit of "one world" seeks a New Deal between the haves and have-nots, reformulating the expansive principles embodied in the original Bretton Woods system so they realistically work for everyone.

Such a system is humanly plausible certainly, though not easily achieved in politics or economics. The deeper tides of history are not changed overnight or by political dictum, but only from serious debate and practical experience. But the largest barrier to a shared prosperity is neither physical nor economic, but the limitations imposed by old ideas, the mental boundaries drawn around what people believe is possible.

Imagine that people and nations were free to think anew. What measures would they undertake? The imperatives for a new world order can be boiled down to a series of mutually reinforcing propositions, each of which in different ways would help to redress the economic imbalances of supply and demand. They might include the following ideas:

1. Tax capital instead of labor. Even a modest shift in tax structures can stimulate the creation of new jobs and wage incomes while it creates the mechanism for making investors and corporations more accountable for their behavior. The tax systems in most advanced industrial societies are tilted against work, focusing regressive payroll taxes on wage earners and their employers, thus raising the real cost for a firm that expands its work-force. Financial wealth is lightly taxed by comparison and, at least in the United States, not subject to the property taxes that people pay on real-property assets of homes and businesses.

Reducing the tax barrier to employment can be done in a progressive manner that favors work for the less skilled—lower payroll tax rates on jobs at the lower end of the wage scale, higher taxes on the high end. This would provide a discrete incentive to multiply jobs for those who need them most—a cheaper and more effective approach than social programs that try to help people after they are already poor or unemployed. The same principle could target the common practice, at least among American companies, of escaping the social overhead of doing business by marginalizing workers in piecemeal jobs—the "temporary" or "contract" work that lacks decent wages or benefits. The supposed efficiency of these measures actually involves pushing the social costs—health care or income support for indigent retirees—onto others, mainly the general public.

Direct taxation of financial capital could also create the mechanism for enforcing social obligations, rewarding the firms and investors that take responsibility for broader economic and social consequences while punishing the free riders. Globalizing corporations, deploying their employment offshore and arbitraging tax concessions from different governments, ought to be treated less favorably than the enterprises that are conscientiously increasing their domestic employment. Capital investors, likewise, have a financial obligation to the commonweal that protects them.*

A direct tax on wealth is not as radical as it may sound to Americans since eleven other OECD nations, including Germany, already have modest versions. The principle is not different from ordinary property taxes or business-license taxes on merchants or professionals: capital owners benefit from the public domain and, if anything, benefit more since they have more wealth to protect. For instance, Edward N. Wolff has proposed that the United States follow the model of Switzerland and adopt a system of modest, graduated rates that would start by exempting the first $100,000 of financial assets, tax the next $100,000 at a rate of only .05 percent and rise to a rate of .3 percent above $1 million. He calculates such a system would have raised only $40 billion in 1994—a lot of money but hardly an onerous burden on the wealthy nor a solution to the fiscal disorders.[2]

A central purpose of taxing capital, however, is to establish the means for defining the responsibility of capital owners to each nation and its people. If capital wants to enjoy record returns from the global system, it must help pay for the economic and social wreckage it leaves behind. Once that principle is established, the tax code can begin to make distinctions among both corporations and investors, based upon their civic behavior. Capital investors and investment funds ought to pay property taxes at a higher rate, for instance, if they are merely using the United States or other nations as a secure sanctuary for their wealth.

"The emerging modern system gives a larger share of income and power to capital, yet the burdens of government and community have steadily been shifted to labor," as one financial economist explained to me. "At some point, we have to ask whether utterly free capital is a benefit to everyone. Free capital is certainly a benefit to the people who own the capital. But they couldn't exist if these governments did not exist to protect them. No one wants to locate the Chicago Board of Trade in Bangkok or

---

* The United States needs a constitutional amendment, based on principles of equitable taxation, that would prohibit all governments—state, local and federal—from granting special tax favors to corporations in exchange for industrial investments. The competition in public subsidies is scandalous, as states bid up their offers for new factories, but the practice probably cannot be halted unless every jurisdiction is compelled to stop.

Jakarta. They want to be in the United States or maybe five or six other countries where their transactions and their wealth will be safe."

Similar logic could change the strategic calculations of multinational corporations as they disperse production, perhaps by making preferential distinctions in the tax code. If the national objective is to stimulate domestic employment, then capital or corporate stocks might get a reduced rate or even exemption from capital gains taxation if the corporate balance sheet confirms that the enterprise is increasing jobs by investment at home. Capital should be taxed at the full rate if it is doing the opposite. The global dispersal of industry would not be stopped—indeed, the process couldn't be stopped by such modest measures—but firms and shareholders would have to help pay for what they left behind.

This approach inevitably favors domestic firms over multinationals, but it also discards the fraudulent political proposition that any tax break or government subsidy to business automatically translates into general benefit for the society at large. If that assumption was ever sound, it is clearly most suspect in the presence of globalizing firms. Governments promoting the trading fortunes of multinational firms have not yet answered the gut question: Who in the nation really benefits from this process, owners or workers, capital or citizens?*

If measures such as these can reduce idle labor and bolster consumption in the older economies, the economic benefit should flow to everyone in the trading system, rich and poor alike, since it expands global demand. The practice of labor arbitrage between high- and low-wage economies might be slowed down, at least modestly, but the wage differential of the poorer labor markets remains enormous and the advantage will not soon be dissipated. In any case, the developing nations have worse prospects in the long run if the trading system is shut down by protectionist measures or implodes from the weakening consumption and burgeoning supply.

The paradox of the global economic dilemma—and its great promise —is that the poor need the rich, just as the rich need the poor, and neither is likely to prosper without the other.

2. Reform the terms of trade to ensure more balanced flows of commerce, compelling exporting nations to become larger consumers of the global production. As Chapter 10 described, the present system is propped up by the persistent trade deficits of wealthier nations, mainly the United States, a condition that will not endure for much longer. Rhetorical promises notwithstanding, global agreements like GATT and the endless rounds of trade disputes have failed utterly to redress the trade imbalances. Indeed,

---

* *The question of national interest is especially acute in the United States, where major multinationals have bluntly declared independence from national loyalties or obligations to workforces and communities. In Japan, by contrast, the level of mutual trust and obligation is much stronger between enterprises and society at large. Yet even in Japan, tensions are building around this question as manufacturing moves more of its production offshore.*

prospects are worsening as China and other major new industrial powers prepare to enter the stream. The fundamental principle, therefore, must be established: an industrial economy cannot expect to construct vast oversupply of production for export while refusing to accept equivalent volumes of imports from others.

The system, in effect, has to provoke a meaningful showdown with the Japanese model of wealth accumulation—the irregular mercantilist practices that exact zero-sum advantage at the expense of trading partners. Those economies that persist in accumulating huge trading surpluses would lose their cost-free access to foreign markets through emergency tariffs or other measures. On the other hand, nations that practice genuine reciprocity of buying and selling, including the aspiring poor nations, would be rewarded with preferences. In short, Japan and other Asian nations like China following Japan's strategic path would face an unsentimental choice: either expand imports or expect to be stuck with excess productive capacity.

The objective of temporary trading barriers would not be to protect domestic industrial sectors, but to force everyone to confront the underlying crisis of surpluses. If a country intends to expand its industrial base for global trade, it must expect as well to expand its share of global consumption—not perfectly, of course, or even right away, but with enough vigor so that the negative trends can be moderated substantially.

Every trading nation, including poor nations hoping to become less poor, has a tangible stake in solving the supply problem because it poses a principal obstacle to adopting a pro-growth regime for the world. Under the present system, older economies may actually suffer from faster growth if their rising consumption simply generates a deluge of imports and larger trade deficits, while the foreign markets remain closed to their production. Until this zero-sum condition is corrected, the potential for greater growth will remain stymied. If it is not corrected—and rather soon—the crisis of overcapacity will bear down on the system until one day it eventually becomes explosive.

3. Bring the bottom up—raising wages on the low end as rapidly as possible—by requiring trading nations to honor labor rights. By defending human freedom, the trading system can establish that the collective right of workers to bid up their wages is sanctioned and protected. Morality aside, the economic objective is straightforward: raising wages at the bottom enlarges the base of consumption for everyone's goods. Even in the best of circumstances, the downward pressures on high-wage labor markets will not abate soon, given the vast sea of available low-wage workers. But every gain in wage levels at the bottom, even modest gains, translates into immediate economic benefit for the global system: more purchasing power.

At present, the system functions in reverse: eroding consumption by replacing high-wage labor with cheap labor. To be sure, the new industrial workers in Asia or Latin America have new wage incomes to spend, but overall the system experiences a net loss in the potential for mass consumption. The challenge, roughly speaking, is to create a global system that functions more energetically by pulling the bottom up instead of the top down. Many poorer nations are naturally hostile to the suggestion, fearing they will lose the comparative advantage of cheap labor or reluctant to relax political control over their workforces. But firms or nations that rely upon repressive exploitation of the weak for trading advantage are not truly ready for membership in a "one world" economy. They should be penalized, even excluded.

The easiest way to accomplish this reform is to insert an enforceable "social clause" in the global trade agreements requiring all trading nations to honor the long-established international rules for labor rights. As a practical matter, that is unlikely to happen at the level of GATT or the World Trade Organization, since both developing countries and multinational corporations are opposed to any labor reforms.

The political opening, therefore, lies in negotiating regional or nation-to-nation compacts that begin to establish networks of mutual social standards and extend trading preferences to those who honor them (the opportunity Bill Clinton failed to act upon in the North American trade agreement with Mexico). Reciprocal trade agreements that link several rich nations with several poor nations would establish a working model that demonstrates the positive economic energies that flow from labor reform. As participants benefit on both ends, other poor nations may see the wisdom of emulating the reform.

Nations are, of course, entitled to their sovereignty—the power to set domestic social standards free of foreigners' interference—but that principle does not require the foreigners to buy their goods. Advanced economies need not meddle in other nations' domestic politics since they can regulate the social behavior of their own multinationals, both at home and abroad. If the national interest lies in bringing up wages worldwide, then governments may withdraw subsidies and tax preferences from firms that, like the U.S. electronics industry in Malaysia, actively seek to block labor rights for their foreign workers.

4. Forgive the debtors—that is, initiate a general write-off of bad debts accumulated by the poorer nations. Extinguishing failed loans issued by the international agencies would free desperately poor economies, especially in Africa, to pursue more viable strategies for domestic development. The gross liquidation of debt obligations is fundamentally a stimulative economic measure since it frees up cash for other pursuits, including active consumption, and socially enlightened in terms of easing global poverty.

Writing off these debts is probably inevitable, in any case, since most of these loans can never possibly be repaid. Right now, the interest costs simply bleed the poor nations further each year and often require new international loans so they can keep up payments on their old loans. Liquidation would free their meager cash flows for genuine development and at least raise the possibility that they may someday become significant consumers in the global system.

To accompany the debt forgiveness, however, the operating purposes of the international lending institutions, the World Bank and the International Monetary Fund, must also be reformed. In essence, both of these public financial powers have to develop greater respect for the indigenous strategies for growth, promoting a more patient development of domestic economic foundations instead of simply enforcing the financial imperatives of the global system. To cite the most obvious contradiction, the World Bank and IMF routinely use their power to suppress wages and consumption in the developing countries when the advanced nations that finance their lending have an interest in achieving the opposite. If the lending institutions are unable to change direction, then sponsoring governments should withdraw funding and abolish them, writing down their loan portfolios in the process.

5. Reform the objectives of central banks so they will support a pro-growth regime instead of thwarting it. The purposes of monetary policy have to be returned to a more balanced and democratic perspective—an understanding that growth, employment and wages are crucial to a sound economy, no less important than the prerogatives of stored wealth. So long as the Federal Reserve and other central banks stand in the way of more vigorous growth that might allow a reinflation of wage incomes, the problem of weakening consumption and oversupply is sure to increase, accompanied by compounding debt burdens.

The policy choices embedded in the regulation of money and credit always involve difficult trade-offs between which risks a society is more willing to accept—inflation or recession, idle capacity or overheated activity, failed debtors or financial speculations. But the consequences of these choices are not distributed evenly throughout the society, especially when the policy is always skewed toward the conservative interests of wealth holders. Most of the leading central banks are ostensibly independent of politics, yet this does not prevent them from adhering faithfully to the narrow constituency of finance capital. Their prejudices are unlikely to change until the competing interests—labor, manufacturing and other sectors—organize concerted counterpressures demanding a more generous policy toward economic growth. To make central banks yield, they should be reformed thoroughly—reconstituted as open and accountable governing institutions.

In practice, central banks remain stuck in the past, still fighting the last war against inflation when the global system now faces the opposite danger —a massive deflation of prices, economic activity, debt. The trade-offs surrounding monetary policy have been profoundly altered by globalized finance and production. Yet central bankers continue to operate in the traditional manner, as if they were still regulating self-contained domestic economies. This anomaly leads them to err repeatedly on the downside—

repressing domestic economic activity and discouraging new investment in the name of stability—while markets meanwhile respond to the global influences of supply and demand. If a new era of growth is to occur, new theoretical understandings must replace the traditional rules of central banking—new operating principles that acknowledge the reality of the globalized industrial base and the globalized financial flows. Above all, central bankers must learn to take some risks for prosperity on the upside.

6. Refocus national economic agendas on the priority of work and wages, rather than trade or multinational competitiveness, as the defining issue for domestic prosperity. Obviously, these objectives are intertwined and interacting, but it makes a great difference as to which is put first. If advanced nations, especially the United States, concentrate on promoting employment and more equitable wage incomes, they can make a great contribution to the global system, in addition to domestic well-being, by boosting mass consumption. If governments continue to be preoccupied with globalization and promotion of the free-market doctrine, then they must inevitably accept the consequences of deepening inequality and deterioration at home.

The storm of global revolution will not soon pass and seems indeed to be accelerating, promising more dislocations and downward wage pressures ahead for the older industrial nations. There is no easy escape from that reality, not even if all these propositions were conscientiously pursued. Yet, if that is the case, it puts an even higher premium on the practical measures nations can undertake at home to ameliorate these forces—measures to support wage levels and to construct new pillars for domestic enterprise.

The actions that governments might take will require new spending, but mainly a purposeful shift in priorities, focusing less on government social aid programs and more on the wage realities in private-sector labor markets. Many of these measures are traditional forms of intervention: raising the floor of minimum-wage levels to promote upward pressures on low-end compensation, strengthening labor laws to encourage firms to share productivity gains with workers, restoring progressive taxation to redistribute incomes, curbing the luxurious corporate subsidies embedded in the tax code and government spending, underwriting major works projects like high-speed rail systems or urban housing rehabilitation.

If it is true that global pressures will tend to drag down wages and employment for at least another generation, then the economic imperative for large-scale subsidized employment is inescapable. If people cannot find jobs that promise a living wage for families, then all of the various social interventions that government undertakes will be futile. Instead, societies will accumulate another generation of marginalized citizens—dispossessed and alienated, lost and unproductive lives.

The same essential question has to be asked of every public measure: Does it genuinely promise to enhance work and wages? In debating that question, people will discover that much of what government presently does is useless or even harmful to broadly shared prosperity. But the answers may also begin to bring the economic future into clearer focus; defining potential new pillars for domestic economic activity that can flourish with or without global cooperation. Financial reform, for instance, might direct credit subsidies to sectors like housing or small-scale business enterprises or a national child-care system—new business activity that becomes a significant employer while filling real social needs. Every such step, of course, tends to distribute the economic returns more broadly through the society and thus creates more buyers for the world's glutted surplus production.

If people can get beyond passivity and insecurity, a new era of economic experimentation lies ahead—ventures that explore new social and economic arrangements, projects that can be encouraged by government, not managed by it. Some of the possibilities will be revisited in the final section of the book, where we examine some dimensions of social upheaval around the world. Among rich and poor, people are already exploring ideas that may change their destiny, social invention that need not wait upon market forces.

The revolutionary implication of the new technologies is about the future of work itself, about the nature of mass consumption and prosperity in industrial societies. The social portents are as dreadful and promising as any other element of the economic transformations. The hard work of exploration is waiting to be done.

None of the propositions I have suggested is especially radical or even new in historical terms, since they have all been actively employed at one time or another in the past. These ideas may disturb those who are utterly innocent of history or so imbued with current dogma they cannot imagine any other possible arrangement beyond the present course of events. But, in fact, the world has been here before, only on a different plane.

In rough outline, the global imperatives I have described are parallel to the economic understandings that gradually emerged on a national level in the United States and Europe during the upheavals crisis of the last great industrial revolution in the early twentieth century. At that time, as corporations achieved national and even international scope and scale, it was the states and provinces that lost control over their economic destinies and social standards. As new industries developed around new technologies, power shifted with them, overrunning the ability of localities to conserve their own values and social arrangements.

Eventually, a new principle of collective interest emerged at national levels. Both prosperous and poor jurisdictions slowly recognized that in a nationalized economy, they could no longer protect themselves against random exploitation of cheap labor or permanent burdens of mass unemployment. They would have to defend each other. In crisis, centralized governments took up responsibility for both economic management and upholding broad social values, by regulating the conduct of enterprise and finance to promote a broadly shared prosperity.

Nations of the world, rich and poor, are now at a similar juncture, except there is no world government to assume collective responsibility for the global system (and none likely to appear anytime soon). Some of the measures I have described can be pursued by nations individually, of course, irrespective of what others do. But the most important propositions require collective action, at least among the major economies. That seems most difficult, if not impossible, given the present impasses and competing commercial interests among societies.

The future, however, does not have to be built in a single stroke. It can be stitched together in smaller pieces—reciprocal agreements fashioned among like-minded nations—networks of nation-states that establish new rules and standards for their own role in the global system and then gradually broaden the ranks of participating economies, both rich and poor. Just as a handful of progressive states led the way to the great economic and social reforms in American history, a few strong nations can lead the way to a fuller realization of "one world." Good intentions will not be established by proclamation, but only by tangible demonstration that everyone may prosper by sharing responsibility for the new order.

The revolutionary machine is awesomely powerful and quick, plowing forward out of control, but the footrace with history is not yet lost.

Part Four

The Social Question

Fifteen

"These Dark Satanic Mills"

REVOLUTIONS, BY THEIR NATURE, do not operate with the consent of the governed. A revolution, whether it is driven by political ideals or economic imperatives, is always the work of a radical few who seize power and impose new values and social arrangements on the many. While the process is inescapably anti-democratic, that complaint is beside the point. Human history does, on occasion, advance by such decisive breaks from the past—epic transformations that destroy the comfortable old identities and compel people, for better or worse, to adopt new understandings of themselves.

If the question were put now to everyone, everywhere—do you wish to become a citizen of the world?—it is safe to assume that most people in most places would answer, no, they wish to remain who they are. With very few exceptions, people think of themselves as belonging to a place, a citizen of France or Malaysia, of Boston or Tokyo or Warsaw, loyally bound to native culture, sovereign nation. The Chinese who aspire to get gloriously rich, as Deng instructed, do not intend to become Japanese or Americans. Americans may like to think of themselves as the world's leader, but not as citizens of "one world."

The deepest social meaning of the global industrial revolution is that people no longer have free choice in this matter of identity. Ready or not, they are already of the world. As producers or consumers, as workers or merchants or investors, they are now bound to distant others through the complex strands of commerce and finance reorganizing the globe as a unified marketplace. The prosperity of South Carolina or Scotland is deeply linked to Stuttgart's or Kuala Lumpur's. The true social values of Californians or Swedes will be determined by what is tolerated in the factories of Thailand or Bangladesh. The energies and brutalities of China will influence community anxieties in Seattle or Toulouse or Nagoya.

That is the essential new fact of everyone's social existence and it is indeed revolutionary: unless one intends to withdraw from modern industrial life, there is no place to hide from the others. Major portions of the earth, to be sure, remain on the periphery of the system, impoverished bystanders still waiting to be included in the action. But the patterns of global interconnectedness are already the dominant reality. Commerce has leapt beyond social consciousness and, in doing so, opened up challenging new vistas for the human potential. Most people, it seems fair to say, are not yet prepared to face the implications.

The economic transformations have engendered a profound identity crisis for peoples and societies everywhere, though the political confusion is as yet only dimly recognized. Traditional expressions of nationhood—amassing great armies, waving flags and deploying troops—are subverted by the borderless marketplace, yet these martial activities still absorb vast public resources. The capacity of nations to control their own affairs has been checked by finance and eroded by free-roving commerce, but politicians continue to pretend they are in charge.

The nation-state faces a crisis of relevance. What remains of its purpose and power if authority over domestic social standards is yielded to disinterested market forces? If governments are reduced to bidding for the favors of multinational enterprises, what basis will citizens have for determining their own destinies? If commerce and finance are free to roam in the borderless world, why should people be restricted by the mere geography of their birthplace? Political leaders are weak and unstable at present because they lack coherent answers to such questions.

When people rebel against these global implications, it reflects the natural human tendency to defend hearth and home, the bonds of community and nation, against outside interference. Their social conservatism is usually dismissed as reactionary, the antiquated nationalist sentiments standing in the way of progress. Public roles have been reversed, so men of commerce are now the radical reformers, proclaiming the progressive goals, while social advocates try to defend a defunct past, longing to restore what has been obliterated.

The social question—how does a society sustain equable relations among its own people?—has been brushed aside by the economic sphere. Social cohesion and consent, even the minimal standards of human decency, are irrelevant to free markets. The essential purpose of deregulation, after all, is to free the market functions of such noneconomic considerations. This arrangement is unnatural and incendiary and cannot endure, not without provoking explosive political reactions. Yet neither can people resign from their new circumstances in "one world."

The social imperative is to think anew rather than retreat inward. Like it or not, this will require people to reimagine themselves as social beings on a larger stage, not helpless cogs in an awesome market system, and to glimpse the all-encompassing possibilities that the global revolution has put before them. The challenge is not to abandon old identities and deeply held values, but to enlarge them. If capitalism is now truly global, what are the global social obligations that accompany it? The wrenching economic changes will be understood in time as a great new opening in history—an invitation to social invention and human advancement—but only when people learn how to think expansively again about their own ideals.

This book's final section is intended to help people undertake that difficult endeavor. Its aim is to clarify and provoke, to pose some difficult questions and suggest some tentative answers. These chapters explore selected glimpses of how the global system tears at the social fabric—upending the peasantry in Thailand, attacking the social state of Germany, suppressing human freedoms in behalf of commerce in Indonesia or China, threatening the foundations of social cohesion of Japan, deepening the social deterioration in the United States and elsewhere.

Ultimately, the purpose is to ask questions and stimulate some forward-looking thinking about the nature of capitalism itself, about the future of work and mass consumption, about the ownership of wealth and its dominion over others, about new opportunities for human fulfillment. I do not claim to have settled answers to any of these, only some suggestions about how people might begin thinking about them.

The gravest danger I perceive at this moment of history is the understandable inclination of people and societies to turn back from the larger questions about the future and, instead, replay the terrible conflicts of the twentieth century. The outlines of that possibility are already visible in many societies, where middle-class security disintegrates and the lumpen ranks of alienated citizens are swelling—peasants gathering in Asian slums, young Europeans or Americans without work or future prospects.

Assuming that the global economic system is not redirected toward a more moderate course, these weary political and class conflicts are sure to ripen, leading toward the same stalemate between markets and society in which fascism arose and flourished nearly a hundred years ago. In that sense, global capitalism is a reactionary system itself despite the dazzling technologies of the so-called information age, for it drives human societies backward to face social questions people thought they had resolved.

The social context of the global revolution is easier to grasp if one understands it as divided into two distinctly different realms that, distant as they are, interact intimately with one another. The realm of the poor, industrializing nation repeats capitalism's tumultuous past but in new territory—liberating millions with new incomes but also reviving the barbarisms and exploitation that industry employed in advanced nations when they were developed eighty or a hundred or even two hundred years before.

The process of industrialization has never been pretty in its primitive stages. Americans or Europeans who draw back in horror at the present brutalities in Asia or Latin America should understand that they are glimpsing repetitions of what happened in their own national histories, practices that were forbidden as inhumane in their own countries only after long political struggle. To make that historical point complicates the moral responses, but does not extinguish the social question.

The other realm, of course, is the wealthy nation where the established social structure is under assault, both from market forces depressing wages and employment and from the political initiatives to dismantle the welfare state. The governments' obligations to social equity were erected during the upheavals of the last century to ameliorate the harsher edges of unfettered capitalism; now they are in question again. The economic pressures to shrink or withdraw public benefits are relentless, yet no one has explained how wealthy industrial nations will maintain the social peace by deepening their inequalities.

A standard response to all these social concerns is the reassuring argument that market forces will eventually correct them—if no one interferes. The new wealth of industrialization, it is said, will lead naturally to middle-class democracy in the poorer countries and the barbarisms will eventually be eradicated. In the older societies, it is assumed that technology will create new realms of work that in time replace the lost employment, restore living wages and spread the prosperity widely again. People need only be patient with the future and not interrupt the revolution.

The global system has more or less been proceeding on these assumptions for at least a generation and one may observe that the unfolding reality has so far gravely disappointed these expectations. Nor does the free-market argument conform with the actual history of how democratic development or social equity was advanced over the last two centuries, neither of which emerged anywhere without titanic political struggles. A more pointed contradiction is the hypocrisy of those who make these arguments. If multinational enterprises truly expect greater human freedom and social equity to emerge from the marketplace, then why do they expend so much political energy to prevent these conditions from developing?

In any case, the theoretical arguments about the future do not satisfy the moral question that exists concretely at present. If one benefits tangibly from the exploitation of others who are weak, is one morally implicated in their predicament? Or are basic rights of human existence confined to those civilized societies wealthy enough to afford them? Everyone's values are defined by what they will tolerate when it is done to others. Everyone's sense of virtue is degraded by the present reality.

A revolutionary principle is embedded in the global economic system, awaiting broader recognition: Human dignity is indivisible. Across the distances of culture and nations, across vast gulfs of wealth and poverty, even the least among us are entitled to their dignity and no justification exists for brutalizing them in the pursuit of commerce. Anyone who claims to hold humane values cannot escape these new connections.

Two centuries ago, when the English industrial revolution dawned with its fantastic invention and productive energies, the prophetic poet William Blake drew back in moral revulsion. Amid the explosion of new wealth, human destruction was spread over England—peasant families displaced from their lands, paupers and poorhouses crowded into London slums, children sent to labor at the belching ironworks or textile looms. Blake delivered a thunderous rebuke to the pious Christians of the English aristocracy with these immortal lines:

> *And was Jerusalem builded here*
> *Among these dark Satanic mills?*

Blake's "dark Satanic mills" have returned now and are flourishing again, accompanied by the same question.[1]

On May 10, 1993, the worst industrial fire in the history of capitalism occurred at a toy factory on the outskirts of Bangkok and was reported on page 25 of the *Washington Post*. The *Financial Times* of London, which styles itself as the daily newspaper of the global economy, ran a brief item on page 6. The *Wall Street Journal* followed a day late with an account on page 11. The *New York Times* also put the story inside, but printed a dramatic photo on its front page: rows of small shrouded bodies on bamboo pallets—dozens of them—lined along the damp pavement, while dazed rescue workers stood awkwardly among the corpses. In the background, one could see the collapsed, smoldering structure of a mammoth factory where the Kader Industrial Toy Company of Thailand had employed three thousand workers manufacturing stuffed toys and plastic dolls, playthings destined for American children.[2]

The official count was 188 dead, 469 injured, but the actual toll was undoubtedly higher since the four-story buildings had collapsed swiftly in the intense heat and many bodies were incinerated. Some of the missing were never found; others fled home to their villages. All but fourteen of the dead were women, most of them young, some as young as thirteen years old. Hundreds of the workers had been trapped on upper floors of the burning building, forced to jump from third- or fourth-floor windows, since the main exit doors were kept locked by the managers, and the narrow stairways became clotted with trampled bodies or collapsed.

When I visited Bangkok about nine months later, physical evidence of the disaster was gone—the site scraped clean by bulldozers—and Kader was already resuming production at a new toy factory, built far from the city in a rural province of northeastern Thailand. When I talked with Thai labor leaders and civic activists, people who had rallied to the cause of the fire victims, some of them were under the impression that a worldwide boycott of Kader products was under way, organized by conscience-stricken Americans and Europeans. I had to inform them that the civilized world had barely noticed their tragedy.

As news accounts pointed out, the Kader fire surpassed what was previously the worst industrial fire in history—the Triangle Shirtwaist Company fire of 1911—when 146 young immigrant women died in similar circumstances at a garment factory on the Lower East Side of Manhattan. The Triangle Shirtwaist fire became a pivotal event in American politics, a public scandal that provoked citizen reform movements and energized the labor organizing that built the International Ladies Garment Workers Union and other unions. The fire in Thailand did not produce meaningful political responses or even shame among consumers. The indifference of the leading newspapers merely reflected the tastes of their readers, who might be moved by human suffering in their own communities but were inured to news of recurring calamities in distant places. A fire in Bangkok was like a typhoon in Bangladesh, an earthquake in Turkey.

The Kader fire might have been more meaningful for Americans if they could have seen the thousands of soot-stained dolls that spilled from the wreckage, macabre litter scattered among the dead. Bugs Bunny, Bart Simpson and the Muppets. Big Bird and other *Sesame Street* dolls. Playskool "Water Pets." Santa Claus. What the initial news accounts did not mention was that Kader's Thai factory produced most of its toys for American companies—Toys "R" Us, Fisher-Price, Hasbro, Tyco, Arco, Kenner, Gund and J. C. Penney—as well as stuffed dolls, slippers and souvenirs for Europe.[3]

Globalized civilization has uncovered an odd parochialism in the American character: Americans worried obsessively over the everyday safety of their children, and the U.S. government's regulators diligently policed the design of toys to avoid injury to young innocents. Yet neither citizens nor government took any interest in the brutal and dangerous conditions imposed on the people who manufactured those same toys, many of whom were mere adolescent children themselves. Indeed, the government position, both in Washington and Bangkok, assumed that there was no social obligation connecting consumers with workers, at least none that governments could enforce without disrupting free trade or invading the sovereignty of other nations.

The toy industry, not surprisingly, felt the same. Hasbro Industries, maker of Playskool, subsequently told the *Boston Globe* that it would no longer do business with Kader, but, in general, the U.S. companies shrugged off responsibility. Kader, a major toy manufacturer based in Hong Kong, "is extremely reputable, not sleaze bags," David Miller, president of the Toy Manufacturers of America, assured *USA Today*. "The responsibility for those factories," Miller told ABC News, "is in the hands of those who are there and managing the factory."[4]

The grisly details of what occurred revealed the casual irresponsibility of both companies and governments. The Kader factory compound consisted of four interconnected, four-story industrial barns on a three-acre lot on Buddhamondhol VI Road in the Sampran district west of Bangkok. It was one among Thailand's thriving new industrial zones for garments, textiles, electronics and toys. More than 50,000 people, most of them migrants from the Thai countryside, worked in the district at 7,500 large and small firms. Thailand's economic boom was based on places such as this, and Bangkok was almost choking on its own fantastic growth, dizzily erecting luxury hotels and office towers.

The fire started late on a Monday afternoon on the ground floor in the first building and spread rapidly upward, jumping to two adjoining buildings, all three of which swiftly collapsed. Investigators noted afterwards that the structures had been cheaply built, without concrete reinforcement, so steel girders and stairways crumpled easily in the heat. Thai law required that in such a large factory, fire-escape stairways must be sixteen to thirty-three feet wide, but Kader's were a mere four and a half feet. Main doors were locked and many windows barred to prevent pilfering by the employees. Flammable raw materials—fabric, stuffing, animal fibers—were stacked everywhere, on walkways and next to electrical boxes. Neither safety drills nor fire alarms and sprinkler systems had been provided.

Let some of the survivors describe what happened.

A young woman named Lampan Taptim: "There was the sound of yelling about a fire. I tried to leave the section but my supervisor told me to get back to work. My sister who worked on the fourth floor with me pulled me away and insisted we try to get out. We tried to go down the stairs and got to the second floor; we found that the stairs had already caved in. There was a lot of yelling and confusion. . . . In desperation, I went back up to the windows and went back and forth, looking down below. The smoke was thick and I picked the best place to jump in a pile of boxes. My sister jumped, too. She died."

A young woman named Cheng: "There is no way out [people were shouting], the security guard has locked the main door out! It was horrifying. I thought I would die. I took off my gold ring and kept it in my pocket and put on my name tag so that my body could be identifiable. I had to decide to die in the fire or from jumping down from a three stories' height." As the walls collapsed around her, Cheng clung to a pipe and fell downward with it, landing on a pile of dead bodies, injured but alive.

An older woman named La-iad Nada-nguen: "Four or five pregnant women jumped before me. They died before my eyes." Her own daughter jumped from the top floor and broke both hips.

Chauweewan Mekpan, who was five months pregnant: "I thought that if I jumped, at least my parents would see my remains, but if I stayed, nothing would be left of me." Though her back was severely injured, she and her unborn child miraculously survived.

An older textile worker named Vilaiwa Satieti, who sewed shirts and pants at a neighboring factory, described to me the carnage she encountered: "I got off work about five and passed by Kader and saw many dead bodies lying around, uncovered. Some of them I knew. I tried to help the workers who had jumped from the factory. They had broken legs and broken arms and broken heads. We tried to keep them alive until they got to the hospital, that's all you could do. Oh, they were teenagers, fifteen to twenty years, no more than that, and so many of them, so many."

This was not the first serious fire at Kader's factory, but the third or fourth. "I heard somebody yelling 'fire, fire,' " Tumthong Podhirun testified, ". . . but I did not take it seriously because it has happened before. Soon I smelled smoke and very quickly it billowed inside the place. I headed for the back door but it was locked. . . . Finally, I had no choice but to join the others and jumped out of the window. I saw many of my friends lying dead on the ground beside me."[5]

In the aftermath of the tragedy, some Bangkok activists circulated an old snapshot of two smiling peasant girls standing arm in arm beside a thicket of palm trees. One of them, Praphai Prayonghorm, died in the 1993 fire at Kader. Her friend, Kammoin Konmanee, had died in the 1989 fire. Some of the Kader workers insisted afterwards that their factory had been haunted by ghosts, that it was built on the site of an old graveyard, disturbing the dead. The folklore expressed raw poetic truth: the fire in Bangkok eerily resembled the now-forgotten details of the Triangle Shirtwaist disaster eighty years before. Perhaps the "ghosts" that some workers felt present were young women from New York who had died in 1911.

Similar tragedies, large and small, were now commonplace across developing Asia and elsewhere. Two months after Kader, another fire at a Bangkok shirt factory killed ten women. Three months after Kader, a six-story hotel collapsed and killed 133 people, injuring 351. The embarrassed minister of industry ordered special inspections of 244 large factories in the Bangkok region and found that 60 percent of them had basic violations similar to Kader's. Thai industry was growing explosively—12 to 15 percent a year—but workplace injuries and illnesses were growing even faster, from 37,000 victims in 1987 to more than 150,000 by 1992 and an estimated 200,000 by 1994.

In China, six months after Kader, eighty-four women died and dozens of others were severely burned at another toy factory fire in the burgeoning industrial zone at Shenzhen. At Dongguan, a Hong Kong–owned raincoat factory burned in 1991, killing more than eighty people (Kader Industries also had a factory at Dongguan where two fires have been reported since 1990). In late 1993, some sixty women died at the Taiwanese-owned Gaofu textile plant in Fuzhou Province, many of them smothered in their dormitory beds by toxic fumes from burning textiles. In 1994, a shoe factory fire killed ten persons at Jiangmen; a textile factory fire killed thirty-eight and injured 160 at the Qianshan industrial zone.[6]

"Why must these tragedies repeat themselves again and again?" the *People's Daily* in Beijing asked. The official *Economic Daily* complained: "The way some of these foreign investors ignore international practice, ignore our own national rules, act completely lawlessly and immorally and lust after wealth is enough to make one's hair stand on end."[7]

America was itself no longer insulated from such brutalities. When a chicken-processing factory at Hamlet, North Carolina, caught fire in 1991, the exit doors there were also locked and twenty-five people died. A garment factory discovered by labor investigators in El Monte, California, held seventy-two Thai immigrants in virtual peonage, working eighteen hours a day in "sub-human conditions." One could not lament the deaths, harsh working conditions, child labor and subminimum wages in Thailand or across Asia and Central America without also recognizing that similar conditions have reappeared in the United States for roughly the same reasons.

Sweatshops, mainly in the garment industry, scandalized Los Angeles, New York and Dallas. The grim, foul assembly lines of the poultry-processing industry were spread across the rural South; the *Wall Street Journal*'s Tony Horwitz won a Pulitzer Prize for his harrowing description of this low-wage work. "In general," the U.S. Government Accounting Office reported in 1994, "the description of today's sweatshops differs little from that at the turn of the century."[8]

That was the real mystery: Why did global commerce, with all of its supposed modernity and wondrous technologies, restore the old barbarisms that had long ago been forbidden by law? If the information age has enabled multinational corporations to manage production and marketing spread across continents, why were their managers unable—or unwilling—to organize such mundane matters as fire prevention?

The short answer, of course, was profits, but the deeper answer was about power: Firms behaved this way because they could, because nobody would stop them. When law and social values retreated before the power of markets, then capitalism's natural drive to maximize returns had no internal governor to check its social behavior. When one enterprise took the low road to gain advantage, others would follow.

The toy fire in Bangkok provided a dramatic illustration for the much broader, less visible forms of human exploitation that were flourishing in the global system, including the widespread use of children in manufacturing, even forced labor camps in China or Burma. These matters were not a buried secret. Indeed, American television has aggressively exposed the "dark Satanic mills" with dramatic reports. ABC's *20/20* broadcast correspondent Lynn Sherr's devastating account of the Kader fire; CNN ran disturbing footage. Mike Wallace of CBS's *60 Minutes* exposed the prison labor exploited in China. NBC's *Dateline* did a piece on Wal-Mart's grim production in Bangladesh. CBS's *Street Stories* toured the shoe factories of Indonesia.

The baffling quality about modern communications was that its images could take us to people in remote corners of the world vividly and instantly, but these images have not as yet created genuine community with them. In terms of human consciousness, the "global village" was still only a picture on the TV screen.

Public opinion, moreover, absorbed contradictory messages about the global reality that were difficult to sort out. The opening stages of industrialization presented, as always, a great paradox: the process was profoundly liberating for millions, freeing them from material scarcity and limited life choices, while it also ensnared other millions in brutal new forms of domination. Both aspects were true, but there was no scale on which these opposing consequences could be easily balanced, since the good and ill effects were not usually apportioned among the same people. Some human beings were set free, while other lives were turned into cheap and expendable commodities.

Workers at Kader, for instance, earned about 100 baht a day for sewing and assembling dolls, the official minimum wage of $4, but the constant stream of new entrants meant that many at the factory actually worked for much less—only $2 or $3 a day—during a required "probationary" period of three to six months that was often extended much longer by the managers. Only one hundred of the three thousand workers at Kader were legally designated employees; the rest were "contract workers" without permanent rights and benefits, the same employment system now popularized in the United States.

"Lint, fabric, dust and animal hair filled the air on the production floor," the International Confederation of Free Trade Unions based in Brussels observed in its investigative report. "Noise, heat, congestion and fumes from various sources were reported by many. Dust control was nonexistent; protective equipment inadequate. Inhaling the dust created respiratory problems and contact with it caused skin diseases." A factory clinic dispensed antihistamines or other drugs and referred the more serious symptoms to outside hospitals. Workers paid for the medication themselves and were reimbursed, up to $6, only if they had contributed 10 baht a month to the company's health fund.

A common response to such facts, even from many sensitive people, was: yes, that was terrible, but wouldn't those workers be even worse off if civil standards were imposed on their employers since they might lose their jobs as a result? This was the same economic rationale offered by American manufacturers a century before to explain why American children must work in the coal mines and textile mills. U.S. industry had survived somehow (and, in fact, flourished) when child labor and the other malpractices were eventually prohibited by social reforms. Furthermore, it was not coincidence that industry always assigned the harshest conditions and lowest pay to the weakest members of a society—women, children, uprooted migrants. Whether the factory was in Thailand or the United States or Mexico's *maquiladora* zone, people who were already quite powerless were less likely to resist, less able to demand decency from their employers.

Nor did these enterprises necessarily consist of small, struggling firms that could not afford to treat their workers better. Small sweatshops, it was true, were numerous in Thailand, and I saw some myself in a working-class neighborhood of Bangkok. Behind iron grillwork, children who looked to be ten to twelve years old squatted on the cement floors of the open-air shops, assembling suitcases, sewing raincoats, packing T-shirts. Across the street, a swarm of adolescents in blue smocks ate dinner at long tables outside a two-story building, then trooped back upstairs to the sewing machines.

Kader Holding Company, Ltd., however, was neither small nor struggling. It was a powerhouse of the global toy industry—headquartered in Hong Kong, incorporated in Bermuda, owned by a wealthy Hong Kong Chinese family named Ting that got its start after World War II making plastic goods and flashlights under procurement contracts from the U.S. military. Now Kader controlled a global maze of factories and interlocking subsidiaries in eight countries, from China and Thailand to Britain and the United States, where it owned Bachmann toys.[9]

After the fire Thai union members, intellectuals and middle-class activists from social rights organizations (the groups known in developing countries as nongovernmental organizations, or NGOs) formed the Committee to Support Kader Workers and began demanding justice from the employer. They sent a delegation to Hong Kong to confront Kader officials and investigate the complex corporate linkages of the enterprise. What they discovered was that Kader's partner in the Bangkok toy factory was actually a fabulously wealthy Thai family, the Chearavanonts, ethnic Chinese merchants who own the Charoen Pokphand Group, Thailand's own leading multinational corporation.

The CP Group owns farms, feed mills, real estate, air-conditioning and motorcycle factories, food-franchise chains—two hundred companies worldwide, several of them listed on the New York Stock Exchange. The patriarch and chairman, Dhanin Chearavanont, was said by *Fortune* magazine to be the seventy-fifth richest man in the world, with personal assets of $2.6 billion (or 65 billion baht, as the *Bangkok Post* put it). Like the other emerging "Chinese multinationals," the Pokphand Group operates through the informal networks of kinfolk and ethnic contacts spread around the world by the Chinese diaspora, while it also participates in the more rigorous accounting systems of Western economies.

In the mother country, China, the conglomerate nurtured political-business alliances and has become the largest outside investor in new factories and joint ventures. In the United States, it maintained superb political connections. The Chearavanonts co-sponsored a much-heralded visit to Bangkok by ex-president George Bush, who delivered a speech before Thai business leaders in early 1994, eight months after the Kader fire. The price tag for Bush's appearance, according to the Bangkok press, was $400,000 (equivalent to one month's payroll for all three thousand workers at Kader). The day after Bush's appearance, the Chearavanonts hosted a banquet for a leading entrepreneur from China—Deng Xiaoping's daughter.[10]

The Pokphand Group at first denied any connection to the Kader fire, but reformers and local reporters dug out the facts of the family's involvement. Dhanin Chearavanont himself owned 11 percent of Honbo Investment Company and with relatives and corporate directors held majority control. Honbo, in turn, owned half of KCP Toys (KCP stood for Kader Charoen Pokphand), which, in turn, owned 80 percent of Kader Industrial (Thailand) Company. Armed with these facts, three hundred workers from the destroyed factory marched on the Pokphand Group's corporate tower on Silom Road, where they staged a gentle sit-down demonstration in the lobby, demanding just compensation for the victims.[11]

In the context of Thai society and politics, the workers' demonstration against Pokphand was itself extraordinary, like peasants confronting the nobility. Under continuing pressures from the support group, the company agreed to pay much larger compensation for victims and their families— $12,000 for each death, a trivial amount in American terms but more than double the Thai standard. "When we worked on Kader," said Professor Voravidh Charoenloet, an economist at Chulalongkorn University, "the government and local entrepreneurs and factory owners didn't want us to challenge these people; even the police tried to obstruct us from making an issue. We were accused of trying to destroy the country's reputation."

The settlement, in fact, required the Thai activists to halt their agitation and fall silent. "Once the extra compensation was paid," Voravidh explained, "we were forced to stop. One of the demands by the government was that everything should stop. Our organization had to accept it. We wanted to link with the international organizations and have a great boycott, but we had to cease."

The global boycott, he assumed, was going forward anyway because he knew that international labor groups like the ICFTU and the AFL-CIO had investigated the Kader fire and issued stinging denunciations. I told him that aside from organized labor, the rest of the world remained indifferent. There was no boycott of Kader toys in America. The professor slumped in his chair and was silent, a twisted expression on his face.

"I feel very bad," Voravidh said at last. "Maybe we should not have accepted it. But when we came away, we felt that was what we could accomplish. The people wanted more. There must be something more."

In the larger context, this tragedy was not explained by the arrogant power of one wealthy family or the elusive complexities of interlocking corporations. The Kader fire was ordained and organized by the free market itself. The toy industry—much like textiles and garments, shoes, electronics assembly and other low-wage sectors—existed (and thrived) by exploiting a crude ladder of desperate competition among the poorest nations. Its factories regularly hopped to new locations where wages were even lower, where the governments would be even more tolerant of abusive practices. The contract work assigned to foreign firms, including thousands of small sweatshops, fitted neatly into the systems of far-flung production of major brand names and distanced the capital owners from personal responsibility.

The "virtual corporation" celebrated by some business futurists already existed in these sectors and, indeed, was now being emulated in some ways by advanced manufacturing—cars, aircraft, computers.

Over the last generation, toy manufacturers and others have moved around the Asian rim in search of the bottom-rung conditions: from Hong Kong, Korea and Taiwan to Thailand and Indonesia, from there to China, Vietnam and Bangladesh, perhaps on next to Burma, Nepal or Cambodia. Since the world had a nearly inexhaustible supply of poor people and supplicant governments, the market would keep driving in search of lower rungs; no one could say where the bottom was located. Industrial conditions were not getting better, as conventional theory assured the innocent consumers, but in many sectors were getting much worse. In America, the U.S. diplomatic opening to Vietnam was celebrated as progressive politics. In Southeast Asia, it merely opened another trapdoor beneath wages and working conditions.

A country like Thailand was caught in the middle: if it conscientiously tried to improve, it would pay a huge price. When Thai unions lobbied to win improvements in minimum-wage standards, textile plants began leaving for Vietnam and elsewhere or even importing cheaper "guest workers" from Burma. When China opened its fast-growing industrial zones in Shenzhen, Dongguan and other locations, the new competition had direct consequences on the factory floors of Bangkok.

Kader, according to the ICFTU, opened two new factories in Shekou and Dongguan where young people were working fourteen-hour days, seven days a week, to fill the U.S. Christmas orders for Mickey Mouse and other American dolls. Why should a company worry about sprinkler systems or fire escapes for a dusty factory in Bangkok when it could hire brand-new workers in China for only $20 a month, one fifth of the labor cost in Thailand?

The ICFTU report described the market forces: "The lower cost of production of toys in China changes the investment climate for countries like Thailand. Thailand competes with China to attract investment capital for local toy production. With this development, Thailand has become sadly lax in enforcing its own legislation. It turns a blind eye to health violations, thus allowing factory owners to ignore safety standards. Since China entered the picture, accidents in Thailand have nearly tripled."

The Thai minister of industry, Sanan Kachornprasart, described the market reality more succinctly: "If we punish them, who will want to invest here?" Thai authorities subsequently filed charges against three Kader factory managers, but none against the company itself nor, of course, the Chearavanont family.[12]

In the aftermath, a deputy managing director of Kader Industrial, Pichet Laokasem, entered a Buddhist monastery "to make merit for the fire victims," *The Nation* of Bangkok reported. Pichet told reporters he would serve as a monk until he felt better emotionally. "Most of the families affected by the fire lost only a loved one," he explained. "I lost nearly two hundred of my workers all at once."

The fire in Bangkok reflected the amorality of the marketplace when it has been freed of social obligations. But the tragedy also mocked the moral claims of three great religions, whose adherents were all implicated. Thais built splendid golden temples exalting Buddha, who taught them to put spiritual being before material wealth. Chinese claimed to have acquired superior social values, reverence for family and community, derived from the teachings of Confucius. Americans bought the toys from Asia to celebrate the birth of Jesus Christ. Their shared complicity was another of the strange convergences made possible by global commerce.

One evening in Bangkok, I went to dine at the luxurious Montien Hotel on Surawong Road, but turned back when I saw the French menu and haute cuisine prices. The lobby was tasteful marble and tropical plants and Pan-Asian businessmen in smart suits. The next morning I read in the newspaper that I had missed the gunfire and murder. A real estate billionaire named Phongsakorn Yarnbenchawongkul swept into the Montien's karaoke lounge later that same evening, accompanied by girlfriends and bodyguards, expecting to sing a few of his favorite songs. He became impatient when a young architect refused to give up the microphone, and Phongsakorn's bodyguards beat the man senseless, then shot him before the horrified customers. Tycoon and entourage fled, police said, in two Mercedes-Benzes and a white sports car.[13]

Every booming Asian city has been described, one place or another, as the Wild West, but Bangkok truly seemed to qualify. The mad, charming tumult in the narrow downtown streets—cars, jitney cabs, people, peddlers —mixed the impatient energies of new money with routine cruelties. Across the road from the glamorous Montien was the city's notorious Patpong district, a neon boulevard of bars and brothels where U.S. soldiers had once taken rest leaves during the war in Vietnam. At night Patpong also turned into a shoppers' bazaar—dozens of stalls selling fine leather, watches, sweaters, all the best designer names at bargain prices.

Prostitution, including sex with children, was the most celebrated aspect of the Thai economy's informal sector. Package tours were arranged in Europe and Japan; the children were consigned and sometimes sold to brothels by impoverished peasant families. The sex has become quite dangerous. By 1994, Thailand had 600,000 HIV-positive citizens and, according to its growth trend, would have four million by the turn of the new century.[14]

The city's streets thumped everywhere with the pounding action of construction pile drivers, and the real estate boom spilled equipment, steel, bricks and dirt into the streets, as in Kuala Lumpur, Jakarta, Singapore, Shanghai and Beijing, all competing for modernity and high-rise office space. "More construction cranes are operating in several of these cities than on the entire North American continent . . . ," an American authority, Anthony Downs, observed. "Nearly all these new properties have been financed mainly with equity funds, often profits from low-wage manufacturing operations." Downs foresaw a great crash ahead in Asian real-estate prices since the construction was piling up a vast oversupply of new, unfilled buildings. Boom and bust was always a feature of the economic frontier. Bangkok was Chicago in the 1920s or perhaps London a century earlier.[15]

The serene, gentle qualities that tourists remembered from a generation ago were still visible, but the fast life was encroaching. Around the corner from the grandiose Peninsula Hotel, Buddhist priests chanted to brass and drums each day at a sidewalk prayer station, the incense overwhelmed by carbon monoxide. Bangkok's traffic jams were routine and monstrous, hours of surging and stalling to get across town, yet the mess was somehow softened by the abundance of blooming orchids spilling down everywhere and also, of course, by the patient, smiling, beautiful faces.

In a working-class quarter by the textile factories, I saw an endearing shrine—a miniature Buddhist temple set on a raised platform, festooned with humble offerings left by neighbors. Around its base, the ground was clotted with the evidence of a higher civilization—bits of plastic—thousands of blue and pink shopping sacks gathered by the wind. These tissue-thin bits of flotsam were ubiquitous in Asian cities, plastic bags clogging gutters, fencerows, swampy fields and drainage canals. Thailand was catching up. NPC, the National Petrochemical Public Company, announced that plastic consumption was approaching forty-four pounds per capita, though still far behind Korea, Japan and Taiwan, which has now surpassed the United States.[16]

The taxi boats still traveled up and down the Chao Phraya River through the heart of the city, tacking from one bank to the other, delivering workers and students or housewives on their way to the open-air vegetable markets. But the network of narrow canals on which the ancient city was originally organized was silting up and stagnant; Toyotas and motorcycles have replaced sampans. The water table was falling in Bangkok and the earth subsiding with it, salinity increasing in the Chao Phraya.

Across Thailand, the monsoons were shorter now and rice farmers experienced recurring droughts. Development, almost everyone agreed, has literally altered the weather. Tropical forests and wetlands were cleared for capital-intensive agriculture, eucalyptus and other industrialized crops, as well as for golf courses and other resort developments. Mangrove swamps by the sea were drained to make the shrimp farms that supply the sushi bars of Tokyo. Rainfall declined, the watery past receded.

As the countryside was transformed by modern roads, dams and electrification, Thai villagers and environmental activists pleaded bitterly for "elephant rights." An elephant required 550 pounds of bamboo and other plants each day, but would not eat any part of the fast-growing eucalyptus trees grown on the new reservations to supply pulp paper for export. Thailand's noble elephants were receding, too, struck by cars or trucks on the highway or, as mahouts complained, starved when the village habitats disappeared.[17]

The gentle loveliness has assumed a cruel and desperate edge. Bangkok was thriving and Bangkok was declining. The city has swelled to more than 6.5 million people, but nearly one third of them were landless squatters, rural refugees drawn to the city or driven there by changed circumstances. In the vast, cluttered slums, many of the hovels had electricity, some even color TV. Yet families sent out squads of children each day to the city's huge garbage pits, where they methodically picked over the new refuse in search of food. Others worked in the sweatshops and factories, more than five million children nationwide. Child labor was an accepted ingredient of booming prosperity.[18]

Thailand, like other nations before it, was in the throes of profound social transformation, the violent reordering of class structures that usually accompanies new industrialization. The vast rural peasantry was being upended, ensnared and eviscerated by the wage economy, stripped of its ancient role as the conservative bedrock for Thai society. A new middle class was gradually emerging, gaining sophistication and wealth. Alongside it, a confused and embittered working class formed, too.

The essential transaction in this transformation involved turning rural peasants into cheap industrial labor. In the countryside, the modernization of agriculture and other developments have displaced millions of small farmers and subverted the basis of their meager livelihoods. Caught in an economic bind, families migrated to Bangkok or sent their children there to earn wage incomes in the factories (or brothels). But none of the foul social conditions arising in Thailand was especially new. All of the inequities and rapacious practices have unfolded before, one place or another, in the histories of the wealthiest nations.*

In fact, the dynamics of Thailand's upheaval eerily resembled what had occurred in England two hundred years before: the infamous Enclosure Movement that accompanied the English industrial revolution, when the ruling interests dispossessed peasants of common lands in the village and effectively drove them to the city's mills and slums. The horrifying facts of Bangkok in the 1990s were the same facts that stirred the poet Blake's indignation in the London of 1800.

What was distinctive in Thailand and many other developing countries was the speed of upheaval and the awesome cultural span they attempted

---

* The underlying struggle—the city versus the countryside—is a very old story in human societies and has been reiterated across millennia, long before the rise of capitalism. The ambitious urban dwellers seek new forms of wealth and progress; the agrarian peasants and yeomanry defend tradition and their own independent self-sufficiency. The city folk promise modernity and it is they who usually win.

to cover: a sudden leap from agrarian feudalism to cosmopolitan capitalism. The world, one could say, was now divided by three different planes of consciousness in terms of how people thought about time. The global financial market and its electronic participants traded continuously around the clock and no longer paused to recognize day or night. Most people in modern society measured time in segments of hours and days, weeks or months. But the primitive among us, still existing in many places, continued to think and function according to the ancient cycles of seasons. A country like Thailand encompassed all three of these time zones. Its furious pace of economic growth has put the three in a lopsided contest for power, one that brutalized the innocent ancients.[19]

Revulsion was the easy, uncomplicated response, but it was much more difficult to come to terms with a deeper understanding of what was occurring. Why would people do this to one another? And what was it about the capitalist system that encouraged them to accept common cruelties?

"What these people want is what the West already has. And why shouldn't they? It is a very nice life, isn't it?"

I heard the remark in Malaysia from a British expatriate and Muslim intellectual, Merrill Wynn Davies, expressing her impatience with self-righteous critics of Asian development. Her point applied to Thailand and almost everywhere across the developing economies. Ancient cultures resisted destruction and needed sympathetic allies who could defend helpless people and the natural environment. But it was also true that, in most places, most people yearned to share in the material comforts that industrial development promised. They would endure gross disturbances, even vicious social conflicts, to acquire them.

Thailand's leaders eagerly seized the Faustian bargain that capitalism offered and were now compelled to struggle with the social consequences of that choice. One could hardly blame people of a very poor nation for lunging at the risks of prosperity, accepting the vulgar excesses and inequities that rich nations had undertaken before them.

The disturbing social question embedded in the new industrialization was why capitalism reverted so readily to its barbaric patterns from the distant past, repeating old brutalities on fresh ground, among new people, and inviting the same explosive conflicts for the future. In that sense, capitalism was still an immature system of social organization since its creativity depended on neurotically repeating its own worst behavior, abandoning and destroying in order to build anew. Did the capitalist system learn nothing from the class warfare of the last two hundred years? Could the raw creative energies ever be schooled to follow a more humane path, one based on greater respect for human differences and dignity?

In Bangkok, like any other tourist, I took the hotel's guided tour of the city's golden temples—stunning and numerous—and listened to the young guide's canned explanations of what we were seeing. Buddhist prayer days are four times a month, he explained, determined by the phases of the

moon. The ornate gates to the temple grounds were built by rich businessmen, honoring their parents, making merit for future life.

"To Buddhists, life is suffering, believe it or not," said the guide, who
was ethnic Chinese himself and sounded slightly amused by these beliefs.
"Hatred, anger, envy, desire of material things—the body is cremated in
order to escape from that, but you can never be free from the good and bad
of your past life. The only way you save the best for your next life is to
build a temple to express these things. That's why there are 30,000 temples
in this country."

Capitalism, I reflected, was attacking the foundations of Buddhism,
just as it had challenged Christianity's five or six centuries before. The
process of material accumulation offered people if not immortality at least
a promise that there was a comforting alternative here on earth to the
suffering and knowledge of certain death. Many Thai people were eagerly
exploring the possibilities, just as Europeans or Americans had before them,
even if it put their eternal souls at risk. And some Thais no doubt embraced
the illusion, as people always have, that accumulations of great wealth
might somehow save them from mortality. The universality of the human
condition is grounded in tragic terms that no one, rich or poor, has ever
escaped.

Looking at the great golden figure of the Reclining Buddha, I saw his
placid, knowing, ancient face surrounded anew by worldly contradictions.
My mind flashed on an old line from Albert King, the American blues
singer: "Everybody wants to get to heaven, but nobody wants to die."

The democracy uprising of May 1992 was remembered fondly in Thailand as the "mobile telephone revolution" because the middle-class rebels
were better equipped technologically than the military troops who put them
down. Army generals had deposed yet another elected government—military coups were a recurring feature of Thai politics—but this time citizens
protested by staging an embarrassing occupation at the national freedom
shrine. Students, businesspeople, intellectuals, labor and social activists
united spontaneously, armed with cell phones, cameras and radios. In the
political tumult, they faxed their daily bulletins to the international news
media and foreign embassies. When the troops moved in and fired on the
demonstrators, fifty-two people were killed. But the military regime was
brought down by the scandal.

A commemorative poster of the uprising, given to me by a university
professor, depicted the drama in the stylized tradition of Thai symbolic art:
a mass of green-jacketed soldiers guided by fiery goddesses aim their rifles
at the assembly of happy democrats, tiny dancing figures who seem protected by an impish genie floating above. Many of the tiny figures are clad
in dark business suits, some holding portable phones and cameras. The
advance of democracy in the new Thailand was embellished by such charming detail.

The birth of popular sovereignty was halting and limited, however, still largely confined to an unstable contest for power between two rival elites. The Thai military has staged eighteen coups since 1932, the year when the king of Siam's absolute power was finally abolished, and an armed presence hovered ominously over every elected government. Most members of parliament were democratically elected, but feudal structures endured and the king continued to have broad, vaguely defined influence in national affairs. Unlike its Asian neighbors, Thailand had a fascist military government during World War II and, reflecting the nationalist hostility toward China and the ethnic Chinese merchants who dominated Thai commerce, was aligned with imperial Japan.[20]

Now the military-bureaucracy alliance defended the old order and waged a continuing seesaw contest for control with the new political force, the politicians and capitalists aligned with business and the emerging middle-class aspirations. The democracy uprising of 1992 prompted a shift from the military to the business elites, but did not alter the basic alignments of power. Both of these political formations practiced crude forms of money corruption—arranging economic favors for business friends, buying votes wholesale in the rural villages. Neither of them represented, in any genuine sense, the popular masses of citizens—the workers and peasants caught up by industrial upheaval.

Professor Lae Dilokvidhyarat, an economist at Chulalongkorn University, described the underlying class tensions: "The middle class has broader political space and no longer feels threatened by the military or bureaucrats, but the middle class also sees that the cheap-labor policy and exploiting the farmers are supportive of their own business expansion. They are much more sensitive to the international community, so their ways have become more sophisticated than the old military suppression. They understand you have to feed a cow in order to milk it, whereas under the military regime the cow was regarded as a dumb animal and beaten with a stick."

In other words, the facile assumption that capitalism would lead inevitably to civil democracy was irrelevant to the complex social realities in a nation like Thailand. If the ruling class based on military power and royal lineage simply broadened to become a nobility based on wealth, then it might be centuries before Thailand could claim to be a modern democracy. Whether a genuine democracy eventually emerged would depend upon many imponderables of Thai history and culture, but especially on the question of social-class formation. The middle class might in time become strong enough to defend its own rights, but would it develop the independent economic base necessary to advance broader reforms, encompassing the interests of peasants and workers? Or would the middle class regard their struggles as antithetical to its own?

Thailand's industrial transformation has so far resembled a "revolution from above"—great changes imposed by powerful ruling groups on a weak and disorganized citizenry. "Industrial development may proceed rapidly under such auspices," political historian Barrington Moore Jr. wrote thirty years ago in his classic study, *Social Origins of Dictatorship and Democracy.* "But the outcome, after a brief and unstable period of democracy, has been fascism." Moore was explaining why industrialization in nineteenth-century Germany and Japan did not lead to democracy.[21]

If, instead, Thailand managed to follow England's example, the road would still be tortuous, bloody and long. Conscientious reformers were beginning to mobilize in Thai society, just as Victorian reformers had campaigned for decades in behalf of England's exploited classes. But it took Britain's aristocracy and gentry a century and a half before they yielded full political rights to everyone; in the meantime, the society was defined by a rigidified class structure and recurring, sometimes violent conflicts between labor and property.

England's failure to address the social consequences of industrial revolution in a timely manner proved fateful for the society it became. The indifference of the ruling class led directly to the subsequent generations of dispiriting ideological struggles, labor versus capital, and produced a cramped social order that two hundred years later is still riven by class conflict and harsh inequalities. Every nation, it seemed, chose its own heaven and hell.

The seeds of a similarly explosive future were already planted for Thailand in the ways that its industrialization has manipulated and dehumanized the weaker groups. As Professor Lae has documented, the Thai development strategy, starting in the 1960s, deliberately knocked the props out from under the rural peasantry, imposing rice taxes that depressed incomes for the small farmers and fostering large-scale consolidations of agricultural lands (the opposite of Japan's or Korea's approach). The World Bank supported this strategy with development loans to finance infrastructure— roads, dams, electrical generation—and the industrialization of agricultural production. Thailand has become a major food exporter (led by the Pokphand Group among others), but small holders in the countryside paid a devastating price.

Uncounted millions of landless peasants were evicted from their ancient farm plots and forests by large dams or eucalyptus reservations, much as English landlords drove off the peasantry by enclosing the commons so they could raise sheep to supply the new textile mills with wool. The Khor Chor Kor forest-development program launched in 1991, for instance, intended to displace 1.5 million Thai people and resettle them on lands half the size —land already occupied by two million other poor farmers. The peasant leaders who resisted were arrested or beaten by soldiers.[22]

As large-scale agriculture developed, the rice growers encountered droughts and debt. Faced with disappointing prices and the more efficient competition of large holders, peasants borrowed each year to buy fertilizers to boost their production and, in time, became ruinously indebted, much the way small farmers in the American South and Midwest were ensnared by creditors during the Populist era of the late nineteenth century. Struggling peasants sent sons or daughters to Bangkok in search of wage incomes or moved there themselves, just as American farms were depopulated by capital-intensive agriculture, only much more swiftly.

"Those who were deprived of their rights, displaced from their lands, were moved somewhere else and told they would be the first to benefit," Professor Lae observed. "Yet, five years later, they still have no electricity, even though the power lines pass over their house on the way to Bangkok. It seems diabolical to them.

"The poverty in the rural areas leads to selling children to the commercialized sector—the sweatshops in Bangkok, the prostitution of Thai children, the beggars. These things should not be seen as separate problems. They are both expressions of the development strategy, the natural result of a strategy in which the majority serve the minority."

While in Bangkok, I came across a small, stunning book entitled *Behind the Smile* that chronicled the human consequences in intimate, wrenching detail. Sanitsuda Ekachai, a reporter-photographer for the *Bangkok Post,* toured Isan, the northeastern quarter that encompasses the poorest and most traditional provinces, and interviewed hundreds of peasants who had encountered the new Thailand. "The giant spider's web has enfolded our village," a woman named Mae Kamkai Sitthiya told her in Lamphun Province. The strands of spider's web were the new power lines overhead that brought electricity, radio and television. "Magic ears and eyes," she called them.[23]

At Baan Teppattana in Buri Ram Province, Sanitsuda saw armed men guarding the eucalyptus saplings because angry villagers had tried to chop them down. "I still remember vividly the bulldozers destroying my orchard, my mangoes, my jackfruits, my sweet tamarind trees," a woman named Mae Kongsri said. There was no compensation for the losses, and her cash income from tapioca planting fell from 8,000 baht a year to 1,500 (from $320 to $60). "We are poor people," she said. "Don't you think we should be able at least to grow what we can eat?"

A village headman named Jamrat in Roi Et Province tried to persuade his villagers not to leave for Bangkok. "No one wants to leave, but we simply have to," he said. "A lot of us have to pay off the cost of the fertilizers we borrowed for rice farming." Fertilizer, Sanitsuda reported, cost 200 baht a bag, but with interest the farmer would have to pay back 340 baht. "I don't know when we're going to learn our lesson," Jamrat said. "Maybe it's our empty stomachs that block our clear heads."

At the village of Srijomjaeng, the reporter encountered a peasant father of eight whose daughter was sent to work in the city as a prostitute in exchange for 1,500 baht. "I didn't sell my daughter," Pon Chaitep insisted. "She saw me suffer. She saw the family suffer. And she wanted to help." The common transaction with brothel owners resembled bonded chattel, in which the girls were required to pay back double the amount their parents had received before they could keep any of their earnings. At another village, Guan Somyong was no longer ashamed that his fifteen-year-old daughter was the first in their village to enter the sex trade. From the money she sent home, the family now had a brick house, refrigerator, TV and stereo. "Now all the girls want to go," her mother said.

Political resistance was building here and there, but the countryside was accustomed to defeat. Peasant uprisings in the early 1970s had produced some concessions from the government, but the farmers' movement was also effectively decapitated when forty-three of its leaders were assassinated. Thai military leaders were haunted by the specter of Maoist revolution—the peasantry surrounding the city—though they have since moderated somewhat, now that the Cold War has ended and even China has entered the global system. Various reforms softened the terms of transformation, but have not altered the basic economics squeezing the rural population.

"The farmers' attitude these days is defensive," Professor Lae said. "They will say: 'We are losing a war—losing a war with the city.' Send their daughter to be a prostitute. Send their boy to work in a factory. Move to a slum in Bangkok. These are all defensive actions. I'm not romantic about the past, but the point is the rural bond that connected these people to one another was broken and they had to move to the city, where no one will help them. They were pushed by poverty more than they were pulled by opportunity. There were not enough jobs for them. They were left by the roadside."

It was conceivable that Thailand had already, irretrievably, chosen its fate. Three decades of rapid growth lifted incomes generally, but also deepened the inequalities. The richest 20 percent now claimed an even greater share of national incomes—56 percent—while the bottom 40 percent had lost ground, from 17 to 12 percent. Labor unions were weak and fractured and severely restricted by law, but a working-class consciousness was slowly, haltingly developing among the former peasants who have become new industrial workers. Yet, as they found voice and pushed for improvement, better wages and working conditions, Thailand bumped up against the market realities—the easy flight of investment capital to cheaper locales.

If Thai wages rose, if the government became vigilant about unlawful factories or child exploitation, production would be moved, the boom would falter. Conceivably, Thailand would find that it was only a transitional stopping place for global industry, and if industry eventually moved on, the country would be left with impossible problems. Under these terms, social collision seemed inescapable. Gentle Thailand would likely repeat in the twenty-first century the same bloody ideological struggles that had engulfed England in the nineteenth century.[24]

Every developing nation was different in its culture and politics, and not every nation has chosen this path. In Mexico, the technocratic reformers were clearly headed down the same road, following a strategy sanctified by

NAFTA that destabilized the Mexican peasantry by withdrawing the subsidies to small-lot corn farmers. If that unfolded, a million or more marginal peasants would become a flood of migrants available as cheap industrial labor (and many would no doubt head north for the United States).

In Asia, on the other hand, the process of industrialization was launched in some places on a more egalitarian basis. In Korea and Taiwan, for instance, the authoritarian governments had brutally repressed labor movements and political rights, but they also protected the small rural holders with price supports for rice, with subsidy and land distribution programs. Thirty years later, those countries struggled still—and sometimes violently—with the basic terms of democracy, but like postwar Japan before them, they had laid a stronger social foundation. A nation that professed the values of social equality and democracy might find itself pulled toward those goals by its own ideals. A nation that recklessly turned its citizens into cheap commodities would eventually face the sinful consequences.

"It's not about money or material wealth," Professor Lae insisted. "It's a question of power—political power—and the fact that some people gain greater benefit from development. Everybody pays the price for change—everybody—but the weaker people pay more than they get in return, much more."

In the modern industrial world, only the ignorant can pretend to self-righteousness since only the primitive are truly innocent. No advanced society has reached that lofty stage without enduring barbaric consequences and despoliation along the way; no one who enjoys the uses of electricity or the internal combustion engine may claim to oppose industrialization for others without indulging in imperious hypocrisy.

Americans, one may recall, built their early national infrastructure and organized large-scale agriculture with slave labor. The developing American nation swept native populations from their ancient lands and drained the swampy prairies to grow grain. It burned forests to make farmland, decimated wildlife, dammed the wild rivers and displaced people who were in the way. It assigned the dirtiest, most dangerous work to immigrants and children. It eventually granted political rights to all, but grudgingly and only after great conflicts, including a terrible civil war.

The actual history of nations is useful to remember when trying to form judgments about the new world. Asian leaders regularly remind Americans and Europeans of exactly how the richest nation-states became wealthy and observe further that, despite their great wealth, those countries have not perfected social relations among rich and poor, weak and powerful. The maldistribution of incomes is worsening in America, too, not yet as extreme as Thailand's, but worse than many less fortunate nations.

Hypocrisies run the other way, too, however. The fashionable pose among some leaders in developing Asia is to lecture the West on its decadent ways and hold up "Asian values" as morally superior, as well as more productive. If their cultural claims sound plausible at a distance, they seem less noble, even duplicitous up close. The Asian societies' supposed reverence for family, for instance, is expressed in the "dark Satanic mills" where the women and children are sent to work. "Family" and "social order" are often mere euphemisms for hierarchy and domination. A system that depends upon rigid control from above or the rank exploitation of weaker groups is not about values, but about power. Nothing distinctive about that. Human societies have struggled to overcome those conditions for centuries.

My point is that any prospect of developing a common global social consciousness will inevitably force people to reexamine themselves first and come to terms with the contradictions and hypocrisies in their own national histories. Americans, in particular, are not especially equipped for that exercise. A distinguished historian, Lawrence Goodwyn of Duke University, once said to me in frustration: You cannot teach American history to American students. You can teach the iconic version, he said, that portrays America as beautiful and unblemished or you can teach a radical version that demonizes the country. But American culture does not equip young people to deal with the "irreconcilable conflicts" embedded in their own history, the past that does not yield to patriotic moralisms. "Race is the most obvious example of what I mean," he said.

Coming to terms with one's own history ought not only to induce a degree of humility toward others and their struggles, but also to clarify what one really believes about human society. No one can undo the past, but that does not relieve people of the burden of making judgments about the living present or facing up to its moral implications. If the global system has truly created a unified marketplace, then every worker, every consumer, every society is already connected to the other. The responsibility exists and invoking history is not an excuse to hide from the new social questions.

Just as Americans cannot claim a higher morality while benefiting from inhumane exploitation, neither can developing countries pretend to become modern "one world" producers and expect exemption from the world's social values. Neither can the global enterprises. The future asks: Can capitalism itself be altered and reformed? Or is the world doomed to keep renewing these inhumanities in the name of economic progress?

The proposition that human dignity is indivisible does not suppose that everyone will become equal or alike or perfectly content in his or her circumstances. It does insist that certain well-understood social principles exist internationally which are enforceable and ought to be the price of admission in the global system. The idea is very simple: every person—man, woman and child—regardless of where he or she exists in time and place or on the chain of economic development, is entitled to respect as an individual being.

For many in the world, life itself is all that they possess; an economic program that deprives them of life's precious possibilities is not only unjust, but also utterly unnecessary. Peasants may not become kings, but they are entitled to be treated with decent regard for their sentient and moral beings, not as cheap commodities. Newly industrialized nations cannot change social patterns overnight, any more than the advanced economies did before them, but they can demonstrate that they are changing.

This proposition is invasive, no question, and will disturb the economic and political arrangements within many societies. But every nation has a sovereign choice in this matter, the sort of choice made in the marketplace every day. If Thailand or China resents the intrusion of global social standards, it does not have to sell its toys to America. And Americans do not have to buy them. If Singapore rejects the idea of basic rights for women, then women in America or Europe may reject Singapore—and multinational firms that profit from the subordination of women. If people do not assert these values in global trade, then their own convictions will be steadily coarsened.

In Bangkok, when I asked Professor Voravidh to step back from Thailand's problems and suggest a broader remedy, he thought for a long time and then said: "We need cooperation among nations because the multinational corporations can shift from one country to another. If they don't like Thailand, they move to Vietnam or China. Right now, we are all competing and the world is getting worse. We need a GATT on labor conditions and on the minimum wage, we need a standard on the minimum conditions for work and a higher standard for children."

The most direct approach, as Voravidh suggested, is an international agreement to incorporate such standards in the terms of trade, with penalties and incentives, even temporary embargoes, that will impose social obligations on the global system, the firms and countries. Most of the leading governments, including the United States, have long claimed to support this idea—a so-called social clause for GATT—but the practical reality is that they do not. Aside from rhetoric, when their negotiators are at the table, they always yield readily to objections from the multinational corporations and developing nations. Both the firms and the governing elites of poor countries have a strong incentive to block the proposition since both profit from a free-running system that exploits the weak. A countering force has to come from concerned citizens. Governments refuse to act, but voters and consumers are not impotent, and, in the meantime, they can begin the political campaign by purposefully targeting the producers—boycotting especially the well-known brand names that depend upon lovable images for their sales. Americans will not stop buying toys at Christmas, but they might single out one or two American toy companies for Yuletide boycotts, based on their scandalous relations with Kader and other manufacturers. Boycotts are difficult to organize and sustain, but every one of the consumer-goods companies is exquisitely vulnerable.

In India, the South Asian Coalition on Child Servitude, led by Kailash Satyarthi, has created a promising model for how to connect the social obligations of consumers and workers. Indian carpet makers are notorious for using small children at their looms—bonded children like Thailand's bonded prostitutes—and have always claimed economic necessity. India is a poor nation and the work gives wage income to extremely poor families, they insist. But these children will never escape poverty if they are deprived of schooling, the compulsory education promised by law.

The reformers created a "no child labor" label that certifies the rugs were made under honorable conditions and they persuaded major importers in Germany to insist upon the label. The exporters in India, in turn, have to allow regular citizen inspections of their workplaces to win the label for their rugs. Since this consumer-led certification system began, the carpet industry's use of children has fallen dramatically. A Textile Ministry official in New Delhi said: "The government is now contemplating the total eradication of child labor in the next few years." [25]

Toys, shoes, electronics, garments—many consumer sectors are vulnerable to similar approaches, though obviously the scope of manufacturing is too diverse and complex for consumers to police it. Governments have to act collectively. If a worldwide agreement is impossible to achieve, then groups of governments can form their own preferential trading systems, introducing social standards that reverse the incentives for developing countries and for capital choosing new locations for production.

The crucial point illustrated by Thailand's predicament is that global social standards will help the poorer countries escape their economic trap. Until a floor is built beneath the market's social behavior, there is no way that a small developing country like Thailand can hope to overcome the downward pull of competition from other, poorer nations. It must debase its citizens to hold on to what it has achieved. The path to improvement is blocked by the economics of an irresponsible marketplace.

Setting standards will undoubtedly slow down the easy movement of capital—and close down the most scandalous operations—but that is not a harmful consequence for people in struggling nations that aspire to industrial prosperity or for a global economy burdened with surpluses and inadequate consumption. When global capital makes a commitment to a developing economy, it ought not to acquire the power to blackmail that nation in perpetuity. Supported by global rules, those nations can begin to improve conditions and stabilize their own social development. At least they would have a chance to avoid the great class conflicts that others have experienced.

In the meantime, the very least that citizens can demand of their own government is that it no longer use public money to finance the brutal upheavals or environmental despoliation that have flowed from large-scale projects of the World Bank and other lending agencies. The social distress in the cities begins in the countryside, and the wealthy nations have often financed it in the name of aiding development. The World Bank repeatedly proclaims its new commitment to strategies that address the development ideas of indigenous peoples and halt the destruction of natural systems. But social critics and the people I encountered in Thailand and elsewhere have not seen much evidence of real change.

The terms of trade are usually thought of as commercial agreements, but they are also an implicit statement of moral values. In its present terms, the global system values property over human life. When a nation like China steals the property of capital, pirating copyrights, films or technology, other governments will take action to stop it and be willing to impose sanctions and penalty tariffs on the offending nation's trade. When human lives are stolen in the "dark Satanic mills," nothing happens to the offenders since, according to the free market's sense of conscience, there is no crime.

Sixteen

Schraube nach Unten[*]

IN MILITARY TERMS, the free-running market has mounted a pincer movement against the modern welfare state and is advancing to disable it. One
flank of the attack is formed by debt, the accumulating indebtedness of the
wealthiest governments as they are unable to keep up with the costs of
long-established social commitments. The other flank is capital exit—the
flight of firms and investors to other locations when nations fail to shrink
the overhead costs that the welfare state imposes on enterprise and labor
markets. As these two flanks tighten, each makes the situation worse for
the societies under attack, swelling the ranks of dependent citizens and the
cost of resistance.

Then the market reformers launch their frontal assault: a principled
ideological argument that government is itself harmful to people and societies, that it is the welfare state, not global economic forces, that has degraded their prosperity and social order. Government protections and
assistance, it is said, have robbed many citizens of their productive spirit and
interfered with the private economy's natural abilities to generate wealth.
By shrinking government's role, by hacking back its social guarantees and
protective laws, society can free the market to create a better world for all.

This open-ended promise, accompanied by the threatening flanks of
debt and capital flight, has become the preeminent political issue for the
nations of advanced capitalism, the central debate preoccupying Bonn,
Washington, Tokyo and numerous other capitals. The underlying terms, of
course, are seldom stated so plainly, and the reform issues vary from nation
to nation since each political culture has produced its own distinctive version of the welfare state—some that are narrow, some broad; some legalistic
and visible, some administered discreetly through the economic structure
itself. Rich nations, nonetheless, are all confronted in different ways by the
same assault, the same question: Must they now undo what the twentieth
century created—the strong social presence of the state?

* German: "ratchet down" like the tightening of a screw or, literally, "twist toward
down."

In historical terms, revolutionary capitalism has circled back to its original fight with socialism a century ago and reopened the ideological argument, but from a much stronger political position. Labor and the left are in retreat almost everywhere; commerce and finance predominate in politics and have adapted centralized government to their own uses. The extremes of deprivation and insecurity that inspired the original welfare systems seem remote to the present economic conditions. But the cost imperatives of globalizing industry are immediate and real, so is the financial-market discipline exerted on governments' deficits and debts (as described in Chapter 13). Furthermore, aside from laissez-faire purists, the market reformers insist they do not intend to dismantle the welfare state entirely, only to shrink its reach and costs.

Yet, despite the powerful logic of this campaign, societies hesitate to act or resist. The mainstream political rhetoric of Europe and America, even Japan, has shifted to the conservative goals of market-driven reforms, but the actual progress toward executing government's retreat has so far been quite limited. Politicians, whatever their ideological persuasion, cannot escape offending their own constituents if they enact this agenda (unless perhaps they target reforms narrowly at the poor). Voters may generally accept the abstract principles of fiscal order and global competition, but they remain quite skeptical about the concrete consequences of yielding social conditions to the marketplace. What happens if government steps back from its obligations and the market does not keep its promise? Aside from committed ideologues, no one is eager to learn the answer.

In France, bolstered by conservative election victories, two successive prime ministers, Edouard Balladur and Alain Juppé, announced purposeful reform programs that swiftly provoked mass demonstrations and general strikes among students, workers, farmers and others. Confronted by crippling disruptions, both leaders retreated, especially when it became clear that public opinion sympathized with the people in the streets, not the regimes that voters had just elected. Balladur reflected after his debacle in 1993: "We all—French, Germans, British, everyone in western Europe— have a big problem: how can we maintain what we have achieved politically, socially, even morally, in an increasingly competitive world? We have built up systems of social protection which are very necessary, but also very costly."[1]

France's blunt tradition of direct-action politics is more fractious (and sometimes more effective) than the formal deliberative processes in other industrial democracies, but the same sorts of struggles were under way generally, accompanied by increasing rancor and class divisions. The dilemma for reform-minded politicians is straightforward: If they announce their intentions explicitly during the election campaign, they may not be elected. If they finesse the issue and try to dismantle social programs once they are in power, they may be accused of betrayal and likely punished at the next election. When this impasse occurs, as it has frequently in the industrial democracies, conservative commentators blame "special-interest groups" and scold the citizenry for flabby self-indulgence.

Many market advocates, especially those in the United States, may underestimate the staying power of the welfare state because they misunderstand its ideological origins. The ideas and programs that formed the modern welfare state originated from the values of the right as well as the left, from the conservative religious impulse to defend the domain of family, community and church against the raw, atomizing effects of market economics as well as from the egalitarianism of anti-capitalist socialism. The welfare state was, in fact, an attempt to devise a fundamental compromise between society and free-market capitalism. The New Deal saved American capitalism from onslaughts of both left and right. The aid programs and labor laws were intended to compensate for the social consequences of unfettered enterprise—the poverty and unemployment and family dissolution—without destroying the energies of the capitalist process.

The first formal social-insurance system of the modern epoch was instituted by Bismarck (a half century before the United States enacted Social Security), when he governed the newly unified German nation swiftly industrializing in the late nineteenth century. "Germany's unity has developed so much new energy and created new interests and points of view," Bismarck once remarked. "But oh! The social question! It makes all governments shudder."

In France, though it is seldom acknowledged by the modern parties, key elements of its comprehensive welfare system—old-age pensions, the universal family allowance and the technocratic supervision of the economy—were implemented by the fascist Vichy regime that collaborated with Hitler during World War II. In the United States, it is also nearly forgotten that New Deal reforms like Social Security were enacted with crucial support from major corporations like du Pont and General Electric as well as progressive-minded investment bankers.[2]

The Cold War contest that subsequently divided the world into realms of free enterprise and communism gave governments another important reason to expand social benefits: to keep the working class from turning Red. In Europe and Asia, it has been observed, the free industrial nations closest to the Soviet empire's borders seemed to develop the most generous welfare states—a discreet form of social bribery that effectively undercut appeals from the hard left. The farther one lived from the active Communist alternatives, the less the political need for this, as in the United States. The end of the Cold War has effectively reopened this unspoken bargain in many Western European societies. With the triumph of capitalism, business interests sense that they no longer need to pay the bribe.

After World War II, Germany and Japan rebuilt their social systems from the bitter ashes of fascism and total defeat—new arrangements inspired not only by their traditional cultural values, but also by the tragic knowledge of what can happen within an industrial society when large groups of citizens are marginalized and pushed into a corner. Each of their social systems is peculiarly ingenious in how it functions, and up until now each has largely succeeded in terms of generating a broad sense of social cohesion and equity. Because of their guilty historical burden, neither Germany nor Japan ever received full recognition for their political inventiveness.

As this chapter explores, both of these welfare-state systems are now under intense pressure from market forces to reform in different ways. The economic model they are expected to emulate is that of the United States. The choice might seem obvious to self-satisfied Americans, but not to many people in other countries who observe the social disintegation underway in the United States and the deepening inequalities of income and wealth. Even the reform advocates I interviewed in Germany and Japan assured me that while they want to copy aspects of the "American system," they do not intend to replicate the social deterioration accepted by Americans.

The German and Japanese systems both manage to distribute the economic returns among all their citizens much more evenly than does the American welfare state (indeed, the same can be said for virtually all of the other advanced economies). In Japan, the incomes received by the highest 20 percent of the population total a little more than four times the incomes of the lowest 20 percent. In Germany, the ratio is a bit less than six times. In America, the top group earns nine times more than the bottom.[3]

The global market's imperatives are, in effect, pushing both of these powerful nations to engineer greater income inequality among their citizens —more like the wider class divisions within the United States. So far, despite much tinkering and rhetorical flourish, Japan and Germany both seem reluctant to move very far in that direction. Income inequality has increased modestly in both countries during the last fifteen years, but nothing like the widening gulf in the United States. American political elites, meanwhile, have embraced the market reformers' goals with renewed vigor and assume that if the debris of the welfare state can be cleared away, the American economy will flourish again.

A terrible potential lurks in these developments, not widely appreciated because it seems so remote: fascism. The collision between society and the free market has the potential to stir a great social disturbance that emanates not from the left, but from the revolutionary right. Fascism arose in the early twentieth century, as economic historian Karl Polanyi explained in *The Great Transformation,* from a fundamental stalemate between the social sphere and the economic sphere: neither realm would yield its claims and priorities, yet neither fully succeeded in overpowering the other. This impasse produced accumulating economic insecurities, social disorder and destabilized politics—a world that to many people seemed out of control, hopeless. "The time was ripe for the fascist solution," Polanyi wrote.[4]

The leading industrial democracies are confronted now with the outlines of the same collision. If it is allowed to deepen and harden into political deadlock, the ground is prepared again for the political impulse known as fascism—a popular movement that promises to resolve the stress and conflict by dictatorial fiat, destroying personal freedom and democratic process in exchange for restoring stability and an orderly prosperity. The suggestion sounds extreme, I know, alongside the pedestrian facts of current political debates, but the symptoms are already visible in many countries—distress signals from the margins of public life that are largely ignored by governments, as the liberated market pushes forward with its social agenda.

The advanced nations have entered a prefascist social condition that will ripen in various ugly ways if the market's imperatives prevail, if commerce and finance refuse to compromise their objectives. By making that assertion, I am not predicting the replay of twentieth-century political history, the rise of a new Hitler or World War III and another Holocaust. But I do observe that the same social-economic forces are in deep collision again, agitating the same irrationalities and extreme reactions that arose from the last great upheaval of industrial revolution.

Fascism is the counterrevolution that developed the last time the market system swept aside social arrangements and transformed everyone's pattern of living. During tumultuous economic changes in the 1920s, fragmentary fascist movements appeared in every industrial nation, including the United States, mainly among the dispossessed working class or bewildered middle-class traditionalists. When economic collapse enveloped the 1930s, the crisis allowed some of those parties to flourish and seize power, imposing their own deadly bargain on society.

Fascism's popular appeal, aside from restoring order, was that it collapsed the two warring realms into one, fusing the social claims and economic imperatives in a corporatist state that Germans called national socialism. "Fascism," Polanyi observed, "was a revolutionary tendency directed as much against conservatism as against the competing revolutionary force of socialism."

When enough people feel cornered—confused and powerless, deprived of security and ignored by authorities—some will be drawn into extreme and violent forms of political expression. Governing elites preoccupied with perfecting the market system and curtailing the old social guarantees seem unaware that they may be stimulating these symptoms—adding to the social stress—in the name of reform. Neofascist political parties, though still small and weak, are active again in the politics of Western Europe—Italy, Austria, France, Germany and others—where mass unemployment has persisted for many years. These groups are renewing the paranoid themes of racial purity and nationalism that always accompany such movements.

But, of course, the portents of social madness are not confined to Old World societies, but have surfaced in American life as well. If Americans are disturbed by the rise of neofascists in Europe, they should understand that most of the Nazi literature circulating in Germany, where it is illegal, is mailed from the United States.[5]

O

In Germany, class resentment was on the rise again, though not always according to the usual stereotypes. The resentments I heard expressed routinely came from people of advanced education and prestigious circumstances. What they resented was the comfortable lifestyle of the German working class.

"Germans are very spoiled," said Dr. Stephanie Wahl, a social scientist at an important think tank in Bonn, the Institute for Economics and Society. "This is the third generation since the war, and we are so lazy and spoiled today, used to a high standard where you get more and more. Even here in this office, they do everything nicely, but if you ask them to start something on a Friday afternoon, they wave bye-bye very nicely and leave. . . . They spend a lot of time organizing their holidays. . . . Germans are very difficult to handle. They know what they want and become very individualistic. Most employees feel they are equal to their bosses."

At ASU, the political organization of independent small businesses, Hanno Bernett, secretary-general of an association for young entrepreneurs, complained that Germany's high wage levels, rigid labor laws and unemployment benefits have destroyed many of the society's traditional grace notes. "Simple work has become too expensive for Germany," he said. "There are so many jobs you can't find any more. There's nobody in Germany to wash your car at the filling station. There's nobody to bring your milk or your bread every day."

In Frankfurt, the center of German finance, the bankers whom I interviewed put the class problem more explicitly. Germany's economic problem, they explained, was excessive equality.

"The price of maintaining equality is too high—we have to allow for more inequality," said Norbert Walter, chief economist of Deutsche Bank. "I'm not minimizing social cohesion. It's something I welcome. But I think we pay dearly for it and I think we can't afford it for the future. I do not speak for a class society. I think it's deadly. But we need more opportunity to move up."

At the Frankfurt offices of Goldman Sachs, the chief economist, Thomas Mayer, waved toward the investment bank's trading desk and remarked: "When I look out on the trading floor, I see no need to get the wages of the traders down. That's beside the point. But the need is to get the cleaning workers' wages down and to widen the spread between them. If we do that, we get more employment, less tax burden on those who are financing the unemployed and, therefore, greater growth."

When I appeared startled by the harsh illustration—cutting wages for janitors, but not for bond traders—Mayer explained his point further. "Compare the situation of German janitors and U.S. janitors," he said. "Why is there such a vast difference? How often does a U.S. janitor go for vacation abroad? Not very often, I think. Here, everybody goes abroad. That would be nice if the productivity of German workers were higher, but it isn't. You can only send your janitor to Majorca for four weeks a year if the higher paid people are willing to pay for it. That's fine, if they are able. But if they aren't, the janitors may have to do without."

Some people, I suggested, thought bond traders were overcompensated themselves. And wouldn't his argument seem unfair to many Germans? Was the society ready to accept reforms that cut from people at the bottom in order to stimulate the productive energies of those at the top?

"Traders get lots of wonderful gains that come out of zero-sum games," Mayer conceded. "But who decides what's fair? That argument assumes that this society is not yet mature enough to live with the same kind of tensions that other countries cope with. I think we are mature. I don't think you need to wrap up the working class and put them in a featherbed so they won't become fascists. I don't think that is any longer the case."

Class implications aside, these comments were all directed at the economic crisis facing the social market economy—*Soziale Marktwirtschaft*—that was modern Germany's proudest accomplishment. For nearly fifty years German prosperity has been widely shared through a complex system of public and private understandings that reduced income inequality and fulfilled the nation's new civic sensibilities. Now the system was under assault—too expensive, too rigid, too centralized—from the relentless arithmetic of price-cost competition in the global marketplace.

The generous benefits of Germany's social safety net, from pensions and universal health-care coverage to the stipends for families and the unemployed, were the most visible aspect of the social-market system, but really only a subset of a larger political apparatus designed to promote consensus and maintain a bedrock of economic equality. German politics was reorganized after World War II (with American tutelage) to require consultation and round-table discussions at virtually every level of public and private governance—forums for continuous bargaining and compromise that kept the conflicting interests engaged in negotiating the decisions.

These dialogues covered every issue from wage levels to broad national political issues to the governmental changes required for unification with Communist East Germany. From the elected workers councils to corporate supervisory boards, the system gave formal voice to groups that had none in other, more purified systems of free-market capitalism. The historic wound of Nazism led Germans from all classes to elaborate a new, more complex design for democratic relations and to accept its terms.

Professor Stephen J. Silvia of American University, an authority on German political economy, explained the heritage: "The Nazis were seen as an excess of ideological extremism, and one of the ways to deal with that is to end this nasty class conflict and try to make a society where everyone can participate and everyone is given a share. The larger idea was to try to keep society uniform and, with good reason, to try to end the class divide. Capitalism can't just be brutal. It has to be inclusive because, if it's not,

those people are going to organize themselves in revolutionary or reactionary parties."

This principle was embedded in the institutional mechanics of both
politics and economic enterprise, encoded in law but also enforced by popular expectations. On labor issues, the works council delegates elected from
the factory floor were consulted before major corporations made any significant change in operations. Strong national unions like the metalworkers'
IG Metall negotiated wages and working hours not by individual factory or
company, but across broad industrial sectors. And they bargained with
all-encompassing employer federations that were legally empowered to hold
their member firms to the terms.

Corporate governance itself followed broader social values, organized
as the so-called stakeholder company that reflected the priorities not just of
the stockholders, but of workers, managers, communities and allied suppliers as well. Corporate ownership was often closely held and centralized in
Germany's three dominant commercial banks, led by Deutsche Bank. As
the principal owner-creditor, the banks exerted intimate influence over corporate strategies and could afford to take a long view of expected returns,
longer than the transient investors in stock markets. Their power allowed
the so-called patient capital that American managers often admired and
envied.

Each of these elements interacted with the others, reinforcing the cooperative ethos, the impulse to compromise and avoid extreme ruptures. Conflict did not disappear, of course, but there were numerous safety valves in
place for talking things out. Germans talked and talked and talked—a
political dialogue that sounded richly detailed, deliberative and rational,
compared to the empty slogans and half-clever sound bites of, say, the
American political dialogue.

In concrete terms, the economic results were envied widely, too. Germany not only had the highest wages and the shortest working hours among
the leading industrial nations, but also one of the lowest rates of income
poverty—one third of the U.S. rate. Wage differences were less extreme
from top to bottom, too. Service-sector wages were about 85 percent of
manufacturing wages in Germany, compared to only two thirds in the
United States.

The German workers admired for their technological skills were supported by an elaborate training system, a responsibility shared among government, companies and unions. The government spent 1.02 percent of the
nation's GDP on labor-market programs—training and retraining, subsidized jobs, vocational rehabilitation and others—compared to .25 percent
in the United States. Unemployment remained at punishing levels—above
10 percent in 1996—but a jobless worker with a family would draw benefits equal to 68 percent of former net earnings.

All families, rich and poor, were supported by monthly child allowances, and these benefits were substantially larger for low-income parents. Given Germany's low birthrate and aging population, the state encouraged people to have larger families and provided bigger allowances for each additional child. Children were supported in this way up to sixteen years old or up to twenty-seven if they were enrolled in college or vocational training. Mothers or fathers drew child-rearing benefits for up to twenty-four months if they chose to take work leaves to stay home with small children. Their job rights were protected for three years.[6]

As these generous terms suggested, a well-developed system of social obligations did not stand in the way of successful capitalism. Germany's postwar economy had gained its preeminent status despite these expensive commitments or, as many Germans would say, because of them. The social options were not limitless, but people in a society would pay for what they regarded as valuable and necessary. Each country's social system reflected its own distinctive cultural values and circumstances, its own historical experience. Germans valued social cohesion much more than, say, Americans.

Condescending comparisons were a bit facile and unfair, however, since Germany had certain implicit advantages in constructing such a system. Aside from immigrants, Germans were ethnically, racially homogeneous—more or less all alike—and geographically compact in how they lived, while Americans were a wildly diverse people and scattered across vastly different territories. More to the point, German social consciousness was anchored in the country's tragic knowledge of guilt and defeat, a humbling encounter with self-doubt that Americans have so far evaded in their national history.*

Germany's social success, in any case, was now its economic burden. Every major component of how the social-market economy functioned was either weakening or under attack from business-minded reformers. The high wage levels and shorter workweek were a barrier to job creation and new investment and, now that Eastern Europe was opened up, an invitation to move production to the neighboring labor markets in Hungary, Slovakia, the Czech Republic and Poland, where wages were 10 to 15 percent of Germany's.

The tax system required to support the social state compounded the squeeze: payroll taxes paid by employers and workers to finance the pensions, unemployment benefits, health care and other programs totaled 40

---

* American history did provide ample basis for humility and social introspection: slavery and the enduring wounds of race, "winning" the West by armed conquest, Hiroshima and the nuclear potential for mass destruction, the bloody failure of neocolonialist war in Vietnam, to name several large and obvious examples. The social meaning of these experiences was usually deflected, however, and repackaged by the optimistic American culture as stories of triumph (or as bureaucratic betrayal in the case of Vietnam). Thus, Americans generally managed to evade any national sense of guilt or defeat. Critical reflection on the national character was discouraged, ridiculed as "un-American."

percent of gross earnings. That was in addition to income taxes and the value-added taxes on consumption. The tax burden on work and enterprise led companies to move production offshore, but, perhaps more important, discouraged foreign capital from investing in Germany.

The government's deficits resembled other industrial nations that could not keep up, but Germany's problems were grossly magnified by the costs of reunification—providing welfare support for the vast unemployment and collapsed industries of the eastern states. A new 7.5 percent "Solidarity tax" was imposed to pay for the historic reunion, but that simply added to the cost-price squeeze.

The government in recent years reformed health benefits and trimmed selected welfare programs on the margins, but hesitated to do more. Chancellor Helmut Kohl scolded Germans for losing their work ethic, but the conservative Christian Democrat was himself denounced by business critics for a failure of nerve. In 1995, Kohl proposed to cut unemployment benefits, but then backed off, influenced perhaps by the popular eruptions in France.

As an economic scheme, the social-market system had worked wondrously well in a self-contained market organized cooperatively by German banking, labor and corporations, but the social bargain was rendered vulnerable once liberalized finance and globalizing production were free of national boundaries. Indeed, the very political mechanisms Germany had created to foster compromise and consensus were now seen as barriers to executing rapid changes.

Meanwhile, there were four million unemployed, multiplying the social overhead for government and enterprise. Some 40 percent of the jobs in traditional sectors like steel and textiles had already fled and larger losses were predicted for advanced industries in the next few years: 100,000 jobs in autos and another 200,000 in supplier industries, 150,000 in mechanical engineering, 100,000 in electrical and electronics manufacturing, 50,000 in chemicals. In the absence of government reform, firms and investors were making their own cost adjustments, exiting from the German system.[7]

"Vertical deindustrialization, I believe, is the order of the day," Norbert Walter of Deutsche Bank observed, "which is nothing else but a functional attempt to reduce the power of unions. I'm not sure of the ability of those labor institutions to learn from their mistakes. If they don't learn, this system will break apart. . . . It's a long, murky road. I don't know if we are going to be fast enough to get out of the trap. I don't know if the country wakes up fast enough to avoid losing its financial strength through capital exit." Walter's pessimism was widely shared among business and financial elites.

In general, what the reformers wanted was frequently described as the "American solution" to globalization—a much smaller welfare system, deregulation across many fronts but especially in labor laws, a weakening of the national collective-bargaining system that promoted a high and uniform wage spectrum, more freedom for employers to hire part-time workers and to modernize business practices. The greater flexibility in the United States, business groups argued, enabled more job creation by firms and much lower unemployment—and, thus, reduced welfare costs.

In particular, the U.S. system's weaker labor-market laws allowed the steady shrinkage of unions, declining real wages, more "temp" jobs without rights or benefits and a much greater spread in incomes between highly educated and less skilled citizens. In America, people were beginning to grasp that these conditions contributed to the social deterioration. In Germany, they were the reform goals.

The social market "has to be substantially corrected," Walter explained. "The state has to have a sound safety net, but it must lower standards, much lower than today and only for those who are unable to care for themselves. It's not a managerial reform—it's a conceptual reform. But to expect that we will have the same disregard for people as in the United States—that's not reasonable to expect."

While the politicians mostly talked about such changes, German companies large and small were executing their own forms of retreat from the old paternalism of the social market. Deutsche Bank, for instance, reduced its ownership stake in Daimler-Benz, and Daimler began offering its shares on the New York Stock Exchange, raising capital from American investors who were much more preoccupied with quarterly returns and quite oblivious to local social questions. This was a small but perhaps meaningful step toward altering the priorities of the stakeholder company.[8]

The social premise of corporate governance, Thomas Mayer of Goldman Sachs predicted, "does not survive, in my view, for a very simple reason: in the stakeholder company, the guy who gave the capital always comes last. . . . You have to put the guy with capital higher up the ladder or he will go somewhere else. You will have to elevate the supplier of capital in the ranking and labor must fall. Look at Daimler—they squandered their capital and they had to go to the U.S."

At the same time, hundreds of small and medium-sized supplier companies—the *Mittelstand* that represented the core of German manufacturing —were resigning their memberships in the large employer federations so they would be legally free to set wages lower than the national wage bargains. Some major American subsidiaries like IBM, never comfortable with the German labor system, were doing the same. Social sentiments aside, the national bargaining system had long served the interests of the largest German manufacturers by discouraging low-wage competition and imposing price discipline on smaller firms. Now the solidarity was fraying and wage levels were beginning to diverge.

"Look at the automobile industry," said Hanno Bernett of ASU. "The level of wages has been set in Baden-Württemberg—when the trade unions push forward the deal, Daimler-Benz, Bosch, Porsche are able to pay. But a hundred miles east of Stuttgart, there are mostly little companies of traditional metalworking, with a hundred to two hundred employees, and they are made to pay those wages, too. If they are flexible enough, they move offshore. If they are not, they simply go bankrupt."

The largest names in German manufacturing were playing hardball themselves, first by withdrawing traditional company perquisites from employees, next by confronting their works councils with hard choices between contract concessions or job losses. At its Sindelfingen plant outside Stuttgart, Mercedes stopped paying for the confirmation dresses of workers' children and canceled the Christmas bonuses. At the Alcatel electronics factory, the French-owned company withdrew the extra week of vacation usually awarded to twenty-five-year veterans. When Mercedes tried to do the same, the works council resisted, 25,000 workers walked out and the next morning the proposal was withdrawn. Yet the union made much larger concessions to keep a new production line from moving to Britain or the Czech Republic.

"There is the fear that in the future there will be more points of attack and more attempts at blackmail," said Erich Klemm of the Mercedes works council. "We read in the newspapers the other day that this was a record year of production for Mercedes. Workers say: this was a record for the company, while we got less. So there is disappointment and anger among many, but others say, let's get going and make it work. Workers share the feeling that without restructuring, the company would be in trouble."

At Alcatel, Alois Süss, chairman of the works council, used a common phrase to describe the pressures: *Schraube nach unten.* "It's like the thread of a screw that turns downward—a constant downward path," Süss said. Blue-collar employment at the factory has already fallen drastically as workers reluctantly granted concessions, but the screw kept turning.

"They use the plant in Slovakia to persuade Germans to accept less," Süss complained. "We are often told if things don't improve they will move all of this to India. I tell people: we can't compete with countries like India because look at their conditions. In Calcutta, they don't even count their dead. Some employers would really like to go back to an earlier, almost forgotten time. We can't follow this constant downward path. The consequences for the country would be disastrous, it would be terrible if there is just this competition of dumping people. It's not right. We must fight it."

In a sense, that was the choice confronting German labor and its political allies: stand and fight or try to work things out. The usual inclination was for bargaining—compromising new social terms that might restore economic stability—rather than provocation and political crisis. Some younger leaders like Erich Klemm thought that compromise was the sensible route because the high skills of German workers would ultimately prove to be too valuable for employers to sacrifice. Alois Süss was older and more skeptical of corporate intentions.

"This is a very tense time," Süss said. "People are feeling very threatened about the future. Partly, it is the fear that more jobs will be moved, but they also fear primitive actions against them. Stuttgart is considered the most aggressive workplace. We're regarded as the troublemakers and people are afraid that the company would like to punish us for that. . . . But German unions are strong and self-confident. We are in a fight and other countries will look to us. We have to stand for the idea that good social relations are important to production and motivation."

IG Metall, resourceful and self-confident (or stubborn, as critics would say), faced the same dilemma. The German metalworkers union employed brief strikes and militance to win significant contract gains in 1994 and 1995, but was then compelled to acknowledge the deepening crisis. With unemployment rising toward 10 percent during a supposed economic recovery, IG Metall began searching for new grounds for compromise. The largest and strongest free trade union in the world was losing hundreds of thousands of members itself. The high density of German unionization reflected the fact that manufacturing was still 32 percent of the national economy (nearly twice the U.S. level), but as manufacturing jobs moved elsewhere, labor's influential position in German politics and society was almost sure to weaken, too.

"The traditional form of the industrial union is growing obsolete in this situation," Helmut Schauer, IG Metall's deputy head of collective bargaining, mused dourly. "We don't have a national economy any more. National unions do not have a future. We must change both the policy and the structure. This is no longer a territorial question. You have not a border any more. The next step must be to go to a serious European movement."

During the recession of 1993, IG Metall had worked out a novel cost-cutting plan with Volkswagen—a twenty-eight-hour workweek designed to save jobs and help the company's balance sheet by reducing labor costs. The union had hoped this would become the model for industry-wide adjustments, but reducing working hours was an inadequate solution. VW did not save much money from the plan and was still stuck with 30,000 surplus workers. No other companies wished to follow.

By late 1995, the union president, Klaus Zwickel, was offering a broader idea: a proposed "alliance for jobs" with government and industry in which unions would guarantee wage restraint in exchange for more job creation, fewer cutbacks in basic benefits. Helmut Kohl seemed interested; business leaders did not. Daimler and the others were pursuing another round of major restructurings.[9]

"The problem is ourselves," Helmut Schauer reflected. "In the spring of the workers movement, it was a more international movement. Now unions are going back to the national level. As their utopian ideas decline, it is a retreat to the parochial. If I say to people in the workplace, it is not possible to have a national solution, they all know this is true. But they still go back to questions of how to solve these problems themselves on a national level. People just can't think in those terms yet. It is a question of social understandings."

In the meantime, the German economy was moving, slowly but ineluctably, toward the kind of two-tiered wage structure familiar to Americans, with a higher top and a lower bottom. While the manufacturing sectors were shrinking, those workers whose jobs survived would be at the high end of the wage structure while others in service sectors and part-time work or unemployed would become the more distant bottom tier. No one expected the institutional arrangements of the social-market system to be dismantled, but the managerial values were shifting toward a harder understanding of what mattered most—closer to the bottom-line mentality of American managers.

Was German society now mature enough to live with these tensions? "It's politically sustainable," Professor Silvia said, "so long as they keep paying out the money for those who have lost. They're reaching the end of their capacity to do that, but the buying of social peace will go on. Whether they can afford it or not, they'll keep trying." Silvia expected German society to display increasing signs of stress, random disorders and aggravations, but he did not think a push toward right-wing fascist politics was likely. "Because World War II did happen," he explained.

Helmut Schauer was somewhat less sanguine. "Yes, it is dangerous," he said. "You can see the problems of right-wing riots and the attacks on minorities in the east. Young people have no prospect of inclusion in the workplace and the social system, no work, no faith in the system. It is possible, in the long run, we will have a very serious decline, more polarization between social groups and destruction of social relations. It's realistic to think it's going to be a little bit like America, even a little bit like Latin America."

The political fight over the social-market system was only just beginning and with immense implications for other societies: if Germany could somehow manage to work out reasonable terms, an economic compromise that did not require the wholesale sacrifice of weaker classes, then other nations might hope to make the same struggle. Germans had no confident answers but were at least talking about how to do this. Meanwhile, they were reluctant to simply throw people over the side.

"This model was very successful for more than forty years," Schauer said, "and it is not going down in five years or ten years. We have many resources to defend the social market. It is planted in the society, in the mentality of the people."

At Deutsche Bank, Norbert Walter more or less agreed. A very hard political fight lies ahead for German society, he predicted, but the nation would pay dearly for its reluctance to reform. "Yes, we can make these changes," he said, "but I don't believe that we will make them until there is a much larger vote by exit—the exit of capital and the exit of people, going elsewhere for greater opportunities."

○

In Tokyo, one could see the homeless beggars encamped in the subway tunnels as evidence that something was changing. Japan was stuck in a long, low-grade recession and experiencing an unprecedented level of unemployment. Its once-stable political order was in chaos, with frequent changes of prime ministers and party control. The massive banking crisis had replaced *kudoka*, the "hollowing out" of manufacturing jobs, as the national preoccupation. Like omens of the stressful changes facing the world's most dynamic economy, a major earthquake in Kobe was followed by the bizarre poison-gas attack launched by an obscure religious cult.

Yet, even in bad times, Japan seemed exempt from the usual social consequences of successful capitalism. While amassing great wealth over the last thirty years and building the efficient production system that others feared, Japan had simultaneously managed to sustain an extraordinary level of social cohesion and economic equality, shared prosperity that was unrivaled among the largest industrial countries. In terms of fairness, Japan's income distribution deteriorated slightly during the last fifteen years but still ranked in the highest class, with much smaller economies like Sweden or Norway.

In terms of full employment, Japan accomplished year after year, even in the worst times, what the economists in America or Europe described as impossible. U.S. financial analysts worried when official unemployment fell below 6 percent; Japanese authorities worried that it had risen above 3 percent. In the United States, economists claimed the stark income-gap widening between the highly educated and the less skilled was the inevitable consequence of the new industrial technologies. Yet in Japan, this gap widened only modestly, notwithstanding Japan's technological prowess.

Japan was different—so different that social and economic scholars from the West often left it out of their comparative studies, despite its centrality in the global system. This was partly explained as a problem of accounting—its national statistics on incomes, government spending and social conditions were too incompatible for reliable comparison. But it was also a difference in systemic values—Japan's different framework for thinking about society and commerce, not as rival entities, but as one unified system. When Japan's superior conditions could not be explained in the usual ways, they were sometimes attributed to the mysterious Eastern culture that values group loyalty over individualism or as the retrograde legacy of feudalism.[10]

These cultural explanations still begged the concrete question: How exactly did the Japanese manage this? Japan's welfare state was based on an ingenious paradox: a system submerged from view and yet fully visible if one knew where to look for it. Unlike in Europe and the United States, the welfare state was not located mainly in the government. Indeed, if one examined the budget statistics for various programs, Japan's social spending looked quite moderate, in some respects more parsimonious than America's.

Japan's welfare state was embedded in enterprise itself—social obligations spread across thousands of firms in every industrial sector and implicitly financed by the export-led structure of the Japanese economy. The welfare system was readily visible on the streets of Tokyo and in the stores.

At night, men in orange coveralls and blue plastic helmets stood impassively by road-construction projects and waved baton lights to caution motorists—work that was done in America by a simple battery-operated flashing signal. In department stores, young women with white gloves operated the elevators with elaborate courtesy. In America, it seemed, the only elevators that still had human operators pushing the buttons were at the U.S. Capitol. Japan's welfare system was most visible in its consumer prices: a $4 apple, a $5 beer, a staggering difference in what people paid for the ordinary staples in life, from clothes to housing.

The essence of Japan's welfare state was jobs—mainly private-sector jobs—and almost every adult could have one. They might be boring and marginal jobs, grossly inefficient and unnecessary, dirty and dead-end jobs, but many millions of Japanese were employed in this manner. That explained why unemployment was always so low and also why government welfare spending could be held to modest levels. With the jobs, employers provided their own social guarantees, formal and informal. The most important of these was the abiding reluctance to dismiss anyone, even people whose functions were clearly not needed, even in bad times when profits were falling. Japanese enterprises carried millions of redundant people on the payroll and it was big news whenever some of them were laid off.

As a result, the overall Japanese economy was extremely inefficient, at least by global standards of productivity. That statement sounded wrong, of course, given Japan's prowess in world trade. After all, Americans and Europeans have been told for years that the superior efficiency of the Japanese production processes explained why Japan was grabbing dominant market shares in one product after another. Didn't Japanese manufacturers pioneer in the applications of automated assembly and other cost-cutting systems? Yes, that was true. But the efficient export-manufacturing sectors were the workhorses carrying everyone else.

Sector by sector, the Japanese economy was the most advanced and, at the same time, the most backward. McKinsey & Company quantified this contradiction in its comparative study of manufacturing productivity rates. Japan's auto industry led America's in productive efficiency by 16 percent (and Germany's by 80 percent). Auto-parts productivity led America by 24 percent; steel, 45 percent; consumer electronics, 15 percent; machine tools, 19 percent. Yet, despite these impressive leads, the overall productivity of Japan was estimated by McKinsey as only 72 percent of the U.S. economy in terms of output per employee.[11]

The explanation, roughly speaking, was the surplus employment—millions of unnecessary workers centered most dramatically in services, domestic manufacturing sectors, real estate and agriculture. Labor productivity in Japan's retailing, for instance, was only 44 percent of American retailing—inefficiency reflected in the profusion of clerks and elevator operators. Productivity in telecommunications was 77 percent of the U.S. industry. Beer was 69 percent. Food processing was a mere 33 percent of American efficiency. These major industries were still organized more or less as old-fashioned crafts—making things by handiwork—while Japan has become rich and famous for the opposite—making things by automated assembly.

The social significance of this contradiction was revealed in this homely reality: more Japanese people worked in the food industry than the total employment of such celebrated export sectors as autos, steel, auto parts and machine tools combined. In other words, export manufacturing conquered global markets and built the nation's wealth through the accumulated trade surpluses while back at home, inefficient domestic sectors provided the abundant jobs and wages for full employment. This peculiar relationship was at the core of Japan's successful economic strategy during the last thirty years and the principal way in which wealth and incomes were broadly distributed.

The social contract was unwritten but well understood. When Japanese consumers paid outrageously inflated prices for ordinary goods, they were effectively subsidizing full employment. When Japan's bureaucracy or collaborative business practices blocked foreign imports from entering the domestic markets, they were defending homespun producers who were major employers from the social disruption of low-priced, global efficiency.

Equity was reinforced by a steeply progressive income tax with high marginal rates that discouraged bloated salaries at the top. Executives of leading Japanese corporations might earn no more than $300,000 to $400,000 a year—a tenth or twentieth or less of what their American counterparts were paid. "It's because of the taxation system," Sony manager Yasunori Kirihara explained. "The Japanese structure is very close to a socialist, Communist scheme. That's why it is nonsense to receive higher salaries. The concept of fairness has made a big difference."

The strategy required, first, broad cultural consensus and a popular deference to the larger social goals—enterprises large and small that willingly accepted their obligations, individuals who would pay the inflated prices without complaint and rely upon company loyalty for their own security. But the system also required the government's active administration of economic life—discreetly supervising the complex market-sharing understandings among rival Japanese firms (cartels, in Western parlance) and defending those inefficient domestic sectors against foreign imports (the informal trade barriers that amounted to protectionism). From packaged foods and retailing to beer and rice, Japan's backward sectors needed protection from the highly efficient producers in America.

Once the Japanese system was understood in these terms, it was easier to grasp the profound social-economic dilemma confronting it: the global market, led by the United States, demanded that Japan fully open up its domestic markets to lower-priced foreign goods and shift from its producer-led strategy to a consumer-based economy. These reforms would arguably improve living conditions for ordinary Japanese citizens by lowering consumer prices. In economic terms, they also offered Japan the greatest prospects for increasing national productivity.

Indeed, the future of the global system itself depended in part on Japan's reform. If Japan became more like other mass-consumption societies, that could mean an important new source of demand for a global economy burdened by gross oversupply. Japan's strategic shift was, likewise, a necessary predicate to establishing more balanced trade among major nations—reducing Japan's perennial trade surpluses and America's perennial trade deficits. That would help staunch the critical hemorrhaging of foreign debt for the United States (though it wouldn't solve the growing trade deficits with the rest of Asia). Americans and others have been making these arguments to Tokyo for many years, but with only limited success.

Government and politicians might acknowledge the logic, but they hesitated to act and for good reason: making these shifts required them to tear up the implicit social contract, dismantling the economic foundations for full employment and social cohesion. That is, millions of Japanese would lose their jobs. Ambitious individuals might find their creativity liberated, but millions of others would experience new economic insecurities. The economy would presumably become more efficient in global terms, but the implicit guarantees that accompanied employment would have to be reduced or withdrawn—reopening the social question for Japan in new and unfamiliar terms.

Were the Japanese people ready for such upheaval? That question was at the heart of the debate between market reformers and traditionalists. Many citizens were eager for reform, especially younger professionals who yearned for the greater individualism expressed in Western cultures and stood to gain most from it. The nation's commercial creativity had been expressed mainly in adapting and perfecting borrowed ideas and systems—not in new invention—and many believed this shortcoming was attributable to the communal value system's stifling of individual inventiveness.

In any case, Japan's new wealth perversely allowed ordinary Japanese to see how others lived. When tourists traveled to New York and bought Japanese cameras there much cheaper than they could buy them at home, doubts were sown. If Japan was so wealthy and its wages were higher, why did Americans seem to live so much better in material terms? Deference was deeply embedded in the national character, but, meanwhile, Madonna was wildy popular among Japanese schoolgirls.

Nevertheless, if market reforms proceeded, the nation's sense of shared enterprise would inevitably be diminished—and, for many, destroyed. Despite the economic imperatives, this was a most difficult transaction for either firms or politicians to embrace. "Many companies, the managers, wish they could change," said Professor Harou Shimada, an economist at Keio University in Tokyo, "but there are so many barriers, including inertia, that they can't really do it. So it's quite an agony."

"The situation is very similar to the U.S.," Shimada said, "when Reagan changed the tax structure and said he would reward people who prefer better production, more work. We can't do this as radically as Reagan did, and American corporations took advantage of that situation, squeezing out middle-level people and the relatively high-paid blue-collar workers. I don't think Japan will go through that kind of transformation, but Japan needs some kind of transformation."

The cost-price pressures were felt by the largest, most efficient export-manufacturing companies, which responded by moving more blue-collar jobs offshore to low-wage markets and by reforming their managerial structures, including efforts to phase out the celebrated lifetime-employment guarantees. Fujitsu shifted to performance promotions, not the automatic pay raises that "salarymen" expected for time in grade. Sony restructured to create independent companies within, more like GM or GE, and management layers were cut from seven or eight to three or four.

"Most of the big Japanese companies were dreaming when they talked proudly during the rapid growth years about maintaining lifetime employment," said Kirihara, manager of corporate human resources at Sony. "I haven't used the phrase for over ten years. Japanese industries began changing the gears some years ago, but not openly. Because of relations with labor unions, they cannot say so openly. The official comment and the private comment are very different."

The really crucial squeeze—and greatest social pain—did not confront the major manufacturers, however, but was aimed at the less productive domestic sectors. Professor Shimada, an advisor to MITI on how to engineer these reforms, cited these sectors as the main problems: food processing, beer, transport, electricity, infrastructure and construction, airlines, communications, financial services and education.

"If we rationalize the sectors of untraded goods and services, at least several million people will lose jobs," Shimada explained. "The Japanese cost-of-living difference with other advanced nations like the U.S. and Germany is about 16–17 percent. My calculation is that if we squeeze that price differential to zero, we will have to lose eleven million jobs. That's why people are against it—they know what it will mean."

As a reform advocate, Shimada argued that Japan would still experience a net gain from this upheaval: "A reduction of prices will increase the real incomes of people, and if that happens, real consumption will increase and produce greater demand for industry and new products. By my calculation, that can lead to twelve million new jobs—one million more than are lost. What we need is the courage, because there is the risk of losing jobs in the process, losing more than are gained." Like the market reformers in America, Shimada was rather vague about where exactly these twelve million new jobs would be created. His confident prediction was derived from the same economic logic—greater efficiency increases growth and incomes—that the White House used to promote its free-trade agreements.

MITI has so far settled on a much less ambitious strategy, reforms designed to eliminate 2 to 2.5 million jobs over the next ten years. Retailing and wholesale distribution networks would lose the most. Daiei, a major retail chain, has announced plans to cut its prices in half during the next ten years, opening its shelves to cheaper American brands. The strategy will require drastic reduction in employment.

"If we try to bring the service industries up to manufacturing productivity, maybe three to four million would lose jobs and four to five million might get jobs by creating new industry, like housing and consumption goods," Shimada speculated. "The bottom line is that if Japan opens the market widely, that's how we can reduce prices and increase productivity. It may not close the trade gap between the U.S. and Japan too much, but it will greatly benefit our other trading partners in Asia."

The reformers' logic sounded familiar and that was the problem with it: Japanese authorities have for years been promising to launch such adjustments, but usually disappointed the trading partners that demanded them. The instability of political leadership made the reforms even harder to accomplish now; so did the banking crisis and general social anxieties. Yet the country's long-term competitive position demanded action.

To carry this out, Japanese firms would have to test the peaceable relations with their own "enterprise unions"—labor organizations that for forty years have been closely allied with the companies and comparatively passive. Many plant managers in overseas factories were actually former union leaders who shifted automatically to the managerial ranks; the deep conflict between capital and labor that existed elsewhere was fused into a more cooperative relationship by the Japanese.

However, as more manufacturing jobs were moved offshore, as wage equity was weakened, Japanese unions began building a huge strike fund that, according to observers like reform advocate and author Kenichi Ohmae, presaged a brutal collision ahead. Like the social question in Germany, Japan had to decide if it was now "mature enough" to live with such tensions.[12]

"If they misjudge company management," Sony's Kirihara said, "there may be a possibility for labor to become very radical. But I think we can find some other way. If the management side takes an extreme position, then unions are forced to be more radical. We will have to find some other way—maybe burden sharing is an answer—so we can avoid conflict."

The Sony executive suggested what would be unthinkable in the United States. "In extreme cases," he said, "maybe we can reduce our own salary level by ten percent. In such ways, union issues can be worked out. One step down, one step ahead."

○

In Washington, the social question was framed in personal terms, not as class conflict or market forces, but as the character weaknesses found in those individuals who failed to prosper on their own. Political debate dwelt upon the foibles of the most desperate, dependent citizens and how to instill in them a greater sense of personal responsibility. Market reformers argued that the welfare state itself has destroyed the incentive for people to rescue themselves from poverty, unemployment or inadequate incomes so the reformers proceeded with the high moral purpose of liberating people from their benefit checks—from food stamps, subsidized health care and housing or the other forms of public assistance.

America was different. Its deepest social value was the autonomy of the individual—people were free to take care of themselves, without government interference or nagging demands from society. Some citizens would succeed spectacularly at this and others would do less well, but reasonable abundance was available to any and all who applied themselves. America was so wealthy as a nation, so large and diverse with opportunity, the culture assumed that anyone who failed to gain a share in this prosperity must have done something wrong.

This idea of upward mobility, though demonstrably not true for everyone, encouraged human potential at all levels and was the inspired core of America's industrious, inventive, acquisitive energies. A spirit of purposeful striving for material self-sufficiency endured in the American character because, across many generations, it had largely been confirmed by experience. Not everyone would get rich, but almost everyone did very nicely. This open-ended promise was itself what implicitly united Americans, from the first pioneers to the waves of new immigrants still arriving. Despite contradictions it was an optimistic social message, free of the fatalistic class assumptions found in older, wearier societies. The social system was defined by individual endeavor, not class or political connections or economic forces.

The American welfare state was, thus, limited in scope and premised on the idea of personal self-improvement. Poverty and unemployment were regarded as temporary conditions that might require temporary assistance, but could be overcome with applied effort. The reverence for communal obligations so strongly expressed in the Japanese system was quite weak in the United States. So was the desire that Germans felt for a grand political bargain that would narrow class differences and avoid social ruptures. Americans, on the whole, were ill equipped to think about such matters or to understand how such basic forces as the labor market of available jobs and incomes created circumstances beyond an individual's control.

America's contemporary liberals and conservatives were more alike in this than they recognized, since both shared the assumption that society's displaced or disadvantaged could be fixed up—trained or motivated or compelled—to make their own way toward middle-class prosperity. They disagreed mainly on how to achieve this. Conservative reformers hacking away at the government's various social programs were convinced that the marketplace itself was the best teacher and government got in the way. Liberals believed in remedial intervention—programs that in various ways would clean up the losers and equip them to get back on the ladder to self-sufficiency. Neither liberals nor conservatives were prepared to question the ladder itself.

Mainstream political perspectives were blinkered to the larger failure of the marketplace—the existing universe of work and incomes that effectively guaranteed that gross inequalities, disappointment and even cruel deprivation would continue to accumulate in the wealthiest nation on earth. Indeed, as Democrats and Republicans argued tenaciously over federal aid to the poor, their debates took on a tone of willful opacity—as if American politics was determined to preserve the old ideal of upward mobility by ignoring the fact that it was no longer functioning for most families.

The larger crisis confronting America's limited version of the welfare state was not about the social pathologies of the poor but about those transcendental assumptions of American life—a crisis that challenged Americans' own onward-and-upward idea of themselves. In that sense, the social question facing the United States was profoundly more threatening than the market's squeeze on European or Japanese social systems. While the U.S. political debate focused on fiscal disorders and how to shrink the welfare state, it was the organizing idea of American life, not its money, that was put in doubt by the market forces. Was the social promise still true? Could most people continue to believe in it?

Across the last twenty years, corrosive self-doubt slowly began creeping into social consciousness, as larger and larger groups of citizens experienced loss or disappointed expectations for themselves or their children. The poor, as always, suffered most from the deteriorating prosperity, but their struggles were not the source of alarm. The broad American middle class was shrinking or else breaking in two, depending on how one defined it, and the psychology of being American was darkening with it. Home ownership, the principal marker of middle-class identity, began declining in 1981, slowly overall but most dramatically among younger families.

The wage erosion and job losses have crept steadily up the ladder— from the working poor to the blue-collar factory workers to the white-collar managerial ranks. These were people who, on the whole, were not dysfunctional or ill motivated but had done the "right things" expected of them— gotten educated, worked earnestly at jobs and careers. Yet their prosperity was shrinking, too. Some people still blamed themselves, as American culture taught them to do. Others began to suspect that the fabled "American dream" was no longer operative, though they were perhaps unsure why or whom to blame.

The future looked explosive. If global economic forces kept advancing as I have described them, another debilitating wave of deindustrialization was in store for America and other high-wage economies when new producers like China eventually came on stream in advanced sectors, with multitudes of low-priced labor. If the rentier regime continued to enforce its slow-growth policy, if U.S. trade debt and the global surpluses of goods and labor kept accumulating, all these factors would—gradually or swiftly—amplify the downdraft on U.S. employment and income levels. In other words, the social stress and class divisions were just beginning.

America was not going to become poor or suddenly without space and opportunity, but how would Americans cope with the idea of steadily becoming less rich? The cramped expectations were perhaps more threatening than any concrete economic losses since the prospect undermined the shared premise of national life. The relaxed understandings that had always bound everyone together, more or less peaceably, were calcifying—poisoned further by the knowledge that some, a relative few, were still gaining fabulously. As the promise of upward mobility faltered for many striving citizens, not just the poor, it became much harder to explain the failure in personal terms or to imagine that the government's selective remedial programs were going to make much difference.

One possibility was the hardening of class-based politics—closer to the traditional political divisions in Europe—that would contest for the public domain and revive the neglected issues of economic inequality. The broad mantle of middle-class identity, ascribed to all but the very richest and poorest families, was disintegrating and, in any case, had always been a convenient political fiction. The American working class still existed and they knew who they were. Regular surveys by the National Opinion Research Center found that the people who by education, income or manual types of work defined themselves as working class were about as numerous as those who called themselves middle class. In a 1993 poll, 45.3 percent of Americans chose middle class as their identity while 44.9 percent said they were working class (only 3.1 percent called themselves upper class, only 6.7 percent lower class).[13]

The working class existed, but its sensibilities and political attachments were scattered randomly from left to right, from the pockets of paranoid alienation to the political activism of the Christian right, from organized labor to the much larger ranks of those in utter resignation. Neither major party really spoke for these people in the bread-and-butter terms of jobs and wages. Deepening class conflict seemed inevitable, perhaps even necessary to challenge the market's ambitions, but this also invited the risk of an ugly, retrograde politics that could draw anxious, confused people into futile nationalistic fantasies.

Indeed, as the economic insecurities spread, resentments toward the dependent poor hardened, too. The burden of public welfare was depicted as sapping the nation's vital juices, encouraging crime and slothfulness. This social scapegoating, laced with racial hostility, was encouraged by the market reformers as a way to advance their radical vision for disassembling the public realm. Almost every public function, they argued, could be privatized, from schools to health care to charity, even police protection if one could afford to hire private guards. Taxation could be reduced drastically, especially for upper-income groups and wealth holders. People would be free to spend their own money, liberated from public responsibilities.

In this vision, society would become as atomized as the free market itself—each one working for oneself—and social obligations would be refashioned as tradable commodities, to be supplied by profit-seeking enterprises or by the private generosity of the fittest. This agenda advanced haltingly in the face of public skepticism, but it did offer a spirited alternative to the social quandary, when other visions seemed unavailable. If cutting off the poor might help, then most politicians were willing to try it. Many Americans grasped that a deeper crisis was before them, but the culture of individualism did not prepare people to understand the failure as systemic, not personal.

Inaction was itself a choice about the future. When American politics, business and financial interests ignored the hardening outlines of economic loss and social division, they were inevitably defining the terms for ugly class conflict in future generations. Just as the elites in Thailand were sowing a terrible future for their country by brutalizing the Thai peasantry, just as the English industrial revolution had two hundred years ago decided England's fate as a class-ridden society, the indifference of America's governing elites to this profound transformation would haunt the national life far into the future. A society unwilling to confront its social reality in a timely manner is doomed to experience the consequences in later generations and possibly forever.

America had no plan for how to cope with this new condition. Aside from the woolly platitudes of political leaders, there was no shared understanding—no long-term vision like Malaysia's "Wawasan 2020"—of what Americans wanted the society to become. The American plan was: "more." In the past, that had always been sufficient to sustain social relations, but what if "more" was no longer in the cards, at least not in the old terms of burgeoning mass consumption? Environmental imperatives argued for a new industrial sensibility that would produce more human satisfaction from less—less waste and despoliation—and a new consumer ethic that recognized the enervating nature of endless material desires. In any case, many Americans were now effectively blocked from realizing their material desires.

Necessity was an opportunity. These new realities suggested that equable social relations would have to be fashioned from a new understanding of what constituted the good life—the basic elements necessary for self-fulfillment and human satisfaction—and how those qualities might be made broadly, equitably available to all citizens. These were hard questions not just of politics and economics, but of social understanding. If the old premise of onward and upward was weakening, perhaps defunct, the nation would have to reinvent the basis for its social cohesion—whatever it was that bound everyone together as Americans. Some critics in Europe and Asia wondered if Americans were mature enough to live with such tensions.

If Americans set aside egotistical presumptions, they could discover useful insights from the social systems of Germany or Japan or elsewhere, not about particular programs so much as their underlying assumptions. In different ways, both countries recognized from bitter experience the dangers to the social order when economics was allowed to destabilize large ranks of citizens, not only the poor and dispossessed. Both countries have managed to integrate market and society in their public thinking and to impose mutual obligations on commerce and finance in a way that American politics has never been able or willing to do. These various measures compromised efficiency certainly, but did not sacrifice successful enterprise or stifle wealth creation, most especially in the case of Japan.

The United States was, of course, much too diverse and spacious, too alive with individual energies and differences, to ever imagine the kind of centralized control exercised by Germany or, much less, the deferential obligations imposed on commerce by Japanese culture. Still, a welfare state that was based narrowly on government benefits for the losers was bound to disappoint social equity when the market reality was simultaneously tearing up the middle class. Government could assist the ethic of self-improvement in various ways, but upward mobility was not going to solve social failure rooted not in individuals but in the marketplace.

The market failure was inadequate jobs and maldistributed incomes. If government intervention focused purposefully on work and wages—that is, assuring jobs for everyone who wanted to work, promoting the broader sharing of economic returns and livable incomes for all working families and their children—then most people could take care of other social problems for themselves, with much less need for the remedial kinds of programs. This much was certain: if society did not confront the issue of work and wages, then all of its various ameliorative programs were bound to be overwhelmed.

The state would have to become stronger, though not necessarily larger. It would have to change the tax incentives and subsidies for private enterprise by rewarding firms that fostered greater employment and penalizing those that did the opposite. It would have to accept the necessity of providing substantial, long-term public subsidy for work—the jobs needed to prevent another marginalized generation from forming, young people deprived of hope and self-respect. All this required more public revenue, of course, but none of it was beyond America's means. The state could begin by taxing capital more and work less.

As Germany and Japan demonstrated, such commitments were basically choices of the social imagination, not limited by national wealth but by what people truly valued for their society, what they were willing to pay for. Both of those social systems now faced their own distinctive crisis, but both also illustrated the range of choices that was possible in a very wealthy

country. Adequate housing, health, education, safe and well-nourished children—these were public goods the market might not deliver unless the
society insisted upon them, social arrangements that the market might destroy if society allowed it.

If Americans wanted safe and pleasing cities like Frankfurt or Tokyo,
free of decrepit public facilities and squads of homeless people, they could
afford that. If they decided that home ownership was the key to a stable
middle class, they could make the promise of home ownership real and
expanding again. If America wanted to build high-speed trains like Japan's
or a national child-care system like France's or provide universal family
allowances like Germany's, it could afford all those. The nation could put
a laptop computer in every home, just as the Speaker of the House suggested, so that every child, rich and poor, could connect with the technological future. It could even send every child abroad for educational travel so
he or she would engage with the diverse and wondrous global reality.

These ideas or others would cost money, but America was a very rich
country. The social question was not really about finance, but about how
America imagined itself as a nation. Americans are a people who greatly
value the autonomy of individuals, but have not yet learned how to value
one another.

"Fascism, like socialism, was rooted in a market society that refused to
function," Karl Polanyi wrote in 1944. During the economic breakdown
that led to World War II, the strange and deadly political movements called
fascism arose to impose order on the chaos, but the symptoms of deep
social disturbance were visible in industrial societies long before the Great
Depression. Polanyi listed some early signs of fascism from the 1920s: "the
spread of irrationalistic philosophies, racialist esthetics, anticapitalistic
demagoguery, heterodox currency views, criticism of the party system,
widespread disparagement of the regime."

In 1995, the Italian novelist and scholar Umberto Eco, who as a child
had experienced Mussolini's national socialism, published a wistful medita-
tion entitled "Ur-Fascism" in which he observed that many of the same
social symptoms have reappeared at century's end. The emotional power of
fascism, Eco wrote, bundled together such disparate, resonant themes as:
"the rejection of modernism . . . action for action's sake . . . fear of difference . . . appeal to a frustrated middle class . . . obsession with a plot . . .
life is permanent warfare . . . contempt for the weak . . . the cult of heroism
. . . selective populism . . . against 'rotten' parliamentary governments.

"We must keep alert . . . ," Eco reflected. "Ur-Fascism is still around us,
sometimes in plainclothes. It would be so much easier, for us, if there appeared on the world scene somebody saying, 'I want to reopen Auschwitz.
I want the Black Shirts to parade again in the Italian squares.' Life is not that
simple. Ur-Fascism can come back under the most innocent of disguises." [14]

In *The Great Transformation,* Polanyi argued for a deeper explanation of why the fascist impulse had flourished: "The origins of the cataclysm lay in the utopian endeavor of economic liberalism to set up a self-regulating market system." The free market, he explained, could not fulfill society's basic requirements, despite its utopian claims, and instead generated social instabilities and the growing presence of marginalized citizens. The two realms of market and society engaged in a deep and unstable political conflict in which neither's power or priorities could prevail. It was this debilitating stalemate, Polanyi said, that prepared people for the irrationalities and brutalities of fascism.

To observe that similar symptoms are present again, that outlines of the same collision between social and economic spheres have surfaced again, predicts nothing about the future. History does not repeat itself slavishly since the circumstances are always new and different, since human agents are capable of learning from the past and altering the outcomes. The rise of fascist politics is most unlikely in Germany, as Stephen Silvia observed, "because World War II did happen." The pressures on societies are intensifying and the breakdown of regular politics is quite visible, but these developments are still mild compared to the wrenching upheavals and suffering in the 1920s. The welfare state does exist now, and though embattled, it serves as an automatic stabilizer for the societies in stress.

The collision between society and the market, nonetheless, seems sure to harden further since neither realm is ready to sacrifice its prerogatives to the other. People and elected governments, whether out of self-interest or morality, are not anxious to vote for greater social suffering unless compelled to do so by the economic imperatives. The market forces, from multinational corporations to global financiers, have no easy means of moderating their behavior as long as sovereign governments do not make them do so. The claims and ambitions of both realms seem beyond obvious compromise. That is the frightening condition and also the great political challenge.

The present conflict differs from the past that Polanyi described in several fundamental ways that make it both harder and easier to imagine a peaceable resolution. For one thing, there is no socialist movement today— at least none like the energetic left-wing parties contesting for power in the early twentieth century and promoting their own social vision. Labor and the left still hold important institutional strength in Europe, much less in the United States or Japan, but their energies are almost entirely defensive. This makes the contest for the public domain seem more one-sided than it was then, at least more fractured. Socialism spoke then for a heretical vision of social arrangements, some of which were eventually incorporated in the welfare state. Alternatives are cloudier today, without the same strong voice.

On the other hand, the modern state does exist now, with skills and powers that most national governments did not possess in the early twentieth century, and capitalism itself has come to depend on it. The old collision between market and society argued over a genuine version of laissez-faire economics that has been thoroughly compromised by the subsequent history. Commerce and finance may wish to disable the social presence of the state but not to do away with the state that subsidizes, protects and promotes the interests of capital. This contradiction will ripen for societies as citizens grasp that government is withdrawing its social protections, but not the commercial kind. The present struggle seems less about abolishing big government than about who gets to use it.

Finally, the global reality squeezes the social choices for all of the older economies and encourages a nationalistic impulse to withdraw from the global system in order to protect society. This condition is not so different from the previous industrial revolution, when international production was also highly developed. As the pressures increased then, nations sought the refuge of protectionism and the trading system imploded. As Polanyi wrote, the final crisis that launched fascism was triggered by the breakdown of the international economic order.

The same threat is present again, for reasons this book has illuminated. The dimensions are now larger and more complex, too diverse and dynamic to imagine that statesmen alone can manage them. The surest way to avert a terrible replay of history, perhaps the only way, is for the rival realms—societies and markets—to pull back from their collision and seek the grounds for compromise. The leaders of business and finance need the courage to moderate their utopian claims before some sort of dreadful resolution is forced upon us.

Seventeen

Buruh Sejahtera*

IN THE GLOBAL MARKETPLACE defined as free trade, everyone is free, it seems, but the people. Multinational enterprise can come and go from one market to the next, investors may insist upon terms for the use of their capital, governments may demand concessions in exchange for commercial opportunities. These contractual rights do not extend to the citizens, however, in large portions of the global system. In many developing countries, people are rigorously regulated by the state as a commodity—wage labor —and often forcibly deprived of the most basic individual freedoms—the right to speak one's mind or associate freely with others.

The general evidence of repression poses an ancient contradiction for capitalism: while it claims to promote human freedom, it profits concretely from the denial of freedom, most especially freedom for the workers employed by capitalist enterprise. Indeed, what draws producers to many locations around the world is the knowledge that labor surpluses allow piteously low industrial wages and that the government will prevent the workers from doing anything about it. In wealthy countries, business interests often complain that labor laws and unions prop up wage levels, but in poorer countries the same companies rely upon heavy-handed labor regulation, including the prohibition of free trade unions, to suppress wages.

The economics of globalization thus relies upon a barbaric transaction —the denial of individual rights—as a vital element of profitability. The fact that this practice is widely accepted and commercially efficient or that it has a long, notorious history from earlier industrial eras does not remove the moral stain. Exploitation involves extracting profit from the inherent weakness of other human beings—people who are unable, for whatever reason, to defend themselves against domination. The presence of exploitative conditions is usually reflected in two complementary facts: First, the industrial wage is so low that it cannot sustain a minimal livelihood, even for young single workers in very poor countries. Second, the power of the state is actively employed to prevent workers from overcoming their weakness.

* Bahasa Indonesia: "worker prosperity."

Exploitation speaks the same language in every age. The rationale offered by modern multinational corporations in defense of these practices is cloaked in public relations euphemisms, but is not essentially very different from what the English mill owners said in the early nineteenth century or even, for that matter, how American slave owners once justified themselves. Commerce, it is explained, helps "civilize" the backward peasants recruited for factory work. These people are not yet equipped for the experience of individual expression, democracy or labor rights, but their jobs and wage incomes will, in time, "educate" them to expect more from life. Meanwhile, they are grateful for the work. Any interference deprives them of opportunity.

This benevolent claim, like some other aspects of the global system, sounds more plausible at a distance than it does up close. The reality on the ground, in one country after another, is swelling conflict—vigorous, often violent clashes between workers and authorities as powerless people attempt to organize their collective voice and demand improvements. These new labor agitators are usually inexperienced young people, most often women since they are the bulk of the low-wage workforces. Their struggles to be heard are indeed sometimes clumsy since many are quite bewildered by their new circumstances as industrial workers. They are also extraordinarily brave, given the forces aligned against them—the companies, the police and military, their own government.

The reality of conflict begs this question for the leaders of multinational commerce and their apologists: if the raw young recruits working in the new factories are so grateful, then why do these young people stage so many strikes—the hundreds, even thousands of wildcat strikes across Southeast Asia and elsewhere? The strikes are usually illegal under the rigid terms of labor law in developing countries, yet the protests occur even in places where this simple act of defiance can risk years of imprisonment. It takes enormous personal courage to try to start a free labor union in China or Indonesia, yet some people still do try.

A fledgling labor movement is struggling to be born across the developing countries, though it is still much too weak and incoherent to threaten the powerful. The development of these labor institutions may be understood, in time, as a pivotal social question for those societies—their best available mechanism for developing civil society and mature social relations as well as more equitable economic terms. The likely alternative is more repression and bloody civil conflicts.

Advanced nations like the United States ostensibly support the idea of free labor, but, in practice, they are on the other side. Major governments like the United States take their cues from the mutinationals and are unwilling to press the labor issue against even the most abusive cases. International organized labor expresses its solidarity with the weak in various forms, but established unions and their members still tend to see the other end of the global economy as an economic threat—not as living, struggling people like themselves. So long as workers in America or Europe regard the exploited others as faceless digits in the global wage system, they too are complicit in the barbaric transaction.

The potential exists, however, for a grand fusion of economic self-interest and public morality—a new social understanding that recognizes why bringing up the bottom of the wage ladder is necessary to sustain prosperity for all, why every worker is entitled to the universal right of self-expression. Labor rights can be understood as an economic strategy—a means of generating greater consumer demand worldwide and thus reversing or at least ameliorating the downward pressures on wages at the top. Labor rights can also be understood as synonymous with the cause of human rights since both require a trading system that insists upon free speech and the right of assembly as prerequisites for entry. Thus, defending human freedom for others is effectively defending one's own economic well-being.

The essential relationship between rising wages and economic development was articulated thirty-five years ago by Walter Reuther, president of the United Auto Workers, when he toured a new Nissan factory in Japan. Reuther looked over the parking lot filled with rows of workers' bicycles and told the Nissan executives: "You will never build an auto economy on bicycle wages." Henry Ford made the same point in 1913 when he took the revolutionary step of paying his factory workers $5 a day. Mass production cannot succeed, Ford reasoned, if the workers cannot afford to buy the things they manufacture.[1]

The global system presently operates on an opposite principle. Multinationals are, in effect, "creaming" the poor countries of the world for cheap and disposable labor, with the collaboration of governing elites in those nations. Firms extract the cost advantage until such time as upward wage pressures may develop. Then they move on to other, poorer nations and repeat the process. Morality aside, the arrangement thwarts the emergence of rising wages and greater consumption, as it enriches local elites and global producers.

A shoe worker in Indonesia, for instance, would have to work three or four months to earn enough cash to buy the sports shoes she assembles (though, of course, she would never be able to save her earnings for such luxury). Typically, she lives in the company dormitory or perhaps in a settlement of bamboo-covered huts near the factory, sharing a tiny living space with five or six other workers who sleep in shifts on humble pallets. The system produces grotesque convergences between great wealth and great poverty. The most famous shoe producer, Nike, was said to pay more in one year's promotional fees to one American basketball star, Michael Jordan, than the entire workforce earned in the Indonesian shoe industry— the 25,000 workers who made Nike, Reebok, L.A. Gear, Adidas and other famous brands.[2]

As an economic transaction, labor repression sustains growth and profits. As a social transaction, it sows the ground for bloody explosion.

○

Jakarta was the Potemkin village of global capitalism, the place that statesmen and business executives regularly visited to exclaim over the miracle of Indonesia's economic growth. The city's main boulevards were alive with commercial energies, lined with palms and flowering trees and with the gleaming glass office towers bearing important nameplates of global commerce, Price Waterhouse and Barclays and the Bank of Hong Kong. The swirling congestions of traffic—big German cars surrounded by armadas of Japanese motorcycles—bespoke new affluence. The rapid growth was made visible by the huge new department stores and construction projects, condominium high-rises with tropical flora draped from every balcony, elevated highways and rapid transit system abuilding.

President Clinton passed through Jakarta himself in November 1994 and posed in a splendid batik shirt with other leaders assembled for a meeting of APEC, the Asia-Pacific Economic Cooperation organization. Clinton, like others, expressed his admiration for what the New Order of President Suharto has accomplished during the general's thirty-year reign. Indonesia has averaged nearly 7 percent annual growth for two decades. Per capita income has tripled to $650 and was expected to triple again; absolute deprivation was reduced dramatically. Indonesia was described by the Clinton administration as one of ten "BEMs"—"Big Emerging Markets" —that were targeted for special attention. U.S. cabinet officers came through regularly to court opportunity.

In the months preceding Clinton's visit, the Indonesian military had cleaned up Jakarta much the way that Soviet authorities used to prettify their Potemkin villages in the 1920s for visits by the starry-eyed foreigners eager to confirm that Communist collectivism was working. Before the APEC delegations arrived, Jakarta's regional military command launched *Operasi Bersih*—"Operation Cleansing"—to clear the streets of beggars, thieves and prostitutes, but also troublesome political dissidents. Security troops were instructed to "watch over possible persons wishing to embarrass the country for the sake of their own group's interests." Some forty alleged criminals were shot and killed in the cleansing process.[3]

A leading academic critic, Dr. George Aditjondro, was charged with "insulting a government authority or body," presumably because he had spoken publicly on the forbidden subject of succession—that is, which general might replace the seventy-five-year-old Suharto if he ever died or retired. Four young activists—an artist, a lawyer, a law student and a human rights advocate—were arrested and tortured with electric prods after they released balloons carrying the subversive message "Uphold the Rights of Workers." Three newsmagazines noted for their reporting on controversial issues—*Tempo, Editor* and *DeTik*—were summarily closed down.

At the same time, criminal prosecution went forward against Muchtar Pakpahan, a young lawyer who had founded an independent workers federation in opposition to the government's official labor organization. After wildcat strikes and rioting in Medan in northern Sumatra, Pakpahan was arrested and charged with inciting the workers to break the law. The particulars cited his demand for an increased minimum wage and official recognition for his federation—known by its initials, SBSI, for Serikat Buruh Sejahtera Indonesia, the Indonesian Worker Prosperity Union. Under Indonesian labor law, SBSI was illegal and, therefore, his advocacy was illegal, too.

"What is on trial here are not my actions, but my ideas," Pakpahan told the trial court. He was subsequently sentenced to three years in prison. When he appealed the verdict, the court increased his sentence to four years.[4]

None of these matters was raised by Clinton or the other heads of state assembled at the APEC meeting or, for that matter, by American reporters who accompanied the President (though the press had been alerted to many of these facts by Amnesty International). A *Washington Post* correspondent, on his return from witnessing the "Suharto miracle," told me his verdict: "Two cheers for authoritarianism."

President Clinton, rather than dwell on the regime's abuses, instead celebrated a supposed diplomatic breakthrough—the promise by Indonesia and the other Asian economies to embrace free trade (though not until twenty-five years later, in 2020). The U.S. ambassador had assured the Indonesian government in advance that while Washington was "concerned" about Pakpahan's arrest, it would not be so impolitic as to bring it up. "APEC is a trade forum," the ambassador explained, "not a forum for discussing human rights or the rights of workers."[5]

This delicate distinction was necessary to sustain the fictional qualities of Indonesia and, indeed, of the global system at large. Economic growth and the human condition were treated as separate subjects. So long as this artifice was maintained, politicians and businessmen could continue to celebrate the amazing progress of places like Indonesia, just as admiring socialists had been blind to reality in the Soviet Union seventy-five years before.

Away from the glamorous Jakarta Hilton and other first-class hotels, the city seemed less promising. Its streets were clotted with uncollected garbage and the reek of broken sewers and smoky buses. Indonesia was undergoing a social transformation much like Thailand's, but perhaps even more extreme. Jakarta and its environs had swollen to thirteen million people and groaned with dense, physical strains. Neighborhoods still had the broken-down look of perennial poverty, and at night the streets were crowded with peddlers and shadowy teenagers hustling for change, the air rancid with burnt cooking oil and the kerosene lanterns that lit curbside food stalls. Guests at the luxury hotels were urged not to attempt an evening stroll, even along the best boulevards.

Despite the fabulous growth statistics, Indonesia's national economy was still itself something of a fiction. The boom existed in Jakarta, Surabaya and a couple of other Javanese cities, but not across the vast archipelago of 13,000 islands and three hundred languages. Sixty percent of the nation's money supply circulated in the Jakarta area alone. Excluding oil and gas, more than 60 percent of the industrial output was clustered in and around the capital, another 20 percent around Surabaya in East Java, according to estimates by Rizal Ramli, a university economist and business consultant.

"Look in the streets: there are so many Mercedes, more than in the city of Boston, where I lived for many years, yet here they cost three times more than in the United States," said Ramli, who had earned his doctorate at Boston University. "I think the upper class of Jakarta has a life much better than the American upper class." How many Indonesian people qualified as upper-class? "About a quarter of a million," he estimated.

The nation had the largest Muslim population in the world, close to 200 million people, but its subcultures ranged from Stone Age tribes on remote islands to the fledgling aircraft industry rising at Bandung. From Sumatra to Irian Jaya, Indonesia spanned territory as distant as Seattle from New York, yet the close details of commerce and politics were all run out of Jakarta, usually by family, friends and military associates of the maximum leader. The top ten business groups, many of them managed by interlocking Suharto kinfolk, accounted for 35 percent of Indonesia's Gross Domestic Product.

"The Indonesian system is more like the Soviet system," Ramli explained. "Of course, there is more freedom, but control of power is still at the center. If you want to be a leader of a social organization, you must have the blessing of the center. If you want to start an enterprise, you must come to Jakarta for permission. The Russians did it in the Communist way. We did it in the right-wing way."

Indeed, though it had gradually moderated repression and allowed political space for independent civic organizations, the Suharto government remained a prototypical fascist regime, a governing system that fused political, military and economic power. The dictatorship promoted its own nationalist ideology—the principles of Pancasila—to reinforce unity of thought and behavior. Its rule was first established during Indonesia's great postcolonial trauma of 1965, a coup d'etat and vicious civil war in which the army (abetted by the U.S. Central Intelligence Agency) swept across the island chain in a systematic massacre of village chiefs, teachers, labor leaders and other left-wing dissidents—literally decapitating local leadership and political opposition. No one knew how many people died; the estimates ranged from 500,000 to one million.

Like other former colonies, Indonesia inherited instability from its European masters, in this case the Dutch, who had fashioned an artificial national identity from many disparate peoples and imposed their own brutal dictatorship in order to extract cheap commodities like oil and rubber.

The continuing insurgencies in provinces like East Timor and Achee reflected the troubled history, as did the deep racial resentments against the ethnic Chinese who dominated commerce. The memory of epic violence still hung over the nation like a shared nightmare and was regularly invoked by the Suharto regime to justify the suppression of free expression.

The Cold War was over for most of the world, but not for Indonesia. Despite two decades of vigorous growth and rising prosperity, Suharto's lieutenants still used the specter of Red conspiracy to explain why it went after freethinkers like Pakpahan and Aditjondro or world-renowned novelist Pramoedya Ananta Toer. Dissidents were using "Communist tactics" to try to destroy the nation, General Sudibyo, chief of military intelligence, explained. "Local human rights groups are all right," he said, "so long as they do not deviate from the official line." The United States, having justified its embrace of right-wing dictators like Suharto as a bulwark against communism, now continued the alliance on commercial grounds.[6]

The awkward question of human freedom—the moral cause that had ostensibly motivated the Cold War struggle—was now reduced to a cynical, bureaucratic charade between the two governments. U.S. leaders periodically expressed their concern and threatened trade sanctions; the Indonesian generals responded with appeasing gestures. American officials investigated the notorious restrictions on workers and set deadlines for reform; Suharto announced reforms and the deadlines passed. The pattern of evasion was so blatant, it was impossible to believe in the sincerity of either party. Washington, in effect, collaborated with Jakarta in sustaining the illusion of progress required by global sensibilities.

In February 1994, when I was visiting Indonesia, another of these theatrical episodes was playing out to predictable conclusion. The Office of the U.S. Trade Representative in Washington threatened to withdraw the special tariff preferences that America extends to goods from poorer countries if Indonesia did not demonstrate a real commitment to international standards for labor rights. This official scrutiny was authorized by U.S. trade law, and a Washington group, the International Labor Rights Education and Research Fund, had filed a formal complaint, triggering the investigation. Withdrawal of the preferential tariffs would not have great economic impact, but might damage Indonesia's good standing in the global system.

Washington announced February 15 as the deadline for action. Jakarta responded with a flurry of reforms. The official minimum wage was raised to 3,800 rupiah, or $1.80, a day. Suharto issued a decree ordering military troops to stop their usual practice of intervening forcibly in labor disputes. In a rare personal message, Suharto warned factory owners they must comply with the new minimum-wage standard or face fines up to 100,000 rupiah (that is, about $50). When the deadline arrived, Washington let it pass without taking action.

Meanwhile, on the ground, the industrial zones of central Java and elsewhere were alive with labor conflicts—hundreds of wildcat strikes. The flash protests were mostly organized by the young women who made shoes and shirts, toys, watches and cordless telephones, without help from any union organizers and despite Muslim culture that disparages women for aggressive behavior. The spontaneous walkouts were mainly directed at a single grievance: thousands of companies simply ignored the government's new wage law, confident nothing would happen to them, knowing many of their young workers were not even aware of the law.

And notwithstanding Suharto's decree, local troops intervened in several dozen strikes, sometimes forcing the young people to return to their factories. The majors and generals took a strong interest in industrial relations because they were partners or board members at so many factories. Indera Nababan, a leading human rights advocate, explained the typical setup in the shoe and garment industry: "You hire three Koreans to run the factory and then you hire generals for the board of directors and they provide protection for the business. If a labor inspector ever files a complaint, the company just tells the guardian and he calls the government and says: 'This is mine.' "

The essential conceit in Indonesia's booming prosperity was the fraudulent nature of private enterprise: all enterprises functioned in a framework of labyrinthine political control, with systemic corruption that imposed enormous costs on commerce. The U.S. Embassy warned American firms about the "irregular fees and/or commissions" required to do business at every stage. "In the event of a legal dispute," the embassy advised, "the judicial system does not yet offer fair, reliable, prompt, effective recourse. The choice of an Indonesian partner is critical . . . Dissolution of a joint venture partnership can be difficult."[7]

The regulation of labor was an important subset of the corrupt business system. The minister of manpower, Abdul Latief, was a millionaire businessman himself whose own factories had been struck by workers complaining they were not being paid the legal minimum. "Agitation and propaganda are methods of the past," the labor minister declared. "Today, workers have to fight by increasing productivity and welfare in their working units."[8]

The chairman of the government-controlled federation of labor unions, SPSI, was Imam Soedarwo, a key executive of the Karwell Group, a garment and textile conglomerate that produced millions of gloves and T-shirts for export to the United States, Japan and Europe. The American equivalent would be if the AFL-CIO chose a leader who was president of General Motors or if the secretary of labor was recruited from an anti-union company like Motorola.

In theory, but only in theory, anyone might start a rival union, except that labor law set impossible hurdles for official status. Only the official unions had a legal right to strike. Even they had to seek government permission in advance. Given these rules, any attempt at independent organizing was, by definition, illegal. Yet workers tried anyway. Given the wages and working conditions, they had very little to lose.*

The suppression of labor was vital to the functioning of Indonesia's economic system, not mainly to counter global wage competition since Indonesian labor was already cheaper than most, but because the depressed wages provided a way to compensate firms for the heavy costs of corruption —the bribes they paid to the bureaucracy, the profits they had to share with local military and business elites. As Professor Ozay Mehmet of Carleton University in Ottawa, Canada, has explained, the "rent-seeking" overhead collected by Indonesia's "gatekeepers" did not injure profit margins "because high transactional costs are offset by exploitative labor policies, so that the workers are paid below their marginal products.

"The exploited factor is the unorganized workers, receiving less than competitive wages," he wrote. ". . . Statistical evidence demonstrates that wage policy administered by the Ministry of Manpower keeps actual wages in Jakarta at levels approximating 70 percent of the daily physical requirements and, at the same time, represses trade union activity in the country." [9]

Rizal Ramli's firm studied the "informal costs" in labor-intensive sectors and found that as a percentage of investment, firms paid an overhead for corruption of 3 to 8 percent, often as large as a firm's total labor costs. Ramli suggested that if international pressure forced the business system to reform, then firms would be able to raise their wage levels substantially— even double wages, in many cases—without damaging their cost structure or profits. "There are a lot of informal costs of doing business in the system that could be removed—that would compensate for rising labor costs," he explained.

Thus, the "Suharto miracle" relied upon a perverse trade-off between government-suppressed wages and government-administered bribery. The fact that foreign governments and multinational firms meekly accepted this arrangement suggested that the high principles of free trade articulated by the global system were perhaps somewhat fictional themselves. International trade agreements like GATT were dedicated to liberating commerce from politics, and when labor organizations demanded new trade rules to protect worker rights, they were told this would constitute an unnatural interference with the marketplace. Yet when regimes like Indonesia's imposed their own unnatural tolls on commerce, the system paid them.

The United States, Ramli thought, might have sufficient cause to file a formal GATT complaint against the corrupt practices. "American corpora-

---

* To win official status, a new union must recruit 100,000 members in one thousand chapters and at least five provinces, then gain membership in a sanctioned labor federation with ten similar unions. Since the only legal federation was the government-controlled one, the rules ensured that any genuinely free trade union would be illegal.

tions are limited by law in the way they can corrupt or bribe foreign governments," he said, "but the Japanese or East Asian multinationals are not bound by this. They can win concessions or contracts, power stations or whatever, because they just bribe everyone. If the U.S. finds a Japanese or Korean or Taiwanese company winning contracts through bribery or collusion, it is in your economic interest to take the case to the World Trade Organization as a violation of GATT."

American leaders and others nonetheless continued to celebrate Suharto as a progressive figure—and the Indonesian president continued to disappoint them with his own corrupt nepotism. In early 1996, he abruptly imposed a 25 percent import tax on foreign-produced propylene and ethylene in order to boost sales by a domestic chemical company owned by his eldest son. His youngest son was exempted by presidential decree from sales taxes and tariffs on auto components to give his "national car" project an advantage. His grandson was granted a special franchise to collect a tax on beer bottles at the popular resorts in Bali. Multinational producers from Europe and America expressed outrage at these irregularities, but this was, in fact, the true nature of the "Suharto miracle." [10]

The two issues—corruption and labor rights—were intertwined in Indonesian economic reality and in many other developing economies. Confronting both, Ramli believed, was crucial to Indonesia's future, both to improve its economic efficiency and to foster political stability. "Clinton is pushing to open up markets, but that misses the point," he said. "It is also important for Indonesia, for our unity, to distribute these benefits among the people. The only way you can do that is through labor rights. Of course, there are problems, but having labor organizations allows for a system of negotiations. If labor is asking too much, management can say, hey, stop. There's an army of surplus labor available if you go too far."

Indonesia, despite its occasional gestures, was not evolving toward such a system. As Professor Mehmet observed, the present system was stable and sustainable "so long as workers remain weak and vulnerable, due to the regulations banning collective rights, legislated by rent-seeking gatekeepers." The only danger, Mehmet thought, was that in time "the burden of exploitation will become so intolerable as to result in unpredicted regime change."

In plainer language, a political upheaval. Many Indonesians expected as much. If nothing changed, they told me, Suharto's "miracle" was leading Indonesia toward another violent explosion.

On the morning I went to interview Muchtar Pakpahan, chairman of the new independent labor federation, the arrangements seemed excessively melodramatic, as though *The Year of Living Dangerously* was being restaged for my benefit. Pakpahan's union, though illegal, had called a national strike for Friday. It would be a symbolic one-hour walkout intended to demonstrate its strength and dramatize the U.S. government's deadline on trade sanctions. A *taksi* took me to an address on Pasa Burung in a seedier section of Jakarta and a shaded courtyard of row houses. When I knocked on several doors, no one seemed to recognize Pakpahan's name.

A young man named Tono, taller and more muscular than most Indonesians, appeared from a doorway and indicated I should follow. "Security," he said. That was all he said. I did follow him, a few paces behind, feeling very conspicuous and faintly ridiculous as Tono led me several blocks along the busy boulevard, then turned into a narrow side street no wider than an alley. We passed a bird market on the corner where scores of bamboo cages were stacked along the wall, filled with sullen-looking birds of exotic color. The bird peddlers looked up hopefully.

A few small shops and shuttered houses lined one side of the alley; on the other side was a drainage canal clogged with driftwood and bits of plastic. A circle of small children was gathered around an open-air stall, watching a butcher skin a freshly slaughtered goat hanging by its hind legs. They turned briefly from the goat to gawk at a tall, pale-skinned foreigner passing through their neighborhood. One of them tagged along, chattering at me in Bahasa, pointing to a homemade basketball backboard. The backboard was painted purple, with words in English: "Phoenix Suns."

Tono turned eventually into an even narrower alleyway and along a path that ran past the dim, open doorways of row houses. The fourth house was the headquarters of Pakpahan's free labor federation, SBSI, its initials painted in rough blue letters on the door frame. Inside, a dozen young men and women sat around a long table under an unshaded light, drinking coffee and smoking cigarettes. I asked for Pakpahan. "He's in jail," one of them said. He led me into a side room, where I was handed a telephone.

"Hello, sir, I am unable to keep our appointment today," the voice said. "I am under arrest. Since yesterday. I don't know how long I will be detained." It was Pakpahan, calling from a police station in Semarang, an industrial city in central Java. He had gone there the day before to address a meeting of workers, but before he could speak the police, accompanied by the central commander of the military district, had come in and arrested him.

"Well, I am accused of violating the terms of the meeting permit, but, of course, it is because I organized a national strike," Pakpahan said. Indonesian law required a police permit for any public assembly of five people or more; the permit designated what subjects could be discussed. A bit flustered, I could only think to ask him if he was all right.

"Yes, but I'm so tired, because for as long as twenty-four hours I was being interrogated and slept only a half hour," Pakpahan replied. "The interrogation is still going on." I lamely wished him well.

When I rejoined the young activists in the other room, they seemed unperturbed. "It is routine," Ara Tampubolan, a thirty-three-year-old organizer, said. "We hear it every day. All of the participants of this organization are subject to arrests." The others around the table laughed, not yet aware that the police and military had simultaneously arrested twenty-one other SBSI leaders in the industrial zones outside Jakarta and elsewhere. The new federation claimed to have 250,000 members in ninety-five branches across Java, Sumatra and all twenty-seven provinces. While this was almost surely a gross exaggeration, the authorities took it most seriously.

"If the government wanted to stop this organization, they did it at the worst possible time," a slight young man, Rekson Silaban, the twenty-seven-year-old vice chairman, said confidently. "This is in contradiction to the laws of freedom of association, so the government always creates many reasons for the future of SBSI. It never wants any competition for the government union."

With Rekson translating, the group talked about the work and working conditions and the possibilities for political change. A woman named Rini, a mother of two in her early thirties, described work in a Korean garment factory where she stitched raincoats, enduring twelve-hour days and frequent scoldings from the foremen, for about $70 a month. Rini earned a bit more than others because she was a skilled graduate of a textile school. "It is our confidence that we will triumph," she said. "That is why we resist, why we do the strike."

Their talk became more contentious when they turned to the question of the U.S. government's deadline for sanctions. Some imagined that American power was on their side; others were skeptical. "I think the American government is with labor, not the companies," Rini said hopefully. "The American government should properly stand on the same side with the workers."

Ara Tampubolan said she was being naive. "There are many fluctuations in the American government," he said. "We always understand that America only acts in a country if America has an interest in doing so. That's the reality."

Looking around the table at the earnest young faces, I wondered if I had perhaps stumbled upon the future—the humble origins of a genuine free labor movement for Indonesia. Perhaps not. Others had tried before them and were eventually crushed. Their self-confidence was impressive, but so was their innocence. They understood well enough the awesome forces they were taking on inside Indonesia. They perhaps did not grasp how very alone they were in their struggle.

Two days later the SBSI's proclaimed national strike was a flop. Six busloads of troops showed up at the national monument grounds to monitor a rally planned by the fledgling union, but the demonstrators all stayed home, perhaps frightened away by the sweep of arrests. Pakpahan was charged with "desecrating the government" and released a few days later on conditional parole. "Don't forget," the Jakarta military commander told reporters, "this government is on the side of the workers." [11]

The following month, 40,000 workers staged wildcat strikes against the garment factories around the city of Medan in north Sumatra, demanding better wages and protesting the mysterious death of one of their leaders, a twenty-two-year-old activist named Rusli (he drowned in a river while being chased by security forces). SBSI was well mobilized in north Sumatra, having made an informal alliance with the Batak Protestant Church, Indonesia's largest Christian congregation, with more than two million members in the region. As the Medan strikes and rallies proliferated, troops were moved into blockade formations, and by April the conflicts were degenerating into sporadic violence.

On April 14, thousands of workers marched peacefully on the governor's office, carrying banners that proclaimed: "Give us the right to organize!" and "We're Not Beasts of Burden." When they were turned away by soldiers, a full-scale riot ensued—workers storming through the streets, smashing windows and luxury cars, looting scores of shops. A Chinese factory manager named Kwok Joe Lip was dragged from his car and beaten to death. The specter of ethnic violence that had haunted Indonesia since 1965 was revived.

The government charged fifty-five SBSI leaders, including Muchtar Pakpahan, with inciting the riot. Pakpahan was arrested a few days later at his home in Jakarta four hundred miles away. He was convicted and sentenced, but released by administrative order in May 1995, after a year of imprisonment. The Indonesian Supreme Court subsequently overturned his conviction—perhaps a rare act of judicial independence but more likely an attempt to defuse the international protests. The government, Pakpahan told others, decided his case was less trouble with him out of jail than in.[12]

In any case, the regime may have felt it accomplished its objective. SBSI was gravely weakened by the arrests and controversy, though it continued to exist. "The organization has indeed been beheaded," an American labor activist, Jeff Ballinger, reported after visiting there. "I went to an SBSI meeting in the Jakarta area and, on the roll call, name after name was missing. Oh, they said, they're afraid to come. Or they don't want to be active any more."

Pakpahan, nonetheless, continued to organize despite various new obstructions put in his way. While the U.S. inquiry was under way, he had managed to launch SBSI and win international recognition as an authentic labor organization. The American government's attention to Indonesian labor rights, however shallow or insincere, had opened up new political space in the society and legitimized a public debate that had not previously existed. Now Suharto was intent on shutting it down.

"This was the beginning of an evolutionary process," said Pharis Harvey, director of the International Labor Rights Education and Research Fund in Washington. "But I don't think that process will continue unless the U.S. establishes some integrity to its own interest in the issue. Sooner or later, people on the ground will see that it's not real."

In November 1994, just before Clinton and the other APEC leaders gathered in Indonesia, the U.S. government announced that it was pleased by the Suharto regime's efforts to improve labor rights. The Office of the U.S. Trade Representative suspended its official review and the matter was closed. Washington was quite deluded if it actually believed Suharto's promises of reform. In the summer of 1996, amid general political unrest, Muchtar Pakpahan was arrested again and, this time, charged with subversion, an offense that carried a possible sentence of death. The State Department limply protested.

President Clinton has piously proposed that the multinational corporations develop their own "codes of conduct" to uphold humane standards in their workplaces. In other words, if the government would not defend workers' rights, perhaps commerce would.[13]

In the factory zone outside Jakarta, the young shoe workers gathered around the table seemed stiff and shy, stealing glances at one another and at me, like embarrassed teenagers not sure they had dressed properly for the occasion. My questions in English drew them forward in their chairs, then they sank back with nervous smiles when they heard the translation in Bahasa. Why did you come here from your villages? "To earn money . . . to be independent." Were your hopes fulfilled? "Not really." Why? "The costs are very big, the pay is very small." Each answer was accompanied by scattered giggles, nodding heads.

This was Sunday afternoon in the dim front room of a small house in the Tangerang district, an hour or so outside Jakarta. The industrial zone was where famous brands like Nike shoes, Arrow shirts and Levi's jeans were manufactured, only these young men and women worked in contractor factories with names like Sung Hwa Dunia, Nasa and Hasi. YAKOMA, a church-supported social foundation, maintained the house as an informal training center for the young people, a place for them to come on their day off for frank discussions about their condition.

"We are trying to organize the workers, to educate them on their rights —to make them aware that they could be strong if they come together," said Indera Nababan, the YAKOMA leader who had arranged the session for me. "This is a paternalistic culture," he explained. "It teaches the people that all that comes from above is good, that you never raise your voice. Some do resist, but most of the workers are rural girls and unsure of themselves. It's only through experience that they learn they must take their destiny in their own hands."

Sadisah, Cicih, Sugeng, Suprato, Hazimah, Eva, Enaf and some others —most of these workers were in their late teens or early twenties, but their hesitant manner made them seem much younger. They were prim and respectful, not at all like hip, shaggy American teenagers pretending to be worldly-wise. The young women were unmarried—still girls in Indonesian social status—and had sweetly beautiful Javanese faces with rich, loosely flowing black hair. They were simply dressed in slacks and bright print blouses or striped cotton shirts. One of the boys, Suprato, wore a crisp T-shirt that declared in English: "Follow the Flag."

What do you expect for the future? A blank pause, then tentative and unfocused answers. "We hope to improve ourselves." Can you do that? No. Yes. Possibly. "If we struggle . . ." There was something painfully innocent in their mien. They seemed so young and unequipped, too frail and vulnerable to be caught up by such heavy questions. Still, they leaned earnestly into the conversation, chins up, trying to answer correctly, bravely.

"If we fight, things may be different," Eva Novitasari offered slowly at last. "I think we will fight."

"We are hopeful," Suprato said. "Right now, we accept what we have, but we would like to change that."

"We hope the company will respect our rights," Cicih said. "But if we don't struggle for that, the company will not give its respect. The company only follows the rules in theory, not in fact."

They were well aware of the risks since a new national heroine had arisen in Indonesia as a courageous symbol of their own aspirations. Marsinah, a twenty-three-year-old worker, tried to organize her fellow workers at a watch factory in east Java. She was abducted, raped and murdered. The brutal details of her death had become a national scandal, and though the military itself was implicated in her murder, the Suharto regime anointed Marsinah posthumously as a "worker hero." Her story inspired these young workers in Tangerang and also reminded them of the dangers of asserting themselves.

Cicih and Sadisah had themselves organized a strike at one of Nike's contractor plants, demanding the legal minimum wage and other improvements. They were fired along with twenty others (suspended, the company said). "I was scared because we were fighting for our rights," Cicih remembered. What about losing your job? "No, I wasn't afraid of that," she said. "The pay is very poor."

But if they were paid so poorly, why didn't they return to their home villages and families? Everyone laughed at the suggestion. "Oh, no, no, no," Suprato said, "only if we had enough money would we go back." "Lots of money," a girl added.

"I expected much higher wages, but I was new," Sadisah explained. "I expected to rise, then I found it was not true. It's no good going back home without success, you don't feel satisfied. First, you have to find a job, accomplish something, then you deal with your dreams later."

Sadisah has signed on with YAKOMA as a community organizer, living in an impoverished settlement near the factories and trying to engage the workers in dialogue about their conditions. Progress was slow and difficult. "The community is too close, they won't take advice," she grumbled. "The women workers I hope will be independent and brave enough to fight for their rights. But, you know, in Indonesia the women are the weak ones, not strong, not brave."

Beyond the question of courage, the young workers lacked basic knowledge about how the industrial world worked and how they might cope with it. What was a union? What rights did they possess to complain? "We have a union at Hasi," Enaf Nafsiah said, "but it is not the union that told us to strike. It is the workers. The union is all from the company." Eva added: "The company told us to choose our union leader from the company staff. We didn't know about the union or what it was."

They were desperate to learn more, also understandably wary. The task of developing self-awareness and confidence would be necessarily slow and required great patience, as Nababan explained. A genuine sense of individualism emerged only from experience, not political texts or ideology. YAKOMA was prominent among the dozens of nongovernmental organizations that have taken hold in Indonesia during the last ten years, as advocates for civil rights, environmental issues and women. Inevitably, many of these groups have converged on the core issue of labor rights since the outcome of that struggle would determine almost everything else—personal dignity and civic democracy, economic justice and individual freedom.

While most of the young women in Tangerang were Muslim, Indera Nababan himself was an old-fashioned kind of Christian. He was a Batak Protestant from Sumatra with skin the color of dark-roasted coffee, a rueful manner that was both tough and playful and an outlook that seemed grimly pragmatic yet also deeply faithful. At one of Nike's fenced factory complexes, Nababan had driven right up to the front gate and conned his way past the guards. We drove around the factory grounds, chatting with workers and snapping pictures. The huge dormitory buildings were festooned with fresh laundry, shirts and jeans hung from the windows to dry in the sun.

"Ten years ago there were only three action groups courageous enough to take on the labor issue," Nababan said. "Now there are many active groups—so many champions that if you pick up the newspaper, it reads like the labor news." He smiled at the thought. The government has turned its repression on some of the more aggressive organizations, but it cannot very well stamp them all out without destroying its own claims to social progress. In Indonesia, labor rights has become a religious cause that united Christians and Muslims, some of them at least.

"We know we cannot change everything and sometimes we feel like Sisyphus rolling the stone up the hill and the stone rolling down again," Nababan said. "Some days we feel like that. Still, we try. We still believe we can achieve democracy and rights. Maybe not in this decade. Maybe in the next decade."

When our meeting adjourned, the young people rushed out to find their friends, to stroll along the dusty streets or hang out at shops for the few hours that remained of their day off. On the long ride back to Jakarta, I kept thinking about the weirdness of the cultural connections in the relationship between consumers and producers. I tried to imagine what young Americans would say to the young people from Tangerang, what commonality they might discover if they were ever brought together in the same room. Neither group, I decided, was quite prepared for such a conversation.

These kids in Indonesia were the people who assembled the basketball shoes and brand-name jeans so valued back in the United States, the goods that were expensive symbols of style and grace for American youth. In their amusing advertising messages, Nike, Reebok and other manufacturers have concocted an artful fantasy of power that the status-conscious young Americans eagerly consumed—the idea of magical shoes that embodied superhuman athletic prowess, images of sports celebrities performing amazing feats.

The young Indonesians who actually made the shoes were still trying to understand real power, as it buffeted their lives in the real world. They thought, perhaps naively, that if the American kids would stop buying Nike shoes, their own grievances might be heard, and some of them had signed a petition asking other young people around the world to boycott a company that collaborated in their oppression. I did not try to explain to them why American young people were oblivious to their plight. In their shy and cautious manner, Cicih, Suprato and the others were already the adults in this relationship.

Indonesia was not the worst case. China was far more systematic and brutal in its labor regulation and, unlike Indonesia, bluntly contemptuous of outside complaints. One might imagine Indonesian society eventually evolving toward greater individual rights or exploding in a power struggle, once Suharto is gone, that opens space for the reformers. But, in China, the system was so powerful—and efficient in its own ingenious way—that it was much more difficult to believe in the idea of gradualism. Chinese authorities, like Indonesia's, suppressed human freedom primarily to protect their own political position, but it was also important to acknowledge that as a cold-blooded economic machine, the system worked.

At Shenzhen on the South China coast, a fantastic new industrial city had arisen almost overnight. The new factories and hotels started just beyond the border-crossing bridge from Hong Kong and stretched on for miles and miles, not dozens or scores of new factories but hundreds of them, drab gray concrete buildings with large red billboards in Chinese characters across their roofs, announcing toys, leather, shirts, semiconductors, TV sets, whatever. A decade ago Shenzhen was a border town of 300,000; now it was nearly three million people and still abuilding. I thought of Chicago rising from the Illinois prairie in the 1840s or California developers paving over the desert with new suburban housing. Shenzhen was as spectacular as that.

As a model for orderly growth, Shenzhen excelled other boomtowns of Asia. Unlike Jakarta or Bangkok, there was no dense, sprawling slum next to the factories, no blight of squalid hovels filled with desperate migrants from the countryside. The workers at Shenzhen lived mainly in company dormitories, usually attached to the factories, entrances and exits controlled by the uniformed guards. The city even had a Disneyesque amusement park called Window on the World, with miniature versions of famous structures like the Eiffel Tower (though admission was much too dear for ordinary workers to afford).

Shenzhen's planners were able to avoid the excesses of rapid urban development because they also regulated the people. One hundred million rural migrants were said to be roaming China's countryside in search of jobs, but none could gain entry to the industrial zones at Shenzhen without an internal passport, the *hukou* system that controlled movements of humanity within China.

Three or four times, while driving around the factory districts, we encountered the internal border stations—highway checkpoints resembling tollbooths where our papers were examined. A U.S. or Hong Kong passport was waved right through, but a Chinese citizen who lacked the proper *hukou* would be driven off or arrested. My guide in Shenzhen was Trini Wing-yue Leung, a labor activist from the Hong Kong Federation of Trade Unions who ironically had more freedom to move about in the country than most of its own citizens.

The *hukou* system has developed a lot of leakage in recent years, owing to the furious pace of economic growth, but it still functioned. At a seaside park, we encountered a young man on a bicycle named Chen Guo Qiang, who had come to Shenzhen from the southeastern province of Fujian without legal papers. Chen said he was a salesman for a small chemical company in Fujian and had biked to the Shenzhen industrial zone to scout for customers. "My *hukou* is still back in the village," Chen explained, "but my sister is very fortunate. Her *hukou* has already moved over here, so I stay with her."

The risks were tolerable, he thought. "You must have a legal residence permit or the public security bureau might come around to round you up," Chen said. "Then they take you to a detention center, and if your relatives don't come and bail you out, you have to do prison labor for half a year. But you two don't have to worry; you have foreign passports. They only do this to people coming here to look for work."

In addition to assuring orderly population growth, the system had the collateral benefit of keeping people under regular scrutiny—and always vulnerable to official discipline. The young girls coming and going from the garment-factory dormitories, all of them migrants from poorer rural provinces, had to flash their identity papers to the guards at the door. Some employers even held the papers of their workers to restrict their movements. As Leung explained, more than 70 percent of the workers in the Shenzhen economic zone were actually temporary residents: if they lost their jobs, they were forced to return to rural villages. Any outsider attempting to persuade workers to organize a union would, of course, be vulnerable, too.

Yet the most startling fact about Shenzhen and China's other burgeoning industrial zones was that people still did try to assert themselves despite the thoroughness of the government's control. Even official statistics acknowledged that the wildcat strikes demanding better treatment and wages have increased dramatically during the 1990s: some 260 labor actions were reported at Shenzhen alone in 1993, though the actual total was undoubtedly higher. "In the absence of an independent and effective trade union, workers in the export-processing zones have been organizing autonomous industrial actions," Leung reported in her study of the EPZs. "However, these initiatives have been met with brutal government repression, often with the collaboration of the official trade union, the All-Chinese Federation of Trade Unions."[14]

A "Workers' Forum" was set up by a group of Shenzhen workers and students who attempted to run an evening school for the young migrants. They published a "Workers' Bulletin" that criticized government abuses and such scandals as the Zhili toy-factory fire of November 1993 in which eighty-four people died. Three of the forum's leaders were arrested, among hundreds of labor activists who have been imprisoned across China.

In March 1994, three thousand Shenzhen workers staged a three-day strike at the Taiwan-owned Yung-feng shoe factory, protesting wage cuts and abusive treatment. The Shenzhen Labor Bureau came in and mediated a settlement but, as Leung reported, "no workers' representatives took part in the negotiation because no workers dared to come out in the open for fear of victimization."

At the Zhuhai economic zone, hundreds of workers were fired after striking the Hong Kong–owned Weiwang Data factory. The same occurred at the Apollo toy factory when a thousand workers had the temerity to stage a sit-in strike at a factory owned by the People's Liberation Army. Why would anyone be so foolhardy as to take such risks?

Because, as Leung reported, "labor exploitation and oppression have progressively worsened over the past fifteen years. Long working hours, unreasonable wage cuts and remuneration, poor living conditions, a dangerous working environment, lack of health provisions, arbitrary dismissals, harsh and abusive treatment are the common problems."

Starting in 1994, Beijing required local governments to establish minimum-wage standards and Shenzhen's was set at 325 renminbi—about $32 a month. But, according to a survey of seventy-five foreign-owned enterprises in Shenzhen, Zhuhai and Shantou zones, more than half of the firms still paid below the local minimum. The lowest factory wage discovered in the survey was $14 a month. Industrialists from Hong Kong, Taiwan, Korea and Japan naturally moved their unskilled assembly work here to take advantage of such cheap human labor. American consumers benefited, too, since goods from these industrial zones fueled China's swelling trade surplus with the United States.

Ironically, Chinese enterprises themselves suffered from the exploitative labor conditions in South China industrial zones like Shenzhen. In general, they blamed "foreign capital" for the abusive practices. Anita Chan, a professor of Asian studies at Australian National University in Canberra, reported: "All of the 23-some shoe factories in Beijing and Shanghai that I visited felt they are losing out in competition with the South. They complained of unfair competition: 'they exploit workers, that is why their shoes are so cheap and why they are invading our market up North.' I am not saying that the factories I visited in the North do not exploit labor, in particular migrant workers who do not have urban residential rights. . . . Managers, officials and trade-union cadres talk about such practices casually, as if these are normal management practices. [But] there is ordinary exploitation; and there is EXPLOITATION. It is all a matter of degree." [15]

Like the elite "gatekeepers" in Indonesia, China's ruling regime has fashioned its own system for skimming profit from the labor exploitation. Most workers were supplied to the factories through an official subsidiary of the Shenzhen Labor Bureau—a kind of state employment agency that recruited the rural migrants and placed them in jobs with temporary employment contracts. The agency collected a lump sum per worker from the foreign employers, covering wages as well as pensions and health benefits plus a 15 percent management fee. The labor bureau converted the companies' payments into renminbi at the higher official exchange rate, rebated 70 percent to the companies to cover wages—and then pocketed the difference. The labor regulators thus had an incentive to promote higher job turnover—more "temp worker" contracts meant larger management fees—and to keep the welfare costs low.

The young workers were disposable for the fundamental reason that China's huge and growing labor surplus—the presence of more than 100 million rural people seeking wage jobs—invited this kind of tumbling exploitation. If anyone complained, send them back to their villages (if not to prison) and fill their slots with someone else. The political irony was stunning: the last great nation governed under the banner of Marxism was offering its impoverished citizens as a low-priced commodity to foreign capitalists—the "reserve army of the unemployed" described by Karl Marx, only on a massive scale.

"People are desperate, really desperate, to find jobs," Trini Leung explained. "That is the ultimate black hole for the workers—this vast number of people who say they are willing to work under any terms. That is why we must talk about international labor standards, why we're trying to set up some standards for fair competition among workers. At the end of the day, the question is whether capital has the option to exploit these peasants who will do anything for work."

○

The examples of China or Indonesia, harsher than the labor systems in most developing countries, illustrate how very far the world remains from a marketplace that anyone might genuinely call free. The idea of labor rights is not, after all, only about the freedom to speak and assemble with others. The core idea has always been the legal right to enter freely into a consenting business contract—a contract that will be protected by law, enforceable in court, like any other self-interested business agreement. Every advanced economy, though the particulars vary widely, recognizes the right of workers to contract collectively on the terms of employment. Yet the global system tolerates—indeed welcomes—new labor markets where the governing powers will systematically deny that basic right.

The lawyerly contradiction in this is profound: global commerce insists on a legal system that will protect the contractual rights of capital but treats the same rights for individual workers as an impediment to economic progress or a luxury that is reserved only for the wealthy nations. The same opinion leaders who celebrate the virtues of free competition among firms are strangely silent on the subject of free labor. The trade lawyers who lobby for liberalizing terms of trade are oblivious to the repressive, manipulative terms on which people are employed in many markets. The lawyers might insist that there is no contradiction since they are serving the interests of their clients, the multinational producers. Whatever the rationale, a barbaric transaction is still barbaric, regardless of local culture and political realities.

The best mechanism for establishing a new social understanding on free labor is the terms of trade—global trading rules that would require producing nations to meet the internationally recognized standards for labor rights and thus establish the basic human rights of self-expression as well. The trading terms might authorize nations to impose penalty tariffs on goods from countries that deny workers the right to organize and bargain or to block goods from the most abusive producers.

No one should imagine that millennial changes would flow from this reform. Progress will be necessarily slow because it depends ultimately on human experience and the development of individual self-awareness in cultures that do not encourage it. But there is no economic reason why every nation that wishes entry in the global system cannot be made to demonstrate real progress toward the global standards. Political charades aside, nations do act in their own self-interest when the terms are clearly put before them. If poor countries wish to become players in the global industrial structure, they will learn to play by the global understanding of civilized conduct.

The usual argument against adopting international trade standards on labor rights—that foreigners must not intrude on the culture and domestic politics of other societies—seems quite fatuous, given that foreign commercial interests have already intruded on those societies. Global capitalism has launched great transformations, for good and for ill, in the way that poorer societies function. The revolution has already invaded the politics and social structures of nations in both positive and damaging ways. So it is disingenuous (and a bit late in the day) for the advocates of a borderless world to hide behind national sovereignty. Like it or not, disparate peoples are already connected by their economic relationships. They are not yet connected by social understandings of what is morally acceptable in their shared economic system.

Multinational firms complain that such a system would require monstrous bureaucracy—investigators and regulators who must examine the social realities in various countries. This argument also seems specious, given the existing reality. In China, for instance, the foreign employers do not object to the computerized file system that the Shenzhen Labor Bureau maintains on every past and present worker in the zone—the government's records of age and gender, education, home village and employment history, even the method of contraception used by women of child-bearing age. Nor do the multinationals complain about the elaborate bureaucracies that regulate labor in developing countries in order to suppress unions.

A more significant objection to international labor standards is the argument that such reforms would injure the very people who are supposedly being helped—depriving the poor nations of an opportunity to industrialize, preventing their peasants from even starting to climb up the wage ladder. Organized labor is accused of promoting a high-minded version of protectionism—trying to shut down the industrial competition and protect high wage levels in advanced economies. Some labor advocates do, no doubt, seek that one-sided result.[16]

If global labor standards stopped new investment and economic growth for the poorer nations, the objection would be well founded, but there is no reason to assume that outcome. The economic results would depend on how the rules are designed and applied in each country, on whether a nation conscientiously responds or simply refuses to accept any improvements at all. Global labor rights would, undeniably, damage the present strategies of certain developing nations—China, obviously, or probably Indonesia—by reducing the power of local elites and global firms to extract profit from the weakness of their workers.

However, other aspiring nations—India, for instance, or perhaps Malaysia and Thailand—could gain important new trading advantages by responding positively to the new rules. Global capital would, in effect, have a different set of incentives when it chooses to invest in some places and not others. The trading system would begin—imperfectly, of course—to pull wage standards and working conditions upward, instead of ratcheting them downward. The firms would have to change their approach, certainly, but multinational commerce has already adapted itself to more hostile conditions than human freedom.

Indeed, imposing international rules for minimal wage and working conditions may be the only way to rescue citizens in the poorest economies from the vicious treadmill they are on now. As China and Indonesia illustrate, the corrupt overhead imposed on exploited labor markets is substantial, so freeing workers to speak for themselves should actually help force the reform of corrupt business systems, too. Rising wage pressures would confront firms and local regimes with an unpleasant choice between paying the systemic bribery or paying their workers better. In any case, so long as the corruption costs endure, a nation cannot claim to be defending "comparative advantage" by suppressing labor. It is defending privilege and profit at the expense of its own people.

As Thailand or Malaysia illustrates, even a government that may want to improve its domestic labor standards is inhibited now by the threat of capital flight—trapped by the food chain of poorer countries eager to accept the new factories on any terms. Global rules would no doubt reduce the easy mobility of capital—at least the advantages of "creaming" cheap-labor markets and moving on. That reform ultimately benefits poorer nations if they are interested in more than enriching the elite "gatekeepers." Likewise, labor rights would inhibit China's internal tumbling of disposable rural labor, a practice that also amounts to "creaming" weak and desperate people and injures the competing nations that are trying to improve. As advanced nations learned in their own early development, organized labor is an important ingredient of genuine national prosperity, forcing the economic system to share returns more broadly and thus create a middle class of consumers.

In the long run, a global floor on labor practices should lead to more positive development strategies and less human wreckage—at least an opportunity for growth that is built on more stable social relations. The popular notion that every country will someday become the next South Korea or Taiwan is suspect on other grounds, but this hope depends on improving education and technology as much as on access to foreign capital. That upward path is discouraged, if not blocked, by the economic forces pulling so many nations downward on wages and working conditions. To put it crudely, a nation that sends its children into the sweatshops is not sending them to school.

Finally, the wage differentials in the global system are so stark that even dramatic wage increases at the bottom are not going to eliminate the developing countries' advantage against highly paid workers in the wealthiest economies. The gulf is so vast between rich and poor, it will take decades of bringing the bottom up before opportunities for wage arbitrage abate. If that is so, one may ask, how can the high-wage workers benefit from solidarity with the poor? Why should they even care?

Morality aside, the economic crucible for general prosperity in the advanced nations lies in what happens to the new workers on the bottom. Professor Stephen J. Silvia of American University described the connection bluntly: "It's going to be bad for the U.S. and Europe, really, until Asia is industrialized. The golden millennium comes when Asian wages creep up and they become real consumers—that is, if Asian wages ever do creep up, if they are not held down by repressive regimes. If the rest of Asia went the way of Korea, we would all be better off, but it's not clear that the others will or can."

In South Korea, when the popular protests and labor agitation finally overpowered the authoritarian regime, spectacular wage increases followed the triumph of democracy: 8.4 percent in real terms in 1988, 15.4 percent in 1989, 10.2 percent in 1990. Conventional opinion often cites Korea as a case for labor suppression—first repression, then political upheaval, then good times for all. This argument implicitly assumes that violent explosions are the only road to prosperity and must lie ahead for all developing countries following the dictatorial model. That is a very cynical view of human society. The relevant point, in any case, is that Korea's economic prospects as a multinational power were not injured by liberation and rising wages. On the contrary, society was strengthened.[17]

The American and European interest—and Japan's, too—is the imperative to create more consumption power for the glutted global marketplace. That requires shifting more of the economic returns from capital to labor so that there will be more buyers—people with the rising incomes and purchasing power that enable them to consume more and better goods of every kind. As an economic fact, it does not really matter whether Indonesian shoe workers ever buy the Nikes they make or even other American-made goods. When they earn more than mere subsistence, their disposable incomes become part of the aggregate demand worldwide, helping to correct the global system's supply-demand imbalances and to boost the demand for production, employment and wages everywhere.

To use Silvia's metaphor, the political question is whether governments should wait patiently for a "golden millennium" that may not arrive on its own, at least not for many decades, or mobilize purposefully to make it happen now, at least much sooner. The introduction of labor rights is the necessary predicate for ever reaching that prosperous future, whether those rights are achieved by orderly global politics or by decades of bloody conflicts and social explosions in poor societies. As a practical matter, the initiative for reform must come from advanced democracies like the United States—demanding that global trade agreements incorporate labor rights or, if that way is blocked, imposing these terms unilaterally as a condition of access to their markets.

The most controversial question is whether the trading system also needs a global minimum wage and whether such a difficult proposition is even possible (assuming governments agreed it was desirable). History suggests that some sort of wage floor will eventually be needed to prop up the bottom, given the endless supply of poor people available in the world, but the vast disparity in wage levels and stages of development makes it improbable that the standard approach could work at present.

The history of the United States illustrates the problem. When a single-nation wage floor was finally established for the United States during the depression years of the 1930s, it covered both the industrial North and the impoverished agricultural states in the South—in effect, accepting the reality that America had become a unified national market. The national minimum wage built a floor under low-wage jobs everywhere (with major exemptions granted to agriculture and other interests), while it also protected industrial labor from the bottomless downdraft of abundant cheap labor.

Business firms were compelled by law to share more of their returns with workers at the bottom and this stimulated consumer demand, even in the poorest states. So long as the U.S. minimum wage was kept in a constant relationship with manufacturing wages, roughly 50 percent of average factory pay, the bottom of the wage ladder rose slowly in step with the top. That relationship was effectively dismantled during the last twenty years as the real value of the minimum wage was allowed to erode dramatically.

Given the much wider disparities of global wages, a global floor could not operate on these same principles, at least not yet. What is possible now is the construction of certain international standards by which the trading system can judge the authenticity of minimum wage laws set in each national labor market, based on each society's own economic conditions and stage of development. A nation's minimum wage law, for instance, is clearly inadequate if it does not even provide subsistence incomes for industrial workers. No one, not even China, should be free to pay workers $14 a month, then export the product of their labor to other markets.

Richard Rothstein, an American labor economist, has proposed various comparative methods for determining a reasonable wage floor for poor nations—standards that would not interrupt their early stages of industrialization, but would compel them to raise the bottom consistent with growth. "Any reasonable standard," Rothstein wrote, "should have as its goals an increase in worldwide purchasing power by encouraging more equal income distributions in developing countries." The wage floor would restrain the wasteful relocation of capital—the "creaming" of low wages—and also reward nations that put a premium on education and technological improvement. As Rothstein said, it would rescue young workers "from lives of needless deprivation and misery."[18]

The global system can afford to do this, just as America and Europe could afford to bring the bottom up during their earlier stages of development. Governments are not likely to try, however, until the day when more people in the richest nations grasp that their fate is now tied to lowly peasants at the other end of the global system, like the young factory workers in Shenzhen and Tangerang.

Several months after my visit to Indonesia, I was meeting with a group of community leaders in Texas and recounted some of what I had seen in Southeast Asia—the bewilderment of the young workers, the terrible

conditions imposed on them by powerlessness. One of the community leaders, a Mexican-American woman named Dora Olivo from the Rio Grande
valley, responded with a personal reflection.

"When you mentioned the young people in Indonesia," Olivo remarked, "it took me back to the days when I was a kid and we used to pick
cotton. Our family lived in a barracks, all of us in one room, and we didn't
have water or toilets or anything. We were very poor, we didn't know to
expect anything else. Then César Chavez came and told us we had dignity.
And that started to change things. People began to recognize their dignity
—that they have a right to dignity—and we began to expect something
better for ourselves. So what I see is that we need to keep organizing, keep
teaching more people to understand this."

Olivo's eloquent comment sounds disarmingly simple, yet she is expressing the vital, universal core of human experience—the possibilities of
self-realization. Across the different cultures, people in different places define the search in wildly various terms, from material accumulation to spiritual awareness, but the unifying thread of mortal existence is the search for
self-discovery. Who am I? What is my purpose here on earth, my true
potential? Where do I fit in the larger scheme of things? The human struggle
seeks answers to those questions, in every time and place, regardless of
wealth and poverty, history or religion. The questions begin anew with each
new being.

When all the economic complexities are set aside, the social question
before the world is really about that word—"dignity"—and the possibilities
for individual self-realization. If the idea of equality is ever to have meaning,
especially on the global plane, it cannot be only about money incomes. It
must begin from the understanding that the human potentiality is universal
and diverse, vast and unfathomable and largely unrealized. The unknown
potential is what makes the future so interesting, so promising in every age,
especially in this one.

The social ideal is an economic system that is measured not by wealthy
abundance alone, but by how well it fosters this process of individual realization for everyone, regardless of where they stand in the order of things
or how they might define their own personal aspirations in terms compatible with their own culture and circumstance. Economic progress—overcoming scarcity, expanding comforts—advances this ideal, but it cannot be
considered progress to tolerate enterprise that, for many, destroys life's
possibilities.

These assertions—basically restating ideas of the individual inherited
from the European Enlightenment—are, of course, fiercely controversial in
most parts of the world. On every continent, many people, rich and poor,
do not share this understanding of human nature. Their cultures, religions
and political systems (including many that call themselves democracies)
promote ideas of a natural ranking in the human order—some people who
are capable and advanced, others who are fated by birth to be backward

and unsuccessful, therefore less aspiring. Race, religion, national identity and material wealth are all used as markers to identify the less worthy "others." Domination, whether it is military empire or economic exploitation, always justifies itself on these grounds.

Addressing the social question in global terms thus requires a spirited argument, both within nations and across national borders, about the nature of individuals and society. Some Asian political leaders regularly belittle the Western understanding of individualism and assure us that their cultures do not share in these assumptions. Those smug Asian leaders, I think, are in for a rude surprise about human aspirations. They may dismiss the concept of personal identity, but ultimately their prospering societies will be unable to hold back the tide of individualism that is carried in on the waves of capitalist enterprise.

Japanese culture is already changed by its impact and wrestles now with the social and economic implications. In Malaysia, the young Muslim women working for Motorola were introduced to the idea when the company installed automatic banking machines and the women, for the first time, gained personal control over their own money. In Indonesia or China, one knows the idea of self-realization is present when brave young people decide to strike their factories. Commerce invades with revolutionary ideas and challenges. Once the concepts are implanted, a regime will need enormous force to keep them down.

The gut question for any new citizen of the world is: Do you believe that every human being has a potential thirst for self-realization and is entitled, in his or her own terms, to the opportunity? Or are those others really lesser beings, incapable of an expanding self-awareness and larger ideas of themselves? The human struggles and aspirations that I encountered around the world make the answer seem obvious to me. This book, I hope, has made the same conclusion obvious to others.

The political problem is: Who speaks for this new social question of indivisible human dignity? Not governments or commerce certainly, not the global financiers or market reformers. The institutions of organized labor were founded in the nineteenth century on international egalitarian convictions—a belief that self-realization was the universal right—but their original social perspective has lost its grandeur in modern times. As workers succeeded in establishing a strong collective presence, many labor organizations evolved toward self-satisfied, bureaucratic goals—defending the economic gains of their own members—and the larger vision atrophied.

Labor's narrowing focus provoked resentments among nonunion citizens, but it also drifted away from the questions of individual fulfillment that were originally about more than economics. The sense of community and internationalism weakened. Many unions, as they grew larger, became distant from their own members and began to see them in the market's own narrow terms—as mere economic cogs, not as richly complicated, aspiring individuals who imagine new and distinctive futures for themselves and their children.

If organized labor does not wither and disappear, as some expect, it will have to reinvent itself. If the established industrial unions expect to speak for exploited others at the far end of the global economy, they will first have to rediscover their own original social conscience and reeducate their own members and societies about what is both right and necessary in this new world.

Different institutional arrangements emerged for labor in the advanced economies—social democracy in Europe, enterprise unions in Japan, the adversarial unions of the United States—but none of these may fit the social reality in developing nations. As new labor movements struggle to gain strength, they may find they have to devise a different model grounded in their own cultures—a labor organization that is perhaps closer to the civic organizations that have sprung up to speak for community and society, for human rights, the environment and economic justice. In any case, if the old version of free trade unions should founder and disappear, then people and societies will have to invent something to take their place—an organized voice that carries the fight for these universal aspirations.

The global system, in other words, is at the dawn of social invention. The economic revolution has given people—forced upon them really—an opportunity to reimagine what is possible. Many will turn away from the opening since it is so daunting and retreat instead to the familiar outlines of the labor-capital struggles that originated 150 years ago. Some people, however, do see the outlines of a different future, even a different kind of capitalism. Those people are the new citizens of the world.

Eighteen

Wlasności Pracowniczej*

THE COMMUNIST EXPERIMENT failed utterly and the alternative system of state ownership collapsed from its own inherent contradictions. Yet the contradictions of capitalism that originally inspired Karl Marx's critique are enduring, largely unchallenged and uncorrected. The greatest of these is the maldistribution of wealth and the grossly concentrated ownership of income-producing property, that is, of capital itself. Left to its usual reflexes, industrial capitalism generates vast stores of new wealth and rising prosperity, but the new assets are accumulated among the relative few, leaving most people in conditions of dependency and subordination much as Marx described.

The Marxist-Leninist solution was to abolish private property and escape the marketplace by collectivizing ownership of the means of production—a fatal misunderstanding of economics as well as human nature. Owning property, as market advocates have always explained, is an important element of individual freedom, an anchor for personal independence that encourages self-realization and responsibility. Yet the free-market system they espouse does not disperse this ingredient of freedom very broadly. In modern industrial society, a small minority ends up owning most of the wealth. Most people wind up with little or none.

So long as this remains true, capitalist societies, new and old, are doomed to replay in one way or another the deep social conflicts and political struggles delineated by Marx. The many will remain dependent on the few, either as wage earners or as welfare cases. Political contests will be drawn to questions of how to redistribute malapportioned economic returns, trying to correct for capitalism's excesses. Democracy itself will always be stunted by the exaggerated political power exercised by concentrated wealth. The problem is not that capital is privately owned, as Marx supposed. The problem is that most people don't own any.

The United States is the most extreme case, though other industrial democracies display the same malady in milder degrees. In America, 35 percent of the household net wealth, everything from land and houses to

* Polish: "owner workers."

stocks and bonds, is owned by a mere one percent of families; 80 percent of the wealth belongs to one fifth of the people. This maldistribution has been obscured in recent years by the enormous surge of middle-class families investing their savings in stocks and bonds through mutual funds, but, in fact, the maldistribution is growing more extreme, rivaling the wealth concentration that developed fatefully during the 1920s.[1]

The ghost of Marx remains influential (if unacknowledged) because his class distinctions still implicitly define how most people—rich and poor alike—think about themselves and society. The unspoken assumption is that these gross disparities of wealth are the natural, immutable order. Workers are workers, living on wage incomes. Owners are owners, collecting profits, rents and dividends from their assets. While some people get from one side to the other, this fault line defines the basic economic and social relationships and underlies every important political question, from taxation to social welfare.

In that sense, the advanced industrial societies remain stunted in their social thinking by a frame of reference that was formed 150 years ago when the great labor-capital conflicts arose in the nineteenth century. Rich nations are joined now in this debility by many newly industrializing economies that encounter the same class struggles and inherit the same distinctions. The great social question for the future is whether capitalism will be reformed to escape the boundaries of the past—the class-ridden vision of society that limits human possibilities—or simply repeat, pathologically, the same contradictions and struggles that Marx identified.

The global industrial revolution, with its wondrously efficient inventions, has sharpened the class question, just as the industrial revolution did in the nineteenth century, because the new capital formation buys the technology that displaces labor—more production from less human input —and this shifts the imbalances further in favor of the capital owners. The owners earn an increased share of the returns, justified by the labor-saving nature of their capital assets, while the displacement of human labor intensifies the problems of wages and work for others and multiplies the social burdens on the welfare state. The class struggle is thus renewed on many fronts, only without Marxism available to blame.

The means exist to escape from this stale past and define a different social reality for the future: by democratizing capitalism, by ensuring that over time the ownership of capital will itself become broadly shared, dispersed among workers, citizens at large and communities, more or less universally. A new social being would emerge from this transformation— the owner worker—who draws income from both wages and capital assets, who is compelled by self-interest and social values to take responsibility for both. A realignment of wealth would certainly alter the outlook and behavior of working people. It is conceivable that, eventually, owner workers might alter the behavior of capitalism itself, including the stateless multinational enterprises.

Achieving this structural reform does not require the expropriation of anyone's existing wealth; it does require changing the rules for capitalism so that newly created capital assets—the factories built to expand production or replace the obsolete—are not simply accumulated by the same narrow class of wealth holders, but are broadly owned among all citizens. If governments were committed to this goal, they would begin by altering their relationships with private enterprise and scrapping the standard premiums—favoring instead the firms that distribute equity shares to their workers or communities, withdrawing tax benefits and subsidies from those that do not.*

The central mechanism for democratizing ownership, however, is reform of the credit system—enabling people without any wealth of their own to borrow the funds to buy shares of capital ownership, loans that will be paid back by future earnings from the very income-producing assets they have acquired. This approach to financing sounds radical only to those who are unfamiliar with how capitalism actually functions. In fact, it is the same means by which families acquire equity in their homes: instead of paying rent to a landlord each month, they pay off the mortgage loan that enabled them to buy the house. It is the standard method of corporations expanding their production: they borrow funds in financial markets to build a new factory and commit the factory's future revenues to paying off the debt.

Nelson Peltz, who used debt in this manner to build Triangle Industries into a large and successful packaging company, described the underlying principle: "The thing about capital is, if you don't inherit it, you have to borrow it."[2]

His remark captures a choice paradox of capitalism: people do not usually get rich by saving money but by borrowing it. Every aspiring entrepreneur or inventor understands this well enough; so do the global financiers whose market plays are so highly leveraged with borrowed money. Yet this practical reality conflicts with the Calvinist ethos of orthodox economics that instructs people and nations to become virtuous savers. That is, they should accumulate wealth by not consuming, by not spending all that they earn.

The savings principle does, of course, encourage virtues of thrift and abstinence, but it also perversely promotes the class system based on wealth. Tax measures described by politicians as "promoting savings" are often merely ways to enhance the status quo—that is, to help the rich get richer. As a practical matter, most people are unable to save much of anything, given their incomes and living costs. The minority of people who are already

---

* Since many firms already include stock shares or profit-sharing in their employee benefits and several thousand firms are employee owned, the political objective would be to accelerate and universalize a practice that already has general approbation.

wealth holders are able to save a lot—and borrow freely to acquire still more of the capital assets.

This factor—the limited access to credit—explains, as powerfully as anything else, why capitalism continues to generate its gross inequalities of wealth, generation after generation, despite the centuries of fabulous expansion and rising prosperity. The wealth holders, including the established firms, are able to borrow to acquire new capital assets because, of course, they have the collateral to guarantee their loans. Most citizens (and new, untested enterprises) have little or no collateral. They are, therefore, ineligible for capital-acquisition loans (though the U.S. credit system does allow them to borrow recklessly for consumption).

The problem, in other words, is not debt per se, as people are led to suppose. After all, the capitalist process relies on debt, continuous lending and borrowing, for its creativity and progress. The problem is that most people cannot get into debt—not the kind of debt that will enable them to become capital owners. This does not sound like an insolvable problem—given the many ingenious innovations generated by modern finance—and, indeed, the problem has been solved. Nearly fifty years ago an American investment banker named Louis O. Kelso invented the employee-ownership trust, better known as ESOP, for "employee stock ownership plan."

Kelso's invention provided a financing mechanism that overcomes the collateral problem of ordinary workers—a trust that borrows in their names, buys stock shares of their company and holds the title until the loan is paid off by the company's earnings and dividends. Ownership of the assets is then distributed directly to the individual workers who, as owners, will collect future dividends themselves or sell the shares, as they choose. The collateral for the originating loan is simply the productive asset itself—the new factory built by the borrowed capital.

If this financial transaction sounds exotic, it is actually quite common in American corporate life. The methodology is essentially the same as the leveraged buyouts, or LBOs, that became famous (and infamous) during the 1980s when many corporate executives bought ownership of their own companies from the shareholders by borrowing millions, then pledging the assets and future profits of the company as the collateral for their loan. If bankers will approve this collateral arrangement so the CEO and other insiders can acquire ownership, why not for the workers on the factory floor or the clerks and engineers and salespeople? In fact, bankers do make such loans for the rank and file, and employee ownership is spreading as a result.

Largely because of Kelso's pioneering efforts, some degree of employee ownership is now present in more than ten thousand American companies, usually through the mechanism of employee stock ownership trusts that Kelso invented or through the company's distribution of stock shares. The largest and most celebrated examples are United Airlines and Avis—successful major companies in which the employees became the majority share-holders through ESOP buyouts. The fifteen hundred U.S. firms that are majority owned by their workers are, more typically, much smaller enter-prises, often family-owned businesses that were sold to the workers when the founder retired.

While these represent only a tiny slice of U.S. business firms, they provide living evidence of how ownership can transform the nature of both work and enterprise. People who labor for years in pedestrian jobs are often able to acquire modest fortunes in the process. (Some even become millionaires.) The shared ownership does not, of course, except the firm from the usual risks and frustrations of market competition—worker own-ers may fail, too—but it does alter the structure of rewards and responsibil-ity within the firm. Every question looks a bit different to an employee who is also a shareholder or to a boss whose shareholders are the workers.

In one variation or another, the idea has gradually spread around the world. In Japan, some measure of worker shareholding has become nearly universal, present in 97 percent of the companies. The workers rank among the ten largest shareholders in 21 percent of Japanese firms.

Russia, the former citadel of world communism, has achieved the high-est level of worker ownership in the world, thanks to the privatization of 16,000 state-owned enterprises. According to an extensive survey by Profes-sor Joseph R. Blasi of Rutgers University, employees and managers now own on average 53 percent of equity in those Russian companies, though their stake will undoubtedly decline as many of the firms fail or are acquired by outside investors. Across Eastern Europe, all of the post-Communist governments have attempted, with mixed results, to broadly distribute own-ership of state enterprises to the general population. Among developing nations, some are experimenting with ventures based on worker ownership. Even China's economic reformers are actively exploring the concept.[3]

Yet Louis Kelso remains a prophetic voice whose radical economic vision is still not widely understood or fully appreciated. The suggestion that some minor stake in a firm should be shared with the workers sounds too wholesome for controversy. But Kelso's larger critique of capitalism (and of Marxism and the welfare state) envisioned a revolutionary transfor-mation. Like most original thinkers, he was disparaged by contemporary authorities—in his case, economists from both left and right—because he was articulating concepts outside their own terms of reference. When Kelso died in 1993, the obituaries cited the contribution of ESOPs, but did not explain that employee trusts were only one device in his grander plan for rescuing capitalism from itself.

Kelso began warning, as early as the 1950s, that the accumulating impact of labor-saving technology was leading to a grave crisis for capital-ism if the problem of concentrated ownership was not addressed. The effi-cient new machines would keep multiplying the output from invested capital and keep shrinking the value of the labor input, thus setting up an impossible confrontation between the two. As labor sought a larger share of returns for its diminishing input, either through wage increases or the government's redistribution of incomes, the market would sooner or later rebel against these distortions—or else be destroyed by them.*

In a sense, that is what appears to be happening now. The globalization of labor can be understood as the market's response to the dilemma that Kelso described, as firms escape from home labor markets and undermine the labor position by moving jobs and production elsewhere. The political assault on the welfare state reflects the same motivation. The consequences may temporarily satisfy capital's complaint—but only temporarily. Because, as Kelso also explained, the technological displacement of wage incomes undermines the base of consumption needed to sustain the capitalist system. As wages and consumption erode, capital will eventually face the even graver crisis of surpluses—too many products chasing buyers without enough income to purchase them.

Present events are confirming his analysis. "Right now, we have a capital boom and a labor depression around the world," said Robert Ashford, a Syracuse University law professor and Kelso scholar. "That's exactly what Kelso predicted." [4]

Kelso's solution was profound: reordering the system of capital accumulation so that virtually everyone would become owners and therefore come to rely upon two streams of income—from wages and from capital assets. The process of distribution would require a generation or two of economic expansion to fully transform society, but as capital assets became more broadly owned, the political and economic benefits would be promptly felt, as a healthier balance in incomes generated greater consumer demand while also moderating wage pressures and the need for compensatory welfare. His theory was distinctive because it linked broadened capital ownership to consumption as an essential platform for sustaining aggregate demand that, he predicted, would generate faster growth in a self-reinforcing manner.

Kelso elaborated many variations on his basic mechanism—community trusts, customer trusts, even ownership trusts for poor people—that collectively would universalize the access to capital credit. The trusts' investments would be backstopped by private reinsurance agencies that, for a fee, provided various forms of hedging insurance to protect both the lenders and borrowers against catastrophic losses.

The risks of private enterprise would still be present, of course; so

---

* *Standard economics evades this dilemma by assigning the increased productivity to the worker, though it is the machine that multiplies the worker's output. Thus, when capital invests in new technology to improve a factory's efficiency, the workers' productivity—output per hours of human labor—is said to increase. This is statistically true, of course, but masks what is really happening and avoids the matter of those displaced workers who no longer have jobs and whose "productivity" has effectively fallen to zero.*

would all the possibilities for human error and folly. But these ventures would be subjected to the same kinds of rigorous market judgments—screened by banks, investors and insurers—that already govern capital formation. Workers would typically have a far stronger base of incomes and family security than they have at present. Over time, they would acquire substantial assets of their own.

Kelso's most radical proposition, however, was that the public's power of money creation, vested in central banks like the Federal Reserve, should be harnessed to the task of democratizing ownership. Without disturbing monetary policy's usual functions, the central bank could force-feed the development of universal ownership by providing low-interest credit directly to these citizen trusts—buying their loans at discount as the preferred method for increasing the money supply, rather than buying government bonds as the Federal Reserve does now.

Every year, as it enlarges the nation's money supply to meet the needs of commerce in an expanding economy, the Federal Reserve creates $30 billion to $40 billion in new money—literally "free money" that is created out of nothing more tangible than the public's shared faith in the currency and the economic system. This new money is now distributed through the private banking system, lent out by commercial banks to people and businesses at market interest rates and for private gain. If the newly created money was instead lent directly to citizen-ownership trusts, it would provide very cheap capital for a large public purpose. Economists who have grudgingly accepted Kelso's other ideas still choke on that proposition, though it is the core of his vision for achieving a synthesis of democracy and capitalism.

Controversial aspects aside, Kelso's general diagnosis has become more convincing to many, from both left and right, as the industrial revolution's deeper consequences become more visible. If technology and labor arbitrage continue to depress wage incomes and employment, with no solution in sight for decades, what will sustain the social order in the meantime? And what will sustain global aggregate demand? If the welfare state can no longer take care of distressed citizens, what will replace it?

In his larger thinking, Kelso was attempting to reconcile the critique of Marx with the creative energies of market capitalism—rejecting the crippling consequences of collectivism, but also the cramped domination of concentrated wealth. Kelso himself was a conscientious libertarian who despised big government and big business's cozy embrace of it. He imagined a future world in which the class conflicts became irrelevant and the welfare state would wither away, once everyone had the financial capacity to take care of himself. The governing artifacts created by the twentieth century's class struggles, he thought, would be replaced by a dynamic and democratic market—truly democratic because the returns of capitalism would be shared among all.

Kelso's grander vision still lies far beyond mainstream political imagination in America and other mature capitalist economies. Yet, ironically, the children of Marxism are perhaps in a better position to achieve it. Because the nations of the former Soviet empire collectivized capital ownership in the state, they all had a one-time opportunity in the 1990s to truly democratize capitalism—when each country privatized its state-owned enterprises and distributed the equity shares to the citizenry and workers. Amid the collapse of their centralized economies, they all launched efforts toward that objective.

It would be nice to report that they have fully succeeded in this, but the results to date are much more ambiguous. In most countries, personal access to credit was not the central problem since, in theory, the people already "owned" the means of production. But the mass privatizations and distributions of ownership shares were gravely compromised by the economic weaknesses of each country and the intense political conflicts, as well as by a desire to conform as swiftly as possible with the conventional assumptions of investors from the triumphant West.

The former Communist nations did, at least, create new dimensions of popular ownership and construct some tangible foundations for the owner worker of the future. In fact, Russia went further in this direction than others, at least on paper, but its enterprises still must face wrenching reforms. Overall, the state monopolies of wealth were broken up and broadly redistributed, but it is not so evident that genuine control will reside ultimately with the citizen owners. Spirited arguments continue over what kind of capitalism may eventually emerge in these countries, but there is a widespread hope it will not be "American hard-style capitalism," as one Polish editor put it.

The most poignant case is Poland—the place where workers first mobilized to free themselves from the state, where the idea of worker self-management was strongest. It was Poland's free labor movement, Solidarity, that ignited the popular revolution that swept across Eastern Europe and eventually unraveled communism. In Poland, they are still fighting over what exactly they have wrought.

On the outskirts of Warsaw, squads of strikers were guarding the iron gates of the Huta Luchini steelworks, refusing entry to the managers or any of the 3,500 workers. They patrolled amiably around the outer fences, their banner spread across the entrance. Inside, the four gray furnaces were stilled. A few days earlier the steelworkers had marched in their hard hats on the Italian Embassy downtown as a way to pressure the Italian conglomerate that had acquired the mill from the Polish government. The demonstrators left a pot of pasta on the embassy steps.

"We know how much the Italians love pasta," said the mill's Solidarity vice chairman. "So we left them a pot of pasta to let them know we don't want it. We want our own. We don't want to be in their pot."

This was in late July 1994, two years after the state-owned steel mill had been sold to Luchini. Huta Warszawa, as it was previously called, was a living remnant of Poland's peculiar economic status during the Cold War. One side of the mill was designed according to German-Italian-Swedish engineering standards and produced world-class steel for export to the free West. The other side was more crude and produced steel for Russia and Poland's own antiquated economy. The mill overall was more modern than much of Poland's heavy industry, but when Luchini took over it was near bankruptcy.

The Solidarity members did not object to foreign ownership itself or the new capital that Luchini intended to invest in modernization. The strike, among other issues, was about the terms of ownership and the fact that the workers had not yet received their stake. They had raised or borrowed some 27 billion zlotys (about $3 million under old currency values) to buy shares, and their money was deposited with a state agency. No one seemed to know what had happened to the transaction.

"The workers are feeling cheated because during the legal conflict between the government and the new owners, the workers haven't been awarded their right to buy 20 percent themselves," said Karol Szadurski, a metallurgical engineer who had been the mill's Solidarity chairman during the heady days of rebellion in 1981. "The employees would absolutely like to be co-partners with the Italian owners. They believe in this company. They've worked here a long time and know it potentially could be a wonderful, successful company."

Solidarity has lost much influence and coherence since its exhilarating origins in 1980, when the shipyard workers at Gdansk unveiled the organization and staged their world-famous sit-in strike, an act of defiance that electrified Poland and swiftly turned into a national movement. Soviet threats and martial law followed, leaders were arrested and the union forced underground again. But when the peaceable revolutions swept Eastern Europe in 1989, everyone agreed that the Solidarity uprising had been the seminal event that inspired the popular dismantlement of the Soviet Union and its satellites. Solidarity's original leader, the shipyard electrician Lech Walesa, became the first elected president of free Poland.

Yet Solidarity locals were staging protests and strikes at various large factories around the country, demanding not only wage increases but also equity shares and a role in company managements. "Capitalism with a human face" was how the *Warsaw Voice* described their agenda. The idea of workers sharing responsibility for decision-making in their own enterprises was a central principle borne aloft by the original Solidarity. The idea lingered stubbornly in public consciousness despite many adverse events.[5]

After forty years of egalitarian poverty under communism, Poles were experiencing the delights and wrenching uncertainties of capitalism. When "shock therapy" economic reforms were introduced in 1990, unemployment soared to 17 percent and real wages began a long decline. Even with a revived economy, expanding robustly by 5 to 7 percent a year, the official unemployment was still at 14 percent and inflation remained above 30 percent. Warsaw was alive with new ventures and hope, especially among younger people, but also disturbed by the recurring banking scandals and privatization deals that went awry. As the state's social benefits were being withdrawn, flamboyant zloty millionaires appeared on the scene, driving big foreign cars. Some of them were former Communist bosses who used to wear the cheap suits.[6]

The popular exhilaration gave way to confusion, resentment and ambivalence. "The problem is that five years ago it was easy—we knew that capitalism was better than socialism," said Dorota Bartzel, the young editor in chief of *Warsaw Voice,* a new American-financed newsweekly. "Now we know that capitalism is not as good as everyone thought. But this is all we know. People fear the foreign capitalists will introduce foreign ways. They only know privatization as a slogan, but they don't really know what it is. People will not allow the primitive capitalism, the American hard-style capitalism. I don't think so. Poles are very proud, even if they are poor."

An American bank executive based in Warsaw described the new ambivalence: "Half of the government is convinced that there's a lot of foreign money out there waiting to buy Poland and the other half is scared that they're right."

"What is happening here, under the skin, is different from what the international financial community would like," said Kris Ludwiniak, a forty-six-year-old lawyer and cable TV entrepreneur. "People are learning fast. They read about all the scandals and they think, maybe we don't want everybody's capital. Maybe the economy won't be as good, but at least it will be ours. People don't intend to become tenants in their own country."

Ludwiniak had emigrated to America twenty years before, then returned to participate in Poland's economic rebirth. In the States, he had met Louis Kelso and became imbued with the idea of employee ownership as the centerpiece for transformation. Back in Warsaw, Ludwiniak ran his small telecommunications importing firm and campaigned with others to advance a new basis for capitalism. In 1990, he helped persuade Louis Kelso to visit Poland, where he spoke to educational meetings for citizens, including the steelworkers from Huta Luchini.

"Poland was made for employee ownership," Ludwiniak insisted, "because we had a system of self-management already in place [under the Communist regime] and people were experienced at running their own companies, with worker councils and management teams. They felt confident and responsible. The whole Solidarity movement grew out of this experience, not just mill workers but the technicians and managers."

Their aspirations collided with financial realities and politics. Poland was an industrial nation without wealth (per capita income was under $2,000, one third of Portugal's, one seventh of Spain's). Like the other post-Communist economies, it desperately needed the infusion of foreign capital to modernize, but outside capital would not come until Poland had undergone harsh reforms—westernizing the government's macroeconomic policies to satisfy lending standards in the global financial market and restructuring more than 8,000 state-owned companies into freestanding and viable private enterprises. Every nation in Eastern Europe, including Russia, faced these twin imperatives and dealt with them in different ways, with vastly different outcomes.

Poland's reformers elected to undergo the cold bath first—macroeconomic reforms imposed in swift, severe terms. Counseled by foreign advisors like Harvard economist Jeffrey Sachs, the new government slashed state budgets and subsidies, decontrolled prices and wages and quickly dismantled the state's centralized control in order to establish the zloty as a reliable currency. Foreign creditors were pleased and agreed to renegotiate Poland's swollen debt burdens, opening the way for new lending and investing.

The advisors trumpeted the success of their "shock therapy" approach and Sachs himself disparaged the popular desires for employee ownership as a new version of "Bolshevism." If workers owned the factories, he warned, they would surely vote to raise their own pay and save everyone's job, when the restructuring demanded the opposite of firms.[7]

Whether "shock therapy" was wise or foolishly arrogant, the political consequences were severe: a popular backlash against the neoliberal economic reforms imported from the West. By 1993, Polish voters had rejected the market reformers and were electing former Communists (reborn as socialists) to parliament, with a new prime minister from the Polish Peasants Party, the most conservative constituency, based in the countryside where farmers and small holders had suffered dramatically from reform. In 1995, President Walesa himself was defeated for reelection, replaced by a former Communist leader who promised to continue economic integration, but more pragmatically.

The larger political consequence of "shock therapy" was that enterprise reform itself was derailed. The swift and brutal economic shifts deepened popular pain and suspicions and fueled a political reluctance to proceed quickly with the privatization of the large state firms. Poland, once the pioneer, fell behind its neighbors in achieving this imperative. Legislation for mass privatization was debated and defeated repeatedly, then finally enacted, then amended and stalled further. It was not until November 1995 that the first significant distribution of share vouchers was completed, covering some 440 state firms.

Meanwhile, the smaller Czech Republic had promptly offered equity vouchers to all of its 8.5 million citizens, entitling them (for a fee of about $35) to acquire shares in privatized companies. Approximately 80 percent of the population participated. Most chose to invest their stake in the scores of semiprivate mutual funds created to hold the actual ownership of some 1,500 state companies. This was not genuine equity ownership of the companies, to be sure, but it did broadly redistribute capital assets virtually overnight.[8]

In Russia, the reformers were anxious to quickly strip the state of its economic assets, fearful that a coup or counterrevolution might seize power and restore the status quo ante. To move fast, they cut a deal with the company managers and agreed to privatize 16,000 firms with 22 million employees, assigning a very large ownership stake to the insiders. Employees and managers held a majority stake averaging 53 percent in these companies, according to Professor Blasi of Rutgers, a democratization of capital unparalleled anywhere else in the world but also compromised by scandal and political favoritism.

The standard view in the Western press (and among many former Soviet subjects) was that the Russian accomplishment was fake. The old Soviet nomenklatura, the managerial class, simply wound up owning everything, it was said. Professor Blasi disagreed. His on-the-ground survey of hundreds of firms in forty-four of Russia's eighty-nine administrative regions convinced him that the distribution of ownership was imperfect, but real and significant.

Russia's private sector, for instance, was now larger than Italy's, as a percentage of the total economy. Russian managers did retain full control, but the 10 percent of equity they acquired was roughly comparable to what America's top managers owned in their companies. Russia's new owner workers, it was true, were denied any real voice in managing their companies, but, in these terms, they were not worse off than American workers or, for that matter, most American stockholders.[9]

The Russian experiment still faced hard times, however, since a large portion of these firms were sure to fail, perhaps a quarter of them by Blasi's estimate. To become viable, the others must sooner or later undergo dramatic restructuring—plant closings, massive layoffs and new foreign investors. All these factors were certain to provoke great controversy and also shrink the workers' stake considerably. With ex-Communists regaining political positions, the ownership of capital would doubtless become more concentrated. No one could say with certainty what these different strategies would produce in the long run. As Blasi pointed out, Russia privatized firms first and put off the cold bath of structural reform until later—roughly the reverse of Poland's approach.

In Poland, despite the government's hesitation, some Poles did succeed in establishing a substantial beachhead for their original idea: workers owning and influencing their own economic destinies. Karol Szadurski, Ludwiniak and others organized the Unia Wlasności Pracowniczej, an association of employee-ownership advocates who managed to win modest legislation authorizing at least limited reform. About a thousand companies took advantage of the law and successfully converted to genuine worker ownership—mainly small and medium-sized firms ranging from thirty to three thousand employees. Another thousand or so companies were born as private spin-offs from larger state enterprises, and these also were said to have majority ownership vested in employees.

These companies became a living model for the idea—and proof that economic experts from the West were perhaps wrong about the Polish workers. As Szadurski explained, the concept of self-responsible employees had been the unifying idea between intelligentsia and workers during the rise of Solidarity, but their mutual understanding was undermined by the newly influential presence of capitalist orthodoxy.

"The political elite that grew out of the Solidarity movement divided into two opposing camps," said Szadurski, now director general of the owner workers association. "One camp was committed to the quintessential Solidarity idea of self-management and it pushed for the legislation. The second camp, which took control of government and followed Jeffrey Sachs, was strongly opposed to employee ownership and opted for the classical view of capitalism. They had this nineteenth-century view of paternalistic owners and employees as employees, in other words, a continuation of class warfare."

Though they were outgunned politically, the advocates of worker ownership had strong popular support. They saw Louis Kelso's model as a good fit with their own aspirations, but they lacked experience and the financial wherewithal to make it universally plausible. "What we did know is that workers did not identify with their place of work," Szadurski said. "They were alienated in the classic Marxist sense. I am a son of the merchant class myself—my father owned a wholesale company—and so I know from my own experience that ownership is a sacred element. It is the way to feel close to your work."

The legislation was disappointing, but it opened the door partway: employees could lease-purchase their state-owned companies, and after five years of payments to the government, the worker shareholders would get full title. This resembled the employee trusts designed by Kelso, but an essential element was missing: access to new credit. As the companies were undergoing their most difficult changes, banks were reluctant to make loans since the owner workers did not hold title to the company assets and thus had no collateral to mortgage. The credit problem discouraged new investment and made it much harder for the companies to expand.

Nevertheless, the first wave of a thousand employee-owned companies generally flourished, and contrary to the expectations of Sachs and others, the workers did not engage in self-indulgent business decisions. In fact, the first hard decision that workers made at most companies was to cut the jobs drastically and fire many of their colleagues. "As a rule, the companies drastically reduced the level of employment, affecting 30 to 50 percent of the total employees," a study by the Polish Academy of Sciences reported. "This indicates both the flexibility of the company management and its pragmatism, not an ideological defense of the employees at all costs."

Pay increases, the academy scholars concluded, were done "fairly rationally" and only following the lay-offs and when real profits appeared. In some firms, individual earnings rose because, for the first time, the owner workers were receiving modest dividends from the company profits—a small initial taste of capital ownership. They expected their incomes to expand further once the lease-purchase debts were paid off and they became fully certified owners. "The concepts of 'we' and 'they' have changed," the academy report added. "Now 'we' is the entire personnel with 'our' management. 'They,' on the other hand, are external factors: the ministry, the government. . . . It is difficult not to notice that social relations appear much better than in state companies. The strike is, practically speaking, not a tool of regulating conflict." [10]

"We had a chance for the future and we took it," said Wlodzimierz Juraszek, slender and harried-looking, the thirty-seven-year-old director of Kragum, a company with 360 employees in Cracow that manufactured rubber products, from tennis balls to hot water bottles. Like the rest of Poland, Kragum was both struggling and, in its own terms, succeeding. Its shabbily appointed offices and darkened hallways reflected the spare circumstances. A plaque with the blue Polish eagle—symbol of the state—still hung on the wall by the front entrance.

Kragum was modestly profitable and gradually consolidating its operations more efficiently, but a shadow of its former self. When the factory was booming in socialist times, there were 1,700 employees, and the downsizing had been harrowing. "If I was ten years older, I would not be able to take it," Juraszek said, "because, as you can see, 360 owners is 360 troubles."

In Cracow, when I visited several of the pioneer firms like Kragum where workers were the principal shareholders, the optimistic report by the Academy of Sciences was more or less confirmed. But the supple reality of their endeavors was, of course, more complicated and ambiguous. No one was bubbling with visions of becoming rich capitalists. Poles were well beyond such fantasies. The firms were inching ahead, not leaping, and still confronted large uncertainties. But the employees and managers expressed the notion that they had accomplished something for themselves and, perhaps by example, for the rest of Poland.

"At the beginning of the transformation, it was like magical thinking —everything will be better," Juraszek said. "Now they know nothing amazing will happen. They know they have to produce by their own hands. There's not any magic."

Kragum was a typical state enterprise that, in addition to work and wages, had provided elaborate social benefits to its employees—assistance with housing, education and health, even with vacations. When it converted to private status in 1992, all that disappeared. "We were scared of losing our jobs and so we decided to make the firm ours and not to follow the usual rules," Juraszek explained. "We lost the houses for workers, the cafe, the health clinic—we gave them up."

Then came the hard part: losing lots of workers. At that point, Kragum's workforce had already fallen to seven hundred people, but it would have to be cut again—roughly in half. "It was a little painful for everyone," he said. "If they couldn't work any more, they felt like they were cheated. Some people started complaining to the general control office and tried to make this out as a dirty business, that we were destroying their beautiful factory."

Foremen and other middle managers, after consultations with the rank and file, had to choose who stayed and who went. "If you asked each one who was the best worker, they say: I am," Juraszek recalled. "But then they have to decide. It wasn't easy. But, of course, they didn't want to choose bad people, like the drinkers, because they would have to work with them."

At Malopolska Spólka Handlowa, a building supply company with 280 employees, the leading shareholder was an assistant office manager at one of the firm's supply yards. "I'm the biggest stockholder—I've got one hundred shares," said Elizabeth Miernczek, a middle-aged woman in tank top and slacks. "I've worked here fifteen years and I believe in the company. I have to believe in something. Besides, I like to gamble. It's a big risk, but Poland is developing now, and in the future, we can make real money."

Did she expect to become wealthy? "Not me," she said. "Maybe my kids." She puffed energetically on a cigarette. Other workers gathered around her in the office and seemed amused by her forwardness, not quite sure of her ebullient optimism. "In the Communist time, we had better morale because it was easier then," she said. "We were more relaxed because the government gave us help and there was no competition. Now we have big competition and we have to be more aggressive. Actually, we are working smarter. We have to."

One of the company's senior managers, Bógdan Wojtowicz, teased Miernczek about her important status. "You have real power," he said. "You can change the managers."

She nodded, with a knowing attitude that made everyone in the office laugh. "Yes, that's true," Miernczek said. "We can call a meeting of shareholders if ten of us demand one and decide to change things."

The MSH workers did vote each year, by secret ballot, on whether to retain the top managers and their policies. They also groused and criticized freely. The managers all claimed to regard this as helpful. The atmosphere, in any case, seemed congenial and open. The status distinctions between bosses and workers did not disappear, but became less freighted when the workers were also owners. "We are like the precursors—the pioneers," Wojtowicz said. "We went our own way, so other firms will follow our example."

At Kragum, Wlodzimierz Juraszek had expressed the same sort of tempered optimism. "Personally, I think the people in Poland are hungry for this kind of success," he said. "They will do a lot to make it happen, but you have to show them what is possible. Nothing kills action like hopelessness."

Back in Warsaw, the band of employee-ownership advocates still nursed the hope that as Poland moved forward with more privatizations, the success of these existing firms would persuade the government to grant a larger role to owner workers. The main problem, of course, was that workers could not afford to buy the larger state companies beyond, perhaps, the 15 or 20 percent stake reserved for them. Those enterprises needed new capital from abroad if they were going to survive. One solution was radical credit reform along the lines suggested by Kelso, but that seemed most unlikely, given that Poland was also trying to convince foreign capital that it was following a straight-and-narrow road to orthodox capitalism.

Marek Kosak, director general of the Polish Agency for Regional Development, summarized the dilemma: "It is still very important for most Poles to feel they have some control of the enterprise. But people would also like to live better. If living better means giving up the idea of control, they will go for it."

Kosak noted that an international paper company had acquired a Polish pulp mill in which employees held 20 percent ownership. "The company offered them more than four times the share price for their stock and they took it," he said. "Overnight they became very rich people, able to acquire American cars and TVs and refrigerators."

The mass distribution of equity vouchers was better than nothing, but it contained the same conflict between present poverty and future ambitions: citizens might like the idea of becoming owners, but scarcity compelled many to quickly resell their shares for ready income. The PKO state bank had one window that dispensed equity vouchers to eligible citizens and another window nearby that bought them back at twice the price. Rather quickly, the voucher approach allowed a reconcentration of wealth —the actual equity accumulated by the investment funds or resold to wealthy speculators and foreign investors.

"Vouchers are not direct ownership of the means of production," Szadurski complained. "It leads to a very diluted, speculative kind of ownership that weakens the bonds of workers. What is important for Poland is to create the owner—to create the middle class out of nowhere. Vouchers are not going to do this. It will be a speculative game and the capital will eventually concentrate in a few hands. In Western societies, the middle class was built over a very long time and it was a foundation for democracy. In Communist countries, this must happen in a very few years. If it doesn't happen quickly, we won't get to democracy. We will wind up with a kind of nineteenth-century capitalism—and with a socialist face."

The Polish advocates believed this had already occurred in countries like the Czech Republic, where the vouchers had been universally distributed: much of the ownership wound up concentrated in investment funds that were closely associated with state-owned banks, so the government might still retain effective control. "From my perspective, privatization by vouchers is a fraud," Ludwiniak said. "For political reasons, it creates a system that says, look, you are owners now. But it's just a piece of paper. It's like communism—you are all owners—but it doesn't mean anything."

Poland seemed headed down the same path, but Poles were a stubborn and independent-minded people. They might yet impose social limits on how much concentration of wealth they were willing to abide. "Every government, if it wants to survive, must confront this question," said Marek Kosak. "People won't tolerate an extreme level of inequality. What has been acceptable in the United States for many years for ideological reasons is not necessarily acceptable in Poland."

Like many others in and out of government, Kosak still hoped for a middle road—a different version of capitalism. "People used to think of America as paradise," he said, "but I'm not tempted by the American paradise. I visited Washington, D.C., a few years ago and I remember the ten or fifteen minutes I spent in the inner city of Washington. It was a very unpleasant feeling."

In the shadow of the old order, a small, spirited group of Americans campaigned audaciously to construct a new order—the U.S. economy reorganized around Louis Kelso's revolutionary principle of universal capital ownership. The revolution, these ambitious activists decided, ought to begin right in the nation's capital—Washington, D.C.—a city mired in financial insolvency, with accelerating social and economic deterioration, with extremes of wealth and poverty as stark as any found in America. Under congressional oversight, the District of Columbia could become the laboratory, they thought, the place where Kelso's ideas were actually applied. If the concept worked for D.C., every city and region in America would want to emulate it.

"I'm not trying to reinvent capitalism, I'm trying to obliterate it," said Norman G. Kurland, a Washington lawyer and business consultant who has tirelessly shopped Kelso's ideas among Washington politicians for three decades. "To me, capitalism has always meant exploitation, greed, domination, concentrated power. The name itself was invented to describe those qualities. What we're talking about is a way of putting capitalism behind us—to create a material foundation for people so they can develop spiritually and intellectually, so we can realize economic and social justice in the age of the robot."

Such talk, of course, sounded hopelessly grandiose to most players in the political establishment and far too marginal to threaten the old order. Washington politics preoccupied itself with smaller ideas—how to shrink the welfare state and balance the federal budget, how to keep the defense industry going with new contracts now that the Cold War was over, how to promote more foreign trade and sales for the multinational corporations.

Any political figure who strayed from these conventional concerns was sure to be labeled eccentric or worse. People like Norm Kurland, with zealous plans for economic justice, were often kept at a polite distance.

The power of Louis Kelso's vision, however, has attracted an odd assortment of converts—idealists from right and left and from across the usual racial and religious divides, people who believed Kelso's thinking held the key for renewing American society. Some of them joined with Kurland and his Center for Economic and Social Justice to promote a daring experiment: Congress should designate the District of Columbia a "super empowerment zone" that would launch new enterprises and industries (and privatize some governmental functions) through Kelso's mechanism of citizen and worker ownership trusts. New economic development would be attracted to D.C., not by tax subsidies or relaxed laws, but because low-interest capital credit would be available to the community trusts—cheap credit provided through the Federal Reserve's discount lending.

If that proposal sounded improbable, their idea for an initial demonstration project seemed even more far-fetched: building a productive prison, a futuristic new prison to house the thousands of young black men who circulated regularly between D.C.'s mean streets and incarceration for drug-peddling or violent crimes. Only, instead of a warehouse for idle humanity, this new prison would produce real value—a beehive of income-generating economic activities, from renewable energy production to allied assembly work. Such a place would reduce costs for government and give genuine work experience to the inmates—and also yield real returns for the owners.

Only, in this design, the owners would not be the government but individual citizens and workers—the 300,000 voters in the District of Columbia, plus the guards and managers who ran the prison, plus even the prisoners themselves. They would all be awarded shares, but their equity would be held by a community trust that borrows the capital—$1.5 billion —to build the prison. The originating loans would come from the private commercial banks in D.C., but they would be authorized to resell the loans to the Federal Reserve at a small fractional discount.

Overall, the total interest cost on this borrowing would be very low, about 3 percent, enough to cover normal profit margins for the private banks and the overhead costs at the central bank. The debt would be paid back by the profits generated by the prison industries and by the government's usual payments for incarceration (now about $30,000 a year per inmate). The capital loan would be collateralized by the new income-producing asset that it builds, in this case the prison itself. When the debt was eventually retired, the citizens and workers would hold clear title to their shares, receiving dividends themselves.

Despite its other innovative features, the real key to making such an unusual enterprise plausible was the low-interest financing provided through the Federal Reserve. The venture would be instantly rejected by financial markets as too risky, and even if private investors decided it was viable, they would still demand an interest rate on the borrowed capital that was at least three or four times greater. Very low interest costs meant the enterprise could pay back the capital loan faster or with a lower rate of profitability than the marketplace would normally require. This favorable financing arrangement could be justified only if it served a larger public purpose—democratizing capital ownership.

This idea was dubbed the "New Birth Transformation Corporation," the name provided by an ex-convict named Joseph Coleman, who during his many years in prison had found Jesus and dreamt of redemption for himself and D.C.'s impoverished black community. A prison chaplain helped him learn to read. When he got out, Coleman started a small self-help enterprise for ex-convicts—the New Birth Project, which did home repair and other jobs—and he was now among the visionaries Kurland had brought together. "Once you come out from the dead, into a brand-new life, a brand-new mind," Coleman explained, "you want to start to do something successful in your life, create something in society, and that's what it is—a new birth."

I have focused on the outlines of the "New Birth" venture not because I think Washington politicians are likely to adopt the project or because I am even sure that it will work, but because it offers a succinct illustration of the expansive new thinking that is possible—if people could free themselves of the inherited boundaries. In political terms, Kelso's thinking discards the conventional framework for thinking about public and private obligations and escapes the usual arguments between left and right.

Could one imagine a prison owned by ordinary citizens? Or a city where every adult became a stockholder in profitable enterprises? A community that undertook the shared risks of introducing promising new technologies? A community that provided real opportunities for renewal to its most despised and troubled citizens? Aside from the Green Bay Packers and various forms of producer or consumer cooperatives, community ownership of enterprise was nearly nonexistent in the United States. The usual examples involved public utilities operated by city or state governments, but the community ownership that Kelso had in mind was utterly different. The originality of Kelso's vision is reflected in the fact that one could not easily assign ideological labels of left or right to these propositions since they borrowed from both.

What Kelso sought, in essence, was a grand synthesis in which the market and society would make peace with one another. Instead of warring destructively for domination, market and government would agree to function on terms that mutually reinforced human satisfaction and a genuine democracy. This was only a vision, of course, utterly unrealized in any advanced industrial societies. But it did offer people a new way to think about the future—a vista beyond the class warfare decreed by Marx and by orthodox capitalism.

Joe Coleman's fellow advocates included conservative Republican businessmen, Catholic priests and social activists, a retired architect and university planner, a veteran civil rights leader who had marched with King. The Reverend Walter E. Fauntroy formerly served as the elected D.C. delegate in Congress and once chaired the Congressional Black Caucus; his congregation, New Bethel Baptist Church, was in the bleak heart of Washington's inner city. Norm Kurland was Jewish and had started out on the political left, as a liberal-labor activist in the anti-poverty and civil rights movements.

Kurland's frustrating experiences during the 1960s convinced him that standard liberal reforms, usually based on income redistribution, would never succeed in overcoming the gross economic inequalities of American life, but that Kelso's more fundamental critique of concentrated wealth offered a genuine opening. During the 1970s, Kurland and Kelso jointly lobbied Congress for a series of business tax incentives for ESOP trusts, and these measures have accelerated the spread of employee ownership.

The ESOP tax breaks were enacted mainly because they had a powerful sponsor, Senator Russell Long of Louisiana, a conservative Democrat who chaired the Senate Finance Committee. He was also the son of Huey Long, the notorious "Share the Wealth" populist of the 1930s who had called for the massive redistribution of assets. Russell Long thought his father had attacked the right problem—the concentration of wealth—but that Kelso offered a more plausible solution.

Kurland found, during his years of lobbying for employee ownership, that most people on the left, including organized labor, were indifferent or hostile to the idea. The prospect of generating more capitalists did not fit neatly with an ideology promoting collective action by workers or a larger presence for the state. Union leaders would ask skeptically: How can workers be mobilized to confront the company in collective bargaining if they are owners themselves? Labor was suspicious that Kelso's scheme would be used by employers to undercut pension rights, Social Security and other hard-won gains for workers (and some business interests did indeed have that objective).

Labor's doubts largely dissipated during the last two decades, however, as unions experienced the withering losses in jobs, wages and bargaining power. Globalization had shifted the battle lines in favor of capital and some labor leaders began rethinking the adversarial assumptions. The United Steelworkers became a pioneer in promoting worker ownership to save troubled steel mills and has won union representation on some company boards. The machinists union, pilots association and others joined to become the majority shareholders of United Airlines.

While employee ownership was expanding slowly but steadily in the American economy, the "New Birth" prison was intended to give provocative visibility to the concept: a working model for Kelso's ideas, infused with advanced technologies that private commerce was not ready to embrace and directed at severe public problems. The federal penitentiary in Lorton, Virginia, where inmates from D.C. were housed, was a scandal itself and scheduled to be replaced. Lorton was inhumanely overcrowded, riddled by drug trafficking, with an extraordinary recidivism rate of 70 percent, with less than one tenth of its seven thousand inmates actually employed in productive work. Fauntroy, Coleman and the others found an ideal site for their model prison beside the Potomac River and near the district's waste-treatment plant, a facility also in need of expansion and renewal.

The "New Birth" prison was conceptualized as a huge geodesic dome, covering 160 acres, that would house both the prison quarters and an array of productive enterprises. The conception came from Dean Price, retired planner at Georgetown University, inspired by the visionary Buckminster Fuller. Price had worked two decades at Georgetown implementing new technologies like solar energy and his scheme incorporated many leading-edge ideas that science has developed but society has not yet implemented.

The dome's huge ribbed surface would collect solar power, while other facilities down below converted sewage and other biomass waste into electric power, generating 225 megawatts a day for sale to the commercial power grid. In addition, the huge space could house related industrial production—assembly work for advanced hardware like fuel cells or alternative-fuel vehicles—as well as commercial gardening and fish farming. The model prison could earn additional millions in revenue by housing several thousand inmates from other jurisdictions, cities and states willing to pay to place their convicts in an ideal setting for rehabilitation.

Prisoners would still be prisoners, but they would also have the chance for genuine work and training. According to Kurland's social blueprint, inmates would receive a minor portion of the income derived from their work, but most of the money would be distributed in socially useful ways: as restitution for crime victims, as income support for their families, as repayment to government for the cost of their incarceration.

But were any of these ideas really feasible? Could a "New Birth" prison actually work? No one, including the sponsors, could say with certainty, not without elaborate studies of design and cost. But these technologies, Price said, have all been developed by research centers like NASA or the Jet Propulsion Laboratory and were already functioning successfully on a pilot scale. The challenge, he explained, was to put them into commercial-scale application. The greater challenge, he thought, was how to integrate the technological possibilities in a new, holistic fashion—a system that synthesized economics and social purpose, the marketplace with democratic goals.

The architect produced a color sketch of the prison that looked as if a huge white spaceship had landed alongside the Potomac. A curled silver ornament was atop the dome. "It's the symbol of the African mother," Price explained, "the mother of us all." The project, the Reverend Fauntroy explained, was really a fusion of three American thinkers—Martin Luther King Jr., Buckminster Fuller and Louis O. Kelso—each of whom, in his own way, imagined a more humane future.

○

The future requires a large imagination if people expect to shape their own destinies. Societies will have to risk failure by undertaking adventurous experiments if they are to avoid replaying the stale past. The Kelso analysis offers one important realm (though not the only one) for experimentation —a way to reengineer the basic mechanics of capitalism, if not to obliterate capitalism as Kurland hopes, at least to civilize its social consequences. Rhetoric aside, political leaders in most industrial nations are not much inclined to bold gambles; they feel embattled by events and insecure about their own power. Political imagination will have to arise from different quarters—the outsiders who are free to believe in new ideas.

If it is theoretically possible for citizens to own stock shares in a public prison, then it is certainly plausible that the same financing principles can be applied to the conventional forms of industrial expansion, fostering the spread of ownership and gradually rearranging the distribution of wealth. This would not achieve the perfect economic equality envisioned by Marx's collectivization. To paraphrase the Bible, the rich will be with us always. But universalizing access to capital ownership would greatly strengthen the economic foundations for society and for individual self-realization.

In the best of circumstances, it would take a generation or longer for every family to accumulate a significant nest egg of capital assets, enough to provide a parallel source of meaningful income. Still, those with modest wage incomes or none would experience immediate and substantial benefit. To give a rough idea of the dimensions, U.S. business investment in new plant and equipment expands each year by about $600 billion—new capital assets that total nearly $2,500 per capita.[11] If a substantial portion of that growth was financed through citizen or worker trusts, broadly distributing the ultimate ownership of those assets, families could gradually build a portfolio from different sources, including their own workplaces. This would enhance economic security for them, but also multiply life's choices for their children.

Home ownership in America was gradually broadened in a similar fashion mainly because reforms in the credit system made it easier for people of modest incomes to borrow through home mortgages. In 1940, fewer than 45 percent of American families owned their own homes. By 1980, thanks to the use of debt, home ownership had been achieved by 65 percent of all families. The other historic precedent, often cited by Kelso and his followers, was the government's massive distribution of free land during the second half of the nineteenth century—Lincoln's Homestead Act, which awarded the title to millions of western acres to new settlers who agreed in exchange to make the land productive. In the modern economy, industrial capital has replaced land as the income-producing asset everyone ought to own.

If governments were to make this a central priority, they would ask this question of every proposal for public spending or subsidy: What does it do to spread the wealth? Faced with this public requirement, firms might be prompted to innovate on Kelso's idea and find new ways to ensure that title to the company's newly created assets was broadly shared with workers or citizens in the communities. The Kelso standard, in other words, could replace the outmoded New Deal assumption that public assistance to almost any business enterprise is bound to benefit the general public indirectly. The age of globalized corporations has already destroyed that assumption. Democratizing ownership provides a new answer to the old political question: Who benefits? The owners or the workers, the company or the nation?

The most controversial element, however, is the use of central bank financing to provide the low-cost capital—a proposition sure to be indignantly opposed by the Federal Reserve and all its influential constituencies in finance. The idea of a central bank purchasing the loans of private commerce, instead of simply buying government bonds, may sound unorthodox, but it is actually the method the Federal Reserve originally used to manage the nation's money supply, and the practice is still employed among European central banks.

There is nothing inherently risky in the approach itself. Bankers would still have to exercise the lender's judgments on the soundness of the ventures, just as they do now, and sometimes they would be wrong. The Federal Reserve would still have to manage the money supply's growth to avoid inflation or economic contraction, just as it does now, and sometimes the Fed would make mistakes, too. In fact, if the Federal Reserve held more business loans in its own portfolio, it might develop a more sober respect for the real economy of production as opposed to its present preoccupation with the financial markets.*

The element that is genuinely new and radical is Kelso's presumption that the central bank's power to create new money represents a public asset that ought to be shared with all—instead of allowing the commercial banking system to distribute this public good through its own private lending and to profit from it. While this seems an obscure theoretical question, knowledge of the potential public benefit inherent in the central bank's money-creation power is beginning to spread in the society, as more people grasp the financial possibilities of applying this power to democratic purposes. Despite influential opposition the radical thought is ripening as a subject for wide-ranging public debate and experiment.†

---

* *The mechanics of monetary policy and credit are too complex for a fuller description here. The operating details and underlying principles are available in my book* Secrets of the Temple *(New York: Simon & Schuster, 1987); see especially Chapter 8, "Democratic Money," which relates the broad political context for Louis Kelso's ideas.*

† *Ken Bohnsack, a small businessman in Freeport, Illinois, has launched the Sovereignty campaign to use Federal Reserve low-interest lending to finance public works projects at city and state levels. Similarly, financier Alan F. Kay and futurist Hazel Henderson have proposed that Fed financing could be responsibly applied to paying down the federal debt in small, steady increments.*

Bankers, not surprisingly, will argue against this proposition. They will claim that it amounts to credit allocation by government or opens the door to political manipulations of monetary policy. But the present system already allocates access to capital credit—mainly to those who already own lots of capital, away from those who have little or none. Nor is the financial system exactly free of corruption and the distortions arising from political influences. Nor is the central bank as aloof from the influence of special interests as it pretends. In any case, one may observe that in terms of fiscal soundness, not to mention equity, the old order is not working very well itself.

The real question is: Can democracy be trusted to act responsibly in this manner? Or must society be resigned to accept whatever the invisible hand delivers as economic justice? Louis Kelso, a wealthy investment banker, believed fervently in the market system of capitalism, but he thought he had located its central flaw, the reason it generated disastrous social consequences, deep political conflict and the economic imbalances that ultimately threatened the system itself. Kelso believed in markets, but he also believed in people.

The question does rest, finally, on what one thinks about human capabilities—whether one believes that societies can alter the economic systems that frame human behavior and that people have the capacity to adjust intelligently to new circumstances, new possibilities. Many, of course, do not believe in this human potential. Their visceral reaction to the idea of universalizing the wealth is that most of their fellow mortals wouldn't be able to handle it.

Poor people would rush out and sell their shares for quick cash, just as impoverished citizens in Eastern Europe have sold their equity vouchers. The security of wealth would make people lazy or greedy, or perhaps both. Wealth that was not directly derived from human toil and savings would encourage people to indulge in wasteful conspicuous consumption or else turn them into miserly misanthropes, nervously counting their money and craving more.

In the fullness of human variety, all of these personal responses to owning wealth are, indeed, sure to occur. We know this with certainty because these are some of the behavioral traits already visible among people who own great wealth. Some of them are foolish and arrogant, some are malevolent and grasping. Yet it is likewise true that some rich people are modest and wise, some are creative and generous, some even saintly. Wealth by itself does not determine human character, nor does the fact of owning wealth exempt one from the human condition.

The illusions surrounding money are so powerful and enticing, it is difficult to escape from them, especially if one has little and needs more. Accumulation has become a totem of spiritual blessing, especially in wealthy secular nations, and many people still implicitly believe in the old

Calvinist fallacy that if one becomes rich, God must have wanted it that way. Owning wealth does allow more choices in life, a more pleasant material existence than being poor, but in the end rich people die, too.

Three generations ago John Maynard Keynes prophesied that only when humanity finally escapes the ancient fears of scarcity and puts the economic problem behind it will people at last be free to discover what it truly means to be human. "For the first time since his creation," Keynes wrote, "man will be faced with his real, his permanent problem—how to use his freedom from pressing economic cares, how to occupy his leisure, which science and compound interest have won for him, to live wisely and agreeably and well."

Keynes was a profound optimist who believed that the day of general abundance was approaching faster than people imagined. He was also a realist who warned that, once freed of their economic preoccupations, people would face a profound reckoning with self-discovery. Who am I? What is my life for? If people are no longer bound to endless toil, what is their real work and purpose here on earth? If survival and accumulation are no longer the challenge, where does one find meaning and pleasure? As wealthy people can attest, these are the hardest questions.[12]

In the spirit of Keynes's optimism, I believe most people would learn to cope with this new condition and that the wealth problem, once resolved, opens new vistas for human development beyond any that societies have yet imagined. If the class struggle can be disarmed, if domination and dependency lose their relevance, human conflict and folly will certainly not disappear from the earth. But people generally will have more space in which to imagine their own individual possibilities and to pursue them, more freedom to build enduring social relations.

In time, perhaps over many generations, people may learn to become social beings on a larger scale, discarding some of the old barbarisms and moving modern societies a step closer to what may rightly be called civilization. At least, people will have a new material confidence that allows them to experience the world's wondrous variety and enjoy their place in it. There is a lot to see and understand in the world, many strange connections to explore. If this thought sounds too wishful, it describes approximately the actual history of how societies and peoples have gradually evolved and expanded social consciousness in the past. Everyone started in a small village somewhere, fearing the unknown others, confined by tribal taboos. Everyone has now—or might have—the chance to become an inquisitive citizen of the world.

The great unanswered question is whether an economy in which almost everyone was an owner might also eventually alter the irresponsible behavior engendered by capitalism itself. The capitalist process, by its nature, encourages infantile responses from every quarter, as people are led to maximize self-interest and evade responsibility for the collateral consequences of their activities, the damage to other people or society or the natural environment. Even if people understand this dilemma, it is very difficult for them to escape from it without suffering immediate disadvantage in the market competition.

The atomizing nature of the marketplace itself thus separates people from responsibility for their own actions, allows them—or even requires them—to detach themselves from the whole. Workers are oblivious to the well-being of their own enterprise when they impose impossible demands on it, but the same narrow-mindedness is, of course, common among managers and disinterested investors, who pursue personal returns regardless of larger consequences. It is for this reason that capitalism remains immature as a social system, unable to get beyond its old destructive habits or to make permanent peace with the society in which it functions.

But would owner workers prove to be any more responsible as capitalists than the absentee owners? Perhaps. The question is unanswered and there is no way ever to know, so long as the present system assigns its divisive roles. However, what is clear, at a minimum, is that universalizing ownership would connect people more directly to the consequences of their own economic activities. In time, people might learn how to weigh the trade-offs between their social values as citizens and personal gain as owners with more responsibility than the present system does. To illustrate the point crudely, factory owners are less likely to dump their toxic wastes in the river if they have to drink the water. Absentee investors wish to maximize the return on their capital assets, but a community of investors also has to defend the well-being of where they live.

This question puts a premium on encouraging the spread of owners who have proximity to their capital assets—that is, the employees in a company or citizens who live in the same community who, as shareholders, will have a stronger incentive to impose social accountability on the enterprises. They would be motivated by the usual desires for economic gain and face the same hardheaded business decisions, but they would also be connected to the countervailing influences of society. Self-interest might converge with broader moral values; at least, the social dilemmas that capitalism typically evades would be brought home to the capitalists.

New laws might grant favored status to "responsible owners"—the employee or community stakeholders who are closely connected to their holdings and willing to serve as active stewards of enterprise. But then government would also have to establish genuine rights for all shareholders, the ability to exercise a real voice in management priorities and decisions. Stockholders are, in a sense, the most infantilized participants in capitalism since, unless they are wealthy and dominant players, their connection to the income-producing asset is a disinterested paper transaction, easily discarded, utterly detached from any real responsibilities of ownership.[13]

In theory, employee ownership trusts will enhance the accountability of owners, but this political dimension has been widely neglected in the spread of ESOPs. Many workers have wound up only as passive owners, as impotent as the regular stockholders. The idea of self-management, whether it is in Poland or America or Russia, requires meaningful legal rights for shareholding—voting on management and policy ratification and formal channels for criticism and representation. But ownership also requires taking responsibility for the assets. Imagine a corporate board with labor and community directors alongside the CEOs and financiers, people who themselves would be accountable to the stakeholders they represent.

Ironically, Louis Kelso's idea of broadened ownership holds greater promise for the new entrants in global capitalism—an opportunity at least for newly industrializing nations to avoid the maldistribution of wealth and class conflicts that are so deeply embedded in the advanced economies. Some poorer nations are experimenting in small ways with how to achieve this, trying to create enterprises owned and managed by employees, and they deserve greater international encouragement for this progressive pursuit.

The distribution of wealth and ownership will determine the class formation and social conflict that emerge in the distant future of these nations. England sealed its fate as a class-ridden society when its ruling class refused to deal with the barbaric social consequences of industrial revolution. Korea and Taiwan, on the other hand, created a better foundation for social stability and equity with their early land-distribution programs. In the same manner, an aspiring industrial nation can shape its future social structure by insisting on the broad distribution of capital assets—shares in the new factories being built by global commerce.

In theory, for instance, there is no reason the young people drawn from peasant villages to work in the shoe factories of Indonesia (or toy factories of Thailand or even garment factories in China) cannot also be made into owners, sharing title to the new wealth their labor helps to create. Political realities argue, of course, that this is not going to happen. The local wealthy elites and their governments have no incentive to empower peasant workers. Neither do the great multinational corporations that relocate to take advantage of the cheap labor.

Nevertheless, if nations can demand that multinationals transfer production and technology as the price of market entry, they can just as readily demand broadened ownership of the new assets. If Boeing or Motorola or AT&T are so willing to shift jobs to poor countries, they can also arrange the financing to redistribute shares of ownership. The global system knows how to turn backward peasants into modern industrial workers. Perhaps it could also turn them into capitalists.

The idea of "responsible owners" also offers at least a possibility for establishing greater social accountability in the stateless corporations. This is far beyond the present reality certainly, but imagine that employee and community owners existed on both ends of the global system, exerting the influence of local values on the multinational firms. If this were the case, it might provide a viable bridge for connecting the mutual social values across the global system—the means for workers and communities on both ends of the system to communicate across the distant borders and to alter the behavior of the global corporations.

These people are now connected only by the actions of markets, utterly dependent on the larger economic forces and blocked by them from discovering their mutuality. If people in distant places became genuine stakeholders in the same institutions of global commerce, they might devise their own forums in which to discuss conflicting interests and shared reality. Conceivably, if a new global labor movement arises in the future, it will be built around borderless networks of organized owner workers—people speaking for themselves and for their own communities.

Can capital and labor ever put an end to the warfare and take up shared responsibilities for enterprise? Is it even possible to imagine "one world" connected by socially responsible capitalism? Perhaps not. But this is no longer an idle question for theoretical discussion. The global system is itself careening toward a moment of reckoning with its own values, propelled by its own success.

So long as only a few were rich and the many were poor, so long as wealthy nations dominated and the rest were hapless bystanders, capitalism did not have to become more responsible to societies. Indeed, it thrived by distancing itself from the social consequences. But now that many new nations are industrializing, claiming greater shares of production and consumption and wealth, the question of responsibility has taken on a new and different urgency. A greater social question now stalks everyone, rich and poor alike: Can the earth survive the triumph of global capitalism?

Nineteen

Oikonomia[*]

EACH DAY AT DUSK in Beijing an engaging spectacle played out along the Avenue of Eternal Peace, Chang An, as silent flocks of bicyclists streamed homeward on the imperial boulevard's tree-lined bicycle lanes. Men and women, some teenage students, in business suits and work clothes, toting briefcases, groceries, schoolbooks—thousands of people on bikes glided past in stately calm, as quiet and effortless as birds in flight. I never tired of watching this, perhaps because it was so different from city streets in the American rush hour, the dehumanized, contentious traffic made possible by affluence.

Of course, it will not survive. At each major intersection along Chang An, a different spectacle unfolded, when the swarms of bicycles met up with rushing cars and other motorized vehicles. The encounter was revealing: The people on bikes surged forward in tight clusters, bold and unblinking, claiming the open space until they converged, nose to nose, with the oncoming streams of cars. Neither gave way. When a break appeared in the gridlock, the flocks of bicycles seized it aggressively, oblivious to traffic lanes or personal risk, a bit like in-your-face New Yorkers. The automobile age is encroaching, though not yet bold enough to prevail.

China intends to build an auto industry as large as America's and Chinese people would like to own cars, for about the same reasons Americans do. The street scene I witnessed in Beijing was not so different, I imagine, from what played out in America's cities nearly a hundred years before, when the first automobiles challenged people and horses for the right-of-way. Everyone knows how that contest ended. The graceful past gives way to industrial modernity for the simple reason that the new machines deliver real value to human existence—speed and comfort, saved time and effort, enhanced choices and status.

Social aesthetics aside, can the world survive such progress? China, at

[*] *Ancient Greek: "the management of the household and husbandry of its valuable assets," the original meaning of "economics" before it focused more narrowly on market exchange.*

present, has 680 people per automobile, compared to 1.7 people per car in the United States. Can one imagine a global prosperity in which China's 1.2 billion citizens have the same wherewithal to consume? And if China's ambitious auto policy should fail, there are still India, Brazil and dozens of other nations pursuing similar aspirations. The hydrocarbon pollution will be staggering, but so will the demand for raw materials, especially oil, to build and operate such an awesome fleet of vehicles.[1]

If one decides the earth cannot stand to have so many automobiles, the question is: Who should give up their cars—the Chinese or the Americans? Must the poorer nations be turned away from their desire to acquire a share of industrial convenience or should rich nations agree to forfeit some portion of their own abundance? The answer seems obvious to most of the world, and their answer, just as obviously, is unacceptable to the minority who are already wealthy. One does not have to embrace the dark Malthusian logic to see the crisis ahead. What appears as endless opportunity for global enterprise begins to look quite threatening to human existence.

The great overbearing irony of the global industrial revolution is that all of its technical wonders and expansive energies are bringing people face-to-face with the central fallacy concealed in the standard idea of industrial progress. The conviction that limitless industrial expansion would eventually lift everyone to the ranks of material affluence seemed plausible so long as there was no chance that it would actually happen. But once commerce achieved the skills to truly globalize production and many more nations began to participate in advanced forms of consumption, the contradictions began to crystallize as anxiety about the finite limits of the earth—the preciousness of air, water, land and resources, the resilience of life-giving systems of nature.

During my travels I saw recurring glimpses of the dilemma. In Thailand, U.S. chemical companies are adding to that country's many other afflictions by shipping toxic wastes there for cheap disposal. The transaction makes sense in the narrow accounting of market economics, but cannot be either wise or just for the Thai people.

In Malaysia, where rain-forest activists campaign to halt logging in the Borneo provinces, the prime minister, Mahathir Mohamad, asks: What has happened to the forests of North America? Mahathir suggests that if rich people in the United States wish to preserve pristine nature in the poor countries, they should pay for it.

In Germany, despite the economic prosperity or rather perhaps because of it, the fabled forests of Bavaria and Baden-Württemberg have been gravely injured by mankind. The Germans call it *Waldsterben*—"forest death." A government ministry reported that 25 to 40 percent of the trees in the southern forests—oak, beech, spruce and pine—have been damaged by air pollution and human traffic.[2]

In Japan, a troubled professor described for me a mysterious environmental affliction known as the *itai-itai*—"painful-painful"—disease. Farm fertilizers leached cadmium into soils and the chemical waste migrated to the sea. People ate the fish and slowly poisoned themselves.

Such stories are now commonplace around the world, of course, and I do not propose to catalogue them again here. Intelligent observers have been sounding environmental alarms for nearly half a century, with varying degrees of apocalyptic warning about what industrialization is doing to the world's ecosystem. These predictions are by now familiar and I do not intend to reargue their details. The conventional faith that producers will solve these problems through routine adjustments and technological innovation remains strong in many quarters, at least among government officials and corporate managers, if not the general public. My own conviction, reinforced by glimpsing the scope and scale of global industrialization, is that a far more profound crisis is at hand.

The nature of this crisis is not simply about the scientific issues that are usually debated. Is the earth's protective ozone mantle disintegrating? Might electric cars solve the problems of hydrocarbon pollution? Can the depleted stocks of fish and forest be replenished? Is the chemical-tainted water still safe to drink? The many technical disputes provide the visible battleground for environmental reform, but important as they are, they also tend to obscure deeper systemic questions about the incomplete nature of industrial capitalism itself.

The capitalist process has always functioned by distancing the consumer from the true costs of consumption. The real costs implicit in production are thrown off on someone else—externalized, in the economist's euphemism—either by discarding the wastes somewhere else or by depleting finite resources that are not renewable. Producers have an unrelenting imperative to do this, intensified by the global cost-price competition. Nature has always been a principal source of profit as well as the dumping ground for the used materials and useless by-products. That is why manufacturers always resist new protective measures for natural resources or demand elaborate scientific proof before they will stop polluting or plead for "common sense" in environmental enforcement.

So long as the producers can keep moving on—locating new "greenfields" for factories, new sites for despoliation—consumers benefit tangibly from the abundance of cheaper goods. The future, it is assumed, will someday clean up the wastes if ever it becomes cost-effective to do so. Future technology, meanwhile, will invent new tools that enable industry to exploit new varieties of raw materials, once the old resources are gone. In rough terms, this describes the actual history of the industrial growth spread across several centuries—an open-ended story of rising prosperity and material comfort driven by the technological discoveries. The notion that the industrial system can continue to expand in this same manner, more or less forever, is the logical fallacy made plain by the globalized system.

The economic luxury hidden in the capitalist process is space—capitalism's ability to move on and re-create itself, abandoning the old for the new, creating and destroying production, while trailing a broad flume of ruined natural assets in its wake. Because globalization has narrowed distances, the luxury has diminished visibly. It is now possible for people to glimpse what was always true: the wasteful nature of their own prosperity. So long as the consequences could be kept afar from the beneficiaries, no one had much incentive—neither producers nor consumers—to face the collective implications.

The brilliant possibility of "one world" is the emerging recognition that there is not going to be anyplace to hide. If Thailand becomes rich, where will it ship its toxic wastes? To Vietnam? To Africa? When every nation has industrialized, will they all dump their refuse in the ocean, as the so-called civilized societies now do? If the rain forests are shrinking, will someone invent machines to purify the air and generate rainfall? When the automobile conquers China, will the world be choking on the polluted atmosphere?

The economic dilemma embedded in these questions revolves around price: global producers are caught up in the desperate competition to reduce costs and prices to hold on to market share, yet the earth's imperative asks the economic system to achieve the opposite—to raise the price of goods so that consumers will begin paying the real production costs of their consumption. The marketplace (including most consumers) is naturally hostile to that imperative since it puts enterprises at immediate disadvantage unless all their competitors in the global system are required to accept the same pricing standards. There is at present no mechanism to achieve such harmony of purpose even if everyone agreed on its wisdom.

The social dilemma grows out of the same facts: If the collective interest requires a transformation of the industrial system's values, the poor will likely be injured more profoundly than the rich since they are the new entrants and least able to pay higher prices for consumption. The developing nations, after all, are emulating the rapacious practices they learned from the advanced economies and are understandably skeptical when high-minded reformers urge them not to repeat the same environmental mistakes —"mistakes" that have made Americans and Europeans quite wealthy. The environmental ethic proposes to alter the basic rules of capitalism at the very moment when some impoverished former colonies are at last enjoying the action.

Mahathir of Malaysia, with his usual acerbic bluntness, put the accusation to a Swiss environmental activist named Bruno Manser, a man who has rallied international opinion in defense of the Borneo rain forests and the people who live there, an indigenous tribe called the Penans, whom Manser lived among for several years. Exasperated by Manser's effective campaign, Mahathir wrote him a bitter letter of rebuke: "As a Swiss living in the lap of luxury with the world's highest standard of living, it is the height of arrogance for you to advocate that the Penans live on maggots and monkeys in their miserable huts, subjected to all kinds of diseases. . . . Do you really expect the Penans to subsist on monkeys until the year 2500 or 3000 or forever? Have they no right to a better life? What right have you to condemn them to a primitive life forever?"[3]

Mahathir's letter crudely finessed the question of informed consent. The Penans, like other peoples whose primitive existence has been overwhelmed by industrial intrusion, were not consulted on whether they wanted their lives and habitat upended. The tribal members have mounted spirited resistance to the logging operations. Mahathir's point, nonetheless, was aimed at a ripe target—the high-minded hypocrisy of wealthy sensibilities. It does not diminish idealistic accomplishments of global environmental activism to observe that some reformers do indeed wish to save the innocents from modern life itself.

If one's real objective is simply to halt the spread of industrialization, then saving the earth will generate its own form of massive injustice. To put the question crudely, are poor people also entitled to electricity? Or must the global system limit access to TV and stereos, refrigerators and washing machines, cars and air conditioning, the material comforts the rest of us now regard as life's routine necessities?

Indigenous peoples, one can argue, do not really wish to enter this realm of mass consumption, but the question of consent is ancient and extremely difficult to resolve. Tribal groups, if they can, often resist the invasion of foreign technology and commerce, as any people would resist the upheaval of their community by powerful outsiders. Yet the mere act of seeking informed consent in advance can itself be corrupting. Once people who hunt with spears have been shown how to use guns, traditional life is already compromised. Once a village is electrified, villagers seldom decide to turn off the lights and TV.

The collective dilemma, shared by rich and poor, fuses these social and economic dimensions: if industrial growth proceeds according to its accepted pattern, everyone is imperiled. Yet, if industrialization is not allowed to proceed, a majority of the world's citizens are consigned to a permanent second-class status, deprived of industrial artifacts that enhance life's comforts, the tools that multiply human choices. Alongside all of the other social tensions and economic disorders recounted in this book, this dilemma constitutes the largest historical challenge. The world has entered new ground, a place where its people have never been before. They will have no choice but to think anew.

Across the last generation, the environmental ethic has described the outlines of how to resolve the dilemma: what is required is nothing less than a radical transformation of the industrial system itself, its production practices and pricing methods, the economic assumptions surrounding enterprise and consumption. These reforms are usually capsulized in a single phrase—"sustainable development"—that carries revolutionary implications, but sounds so wholesome that almost everybody can endorse it. Every enlightened politician now supports the goal of sustainable development; so does every leading corporation and financial institution that is sensitive to popular opinion. Meanwhile, the global system plunges forward along its usual path, building toward some sort of epic showdown with nature.

The revolutionary content of "sustainable development" is difficult for most people to digest because it upends the inherited understandings of how the world is meant to work. Yet the industrial system is unlikely to be changed fundamentally until people learn to think about it in this new way. The barriers to change are thus enormous. The good news is that some optimistic revolutionaries are already present among us, trying to make their ideas heard.

In Tokyo, I went around to see an engineering professor named Hiro-yuki Yoshikawa at Tokyo University because he was an authority on advanced robotics and I was exploring the implications of technology for the future of work. Yoshikawa did talk about robots and some futuristic ideas for their application, but the conversation swiftly escalated to his larger theme: the problem of mass unemployment would be solved, he said, by saving the earth, since both require a transformation of the industrial system itself.

"It is time for a new revolution—a kind of humanized process of change that offers the only solution for our problems," he said. "From this time on, maybe for the next hundred years, everything should be devoted to changing everything—the physical structure, the type of products, the economic system, the value system. My message to politicians is that we must convert the target of investment from the road system and bridges to the brain system."

The apocalyptic language sounded familiar, vaguely like the visionary rhetoric of various environmental thinkers, except that Yoshikawa was an industrial engineer and with exalted status in the Japanese establishment. When I interviewed him, he was serving as the president of Tokyo University, a position that in American terms would be roughly equivalent to the president of Harvard, MIT and Berkeley combined. Yet Professor Yoshikawa sounded like an anxious radical.

"It's my feeling that, yes, the companies can survive but the people cannot survive," he went on. "Globalization, relying on offshore production, is inevitable, and, of course, the companies are going to do it. But with many factories going out of Japan, we then have no incentive to invest in robotics, to devise new systems, and it reduces our ability to develop new jobs. The only solution in my opinion is to invent new products which will satisfy human beings. Otherwise, we are just fooling around with the same industrial structure from the last industrial revolution. It was a gift that we are still living on and wasting our assets."

Yoshikawa's idea of "new products" was not meant as the usual engineering challenge of designing better cars or new entertaining electronic gadgets. He meant products that would come from a new system of production that is fundamentally different from the industrial system that has existed for three hundred years. A factory that cleans up its own mess and uses the materials over and over again. Consumers who do not throw things away, but send them back to the factory as raw materials for conversion into new products. Workers who merge their skills with robotic machines to do the dirty, dangerous work of saving the earth.

"From the environmental point of view, the present manufacturing industry is only part of the actual industry," the professor said. "They take up materials from somewhere else and they convert the materials into useful products and these are distributed and consumed—from material output to manufacturing to consumption to waste. But now we are confronted with limited space on earth and limited materials and limited places to waste things.

"We should design a new type of manufacturing activity which is not an open pass-through system, but is a closed loop. Then the waste material should be recovered and input into some new type of factory that translates waste into new materials. We will have a plus factory and a minus factory —a normal factory and an inverse factory."

The "inverse factory," Yoshikawa imagined, would effectively solve the global problem of surplus labor since it would necessarily broaden the work requirements of the industrial process itself. "If manufacturing industry becomes a closed circle, then the work will be multiplied, too," he thought. "Normal factories should be supplanted by highly sophisticated technology, and we need a new robotics to do this very hard, very dirty work—a new robotics and a new kind of thermodynamics for materials, for recovery and conversion. Very simply, if we develop this inverse industry, the size of industry will be doubled."

If the vision seemed naively beyond present reality, Yoshikawa has had practical experience experimenting at the margins. He led a small research group that developed robots to do the dangerous work of cleaning containment vessels at nuclear power plants, a project that did not succeed commercially but convinced him of the broader potential for transformation. MITI has sponsored limited research on a "dirty work robot" system that would clean the streets and collect garbage. Yoshikawa imagined "social robots" that did housework and "intelligent robots" that amplified the human skills of nurses and other kinds of service workers—raising wages by making the people more productive.

"Of course, the social robot or the home robot is the same kind of dream at this point," he said. "But the by-product will be the long-term goal of devising the technology that makes it possible to develop the inverse factory. If we develop recycling without new technology, then the industry will be very dirty, very dangerous, very bad. The people must be equipped to do these jobs that are very necessary. The process should be harmonized development, which means to improve the quality of life and also to develop this new kind of industry. If we do this, if we develop this new dimension, we shall be free. We will invent a new industrial system and also solve our deepest social problems."

Despite Yoshikawa's optimism neither the economic system nor his academic colleagues were prepared to pursue such a vision with the resources that would be required. "Our knowledge is very, very flawed in this field," he conceded. "There's no academic framework for it, no kind of faculty to deal with it. From an academic point of view, we have reached only halfway. There's study to support the normal factory, but none to support the inverse factory."

The marketplace was even more resistant to this new frontier and with good reason. On its face, Yoshikawa's plus-minus industry might theoretically double the cost of a product, at least initially, and thus injure consumer standards of living. "Of course, we must be patient," he allowed, "because maybe we lose some level of income at first. But if we introduce this approach, then eventually it will be improved as we learn how to create this type of closed-loop system and make it work to everyone's benefit."

I came away from the interview enthralled by Yoshikawa's confident optimism. Was he another starry-eyed professor dreaming of utopian solutions? Or a practical man who sees the future clearly? Some of what he envisioned has already occurred in limited ways, as new industrial centers are being developed on the closed-loop principle, recovering their own chemical wastes and reprocessing them into raw materials for new production. The development of renewable energy systems has advanced dramatically in the last two decades, though still not widely commercialized. Scientists are working on robotics and the materials processes, though not as energetically as Yoshikawa thinks is necessary.

His vision perhaps appealed to me because it seemed to reconcile so much of what I had glimpsed around the world—the awesome technological capabilities that now exist and the terrible social-economic destruction that has accompanied these new inventions. Yoshikawa, the engineer, believes that these two realities can be harmonized—that the technology will serve society, instead of threatening it. Achieving harmony, he said, is the great work of the future.

"Very soon," he concluded, "this will be necessary in any case—perhaps in the next five or ten years—because it can't go on like this. The unemployment will continue forever if we maintain the manufacturing system as it is. At the same time, we can't go on like this. There will be some kind of disaster. We've already had several kinds of tragedy here in Japan. We can't escape."

At the University of Maryland in the suburbs outside Washington, D.C., an economist named Herman E. Daly was something of a pariah in his own profession. Daly taught at the university's School of Public Affairs, not the economics department, though he had co-authored an important book on sustainable development, *For the Common Good*. His views were equally unwelcome at the department of agricultural and resource economics, though Daly had worked in that field as a senior economist at the World Bank. "I am regarded with bemused tolerance and mild interest and occasional anger," he explained amiably. "How the hell can you say these things and call yourself an economist?"

The heresy that Daly and his co-author, theologian John B. Cobb Jr., committed was to attack the accounting assumptions at the very heart of industrial capitalism, the totemic statistic known as the Gross National Product. What orthodox economics described as growth, Daly and Cobb argued, was actually decline. What appeared in the standard statistics as gain was actually loss. The data on accumulating capital, in fact, concealed the destruction of assets. Poor countries were deluded by these numbers, but so were wealthy nations like the United States. By Daly and Cobb's calculations, American citizens were collectively becoming steadily poorer.

These insights were derived from a basic shift in perspective that was so straightforward and obvious one might wonder why the science of modern economics persisted in ignoring it. The standard accounting of economists regarded the market activities of production and consumption as a self-contained system, distinct and separate from its external surroundings. "My scheme," Daly explained, "is to see the economy as a subsystem of the larger ecosystem and ask: How does the economy depend on the larger system? It depends on it as a source of raw materials and as a sink for wastes. So that obviously means there's a scale limit on the economy since we can't overburden the ecosystem. That's a physical limit that economics doesn't understand. The idea that you can draw on it endlessly is simply wrong."

Daly and Cobb started with an assumption that everyone, living at present and in the future, shared a collective economic interest in the balance sheet of the larger natural world, not just those workers, owners and consumers who were active now in the subsystem of the marketplace. So they tried to construct a new way of measuring prosperity that incorporates the collective interest—an Index of Sustainable Economic Welfare—that counts things the economists leave out of their GNP calculations. "When we measure growth as growth in GNP, we don't subtract anything," Daly said. "We assume it's all good."

Their index subtracted the obvious losses—the collective costs of air and water pollution, the destruction of wetlands, the deterioration of farmland, long-term environmental damage such as ozone depletion and the consumption of nonrenewable resources. When these negative factors and other social losses like auto accidents or foreign debt were included in the calculation, the picture of American prosperity looked quite different.

The standard GNP statistics indicated that U.S. income per capita has increased in real value by about 25 percent since the mid-1970s. Daly's index found that despite progress in reducing pollution costs, economic well-being in sustainable terms has been gradually declining for Americans, down about 10 percent per capita since 1976, receding to the levels of the mid-1960s.

"Despite the year-to-year variations in the ISEW, it indicates a long-term trend . . . that is indeed bleak," the authors concluded. ". . . Clearly the important question then becomes whether our nation is going to continue in its efforts to increase total output or whether we are going to redirect our focus towards the enhancement of sustainable economic welfare."[4]

Daly, the economist, was offering a framework for thinking about the industrial system that parallels the vision of Yoshikawa, the engineer. Only Daly's perspective was larger in scope and far gloomier in outlook. Many other environmental thinkers have articulated similar arguments for sustainable development in recent decades; *For the Common Good* was distinctive because Daly and Cobb took on the economics profession in the discipline's own language and methodologies. As the authors readily conceded, their index was only a beginning effort and contained scores of disputable assumptions that would require further debate and refinement. But what they produced was a rough first draft for thinking clearly about the future—free of the deceptive assumptions cherished by modern economics.[5]

Orthodox economics, for instance, defined "capital" as the man-made assets that produce a flow of goods and services, machines and buildings, and so forth. But, as Daly and Cobb pointed out, this narrow definition left out the most important assets—the "natural capital" upon which all economic activity depends.

Economists, though they presumably knew better, effectively assumed that the earth's store of raw resources was infinite so long as the market price was high enough to make extraction profitable. This assumption might make sense for the purpose of describing market functions, Daly acknowledged, but it was dangerously out of touch with the reality.

Economics further assumed that future generations would enjoy a net gain whenever raw materials were converted into man-made capital assets —that is, ore and energy resources consumed to make the machines of steel. But this assumption begged the question of lost value in "natural capital" that would never be recovered and the future costs of cleaning up despoliation.

Indeed, as Daly argued, the depletion of natural capital often devalued the man-made assets as well. "As we are depleting the fish in the ocean, we are rapidly devaluing the fishing boats too," he explained. Instead of assuming an undiluted benefit when raw nature is converted into productive artifacts, economists should acknowledge the complementary nature of the two systems and begin to define the actual trade-offs embedded in these exchanges.

Once this profit-and-loss accounting was reliably established, Daly predicted, the real economic gains would be found in productive activities that nurture nature's ability to renew itself and to regenerate resources. Solar power and similar renewable-energy systems, for instance, were effectively blocked by the cost-price incentives of market economics. But if the true costs of production and consumption were calculated, these innovations would begin to look like bargains.

Many developing nations, Daly and Cobb pointed out, were caught in the same illusion of self-defeating growth—depleting resources and accumulating environmental damage at a pace that would look like "negative growth" if all the true costs were calculated. The political problem with adopting an honest system of accounting was obvious. "No politician wants to be known as the minister under whom the country went from growth to decline in one year," they wrote. "Yet there is an opportunity for someone to be known as the leader who finally introduced the income accounting system that saved the nation from eventual impoverishment."

A much more forbidding message, however, was at the center of their analysis: the natural limits on conventional economic growth itself. "If you're really poor, you need food and housing and much of the world still needs growth in that sense," Daly said. "But I think we've reached the point —the American middle class and above—where growth costs us more than we gain in terms of human welfare and actually makes us poorer. What hinders us from seeing this is that we don't pay the costs as individuals. We get the benefits, but the costs are spread out over the whole society."

The Index of Sustainable Economic Welfare was intended to help people see this more clearly, but Daly conceded that his perspective collided with the universal expectations of society and politics, not just narrowminded economists. The GNP numbers might rest on erroneous assumptions, but they provided the convenient emblem of "progress and prosperity." The problem was grounded not only in language and habits of thought, but also involved a deeper argument over what constituted the good life.

"We have to push the path of progress toward qualitative improvement in resource efficiency, either through technological means or by better ordering of our priorities and institutions in the face of scarcity," Daly explained. "I have tried to make a distinction between growth and development. Growth is increase in physical size. Development is enhanced quality. In standard usage, those two meanings are mixed up."

In conventional terms, proposing to halt "GNP growth" sounded like a plan for permanent depression. Not surprisingly, people and politicians were uninterested in pursuing such an agenda and Daly struggled to overcome the language barrier. "We have to get away from this 'zero growth' thing that economists talk about because that's not the thrust of it," he said. "What we are talking about is zero growth in the energy and material throughput. Whatever gains you can get out of greater efficiencies in energy productivity will naturally become gains to be distributed. Sustainable de-

velopment means qualitative improvement without quantitative growth beyond the point where the ecosystem cannot regenerate."

In theory, at least, no one was for "growth" that threatened life itself.
At the Rio de Janeiro conference on the global environment in 1992, all
the leading governments gathered to endorse the principles of sustainable
development. Professor Daly saw a banner at the booth sponsored by ENI,
the Italian energy company, that proclaimed in Italian and English: "We're
Growing with the Planet."

"That's fine," Daly said, "except the planet isn't growing. That shows
you the level of thought about sustainable development at present. You
grab a slogan without thinking it through."

The World Bank has embraced the concept of "environmentally sustainable development" for its industrial projects in poor countries and in
1995 produced a study on the true wealth of nations that applied an analytical approach similar to Daly's. "Within the World Bank, this idea has won
the day in terms of lip service," Daly continued, "but when you start to
institutionalize the idea operationally, then you run into the growth ethic
concretely. They want to do some good, but they've learned a bad theology.
For all the practical experience and doubts that individuals at the bank may
have, they're still in thrall of endless growth."[6]

Daly's frustrations at the World Bank deepened because its commitment to "sustainable development" implicitly assumed that as poor people
became wealthier and better educated, they too would develop heightened
sensibilities about the environment and thus curb their destructive practices.
"There's a grain of truth in that," he said, "but it exempts affluence as a
source of the degradation."

The nettlesome assertion that governing authorities did not wish to
grasp was that rising affluence itself, at least as it was presently defined
and achieved, faced finite limits. The global system, as it generated new
wealth-producing activity, was hurtling toward a wall, an unidentified point
in time when economic expansion would collectively collide with the physical capacity of the ecosystem. Daly acknowledged it was impossible to say
when or how this might occur since human beings have great capacity for
invention and for changing their patterns of consumption or their birthrates, all of which can alter the trend lines in positive ways. Nevertheless,
the wall existed somewhere in the future—and was approaching much
faster than many people imagined. A terrible collision, Daly figured, may
be no more than a generation or two away.

The logic of this assertion did not rely upon the scientific claims about
global warming or other specific dangers, but was based on the straightforward arithmetic of the human economic subsystem expanding in relation
to the larger natural system. For example, according to studies cited by
Daly, human activity now appropriated in different ways an estimated 25
percent of the world's primary energy source—the photosynthesis of sun-

light that is potentially available on the earth's total surface. This appropriation included not only the direct uses for agriculture and other productive purposes, but also the man-made destruction through deforestation, desertification, urbanization and other activities that, so to speak, paved over the natural world.

If this estimate was correct, the growth of human economic activity and population could logically expand until it has doubled two more times —and then must stop since it would occupy 100 percent of the whole. But, of course, the expansion had to stop long before it reached a point of 100 percent saturation. "Since this would mean zero energy left for all non-human and non-domesticated species, and since humans cannot survive without the services of the ecosystems which are made up of other species, it is clear that two more doublings of the human scale would be an ecological impossibility, even if it were arithmetically possible," Daly and Cobb write.[7]

If the per capita consumption of resources was held to present levels, Daly noted, then expansion of the economic sphere would be driven by population growth alone, which has been doubling on the order of every forty years or so. But, of course, the level of per capita consumption did not remain constant, but expanded at its own compounding rates. In the wealthy United States, per capita consumption has more than doubled in the last thirty years, though natural resources were being consumed with increasing efficiency. China's GNP per capita, though still desperately low, has tripled in the past twenty years, but its population growth has decelerated. The economic subsystem, one might argue, was at least changing in the right direction. But was it changing fast enough to avoid hitting the wall?

"Unless we awaken to the existence and nearness of scale limits," Daly and Cobb wrote, "then the greenhouse effect, ozone layer depletion and acid rain will be just a preview of disasters to come, not in the vague distant future but in the next generation."

The ominous trend lines put one face-to-face with the excruciating paradox of the industrial age and its triumphs. Human experience was spread across four or five million years, but for most of that time, so long as societies survived by primitive means of hunting and gathering, population grew quite slowly. As human inventions expanded the means of production and eased the burdens of scarcity, people lived longer and population grew more rapidly. This process of expansion started with the practice of settled agriculture and has been under way across many millennia. But during the last three hundred years of industrial technologies, it exploded.

As economist Douglass C. North recounted in his Nobel laureate's address in 1993, the world's population was probably no more than 300 million people two thousand years ago. By 1750, at the dawn of modern industrialization, it had grown to 800 million people. Since then, thanks to growing abundance and science's conquest of disease, global population has grown to nearly six billion people.[8]

The facts seemed terrifying, yet also wondrous. The human species, it appeared, was in a footrace with its own ingenuity, inventing and producing and prospering, thereby creating the predicate for its own oblivion. Could mankind invent its way out of this trap? Many have grimly concluded that the race was already lost—that the propensity for accumulation was a fatal impulse that would eventually drown human beings in the excess of their own desire. People wanted "stuff" and, when they got some, wanted more. If appetites were sated, new stuff was invented and the need to consume expanded further. Meanwhile, the poor people of the world were having more babies and they wanted stuff, too.

Perhaps gloom was justified, but the paradox of industrial abundance was deeper and more complicated than that. As advanced societies have discovered, when people achieved a certain level of stable prosperity, their birthrates leveled off and declined. Population growth moderated or even turned negative in some wealthy countries. If one wanted the poor people around the world to stop having so many babies, perhaps the solution was to make them less poor. The globalization advanced toward that goal, at least in some places, albeit with grossly unequal results and various injustices for poor people.

Yet industrial growth, as it was now practiced, also pushed up the curve of global consumption and devoured still more of the "natural capital." So was economic growth the solution or was it the problem? The paradox was dizzying. In terms of the common good, economic growth appeared to be both.

Prophetic voices like Daly and Cobb and Yoshikawa were enunciating, in different ways, the same warning: if people hoped to escape this historic dilemma, they would have no choice but to alter the fundamental nature of both production and consumption. One might argue with specific projections and assumptions, but the logic was bearing down ominously on the conventional idea of industrial progress. As Yoshikawa said: "We can't go on like this. . . . We can't escape."

The way out was not beyond human possibility. If the human species could "learn" in prosperous circumstances to have fewer offspring, then human society could perhaps "unlearn" wasteful tastes and economic practices picked up during humanity's relatively brief exposure to industrial abundance. The modern age of mass consumption, after all, was less than a century old, no more than a flickering moment in the long saga of human existence. The industrial system itself was quite young compared to the full sweep of history and, as Yoshikawa suggested, only half completed.

The imperative, roughly speaking, had two parallel dimensions. One was the engineering challenge described by Yoshikawa: designing the waste out of the production process itself, completing the other half of the industrial system so it would swallow the costs it now externalized. Herman Daly suggested a smart way to visualize Yoshikawa's proposition: "Put a factory's input pipe downstream from its output pipe. That's going to increase costs for the company because it will have to clean up its own wastes."

The engineering problems were formidable, of course, but not more fantastic than what engineers have already accomplished. Consider, for instance, that mortals discovered the mechanisms of human flight at the dawn of the twentieth century, and three generations later engineers designed and built an awesome works like Boeing's assembly plant at Everett, Washington —a monumental factory where men and women make gigantic aircraft that will carry three hundred and four hundred people across oceans and continents. My example suggested a faith in technology that many people do not share, but the great industrial sites I saw around the world deepened my respect for engineers and what they might achieve. The semiconductor chip, with all the multiplying capabilities that flowed from its invention, seemed exquisitely suited to the engineering challenge of our age: reinventing the industrial system itself.

The other dimension of reform, Daly and Cobb's version, was more difficult, in a sense, because it required a profound shift in everyone's habits of thought, the same shift in perspective that the two scholars had applied to the Gross National Product: a recognition that the common good may be endangered by individual appetites, that more was not leading to better. Could human societies decide that accumulation of more "stuff" was not the only meaning of economic progress? Would people pay for greater quality in life as a trade-off for endless quantity? The physical difficulties seemed a less formidable barrier than the mental habits of modern life.

The "new economics" vision of Daly and Cobb has a historical symmetry that appealed to me since the sensibility described by their scheme was actually the wisdom of the ancients. As they explained, the root word of economics—*oikonomia*—was a term that, in ancient and modern Greek, meant "the management of a household's valuable assets," with a sense of prudent husbandry for the future. That meaning has been lost in modern economics, pushed aside by the economists' preoccupation with markets and the exchange mechanisms for maximizing return.

Indeed, modern economists have become the "thought police" in advanced societies, as futurist Hazel Henderson observed. Despite their scientific pretensions they acted more like priests defending the true faith against heretics. Their religion was the marketplace, and in the political dialogue, they were the arbiters of sound thinking, ridiculing any ideas that conflicted with orthodox theology. The media embraced the economists' creed and amplified it, scolding any politician who seemed to deviate from correct thoughts. Heretics like Herman Daly would naturally be ignored, at least until society learned from painful experience that they had been right.[9]

Still, if the Greeks could understand the importance of *oikonomia*, then perhaps Americans and Chinese and other peoples might also grasp its meaning before it was too late. In the abstract, one could see the logic of what Daly and Cobb are saying. In the actual world, it was not just the economists who were reluctant to pay the price.

Now we come to the hard part of this global dilemma: the realization that the poor cannot save the earth, only the affluent minority can do that. If the wealthier nations choose not to face the portents of industrial disaster, then the global system will proceed forward to meet whatever wall of calamities may lie ahead. This statement is not based on moral sensibilities, though it would seem immoral to expect impoverished peoples to solve a problem born of the affluence elsewhere in the world. This is a matter of practical reality. The road to industrial reform, in behalf of the common good, is blocked by the divisive fact of wealth and poverty.

As a practical matter, the world's poor people do not have the capacity to alter the industrial system for the simple reason that they do not consume most of the world's resources or throw off most of the industrial waste and pollution. That role belongs to the wealthy nations. Furthermore, the poor cannot afford it. Industrializing nations are put at an economic disadvantage if the global regime sets out to incorporate the true costs of production into the price of goods. Poor people, aspiring to increase their meager levels of consumption, are least able to pay the price for this transformation. Even if their governments choose wisely and insist upon high standards of environmental protection, they are unlikely to cooperate with an agenda that threatens their chance to claim a share in the industrial prosperity.

In another time in history, when the rich and powerful nations routinely colonized the weak and poor, these systemic reforms might simply have been imposed on others by military or economic force. But, in present circumstances, the rich nations need the poor, as earlier chapters have described. The global system of enterprise desperately needs the energy of the developing markets—the new pools of consumers with rising incomes—to help mop up its own burgeoning surpluses of goods. Furthermore, developing nations that have already acquired a share of the global industrial base have some market leverage on these questions now. They may refuse to forfeit a portion of their own economic growth in order to correct the profligacy of others.

All these factors argue that if industrial transformation is to occur, it will have to be led by the people, governments and enterprises in the advanced economies, transforming their own values first. The wealthy can best afford to pay the higher prices required by the disruptions of regular business assumptions. They have the consumer power to make a new market for quality and to insist upon it in their goods and production systems. The rich nations must lead the way, in any case, because they possess the advanced technologies and design capabilities needed to complete the industrial system's other half. If the affluent minority refuses to take up this responsibility, then probably no one will.

That does not exempt the poorer nations from the problem, of course. They can be prodded—and tangibly assisted—to adopt higher production and consumption values, too. Given globalized production systems, environmental standards cannot be meaningful unless they are incorporated in the terms of trade—a positive incentive, like labor rights, to reward nations that are pulling upward and penalize those whose price margins are based on rank despoliation. Still, it is epic hypocrisy for Americans to scold the poor for destroying nature while U.S. companies are still free to dump toxic wastes from American consumption in poor countries. If they intend to reform the world, America and other advanced nations have to take care of their own mess first.

The dilemma posed by wealth and poverty is even more difficult, however, because this division of interests does not just exist internationally, but is also found within the wealthiest societies. Raising the real price of consumption may describe the right thing to do, but it can also generate immediate social injustices since the impact will be devastating for those of modest means while it seems trivial to those with wealth and abundant incomes. As politicians often grasp more clearly than reformers, these unequal social costs surface whenever meaningful environmental measures are proposed.

A "green tax" on the fuel efficiency of cars, for instance, effectively pushes both consumers and producers to embrace conservation by raising the market price of vehicles that consume energy wantonly. It may also price many people out of owning a car. Higher taxes on oil and gasoline offer a direct means of curbing reckless energy consumption, but would punish people with limited incomes, especially those whose livelihoods commit them to long-distance commuting. An arbitrary "cap" on total pollution would create a market incentive for power companies and other producers to cut their wastes internally since, if they don't, they will have to purchase "pollution rights" at auction, competing with other bidders for a scarce privilege. Society benefits overall, while some citizens struggle with electric bills they cannot afford.

What I am trying to suggest with these examples is a powerful conjunction of social purposes: The collective interest of achieving industrial transformation also requires societies to confront the questions of economic inequality, domestically as well as globally. I have already described in earlier chapters why reducing the maldistribution of wealth and incomes is a crucial predicate for rescuing the global system from its own economic disorders. The accumulating market surpluses, feeding the continuing destruction and social erosion, cannot possibly be absorbed unless consumer demand is stimulated from the bottom up, through policies that address work and wages, among other things.

But there is another, parallel dimension to this economic imperative: The challenge of saving the earth is not likely to succeed as a practical political matter unless advanced societies also achieve a greater degree of economic equity and social cohesion. Everyone, rich and poor, wishes to protect nature, but if the broad ranks of working families lack the wherewithal to defend hearth and home, they are unlikely to welcome environmental measures that threaten to make their economic situation even worse. If only the well-to-do can afford to pay the price for quality, then the environmental quality will remain a niche market, reserved for the virtuous few with ample surplus income.

This proposition is about more than prices and incomes, however. The common good, as envisioned by thinkers like Daly and Cobb and Yoshikawa, assumes a sense of shared social purpose—a general understanding among people of every rank that "we are all in this together." This sense of unity is visibly weakening in the wealthiest nations, but most dramatically in the United States, as the global industrial revolution deals out the returns with increasing inequality. As the unwritten social contract that underlies American prosperity is gradually nullified, social attitudes naturally coarsen and a raw, mean-spirited contest of self-defense ensues—the very opposite of the social cohesion required for the great task ahead.

The common good, in other words, must exist as an economic and social reality—the promise of shared, equitable sacrifice and rewards—if societies are to undertake the larger challenge of reforming their conventional ideas of progress and prosperity. Economic equality and the environmental ethic, usually regarded as separate or even conflicting ideals, have to be understood as mutually reinforcing in pursuit of the collective interest. If environmental reformers hope to raise the price of consumption, they must also address the question of whether people are able to pay that price —that is, the questions of jobs, incomes and ownership.

The idea that environmental values and social cohesion are closely interdependent may offend many Americans, but there is considerable evidence around the world to support the proposition. It is not a coincidence, I think, that the wealthy nations with the highest environmental values and most rigorous enforcement standards are also the countries that have achieved the greatest degrees of economic equality and social cohesion— that is, countries like Japan, Germany, Sweden and some other European nations. Europeans pay taxes on energy consumption that would be unthinkable in the United States, but then Europeans of every class enjoy social protections that would also be unthinkable in the United States.

Many Americans are under the illusion that their country is the world leader in advancing the environmental ethic. Indeed, the steady torrent of business-financed propaganda argues the United States has already gone too far (a claim the American public does not believe). Meanwhile, in Europe and Japan, industries are operating under stringent recovery-and-recycling laws that at least start down the road described by Yoshikawa. No one has yet solved the larger problems of transformation, but America's industrial allies at least recognize that they exist.

Germany embarked on a crash program to reduce acid-rain pollution from power plants by 90 percent in six years (compared to the loosely drawn U.S. air-pollution laws that give some industrial sectors twenty to thirty years to reform). Sweden has adopted a variety of new "green taxes." The Dutch plan to generate electricity from sewage. Japan produces steel that, on average, requires 40 percent less energy expenditure per ton than American-produced steel.

These and scores of other startling comparisons are reported by Curtis Moore and Alan Miller in *Green Gold*, a book that describes how environmental technology has become a hot, new growth sector in the global system and how the United States has fallen behind nations like Germany and Japan, often because the others commercialized inventions that originated in the United States. Michael E. Porter of the Harvard Business School summarized the competition in his book *The Competitive Advantage of Nations:* "Although the United States once clearly led in setting [environmental] standards, that position has been slipping away. Today the United States remains the only industrialized country without a policy on carbon dioxide, and our leadership in setting environmental standards has been lost in many areas."

Germany, Porter noted, "has had perhaps the world's tightest regulations in stationary air-pollution control and German companies appear to hold a wide lead in patenting—and exporting—air pollution and other environmental technologies." These other nations, it is true, have a much stronger incentive to take care—given their limited space and higher densities of population. Still, the aggressive response of German and Japanese industry to the environmental problem also reflects the fact that their corporations are governed by a stronger sense of social obligation.[10]

If the environmentalists are right about the shape of the future, saving the earth will become a major field of opportunity for advanced producers. American industrialists, despite frequent pep talks about "competitiveness," are still mostly fighting a rearguard battle against this emerging market reality—still trying to gut America's environmental laws, still dumping wastes in the land, air and water or shipping their toxics to benighted countries like Thailand. When American companies decide to clean up their production systems, they often must do it with foreign-made machinery.

The larger question, nonetheless, is whether rising economic prosperity can be reconciled with the imperative to transform the values of production and consumption. Most of this book, after all, has been devoted to the shifting fortunes of people, enterprise and nations in the traditional terms of economic growth. Can growth be made compatible with saving the earth? As the emerging market for environmental technology suggests, the two goals need not collide—if the terms of growth are redefined as steady-state equilibrium with the natural world. Growth in those terms means enhancing the general well-being, including a promise of rising prosperity for those who do not share in the standard comforts of modern life. The quality of life—as opposed to mere accumulation—can drive the economic engine as effectively as profligate habits of mass consumption, if people choose.

Economic value, as John Maynard Keynes taught, is actually an intangible quality because it is ultimately determined by whatever people are willing to pay for—that is, whatever people subjectively believe is valuable. That intangible quality explains why modern advertising works so imaginatively to associate illusory fantasies with ordinary products, from athletic shoes to deodorants. A society, Keynes observed, could pay people to dig a deep hole in the ground and bury precious metal there, then pay other people to dig it up. This activity, though quite pointless, would constitute real economic value (if people were silly enough to pay for it). Right now, one could say, modern consumers are paying to dig a very deep hole for themselves.

The experience of German and Japanese producers, as well as some sectors in the United States, demonstrates that improving the efficient use of resources delivers its own economic bonus—rising productivity. The increased productivity derives mainly from reducing the material inputs in the industrial process and salvaging wastes that were once regarded as useless burden. One can also see this process at work in society, at least in limited ways. Recycling of old newspapers was mocked a few years ago as the feel-good indulgence of idealists; now it is public policy in most major cities.

The improved returns for a responsible enterprise can be distributed among all its stakeholders, from owners to workers to consumers, either as cash or quality. With a little imagination, one may glimpse the possibility that a new version of the "virtuous circle" might emerge, a mutuality of interests in which the returns are shared in different ways, including as personal satisfaction for defending the common good. But in order for firms to ever reach that happy condition, they must be able to see a market that rewards their responsible behavior. That requires a profound reordering not only in the tastes and values of individual consumption, but also in public priorities.

"The solution is waste," American economist Douglas Dowd wrote. "The waste is systematic and institutionalized, as measured by what is produced and how and by what is withheld from use and/or is destroyed."[11]

Consumer markets, for instance, still function on business strategies of planned obsolescence—products designed not to last very long, so people must buy more of them. Industrial sectors compete by accumulating strategic overcapacity in production—building surplus factories that eventually must be abandoned. Governments subsidize waste in numerous large ways, not just in their bureaucracies, but in the marketplace, too. Farm price-support programs idle productive acreage and thereby encourage the high-yield, chemical-intensive agriculture that damages the land and water supply, rivers and oceans. Defense spending piles up massive arsenals of surplus weaponry, armaments that governments must then try to sell to the rest of the world.

When the economic dilemma is understood in those broad terms—as a problem of institutionalized wastefulness—the prospect of industrial transformation does not seem so threatening to the general prosperity (though reform will, of course, deprive some people of their profitable activities). U.S. tax law, for instance, is tilted now to favor the exploitation of virgin resources against the recovery of used materials. The mortgage-interest deduction rewards rich people who acquire two or three or even more homes, the bigger the better for tax purposes. There are literally thousands of public policies, large and small, that need to be reversed.

Consumers can and do apply their own market pressures for change. Indeed, some portion of American citizens has drawn back from the frenzy of acquiring more "stuff" to redefine the good life in their own terms. Even the erosion of wage incomes and job opportunities has a bittersweet reward in that it has led many people to sort out their personal priorities more carefully. Some young people especially find themselves making choices about their life's work that put personal satisfaction ahead of income or security since both of those prospects seem in doubt anyway.

The waves of corporate restructuring and dismissals have reminded many Americans that they are not as free and independent as they supposed. The dislocations expose a vague, unexpressed sense of terror that, I suspect, has always dwelt at the core of modern consciousness—an anxiety that originates in people's knowledge of how utterly dependent they have become on these abstract forces, the marketplace and the corporation, both of which are functionally indifferent to their human concerns. Many of us have acquired awesome levels of prosperity from the complexities of the modern industrial system, yet also lost the skills and confidence that made our ancestors self-reliant. How to make things of quality with one's own hands. How to fill leisure hours if the electricity fails and the TV goes off. How to survive by one's own labor and ingenuity if it should come to that.

This peculiar sense of frailty is an unpleasant corollary to modern abundance, a condition reserved for the affluent few and one that probably many poor people would happily settle for. The sense of personal loss, after all, seems trivial in economic terms since capitalism's division of labor brilliantly does the homely chores for us now. Yet some people are discovering that the deepest human longings—the desire to fully realize the experience of life itself—can be fulfilled not by more accumulation, but by exploring what was lost, relearning some of the human-scale activities that lie beyond the market forces. These are all minor trends, to be sure, but perhaps harbingers of larger social change ahead.[12]

As a practical reality, however, the imperative for industrial transformation is too urgent to wait upon market forces. Global enterprises, even the most enlightened firms, are caught up in a price contest that undermines the new values and seeks to degrade the environmental standards already established in law. The atomizing incentives of the marketplace—self for self—naturally war with the common good and inhibit the pursuit of collective goals.

For instance, if the advanced technologies already developed, such as solar power and hydrogen fuel cells, were widely commercialized, the outlook for nature would be dramatically improved and rather quickly. Yet that is unlikely to happen anytime soon if left to private commerce. The market mechanism that governs enterprise and is enforced by financial markets assumes that resources are infinite, that there is no point in moving on to new sources of renewable energy until the price is right—that is, until the old resources are scarce or depleted.

Society, therefore, has to take a more aggressive role not only in effecting environmental enforcement, but also in making a market for reformed products and processes. Environmental taxes, if they can be equitably applied, will move the market behavior, but government procurement can also be a major force in industrial reform, just as government procurement brought new technologies and industries on stream during the dramatic industrial transformation of World War II, from electronics to petrochemical synthetics. Local governments need not wait upon national authority to do this since they represent a major market themselves. If Washington will not act, then Chicago, New York and Los Angeles might act collectively. Like any new market, the initial price is higher, but the price comes down as producers discover there are buyers and begin competing for them.

Governments and communities can also advance the technological frontier, independent of regular commerce, by fostering "pioneer firms" that will develop the new operating principles and products, leaping beyond the market's hesitation. Instead of devoting so much care and public subsidy to the fortunes of multinational corporations, taxpayers can focus their attention closer to home—subsidizing community-based employers that, in exchange for certain benefits and protective measures, will take big risks for the common good and address the community's tangible social concerns.

These pioneers would encompass new values and apply new technologies the public has already paid for through government-financed research, but that private commerce does not yet find profitable to adopt. The New Birth prison project, described in the previous chapter, provides a vivid example of what is possible with imagination. The pioneer firms, though perhaps quite small, would provide another effective setting for subsidized employment, but the jobs would be anchored in a larger public purpose and incorporate numerous social innovations, from flexible working schedules to continuing on-the-job education.

Unlike socialism, the companies would be privately owned and intended to become profitable, but the ownership would be vested among workers and citizens—owners required to take greater responsibility for their assets. Unlike the usual industrial policies, the focus would be on innovation in work and production, not on protecting the competitive position of existing firms or sectors. Many ventures would doubtless fail (and some entrepreneurs would abuse the public interest). But taxpayers would at least be financing risk-taking to advance their own collective interest, not simply to improve the private gain for some.

What these observations also suggest is that the conventional notions of mass consumption, the twentieth century's distinctive contribution to modern life, may no longer provide a viable economic solution either to the problem of future work or in the event of a market catastrophe. If the global system breaks down, the road back to general prosperity cannot rely upon simply reviving the same wasteful practices. If technology and the shifting industrial base continue to generate mass unemployment and wage decline, the new jobs will not be created by restoring the old status quo. In other words, the great transition that many are counting on to provide an eventual millennium—a transition like the early twentieth century's shift from agriculture to mass-production manufacturing—is unlikely to be repeated.

If so, the great problem of ensuring work and well-being for all will likely be solved more by social invention than by new variations on mass production. The usual labor-market remedies—legislating a shorter workweek, more equitable terms of pay and taxation—address part of the problem, but cannot possibly fill the growing void. The new jobs, as Yoshikawa said, have to be discovered by pursuing industrial transformation. The work of the future, as Daly suggested, will be revealed by establishing the new patterns of living—a good life that is perhaps less intense and less dependent on the corporation, but can be more satisfying in human terms, more sustainable in nature. These social visions are quite vague, of course, but a society looking at the future rather than the past will use its resources to explore them.

In the present climate, visions of grand public experiments sound quite fanciful, I know. The leading governments are mired in debt and struggling to cut back social commitments, not to expand them. Public spending, however, is always a choice of priorities—deciding what matters most to the society. If a society decides to reconsider its public spending in terms of true value versus institutionalized waste, it will discover there is lots of money available for experimentation.

An obvious source is the military establishment. While I was writing this final chapter, the newspapers reported on a new competition the Pentagon has organized among defense manufacturers to decide who gets to build the next generation of all-purpose fighter planes. This contest will be worth $750 billion to the winners. Half of that money will be provided by American taxpayers across the next twenty years, the rest from foreign taxpayers whose governments are expected to buy the new fighter planes. The price tag is astounding, especially for a government that claims to be broke, but this sort of long-term commitment of public capital is routine to the old order. [13]

Now imagine, for a moment, a new order that asks the military services to do without their new fighter plane and instead devotes the $750 billion to inventing the future. That money could launch tens of thousands of pioneer firms in America and abroad, committed to creating new and durable products and processes, to remaking the industrial economy in terms that will sustain life rather than threaten it. That money could make a commercial market for renewable energy sources or closed-loop factories; it could mobilize research and development to realize the visionary innovations, from robots to thermodynamics, and social inventions as well.

A democratic society makes choices and those choices will reflect what its people truly value. And every society, even a very rich one, has to live with the consequences, wise or foolish.

At last, we return once again to the original problem of capitalist enterprise—the market problem of matching supply to demand, of creating the new productive capacity needed to capture market shares but without generating surpluses that overrun the pool of available buyers. Capitalism's critics, from Marx to Gandhi to Thorstein Veblen, all focused on that dilemma and the obvious social contradiction it generates. Gandhi asked why the jute mills must close down in slack times and dismiss the workers when people still needed the goods they produced. This seemed inhumane to him, and he tried to imagine a steady-state enterprise that would balance its obligations and resources better—keep the mills running and producing goods for the future in order to reduce the human suffering imposed by market forces. Gandhi's jute mill did not succeed. Neither did Karl Marx's collective state ownership nor many other utopian experiments attempted across the centuries to get around the market.

Nor has anything in this book offered any solution to this core problem of capitalism. The market process is, as its advocates proclaim, a source of vast creative energies—the sales-and-profit incentive that leads individuals and enterprise to invent and multiply output. Yet this same mechanism also generates the brutal swings and manic excesses—the herds of reckless investors, the false hopes of producers, the relentless drive to maximize return—that create so much destruction and human suffering, subordination and insecurity.

The terms of the market incentives may be altered by society and government, but only on the margins. I can imagine, for instance, a reformed tax-depreciation structure that discourages firms from the wasteful practice of creating so much excess production. Or perhaps a system of forfeitable bonds could hold investors more accountable to the communities where their productive assets are located. These reforms might ameliorate the tides of creative destruction. They would not alter the fundamental social dilemma posed by markets.

Perhaps, in this next age of capitalism, an original thinker will arise somewhere in the world with a new theory that reconciles the market's imperatives with unfilled human needs, without having to destroy the marketplace to do so. This would be an intellectual achievement for the ages— reordering economic rhythms that have governed for five or six centuries and offering capitalist enterprise a way out of its own destructive pathologies. Though many have failed previously, it is not inconceivable that someone might someday solve this problem.

The need for such a theoretical breakthrough becomes more compelling, I think, as commerce globalizes toward the "one world" market. As the global system has extended its reach, the ancient paradox of poverty amid plenty becomes more acute and obvious because even though many prosper, the extremes between wealth and the unfilled human needs grow wider. Capitalism's problem of surpluses was portrayed by Gandhi, Marx and Veblen as its enduring barbarism: Why must so many human beings suffer from scarcity when the world is awash in abundance? How can factories refuse to produce when the need for their production remains so stark?

In our own time, these questions have resurfaced in tangible form as the immense surpluses of abundance accumulate alongside growing ranks of the destitute. For several decades the world's capacity to produce food, for instance, has far exceeded the entire human population's need for nourishment. Yet the stockpiles of unused foodstuffs pile up unsold each year in producing nations while somewhere else in the world hundreds of millions of others are malnourished, if not actually starving to death. The paradox is explained away easily enough in market terms. Indeed, the market insists that feeding impoverished people would be harmful to them, indulging their backwardness and postponing their eventual self-sufficiency.

That answer may satisfy the marketplace, but for humanity it constitutes another great, unanswered social question. Capitalism, for all its wondrous creativity and wealth, has not yet found a way to clothe the poor and feed the hungry unless they can pay for it.

Traveling around the world, between moments of euphoric wonder and dread I began to sense that a new ideology is struggling to be born—a new global consciousness that I heard expressed now and then in scattered fragments, but that is still weak and unformed, too undefined to even have a name. One cannot properly call it socialism, though this new understanding shares many of socialism's original ideals. The global future is too diverse and complex to be defined by socialism's origins in European class conflict or by the failed economic arrangements derived from Marx. The environmental ethic represents a core perspective of this nascent ideology, but does not adequately describe it either. Environmentalism is too narrow and precious in its present voice to speak for the global social reality.

Revolutionary energy emanates from feminism's ideas of justice since women are the most exploited class in the global industrial system, but women's advocates are also handicapped by vast differences in wealth and culture. Organized labor expresses universal values that speak to the global condition, yet its institutions are still burdened by the parochialism of national identity. Likewise, the world's great religions might contribute important elements to this new way of thinking, except their theologies still often reflect the tribalism that exalts faithful followers and demonizes the nonbelievers.

What I am suggesting is that these various strands of human thought are compatible and their perspectives might somehow converge in a new framework for understanding this new world. Yet even expressing the thought also makes obvious the immense difficulties of their ever finding common ground across the distant borders—that is, of societies ever accomplishing what commerce and finance have already achieved. Discovering the unknown other—stripping away the ancient fears and accepting that humanity is now a shared enterprise—is perhaps the hardest struggle posed by the global system.

Yet many people have, in fact, already made this leap of consciousness, including many of the managers, engineers and financial analysts who are dispersed around the global marketplace. If business can see the world as a unified whole, then surely societies can do the same. When social thinkers and citizens at large learn to overcome limitations of thought and to synthesize a concrete understanding of what the world should become, then a powerful new ideology may be born. For lack of a better name, it might be called global humanism.

If this new consciousness does gather force, it will start from a shared understanding that the market cannot deliver certain values to people and must be governed by them. At present, societies are yielding their social claims to the market little by little, in response to the economic pressures and in the hope that somehow the global system will eventually reward them for this retreat. If the arguments of this book are correct, the global system cannot possibly do that since it is driven by its own harsh imperatives and running ahead recklessly to collide with its own economic contradictions. So long as nations preoccupy themselves with the head-to-head footrace for competitive advantage, none can draw back and face these larger portents. A new global ideology starts by accepting that, ready or not, we are all in this together.

For fifty years, the world's affairs were organized by a blunt choice between the competing alternatives—market capitalism or the centralized command economies of the Communist realm. That choice is now irrelevant. The future will be determined by whether people can confront capitalism's repetitive pathologies and organize a new system that genuinely merges the market with democracy. This future is impossible to describe concretely, but it will be guided by certain basic guideposts—principles that will alter capitalism fundamentally when they are realized. Some of these principles have been described in these pages; others could be added.

Human dignity is indivisible, everywhere. The ownership of productive capital must be broadly shared in societies as the predicate for discovering genuine democracy and general social well-being. The industrial system must be reinvented to save the earth. The social values that are precious to most people must be freed from the confinements of economic imperatives and allowed to find fuller expression. These ideas are not utopian platitudes but the hard, practical work of the future.

Are such goals beyond human capacities, as many assume? Obviously, I do not think so. As I read history, human nature does not change over the millennia, but human behavior has changed—when people applied their natural inventiveness to constructing a new context for their lives, freeing themselves of narrow, debilitating habits that the old system required of them. This means thinking outside the framework of what is—imagining new economic and social understandings that deliver real value to the human experience, instead of destructive repetitions. Capitalism is in need of such examination. The world is new. The story of human aspirations begins again.

While everyone is not going to become alike (or even necessarily come to like each other), everyone is entitled to the respect and dignity inherent in being human. That means, most obviously, striving to get beyond the categories of race and culture and religious superiority that have defined so much of human history. The global system of production is teaching a powerful lesson: people are capable, everywhere in the world. Every nation, especially the wealthier ones, promotes its own version of national arrogance, a natural self-centeredness that is very difficult to set aside. But global commerce undermines—and perhaps will someday destroy—the ancient, nativist stereotypes by which different peoples are ranked and rank themselves.

The idea of empire and dominion is also undermined by these new realities. The history of nation-states, especially during the bloody twentieth century, has been a series of armed contests for territory and domination, but the traditional geopolitical assumptions are now quite confused as global commerce dilutes the meaning of national borders and constructs complex webs of interdependence. Nations keep acquiring armaments as though nothing has changed, without asking how gunboats and bombers are supposed to enforce the terms of trade or acquire market access for them. While it is most unlikely that warfare will disappear from human affairs, it becomes increasingly difficult to select a proper enemy—someone who is not also a major customer or co-producer. When foreign policy catches up with economic reality, the superpowers can abandon their illusions of dominance and the world may at last be ready to accept the end of empire.

The problem of political domination has shifted, in any case, to the free-running system of global enterprise itself. The nation-state is not going to disappear anytime soon for the good reason that citizens need some way to assert control over multinational corporations and capital. The dim prospect that supranational government might fulfill that role is neither plausible nor especially reassuring since global commerce and finance manipulate the international organizations to their own ends, at least as easily as they influence national governments. Mere citizens count for very little in the global system's decision-making, and if they do not try to reformulate the power of their own governments, they will have no power whatever to decide their own destinies.

The new question for democracy, one might say, is: Who elected George Soros? Or IBM-Siemens-Toshiba? If the nation-state will not defend the economic well-being of its own citizens or can no longer use military power for that purpose, then what exactly is it for? Americans and their allies surely did not win the Cold War in order to cede sovereignty over national economic policy to Motorola and Daimler-Benz, Toyota and Goldman Sachs. As global firms elaborate their own partnerships, sharing production and markets, the question of concentrated power will intensify the crisis for nations and domestic political leaders. The reactionary impulse to withdraw from the world—to defend the homeland against the future—is certain to grow stronger and perhaps quite dangerous.

The political task, therefore, is tricky: to re-create a national governance that asserts its power to regulate players in the global market and yet, at the same time, recognizes the necessity of embracing the internationalist perspective. This does not ask people to abandon national interest, but to accept that national interest must now find expression in the far more complex context of the collective global interest. The real political challenge is to confront the internationalists of commerce and finance on their own ground and compel them to accept larger social values. The United States cannot save the world or even save itself unless it learns to think in this manner, but then neither can Japan or Germany, China or Sweden or Indonesia. Citizens naturally feel a sense of loss, but this is the new reality. There is no way of turning back from it that does not invite its own form of calamity.

Earlier on, I sketched some of the political ideas that, if mutually asserted by major nations, could moderate the pace of industrial revolution and push the global system toward more positive and equitable outcomes, with less danger of a tragic breakdown. None of these propositions violates the existing rules of global trade, but all of them challenge the laissez-faire presumptions of the global system, pretensions of free trade that are largely fraudulent in any case:

Restore national controls over global capital. Tax wealth more, labor less. Stimulate global growth by boosting consumer demand from the bottom up. Compel trading nations to accept more balanced trade relations and absorb more surplus production. Forgive the debtors, especially the hopeless cases among the very poorest nations. Reorganize monetary policy to confront the realities of a globalized money supply, both to achieve greater stability and open the way to greater growth. Defend labor rights in all markets, prohibit the ancient abuses renewed in the "dark Satanic mills." Withdraw from the old labor-capital battleground by universalizing access to capital ownership. Reformulate the idea of economic growth to escape the wasteful nature of consumption. And, in the meantime, defend work and wages and social protections against assaults by the marketplace.

It is my conviction that all of these reforms are plausible and possible to achieve if people can free themselves of the usual bromides and reassurances and begin to examine the bewildering facts with more clarity and purpose. This book, I hope, has helped people to do that or at least provoked them to reconsider what they have been taught about the world.

Any reader who has come this far already knows that I am, by nature, abundantly optimistic about the human condition and its possibilities but not a fool, I hope, about the present political realities. It would be dishonest to leave the impression that I think these reforms and other new ideas are likely to prevail in a prompt and rational manner. I am not so sanguine about the future. I think there will be more pain, more destabilizing disruptions and loss, before people find the courage to rebel and take control of their destinies.

This wondrous machine I have described is too awesome and self-confident to yield to mere facts or gentle persuasion. In the history of revolutionary eras, when moderate voices come forward to plead for moderate reforms, they are typically brushed aside. Eventually, more radical solutions arise and advance because the reigning system would not pause to listen to dissenting voices.

The blunt truth is that the political power arrayed against reform visions is overwhelming, while the people who support these new directions are everywhere quite weak. The inertial momentum of the status quo—the insecurity of political leaders, intimidated as they are by the overbearing influence of business and finance—makes it quite difficult, if not impossible, to imagine that the alternatives will receive rational consideration and timely response.

This seems especially the case in America, where opinion leaders, despite the facts, still see themselves as the confident leaders of the global system. American politics is steeped in ignorance about the global reality, and any who question the reigning mantra of economic orthodoxy will be harshly disciplined by the press and multinational interests. Other great nations are, likewise, not exempt from ignorance and indulge in their own forms of blindness and evasion.

In short, if I am compelled to guess the future, I would estimate that the global system will, indeed, probably experience a series of terrible events —wrenching calamities that are economic or social or environmental in nature—before common sense can prevail. It would be pleasing to believe otherwise, but the global system so dominates and intimidates present thinking that I expect societies will be taught still more painful lessons before they find the will to act.

The utopian vision of the marketplace offers, after all, an enthralling religion, a self-satisfied belief system that attracts fervent and influential adherents. The wondrous machine of free-running enterprise has fantastic capabilities and people defer to its powers, persuaded it will carry them forward to millennial outcomes. Abstracted from human reality, the market's intricate mechanisms convey an entrancing sense of perfection, logical and self-correcting. Many intelligent people have come to worship these market principles, like a spiritual code that will resolve all the larger questions for us, social and moral and otherwise, so long as no one interferes with its authority. In this modern secular age, many who think of themselves as rational and urbane have put their faith in this idea of the self-regulating market as piously as others put their trust in God.

When this god fails, as I think it must, people around the world may at last be free to see things more clearly again, and to reclaim responsibility for their own lives and begin organizing the future in its more promising terms.

Notes

As these notes reflect, I have relied on many diverse sources, but none was more valuable than the *Financial Times* of London. The *Financial Times* provides an authoritative snapshot of action in the global economy every day, with superb reporting and analysis, much more comprehensive than anything published in the United States.

ONE: *The Storm Upon Us*

1. The elephant population of Thailand has declined to 1,975 in the wild and 2,938 domesticated animals, according to Rodney Tasker, *Far Eastern Economic Review*, April 29, 1993. Daily commuting time in Thailand is the longest in Asia, according to a survey of affluent consumers: *Far Eastern Economic Review*, August 27, 1992. Thai auto sales and traffic jams: Victor Mallet, *Financial Times*, November 27, 1993.

2. The Warsaw stock market crash: *Warsaw Voice*, April 24, 1994.

3. Willkie made the crucial connection, quite radical in his time, between European colonialism and America's own system of racial segregation: "It has been a long while since the United States had any imperialistic designs toward the outside world. But we have practiced within our own boundaries something that amounts to race imperialism. The attitude of the white citizens of this country toward the Negroes has undeniably had some of the unlovely characteristics of an alien imperialism—a smug racial superiority, a willingness to exploit an unprotected people." Wendell L. Willkie, *One World* (New York: Simon & Schuster, 1943; reprint, Urbana-Champaign, University of Illinois Press, 1966).

4. Edward W. Said, *Representations of the Intellectual* (New York: Pantheon, 1994).

5. Economist Lester Thurow wrote as recently as 1992: "History and human nature tells us that it will be far easier for the Americans and the Japanese to avoid doing what they must do if they are to win. Future historians will record that the twenty-first century belonged to the House of Europe!" *Head to Head: Coming Economic Battles Among Japan, Europe, and America* (New York: Morrow, 1992).

6. The fastest elevator, built by Mitsubishi in the 70-story Yokohama Landmark Tower, travels 3,461 feet a minute, about 28 miles an hour: *New York Times*, September 22, 1993. Asian "affluents" were described in a survey report by *Far Eastern Economic Review*, August 27, 1992.

7. Anheuser-Busch: *Financial Times*, June 29 and July 30, 1993, and February 23, 1995; Siemens: *Financial Times*, July 21, 1993; Taiwan Aerospace: *Financial Times*, July 24, 1993; drug company mergers: *Financial Times*, May 4, 1994; NEC-

Samsung: *Financial Times,* February 7, 1995; IBM losses: *Wall Street Journal,* July 28, 1993; Bausch & Lomb, Colgate-Palmolive: *Wall Street Journal,* August 4, 1993; AT&T: *Financial Times,* June 24, 1994; Coca-Cola: *Financial Times,* July 22, 1993.

8. John F. Welch Jr., *Wall Street Journal,* June 21, 1994.

9. The 500 largest global firms are described in *Multinationals and the National Interest: Playing by Different Rules,* Office of Technology Assessment, U.S. Congress, September 1993. American firms still dominate among the largest, accounting for 7 of the 20 biggest multinationals, as ranked by foreign assets.

The top 20 are, in order: Royal Dutch Shell (UK/Netherlands), Ford, GM, Exxon, IBM (U.S.), British Petroleum (UK), Asea Brown Boveri (Switzerland/Sweden), Nestlé (Switzerland), Philips Electronics (Netherlands), Mobil (U.S.), Unilever (UK, Netherlands), Matsushita Electric (Japan), Fiat (Italy), Siemens (Germany), Sony (Japan), Volkswagen (Germany), Elf Aquitaine (France), Mitsubishi (Japan), GE and du Pont (U.S.). Cited in "World Investment Report 1993: Transnational Corporations and Integrated International Production," United Nations, from *Financial Times,* July 21, 1993.

10. *Multinationals and the National Interest,* OTA. The biggest owners of the $2 trillion in foreign productive assets continue to be U.S. firms, with a total of $474 billion, followed by Britain, $259 billion, and Japan, $251 billion: *Financial Times,* July 21, 1993.

11. The intrafirm trade patterns vary from country to country. For Japanese manufacturing, 51 percent of all exports from affiliates were to the parent companies or other sister affiliates in 1989, according to John H. Dunning, *Multinational Enterprises and the Global Economy* (Reading, Mass.: Addison-Wesley, 1993).

12. Bank lending growth is from the annual reports of the Bank for International Settlements. Other financial data is from "International Capital Markets, Part I," International Monetary Fund, 1993.

13. William H. Davidow and Michael S. Malone, *The Virtual Corporation: Structuring and Revitalizing the Corporation for the 21st Century* (New York: HarperCollins, 1992).

TWO: *The New Against the Old*

1. Robert Noyce co-founded Intel Corporation, a worldwide pioneer and dominant producer of microprocessing semiconductors, and became quite wealthy. Jack Kilby continued with Texas Instruments and eventually became an independent inventor. T. R. Reid, *The Chip: How Two Americans Invented the Microchip and Launched a Revolution* (New York: Simon & Schuster, 1984).

2. Before his death, Braudel recognized that the U.S. might lose its economic hegemony to Japan and Asia, but he thought it was just as likely that American enterprise would be strengthened by the contest and retain its dominance. His musings are contained in lectures delivered in 1976 at Johns Hopkins University, where Braudel reflected upon his life's great work, the three-volume history of capitalism. Fernand Braudel, *Afterthoughts on Material Civilization and Capitalism* (Baltimore: Johns Hopkins University Press, 1977).

3. China's GNP comparisons for 1993 are from *The World Bank Atlas, 1995* (Washington, D.C.: World Bank, 1994), and the *Statistical Abstract of the United States* (Washington, D.C.: U.S. Commerce Department, 1994). The so-called purchasing power parity comparisons attempt to reflect the vast economic activities of a nation, from food production to housing, that are not fully reflected in market transaction accounts. This approach may eliminate currency-exchange distortion and reflect the broader reality of a nation's living standards, but it encourages exaggerated ideas of a nation's economic prowess. According to the World Bank's PPP calculations, China's per capita income is $2,100, still extremely poor.

4. OECD countries' share of global trade: "World Economic Survey," United Nations, 1993.

5. "Report on the Measurement of International Capital Flows," International Monetary Fund, September 1993. The Grand Cayman Island ranks behind the United Kingdom, Belgium, Hong Kong and Japan: "International Financial Statistics," International Monetary Fund, February 1995.

6. Singapore's notoriously harsh criminal-justice system includes the death penalty for drug-peddling and the celebrated caning of youthful offenders. But, in fact, all of its citizens are confined by harsh laws, the rigid one-party political rule, strict government control of press and speech. Singapore's $19,300 per capita income for 1993 compares to $18,000 in the United Kingdom: *World Bank Atlas, 1995.*

7. The *International Herald Tribune,* jointly owned by the *Washington Post* and the *New York Times,* was compelled to publish apologies three times in 1994 for various "libels" against Singapore's rulers. Some editors objected, but corporate officers "believe the paper can operate successfully in Singapore with judicious editing to avoid future confrontations with the Singaporean establishment," according to Richard Harwood, *Washington Post,* February 17, 1995.

8. My point is not to reopen historical arguments about why class conflicts in industrial England or France produced different dynamics than in Germany or Japan or Russia. The point is that simple generalities about the emerging nations are useless without examining the broad structures of social classes and the inherited power relationships among them. For a classic study of these questions, see Barrington Moore Jr., *Social Origins of Dictatorship and Democracy: Lord and Peasant in the Making of the Modern World* (Boston: Beacon, 1966).

THREE: *The Ghost of Marx*

1. The twenty-seven advanced economies in the Organization for Economic Cooperation and Development officially recorded 35 million unemployed in 1994 and an unemployment rate of 8.5 percent. But, as the Bank for International Settlements has noted, this is artificially low because of all those arbitrarily excluded from the count. The actual unemployment rate, BIS estimated, was as high as 12.5 percent and 2 to 3 percent higher than that if workers temporarily supported by government training are included. Thus, the total may be nearly twice 35 million. A much larger number exists, of course, throughout the rest of the world. *Bank for International Settlements Annual Report,* 1994.

2. John Ralston Saul, who is both experienced in global business and a prize-winning novelist, has elaborated on these themes in *Voltaire's Bastards: The Dictatorship of Reason in the West* (New York: Free Press, 1992) and *The Doubter's Companion: A Dictionary of Aggressive Common Sense* (New York: Free Press, 1994).

3. Peter F. Drucker, "The Age of Social Transformation," *Atlantic Monthly,* November 1994.

4. My analytical approach to the realm of business decision-making is informed by the great American economist Thorstein Veblen, who wrote about business institutions early in the twentieth century, when similar industrialization was under way. Veblen's sociological perspective has been largely eclipsed by the scientific pretensions of modern economics, but ironically his acerbic analysis of how things actually work in business remains much closer to the way businesspeople understand their own world. See, for instance, Veblen's *Absentee Ownership, And Business Enterprise in Recent Times: The Case of America* (1923; reprint, New York: Viking, 1964).

5. My understanding of the past, particularly the collision between markets and societies in the early twentieth century, has been greatly informed by Karl

Polanyi's important work *The Great Transformation: The Political and Economic Origins of Our Time* (Boston: Beacon, 1994).

FOUR: "Gleiche Arbeit, gleicher Lohn"

1. For instance, the *Financial Times* on March 7, 1994, reported the following comparisons of manufacturing labor costs per hour:

West Germany	$24.90	Singapore	$5.10
Former East Germany	$17.30	South Korea	$4.90
Japan	$16.90	Hong Kong	$4.20
United States	$16.40	Hungary	$1.80
France	$16.30	Czech Republic	$1.10
United Kingdom	$12.40	China	50 cents

2. Arunasalam, leader of the Malaysian Electrical Workers Union, described a French-owned electronics plant that moved to Vietnam for wages of $10 to $15 a month. The Shanghai minimum wage was reported in the *Wall Street Journal,* January 10, 1994.

3. James Goldsmith, *The Trap (Le Piège)* (New York: Carroll & Graf, 1994).

4. "International Comparisons of Hourly Compensation Costs for Production Workers in Manufacturing, 1975–1993," U.S. Bureau of Labor Statistics, May 1994. Wage statistics vary in comparisons because of different definitions of who is covered in the averages and what are counted as benefits or wages.

5. ABB details are from David de Pury, "Can Europe Keep Up?" *International Economy,* January 1994. Swissair and Edzard Reuter comment from Hans-Peter Martin and Harald Schumann, "All Hindrances Removed," *Der Spiegel,* December 1993 (translated by Justin Fox). IBM disc-drive shift: Dow-Jones News Service, August 4, 1994. Intra-Europe movements: *Multinationals and the National Interest: Playing by Different Rules,* Office of Technology Assessment, U.S. Congress, September 1993. Ikea in Poland: *Wall Street Journal,* June 28, 1993. Daimler-Benz site contest: *Financial Times,* December 20, 1993, and interviews with IG Metall officials. Daimler's total job reduction: *Wall Street Journal,* April 13, 1995.

6. Charles I. Clough Jr., "The Meek Inherit the Earth," Merrill Lynch Investment Strategy Department, September 1993.

7. Japanese job losses: *Financial Times,* December 3, 1993.

8. Thomas Mayer: *Wall Street Journal,* December 1, 1993. Etienne Davignon: *Financial Times,* June 16, 1994.

9. Wood found that changes in trade created more than 20 million manufacturing jobs in the developing countries, mostly as their exports increased in the 1980s. Adrian Wood, *North-South Trade, Employment and Inequality: Changing Fortunes in a Skill-Driven World* (New York, Oxford: Oxford University Press, 1994).

10. Jeffrey Henderson, *The Globalisation of High Technology Production: Society, Space and Semiconductors in the Restructuring of the Modern World* (London: Routledge, 1989).

11. David R. Howell, "The Skills Myth," *American Prospect,* Summer 1994. The wage declines were much more severe in some nonmanufacturing sectors like retailing and were not spread uniformly across manufacturing.

12. Harley Shaiken's remarks were at an Economic Strategy Institute conference, March 9, 1994.

13. The wage and productivity comparisons were cited by Richard Rothstein of the Economic Policy Institute, "Workforce Globalization: A Policy Response," for the Women's Bureau, U.S. Labor Department, 1994.

14. Earnings as a percentage of value added are listed country by country in *World Bank Tables, 1993.*

15. For a lucid explication of the "virtuous circle" and how it was effectively dismantled by new production systems, see Eileen Appelbaum and Rosemary Batt, *The New American Workplace: Transforming Work Systems in the United States* (Ithaca, N.Y.: ILR Press, 1994).

16. Wages as a percentage of total personal income and total sales: *Economic Report of the President,* February 1995, calculations by Per-Kristian Nelson. If transfer payments were excluded, the wage share would be larger, but still declining.

FIVE: "Wawasan 2020"

1. Details on Proton and Kancil: Kieran Cooke and Jenny Luesby in the *Financial Times,* August 31, 1993, and September 28, 1994. Vietnam deal: *Financial Times,* May 16, 1994. Tallest building: *Wall Street Journal,* November 23, 1993.

2. Growth statistics and projections: *World Bank Tables, 1993* (Baltimore: Johns Hopkins University Press, 1993) and Mahathir Mohamad, "Malaysia: The Way Forward," speech given February 28, 1994.

3. Mahathir speech, UN General Assembly, October 1, 1993.

4. Social progress in Malaysia: *UN Human Development Report,* 1994.

5. Mahathir speech, 1994 China summit meeting, May 11, 1994.

6. Chandra Muzaffar, *Human Rights and the New World Order* (Penang, Malaysia: Just World Trust, 1993).

7. Electronics held a 50 percent share of all manufacturing, according to Mahathir, who said that with textiles included, the figure rose to 63 percent; Mahathir, "The Way Forward." The *Financial Times* reported that electrical and electronics goods accounted for 27.4 percent of all exports in 1983, up to 41.7 percent by 1993.

8. Mahathir, "The Way Forward."

9. "Crude oil of the information age": William H. Davidow and Michael S. Malone, *The Virtual Corporation: Structuring and Revitalizing the Corporation for the 21st Century* (New York: HarperCollins, 1992).

10. Employment in semiconductors included both domestic and multinational companies, as reported by the U.S. Labor Department in "Employment, Hours, and Earnings: United States, 1909–94," September 1994. The multinational employment in electronics components at both American and foreign firms declined from 375,000 to 236,000 over ten years, as reported in "U.S. Direct Investment Abroad" and "Foreign Direct Investment in U.S.," 1982–1992, U.S. Commerce Department.

11. In 1993, Japan's trade surplus with the U.S. was $59 billion while the rest of Asia's was $50 billion, driven mainly by China with a surplus of $23 billion. Malaysia's surplus went from $1 billion to $4.5 billion from 1987 to 1993. Trade data from U.S. Commerce Department.

12. The AFL-CIO and others had petitioned the U.S. government to withdraw the preferential trading terms granted to developing nations on the grounds that Malaysia violated international standards for labor rights. The petition was rejected.

Details on the union ban are drawn from interviews with Malaysian trade-union leaders Rajasekaran and Arunasalam, as well as from various industry documents including discussion notes on meeting with Minister of Labor Lee Kim Sai, October 27, 1986; press release from the Malaysian-American Electronics Industry Association, October 1, 1988, an American Business Council fax to all MAEI members, September 27, 1988.

13. Harris officials claimed that no one was fired, which may have been technically correct but was not meaningful. The company reorganized and offered benefits to all workers who shifted to a newly titled corporate entity, leaving the new union

and its leaders behind in the old entity, which was then discontinued. The women continued in the same factory, doing the same work, but without a union.

14. Details on Alabama-Daimler deal: *Birmingham News,* October 12, 1993, and January 21, 1994.

15. Daimler's Vietnam plant: *Financial Times,* July 27, 1994.

16. Ford-Jaguar threat: *Financial Times,* January 6, 1995.

17. Bidding war: *Multinationals and the National Interest: Playing by Different Rules;* Office of Technology Assessment, U.S. Congress, September 1993; Bill Bishop, "Kentucky Ties Its Future to a Failed Idea," *Lexington Herald-Leader,* March 28, 1993, and Greg LeRoy, "No More Candy Store: States and Cities Making Job Subsidies Accountable," Federation for Industrial Retention and Renewal, Chicago, 1994.

18. Mark Waterhouse was quoted by Fred R. Bleakley in the *Wall Street Journal,* March 8, 1995. IBM's return to Manassas, Virginia, in a joint venture with Toshiba was reported in the *Washington Post,* August 9, 1995.

19. Greg LeRoy, in "No More Candy Store," details the efforts of state and local governments to establish corporate accountability for the tax subsidies. As a practical matter, it would require federal action—perhaps even a constitutional amendment—to shut down the practice.

20. BMW taxes: "All Hindrances Removed," *Der Spiegel,* December 1993.

21. IBM's tax avoidance was cited by Robert S. McIntyre, "The Hidden Entitlements," Citizens for Tax Justice, April 1995. Intel's case was described by Michael J. McIntyre, "Overruling Intel to Pay for GATS," *Tax Notes International,* September 26, 1994. Intel had won a U.S. tax court ruling that effectively upheld its "nowhere income," and as McIntyre explained, reformers were campaigning to get it corrected by congressional action but "did not yet have the political horses to repeal the underlying tax break." The McIntyres are brothers who both pursue public-spirited reform in the densely complicated area of corporate taxation, domestic and international.

22. Foreign firms' tax avoidance, amicus brief by Representatives Don Edwards, Howard L. Berman and Xavier Becerra in *Barclays Bank* v. *Franchise Tax Board of California,* Supreme Court, October Term, 1993.

23. Nissan tax penalty: *Financial Times,* November 11, 1993.

24. See David Harris, Randall Morck, Joel Slemrod and Bernard Yeung, "Income Shifting in U.S. Multinational Corporations," in Alberto Giovannini, R. Glenn Hubbard and Joel Slemrod, editors, *Studies in International Taxation* (Chicago: University of Chicago Press, 1993).

25. As a candidate, Bill Clinton had made an issue of tax evasion by foreign (though not American) multinationals and promised to gain $40 billion in lost revenue over four years. Once in office, he backed off the reforms and offered a mild measure that accomplished very little. Cynics suggested that this change of heart occurred when it was explained to him that tax reform aimed at foreigners was bound to hit the U.S. companies, too.

The state of California applies a unitary tax system to multinational corporations, an approach upheld by the Supreme Court in 1994 despite vigorous challenges by multinationals. The victory was diminished because other states, under pressure from business lobbies, had backed away from the unitary system, and California itself has legislated an "opt out" provision in 1993. *Wall Street Journal* and *Financial Times,* June 21, 1994.

26. BMW wages: *Financial Times,* October 1, 1993.

27. Jeffrey Henderson, *The Globalisation of High Technology Production: Society, Space and Semiconductors in the Restructuring of the Modern World* (London: Routledge, 1989).

28. I have obscured the identities of these young women at their request, for they feared retaliation from employers. Three older women, Betty Yeoh, Asah Ibrahim and Veronica Leo, union members who served as counselors at the hostel supported by the Malaysian Trade Union Congress, assisted with translations.

29. Mahathir, Beijing speech.

30. "Foreign Economic Trends: Malaysia," U.S. Embassy, Kuala Lumpur, December 1993.

six: Jidoka

1. Labor input data are derived from several sources, and the comparisons inevitably contain some distortions due to different methods of measurement. The Tahara No. 4 line, as of November 1994, was producing 450 cars a day with two shifts of 520 workers. This translates into 2.3 worker-days per vehicle, or 18.4 hours each. The labor hours at U.S. plants are from *The Harbour Report 1994*, an authoritative study of manufacturing productivity in the North American auto plants, produced by Harbour & Associates Inc., Troy, Michigan. The Volvo statistics are from the company, cited by Richard W. Stevenson, *New York Times*, October 4, 1994. James E. Harbour provided his own approximate estimates for Volkswagen, Mercedes, BMW and Audi.

2. Japanese transplants and U.S. companies: *Harbour Report 1994*.

3. Toyota's corporate history is described by Yukiyasu Togo and William Wartman, *Against All Odds: The Story of the Toyota Motor Corporation and the Family That Created It* (New York: St. Martin's, 1993). The technological concepts are explained in "Toyota Production System," Toyota Motor Corporation, 1992.

4. VW was derided as a fat duck by its chairman, Ferdinand Piëch, in the *Financial Times*, September 8, 1993. Details on Wolfsburg's "industrial dinosaur": *Wall Street Journal*, April 1, 1993. López's vision was described by Kevin Done, *Financial Times*, September 9, 1994.

5. The VW estimates were from James Harbour of Harbour & Associates.

6. The U.S. improvements are from *The Harbour Report 1994* and *The Harbour Report: A Decade Later, Competitive Assessment of the North American Automotive Industry, 1979–1989* (Troy, Mich.: Harbour & Associates, 1990).

7. Alex Trotman quoted in *Financial Times*, October 6, 1993.

8. India auto deals: *Financial Times*, September 6, 1994.

9. U.S. plant closings from economics department, Chrysler, November 1994. Job decline: "Employment, Hours, and Earnings: United States, 1909–94," U.S. Labor Department, September 1994.

10. Toyota announced in May 1995 that it was considering permanent domestic plant closings as a "last resort" and its capacity was 700,000 to 800,000 vehicles in surplus. Nissan had already announced the closing of its 30-year-old Zama plant. Mazda and others were expected to follow. *Financial Times*, May 11, 1995.

11. Michelin's development: John Griffiths in *Financial Times*, March 4, 1994, and Marlise Simons in the *New York Times*, May 12, 1994.

12. Bayer: *Financial Times*, March 4, 1994.

13. Allen J. Lenz, "The U.S. Chemical Industry: Performance in 1994 and Outlook," Chemical Manufacturers Association, November 1994. His commentary was quoted by Bloomberg Business News, *New York Times*, May 11, 1994.

14. Pharmaceuticals: Paul Abrahams in the *Financial Times*, March 23, 1994.

15. Dean Thornton testified for Boeing at hearings of the National Commission to Ensure a Strong Competitive Airline Industry, Washington, D.C., June 4, 1993.

16. J. H. Hotson, "Financing Sustainable Development," Économies et Sociétés, ISMÉA, Paris, January 1994.

17. Car prices and incomes: Wynn Van Bussman, "Outlook for the Auto Industry," Chrysler Corporation, January 5, 1995.

18. VW's eventual goal, according to Ferdinand Piëch, was a break-even point of 65 percent: *Financial Times,* March 30, 1995.

19. Charles I. Clough Jr., "The Meek Inherit the Earth," Merrill Lynch Investment Strategy Department, September 1993.

SEVEN: *"Scratching Their Itch"*

1. Orders for 777: *Boeing News,* April 8, 1994.

2. On March 21, 1996, Reuters reported the Boeing commitment to make 1,500 tail sections for the 737 in China.

3. The foreign-content trend for Boeing aircraft was described by industry analyst Randy Barber of the Center for Economic Organizing, a labor-supported policy group in Washington, D.C.

4. Engineering collaboration on 777: The technology transfers to Japan by Boeing and other American aerospace manufacturers are described in alarming detail by MIT political scientist Richard J. Samuels in his book *"Rich Nation, Strong Army": National Security and the Technological Transformation of Japan* (Ithaca, N.Y.: Cornell University Press, 1994).

5. Peter K. Chapman was quoted by Patrick E. Tyler, *New York Times,* February 25, 1995. Details on McDonnell's 1985 and 1994 assembly deals in China are from Randy Barber and Robert E. Scott, "Jobs on the Wing: Trading Away the Future of the U.S. Aerospace Industry," Economic Policy Institute, August 1995.

6. Boeing objected to the U.S. financial support requested by Pratt & Whitney for the Aeroflot aircraft: *Wall Street Journal,* March 6, 1995.

7. Boeing generally claims that for every job it relocates offshore, six or seven jobs are sustained in the U.S. The calculation is narrowly correct only if Boeing cannot sell the airplanes on any other terms. In any case, the larger long-term consequences for U.S. employment remain the same: as the industrial structure is moved elsewhere, the local content declines. The value-added share potentially available for American workers becomes smaller.

8. The 20 to 23 percent average for offsets was calculated from remarks by Ron Woodard, president of the commercial group, before the Aerospace Industries Association of Canada, September 26, 1994. Woodard displayed a chart of Boeing's typical "orders and buy levels" from four representative nations over the previous six years. Based on this, he explained, Canada's $800 million in subcontracting work ought to yield $3.5 billion to $4 billion in aircraft sales.

9. Richard J. Samuels, *"Rich Nation, Strong Army."*

10. Acknowledging that more such outsourcing was likely, Mitsubishi designated China's Shenyang Aircraft to produce machine parts for the 777 and Indonesia's IPTN to make fuselage parts for the 777 and 767. *Aviation Week & Space Technology,* April 24, 1995.

11. Boeing discounts: Jeff Cole in the *Wall Street Journal,* April 24, 1995. The sale to SAS of 30 planes replaced aging McDonnell Douglas aircraft.

12. Airbus dispersal details: *New York Times,* February 15, 1995, and the *Financial Times,* August 8 and November 10, 1994.

13. Fuji and Kawasaki technology transfers were described by Samuels, *"Rich Nation, Strong Army."*

14. GM-India transaction: David Bodkin, Delphi Automotive Systems.

15. France-Korea fast trains: James Goldsmith, *The Trap* (New York: Carroll & Graf, 1994). IBM-Intel agreements in China: *New York Times,* May 4, 1994.

16. European auto-import limits: *Financial Times,* September 6, 1993, and May 19, 1994. Details on EC import regulations are from Peter F. Cowhey and

Jonathan D. Aronson, *Managing the World Economy: The Consequences of Corporate Alliances* (New York: Council on Foreign Relations Press, 1993).

17. The aluminum crisis and subsequent cartel agreement played out during the same season that the U.S. Congress was debating approval of the North American Free Trade Agreement, yet the contradiction never arose in the debate, partly because the U.S. press mostly ignored it at the time. Details are drawn from interviews and the *Financial Times,* September 30, October 19 and November 5, 1993, as well as from a definitive account by Erle Norton and Martin du Bois in the *Wall Street Journal,* June 9, 1994. The subsequent price recovery was reported by the *Journal,* November 18, 1994, in a story that failed to mention the cartelized production.

18. Lawrence B. Krause, "Managed Trade: The Regime of Today and Tomorrow," *Journal of Asian Economics,* 3, no. 2 (1992).

19. The Council on Competitiveness in Washington has documented a series of episodes in which Boeing, McDonnell Douglas and some U.S. airlines told the U.S. government not to press its unfair trading complaints against the government-subsidized Airbus. The first was in 1978, the most recent in 1987. "Government officials were unwilling to take trade measures opposed by U.S. industry," the council reported in "Commercial Aircraft Case Study," 1994.

20. I have briefly summarized what is, of course, a complicated point of historical contention. The so-called revisionists in the American trade debate have argued the peculiarity of the Japanese system, based on national culture and the country's authoritarian political legacy. James Fallows, for example, cited the central influence of a nineteenth-century German economist, Friedrich List, on how Japan decided to shape and steer its developing industries with protectionist measures. See Fallows, *Looking at the Sun: The Rise of the New East Asian Economic and Political System* (New York: Pantheon, 1994).

Yet, as others have pointed out, List was himself influenced by the American experience—government-promoted development in the U.S. and the leading figures from Alexander Hamilton to Henry C. Carey, an advisor to Lincoln, whose thinking helped shape a doctrine then known as the American System of Political Economy. See Peter Ennis and Richard Katz, "The System That Never Was," *Tokyo Business,* November 1994. It is not that every industrial nation behaves exactly alike or that Japan is exempt from criticism, but that historical similarities are sufficient to deflate anyone's nationalist moral claims.

21. My visit to Hongyuan Forging was suggested by Newton L. Simmons of Boeing.

EIGHT: "Facai zhifu shi guangrong de"

1. The Japanese loans were described by Zhang Hongbiao, president of Aviation Industries of China (AVIC) in "China Aero Information," China Aero Information Centre, Beijing, October 1994.

2. Details on China's growing state sector: Nicholas R. Lardy, *China in the World Economy,* (Washington, D.C.: Institute for International Economics, April 1994); Harry G. Broadman, "Meeting the Challenge of Chinese Enterprise Reform," World Bank, October 27, 1994; and Patrick E. Tyler in the *New York Times,* December 16, 1994.

3. Communist Party in Chinese factories: *Wall Street Journal,* December 10, 1993.

4. Market potential statistics are drawn from "Chinese Economic Area: America's Commercial Interests, 1993–2000," U.S. Commerce Department, August 1993; "China Trade & Investment," *Far Eastern Economic Review,* September 1, 1994; Tony Walker and Kevin Done in the *Financial Times,* November 23, 1994.

5. U.S.-China consumption comparisons are from Richard Parker, "The Future of Global TV News," Joan Shorenstein Center, Harvard, September 1994, and *Business Week,* February 14, 1994.

6. China's GNP, measured in yuan, rose from 506 billion in 1978 to 1,469 billion in 1991. Per capita income in U.S. dollars rose from $220 to $370: *World Bank Tables 1993,* World Bank. Mahathir's comment was from his Beijing summit speech, May 11, 1994.

7. Lawrence B. Krause, "Managed Trade: The Regime of Today and Tomorrow," *Journal of Asian Economics* 3, no. 2 (1992).

8. Wu Jichuan was quoted in the *Wall Street Journal,* December 19, 1995.

9. Joint ventures: *Asian Wall Street Journal,* August 29, 1994.

10. The IMF estimated total capital flight of $9.4 billion, but state enterprises and some provincial governments were also setting up shell companies in Hong Kong to hold their investments abroad, holdings estimated at $30 billion. Friedrich Wu, "China's Dirty Little Secret," *The International Economy,* May/June 1994.

11. Chinese exports to U.S. have already eclipsed Japan's if one considers the Chinese economic area of China, Taiwan and Hong Kong as one entity. In 1992, those interrelated economies accounted for $60 billion, or 11 percent of all U.S. imports. "Chinese Economic Area: America's Commercial Interests 1993–2000," U.S. Commerce Department, August 1993.

12. The unemployment projection was reported by Agence France Presse, Beijing, August 16, 1994. Data on China's progress is from Vaclav Smil, *China's Environmental Crisis: An Inquiry into the Limits of National Development* (Armonk, N.Y.: M. E. Sharpe, 1993), and the World Bank's *World Bank Tables 1993.*

13. China's auto industrial policy was published in the official *People's Daily,* July 4, 1994. I have also relied on a U.S. State Department "subsector analysis" dated June 1994.

14. Details on the auto competition in China are drawn from the *Wall Street Journal,* July 11, 1995; *New York Times,* September 22, 1994; *Financial Times,* May 2 and June 23, 1995. The 1995 winners were reported in the *Wall Street Journal,* October 24, 1995.

NINE: *Cooperative Capitalism*

1. The Semiconductor Industry Association's 1994 edition of *The National Technology Roadmap for Semiconductors* reports: "A key question is when will the industry forecast depart from Moore's Law? The probable, yet controversial answer is by the end of 2010." *The Economist,* July 15, 1995, predicted that "the end is nigh" and the curve of innovation would break down within five or six years. *Business Week,* July 4, 1994, took a much more optimistic view of the technological possibilities.

2. Cost to end users of each generation of memory chips was reported in *The National Technology Roadmap.*

3. Walter Kunerth of Siemens was interviewed by Tony Jackson in the *Financial Times,* September 10, 1993.

4. Cross-cultural misunderstandings among the researchers were described by E. S. Browning in the *Wall Street Journal,* May 3, 1994. A Siemens manager briefed German engineers on the Americans' "hamburger style of management" in which conversational small talk represents the bun and the meat of criticism is slipped in between. "With Germans," he told Browning, "all you get is the meat. And with Japanese, it's all the soft stuff—you have to smell the meat."

5. The technology-capital curve driving the semiconductor industry may be visualized as three interrelated trend lines, each moving in generational leaps as the technology is improved: the multiplying memory power of the DRAM chip itself,

the declining cost of production per databit (and the accompanying cost decline for end users) and the rising volume of capital required for each new generation's R&D and factories.

The history of magnifying power has unfolded by these leaps in databit power per chip:

1980:	64,000 (64 kilobit)
1985:	256,000
1988:	1 million (1 megabit)
1990:	4 million
1993:	16 million
1995:	64 million

If Moore's Law continues to hold true, technologists expect the future power curve to follow roughly this schedule:

1998:	256 million
2001:	1 billion (1 gigabit)
2004:	4 billion
2007:	16 billion
2010:	64 billion

At each stage of advancement, as a rule of thumb, the production cost per databit falls by more than half while the cost per function to end users falls with it. Thus, the manufacturing cost was 17 cents per million databits for the 64M chip in 1995. The cost of manufacturing the same computing power would fall to 7 cents by 1998, 3 cents by 2001, 1 cent by 2004, half a cent by 2007 and two tenths of a cent by 2010.

The industrial paradox, however, is that in order to achieve these advancements in power multiplication and cost reduction, the companies must assemble increasing volumes of investment capital for the research and development and construction of the new factories. Thus, for instance, a factory for 64k chips in 1980 cost about $100 million to build, the 256k factory in 1985 cost $200 million, the 1m factory in 1988 cost $300 million, the 4m factory in 1990 cost $400 million and the 16m factory in 1993 cost $700 million. A fully automated 64m factory in 1995 cost $1.2 billion and several new factories have been announced that will cost $2 billion. If the capital curve continues in this manner, companies may soon be spending $5 billion or more per factory to keep up with Moore's Law.

These data are derived from *The National Technology Roadmap for Semiconductors, 1994,* and "The New Economics of Semiconductor Manufacturing," Dataquest 1995.

6. *Multinationals and the National Interest: Playing by Different Rules,* Office of Technology Assessment, U.S. Congress, September 1993.

7. John Kanz, professor of management at the University of Calgary, wrote: "The typical new U.S. semiconductor company now forgoes a wafer fabrication facility or 'fab' in favor of 'foundry agreements' with other suppliers, frequently foreign. This is scarcely without risk, but avoids the enormous entry barriers of new manufacturing plant investment, especially when venture capital for semiconductor start-up's is scarce." Kanz, "Strategy Evolution and Structural Consequences in the U.S. Semiconductor Industry," *Technovation* 14, no. 4 (1994). Texas Instruments' alliances were described in *Business Week,* August 7, 1995.

8. The NEC-Samsung alliance: *Financial Times,* February 7, 1995.

9. The Motorola partnership with IBM-Siemens-Toshiba and AT&T's new relationship with NEC-Samsung were reported by the *Financial Times,* October 20 and December 12, 1995.

10. "A cartel is a group of producers in an industry who act together in an attempt to increase combined and individual profit": Stephen Martin in *Encyclopedia of Economics* (New York: McGraw-Hill, 1982). In broad terms, any joint production shared by competitors is bound to have a direct impact on price competition —though not necessarily market control—since the purpose of the alliance is to reduce the manufacturing costs for all of the partners against their other rivals.

11. The aerospace relationships of Mitsubishi are described by Richard J. Samuels in *"Rich Nation, Strong Army": National Security and the Technological Transformation of Japan* (Ithaca, N.Y.: Cornell University Press, 1994). A series of Daimler-Mitsubishi meetings began in early 1990 and were reported in *The Japan Economic Journal*, March 17, 1990. No important results have yet emerged from their talks, beyond inducing nervousness among the Americans. GE–Pratt & Whitney–Daimler alliance: *Wall Street Journal*, June 14, 1995. Boeing and Airbus companies had previously explored an alliance to make a jumbo airliner with 800 seats, but the project was shelved in 1995: *Financial Times*, July 11, 1995.

12. The U.S.-Japan auto alliances: Michiyo Nakamoto in the *Financial Times*, August 19, 1993. VW-Mercedes partnership: *Financial Times*, April 25, 1994.

13. ADM-Fujitsu and Intel-Sharp: John Burgess in the *Washington Post*, September 6, 1992; other electronic alliances cited by Eamonn Fingleton, *Blindside: Why Japan Is Still on Track to Overtake the U.S. by the Year 2000* (Boston: Houghton Mifflin, 1995); NEC-Bull-Honeywell linkages: *Financial Times*, May 12, 1994, and Peter F. Cowhey and Jonathan D. Aronson, *Managing the World Economy: The Consequences of Corporate Alliances* (New York: Council on Foreign Relations Press, 1993). IBM-NEC stake in Bull: OTA, *Multinationals and the National Interest*.

14. Profit turnaround: Dean Baker and Larry Mishel, "Profits Up, Wages Down," Economic Policy Institute, Washington, D.C., September 1995.

15. The profit and retained earnings were calculated from the tables in the annual report of the Council of Economic Advisers. The profit-to-debt ratios are from the "Flow of Funds Account," Federal Reserve Board.

16. Alfred D. Chandler Jr., *Scale and Scope: The Dynamics of Industrial Capitalism* (Cambridge, Mass.: Harvard University Press, 1990).

17. I am indebted to the works of many for my understanding of the Japanese system, but especially Chalmers Johnson, *MITI and the Japanese Miracle: The Growth of Industrial Policy, 1925–1975* (Stanford, Calif.: Stanford University Press, 1982); Clyde V. Prestowitz Jr., *Trading Places: How We Allowed Japan to Take the Lead* (New York: Basic Books, 1988); Karel van Wolferen, *The Enigma of Japanese Power: People and Politics in a Stateless Nation* (New York: Alfred A. Knopf, 1989); and most recently, Fingleton, *Blindside*.

18. The U.S. steel producers filed formal anti-dumping complaints against nearly 20 countries, alleging that American firms were injured by the European-Japanese cartel because its members dumped their surpluses in the U.S. at predatory prices. See Katsuji Nakazawa and Eiji Furukawa in the *Nikkei Weekly*, December 19, 1994, and Laura Viani in *American Metal Market*, July 27, 1993.

19. The Asian share of world exports rose from 8.7 to 14.9 percent from 1980 to 1991: "The Employment Challenge," United Nations Development Program, March 1995.

20. Cowhey and Aronson, in *Managing the World Economy*, call what the Japanese are proposing "cooperative mercantilism."

21. The idea for a new global council of semiconductor producers was launched by the Electronics Industries Association of Japan after "close consultation" between the European Commission and Japan's Ministry of International Trade and Industry, as reported in the *Financial Times*, June 7, 1996.

TEN: *The Buyer of Last Resort*

1. Clinton's American University speech, *Weekly Compilation of Presidential Documents,* National Archives, February 26, 1993.

2. According to David Walters, chief economist for the U.S. Trade Representative's office, a joint study by USTR and George Bush's Council of Economic Advisers concluded that the increased efficiency and lower prices from GATT's tariff reductions would cumulatively over ten years stimulate an additional 3 percent of U.S. growth. The added output—assuming it was distributed to family incomes—would mean an average gain of $17,000 over ten years, or $1,700 a year per family of four. When I asked Walters to reconcile these assumptions with the current maldistribution of economic gains, he replied: "Distribution of incomes—that's entirely different. That statement is entirely neutral on the question of who gets what."

Clinton spoke at a White House ceremony promoting GATT, flanked by James A. Baker III, Treasury secretary in the Reagan and Bush administrations; James Miller, budget director under George Bush; and other Republican notables. *Presidential Documents,* November 28, 1994.

3. The U.S. Labor Department reported that labor costs—wages and benefits —rose 3 percent in 1994, the lowest increase since the recessionary year of 1981, and was effectively canceled in real value by inflation. *New York Times* and *Wall Street Journal,* February 1, 1995.

4. Slower growth in the OECD nations: *Bretton Woods: Looking to the Future* (Washington, D.C.: Bretton Woods Commission, July 1994).

5. Census Bureau report: *Wall Street Journal,* January 25, 1995; record profits and declining wages: Dean Baker and Larry Mishel, "Profits Up, Wages Down," Economic Policy Institute, Washington, D.C., September 1995; job security; *Fortune,* June 13, 1994.

6. Clinton spoke at the White House Community Empowerment Conference, July 26, 1995.

7. Clinton at Georgetown, July 6, 1995.

8. Speaking before the American Federation of Teachers, July 28, 1995, the President blamed the global economy for sowing insecurities among families and then offered a 14-point agenda for helping them. The only economic proposal on his list was a very small increase in the federal minimum wage standard, to $5 an hour.

9. A series of anti-trust consent decrees that the U.S. Justice Department won in the 1950s against major American innovators like AT&T and IBM ensured liberal access to new technological inventions, enabling smaller competitors at home and abroad to catch up and sometimes leapfrog ahead in semiconductors and other advanced fields. Kenneth Flamm, *Creating the Computer: Government, Industry, and High Technology* (Washington, D.C.: Brookings Institution, 1988). The story of how U.S. military procurement launched Japan's rebirth is recounted by Richard J. Samuels, *"Rich Nation, Strong Army": National Security and the Technological Transformation of Japan* (Ithaca, N.Y.: Cornell University Press, 1994).

10. I am indebted to Robert A. Johnson for emphasizing the importance of the core domestic pillars in the American economy.

11. Chrysler economists cut 500,000 vehicles from its assumption that in a normal year Americans will buy 15.1 million units: Robert L. Simison in the *Wall Street Journal,* August 7, 1995.

12. British historians P. J. Cain and A. G. Hopkins describe the myopia and arrogance of Britain's "gentlemanly capitalism" in *British Imperialism: Crisis and Deconstruction 1914–1990* (London: Longman, 1993).

13. Wynne Godley, "The U.S. Balance of Payments, International Indebtedness

and Economic Policy: A Policy Brief," Jerome Levy Economics Institute of Bard College, August 1995.

14. Japan and Asian surpluses: *OECD Economic Outlook,* June 1994; "Big Emerging Markets: The New Economic Frontier" and other briefing bulletins, June 1995, and *Survey of Current Business, 1995,* U.S. Commerce Department.

15. Utsumi's 2 percent solution was described by Eamonn Fingleton, *Blindside: Why Japan Is Still on Track to Overtake the U.S. by the Year 2000* (Boston: Houghton Mifflin, 1995).

16. Japan-U.S. auto-parts agreement: Helene Cooper and Valerie Reitman in the *Wall Street Journal,* May 18, 1995; U.S. companies moving to Japan: Michiyo Nakamoto in the *Financial Times,* March 17, 1995.

17. China's agreement on CD piracy: Martha M. Hamilton and Steven Mufson, *Washington Post,* February 27, 1995. Mitsubishi's purchase of Chinese CD plant: *Financial Times,* August 25, 1995.

18. Early in Clinton's term, cabinet officials privately debated the question of whether U.S. policy should favor American-owned multinationals over foreign firms that invested in the U.S., but they backed away from resolving the nettlesome issue when they grasped the political risks involved. On closer examination, it was not self-evident that American companies were always better for Americans. However, the fundamental question is deeper than the one they were asking: Should the U.S. defend its domestic employment base against erosion by globalizing firms, regardless of their nationality? See contradictory reports on the policy debate in the *New York Times,* June 2, 1993, and *Wall Street Journal,* July 2, 1993. The AT&T deal in China was described in the *Wall Street Journal,* April 29, 1994.

19. See my article "The Ex-Im Files," *Rolling Stone,* August 8, 1996.

20. Kenichi Ohmae argued that U.S. trade negotiations are phony exercises because companies will ignore national accounting anyway. The 1986 semiconductor agreement, he pointed out, was partially fulfilled by counting U.S. chips manufactured in Japan as contributing to America's market share: *Japan Times,* October 25, 1994.

21. Walter Wriston wrote in the *Washington Post,* August 4, 1994. DeAnne Julius's claim of U.S. trade surpluses was based on 1986 sales by U.S. multinationals, before the outflow of profits and other returns turned negative: Julius, *Global Companies and Public Policy: The Growing Challenge of Foreign Direct Investment* (London: Royal Institute of International Affairs, 1990).

22. Frank P. Doyle, "Changes in the Workplace: What's Really Going On," at a conference of the Jerome Levy Economic Institute, April 28, 1995.

23. The auto industry alone created 691 jobs for every 100 of its own: *The State of Working America* (Washington, D.C.: Economic Policy Institute, 1993).

24. Eliot Janeway's proposal for sectoral tariffs was patterned after the reciprocal trade agreements the U.S. fashioned with other nations in the 1930s in an effort to revive global growth. These nation-to-nation agreements offer a political model for the present, a way to begin reforming the global system without waiting upon the tortuous kind of worldwide negotiating marathons associated with GATT. Janeway also suggested that foreign importers be given a choice: either invest their overages in American production or buy an equivalent volume of other American-made products and sell them somewhere else in the world—a reverse version of the "offsets" described in Chapter 7. Thus, foreign producers who took unreasonable advantage of America's open market would have to share responsibility for coping with the consequences. Janeway, *The Economics of Chaos: On Revitalizing the American Economy* (New York: Dutton, 1989).

ELEVEN: *The Alchemists*

1. See, for instance, Charles P. Kindleberger, *Manias, Panics, and Crashes* (New York: Basic Books, 1978), and John Kenneth Galbraith, *The Great Crash, 1929* (Boston: Houghton Mifflin, 1961), and *Money: Whence It Came, Where It Went* (Boston: Houghton Mifflin, 1975).

2. In nominal dollars, not adjusted for inflation, total financial assets will equal $83 trillion by 2000, according to the McKinsey study. *The Global Capital Market: Supply, Demand, Pricing and Allocation* (Washington, D.C.: McKinsey Global Institute, November 1994).

3. I am indebted to Robert Dugger for the metaphor of three great "auctions" to describe the complexities of global finance.

4. In foreign-exchange trading, New York has a daily turnover averaging about $250 billion; Tokyo, $160 billion; Singapore, $100 billion; Hong Kong, Zurich and Frankfurt, $80 to 90 billion each: Philip Gawith in the *Financial Times,* September 20, 1995.

5. The study for the Group of Ten finance ministers reported real interest rates for the G-10 and blamed the decline in savings: *Financial Times,* October 9, 1995.

6. The stock-market returns from Hong Kong, India and Argentina are from Jess Lederman and Robert A. Klein, editors, *Global Asset Location: Techniques for Optimizing Portfolio Management* (New York: Wiley, 1994).

7. An example of how debt was shifted from private to public obligations is the lending to developing nations. In 1982, when the Third World debt crisis surfaced, commercial banks held $390 billion in loans to developing nations while the public agencies held $239 billion. A decade later the banks' lending totaled $473 billion, but the public lending had more than doubled to $591 billion. Peter B. Kenen, editor, *Managing the World Economy: Fifty Years After Bretton Woods* (Washington, D.C.: Institute for International Economics, September 1994).

8. The 1993 ERM crisis was a major upheaval that received only passing notice in the U.S. The *Wall Street Journal* on August 5, 1993, summarized it as a business story: "Currency Traders Welcome Upheaval/Europe's Turmoil Means Jobs, Chance for Big Profits." Details on the crisis are from the *Financial Times,* July 30 and August 4, 1993.

9. Jacques Delors was quoted in the *Financial Times,* September 20, 1993.

10. A month after Black Wednesday, Soros gave a London interview in which he described the triumph to Anatole Kaletsky, "The Man Who Broke the Bank of England," *Times* of London, October 26, 1992. Some other details are from *Soros on Soros: Staying Ahead of the Curve* (New York: Wiley, 1995).

11. Soros's 1987 book elaborated a more complicated version of the perception-reality interactions he called "reflexivity," an analysis of how the observer and the observed continuously interact that echoed Einstein's theory of relativity in physics. Soros, *The Alchemy of Finance: Reading the Mind of the Market* (New York: Simon & Schuster, 1987).

12. George Soros recounted the "message" from the Bundesbank president in *Soros on Soros.*

13. Foreign-exchange turnover in 1973, estimated by McKinsey & Company in *The Global Capital Market.*

14. Following the global bond crash in 1994, Soros testified before the House Banking Committee, April 13, 1994, and explained that the Quantum Fund and other hedge funds had as much in common as "a hedgehog and the people who cut hedges in the summer." Derivatives, he said at that time, did not require government regulation, a position he later reversed as speculative losses mounted.

15. Citicorp profits: Charles P. Kindleberger, "Dollar Darkness," *International*

Economy, May 1995. Bankers Trust and other banks' off-balance-sheet activity: John Plender in the *Financial Times,* May 18, 1994.

16. Losses from derivatives: *Financial Times,* March 21 and August 15, 1994; *Wall Street Journal,* April 13, 1994; *International Herald Tribune,* July 15, 1994. The losses by Malaysia's central bank could not actually be blamed on derivatives but on its own speculative games in the foreign-exchange markets. At the end of 1993, the Bank Negara began devaluing its own currency, the ringgit, in order to reduce the size of foreign-exchange losses reported in year-end balances. Foreign speculators, including Soros's Quantum Fund, recognized what was happening and began pushing the ringgit up, forcing the Malaysian government to expend more and more to counter them. Procter & Gamble's successful claim against Bankers Trust was reported in the *Wall Street Journal,* May 10, 1996.

17. George Soros discussed the portents of disaster in *Soros on Soros.*

18. Dollar/deutschemark volatility: *Bretton Woods: Looking to the Future* (Washington, D.C.: Bretton Woods Commission, July 1994).

19. Kenichi Ohno, "The Case for a New System," in *Bretton Woods: Looking to the Future.*

20. Richard Koo spoke at a Washington conference of the Economic Strategy Institute, March 9, 1994.

21. Some elements of the U.S.-Japan mutual assistance agreements were reported at the time; others I learned from various sources. The Federal Reserve's offer of liquidity aid was reported by Keith Bradsher, *New York Times,* October 17, 1995.

22. Three major reserve currencies: *Bretton Woods: Looking to the Future.*

23. Foreign-currency reserves: *The Economist,* September 16, 1995. The leading wealth holders in Asia are Taiwan, $100 billion; Singapore, $66 billion; China, $64 billion; Thailand, $33 billion; South Korea, $30 billion. Hong Kong holds $53 billion and, it could be argued, should not be included in Asia's total since much of Hong Kong's wealth there is actually from the West, but much of it is also the offshore capital that leaks out from Chinese enterprises and even provincial governments.

TWELVE: El Barzón

1. Some economists estimated the job losses as high as two million. See Alejandro Nadal Egea, "An Alternative Economic Strategy for Mexico: A Commentary," *Referendum de la Libertad,* September 1995.

2. For a dramatic account of Mexico's bloody political intrigues see Andres Oppenheimer, *Bordering on Chaos: Guerrillas, Stockbrokers, Politicians, and Mexico's Road to Prosperity* (Boston: Little, Brown, 1996).

3. The collapse of emerging markets was described in the *Financial Times,* March 16, 1995. Mexico's stock market fell 48 percent in less than three months, Argentina's 31 percent, Brazil's 37 percent, China's 10 percent, India's 13 percent, the Philippines' 21 percent. Even Chile, regarded as the most stable economy in Latin America, lost 18 percent in the panic.

4. Michel Camdessus was quoted in the *Financial Times,* February 8, 1995, and Lawrence Summers in "The United States and Mexico: The Crisis and the Pain of Ordinary People," Alliance for Responsible Trade, Washington, D.C., April 4, 1995.

5. In its annual report on global capital, the IMF surprised many when it conceded that Mexico might have dealt with the peso crisis by imposing temporary capital controls or other types of "prudential" restrictions on capital flows into domestic financial markets. See "International Capital Markets, Developments, Prospects, and Policy Issues" (Washington, D.C.: IMF, August 1995).

6. The opinion survey asked Mexicans what explained the rising assaults: 42 percent said hunger, 27 percent blamed drugs, 17 percent said the need for money. Ninety percent said they expect more and more violence. *El Universal,* April 14, 1996.

7. Some 60 police officers were arrested for the Morelos shootings. *The News,* Mexico City, April 12 and 14, 1996.

8. For an authoritative account of Mexico's economic struggle and the triumph of neoliberalism in Latin America, see Jorge G. Castañeda, *Utopia Unarmed: The Latin American Left After the Cold War* (New York: Knopf, 1993).

9. *El Financiero* reported from its own calculations that Mexico's foreign debt, both public and private, had reached $173.4 billion—60 percent of GDP. The annual interest payments were $27.7 billion. *El Financiero,* April 6, 1994.

10. The growth comparisons are from *The East Asian Miracle: Economic Growth and Public Policy* (Washington, D.C.: World Bank, 1993). The eight "high performance" Asian economies covered by the study are Japan, South Korea, Taiwan, Hong Kong, Singapore, Malaysia, Indonesia and Thailand.

11. Japan's rebuttal was entitled "Issues Related to the World Bank's Approach to Structural Adjustment—Proposal from a Major Partner" (Tokyo: Overseas Economic Cooperation Fund, October 1991).

12. For a fuller description of the Asian alternative, see Lal Jayawardena, "The Bretton Woods Institutions and the Development Problems of the Poorer Developing Countries," in *Bretton Woods: Looking to the Future* (Washington, D.C.: Bretton Woods Commission, 1994). Professor Lance Taylor addressed the same theoretical questions in "Back to the Future Yet Again?" at a World Bank conference on the Mexican crisis, October 13, 1995, and more fully in "Social Implications of Structural Adjustment: A Critical Survey," a paper for a United Nations Development Program conference, New York, June 29, 1995.

13. Free-market advocates in the U.S. sometimes cite Chile's rapid growth as evidence for their model, but the Chilean regime is actually much closer to Asia's. Its forced savings program has produced a national savings rate of 27 percent of GDP. Its capital controls insulate domestic finance from the transient storms of global finance. The government restricts foreign capital to the investment opportunities it selects and prohibits rapid turnover of assets. The *Financial Times,* for instance, described elements of the program: "The central bank is convinced that its restrictions on capital inflows, though unpopular with Chilean financial institutions, helped prevent violent swings in stock-market prices in 1995. So foreign portfolio investment, for example, will remain limited to authorized investment companies, with a one-year lock-in period and a 35 percent capital gains tax." *Financial Times,* March 25, 1996.

14. The religious metaphor for the World Bank offered by Susan George and Fabrizio Sabelli continues: "Debt payments are one offering, a kind of tribute; the structural adjustment measures which insure that these debts can and will be paid, act as a kind of ritual cleansing through sacrifice." George and Sabelli, *Faith and Credit: The World Bank's Secular Empire* (New York: Penguin, 1994).

15. Developing-country debt statistics are from Ashwini Deshpande, "Rethinking Strategy for Global Debt Crisis," *Economic and Political Weekly,* May 27, 1995.

16. The case for debt forgiveness was spelled out by William F. Darity Jr., "Is to Forgive the Debt Divine?" in John F. Weeks, editor, *Debt Disaster? Banks, Governments, and Multilaterals Confront the Crisis* (New York: New York University Press, 1989).

17. The World Bank's original proposal for debt relief was for $11 billion, but was whittled down in subsequent negotiations with private banks, the IMF and leading governments who would share the cost of debt forgiveness. *Financial Times,* June 10, 1996.

THIRTEEN: *The Rentiers' Regime*

1. U.S. debt/GDP ratio is from 1975 to 1995. The European ratios are from the *Financial Times*, June 21, 1995.

2. McKinsey & Company: *The Global Capital Market: Supply, Demand, Pricing and Allocation* (Washington, D.C.: McKinsey Global Institute, November 1994).

3. Alain Parguez, "Debts and Savings or the Scourge of the Search for Sound Finance," in *Économies et Sociétés: Le Rôle de la Dette dans l'Économie Capitaliste* (Paris: Cahiers de l'ISMEA, 1994) and "Keynesianism and the Politics of Austerity," presented at the International Studies Association, London, 1989. The quotation is from Parguez and Mario Seccareccia, "Taking on Interest-Inflated Deficits: Progressives Must Make Interest-Rate Reduction an Important Priority," unpublished.

4. The Council of Economic Advisers' speculations on why interest rates rose are contained in the *Economic Report of the President*, February 1995.

5. During this period Alan Greenspan was uncharacteristically blunt in his public hints of possible interest-rate increases. In late July 1993, he testified about the "disappointing" progress on reducing price inflation. "The signal we are endeavoring to send here," he said, "is, at some point, rates are going to have to move up." See my article "Will the Fed Stiff Clinton?" *Rolling Stone*, September 16, 1993.

6. S. Jay Levy and David A. Levy coined the phrase in "Outlook for the 1990's: The Contained Depression," Jerome Levy Economics Institute of Bard College, 1991. Wallace Peterson made a similar observation in *The Silent Depression: The Fate of the American Dream* (New York: Norton, 1994).

7. The "historical real holding-period returns" on debt and equity investments were calculated in "Savings, Investment and Real Interest Rates," Group of Ten, October 1995. The return on equity holdings in the 1990s was 6.5 percent, below the 10.7 percent return in the 1980s. The report listed these returns on long-term U.S. debt for the twentieth century:

1890s	4.5	1950s	−3.3
1900s	0.5	1960s	−0.7
1910s	−4.0	1970s	−2.1
1920s	8.8	1980s	6.7
1930s	6.9	1990s	8.2
1940s	−2.9	Average:	1.6

8. Alan Greenspan's remarks were quoted by Dimitri B. Papadimitriou and L. Randall Wray in "Monetary Policy Uncovered, Flying Blind: The Federal Reserve's Experiment with Unobservables," Jerome Levy Economics Institute of Bard College, September 1994.

9. UAW's Flint strike: *Wall Street Journal*, October 3, 1994, and January 19, 1995.

10. *Global Research Highlights*, Merrill Lynch, March 11, 1994.

11. The median family income's last peak was in 1989 and fell by 7 percent during the subsequent recession. Despite the supposedly healthy economy it had not surpassed the 1989 level by the end of 1995. The implications for American politics were discussed in my article "Middle-Class Funk," *Rolling Stone*, November 2, 1995.

12. Laura Tyson spoke at a conference on monetary policy sponsored by the Levy Economics Institute, November 17, 1994.

13. The G-10 study on interest rates was prepared by an international working party of government economists, chaired by Mervyn King, chief economist at the Bank of England, with others from the Federal Reserve, IMF and Bank of Italy. "Savings, Investment and Real Interest Rates," Group of Ten, October 1995.

Though the *Financial Times* cited some aspects on October 9, 1995, the G-10 study was apparently never formally released and its important and controversial conclusions were not reported in the U.S. press.

14. Greenspan's rationale for slow growth is described in a letter to Representative Bennie G. Thompson of Mississippi, April 7, 1995. His statement on "maximal growth" was cited by Papadimitriou and Wray in "Monetary Policy Uncovered."

15. W. R. Smyser, "The Bundesbank: America's German Central Bank," *The Washington Quarterly*, Spring 1994.

16. Charles I. Clough Jr., "The Meek Inherit the Earth," Merrill Lynch Investment Strategy Department, September 1993.

17. "Swedish bond boycott": *Financial Times*, July 4 and July 6, 1994.

18. The irony of the German fiscal disorder was that the Maastricht fiscal criteria had been adopted to reassure Germany and guarantee that a unified currency system, managed by a new European central bank, would not undermine the stable-money discipline that the Bundesbank imposed single-handedly. Data on the nations' failing to meet the criteria was cited by Lionel Barber in the *Financial Times*, June 21, 1995.

19. Despite Clinton's deficit reductions the debt as a percentage of GDP was still rising, 3.5 percent in 1996, thus still deepening the dilemma. The primary balances, debt and deficit ratios and other statistics are from the G-10 study "Savings, Investment and Real Interest Rates" or calculated from other data such as the *Economic Report of the President*, February 1995.

20. The Federal Reserve, in its "Survey of Consumer Finances, 1983," reported that 55 percent of American households were net debtors: *Federal Reserve Bulletin*, December 1984. Though Federal Reserve economists did not repeat this analysis in a subsequent survey, the distribution of net financial wealth worsened steadily after 1983, so the percentage is likely even higher.

The holders of long-term U.S. debt, both government and corporate, included in 1993: 8 percent by foreign institutions, 17 percent by commercial banks, 16 percent by insurance companies, 13 percent by wealthy individuals and nonprofit institutions like foundations, 33 percent by nonfinancial corporations, brokerages and governments at every level. Their influence was described by Louis Uchitelle in the *New York Times*, June 12, 1994.

21. Edward N. Wolff, *Top Heavy: A Study of the Increasing Inequality of Wealth in America* (New York: Twentieth Century Fund, 1995).

FOURTEEN: *The Economic Question*

1. George Soros on financial regulation: *The Alchemy of Finance: Reading the Mind of the Market* (New York: Simon & Schuster, 1987).

2. Professor Wolff notes that the standard argument against wealth taxes— that they discourage savings—is not borne out by reality. Some nations with wealth taxes have higher savings rates than the U.S. and some do not. Edward N. Wolff, *Top Heavy: A Study of the Increasing Inequality of Wealth in America* (New York: Twentieth Century Fund, 1995).

FIFTEEN: *"These Dark Satanic Mills"*

1. William Blake's immortal lines are from "Milton," one of his "prophetic books" written between 1804 and 1808. *The Portable Blake*, Alfred Kazin, editor (New York: Penguin Books, 1976).

2. *Washington Post*, *Financial Times* and *New York Times*, May 12, 1993, and *Wall Street Journal*, May 13, 1993.

3. The U.S. contract clients for Kader's Bangkok factory were cited by the International Confederation of Free Trade Unions headquartered in Brussels in its investigatory report, "From the Ashes: A Toy Factory Fire in Thailand," December 1994. In the aftermath, the ICFTU and some nongovernmental organizations attempted to mount an "international toy campaign" and a few sporadic demonstrations occurred in Hong Kong and London, but there never was a general boycott of the industry or any of its individual companies. The labor federation met with associations of British and American toy manufacturers and urged them to adopt a "code of conduct" that might discourage the abuses. The proposed codes were inadequate, the ICFTU acknowledged, but it was optimistic about their general adoption by the international industry.

4. Mitchell Zuckoff of the *Boston Globe* produced a powerful series of stories on labor conditions in developing Asia and reported Hasbro's reaction to the Kader fire, July 10, 1994. David Miller was quoted in *USA Today,* May 13, 1993, and on ABC News *20/20,* July 30, 1993.

5. The first-person descriptions of the Kader fire are but a small sampling from survivors' horrifying accounts, collected by investigators and reporters at the scene. My account of the disaster is especially indebted to the investigative report by the International Confederation of Free Trade Unions; Bangkok's English-language newspapers, the *Post* and *The Nation;* the Asia Monitor Resource Center of Hong Kong; and Lynn Sherr's devastating report on ABC's *20/20,* July 30, 1993. Lampan Taptim and Tumthong Podhirun, "From the Ashes," ICFTU, December 1994; Cheng: *Asian Labour Update,* Asia Monitor Resource Center, Hong Kong, July 1993; La-iad Nads-nguen: *The Nation,* Bangkok, May 12, 1993; and Chaweewan Mekpan: *20/20.*

6. Details on Thailand's worker injuries and the litany of fires in China are from the ICFTU report and other labor bulletins, as well as interviews in Bangkok.

7. The *People's Daily* and *Economic Daily* were quoted by Andrew Quinn of Reuters in *The Daily Citizen* of Washington, D.C., January 18, 1994.

8. Tony Horwitz described chicken-processing employment as the second fastest growing manufacturing job in America: *Wall Street Journal,* December 1, 1994. U.S. sweatshops were reviewed in "Garment Industry: Efforts to Address the Prevalence and Conditions of Sweatshops," U.S. Government Accounting Office, November 1994.

9. Corporate details on Kader are from the ICFTU and the Asia Monitor Resource Center's *Asian Labour Update,* July 1993.

10. Dhanin Chearavanont's wealth: *Bangkok Post,* June 15, 1993; Pokphand Group ventures in China and elsewhere: *Far Eastern Economic Review,* October 21, 1993; George Bush's appearance in Bangkok: *Bangkok Post,* January 22, 1994. The dinner for Deng's daughter, Deng Nan, was reported in *The Nation,* Bangkok, January 28, 1994.

11. The complex structure of ownership was used to deflect corporate responsibility. Kader's Kenneth Ting protested after the fire that his family's firm owned only a 40 percent stake in the Thai factory, but people blamed them "because we have our name on it. That's the whole problem." The lesson, he said, was to "never lend your name or logo to any company if you don't have managing control in the company." That lesson, of course, contradicted the basic structure of how the global toy industry was organized: *Bangkok Post,* May 17, 1993. The chain of ownership was reported in several places, including *The Nation* of Bangkok, May 28, 1993. Details of the Kader workers' sit-in: *Bangkok Post,* July 13, 1993.

12. Sanan was quoted in the *Bangkok Post,* May 29, 1993.

13. The shooting was reported in *The Nation,* February 23, 1994.

14. Thailand has become known as "Disneyland for pedophiles": *Freedom Review,* March 1994. If the educational campaign to slow the spread of AIDS

does not succeed, officials expect six million HIV-positive victims by 2000: Ronald Busarakamwongs in the *Bangkok Sunday Post,* February 20, 1994.

15. Anthony Downs of the Brookings Institution in Washington, "The Coming Crash in Asian Real Estate," *Asian Wall Street Journal,* November 25, 1995.

16. Plastic consumption: "NPC: Dynamic Growth Leading the Thai Petrochemical Industry into the Prosperous 21st Century," special section, *The Nation,* February 1994.

17. The campaign for the elephants and against further forest encroachment sometimes turned violent. Two protesters were killed and a third wounded in a 1992 confrontation in Surin Province: *Bangkok Sunday Post,* February 20, 1994.

18. According to government statistics, Thailand has 5.4 million children, age 13 to 19, working legally and 100,000 under 13 working illegally. Lae Dilokvidhyarat, "National Economic Development and Marginalization of Social Groups in Thailand," Chulalongkorn University, 1994.

19. I first heard the world's three realms of time consciousness elaborated in these terms by a French financial economist, Albert Bressand, at a Washington conference on exchange rates sponsored by Smick-Medley & Associates, November 12, 1985.

20. Thailand's modern political development is analyzed in essays published by the Centre of Southeast Asian Studies at Monash University in Australia and edited by Craig J. Reynolds, *National Identity and Its Defenders: Thailand, 1939–1989* (Thailand: Silkworm Books, 1991). Military coups in Thailand: Rodney Tasker and Gordon Fairlough, *Far Eastern Economic Review,* May 20, 1993.

21. Moore's historic examples of industrial "revolution from above" that led eventually to fascism are Japan and Germany. Barrington Moore Jr., *Social Origins of Dictatorship and Democracy: Lord and Peasant in the Making of the Modern World* (Boston: Beacon, 1966).

22. The profound disruptions to ecology and human society caused by World Bank projects in Thailand, such as the Khor Chor Kor project, are described by Bruce Rich, in *Mortgaging the Earth: The World Bank, Environmental Impoverishment, and the Crisis of Development* (Boston: Beacon, 1994).

23. Sanitsuda Ekachai's book, *Behind the Smile: Voices of Thailand,* was published in 1990 by the Thai Development Support Committee, 530 Soi St. Louis 3, South Sathorn Road, Yannawa, Bangkok 10120, Thailand.

24. Like other fast-growing economies, Thailand celebrated the rapid rise of per capita incomes—from $210 in 1971 to $1,570 in 1991—and a sharp decline in what was described as absolute poverty. These statistics masked the social realities, however. One study cited by Lae found that in the 1980s family incomes rose overall by only 7.5 percent while their spending rose 12 percent, driven by inflation and the concentration of wealth and incomes. Lae Dilokvidhyarat, "National Economic Development and Marginalization of Social Groups in Thailand," and Voravidh Charoenloet, "Report on Technological Development and Its Impact on Employment," Thai Labor Development Institute and Asian-American Free Labor Institute, 1994.

25. The New Delhi–based campaign against child labor in the carpet industry is admittedly limited to a narrow market and expensive product, but its essential value is demonstrating how retailers and their customers can be connected to a distant factory floor. See, for instance, Hugh Williamson, "Stamp of Approval," *Far Eastern Economic Review,* February 2, 1995, and N. Vasuk Rao in the *Journal of Commerce,* March 1, 1995.

SIXTEEN: Schraube nach Unten

1. French Prime Minister Edouard Balladur tried to cut minimum-wage standards for young people and 4,000 jobs at the state-owned Air France, among other

things, in September 1993. His successor, Alain Juppé, announced pension cuts and other reforms, including taxing the family allowance, in November 1995. Both retreated before popular protests, though Juppé insisted he would go forward with the main elements of his agenda. See, for instance, the *Financial Times,* October 26, 1993; December 31, 1993; and December 18, 1995.

2. Bismarck's remark was cited by Hugh Heclo, "The Social Question," in Katherine McFate, Roger Lawson and William Julius Wilson, editors, *Poverty, Inequality and the Future of Social Policy: Western States in the New World Order* (New York: Russell Sage Foundation, 1995). The Vichy government's right-wing social reforms in France were intended to restore Catholic moral order—opposing divorce and abortion, encouraging maternity and family—and were supported by the church. Robert O. Paxton, *Vichy France: Old Guard and New Order, 1940–1944* (New York: Columbia University Press, 1972). Corporate and Wall Street support for the New Deal is described by Thomas Ferguson, *Golden Rule: The Investment Theory of Party Competition and the Logic of Money-Driven Political Systems* (Chicago: University of Chicago Press, 1995).

3. The income-distribution comparisons are from the *1993 Human Development Report,* United Nations Development Program, and provide the following ratios between the top 20 percent and the bottom 20 percent for 1985–1989: Japan, 4.3; U.S., 8.9; Germany, 5.7; Sweden, 4.6; Italy, 6.0; Spain, 5.8; Britain, 6.8. A 1995 study by the Organization for Economic Cooperation and Development, "Income Distribution in OECD Countries," made more sophisticated comparisons, taking into account differences in taxation and inflation, and reached the same conclusion: the U.S. income inequality was worst among 15 nations. See also Keith Bradsher in the *New York Times,* October 27, 1995.

4. Karl Polanyi, an Austrian, was a teacher and financial editor in Vienna who fled the rise of fascist persecution there in 1934 and became a British citizen and scholar at Oxford University. His seminal work on the social consequences of industrial revolution was written in the U.S. during World War II and first published in 1944. *The Great Transformation: The Political and Economic Origins of Our Time* (reprint, Boston: Beacon, 1957).

5. Neo-Nazi materials are illegal in Germany, but German authorities have frequently complained that most of the publications are mailed from the U.S. A new law enacted in 1994 allows postal officials to confiscate Nazi literature mailed from abroad. "This Week in Germany," German Information Center, September 23, 1994.

6. Germany's poverty rate compared to others and service wages: McFate, Lawson and Wilson, *Poverty, Inequality and the Future of Social Policy.* The spending on labor-market programs: Ronald G. Ehrenberg, *Labor Markets and Integrating National Economies* (Washington, D.C.: Brookings Institution, 1994). Terms of social benefits: "Foreign Labor Trends Report: Federal Republic of Germany," U.S. Embassy, Bonn, October 1992.

7. Helmut Kohl warned: "The high level of prosperity in Germany has given many people the illusion that material security is automatically guaranteed": *Wall Street Journal,* October 9, 1995. The prospective job losses were cited in "Focus on Unemployment in Germany," German Information Center, March 1994.

8. Daimler-Benz's move to Wall Street was not widely emulated by other German companies, and it was not yet clear that it would become a general trend that alters the nature of the stakeholder company. In order to participate in American financial markets, Daimler had to adapt its balance sheet to the more transparent corporate accounting required in the U.S., and it thus revealed a weaker profit position. Germany's "patient capital" functioned in part by concealing such unpleasant realities from shareholders. Those who frequently urged American banking reforms modeled on the German system were quite oblivious to this and other contradictions.

9. Klaus Zwickel's "alliance for jobs" was described by Wolfgang Münchau, *Financial Times,* November 12, 1995.

10. Japan was not covered in the OECD's 1995 comparative study, "Income Distribution in OECD Countries," though it did cite older data suggesting that Japan had an income-equality rating quite close to Sweden and Norway and dramatically better than Germany, the U.S. and other major economies. Studies of income inequality in Japan and the U.S. between educated, experienced workers and the unskilled or young new entrants found that while the income gap widened dramatically for these groups in the U.S. during the 1970s and 1980s, the gap grew only moderately in Japan and not at all in terms of work experience. Young, new workers in the U.S. continued to lose ground in the 1980s, even though this group would begin shrinking in demographic terms. See McFate, Lawson and Wilson, *Poverty, Inequality and the Future of Social Policy.*

11. Overall productivity was measured as GDP per equivalent full-time employee. Measured for the "market economy," which McKinsey described as every sector except government, health services, real estate, education and nonprofit organizations, Japan's productivity was even lower—only 61 percent of that of the U.S. See *Manufacturing Productivity* (Washington, D.C.: McKinsey Global Institute, October 1993).

12. Kenichi Ohmae, McKinsey & Company consultant and author of *The Borderless World,* was now active in a reform political movement. He described a half-billion-dollar strike fund amassed by Japanese unions and predicted labor conflicts ahead: *Japan Times,* October 25, 1994.

13. Working-class identity, as one would expect, generally correlated with education and income levels and the kinds of work that one did. The language of class distinctions virtually disappeared from American political dialogue in the prosperity that followed World War II, but the NORC survey results from the 1990s are almost identical to findings in the 1940s. These realities were described by S. M. Miller and Karen Marie Ferrogiaro, "Class Dismissed?" *The American Prospect,* Spring 1995.

14. Umberto Eco related how, at age ten, he won a compulsory oratorical contest on the subject: "Shall we die for the glory of Mussolini and the immortal destiny of Italy?" "My answer was positive. I was a smart boy," Eco wrote. "Ur-Fascism," *New York Review of Books,* June 22, 1995.

SEVENTEEN: Buruh Sejahtera

1. Walter Reuther's remark was quoted by Denis MacShane in *Pacific Review,* no. 1 (1993).

2. The estimate of Michael Jordan's income from Nike compared to Indonesian shoe workers was made by Pharis Harvey, executive director of the International Labor Rights Education and Research Fund in Washington. In 1992, Jordan reportedly earned $20 million from Nike, according to *Forbes,* November 23, 1992. The 25,000 workers each earned $400 to $500 a year at most, or about $12.5 million in total.

3. Details on the Jakarta repression are from "Indonesia: Operation Cleansing, Human Rights and APEC," Amnesty International, November 3, 1994.

4. Pakpahan's increased sentence was reported in the *Indonesian Observer,* January 31, 1995. He was imprisoned but abruptly released four months later by administrative order.

5. According to Muchtar Pakpahan, President Clinton did raise the question of his imprisonment privately with Suharto, though this was not reported at the time. "Clinton asked Suharto, what about Muchtar Pakpahan?" the labor leader related in May 1996, while he was in Washington seeking support for his labor

organization. "It was just a flash," Pakpahan said, "but it makes a difference to us when your government asks the question."

6. In the fall of 1995, Suharto himself complained about a "certain formless organization" that was still spreading Communist teachings. Army Chief of Staff General Soeyono singled out Pakpahan, Aditjondro and a banned author, world-renowned novelist Pramoedya Ananta Toer, as ringleaders. "Their objective is clear: to topple the government, split the Indonesian armed forces . . . and destroy the nation," he said: Manuela Saragosa in the *Financial Times,* October 18, 1995. General Sudibyo was quoted in the *Jakarta Post,* February 8, 1994.

7. Business practices were described in "Investment Climate Statement for Indonesia," U.S. Embassy, Jakarta, December 1992.

8. Minister of Manpower Abdul Latief, quoted in the *Jakarta Post,* February 11, 1994.

9. Ozay Mehmet, "Rent-Seeking and Gate-Keeping in Indonesia: A Cultural and Empirical Analysis," Carleton University, Ottawa, Canada, January 1994.

10. Suharto's business nepotism and the multinational complaints were reported in the *Financial Times,* March 15, 1996.

11. The Jakarta military commander, Major General Henroprijono, was quoted in the *Jakarta Post,* February 11, 1994.

12. Details on the Medan strikes and riot are drawn from interviews and these reports: "Indonesia: The Medan Demonstrations and Beyond," Human Rights Watch Asia, May 16, 1994; *Southeast Asia Labor Notes,* Summer 1994; *Indonesia Observer,* January 31, 1995; "Indonesia Human Rights Practices," U.S. State Department, February 1995.

13. Reebok, Levi Strauss and some other firms, sensitive to public complaints about exploitation and environmental abuses, have developed their own codes of conduct on human rights, covering working conditions in their factories. But even if one assumes these public relations gestures are sincere, the companies are not going to challenge the repressive labor-regulation systems that suppress the rights of their workforces. After all, these companies moved their production to countries like Indonesia in order to take advantage of the cheap labor and they have no incentive to push for genuine reform.

In the course of my reporting, I accumulated many ugly facts about abusive conditions in the factories producing for Nike and other American shoe and garment companies—including companies like Reebok that profess their concern for human rights. I chose not to elaborate these facts in the text, not to excuse these firms for their complicity, but because I think that focusing on the moral values of particular companies—or their immorality—invites a self-righteous response among readers that is too easy and undeserved.

The focus for outrage and political action ought to be the larger reality of labor-control systems that exist in countries like Indonesia, systems designed to benefit multinational producers and consumers as well as local elites. Reebok, Nike and the other shoe companies are indistinguishable in that they have all chosen to take advantage of the labor repression in Indonesia and elsewhere, but then so have General Motors, Boeing, General Electric and many other major U.S. manufacturers, not to mention all the Japanese, German, Korean and Taiwanese producers.

Nike has concocted a particularly sick ideology to sell its shoes—glamorous images of superstar athletics concealing the human brutalities—but why single out Nike or Michael Jordan when the U.S. government itself is implicated in the same sickness? Consumer boycotts of Nike and the others can be an effective way to mobilize the political issue, but the true target should be the systems of human repression.

A new complaint on Indonesian labor rights was filed by International Labor Rights Education and Research Fund in June 1995.

14. Details on labor regulation in Shenzhen are from Trini Wing-yue Leung, "EPZ's in China," a report prepared for the International Confederation of Free Trade Unions, August 1994.

15. China has launched rapid development of labor organizations in the industrial zones primarily as a management-control tool, according to Anita Chan of Australian National University. She reported her findings in "Setting Up New Trade Unions and Collective Bargaining in South China," a paper delivered at a workshop on labor resources and economic development at Shantou University, December 8, 1995, co-sponsored by the Center for Labor Studies at the University of Adelaide. The Chinese, Chan noted, like to portray foreign capital in terms of "white man as slave driver" when, in fact, the abuses are led by Asian managers—Koreans and Taiwan Chinese.

16. For an informative exchange on this question between two economists who are both sympathetic to labor's dilemma, see "International Labor Standards: Protectionism or Simple Decency? A Debate with Alice Amsden and Richard Rothstein," *Boston Review,* December 1995.

17. Korean wage increases: *Financial Times,* July 26, 1993.

18. Richard Rothstein, "Developing Reasonable Standards for Judging Whether Minimum Wage Levels in Developing Nations Are Acceptable," draft paper for the U.S. Department of Labor, January 4, 1995.

EIGHTEEN: Wlasności Pracowniczej

1. Edward N. Wolff of New York University has documented the increasing wealth inequality in "International Comparisons of Personal Wealth Inequality," presented to the conference of the International Association for Research in Income and Wealth, St. Andrews, Canada, August 21, 1994, and *Top Heavy: A Study of the Increasing Inequality of Wealth in America* (New York: Twentieth Century Fund, 1995). Wolff's comparisons with Sweden, Britain, France and Canada make the point that U.S. maldistribution increased much more dramatically in recent decades, but even egalitarian Sweden experienced the same trend and the others all had high degrees of wealth inequality. In West Germany, a study from 1973 found that 54 percent of "productive assets" were owned by one percent of the families, according to Fritz W. Scharpf, *Crisis and Choice in European Social Democracy* (Ithaca, N.Y.: Cornell University Press, 1991).

2. Nelson Peltz was quoted by Glenn Yago in *Junk Bonds: How High Yield Securities Restructured Corporate America* (New York; Oxford: Oxford University Press, 1991).

3. Louis Kelso originally described "binary economics," as he called an economic system based on wage and capital incomes, in *The Capitalist Manifesto* (New York: Random House, 1958), co-authored with philosopher Mortimer Adler. Many books and articles followed over the years, often written with his wife, Patricia Hetter. For a contemporary collection of global essays connecting Kelso's economic ideas with Christian social morality, see John H. Miller, editor, *Curing World Poverty: The New Role of Property* (St. Louis: Social Justice Review; Washington, D.C.: Center for Economic and Social Justice, 1994).

4. For a discussion of Kelso's theoretical disputes with orthodox economics on productivity and other issues, see Robert Ashford, "Louis Kelso's Binary Economics," *Journal of Socio-Economics,* Winter 1996.

5. Some details on Solidarity's 1994 strikes are from the *Warsaw Voice,* May 22 and July 17, 1994.

6. By 1994, Poland's economy was expanding by 5.5 percent a year and exports surged by 20 percent, but still less than imports. Incomes continued to decline in real terms, given the high inflation, though a vigorous "gray economy" of unre-

ported private enterprises made economic conditions better than the official statistics reflected. Data from the *Financial Times,* March 28, 1995.

7. A self-congratulatory account of the "shock therapy" reform program is provided by Jeffrey Sachs in *Poland's Jump to the Market Economy* (Cambridge, Mass.: MIT Press, 1994).

8. My example of the Czech voucher program is a very simplified sample from the vastly complicated story of how ex-Communist nations privatized state holdings. For a survey account of the action, see "Mass Privatization in Central and Eastern Europe and the Former Soviet Union," World Bank, 1995.

9. Joseph R. Blasi, who served as an advisor to the Russian reformers, noted that proposals to establish firm legal rights for owner workers to participate in company management were rejected by the national assembly, so the managers retained full control within firms despite the broadened ownership. See Blasi's paper "Russian Enterprise After Privatization," presented to the Association for Comparative Economic Studies, San Francisco, January 5, 1996.

10. The first wave of privatized firms was analyzed in *Employee-Owned Companies in Poland* (Warsaw: Institute of Political Studies, Polish Academy of Sciences, 1994).

11. The total volume of new capital assets created each year in the U.S. is actually much larger, closer to $1 trillion, if one includes residential construction and government investments in infrastructure and other permanent goods. Much of this new capital could also be channeled through citizen ownership financing, though not all of it unless one imagined citizens owning title to bombers and submarines, highways and federal office buildings.

12. John Maynard Keynes's profoundly provocative essay "Economic Possibilities for Our Grandchildren," written in 1930, tours the moral landscape of capitalism in terms that are exquisitely relevant to the twenty-first century. See *Essays in Persuasion* (New York: Harcourt Brace, 1932).

13. Robert A. G. Monks and Nell Minow have provided a persuasive blueprint for reforming shareholder rights in *Power and Accountability* (Champaign, Ill.: HarperBusiness, 1991). "Corporations," Monks and Minow declare, "determine far more than any other institution the air we breathe, the quality of the water we drink, even where we live. Yet they are not accountable to anyone."

NINETEEN: Oikonomia

1. China's new wealth holders, notwithstanding cultural and political differences, are displaying the same flourishes of conspicuous consumption that Americans have made world-famous. *Car Fan,* a new magazine, celebrates the owners of luxury cars like Li Xiahua, the first Chinese to own a Ferrari. A restaurant owner in Beijing parks his Rolls-Royce out front to attract customers. Chairman Mao's grandson, a college student, told the *People's Daily* that his "biggest wish" was to own his own car. See details from Daluo Jia, *Toronto Globe and Mail,* August 18, 1994. Per capita autos in China and U.S.: *Business Week,* February 14, 1994.

2. Germany has pursued aggressive controls of air pollution, but has still not reversed the damage: "Death of the Christmas Tree? Report Indicates Widespread Tree Damage," *The Week in Germany,* December 16, 1994.

3. The exchange between Mahathir and Bruno Manser was reported by Doug Tsuruoka in the *Far Eastern Economic Review,* August 27, 1992. Manser responded by pointing out that the Malaysian government had arrested—and sometimes beaten—more than 450 native people for resisting the logging companies. "Is this respect? Is this allowing them to choose their own destiny?" Manser asked.

4. The Daly-Cobb Index of Sustainable Economic Welfare modified and extended the reach of a formulation done originally by economists James Tobin and

William Nordhaus in the early 1970s. Daly and Cobb's first version, published in 1989, was slightly more pessimistic than the recalculations done for the paperback edition of their book in 1994. Among other controversial elements, their index included income inequality since, they argued, social well-being was degraded as inequality increased. Herman E. Daly and John B. Cobb Jr., *For the Common Good: Redirecting the Economy Toward Community, the Environment, and a Sustainable Future* (Boston: Beacon).

5. The United Nations Development Program has developed a "human development index" that approaches the question of collective welfare from a different angle, including data on life spans, infant mortality, education and health and other factors to appraise each nation's well-being. The 1993 rankings, for instance, put Japan first among industrial countries, followed by Canada, Norway, Switzerland, Sweden, the U.S., Australia, France, the Netherlands and the UK. *Human Development Report 1993*, UN Development Program.

6. The World Bank's study on national wealth and environmentally sustainable development suggests that eliminating poverty would itself help to correct abusive practices, as people developed greater sensitivity and the wherewithal to adopt protective measures. See "Monitoring Environmental Progress: A Report on Work in Progress," World Bank, 1995.

7. The calculations of scale limits are actually more threatening since if one counts only land surfaces and not oceans, human activity has already appropriated 40 percent of the earth's total.

8. Professor North explained that if the full span of human existence was represented as a 24-hour clock, then what is called civilization, starting with the development of agriculture and settlement around 8000 B.C., involved only the last three or four minutes on the clock. If the 24-hour metaphor was applied to the 10,000-year span of so-called civilization, then the industrial age of inventions that started around 1750 has occupied only the last 35 minutes. See Douglass C. North, "Economic Performance Through Time," *The American Economic Review*, June 1994.

9. Hazel Henderson is among the visionaries who for a generation have attacked the conventional economic assumptions and promoted ideas for sustainable development. Her latest book is *Building a Win-Win World: Life Beyond Global Economic Warfare* (San Francisco: Berrett-Koehler, 1996).

10. Michael E. Porter, *The Competitive Advantage of Nations* (New York: Free Press, 1990), was quoted by Curtis Moore and Alan Miller in *Green Gold: Japan, Germany, the United States, and the Race for Environmental Technology* (Boston: Beacon, 1994).

11. For an economist's cogent brief on the wasteful nature of modern society and its misplaced economic priorities, read Douglas Dowd, *The Waste of Nations: Dysfunction in the World Economy* (Boulder, Colo.: Westview, 1989).

12. The work of the future also centers on engaging the social realm, not just wage employment, Jeremy Rifkin argues in *The End of Work: The Decline of the Global Labor Force and the Dawn of the Post-Market Era* (New York: Tarcher/ Putnam, 1995).

13. I am indebted to Robert Borosage of the Campaign for New Priorities for pointing out the Pentagon's $750 billion contest. See John Mintz in the *Washington Post*, February 27, 1996.

Acknowledgments

KNOWING MY OWN limitations, I was naturally hesitant to take on the enormity of the global economy as the subject for a book, but was persuaded to do so in early 1993 by a strange convergence of old friends—each of them telling me I must. One was Rob Johnson, who kept startling me with the larger dynamics of global finance he then encountered every day at the Quantum Fund. Another friend, Rob Dugger, who gathers political and economic intelligence for the Tudor Fund, delivered the same message.

Meanwhile, Barbara Shailor, a political activist I've known for almost twenty-five years, had become the international representative for the machinists' union and kept returning from her own travels with amazing stories and insights. Barbara talked me into going to Zurich to witness the International Metalworkers Federation's centennial congress—a glimpse of the global reality that more or less hooked me on the project. A fourth friend, Ernesto Cortes Jr., a national organizer with the Industrial Areas Foundation's network of community organizations, also insisted that I engage this daunting subject.

I might still have resisted these urgings except that Bill Keller of the U.S. Office of Technology Assessment came along at about the same time and invited me to serve on an advisory committee for OTA's major study of multinational enterprise. The appointment seemed a bit impish on Bill's part, since it put a writer from *Rolling Stone* magazine at the conference table amidst the corporate managers and strategists from Motorola, IBM, Ford, Merck and some others. The experience was deeply instructive because I got to listen to the anxieties of men who run the multinationals in an informal, frank and off-the-record setting. The global system they described was very different from the one portrayed in the newspapers or in the classical economic theory that purports to explain it.

I take this opportunity to thank all of those people who, from their very different perspectives, informed my thinking and motivated me to write this book. Some of them will no doubt be disappointed with the result, but I hope they recognize that I have tried to approach the subject whole, with respect for the facts and for history, with fairness to their own experiences.

Along the way, I was helped by so many people from business, labor, academia, politics and communities that I will not attempt to name them all. I do wish to express special gratitude to those who lent a guiding hand when I was traveling in strange, new places: Merrill Wynn Davies in Kuala Lumpur (and Hazel Henderson, who put me in touch with her and with many visionary ideas); Valentin B. Suazo Jr. and Vicky Aliamo of the Asian-American Free Labor Institute in Jakarta; John Osolnick and Ubon Kompipote of AFFLI in Bangkok; Trini Leung in Hong Kong; Patrick E. Tyler of the *New York Times* in Beijing; William Dawkins of the *Financial Times* in Tokyo; Robert Steier of IG Metall in Frankfurt; Kris Ludwiniak in Warsaw; Tokya E. Dammond and Olga Tyminska in Kraków; Jorge Castañeda, Carlos Heredia and Mary Purcell in Mexico City; and the many others who were so generous and helpful.

I do not exaggerate when I say the scope of this project might have defeated me if I had not had the advantage of sophisticated tutoring and moral support from Rob Johnson and Rob Dugger. I returned to both of them regularly with questions, large and small, about how this new world works; they challenged my own perspective toward it and critiqued my conclusions. Both have the authority to explain high finance and the broad economic forces, but what was most important to me was their larger historical understanding and social sensibility.

In a similar vein, Clyde Prestowitz of the Economic Strategy Institute provided many insights on trade and the industrial system and also provided many critical reactions to the manuscript. My grasp of how other peoples see the global system was enlarged in conversations with Dirk Philipsen, a brilliant young German-born historian at Virginia Commonwealth University, who also gave me a critical reading of the manuscript. All four, it is safe to assume, dissent in different ways from portions of what I have written.

It takes a large measure of luck to complete a project of this scale and I was blessed in multiple ways, mostly importantly by my wife, Linda Furry Greider. She has learned from previous books not to indulge my exaggerated anxieties, but also to bring me back to earth with intelligent questions and comment, in effect helping me to understand what it is I have seen and what I think it means.

I was also lucky to have Per-Kristian Nelson alongside as an intelligent young research assistant, testing my facts and thinking with his own inquiry and reflection. Pete Nelson is a rare type—a sentient economist—who is fully at home with the abstract theory while retaining his own strong moral compass.

My good fortune includes my long-standing connection to Simon & Schuster and, especially, working with Alice Mayhew as editor. Alice combines the intellect of an uncompromising scholar with the market savvy of a very successful publisher; one's books are subject to rigorous scrutiny by both. This time, my work was read by Alice and associate editor Roger

Labrie, backed up once again by a superb copy editor, Charlotte Gross. My relationship with the publisher has been smartly supervised over the years by my agent, Lynn Nesbit, who keeps us both on track.

I owe an enormous debt as well to Jann Wenner, editor and publisher of *Rolling Stone,* a friend and supporter whose patience when I disappear to Indonesia or elsewhere has been very important to me. Jann is well recognized as a brilliant editor and fabulously successful entrepreneur in magazines; he is underappreciated as a creative citizen, one who still believes in America's best possibilities and works astutely in various ways to help the country fulfill them.

Finally, my family at large: my grown-up children and their spouses, Katharine Greider and David Andrews, Cameron Greider and Lalou Dammond, and all the brothers and sisters to whom the book is dedicated. My sister Nancy, in particular, helped to educate me on the nineteenth-century industrial reality by sharing great literature of that time. The others were supportive and patient, always loving.

My brother David, who died at an early age in 1966, was the oldest child in our family (and the smartest) and looked out for all of us in different ways. He was the editor of a weekly newspaper in the suburbs of Cincinnati, Ohio, and was revered in his community for decency, fairness and his intelligent concern for people and their affairs. The older I get, the more deeply I appreciate that, despite travels far from home, I am still trying to follow David's example.

Index